Also by HOWARD M. SACHAR

The Course of Modern Jewish History
Aliyah: The Peoples of Israel
From the Ends of the Earth: The Peoples of Israel

THE EMERGENCE
OF THE MIDDLE EAST:

1914–1924

THE
EMERGENCE
OF THE
MIDDLE EAST:
1914-1924

HOWARD M.
SACHAR

New York: ALFRED · A · KNOPF

1969

THIS IS A BORZOI BOOK
PUBLISHED BY ALFRED A. KNOPF, INC.

For Eliana

Preface

THIS VOLUME deals with the lands and peoples of western
Asia. At the opening of our chronicle, the territory is encompassed by the Ottoman Empire. At the end, it is fragmentized
into the individual nations of Turkey, Syria, Lebanon, Palestine, the Hejaz, and Iraq. In either case it extends from the
Black and Mediterranean seas to the Persian Gulf, embracing
nearly two million square miles and, in the ten-year period
under discussion, between twenty-five and thirty million inhabitants. Once this sprawling land mass, which nurtured the
majority of the world's civilizations until the late Middle Ages,
was the very cradle of the human heritage. By 1914, however,
or indeed even later, it would have been all but impossible to
adduce evidence of historic fecundity in this deforested,
bleached, and arid terrain, among populations impoverished,
disease-ridden, and backward to the narrowest margin of sheer
survival. If, in modern times, therefore, the Middle East has
regained its ancient importance in world affairs, the reason
can hardly be found in the productivity of its economy or the
creativity of its peoples. Instead, its role in contemporary history has been almost exclusively geographic and strategic,
the consequence of that expansion of nineteenth-century
Europe which transformed the entire globe into the theater of
power politics. A glance at the map immediately reveals the
area's magisterial importance: the Ottoman Empire and its
successors comprised the land bridge joining Europe, Asia,
and Africa. When the land bridge remained in the comparatively enfeebled possession of Turks or Arabs alone, the equilibrium of European politics could be assured. Russia then
was restricted to its Eurasian land mass, Britain to its sea

lanes between the Mediterranean and the Persian Gulf, Germany to its solid emplacement astride central Europe. Conversely, in the hands of any of the major European powers, the Middle East represented the key to near-world supremacy.

Perhaps inevitably, then, the history of our times has been strewn with crises originating in this unique nexus of three continents. Winston Churchill dramatized the region's critical importance, in the immediate aftermath of Dunkirk, by stripping his denuded and vulnerable island of two of its last four divisions and rushing them off to Suez. This decision was hardly more crucial, however, than Napoleon's effort, in 1798, to strike England a mortal blow by landing a French expeditionary force in Egypt; or Russia's plan to swallow the Middle East whole, in 1853, by claiming a treaty protectorate over the Ottoman Empire's Greek Orthodox minorities; or the kaiser's scheme to break the back of England's sea empire by constructing a railroad from Constantinople to Baghdad in the decade and a half before World War I. Surely, against this background of international intrigue, it is not an exaggeration to chart the very fate of modern Europe through the historic and ancient Middle Eastern battleground.

Accordingly, the political orientation of the Sublime Porte, the government which presided over this strategic agglomeration of deserts, mountains, canals, and peninsulas, was a matter of far-reaching consequence to statesmen in Western nations. By the same token, so was the diplomatic stance of the successor nations fashioned out of the Ottoman debris in the postwar era. If European ambassadors after 1919 no longer found it necessary to jockey for position in Constantinople, they soon discovered that their national security had now to be anchored instead in a consecutive series of ha'penny capitals extending from Beirut to Baghdad. The task was accomplished, to be sure, both by treaty and by force of arms; and in the process, the West made little serious pretense to moral or legal refinement. In fact, much has been written of the brutality and duplicity with which the Allies took possession of Ottoman territories. But it may be worth examining the prodigious effort it cost the Entente powers, in lives and treasure, to crack the grip of the Turk on the peoples of the Middle East, and thereby to stake their own postwar claims to the region. It is possibly relevant, too, to explore once again the political and military circumstances under which Britain and France invoked the dormant national aspirations of Middle Eastern peoples, the premises and promises upon which these client nations were induced to link their fate to the Allied cause, as well as the qualifications that were imposed upon the ideal of native independence, both during and after the war. The misunderstandings that later arose as a consequence of those early negotiations have influenced, and in many instances have poisoned, relations between the Middle East and the Western world to this day, often with serious implications for European security. Indeed, one legacy of the First World War, the Palestine question, threatened both in 1956 and 1967 to provoke armed Russian intrusion into the Mediterranean and painfully to strain the NATO alliance. It is of more than passing interest, finally, to recall that a vibrant and creative minority race, the Armenians, once shared the heritage of Middle Eastern civilization; and that, but for the unprecedented tragedy of their genocide (the first of modern times, and now, unaccountably, all but forgotten), the People of Ararat might even today be playing a vital role in the cultural revival of western Asia.

In the preparation of this brief study, I was favored with the thoughtful suggestions of a number of esteemed friends and colleagues. Among them, Professor Harry N. Howard of American University, dean of Middle Eastern diplomatic historians in this country, kindly shared with me the fruits of his matchless scholarship and of his extensive governmental experience in Middle Eastern affairs. Professor Kerim Key, also of American University, read through the entire manuscript to ferret out errors of fact and emphasis, particularly in those sections relating to Turkey, his homeland and the subject of his own extensive writings. Mr. Moshe Medzini, former chief diplomatic correspondent for the leading Israeli morning newspaper, *HaAretz*, diligently perused and annotated the chapters dealing with Palestine and British mandatory policy; my gratitude to him is very great. So it is also to my father, Dr. A. L. Sachar of Brandeis University, whose marginal comments as a historian of British imperialism were extremely useful in clarifying my perspective on the period. The book's point of view is my own, of course.

I should like also to express my especial thanks to the Faculty Research Committee of George Washington University, which generously helped underwrite many of the expenses attendant upon the preparation of this volume; to Professor Neil Klenke, of the University of Virginia, who graciously reviewed my German translations and citations; to Mr. Dudley Ball, Chief of the Stack and Reader Division of the Library of Congress, and to his associates, Mr. William Sartain and Miss Grey Powers, whose helpfulness in making special research facilities available to me much enriched my three years in the one incomparable library of the world. A last word of appreciation must also be tendered my department secretaries, Mrs. Charlene Dougherty and Miss Ginger Worthington, who loyally and accurately typed several of the earliest and least decipherable drafts of this manuscript.

Washington, D.C.
August 1968

[xi]

Contents

Maps and Diagrams

THE EMERGENCE
OF THE MIDDLE EAST:

1914–1924

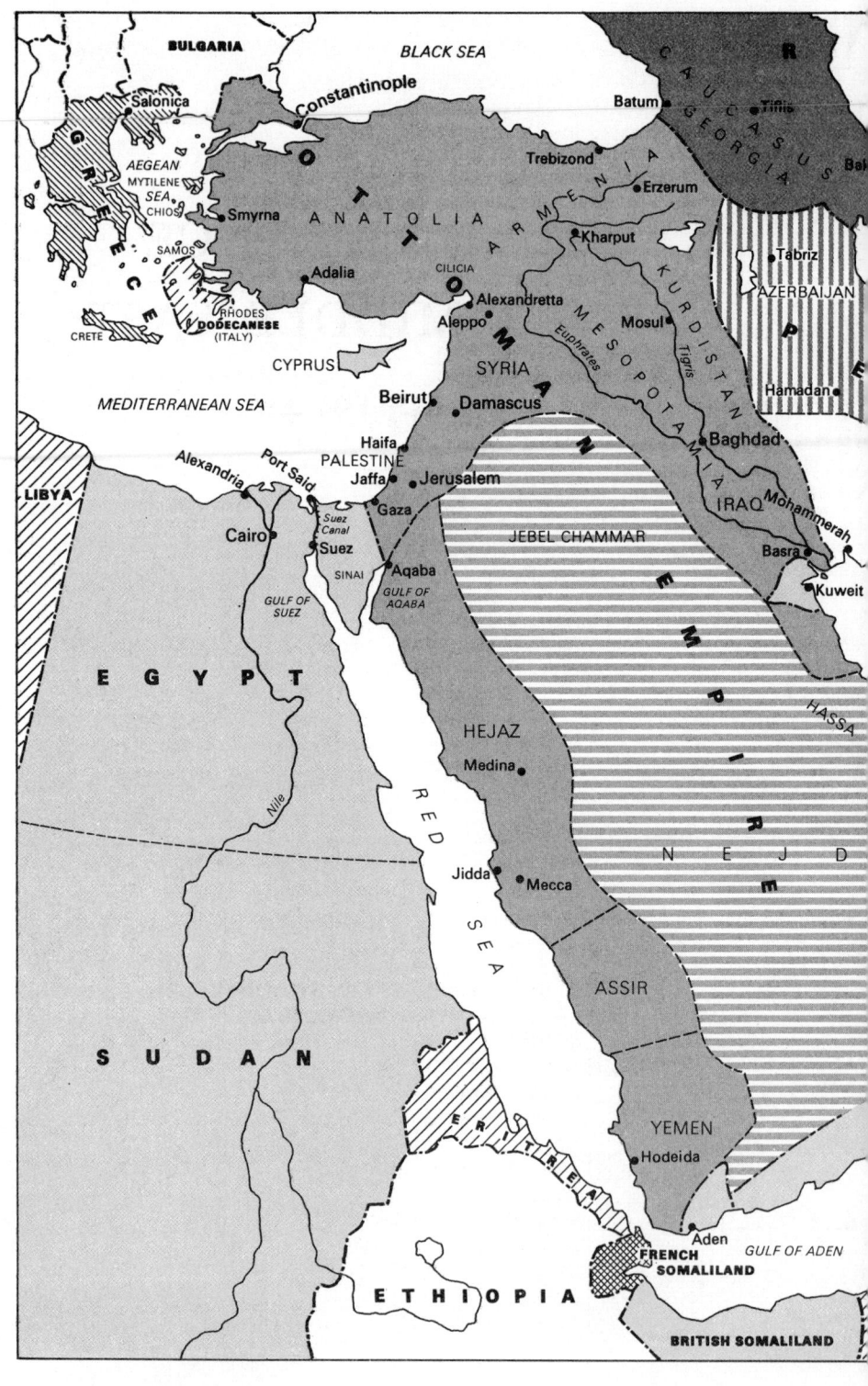

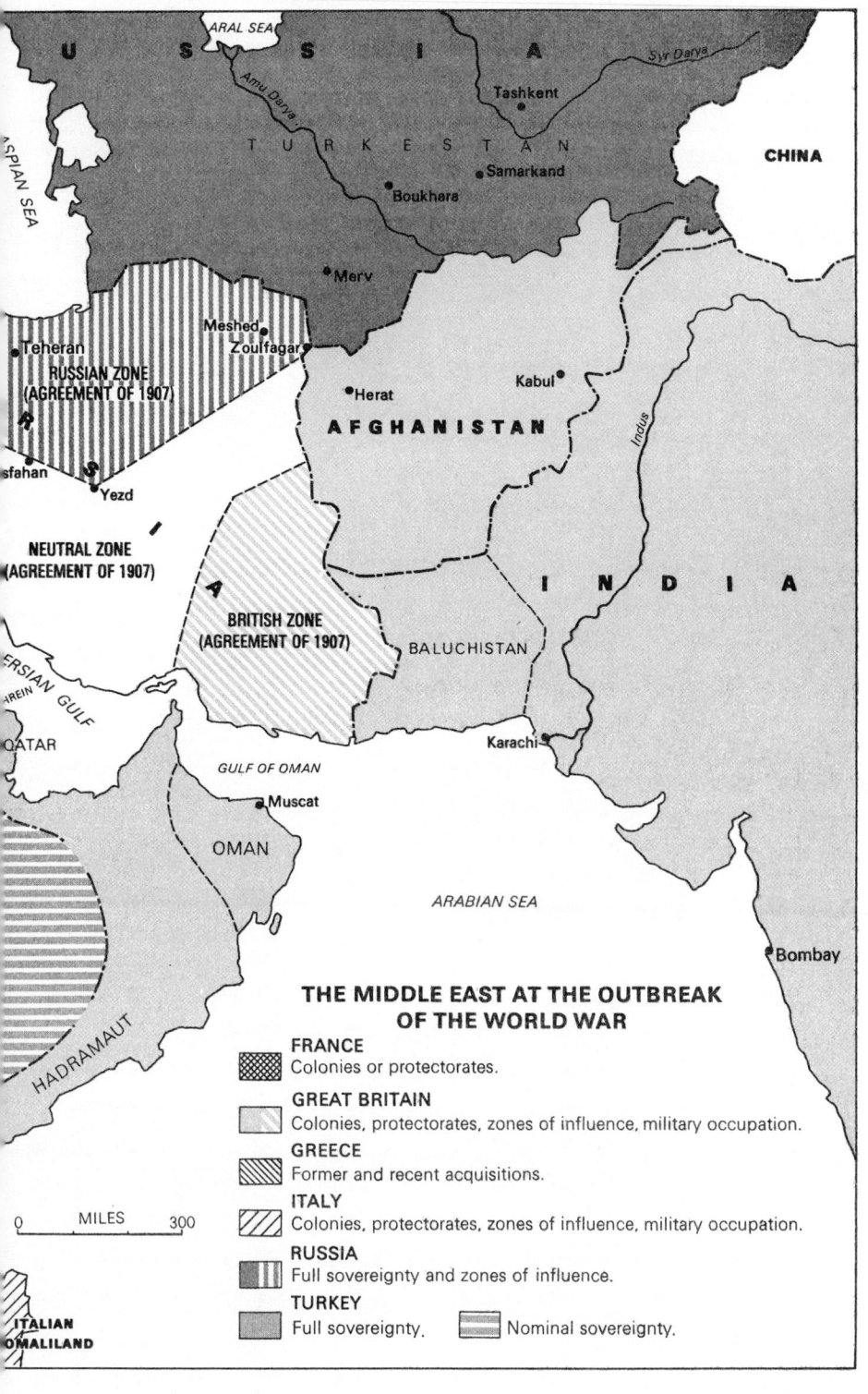

THE MIDDLE EAST AT THE OUTBREAK
OF THE WORLD WAR

FRANCE
Colonies or protectorates.

GREAT BRITAIN
Colonies, protectorates, zones of influence, military occupation.

GREECE
Former and recent acquisitions.

ITALY
Colonies, protectorates, zones of influence, military occupation.

RUSSIA
Full sovereignty and zones of influence.

TURKEY
Full sovereignty.   Nominal sovereignty.

CHAPTER I

THE SICK MAN'S LAST ADVENTURE

The Germans Fill a Vacuum

ON THE MORNING of August 10, 1914, an Italian ocean liner carefully nestled into berth in the Golden Horn, the port of Constantinople. One of the first of its passengers to disembark was a woman in her late twenties. She was Mrs. Maurice Wertheim, daughter of Henry Morgenthau, the American ambassador to Turkey. Driving back to the embassy soon afterward with her father, Mrs. Wertheim described an extraordinary naval encounter she had witnessed at sea three days before. Two German war cruisers had sailed into view from the west, she said, firing their heavy guns at a smaller British naval vessel several miles off on the horizon. The salvoes had evidently accomplished little except to keep the British ship at a respectful distance, and the Germans then had steamed on rapidly, overtaking the passenger liner en route to the eastern Mediterranean. The episode had been quite brief, although Mrs. Wertheim was still flushed with excitement as she recalled it, her first glimpse of actual warfare. Fascinated by his daughter's tale, Morgenthau repeated it later in the morning to his good friend Baron von Wangenheim, the German ambassador. The German's reaction, in turn, was one of agitated, almost uncontrollable curiosity. Indeed, for the next two hours both he and Count Pallavicini, the Austrian ambassador, insisted upon politely but thoroughly cross-examining Mrs. Wertheim. When the interview ended, both men were jubilant. They had received the first authentic information that the battle cruiser *Goeben* and the light cruiser *Breslau* had escaped their British pursuers, and were even then approaching the Dardanelles and the possible sanctuary of Turkish waters.

At this point, Wangenheim rushed back to his own embassy and dispatched an urgent message to Berlin via the chancery radio transmitter. Within minutes a return signal came through on the receiver. The diplomat jotted the code down, then drove off immediately to the residence of Saïd Halim, the Turkish grand vizier. It was an eminently productive visit. At 5:17 p.m. that day, a squadron of Ottoman torpedo boats conducted the two fugitive German naval craft safely through the mine fields of the Dardanelles. The next morning, the battle cruisers dropped anchor in the Golden Horn. The *Breslau*, a small, lean greyhound of a boat, was notable primarily as the flagship of Admiral Souchon, commander of the German Mediterranean task force. The *Goeben* was something else. Constructed recently in Germany, with a displacement of 22,640 tons and boasting the unprecedented speed of twenty-six knots, it was the fastest naval vessel of its size afloat. Moreover, with its formidable armament of ten eleven-inch guns, the cruiser carried substantially heavier firepower than any Russian ship in the Black Sea. Now, too, anchored in the Golden Horn, the *Goeben* was in the unimaginable position of being able to influence the government policy, in fact the very political existence, of one of the largest empires on the face of the earth. Perhaps the significance of the cruisers' arrival was best conveyed by Morgenthau:

> A few weeks after the *Goeben* and the *Breslau* had taken up permanent headquarters in the Bosphorus, Djavid Bey, Minister of Finance, happened to meet a distinguished Belgian jurist, then in Constantinople. "I have terrible news for you," said the sympathetic Turkish statesman. "The Germans have captured Brussels." The Belgian . . . put his arm soothingly over the shoulder of the diminutive Turk. "I have even more terrible news for you," he said, pointing out to the stream where the *Goeben* and the *Breslau* lay anchored. "The Germans have captured Turkey."

Actually, the "capture" of Ottoman political initiative by a foreign power should hardly have been occasion for aston-

6

ishment. The Porte had long since demonstrated its inability to protect its imperial interests on its own. During the preceding two centuries, the very leitmotif of Turkish history had been incompetence and decay. Most of the empire's subject races—Greeks, Slavs, Armenians, Berbers, Jews, Arabs—governed themselves in effect, paying the tribute of their sons or their taxes into the Ottoman military and financial administration. The system was a pitiably inefficient anachronism in modern times, all the more so by contrast with Western progress. The sultans, ostensible rulers of this putrefying regime, were hopelessly effete, stunted mentally and morally by harem politics and by illimitable personal indulgence. The desiccated Islamic religious hierarchy all but precluded administrative and intellectual progress in the empire by anathematizing dynamism in both thought and deed. Even the Ottoman army—its supply services corroded by graft and corruption, its ill-nourished soldiery still recruited by quasi-feudal methods—was incapable any longer of intimidating the gestating Balkan nations on the very doorstep of Turkey itself. As early as the first decade of the nineteenth century, therefore, the Serbs and Montenegrins wrested themselves free from the Turkish grip, as did the Greeks in the third decade, the Rumanians at mid-century, the Bulgarians, Bosnians, and Herzegovinians in the 1870's, the Cretans at the turn of the century, the Macedonians and Albanians in the years immediately preceding the World War.

The empire that suffered the ignominy of these losses plainly bore little resemblance to that fearsome Turanian avalanche which once had overrun Asia and Africa from western Persia to the Strait of Gibraltar, and southern Europe from the Balkans to the gates of Vienna. "The Turk in a very sick man," was Tsar Nicholas's contemptuous description of this emaciated realm in a conversation with the British ambassador in 1853. "A decision must be made on the future of his territories before he dies on our hands." Nor did the Russian government then, or in succeeding years, veil its intention of encouraging Turkey's demise at every opportunity. The straits of the Bos-

7

porus and the Dardanelles, linking the Black Sea with the Mediterranean, still remained under Ottoman sovereignty; and with tsarist maritime commerce immobilized for two thirds of the year in frozen Russian waters, it not unnaturally became an *idée fixe* in St. Petersburg to win permanent naval access to the ice-free trading routes of the Mediterranean. Various techniques were successively employed. In the 1830's, for example, the Russian government posed as Turkey's avuncular guardian against Mehemet Ali, a rebellious Egyptian vassal, and claimed the reward of virtual monopoly over the Turkish straits. The Western powers blocked that maneuver, closing the waterway to vessels of war by the Convention of London of 1841. Altering its approach in the late 1840's and 1850's, St. Petersburg posed as "guarantor" of Turkey's Greek Orthodox minorities, whom it viewed as likely *agents provocateurs* for Russian imperial purposes. Clearly, neither the Turks nor the Western nations were prepared to countenance this tactic. The danger was eventually met and smashed on the battlefields of the Crimea in 1854 and 1855.

Still, the fundamental threat of recurrent tsarist movement toward the Mediterranean was by no means eliminated. Within the space of a single generation it flared up again with renewed intensity. This time Pan-Slavism was the technique, an ideology with which Russian statesmen shrewdly exploited the nationalism of Slavic client-peoples in the Balkan Peninsula, the land bridge between the Black Sea and the Aegean. In the 1870's, St. Petersburg encouraged Bulgarian, Bosnian, and Herzegovinian unrest, providing funds and weapons for guerrilla attacks against Ottoman garrisons, and finally launching a "punitive" war of its own against the Turks in 1877. By March of the following year, its armies cruelly battered, the Ottoman regime was obliged to sue for an armistice. Russia's peace terms envisaged an independent Bulgarian state engorged with some two thirds of the south Balkan Peninsula, including the vital port of Salonica, outlet to the Aegean. Detecting in these provisions yet another tsarist maneuver for access to the Mediterranean, the Western maritime powers

8

were again obliged to threaten St. Petersburg with force. Afterward, too, months of diplomatic negotiations were required to produce a compromise peace treaty at the Congress of Berlin.

Significantly, in every instance of Russian pressure on the Ottoman Empire, it was Britain that played the crucial role of mobilizing Western opposition. For no other European nation, not even other maritime countries, nurtured as vital a strategic interest in keeping the Russian fleet locked in the waters of the Black Sea. Through the Mediterranean flowed Britain's historic routes of supply to the vast subcontinent of India, pearl of the Victorian empire, immense reservoir of British imperial manpower, of raw materials and markets for British industry. The traffic lanes entered the great middle sea at Gibraltar, spanned its entire length up to Alexandria and Beirut, then crossed by land alternatively to the Red Sea or to the Tigris and Euphrates rivers, and from either vantage point directly on to the Persian Gulf and India. By 1869, the opening of the Suez Canal had foreshortened the route, eliminated the need for portage, and profoundly augmented the Mediterranean's value as artery to the East. It was hardly surprising, under these circumstances, that London's obsession in foreign affairs remained the territorial integrity of the Ottoman realm; debilitated though the Turkish regime was, it served Britain as an indispensable buffer against Russian expansion. Accordingly, during the largest part of the nineteenth century, Britain's ambassadors in Constantinople—Ponsonby, Stratford-Canning, Elliott—spoke with near-messianic authority in Ottoman government councils. British troops at Sevastopol and Balaclava spilled their life blood to ensure the continued rule of the sultan in the Middle East. British naval transports rushed battalions of Sikh warriors to Malta in 1878 as a warning to the Russian army, ensconced at San Stefano, not to risk advancing the last twenty miles to Constantinople. As late as the last decade of the century, therefore, no responsible statesman would have ventured a premonitory vision of Turkey in the embrace of one of Britain's enemies.

But who could then have prophesied that Russia and

Britain would themselves become allies in the not distant future? Nevertheless, it was precisely this unlikely contingency which in fact took place. By the early twentieth century, the Russian bear's classic challenge to British imperial security had been largely pre-empted by the German Reich. It was Germany now that competed aggressively with British industry in every world market, and that imperiled Britain's supremacy of the seas by launching a naval construction program of major dimensions. Thereupon, responding in alarm to this entirely unanticipated new menace, Whitehall hurriedly began rethinking the basic, well-seasoned tenets of its foreign policy. France, traditionally Britain's irascible competitor for African territory, was regarded in a new light—as a potential ally. Remarkably enough, so was Russia. After all, tsarist strength had always been judged a potential danger, but a future danger. The burgeoning German fleet, on the other hand, was a sinister contemporary reality. The Turks sensed the shift in Britain's priority of interests well before a common fear of Germany drew London and St. Petersburg together in the Entente of 1907. Indeed, England had compromised its relationship with the Porte in the very aftermath of the Congress of Berlin by occupying Cyprus, in 1878, and Egypt four years after that. France, another erstwhile ally of the Turks, had followed Britain's lead by establishing a *de facto* protectorate over Ottoman Tunis in 1881. Intently watching this subtle realignment of loyalties, the German government was not laggard in divining Constantinople's susceptibility to overtures from other, less traditional quarters. A railway was Berlin's opening wedge.

It happened that Sultan Abdul Hamid II was acutely conscious of the difficulty of governing his conglomerate empire, of transporting grains, collecting taxes, and conscripting soldiers, without adequate rail communications. The Deutsche Bank, one of Germany's largest holding companies, offered to provide those communications for the substantial remuneration of 15,000 francs a kilometer. The Porte accepted the offer. By the end of the century the Anatolian Railway Company, German-financed and German-controlled, had sprouted six hundred miles of rail lines across the breadth of Anatolia to the foothills of the Caucasus. A subsidiary of the project, the Baghdad Railway Company, pushed on toward the Euphrates, and by 1905 had crossed the tip of Mesopotamia. The rail network opened a prodigiously expanding market for German exports, which soared from less than 12,000,000 marks in 1888 to 71,000,000 in 1905. The possibilities of this new economic relationship were not lost on Count Hatzfeld, German ambassador at the Porte, who advocated its use to draw Turkey into the German imperial sphere of influence. Kaiser Wilhelm II heartily agreed. Unlike Bismarck, his former chancellor, Wilhelm was convinced that the time was ripe for his great clattering workshop of a nation to assert itself vigorously in the struggle for empire. In the young monarch's view, it would be useful to remind Britain and France that an industrious and disciplined land animal like Germany had its own methods for winning "a place in the sun." The Austrian government, in fact, had already embarked on its own *Drang nach Osten* through the Balkans; working in tandem, the two Central Powers hopefully might fulfill Wilhelm's cherished goal of outflanking Britain's naval lifeline to the Middle East. What better method, then, for achieving this ambition than to flood the Ottoman Empire with investments and advisers, to link the Turkish market directly to German industrial production?

In 1889 and in 1898, Wilhelm paid ceremonial visits to Constantinople. There he unhesitatingly proclaimed his fraternal affection for Abdul Hamid II—in 1898, at the very moment when an especially odious series of anti-Armenian massacres had placed the "Red Sultan" in virtual diplomatic quarantine. In the wake of the Kaiser's visit, moreover, a heavy infusion of German investments reinforced Berlin's political and economic ascendancy in the Ottoman realm, as did the swelling complex of German Protestant and Catholic missions, convents, monasteries, hospices, and churches, and the German Zionist Society's network of German-speaking schools in Palestine. At home, Pan-Germanist circles discovered new imperial potentialities in the sprawling Ottoman realm. A series of articles by Sprenger, the orientalist, discussing Germany's "mission" in the Levant, commanded a rapt, enthusiastic audience, as did Kannenberg's extraordinarily popular volume, *Asia Minor's Natural Riches*. In truth, by the first decade of the twentieth century, German influence in the Ottoman Empire had become a matter of national prestige, almost a state of mind. Marshal von Bieberstein, Hatzfeld's successor in Constantinople, boasted proudly that Turkey had become "Germany's Canada."

The Ottoman Revolution of 1908 added a significant dimension to the German-Turkish relationship. At first, to be sure, the uprising of that year appeared to be a purely domestic change, unrelated to foreign affairs, and directed primarily against the corruption and brutality of Abdul Hamid's regime. During the initial palmy days following the triumph of the Committee of Union and Progress (the society of "Young Turk" revolutionaries), promises of racial and religious equality echoed jubilantly throughout the empire. Exhilarated by assurances of a new era of brotherhood and toleration, Turks, Greeks, Arabs, Jews, and Armenians embraced each other in the streets, in public meetings, in joint thanksgiving services. European journalists of the time, witnessing the unprecedented display of fraternity, quite understandably emphasized the pan-sectarian and broadly Ottoman nature of the CUP. The most influential of these Young Turks were in fact described not as ethnic Turks at all, but rather as Albanians, Circassians, Greeks, or Salonican Jews. This appraisal was inaccurate. The largest portion of the society's members did consist of Turks, many of them army officers. And their revolt in 1908 was animated not merely by hatred of Abdul Hamid's oppression, but also by outrage at the nerveless extinction of Ottoman sovereignty in the non-Turkish provinces of the realm.

In its first pronunciamento, significantly, the new regime served notice that the empire was no longer fair game for European exploitation. Acidly, it reviled the sultan's former ministers and pashas for subjecting the Ottoman peoples to the "Frankish yoke." (One CUP newspaper described these officials as "scorpions, snakes and hyenas preying upon the land, so lost to all sense of decency that they had been prepared in their lust for profit to export even the droppings of dogs.") And yet, in the end, this defiant warning to the West availed little, for the Young Turks ironically proved even less effective than the defunct Hamidian regime in blocking territorial incursions by the European powers. In 1908, the very year of the revolution, the Habsburg government arrogantly declared the annexation of Bosnia and Herzegovina, while Bulgaria proclaimed her final independence, and Crete her union with Greece. In 1911 Italy attacked, and in 1912 annexed, a large portion of Tripolitania. During the latter year, in the First Balkan War, Greece, Bulgaria, and Serbia devoured Thrace and Macedonia, reducing Turkish sovereignty in Europe to a thin buffer zone on the doorstep of Constantinople itself.

It should not have been remarkable under these circumstances that the CUP government decided to vent upon the empire's non-Moslem minorities its own bitterly frustrated Turkish ethnocentrism. Increasing numbers of Greek, Armenian, and other millet newspapers and clubs were closed down. For the first time, too, non-Moslems were conscripted into the Ottoman armed forces. Turkish became an obligatory language for the public transaction of business even in the most densely inhabited minority areas. Preoccupied, too, with the need for national security, the three leading members of the Young Turk government—Enver Pasha, minister of war, Talaat Pasha, minister of the interior, and Djemal Pasha, minister of marine—abandoned their former deference to constitutional procedure, and by 1913 had fastened a tight, increasingly reactionary grip upon the imperial administration. Suspected traitors and "counterrevolutionaries" were arrested and deported by the hundreds; execution of political opponents was not uncommon. Instead of one Abdul Hamid, the empire was now governed by several. The CUP regime was untroubled by charges of brutality. As far as it was concerned, the empire was under siege. Any measures were justified that would guarantee its security. Any friends that could offer it protection were worth having.

It was precisely this infuriated Young Turk nationalism which solidified German influence in Constantinople. The revolutionary Cabinet was not unaware that Germany was actually the only European great power to refrain from gorging itself on Ottoman territory, that Germany was the only European nation prepared to buy up the Ottoman bond issue in 1909–10 after negotiations with France had collapsed in the public uproar following a series of anti-Armenian pogroms. The Anatolian-Baghdad Railway complex, too, however profitable for Berlin, was also of unquestionable value to the Turkish government. Moreover, as far as the CUP was concerned, the highly disciplined German army was the most effective barrier in Europe to Russian expansionism; and the Turks had learned to fear tsarist imperialism far more than any piecemeal annexation by the West. Indeed, the glittering efficiency of the German military machine all but hypnotized the Young Turk government, and particularly the war minister, Enver Pasha, a soldier himself, who had spent several years in Berlin as Ottoman military attaché. Exposed to the Prussian martial tradition during that period, Enver was convinced that the German army represented the ideal model for the Ottoman armed forces, and probably the last best hope for defending the empire's collapsing frontiers.

A Mission and an Alliance

IT WAS AT ENVER'S INSISTENCE, therefore, that the CUP government decided to take inspiration from the Wilhelmine model. A precedent existed. As far back as 1883, a small German military mission had arrived in Constantinople to help train officers for the Ottoman defense forces. The instructional effort had not been entirely unsuccessful, despite later Turkish military reverses; a number of good company commanders had been turned out. Yet it was equally plain, after the disaster of the Balkan Wars of 1912–13, that more far-reaching help would be needed. In April 1913, the Turkish government asked Berlin for "a suitable Prussian officer" to supervise the training of the Ottoman general staff and to organize new plans for the defense of the Straits. In transmitting the request to the Wilhelmstrasse, Ambassador von Wangenheim noted that such a German officer would be ideally situated for "mobilization and operation in a future war." The implication was not lost on Foreign Minister von Jägow. Control of the Ottoman armed forces, he agreed, would serve as Germany's most effective guarantee for protecting her stake in Anatolia and Mesopotamia. Nor were the imperial possibilities lost on the kaiser, who personally and enthusiastically approved the mission. The task was too important for some obscure brigadier, of course. What was required was nothing less than a senior division commander.

Such a man was found in O. V. K. Liman von Sanders, commander of the Twenty-second Division in Cassel, a stocky, bespectacled, fifty-five-year-old career officer with a superior record in both administrative organization and field training. By September 1913 the terms of his assignment were formulated. Assisted by a staff of forty-two German officers, Liman von Sanders would be charged with exclusive supervision over the entire system of Ottoman military schools. He would serve as a member of the Ottoman supreme war council, and in this capacity exert a "definitive" influence on Turkish promotions. Most important, as commander of the Ottoman First Army Corps, the general would assume personal responsibility for defending Constantinople and the Straits. It was this latter responsibility that turned out to be loaded with political dynamite, for command of the Straits manifestly affected the vital strategic interests of the Triple Entente. Thus, only hours after learning of the Turco-German agreement, St. Petersburg issued an urgent warning to the Ottoman government, charging that Liman's assignment was a direct threat to Russian maritime interests. Indeed, Count Giers, Russian ambassador to the Porte, announced his refusal to stay in Constantinople as long as the capital remained under the "protection" of a German officer. The British and French fully shared this anxiety. As French Foreign Minister Pichon grimly reminded Berlin, a major army under German control in this uniquely strategic city would "put the diplomatic corps in Constantinople under the guard of Germany; it would virtually deliver the key to the Straits to that Power . . . it would break the balance of the Powers which is the guarantee of the existence of the Ottoman Empire."

As the diplomatic exchange between the powers grew more heated, it soon became apparent that the Liman mission threatened to cause one of the most serious crises between Russia and Germany in several decades. At first the kaiser insisted upon holding firm. He allowed it to be known that he valued the Turkish alliance more than the goodwill of the Entente. Thus supported, Ottoman Grand Vizier Mahmud Shevket firmly, even arrogantly, rejected a joint protest delivered by the Entente ambassadors on December 13. ("Bravo," scribbled Kaiser Wilhelm on the margin of Wangenheim's report.) But eventually, cooler heads prevailed in Berlin. Foreign Minister von Jägow, sobered by the intensity of Allied recriminations, devised a face-saving compromise by which Liman would be appointed inspector general of the Turkish army with the rank of Ottoman field marshal rather than commander of the First Army Corps in Constantinople. In this new capacity, the German's substantive influence actually would be enlarged. But at least the sensitive Constantinople-Straits area would remain under direct Turkish command, and it was this assurance which the Entente powers had insisted was crucial. On December 21, St. Petersburg, London, and Paris jointly announced their acceptance of the compromise; Mahmud Shevket and Wangenheim initialed it two days later.

The incident was closed, but the scars did not heal. For the Entente, the Liman affair was an alarming revelation of the magnitude of German influence at the Sublime Porte.

Berlin had made no secret of its intention to draw the Ottoman Empire irretrievably into Germany's orbit. Indeed, this ambition was plain not merely in the vocal and belligerent pan-German press, but also in the increasingly militant stance of the German government. The kaiser, for example, insisted on the last word in the Liman affair by appointing the marshal his personal envoy to the sultan, actually outranking Wangenheim. Presumably the ambassador concurred in this. "The Power which controls the army would always be the strongest in Turkey," he had written prophetically to Chancellor von Bethmann-Hollweg on April 26, 1913, during the Liman negotiations. It was Wangenheim's proposal that Germany duplicate in the Ottoman Empire the role England played in Egypt, that Turkish officers be placed "completely under the direction of German instructors with the most extensive powers." Foreign Secretary Zimmerman heartily agreed. As we shall see (Chapter II), those powers were exceptionally far-reaching.

It is worth noting, however, that the Young Turk Cabinet still believed it possible to exploit German help without becoming altogether a German dependency. To that end, in the last year before the war, the Ottoman government went to extraordinary lengths to accommodate the Entente powers. France was awarded several important railway concessions in Syria. The priority of British influence was recognized in the Persian Gulf area. In a separate, but related, Anglo-German agreement, London was invited to share the concession for the final leg of the Baghdad Railway from Basra to the Persian Gulf. Similarly, a consortium of English firms was granted the rights for oil-drilling in Mesopotamia, for extending the Aidin Railway, for enlarging the harbors of Trebizond and Samsum. An English inspector general was engaged to reform the Ottoman ministry of interior and civil service. A British naval officer, Admiral Limpus, was invested with full authority to renovate the Ottoman fleet; a French general was placed in charge of the Turkish national police force, and yet another Frenchman was hired as inspector general of finance. These concessions and appointments were not entirely grudging. Several members of the royal family and of the Young Turk Cabinet, including the grand vizier and the minister of marine, were widely known for their pro-French sympathies. The Turkish government had not altogether bartered its soul to the Germans. "We followed the exigencies of the hour," recalled Talaat Pasha, minister of the interior, "trying to be equally good [sic] to all the European Powers."

But the tightrope became far more difficult to walk after the assassination of Franz Ferdinand at Sarajevo. Enver and Talaat were quite aware that in the event of war the Western members of the Entente eventually would be compelled to ship munitions to their Russian ally through the Bosphorus and Dardanelles. In peacetime, fifty per cent of Russian trade with the West passed through the Straits, and no less than ninety per cent of Russia's grain trade. It was unthinkable that the Entente would risk German domination of this vital channel. The inescapable possibility of Russian aggression had to be reckoned with. And so now, too, did the need for a defense alliance with Germany. In late June, the Ottoman government made its first tentative overtures to the Wilhelmstrasse. They were received eagerly and were officially approved in July. Wangenheim hammered out the details with Enver and the war minister's close associates, and the treaty was signed on August 2. It was a secret agreement—so secret, in fact, that of the Turkish Cabinet only Enver, Talaat, and Saïd Halim, the new grand vizier, were fully informed of its text. The document unquestionably met Constantinople's first requirement of German military help in the event of a Russian attack on Turkey. But the price was high. The Turks, for their part, were pledged to fight at the side of Germany "if Russia intervenes and takes active military measures, and the necessity arises for Germany to carry out her pledges of alliance to Austria. . . ." Moreover, the agreement was drastically one-sided. It offered the Ottoman government no protection from attack by England, nor did the text specify that Germany actually had to *be* attacked by Russia for the Porte to be committed. Even the promise of territorial acquisitions was at best implicit. As the

18

experts in the Wilhelmstrasse viewed it, therefore, the treaty seemingly transformed the Ottoman Empire into a helpless pawn of German military policy. They did not know their Turks.

By the end of the first week in August, the war had engulfed Germany, Russia, France, Britain, Belgium—but not Turkey. The Austrian army had invaded Serbia, to be sure. Yet even before the Russians moved against Austria, Berlin had unilaterally declared war on Russia. The Sublime Porte had found its loophole. Technically, the "necessity" had not arisen for Germany to carry out her pledge to the Habsburg government. It was still by no means certain which way the Turks ultimately would jump. Craving emancipation from the endemic, familiar threat of partition, the Ottoman government was quite ready, even at this eleventh hour, to negotiate with either coalition of powers.

The ineptitude of Entente diplomacy was at least partly responsible for the Turks' opportunism. Allied propaganda services in Constantinople were all but immobilized, the Allied ambassadors being entirely unwilling to match Berlin's assurance of territorial guarantees and "adjustments." On August 23, a joint Entente note promised to defend the integrity of the Ottoman Empire in return for Turkish neutrality and the dismissal of all German officers. Yet when Enver inquired directly whether the Entente was prepared to recognize Ottoman sovereignty in Tunisia, Morocco, and Egypt (Allied-occupied territories still claimed by the Porte), the answers were noncommittal. Nor were the Entente ambassadors willing to discuss more than fractional abrogation of the Capitulations— those extraterritorial judicial and financial privileges historically enjoyed by Europeans in Ottoman territory. "They never went further in their proposal than that," Talaat complained later, "and never proposed anything else."

It was improbable by then, however, that any Allied inducement, no matter how generous, would have sufficed to assure Ottoman friendship. For most of the Young Turk Cabinet the opportunity of striking a possibly decisive blow against Russia, the *bête noire* of modern Ottoman history, was becoming irresistible. Indeed, the Germans made it irresistible. On August 4, two days after the secret Turco-German Treaty was signed, Enver solicited the Wilhelmstrasse for immediate delivery of 500,000 artillery shells, 200,000 rifles, and other military supplies. Berlin approved the request without hesitation; on August 14 the war minister, General Erich von Falkenhayn, agreed to cover part of the bill from unearmarked army funds. Almost simultaneously, too, the German government contrived a method for augmenting Ottoman naval strength that in audacity and timing proved to be the single most decisive factor in catapulting Turkey into the war.

A Tale of Two Cruisers

IT HAPPENED THAT as early as 1912 the balance of naval strength among the eastern Mediterranean nations began shifting pronouncedly in favor of the Greeks. Reacting to this imbalance, the Young Turk regime that year commissioned a group of British and French shipyards to supply the Ottoman navy with no less than six destroyers, two submarines, and two battleships of the new dreadnought class. The order for the battleships, to be named the *Sultan Osman* and the *Reshadiye*, was placed with the British firm of Armstrong's-on-the-Tyne. The vessels were due for completion by the beginning of August 1914. Then, literally at the last moment, on August 3, Britain's first lord of the admiralty, Winston Churchill, announced the requisitioning of the two ships for the Royal Navy—"in the interests of national security." Whitehall had decided against strengthening Turkish sea power at a moment when German influence at the Porte was at its apogee. However understandable, Churchill's announcement sent shock waves throughout all corners of the Ottoman Empire. To finance the construction of the dreadnoughts, the Turkish government had resorted to popular subscription, including house-to-house solicitations, lotteries, and fairs. Turkish women had actually sold their hair for the "battleship fund." Ottoman prestige as well as Ottoman naval parity was riding on the two ships. Now, after Churchill's announcement, Talaat recalled that "we could hardly believe that England would fulfill her assurance" of respect for Turkish integrity. "Never, never shall I forget my mental anguish when I heard this frightful news," wrote Djemal Pasha, minister of marine.

Never, too, did German diplomacy react to a crisis with more imagination or to better national advantage. At the very moment the British canceled the sale, two German cruisers, the *Goeben* and the *Breslau,* were churning through the waters off the southwestern Sicilian coast. Both ships had been refueling in Haifa on the day of the Sarajevo assassination, and had promptly sailed off at full speed to assume action stations in the western Mediterranean. Their mission now was to evade the powerful British task force bearing down on them toward the Strait of Messina, and at all costs to reach the open sea. Fatefully, on the morning of August 4, the two cruisers picked up a radio message from naval headquarters announcing the Turco-German alliance and instructing the ships to proceed immediately to the Dardanelles, and from there to Constantinople. It was a daring gamble. By international agreement the Turks were obliged to keep the Straits closed to the warships of all nations except their own, and there was accordingly a strong likelihood that the Porte would turn the cruisers back. Admiral Souchon, commanding the two vessels, was perfectly aware of this likelihood. He accepted the radio message at face value, however, and prepared to carry out his orders.

Souchon, described by one American diplomat as a "droop-jawed, determined little man in a long, ill-fitting frock coat, looking more like a parson than an admiral," was also an experienced Mediterranean sailor who knew every tiny cove and inlet of the eastern sea as did few of his contemporaries. His first task was to outspeed his British pursuers and reach the port of Messina for refueling. The admiral's crews responded heroically to the challenge, grimly shoveling coal into the cruisers' furnaces until the ships boiled through the water, leaving the British flotilla well astern. On the afternoon of August 5, the *Goeben* and the *Breslau* reached Messina, apparently out of danger. But there Souchon had an unpleasant surprise awaiting him. The Italian government, ostensibly an ally of the Central Powers, refused to supply fuel—in fact, refused to allow the Germans port hospitality for more than twenty-four hours. Yet the little admiral was nothing if not resourceful. He ordered his crews to requisition coal from the several German passenger liners docked nearby. Thus, racing the clock, officers and sailors sweated frantically side by side, loading the fuel by hand. The task was completed by late afternoon of August 5, and the cruisers steamed out of the harbor within twenty minutes of their deadline.

Souchon's troubles were not over. Once in international waters, his warships were trailed by the British cruiser *Gloucester,* on reconnaissance for the larger squadron. There was no urgency in the chase this time. Admiral Milne, commander of the British Mediterranean Fleet, was certain that the Germans would bear north toward the Adriatic, and the internal protection of the Habsburg coast (Austria was not yet at war with Britain). In any event, it was unthinkable that the cruisers would head eastward and attempt entrance into the Dardanelles, closed to warships since 1841. Souchon disguised the flight effectively, maneuvering north by northwest as if his destination were the Strait of Otranto, then speeding due east at nightfall. But in the morning light of August 7 the *Gloucester* was still hanging on like a leech. Souchon ordered his men to double their efforts. By afternoon the stoker holds were an inferno; four sailors were scalded to death. Finally, after a brief parting exchange of gunfire (witnessed by Morgenthau's daughter on the Italian liner), the two cruisers succeeded in pulling out of the English ship's range.

Milne was by now fully alerted to the Germans' eastward course, but assumed that their destination would be the Greek archipelago. He decided against continuing the chase. Vienna was hourly expected to declare war on Britain, and Milne's fleet would be needed in the central Mediterranean against the more substantial Habsburg navy. The assumption was premature. On August 9 a radiogram from the admiralty canceled earlier reports of Austria's intervention. The chase was therefore immediately resumed; the British flotilla began sweeping along the Aegean coastline in dogged search for the vanished cruisers. It was wasted effort. Milne had already lost a crucial twenty-four hours. The *Goeben* and the *Breslau* were even then threading their way among the Greek islands, and by midafternoon of the 10th had finally reached the mouth of the Dardanelles, where they temporarily dropped anchor. Here also, however, the respite was a brief one. Within two hours the sound of British radio transmissions began to grow louder on the German receivers. For Souchon, everything now depended upon the willingness of the Turks to grant his cruisers entry. And this, in turn, depended upon the diplomatic skill of Wangenheim.

The burly, crew-cut ambassador, an arrogant and fanatical apostle of Pan-Germanism, was then in his mid-fifties, in the full maturity of his physical and intellectual powers, and richly endowed with twenty-five years of experience in the diplomatic corps. He knew every trick in his trade, not excluding the appropriate moment to play the bully. Two days earlier he had radioed Berlin, shrewdly suggesting that the *Goeben* and the *Breslau* be "sold" to the Turks in exchange for the dreadnoughts confiscated by the British. The Wilhelmstrasse had approved. So had Enver and Djemal when the suggestion was made to them the next day. But now, in the late afternoon of the 10th, with a British flotilla perhaps less than an hour away, the Ottoman government had to be persuaded to carry out the sham agreement in the face of possible Allied retaliation. It was a measure of Wangenheim's skill and forcefulness that he talked the Young Turk Cabinet into accepting that risk. At 5:17 p.m. on August 10, two Ottoman torpedo boats sped out of the Dardanelles and signaled the *Goeben* and the *Breslau* to follow. Thirty-five minutes later, when the British cruiser *Weymouth* hove into view, the waters were empty. A

blank charge fired from a Turkish fort warned the English vessel off. Early the next morning the German warships, now bearing the names *Yavuz Sultan Selim* and *Midilli,* dropped anchor
in the Golden Horn. Their arrival was a diplomatic bombshell.
Immediately the Allied governments dispatched an infuriated protest to Constantinople. The Sublime Porte calmly
brazened it out, insisting that the ships were Ottoman.
Indeed their crews dutifully wore fezzes now, and once in
this guise even serenaded the Russian ambassador from
beneath his villa on the Bosphorus to the strains of *Deutschland über Alles.* It was not a laughing matter to the Allies,
and all the less so as Djemal shortly thereafter appointed
Admiral Souchon commander in chief of the Ottoman fleet.
Neither was it a laughing matter to the Turks, as the huge
eleven-inch guns of the *Goeben* were now casually trained
on their capital.

The Decision to Intervene

THE ARRIVAL OF THE CRUISERS emphasized Germany's
mounting interventionist pressure on the Young Turk Cabinet. Wangenheim managed to bring Constantinople's most
influential newspapers under German control by the simple
expedient of purchasing them. Thereafter the press widely
exaggerated the victories of the Central Powers. Germany
was presented as Turkey's friend, and the kaiser suddenly
became "Hadji Wilhelm," the worshipful protector of Islam.
The newspaper campaign became particularly intense in
the late summer of 1914, for by then Berlin urgently coveted
access to Ottoman military resources. "English fleet is at
Pola," the kaiser personally cabled Wangenheim on August
15. "As soon as mines are laid, Dardanelles cannot be penetrated by any military or naval force in the Mediterranean.
Turkey must strike. His Majesty the Sultan must summon
Mussulmans in Asia, India, Egypt, and Africa to holy war
for Caliphate." Talaat recalled that the German and Austrian

ambassadors visited the Porte at least once daily, insisting
upon immediate Ottoman intervention at the side of the
Central Powers. "Every day we were pressed to answer such
questions as these: 'When will you join us? When will you
show your good will by fulfilling the terms of your agreement?'" The response of the Young Turk ministers was
equally unvarying: everything depended upon the attitude
of Bulgaria, they insisted; and they reminded the ambassadors that the Balkan Wars had left Constantinople
defenseless before a serious Bulgarian attack. Perhaps
fortunately for the Turks, German pressure on Bulgaria
evoked no immediate response one way or the other.

Although Wangenheim carried out his orders to the
letter, he entertained mixed emotions about the interventionist effort. The German diplomat knew his Turks well,
and was convinced that their principal value lay in benevolent neutrality, a stance which pinned down several Russian
army corps on the Asia Minor front. Conversely, an Ottoman
declaration of war might well provoke a disastrous Russian
counterstroke in Armenia. This view was shared by General
Joseph Pomiankowski, the Austrian military attaché in
Constantinople, who was fearful that premature Turkish intervention might induce Italy to attack the Dual Monarchy. It
was shared, too, by Liman von Sanders and his officers. To
their experienced eyes, the Ottoman armed forces were
woefully unprepared for modern warfare (see Chapter II),
and the effort to strengthen Turkish defenses appeared
largely wasted. For example, the transfer of German military
personnel and equipment to Turkey during the summer
of 1914 involved an almost hopeless struggle against time
and diplomatic obstacles. The one feasible transportation route
between Europe and Constantinople was through neutral
Rumania; and notwithstanding the fact that the Ottoman
Empire was ostensibly a nonbelligerent, Rumanian Prime
Minister Ion Bratianu sealed his country's frontier against all
military shipments. The Germans feverishly tried every expedient, not excluding massive bribe offers to the generally recep-

tive Rumanian Cabinet ministers. This time their efforts were unsuccessful. Not more than eight freight cars of military goods a day were permitted transit. As late as the final week in October, approximately two hundred freight cars packed with vital howitzers, mines, and ammunition stood idle on German and Hungarian railway sidings, unable to proceed to Constantinople. The Ottoman defense forces continued to be severely underequipped, and the risks of their military intervention at the side of Germany appeared all but suicidal.

Surely if the decision had been made by the common citizens of the empire, the Ottoman government would never have so much as contemplated entering the war. Forty thousand casualties had been suffered in the Balkan fighting only a year and a half before. To the long-suffering Turkish peasantry, the merest suggestion of yet additional taxes and confiscations was profoundly unnerving. The arrogance, too, of the German officers and technicians who flocked to Constantinople in rising numbers was galling even to the most fervent partisans of Young Turk nationalism. Morgenthau recalled that many of Liman's staff drove through the streets in huge automobiles, packed the best restaurants at night, and behaved altogether as if they were the masters of the city. Establishing an exclusive "yachting club" on Prinkipo Island, the Germans blackballed even the highest members of the Ottoman Cabinet. By the autumn of 1914, the Turks were speaking anxiously of the "German Egyptianization of Turkey." It was a legitimate fear. The German naval attaché in Constantinople, Lieutenant Hans Humann, had spent much of his life in Asia Minor and spoke perfect Turkish. Humann's influence, even more than Wangenheim's, proved critical in the summer of 1914, for he was Enver's closest friend, and had access to the war minister night and day. So, too, did the Pan-Germanist Paul Weitz, for thirty years a correspondent in Turkey of the *Frankfurter Zeitung,* and now an unofficial member of the German embassy staff. They knew their man. Whatever the instincts of the Turkish people, Enver himself had long since been disposed in Germany's favor.

He was the stormy petrel of the Young Turk group. The son of an impoverished Turkish clerk and an Albanian mother who had dressed corpses to help feed her family, Enver had fought his way up the professional and social ladder by sheer force of brainpower, stamina, and opportunism. As a young officer in the Ottoman army, he had led the CUP uprising in Constantinople in 1908, then hounded Sultan Abdul Hamid into exile the following year. It was typical of Enver that, on the way up, he calculatingly married an imperial princess and afterward made his residence in a royal palace. The man was not without courage. He had fought well in both the Tripolitanian and the Balkan wars, then had returned to Constantinople to purge the army from top to bottom, replacing "unreliables" with his own followers. In 1914, at the age of thirty-four, Enver was unquestionably the most powerful figure in Turkey. He played the role. Short, dainty-featured, financially corrupt, and inordinately vain, he thrust his ambition before him like a ship's prow. Wangenheim and his colleagues knew Enver's susceptibilities thoroughly and exploited them to the limit. The members of the embassy staff were aware, for example, that Enver's personal sympathies had lain with Germany ever since his earlier two-year stint in Berlin as the Ottoman military attaché. They sensed his awe before the efficiency of the German army, his deep personal admiration for Wilhelm II—indeed, Enver's waxed mustache was a precise imitation of the kaiser's. Wangenheim, Humann, Weitz, and others flattered the war minister incessantly, therefore, conjuring up for him the visions of imperial vengeance and aggrandizement implicit in a German-Ottoman partnership.

The effort was rewarded on September 27. A Turkish torpedo boat passing through the Dardanelles that day en route to the Aegean was stopped and searched by British warships. Discovering German sailors on board, the British quite legally ordered the vessel back into the Straits. At this point, General Weber, a German officer in command of the Dardanelles fortifications, arbitrarily ordered the Straits closed to all

27

maritime commerce. Whereupon the nets and mines were promptly lowered, and the beacons in the lighthouses extinguished. The closure was a patent violation of international law. Nevertheless, when Enver learned of it by telegram an hour later, he concurred on the spot. Djemal and Talaat decided not to protest their colleague's decision, although their acquiescence was somewhat tentative and not uninfluenced by the shadow of the *Goeben*'s guns. In succeeding weeks the Bosphorus began to resemble a harbor in quarantine. Hundreds of Russian ships arrived with grain and lumber for the Allies in the West, only to discover that they could proceed no further. "The waters were a cluster of masts and smoke stacks," Morgenthau wrote, "and the crowded vessels became so dense that a motor boat had difficulty picking its way through the tangled forest. . . . In a few weeks the Bosphorus and adjoining waters had become a desolate waste." The Russian Empire was now effectively cut off from its European partners, the source of its munitions and the market for its agricultural surpluses. It is not unlikely that this fateful move by itself probably would have compelled the Allies to declare war on the Porte.

The Ottoman Cabinet was of course aware that it had irretrievably compromised itself. Somewhat hysterically now, Enver appealed to the Germans for additional funds and war matériel. On orders from Berlin, however, Wangenheim demanded that the Turks first commit themselves to entering the war. Indeed, from the Ottoman point of view, there appeared to be little sensible reason for procrastinating any longer: the die had been cast with the closure of the Straits. On October 11, therefore, the German ambassador was able to radio his government that Enver, Talaat, and Djemal had agreed to announce their nation's belligerency the moment two million Turkish pounds in ingot were forthcoming from Germany. Within hours, a telegraphed reply arrived from Foreign Minister von Jägow, promising immediate dispatch of the money. The gold shipment duly reached Constantinople on October 21. The following day, Enver submitted his master war plan to Liman von Sanders, who transmitted it to German imperial headquarters. It was a blueprint for a surprise Ottoman naval attack on the Russian Black Sea Fleet. Orders for this operation had in fact already been drawn up in Constantinople for delivery to Souchon. Additionally, "defensive" land operations would be carried out in Transcaucasia, while an Ottoman expeditionary force would advance against Egypt. The plan did not lack for audacity. On October 24, Falkenhayn and his staff fully endorsed it. The next day, with the complete approval of Djemal and Talaat, Enver instructed Souchon to proceed with the naval offensive against the Russians.

Thirty-six hours later, the *Goeben* and the *Breslau* duly led a mixed force of Ottoman cruisers and destroyers through the Bosphorus and into the Black Sea. Maintaining radio silence, the armada cruised unheard and unseen for the next two days toward the Russian coast. In the early morning hours of October 29, the *Goeben* suddenly materialized out of the fog off the naval base of Sevastopol. During the ensuing twenty-two minutes the cruiser's huge guns severely battered the harbor's fortifications. A few hours later, the *Goeben* sank the Russian mine layer *Pruth* with 250 men aboard. Simultaneously the *Breslau* and the Ottoman cruiser *Berk* bombarded the port of Novorossisk. By the end of the day, twenty-one Russian vessels had been destroyed, the fifty-five oil tanks and many grain warehouses sent up in flames. Souchon's fleet then returned safely to Constantinople.

News of this raid aroused consternation and dread among the Young Turk Cabinet. Except for the "triumvirate," none of its members had been informed in advance. Grand Vizier Saïd Halim, an Egyptian prince who had only recently assumed his post, furiously rebuked Enver and demanded an immediate cessation of hostilities. The war minister acquiesced to this demand without protest, and even dispatched the necessary orders to Souchon. At the same time, however, according to prearrangement, Enver informed the German admiral privately that the order might be disregarded. Turkish destroyers continued to shell Russian freighters in the Black

Sea. An emergency Cabinet meeting was immediately convened in the home of the grand vizier on October 30, and four
ministers, including Saïd Halim himself, announced their
resignations. Here Enver shrewdly riposted by calling the entire executive committee of the Committee of Union and Progress into session. With full support from Talaat and Djemal,
the little war minister eloquently defended Souchon's raid as a
"necessary" preventive measure; the Russians had intended
to mine the Bosphorus, he insisted. After several hours of debate, the assembled political leaders were finally won over,
and they in turn persuaded the grand vizier and his colleagues
to withdraw their resignations. For his part, Enver agreed to
dispatch a conciliatory note to St. Petersburg. He was perfectly aware that the gesture would be meaningless.

The plain fact was that the inner circle of the CUP was
hardly interested any longer in maintaining a pretense of
neutrality. "If we had insisted upon keeping our neutrality
until the end of the war," Talaat wrote, "refusing aid to our
allies in the time of their necessity, Germany and Austria also
would reasonably refuse to help us in case they were victorious." That was the heart of the matter. The opportunity,
with powerful allies, to redress the consequences of earlier
tsarist depredations was too appealing to be spurned. Late in
the afternoon of the 30th, the Russian ambassador, Count
Giers, icily demanded the immediate dismissal of all German
officers in the Ottoman military and naval services. He was
rebuffed on the spot. Giers thereupon demanded his passport.
London and Paris severed diplomatic relations with Constantinople the same day.

So ended, ingloriously, the widely heralded Young Turk
experiment of 1908, the determined effort of a handful of
courageous reformers to salvage a moribund empire from its
final political and territorial demise. In Western eyes, of course,
the Ottoman government had long since become the incarnation of corruption and despotism. Yet throughout all the preceding decades of ineptitude and reaction, the Sublime Porte
had at least managed to avoid the disaster of simultaneous

conflict with the tsarist land monolith to the north and the great maritime powers to the west. On November 4, 1914, the Committee on Union and Progress chose to walk into that classic trap, and the vise closed irretrievably on the Sublime Porte. This time there would be no recovery for the Sick Man.

CHAPTER II

THE STAGE OF BATTLE

The Germans Win an Ally

Berlin's coup in maneuvering the Ottoman Empire into the war unquestionably was a stupendous one. It was only later, when hostilities in Asia were well begun, that the German general staff began to wonder what it had actually acquired for its efforts. The Turks were exhausted after six years of almost uninterrupted fighting. In the Balkan campaigns of 1912 and 1913, some 40,000 troops had been lost in the hell of Macedonia and Thrace. The most optimistic estimate of the empire's population in 1914 was 25,000,000. Of these, the Turks themselves, comprising less than 10,000,000, remained the only dependable source of military recruits. Even this supply was becoming increasingly uncertain by 1914, for the urban classes often managed to buy their way out of army service, and the peasantry was impoverished, illiterate, and mechanically inept. Many of the soldiers did not own shoes. Dysentery and venereal disease were rampant among them. "Usually sick officers were the only persons whose temperatures were taken [in clinics]," wrote Liman von Sanders. "For the ordinary soldier it was not considered worthwhile." Moreover, the officers' lot was little better. Their wages were inadequate to purchase decent uniforms, and their wives not infrequently resorted to menial work. It was the wry opinion of German Major Kubel, a member of Liman's staff, that "the humble Turkish soldier should be able to live without eating."

Ottoman military equipment was in no way superior to the physical condition of the army. As late as September 1915, the cannon in most of the fortresses were ancient and slow-loading. Fully half of the artillery ammunition was defective. The railway network over which these questionable troops and supplies were to travel was far from complete. In August 1914, for example, no rail link existed between Anatolia and Syria or between Anatolia and central Mesopotamia. The vital tunnel through the Taurus mountain range was not finished until the end of September 1917. The roads generally were inadequate for motor vehicles. Girdled by an extensive coastline, the empire had managed to sustain itself in peacetime primarily by water transport. But with the outbreak of war, the Allies fastened a relentless blockade around the Ottoman littoral, and the Aegean and Mediterranean seas were entirely closed. In fact, until Bulgaria entered the war months later and opened the Balkan land route, no direct means of transportation existed between Constantinople and the Central Powers. This isolation worked a grave hardship on the Turks, for they were almost completely dependent upon Germany and Austria for coal and munitions. Even in the Black Sea, transporation was severely restricted: the entire Ottoman maritime fleet totaled only fifty thousand tons, and the imperial navy consisted of less than a dozen cruisers and destroyers—barely a third the size of the Russian fleet. As a result, the *Goeben* and the *Breslau* abandoned the initial effort to dominate the great inland waterway alone, and instead remained close to the Straits in an effort to block Allied penetration there. Under these circumstances of pitiful physical inadequacy, Germany military officials could not resist the temptation to describe their Ottoman ally contemptuously as *Das Sorgenkind*—"the problem child"—and to discount his combat value in advance.

With grim perseverance, nevertheless, a host of German engineers, economists, and financial agents set about overhauling Ottoman production and communications facilities, reorganizing the Turkish banking system, supervising irrigation and antilocust projects, building munitions factories, and, not least of all, training and modernizing the Ottoman army. In fact, if not in name, the Germans assumed full control of the Turkish armed forces. Exercising their authority just below

33

the command level, approximately a hundred German officers simply became chiefs of staff of corps and divisions, while others directed the noncombatant services, the engineering, radio, and various other technical branches. There were occasions, too, when influence was exerted on the primary level. Liman von Sanders, for example, resumed command of the Ottoman First Army. General Fritz Bronsart von Schellendorf became chief of staff of the Ottoman army, answerable to Enver alone. The Pasha formations, the elite of the Ottoman infantry, were under the personal command of Freiherr Kress von Kressenstein—who doubled as chief of Ottoman Intelligence—and were salted with Germans of all ranks. A Prussian officer, Major Serno, organized and commanded the Turkish air force. A submarine school was established and directed by Germans on the island of Prinkipo, in the Sea of Marmora. By the beginning of 1915 no less than 25,000 German officers and NCO's were assigned to the Ottoman defense effort, representing a fifth of the entire Turkish officer corps. To be sure, matters of highest military policy were almost invariably decided by Enver and his Turkish colleagues; the Ottoman armed forces never became a mere instrument of German policy. Even Liman von Sanders's advisory relationship with the Porte became increasingly acrimonious as the war continued. But on the tactical and technical level German influence was always paramount—evoking Philip Guedalla's memorable epigram "Deutschland über Allah."

At the outbreak of the war, the Ottoman ground forces consisted of thirty-eight divisions scattered somewhat haphazardly throughout the empire. Of the three major Turkish armies, the largest had been returned to the command of Liman von Sanders. This was the First Army, concentrated in European Turkey for the defense of the capital and the Straits, and totaling 250,000 men. The Second Army, half the size of Liman's, was based on the Asian shore of the Sea of Marmora. The Third Army, numbering 150,000 troops, was stationed in the Transcaucasus, along the Russian border. Yet another 100,000 men were distributed in four army corps located at Damascus, Mosul, and Baghdad, and in the Hejaz. Shortly after the beginning of hostilities, a Fourth Army was organized in the Syrian vilayets (provinces) under the personal command of Djemal Pasha, minister of marine. And there it was: slightly more than 600,000 undernourished, tatterdemalion troops, by no stretch of the imagination the military machine of a first-class power. Yet this unimpressive soldiery at least provided the base of an exhaustive recruitment effort which swelled the Turkish armed forces to 730,000 by the opening days of 1915, and to nearly a million by the end of that year. Ill equipped and ill trained as it was, the army full-blown represented a force well beyond the supportive capacity of the nation's economy. It demonstrated Enver's pathetic eagerness to meet the demands of the German high command and pull his country's weight in the war. At one point, indeed, late in 1916, Enver actually had assigned no less than 100,000 Turkish soldiers to share the military burden on other fronts—three divisions in Rumania, two divisions in Galicia, and another two in Macedonia.

To be sure, under the influence of Liman von Sanders, Enver conceived Turkey's essential role as defensive—that of blocking communications between Russia and her Western allies. But this task was not without formidable difficulties. Three of the principal routes connecting Europe with the Middle East ran through Ottoman-dominated territory. These were the maritime artery through the Mediterranean Sea and the Turkish straits; the still uncompleted Berlin-to-Baghdad Railway, parallel to the Tigris-Euphrates paddle-steamer lines; and the complex of Pan-Turanian routes to Constantinople via the Caucasus, including the upland mountain gaps through Persia (Erzerum-Trebizond), Armenia (Erzerum-Cilicia), and Kurdistan (Erzerum-Mosul). Enver and his German colleagues viewed it as the function of the Ottoman armed forces to deny these great communications lines to the Entente at all costs, to protect them until they might ultimately serve as offensive highways for a concerted Turco-German drive against the Allied empires.

35

Precisely in anticiptation of the latter danger, the British decided to make the first move against Ottoman positions. The step was taken with some misgivings, for the Allied high command was convinced that the war eventually would have to be resolved in Europe. Indeed, the French were not represented in the Middle East at all. The Russian general staff, disdainful of Ottoman offensive capabilities, was satisfied to leave a mere eight divisions along the entire Transcaucasian frontier. Even the British at first stationed the rather limited force of 150,000 colonial troops in Egypt, and these to serve chiefly as a revolving training corps for the European front. Yet, despite this lack of emphasis on the Middle East, it was not possible for London to ignore the area altogether. The refineries of the Anglo-Persian Petroleum Company were located in Abadan, an Ottoman-owned island in the Persian Gulf, and the fuel produced by this huge complex of vats and cracking towers was indispensable to the British navy. As early as September 1914, in fact, the India Office had recommended that both Abadan and the Mesopotamian port of Basra be acquired as a defensive buffer against any Turkish threat to the oil installations. Such a move would similarly reinforce the loyalties of the numerous Arab sheikdoms in the Persian Gulf area. Although nominally Ottoman, most of these tiny principalities had belonged to the British sphere of influence for several decades; it would be useful to ensure that they remained so. Because the suggestion did not project a major deployment of troops, it was accepted by the imperial general staff and the British Cabinet. Accordingly the Sixth Indian Division, under the command of Lieutenant General A. A. Barrett, was shipped out forthwith from Poonah to the Gulf area.

The decision to launch this expedition actually was taken in mid-October 1914, more than a fortnight before Turkey's official entry into the war. Yet, in the remote and twilight world of the Persian Gulf, the movement of Indian troops along the periphery of a recognized sphere of British influence would not necessarily have been regarded as an act of war. At any event, the Shatt-el-Arab peninsula—the junc-

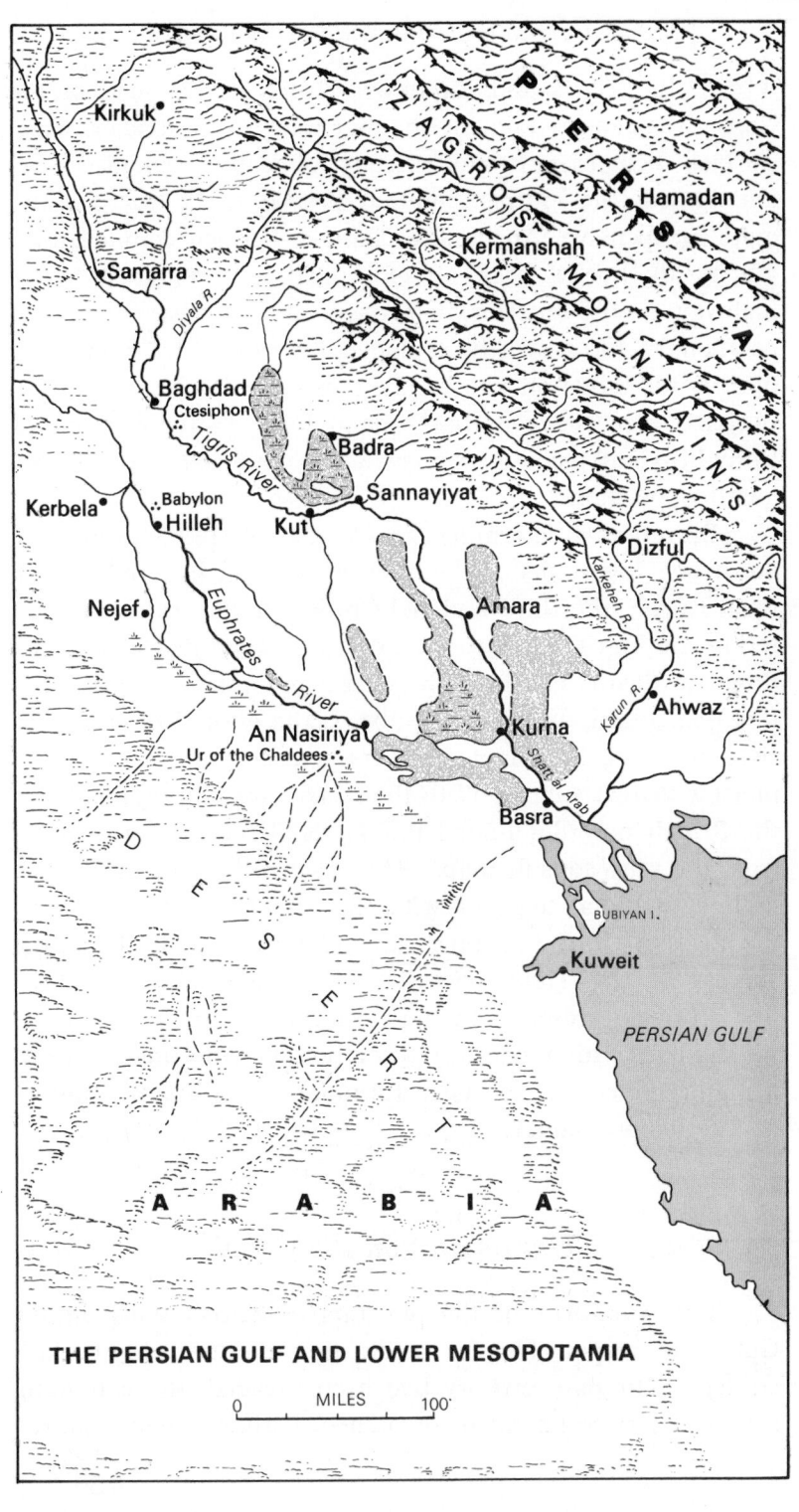

THE PERSIAN GULF AND LOWER MESOPOTAMIA

MILES
0 ———————— 100'

ture of the Tigris and Euphrates rivers at the head of the Gulf—was captured during the first week in November, when Turkish belligerency was already officially recognized. As anticipated, the entire operation proved to be routine and quite inexpensive. An ineptly planned Turkish counterattack was easily hurled back on November 15. With the water highway to the interior now open, the modest Indian expeditionary force swiftly exploited its victory by embarking upriver for Basra on two paddle steamers. On November 23, Barrett's men reached that squalid little Arab town, effortlessly brushing aside the somewhat demoralized Turkish rearguard opposition.

Barrett was determined to enlarge this bridgehead without delay. Remnants of the Turkish division had fallen back upon Kurna, the third and right prong of the water fork entering the Tigris; from there they still constituted a potential threat to Basra. The English general promptly bore down on this rear guard, and on December 9 the entire Ottoman garrison of 1,200 men laid down its arms. It was a not insignificant British victory. With their maritime communications, the British now dominated the Tigris River fully 120 miles from the sea (consult map). The eastern flank of the British lifeline to India, together with the immense oil reserves of the Persian Gulf, was now safe. Moreover, with the initial success of the Tigris operation, England had attained its first strategic presence on the actual soil of middle Asia. As we shall see, this modest land foothold was destined to exert a major impact on the later formulation of British military and diplomatic policy.

The Assault on the Canal

THE AUDACITY of the pre-emptive British move in the Gulf was responsible for a drastic alteration in Turkish strategy. Ottoman territory had been invaded, the communications artery to Baghdad threatened. Perhaps, then, counter-pressure could be applied in an area of British vulnerability. The Turkish and German governments had convinced themselves that the British Empire's innumerable millions of Islamic subjects in Egypt and India were seething with unrest and ripe for insurrection. It was a myth, but one which foreign-ministry "experts" in Constantinople and Berlin chose to believe. Thus, on November 23, 1914, with great solemnity, the sultan-caliph issued an appeal for Moslems everywhere to rise up in jihad against their Entente overlords. The Sheikh-ul-Islam, "spiritual" deputy to the caliph, endorsed this plea in terms that were sadistic and even pornographic. The appeal for holy war did not set Moslems to dancing in the streets, as it happened; the Turks had long since compromised themselves by taking the infidel Central Powers as their partners. Nevertheless, the CUP cabinet and the Wilhelmstrasse persisted. Harry Stuermer, a German journalist assigned to Constantinople in the early years of the war, described the spell of the jihad illusion over otherwise sober German officers and career officials:

> First one [German] would appear on the scene who announced himself as the one man to cope with Afghanistan, then another would come along on his way to Persia and play the great man "on a special mission" for a time in Pera while money belonging to the German Empire would find its way into all sorts of low haunts. It is unbelievable what a mob of low characters frequent the German Embassy now. The scum of the earth, people who would never have dared before the war to have been seen on the pavements of Ayas-Pasha [German Embassy Street], have now free entry. . . . There [one such petitioner] gives wonderful assurances of what he can do, and promises to stir up some Mohammedan people for the "jihad."

It was the notion in Berlin that Egypt was particularly susceptible to an explosive mass uprising, for in Egypt the precedents of the Arabi and Mahdist revolts already existed. Kaiser Wilhelm, flamboyant as always in his geopolitical visions, was unshakably convinced that a surprise offensive against Suez would touch off enough unrest to disrupt British communications throughout the entire Middle East. This view was supported with some pertinacity by Lieutenant Colonel von Kressenstein, the Intelligence chief, and by the former Egyptian khedive, Abbas Hilmi II, a refugee in Constantinople since he had been deposed by the British. It was even conceivable that the Senussi tribesmen, sullen and restive along the upper Nile, would lend their support to a jihad. But whether or not the revolt gained momentum, the German high command favored any offensive capable of paralyzing the Canal even temporarily, thereby undermining the Allied war effort in Europe—their major concern.

The possibility of such a Turkish move had occasionally been considered by the British general staff, but hardly seriously. After all, the Allied navies dominated both the Mediterranean and the Red seas. At least four naval vessels equipped with guns of unchallengeable power and range were regularly passing through the Canal. By December 1915, Lieutenant General Sir John Maxwell, military commander in Egypt, had at his disposal 150,000 British imperial troops, most of them in training for Europe, but certainly available for the defense of Suez. In addition, 35,000 British soldiers were permanently deployed along the vital eighty-five-mile waterway. The ultimate barrier against invasion, however, was the presumably waterless, trackless Sinai Desert. It was axiomatic to old Egyptian hands like Maxwell that the Sinai was a natural death trap and that defensive measures east of the Canal were superfluous. Accordingly, reconnaissance of the desert was left to a couple of seaplanes and occasional camel patrols.

The opportunity for surprise was the single, critical factor which persuaded the Ottoman general staff that the risk of invasion was worth taking. Djemal Pasha, commanding the Fourth Army from his headquarters in Aleppo, was placed in complete charge of the expedition, as befitted his dignity and station. Although the detailed planning of the campaign was the work of Germans—of Djemal's chief of staff, Colonel von Frankenberg, and of Kressenstein, temporarily assigned as chief of staff of the Eighth Corps—it was uniquely Djemal who supplied his army with its discipline and *élan*. The man's personal dynamism and sense of mission were instantly communicated to the most disparate units in his Suez army—even to companies of Druses, Kurds, Circassians, and Bulgarian Moslems. Moreover, with his shrewdly calculating mind, Djemal never really questioned his essentially inspirational role, and he fulfilled it brilliantly. Thus, upon reaching his headquarters in Aleppo and finding that Kressenstein and Frankenberg had already drawn up the plans of the expedition, Djemal characteristically accepted the arrangements without demurrer.

The scheme was for an initial division, some twelve thousand men, to cross the desert first and to force the Canal passage by surprise. If the crossing succeeded, a second division would follow to consolidate the bridgehead on the Canal's western bank. It was not the intention of the Ottoman general staff actually to conquer and hold the Suez. The Turkish and German planners cherished the hope, at most, of igniting a revolt; at the least, of destroying a section of the Canal, possibly by sinking a few vessels there and immobilizing shipping for several crucial weeks. Actually, the most serious challenge was not that of getting over the Canal, but of crossing the blazing, uncharted Sinai wilderness. Kressenstein and Frankenberg had made their preparations well, however, devising plans for the sinking of artesian wells in the desert and the construction of cisterns along an inland bedouin route where patrols had reported the existence of water. It was the rainy season. The water levels were expected to be high. They were. The Twenty-fifth Division marched out of Beersheba on January 14, 1915, crossed over into Sinai and found springs within yards of where they were supposed to be. Detailed advance planning had calculated the rationing exactly. All guns and pontoons were dragged undamaged through the sea of dunes and scrub. The Fourth Army's achievement was unquestionably a remarkable one. Djemal picked the night of February 2 for his crossing.

By then Generals Maxwell and Wilson realized that detachments of Turkish soldiers were in Sinai. Allied seaplanes, sputtering over the desert on eighty-horsepower engines, had detected caravans of men and camels. British gunboats immediately took up positions in the Canal; several detachments of Australian and English yeomanry were hurried to the eastern side of the waterway. As the Ottoman column approached the east bank of the Suez on the evening of February 2, a dust storm unexpectedly whirled out of the desert. The Indian sentries, faces wrapped in stockings, peered unavailingly into the murk. This was Djemal's chance. He launched his main attack south of Lake Timsah, intending to cut the railway from Ismailia to Suez. By morning the Turks had constructed a bridge of pontoons and ferried six hundred men across the Canal, where they dug in along the west bank. But just at that moment, ironically, the sandstorm died out as suddenly as it had begun. The Ottoman advance units were clearly visible now against the silver sheen of the sand. Without further reinforcements, their position soon became untenable. By midmorning of February 3, British gunboats on the waterway had converged on the Turkish beachhead and pinned down the rest of the invading party on the east bank opposite Serapeum. Thoroughly unnerved by this reverse, Kressenstein ordered his remaining companies to launch frontal assaults at El Kantara and Chalouf, near Suez. The diversions were without effect; the exploding shells of the British gunboats soon tore through the ranks of the attackers. After enduring two hours of this bombardment, unable to press their offensive further, the shattered Ottoman troops withdrew to the hills early in the afternoon. Meanwhile, a large party of Punjabi infantry charged the six hundred unfortunate soldiers (most of them Arabs) who had crossed over to the western embankment. The latter surrendered outright. At 4:00 p.m. Djemal ordered a general retreat. Simultaneously the Turkish commander issued a bombastic order of the day, congratulating his troops for having successfully carried out an "offensive reconnaissance against the Canal."

There was an unwitting kernel of truth in the proclamation. For one thing, the retreat was executed at least as skillfully as the original advance. By February 9, the bulk of the expeditionary force had returned to Palestine after suffering 1,300 casualties, including 192 killed and 727 missing. Obviously, no mass uprising occurred among the Egyptians, few of whom were aware of the attack until long after it had failed; and Canal traffic had been suspended at most for two nights. But in the long run the abortive Sinai expedition distinctly served Turkey's advantage. From the purely logistical standpoint, the "offensive reconnaissance" enabled Djemal, Frankenberg, and Kressenstein to study the desert's water resources, and thus to anticipate precisely the route of march the British would eventually take against them. More significantly, it enabled the Turks to hold the frontier between Palestine and Sinai with great economy, deploying there only a single brigade of three thousand men.

Perhaps of greatest importance, the expedition threw a fright into the English which distorted their Middle East strategy for the next two years. Aware now that the desert could be traversed, Maxwell was deeply sobered by the prospect of future Turkish invasions. For a while he estimated the numbers of Turks in Palestine as a fantastic 200,000 or even 300,000. On the basis of this wildly exaggerated appraisal, Maxwell persuaded Kitchener, the war secretary, to dispatch a virtually unending stream of troops to the defense of Suez. By the end of the year, fully 250,000 British and colonial soldiers were stationed permanently in Egypt, drained from other, more crucial fronts. For a while, too, their defensive posture was entirely static, for they manned an elaborate system of trenches, bunkers, and barricades along both embankments of the Canal, a complex so elaborate that Kitchener once quipped sarcastically, upon inspecting the defenses in 1915: "Are you defending the Canal, or is the Canal defending you?" The effort to protect the seventy-mile artery was unprecedented in the sheer magnitude of its logistics, involving water supply, metaled roadways in the sand, floating bridges on the Canal

43

itself, railway extensions, and entrenchment and wiring on an enormous scale. Until nearly halfway through the war, the barricaded encampment in Egypt represented a bottomless sinkhole for imperial resources and manpower. As we shall see, exaggerated concern for the defense of Suez warped British diplomacy no less than British strategy. The promises made to Arabs and Jews, the provisions extracted in secret and occasionally acrimonious negotiations with allies, all reflected a Suez-fixation which, in its political consequences, was destined to be significantly more far-reaching than the actual or potential military danger to the Canal itself.

Icy Hell in the Transcaucasus

PREPARATIONS for the Suez venture had begun within days after Turkey's entrance into the war. Yet the first Ottoman military campaign actually antedated the Sinai offensive by several weeks. It developed, in part spontaneously, as an effort to exploit a minor Russian fiasco. The territory was the Transcaucasus, the highland south of the Caucasus mountain range, which extended from the Black Sea to the Caspian. It formed the border region between the tsarist and Ottoman empires, and embraced the homelands not merely of Turks and Russians, but also of a festering ethnic heterogeneity of Georgians, Armenians, Tatars, and Lazes. The terrain was among the most fearsome in the world, a vast, twisted, tortured ganglion of saw-toothed peaks, some of them rising to eleven thousand feet in the Anti-Taurus range of the Armenian plateau. The angulated, barren upland was continually swept by violent gales, the cold so intense that the natives burrowed underground during winter, in inverted igloos, leaving not a sign of life in the limitless, snowbound emptiness except, at rare intervals, smoke from the fires of subterranean villages.

This tangled knot of ridges in the Anti-Taurus chain was broken in only one place, by the volcanic plateau of Kars and Erzerum. Here, therefore, lay the crucial link in the Turkish-

44

Russian frontier, established at Turkish expense after the victorious Russian campaign of 1877–8. By annexing the powerful Ottoman fortress of Kars, the tsarist government hopefully blocked any future counterinvasion of its Transcaucasian territories. The Turks based their defensive hopes on

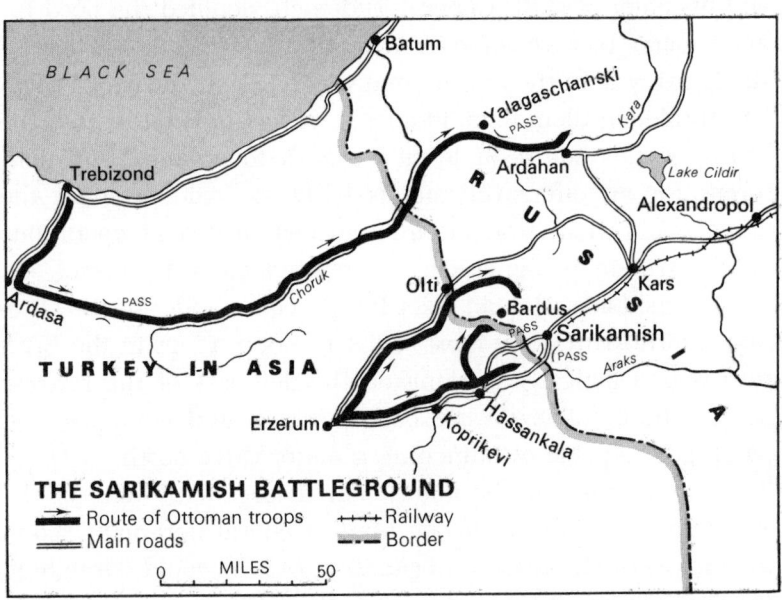

THE SARIKAMISH BATTLEGROUND
→ Route of Ottoman troops ┼┼┼ Railway
═══ Main roads ▬▬ Border
0 MILES 50

Erzerum, an equally imposing fortress (see Chapter IV) only fifty-two miles from Kars. These two citadels accordingly became the pivots upon which the Russian Caucasus Army and the Ottoman Third Army hinged their operations, and the task of outflanking the enemy position inevitably became the central preoccupation of the Russian and Ottoman staffs in the Transcaucasus. If the Turks succeeded, breaking through to Azerbaijan, their armies would be in an enviable position to threaten the industrial heart of the Russian Caucasus, and possibly even the Ukraine beyond. If the Russians succeeded, the next step for them was to open the road to Mesopotamia, forging the link between the British and Russian empires in Asia, and in this manner outflanking the Turkish straits.

But neither side was willing initially to make a serious offensive effort. The tsarist high command entirely shared the conviction of its French counterpart that "all roads pass through Berlin." The total strength of the Russian Army of the Caucasus in October 1914 was about 115,000 men, half of them local conscripts of dubious training. Russian Caucasus headquarters, under the command of General Myshlayevski and his chief of staff, General Yudenich, doubted the need for more than a passive defense. After all, the Turks did not own a single railway in the entire area; the Treaty of Berlin of 1878 had forbidden them to build one. It was assumed, too, that the Turks would require at least a month to organize sufficient forces for an offensive, and as early as mid-November the fiercely cold weather apparently blocked large-scale operations in the Armenian highlands. The assessment was correct. On the Turkish side, Hassan Izzet Pasha, commander of the Ottoman Third Army, kept most of his 120,000 troops in the Erzerum region listlessly working on the defenses of the fortress itself. These soldiers were badly trained and equipped and patently incapable of launching a major drive north.

Actually it was the notoriously disorganized state of the Third Army which persuaded Major General Bergmann, commander of the Russian Kars garrison, that he could "straighten his lines" by occupying a thin stretch of Ottoman territory extending from Alachgert to Kara Killissee (see map). He tried to do so on November 8, and his Thirty-ninth Division was badly mauled by machine gun and artillery fire; Russian casualties totaled seven thousand killed and wounded. The victory was a minor one for the Turks, but it surprised and delighted the Ottoman General Staff and their German advisers. A German officer serving under Major Guse, Izzet Pasha's chief of staff, voiced the awakening speculation that the Third Army might actually possess offensive capabilities: "Until now it was not certain that the Turks actually had the capacity to open a military offensive."

As in the case of the Sinai offensive, moreover, the Ottoman high command pinned its emergent hope upon ties of solidarity between the Turks and pro-Turkish elements in Russian territory. In this case the solidarity was ethnic rather than

46

purely religious, and was based upon the nineteen million Tatars and Turkmenians of central Russia. Most of these Turanian peoples had been conquered by the tsarist armies only during the previous fifty or sixty years. Far from assimilating the traditions and culture of their Russian overlords, they clung tenaciously to their ethnic autonomy and to the common Turanian language (with only minor variations in dialect) they shared with their kinsmen in the Ottoman Empire. Before the war, too, repelled by Pan-Slavist oppression, large numbers of Tatar youths had become deeply imbued with the corresponding ideal of Pan-Turkish solidarity—and not a few of them had migrated to Constantinople, where they became active partisans of the Committee of Union and Progress. In Turkey itself, Pan-Turanianism had been assiduously cultivated for the past decade by a growing number of academies, institutes, and journals. The concept's most influential intellectual exponent was Ziya Gökalp, critic, publicist, and later professor of sociology at the University of Constantinople. A forceful writer, Ziya Bey summarized his vision of Turanian history and culture in the prophetic declaration: "The country of the Turks is not Turkey, it is not Turkestan. It is a vast and eternal region: Turan!" The political version of this dream was initially an awakened Turkish nationalism, indeed a near-xenophobia which threatened the empire's non-Turkish minorities and, in the case of the Armenians, caused their extermination (see Chapter IV). Its military version was an emerging scheme to invade the Transcaucasus, thus inciting revolt among the two million Tatars of the region, and possibly among the entire Turanian population of central Russia. The question was one of timing.

Enver, deeply exhilarated by Izzet Pasha's November victory, was certain that the time to strike was immediately, while the Russians were still licking their wounds. There was evidence to support his view. Several years before the war, a German consul in Tiflis, Count von der Schulenberg (later hanged after the anti-Hitler plot of World War II), had made a detailed study of the terrain of Transcaucasia and had discovered a sizable rift in the plateau which led directly from Erzerum to a small Russian military base, Sarikamish. This base alone blocked the roadway to the mighty fortress of Kars, twenty-eight miles away, and to Ardahan, twenty-six miles away. If it were possible to seize these two key Russian citadels in a rapid surprise thrust, all Georgia would be open before the Ottoman armies, and the tribal khans of the surrounding region hopefully would rise in insurrection. The scheme did not go unchallenged. Liman von Sanders reminded Enver that the weather during the Transcaucasian winter was lethal, that communications were all but nonexistent there, and that the Turks were inadequately supplied with winter clothing. The war minister was unmoved. As he saw it, the Russian high command was counting upon these very uncertainties of weather and communication to preclude military activity in the area; precisely for this reason the opportunity for surprise was greater. Other German staff officers shared this enthusiasm, notably the chief of the Ottoman general staff in Constantinople, General Fritz Bronsart von Schellendorf, who prepared the master plan of the campaign.

Enver decided to assume command of the offensive himself. At the beginning of December 1914, he sailed the Black Sea coastal route from Constantinople to Trebizond, and then continued by road to Ottoman field headquarters in Erzerum. Ironically, even as his troops were gathering in northern Erzerum province, the war minister lost his principal advantage of surprise. Across the hills, General Yudenich's Armenian agents detected the Turkish concentration. Immediately the Russian general began preparing his defenses. One of them, the weather, was ready-made. The six thinly clad Ottoman divisions were inundated by heavy snow from December 23 onward. Half of one division became stragglers en route to Sarikamish. Conversely, Yudenich ensured that his own four brigades were well dug in, well dressed, and well fed.

The town of Sarikamish itself (population 12,000) was reasonably well supplied and served as a major depot on the Kars-Tiflis railway. At its disposal were a fairly good motor road leading back to the interior and a well-sited defensive ridge commanding one of the valleys. On the night of December 24, the local commander, Colonel Bukretov, spotted Turkish campfires on a distant hill. The very next morning, four thousand Ottoman troops threw themselves against the Russian positions and were cut down with heavy losses. Nor were they replaced in time, for Turkish reinforcements arrived only after agonizing delays; they had been compelled to cross ridges ten thousand feet high in a howling blizzard. On December 27 the commander of the under-strength Ottoman division decided in favor of an immediate renewed assault lest even these surviving troops die of exposure. He ordered them forward. The men attacked without hesitation, moving forward into crashing Russian fusillades, groping blindly toward the enemy positions through wild snow flurries. Upper Sarikamish twice changed hands: in the afternoon the Turks established themselves on a bluff overlooking the town; by that evening Russian bayonets had driven them back again. A single last glimmer of hope remained for Enver. On the morning of the 29th, elements of the Ottoman Tenth Corps arrived to reinforce the exhausted men on the line. They launched a new attack at 10:00 p.m., the fresh troops climbing over the bodies of their comrades, pressing into the center of town with nerveless gallantry. The Russians matched their heroism, fighting back in the darkness in hand-to-hand encounters. By dawn of the next day, the surviving Turks were battered into surrender or flight by massive close-range Russian artillery. From then on the offensive passed to the Russians, and by the morning of January 1, 1915, the Turks had been driven out of Sarikamish permanently.

At this point, sensing the desperation of the Turkish position, Yudenich decided to throw in his last reserves from Kars in an effort to surround the entire Ottoman Third Army. The tactic was brilliantly successful. Fully 75,000 of Enver's men were entirely cut off from their communications in the triangle formed by Bardiz, Sarikamish, and the Eskmeydan Pass (see map), and on January 2 Enver himself narrowly escaped capture by a Russian patrol as he retreated toward Erzerum. By January 5, the Russian pincers had closed slowly on the frozen, exhausted remnants of the Ottoman Ninth Corps outside Sarikamish. The Turks fought on until hardly a thousand of them remained to surrender; most of the rest were discovered frozen in upright positions resembling the vegetation of this lunar landscape. Within the week, the Ottoman Tenth Corps was similarly decimated. Of the entire Ottoman Third Army, only 18,000 troops succeeded in making their way back to Erzerum; fully a third of them had limbs amputated in military hospitals. Some 80,000 men of the Third Army had been lost, with most of their artillery. The Russians in turn had lost 16,000 troops killed and wounded; an additional 12,000 had been crippled by frostbite. It was an overwhelming personal victory for Yudenich, who emerged now as one of the ablest commanders of the war.

Enver himself had slunk off from Erzerum to Constantinople as early as January 7, 1915, while the Russian pincers were still closing on his men. Returning to the captial, the war minister blandly concealed the facts of the battle, representing the catastrophe of Sarikamish as nothing more than a local setback to the Third Army. He forbade his officers to speak of the campaign and severely punished those who violated this order. As a result, news of the disaster leaked out to the Turkish people only months later, and even then as unconfirmed rumor. It was the German high command which first learned of Sarikamish. Curiously, Berlin did not take its ally's defeat in bad spirit. During the early winter of 1915, Minister of War von Falkenhayn was too preoccupied with the Western and Balkan theaters to bother with other fronts. It was typical of this general, moreover, that his reaction should not have been one of horror that an entire Ottoman army had been wiped out, but rather of composed satisfaction that the unsuccessful operation had been useful in immobilizing the Russians and in preventing them from sending reinforcements to the Eastern front. The defeat also made Enver somewhat

easier to deal with. For example, when the war minister demanded that troops under Liman von Sanders's personal command be shipped at once via Trebizond to support the shattered
Third Army, the German refused, and successfully faced
Enver down.

Through the perversities of military psychology, however,
the Transcaucasian disaster also afforded the Young Turk
Cabinet a certain degree of leverage against its German ally.
After all, Turkish weakness had been the Porte's major bargaining point throughout the entire nineteenth century. Enver
later was able to remind Berlin of the commitment by which
it had persuaded Turkey to enter the war: a formal promise to
open a direct route between Constantinople and central Europe
across Serbia and Bulgaria. The first Habsburg offensive
against Serbia had in fact collapsed in November and December 1914. The Turks now insisted on a resumption of this
undertaking. They warned that the losses of equipment suffered in the Pan-Turanian offensive had to be recovered, that
the weapons now being smuggled in driblets through neutral
Rumania were insufficient. The kaiser manfully accepted this
reproach. At his orders, pressure was immediately exerted on
Vienna for a second, and ultimately successful, offensive
against the Serbs. The consequence of this renewed drive was
at last to bring Bulgaria into the war and to open the long-
obstructed direct route between Berlin and Constantinople.
Similarly, continuous and urgent Ottoman appeals for financial
assistance had to be honored. Hundreds of millions of German
marks were advanced to Constantinople as reserve for the
Ottoman currency, together with not less than half a billion
marks' worth of direct military supplies. In the ensuing two
and a half years, moreover, the Ottoman government successfully exerted pressure on Berlin to revise in Turkey's favor
the original treaty of alliance between the two countries. By
subsequent agreements, the Germans were precluded from
signing a separate peace; they agreed to recognize the Porte's
demands for abolition of the Capitulations; and, in the event

51

of victory, Germany promised the Turks territorial concessions in Thrace, Macedonia, and Transcaucasia commensurate with Turkish sacrifices.

Yet perhaps the most far-reaching result of these initial Turkish disasters in Sinai and the Transcaucasus was their cumulative effect upon the British. Kitchener and other members of the government were now convinced that the moment had come to wrest the strategic initiative from the Turks, both in the Mediterranean and in the Persian Gulf. On the one hand, the debacle at Sarikamish had evidently rendered the Ottoman Empire vulnerable to a swift and imaginative offensive drive. On the other, Turkey's manifest ability to send troops across the Sinai wilderness was a sword of Damocles poised at the jugular vein of Britain's imperial communications. Either way, London accepted the premise that a major effort ought to be launched immediately to strike the Ottoman enemy, the weakest of the Central Powers, a smashing and, possibly, a fatal blow. With the Turks *hors de combat,* the Western Allies and Russia would then find themselves in the strategically ideal position of linking hands across the Straits, and afterward, hopefully, of coming to grips with the encircled Germans and Austrians on the climactic battlefield of Europe itself.

CHAPTER III

ALLIED
CATASTROPHES
IN THE MIDDLE EAST

Overture to Disaster

Even as the Turks were suffering two galling defeats in their efforts to arouse the Moslem world against the Entente, the Germans were proving to be rather more effective in the same endeavor. Unlike the dreamers and adventurers who floated through Constantinople, however, the Middle East experts of the Wilhelmstrasse preferred to concentrate on Persia, gateway to India and repository of Britain's oil holdings. It was a shrewd choice. For several years, the Persian royal family and the nation's religious hierarchy had chafed helplessly as the Anglo-Russian Agreement of 1907 parceled out "spheres of influence" in their territory. Moreover, at least forty per cent of the nation's inhabitants were Arabs, Turanians, and Buluchis, tribes who lived in the southern provinces of Khuzistan and Tangistan, and whose sympathies with the Turks rose in inverse ratio to their practical acquaintance with Ottoman administrative methods. The catalyst of their unrest was Wilhelm Wassmuss, a former German career official who had served as consul in the Persian Gulf area just before the war. Fluent in Persian and Arabic, in the customs and dialects of the South Persian tribes, the eloquent forty-year-old German dressed himself in native costume and made his way by camel and by foot from one Tangistani community to the next, distributing funds and propaganda, artfully stimulating native hatred against the British garrisons in the Persian Gulf. His success was remarkable. Lashed to a fury by Wassmuss's appeal to jihad, the tribes penetrated to the outskirts of Bushire, sniping at the British garrison there, cutting the Anglo-Persian Oil Company's pipelines and telegraph wires northeast of Ahwaz, and by the close of 1914 presenting a major threat to the British flank in the Persian Gulf area. A method had to be found to extinguish these brushfires before they flared into an uncontrollable guerrilla campaign.

The key was prestige. Sir Percy Cox, political adviser to the Indian forces in the Gulf, repeatedly warned against dissipating the Indian Army's limited strength in the foothills and swamps of southern Persia. He insisted, rather, that stability in the Gulf area would be achieved only as a direct consequence of Allied successes against the Turks in Mesopotamia. Admittedly, the latter was not a simple alternative. Further offensive action through the suffocating furnace of the Mesopotamian plain was all but impossible, and the ordeal of navigating the shallow, treacherous currents of the Tigris did not recommend itself to the imperial general staff. On the other hand, the approval of the imperial high command in London was by no means essential to strategic decisions in this part of the world. The Persian Gulf campaign lay almost entirely within the jurisdiction of the Government of India, a semi-independent administration, with its own viceroy (Lord Hardinge), its own Indian Army commander (Sir Beauchamps Duff), its own secretary of state in London (Austen Chamberlain), and not least of all, its own *raison d'être*—the ironclad security of India, jewel of the empire, together with the network of India's surrounding communications. If Sir Percy Cox, in his infinite wisdom, was convinced that a renewed offensive up the Tigris would secure those communications, the Government of India was not disposed to object. Nor was the War Cabinet in London, the last court of appeal from New Delhi, when the decision was referred to it. On November 27, 1914, as we recall, General Barrett was ordered to load his Sixth Indian Division on river steamers and embark for Kurna, another fifty miles up the Tigris from Basra. The operation

54

was as much a success as its predecessor; after several hard clashes with the Turks, Kurna fell to the British on December 9. It appeared a logical place to stop, for British influence in lower Mesopotamia was now clearly in the ascendant.

Then, in February 1915, Wassmuss's Arab auxiliaries in southwestern Persia again cut the British pipeline, and indeed also effectively cut up a battalion of Indian troops who were rushed to the scene. Immediately the alarmed Indian government shipped yet another division to the Tigris Expeditionary Force. Whereupon Enver, who until now had stripped Mesopotamia of all but a handful of comparatively feeble garrisons, placed another twenty thousand troops at the disposal of Suleiman Pasha, the vali (governor) of Baghdad. Although these reinforcements were inadequate to stop the Anglo-Indian force in a hard-fought initial clash on April 13, Barrett lost nearly twenty percent of his effective troops in the battle. He therefore appealed to headquarters in New Delhi for a chance to rest and consolidate his position. Here the general's earlier, comparatively easy successes proved to be his undoing. Smelling "defeatism" in Barrett's request, the Indian government peremptorily replaced him as commander of Indian forces in Mesopotamia, appointing in his stead Lieutenant General Sir John Nixon. It seemed an appropriate choice. Nixon was a hearty cavalry soldier in his mid-fifties, a polo player and pig sticker, who had earned a certain reputation for dash in Indian border warfare. Convinced now that the opportunity of his career lay within his grasp, Nixon immediately began laying plans for a dazzling offensive against Baghdad itself. Although the notion was seemingly too ambitious for the Government of India, Nixon's eloquence and the support of Cox eventually won permission for a limited offensive on Amara, another seventy-two miles up the Tigris.

Once the decision was made, field command of the expedition was promptly turned over to Major General Sir Charles Townshend, a seasoned veteran of Indian warfare. The latter systematically pressed into service every paddle steamer, barge, and makeshift gondola that would float. On May 21,

"Townshend's Flotilla," a single division of twelve thousand men, set out upriver and reached the vicinity of Amara two days later. The Turks were not equal to pitched battle against a force of this size. After enduring two hours of spirited British artillery bombardment, they decided once again to withdraw. Several days later, Townshend's men peacefully entered the lethargic, half-abandoned Arab town. When the news reached Basra, the delighted Nixon immediately shipped another division to the northwest in a parallel offensive to clear the Turks out of the lower Euphrates Valley. By July 25, he had secured his principal goal, the occupation of the entire Basra vilayet. As Cox had predicted, moreover, sabotage in southern Persia diminished; the oil lines were secured. And apparently in the nick of time, for the Tigris Army had by then fought its way nearly two hundred miles from the sea, and its supply line was stretched to its critical limit.

Churchill's Inspiration

ALTHOUGH THE SUCCESS of the Mesopotamian expedition elated Sir Percy Cox and the Government of India, it did not exert any significant influence on Allied fortunes elsewhere. The presence of an Ottoman army in northwestern Turkey continued to immobilize the Russians in the Transcaucasus. Scores of well-equipped German divisions in the west pinned a million Allied soldiers to their trenches from Switzerland to the English Channel. It was against the bleak prospect of a war of attrition, therefore, no less than against the reputed Ottoman threat to Egypt, that the Western Allies first gave detailed attention to an offensive against the Turkish straits. The strategic value of this prewar lifeline between the Western Allies and Russia was immense. Its closure in the autumn of 1914, as we recall, was a strategic triumph of the first magnitude for the Central Powers. Indeed, if the Turks had succeeded in closing the Straits permanently, the Russian war effort might conceivably have been emasculated altogether. Archangel and Vladivostok, to be sure, still remained open as Russian ports of access to the West; but the former was frozen over in winter, the latter fully half a world away at the end of five thousand miles of tenuous railroad line from Moscow. Conversely, a successful offensive to breach the Straits would have represented a major disaster for Berlin and Constantinople. "If the Straits . . . were not permanently closed to Entente traffic," General von Falkenhayn warned, "all hopes of a successful course of the war would be very considerably diminished." Grand Admiral von Tirpitz agreed. "Should the Dardanelles fall then the World War has been decided against us," he stated emphatically.

The possibility of forcing the crucial waterway had been studied by the British naval staff before the war and rejected as impractial. Only Winston Churchill, first lord of the admiralty, continued to be fascinated by the idea. For a while he entertained the hope that a Greek army might participate with the Royal Navy in a massive amphibious operation. That notion was quashed early in September 1914, when King Constantine announced his firm intention of keeping his country neutral. In any case, the Russians vetoed all suggestions of allowing Greek troops in the Ottoman capital (see Chapter VI). Churchill still remained captivated by his grandoise dream, however. He visualized Constantinople as a ripe apple wating to be plucked. Half the city's population was non-Turkish, after all, and thus a source of potential collaborators for the Entente. Moreover, on November 3, 1914, a squadron of British cruisers had perfunctorily bombarded Turkish forts at the southern entrance to the Straits, and thus had apparently proved the superiority of naval guns over shorter-range Turkish artillery.

Churchill's plan, however, overlooked a basic fact of geography. Although the Dardanelles, the strip of water linking the Aegean and the Sea of Marmora, was four thousand yards wide at its western mouth, it constricted to a mere thirteen hundred yards some thirteen miles up the Narrows. A naval squadron attempting to pass through this bottleneck would accordingly run the mortal risk of short-range artillery bombardment. Presumably Churchill counted on the obsolescence of Turkish defenses, for it was known that the three lines of fortifications guarding the entrance to the Dardanelles were very antiquated. His appeal for the operation was strengthened on January 2, 1915: under the pressure of Enver's offensive in Transcaucasia, Grand Duke Nicholas, the Russian commander in chief, implored the Allies on that day to launch an immediate counteraction against the Turks "at their most vulnerable and sensitive point." Ironically, the grand duke withdrew his request only a week later, upon learning of the Turkish defeat at Sarikamish. By then, however, Churchill had already won Kitchener's approval. The war secretary liked the idea of a predominantly naval action. As Churchill reminded him, the heavy guns even of obsolescent vessels would suffice to blast open the entrance to the Straits. Preoccupied with demands for manpower on every front, Kitchener was gratified that "his worries in this quarter would be shouldered for two or three months by the Admirals."

The admiral who counted most, Sir John Fisher, the first sea lord, was in fact chilly to the idea. He had been impressed by a confidential and detailed memorandum recently transmitted by the Greek general staff to the British naval mission in Athens. It suggested that a Dardanelles expedition required not merely a powerful fleet, but a powerful army as well. The report indicated that Ottoman defenses were so arranged that ships would be unable to close with the forts in the Narrows until the mines were swept. Until the guns were silenced, on the other hand, mine sweepers were barred from entering to clear the mine fields. The memorandum warned that strong landing parties appeared to be the only conceivable alternative. It was an alternative that Churchill, Kitchener, and the rest of the War Cabinet decided to reject. They would take the gamble of a purely naval action. Any front offering more dramatic possibilities than the Western stalemate looked good to them. So did the hope of ending once and for all the threat to the Suez Canal and the British lifeline to India.

The organization of the naval attack was entrusted to Admiral Carden, commander of the Aegean Fleet. The mandate was anything but clear. Kitchener's orders stated that "the Admiralty should . . . prepare for a naval expedition in February to bombard and take the Gallipoli Peninsula, with Constantinople as its objective. . . ." "Take"—did it mean with or without troops? Carden assumed the emphasis was primarily naval. Within a few weeks, therefore, he managed to assemble an impressive fleet of battleships, cruisers, destroyers, submarines, mine sweepers, and miscellaneous other craft. With tacit consent from Athens, the powerful flotilla was assembled off the Greek island of Lemnos on February 7, 1915, and orders were circulated for an opening bombardment on February 15. Alerted by reports of this naval concentration, the Turks were equally busy preparing for attack. Throughout the latter part of February a German artillery expert, General Weber, organized a special force of engineers and imported gunners from the Juterborg artillery school and the Kiel Arsenal. Elaborate improvements were carried out in the channel's defenses. By March, 239 guns of heavy caliber had been trundled into the mouth of the Straits and supplemented by torpedo tubes packed in on each side of the Narrows. Extensive mine fields were similarly laid at the neck of the Dardanelles. The Allies were alerted to these dispositions by Greek spies on the Gallipoli Peninsula, and in February Kitchener agreed that the British Twenty-ninth Division and a number of Australian and New Zealand (Anzac) units in Egypt might appropriately be dispatched to Lemnos for a possible supplementary landing. But no final decision was made on this point.

Admiral Carden opened his attack on February 19. The heavier ships, moving as they fired, attempted to flatten the outer defenses of the Dardanelles and enable the mine sweepers to enter. The bombardment did little initial damage, although a second attempt on February 25 finally silenced the outer forts. The next morning at dawn, Carden sent three battleships churning into the mouth of the Dardanelles to pulverize the inner ring of artillery. The flat trajectory of the naval guns proved ineffective; most of the shells missed. Simultaneously with the effort by sea, parties of marines were landed on the southern inner coast of Gallipoli, and during the following ten days of naval shelling these troops successfully grenaded nearly fifty Turkish guns and their crews. Nevertheless, on March 11 the fleet encountered heavier fire as it attempted to penetrate the inner neck of the Dardanelles funnel. The intermediate Turkish howitzer defenses remained intact. At this point Kitchener ordered troop reinforcements to the eastern Mediterranean, bringing the Allied expeditionary forces there to nearly 70,000 men. Yet the war secretary persisted in viewing this quite substantial army essentially as an oversized landing party, and indeed still hoped to do without it altogether.

It was a vain hope, although the British did not yet know it. Neither did the enemy. In Constantinople despair settled on the German colony like a fog. Wangenheim confided to Morgenthau that the war itself ought to be concluded without delay. ". . . The German General Staff, and practically all military and naval experts in Constantinople," the American ambassador wrote, "believed that the Allied fleets could force their way through and capture the city." Those experts included the veteran General Colmar von der Goltz, commander of the original German mission in the nineteenth century, who was quite certain that the Allied fleet would be in the Marmora within ten hours. As British invasion forces gathered, the unnerved Wangenheim asked Morgenthau for permission to store his valuables in the American embassy. Dr. Richard von Kühlman, councillor of the German embassy, discussed the fall of the capital as if it were a *fait accompli.* The Turks themselves entirely shared this despondency. The Ottoman government had already prepared special trains for the evacuation of important personages. In March, a general exodus from the capital began. Women and children were transported into the interior; banks shipped their gold to Asia Minor. Criticism against the Young Turk regime rose ominously, and the prefect of police began shipping unemployed men out of the city to minimize the dangers of revolution.

By mid-March, Vice Admiral de Robeck, who had replaced Carden as commander of the British Aegean Fleet, was determined to mount a final, surprise naval effort to blast open the Straits. He decided to reverse his predecessor's strategy by sending the battleships on a daring straight run rather than depend upon the mine sweepers to clear the entrance to the Dardanelles. On March 18, a full naval task force of eighteen battleships, flanked by squadrons of cruisers and destroyers, bore head-on toward the entrance of the waterway. Within minutes the fleet's heavy guns knocked out the advance forts guarding the approaches to the Straits. At this point, suddenly, the Turkish howitzers inside the mouth of the Dardanelles began firing. Their aim was devastatingly accurate. The French battleship *Bouvet* exploded and sank with six hundred men. The British *Inflexible* and *Irresistible* were hit moments later and began listing sharply. Soon three other battleships were crippled. Under this rain of howitzer shells, the mine sweepers reversed their course and fled for the open sea. As two of his wounded battleships began to sink, De Robeck succumbed to the general panic and ordered the entire fleet to withdraw.

The admiral had actually come within a hair's breadth of success. The Turks by then were in mortal peril. Nearly all their ammunition was expended. A last decisive British push undoubtedly would have forced the Straits. Such an effort was in fact contemplated. In London, Sir John Fisher ordered four more battleships to the Dardanelles, and the French dispatched one of theirs. Rather, it was the generals whose nerve broke first. General Ian Hamilton wired Kitchener on March 19:

I am being most reluctantly driven to the conclusion that the Straits are not likely to be forced by battleships as at one time seemed probable and that, if my troops are to take part, it will not take the subsidiary form anticipated. The Army's part will not be a case of landing parties for the destruction of forts, but rather a case of a deliberate and progressive military operation carried out in force in order to make a passage for the Navy.

Kitchener called back the same day, agreeing, and De Robeck noted with relief that a military expedition was now probably a necessity.

Armageddon on the Beaches

ENVER REACHED the identical conclusion after the successful Turkish defense of March 18. He began making his troop dispositions accordingly. Pulling reinforcements up from Syria, he stationed ten divisions around Constantinople to defend the capital against a possible Russian attack from the north. On March 26 the war minister decreed the creation of an entirely new army of six divisions, the Fifth Army, which he placed under the direct command of Liman von Sanders. For the German, time was now the critical factor. Liman hoped the British would let him have eight days to prepare his defenses. As it turned out, in one of the most serious Allied blunders of the war, he was granted not eight days, but five weeks. De Robeck had decided to withdraw his fleet and not to waste ammunition on the forts until the army had fully occupied the heights of Gallipoli.

The Gallipoli Peninsula, comprising the western flank of the Straits, thrusts out fifty-two miles into the Aegean Sea. Tapering and bladelike at the entrance, it widens to nearly twelve miles in the center, then narrows again to a pointed tip. An almost uninterrupted spinal column of hills runs down the middle of the peninsula and dominates all its shores. As Liman studied the terrain of this appendixlike protrusion, he became increasingly confident of his ability to block a military conquest there, provided the landings could be restricted to the beaches. The peninsula's sparse, arid vegetation and depleted wells would effectively prevent an invading force from sustaining itself. Everything now depended on the mobility of Turkish forces, their capacity to respond swiftly and decisively to the first amphibious assaults. The German commander diagnosed three danger spots. The first was Mount Achi Baba, a promontory 709 feet high overlooking Gallipoli's southern tip. The second was the western coastline on both sides of the Gaba Tepe foothills; its flat terrain would permit an easy landing, and control of its higher inland ridge of Sari Bair—1,000 feet high—would similarly threaten the Turkish coastal batteries. Finally, there was Bulair, on the upper Gulf of Xernos, the narrow waist of the peninsula and its most vulnerable sector. Liman assigned two divisions to each area, but concentrated them inland, away from the beaches. While this left the coastal defense line open, it avoided exposing the defending troops to naval gunfire. As events developed, the German's strategy proved to be sound in every detail.

Liman's counterpart on the Allied side was a man of equal ability and experience. Ian Hamilton had seen more active duty—in India, the Sudan, and South Africa—than any other senior British officer, and had been repeatedly decorated for courage. Sixty-two years old in 1915, a slim, delicate-featured man whose poetic instincts belied his martial reputation, he enjoyed the undeniable advantage of being a close friend of Winston Churchill, who had recommended him to Kitchener for the task. Unfortunately for Hamilton, his army-to-be was scattered around the eastern Mediterranean. His administrative staff did not arrive in Egypt until April 11, by which time his field officers, possessing no experience in this line, had already drawn up make-shift organizational plans for the operation. Somewhat uncertainly, meanwhile, Hamilton decided that Cape Helles, on the southern tip of the peninsula, would be the site of his first landings. A single British division would be selected for this operation, and its task would be to occupy the Achi Baba ridge overlooking Cape Helles, thus isolating the Ottoman troop concentrations in the south. Simultaneously, two Anzac divisions would be disembarked about a mile to the north of the Baba Tepe ridge, up the southwest coast of Gallipoli. Once unloaded, the Anzacs would secure the Sari Bair heights and drive across the peninsula. There would be diversions, too. Companies of marines would land at Bulair,

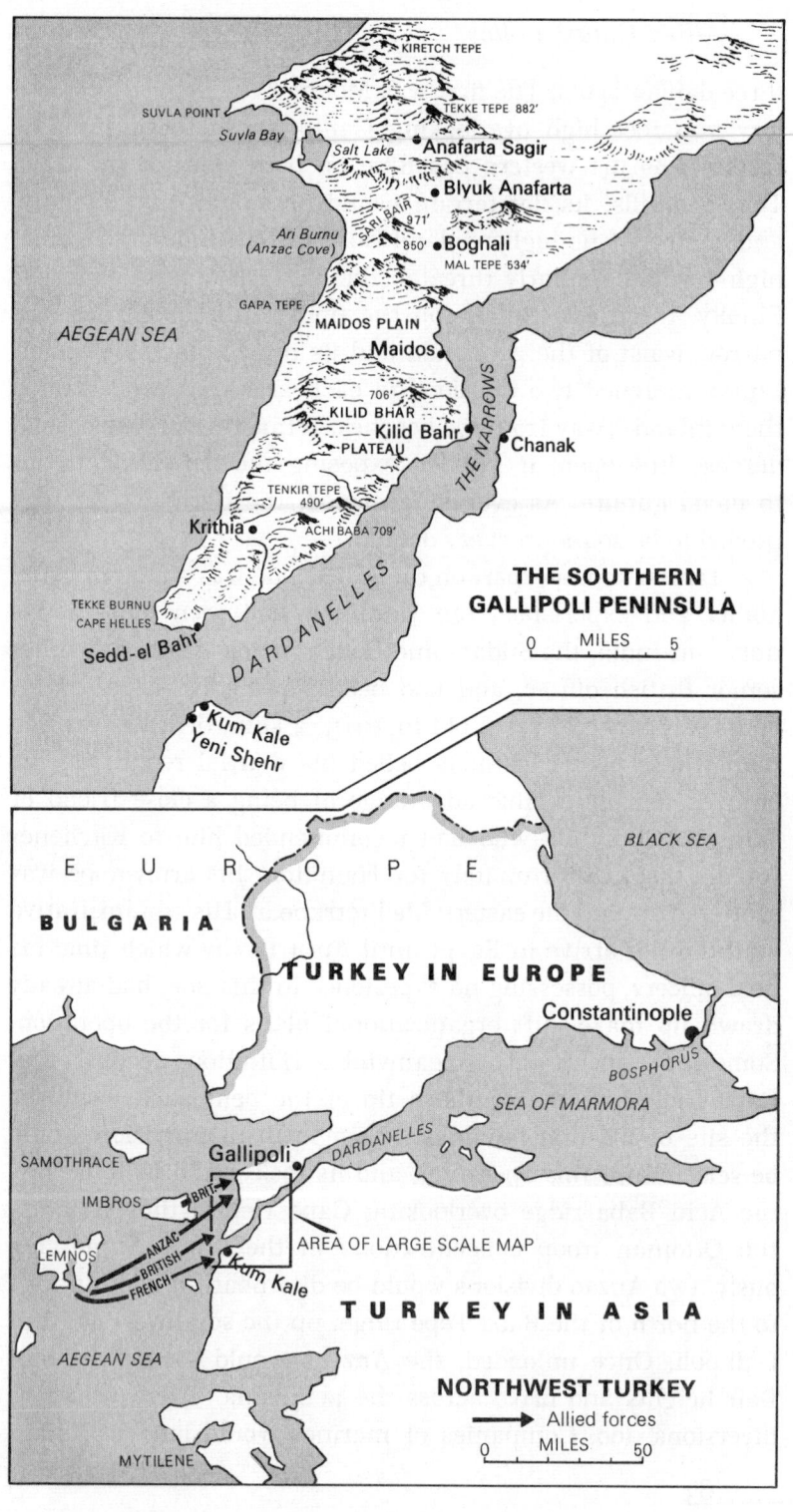

THE SOUTHERN GALLIPOLI PENINSULA

KIRETCH TEPE

SUVLA POINT

TEKKE TEPE 882'

Suvla Bay

Salt Lake

Anafarta Sagir

Blyuk Anafarta

Ari Burnu (Anzac Cove)

SARI BAIR

971'

850'

Boghali

MAL TEPE 534'

GAPA TEPE

MAIDOS PLAIN

AEGEAN SEA

Maidos

706'

KILID BHAR

Kilid Bahr

PLATEAU

THE NARROWS

Chanak

TENKIR TEPE 490'

ACHI BABA 709'

Krithia

0   MILES   5

TEKKE BURNU

CAPE HELLES

Sedd-el Bahr

DARDANELLES

Kum Kale
Yeni Shehr

BLACK SEA

E U R O P E

BULGARIA

TURKEY IN EUROPE

Constantinople

BOSPHORUS

SEA OF MARMORA

SAMOTHRACE

Gallipoli

DARDANELLES

IMBROS

BRIT

ANZAC

AREA OF LARGE SCALE MAP

LEMNOS

BRITISH

FRENCH

Kum Kale

TURKEY IN ASIA

AEGEAN SEA

NORTHWEST TURKEY

→ Allied forces

MYTILENE

0   MILES   50

to the north, in an effort to delay the arrival of enemy reinforcements; the French would disembark at Chanak, across the mouth of the Dardanelles on the Asian side. In conception, the plan unquestionably was bold, intelligent, and ambitious.

The initial difficulty would be getting the men ashore. Intelligence information was sparse, and consequently too much reliance was placed on the ability of a naval bombardment to flatten the defenses. Moreover, the supply, communications, and fire-control arrangements were chaotic. Yet these difficulties and dangers were all but ignored in the initial exhilaration of departure. On April 24 Admiral de Robeck's fleet sailed out of Mudros, an enormous armada of two hundred vessels, including fifteen battleships. John Masefield, who was present, recalled:

> No such gathering of fine ships had ever been seen upon this earth, and the beauty and the exultation of the youth upon them made them seem like sacred things as they moved away. All the thousands of the men aboard them gathered on deck to see, till each rail was thronged. These men had come from all parts of the British world, from Africa, Australia, Canada, India and the Mother Country, New Zealand, and remote islands in the sea. . . . As each ship crammed with soldiers drew near the battleships the men swung their caps and cheered . . . and the sailors answered, and the noise of cheering swelled, and men on the ships not yet moving joined in, till all the life in the harbour was thinking thanks that it could go to death rejoicing. . . . They left the harbour very, very slowly; this tumult of cheering lasted a long time; no one who heard it will ever forget it or think of it unshaken. It broke the hearts of all there with pity and pride.

The sea was dead calm and oily. At 2:00 p.m. on April 25 the flotilla reached its destination. In the predawn darkness the ships glided forward, each with its covey of tows behind, each small boat packed with men. And they reached the shore uneventfully at Cape Helles and near Gaba Tepe, with more landings imminent at Kum Kale, Besika Bay in Asia, and Bulair (see map). Liman, who was notified immediately at his headquarters in the town of Gallipoli, was astonished at the scope of the amphibious operation. Nevertheless, with his usual iron self-control, he decided to wait until it became clear which landings were feints and which were authentic. Twenty-four hours passed before he received definite information.

It was on the west coast of Gallipoli that things began to go wrong for the Anzacs. A navigational error put them ashore at Ari Burnu, a mile north of their intended destination at Gaba Tepe. The beach at Ari Burnu was tiny, hardly more than four hundred yards long. Cramped in disembarkation and unloading, the troops did not reach their objective until mid-morning. It was the ridge of Sari Bair. From its crest the men looked down on the gleaming waters of the Narrows, barely three miles away. At this very moment of apparently effortless Allied triumph, the Ottoman Nineteenth Division ascended the ridge a few hundred feet to the north of the Anzacs. Led by a decisive young brigadier, Mustafa Kemal, the Turks hurriedly set up their mountain artillery and began pouring a hail of shells and small-arms fire into the Allied ranks, mowing the invaders down by the scores, then by the hundreds. The survivors clung desperately to their footholds. A few units even launched attacks, for the Anzacs outnumbered the Turks, twelve thousand to four thousand. In the next few hours the ridge changed hands five times. It was Kemal's leadership alone which kept his men from breaking under the weight of the Anzac drive. Mounting a series of furious counteradvances, the Turkish commander ordered the troops "not to attack, but to die." By late afternoon Kemal had personally led his division in a savage, bellowing, hacking assault that broke the Anzac ranks, driving them off the ridge and down to the beach itself.

The Allied landing at Cape Helles in the south did not enjoy a happier fate. Although shell-shocked by hours of naval bombardment, a thousand Turkish soldiers dazedly regrouped along the tip of the peninsula and managed to resume firing as the English set foot on the beach. Colonel Hans Kannengiesser, who commanded the defense, recalled that "at the moment from the apparently dead ground a totally unexpected and intensely heavy fire from guns, rifles, and flanking machine guns fell on the landing parties. The torpedo heads which had been buried as ground mines exploded. The men stumbled on barbed wire in the water." The German officer marveled at the gallantry of the British, climbing through the hail of steel and fire over their dying comrades. The beach was soon littered with English corpses; the shore ran red with blood. After several hours, however, the Turks temporarily exhausted their ammunition. In the brief lull of firing, the invaders secured a precarious foothold. Twenty-four hours later the men on the beaches finally began to link up.

British and Anzac endurance was fully matched by that of the Turks. The naval barrage whistling in upon the defenders was unending, a torrential nightmare of heavy-caliber shells. The bombardment ranged over the Ottoman Fifth Army's entire supply route, both to Cape Helles and to Anzac Cove (Ari Burnu), and descended with lethal accuracy upon pack animals and quartermaster troops struggling to the front lines. The Turks were swiftly reduced to the uncertain perils of water transportation. It was the strangulation of Ottoman supply lines that eventually permitted the British to land 20,000 troops at Cape Helles against the southern sector's 6,300 Turkish defenders. Yet even with this bridgehead, Allied leadership was curiously indecisive. During forty-eight crucial hours, the officers on the southern beach failed to order a movement forward, and by the end of the second day Turkish reinforcements were well entrenched on the crest of Achi Baba, inflicting fearsome casualties on the invaders. Indeed, failure to attain the ridge signified the initial collapse of Hamilton's strategy. So did the retreat of the Australians and New Zealanders, who found themselves under siege in the northwest as Kemal's Nineteenth Division descended upon them in a continuing series of frontal assaults. The Anzacs who unloaded supplies on the compressed and naked beach were as vulnerable as those in the front line. Turkish shrapnel and bullets scoured their ranks mercilessly, almost literally pinning them to the water's edge.

The final crisis on the Helles front in the south came on May 1, when Colonel von Soderstern, commander of Ottoman forces south of Achi Baba, ordered his troops to mount a last supreme effort to drive the enemy into the sea. Invoking the blessings of paradise on those about to fall, the German buttressed his appeal by ordering regimental commanders to shoot dead anyone who faltered. At 10:00 p.m., a pulverizing Ottoman artillery barrage was followed by the attack of thousands of Turkish soldiers, cascading down on Allied trenches. The ensuing battle in the darkness was almost surrealistic: no one was certain who was friend or foe; bayonets were used by both sides. Somehow the British hurled the Turks back. Two nights later the Turks renewed the assault. The results were identical. This time Allied artillery proved so shatteringly effective that Liman intervened personally to halt the carnage. But Allied losses, too, although half those of the Turks, were appalling enough to limit Hamilton to one final offensive. He launched it on May 6. It sustained its momentum for three days and cost the British six thousand casualties, nearly a third of their total force on Cape Helles. When the smoke settled, the English had gained a total of six hundred yards. It was not enough to secure a foothold on the crest of Achi Baba. At this point Hamilton abandoned all hope of a renewed effort at Helles. Desultory sniping continued for the next three weeks. The Allied offensive was broken.

The operation had been a slaughterhouse beyond the wildest nightmare of Hamilton or of Kitchener or Churchill. So it proved, too, for Liman. On May 18, he ordered Mustafa Kemal to drive the Anzacs off Ari Burnu, the northernmost beach at Anzac Cove, and to accomplish this task at any cost. Reinforcements were sent down from Constantinople. Two days later, Kemal attacked frontally—there was no other way —with some forty thousand men galloping down the slopes of Sari Bair. Within the space of twenty-four hours, Anzac machine gun and rifle fire piled up ten thousand Turkish corpses in the single bloodiest encounter of the Gallipoli campaign. By now, Liman had abandoned all hope of driving the

Allies off the peninsula. Each side fully recognized that the other's position was impregnable: the campaign was stalemated. A lethargic quasi-truce descended upon the battlefields. Winston Churchill, distraught and chagrined, initially refused to accept the manifest failure of his cherished strategic vision for instant victory. Without consulting his subordinates, he ordered additional warships dispatched to the Dardanelles fleet. Sir John Fisher, the first sea lord, learned of this action only afterward. Understandably outraged, he immediately tendered his resignation. By then, Churchill had served himself up as the ideal scapegoat for the Gallipoli disaster, and on May 17 the Cabinet rather peremptorily deprived him of his ministry.

Stalemate and Final Effort

By May, too, the weather on the peninsula had become infernally hot, as the rival armies tunneled themselves deeply into the earth. The stench of shell smoke and decaying flesh and the onslaught of lice and flies corroded morale, particularly on the Allied side. Without access to wells, the British had to ship water in tanks from Malta and Egypt, even from England. Troops often went mad with thirst. By July a thousand Allied soldiers a week were being evacuated with dysentery. The Turks withstood the ordeal somewhat better, for they were accustomed to brutal conditions equally in civilian and in army life. Their position was far from enviable, however. The neutrality of Bulgaria, combined with the Allied naval barrage, still choked off supplies of heavy German artillery and large-caliber shells. Provisions were so inadequate that not even enough sacking existed for sandbags.

Throughout the Gallipoli campaign, in fact, the central problem for the Turks continued to be supply. The land route from Thrace required a week's march, and was vulnerable to naval bombardment nearly every mile of the way. The sea route, ordinarily a mere twelve hours from Constantinople, was in equal jeopardy from British submarines. Several of these, particularly the E-11 under the intrepid Lieutenant Commander Nasmith, managed repeatedly to evade the mine fields at the entrance to the Dardanelles, and throughout the spring and summer of 1915 terrorized Ottoman shipping, destroying over a hundred vessels, including five troopships and nine other large steamers. By the end of July Turkish navigation to the front was drastically reduced. The blockade's psychological effect on the population of Constantinople was quite traumatic. By the end of July 1915, the military situation of the Turks in Gallipoli was unquestionably graver than that of the Allies. Their casualties had been much heavier, and some eighty thousand of their troops in the Straits area had been evacuated with wounds or disease. The impact of these losses created a severe crisis of morale in the Ottoman High Command. On one occasion an effort was made (unsuccessfully) to have Liman replaced—even poisoned!

Evidently the British learned of these developments through American sources, and it was this information that helped persuade them to renew the effort in the Dardanelles. In the late summer the "Mediterranean Expeditionary Force" actually was given priority over the Western front in the shipment of ammunition. Three new divisions were dispatched to Lemnos, restoring Hamilton's depleted army to 120,000 men, and Kitchener promised yet six more divisions in the near future. This time, too, a glimmer of optimism appeared in a report from General Birdwood at Anzac Cove, on the western coast of the peninsula. It suggested a new route to the Sari Bair ridge which might bypass the apparently impregnable Turkish defensive positions. Birdwood's idea was first to launch a renewed diversionary offensive from Anzac Cove itself, and then to outflank the enemy heights by a landing at a new beachhead several miles farther up the coast, at Suvla Bay. Again, surprise was the crucial ingredient. If the plan worked and the troops reached the summit of Sari Bair, the army needed only to advance three or four miles up the inner coast to clear the forts at the Narrows. After that it would be clear sailing for the fleet.

The imperial general staff was fascinated by the ruse, and Hamilton was immediately instructed to work out the details. Unfortunately for the Allies, the man Hamilton picked to lead the Suvla Bay offensive was Lieutenant General Sir Frederick Stopford, an administrative officer in his early sixties, so inexperienced in modern warfare that, on the very eve of the invasion, he refused to divulge to his senior officers information on precisely where they were going or what their objective was. Only Liman von Sanders's uncertainty of Allied intentions saved the landing from initial disaster; a mere two thousand Ottoman troops were located in the area of Suvla Bay. On the night of August 6, therefore, twenty thousand British soldiers managed to wade ashore at the beach site of Suvla Bay—unopposed. Everything now depended on speed in ascending the heights of Sari Bair before Turkish reinforcements arrived. And here Stopford's obsession with secrecy was his undoing. Led by middle-aged, confused officers without map information, the men blundered aimlessly among the snarl of equipment, and then became lost. Finally, too weary and dispirited to continue in the darkness, they spent the night on the beach. Only two and a half miles of deserted salt lake bed remained between them and the ridge. Yet during the next forty-eight hours the troops milled about in confusion, occasionally making for the wrong hills, then retreating under isolated sniper fire to the security of the shore.

Meanwhile, the Australians and New Zealanders at Anzac Cove, the southern arm of the pincers, were fighting with their characteristic gallantry. Repeatedly they mounted frontal attacks against the Turkish lines. In the first three days of battle four thousand Anzacs paid with their lives; at one hill alone, "Lone Pine," seven Victoria Crosses were won. Although these assaults were intended as essentially diversionary to the Suvla Bay landing, they very nearly captured the ridge of Sari Bair. In one unforgettable episode, several hundred Australians and New Zealanders momentarily reached the top and looked down on Stopford's troops leisurely walking about in the brilliant sunshine of Suvla Bay to the northwest. The glimpse was a brief one; the Anzacs were driven off the ridge almost instantly. And when, at last, two days after the offensive began, a few of the Suvla detachments to the north reached the heights of Sari Bair, they were blasted off the crest by an ill-timed artillery barrage from their own men on the shore below.

By the afternoon of August 8, Liman von Sanders had rushed two divisions to the Suvla Bay area. Appointing Mustafa Kemal field commander, he ordered the Turkish brigadier to counterattack without delay, to drive the British down to the very water's edge. Kemal fulfilled the assignment with his usual *élan*. At dawn on August 9 he launched one of his typical frontal attacks. It caught the British off balance. Indeed, it sent them fleeing, terrified, back down the foothills. Turkish machine gun fire laced through the English from above, then set fire to the brush and incinerated additional hundreds of Allied troops. By midday the British were clustered on the beaches again, having sustained fully eight thousand casualties. Whereupon Kemal immediately dashed off for the southern edge of Sari Bair to cope with the Anzac offensive. Both sides had been locked there in mortal combat for three days and nights, and in this last spasm of battle the Australians and New Zealanders were hanging on just under the ridge area. Once again, Kemal ordered six battalions to prepare for a surprise counterattack. The gamble succeeded. At dawn on August 10, the Anzacs were caught off guard as Kemal's men charged down on them with fixed bayonets. Thousands of troops on both sides died horribly, but at day's end not a single height of any importance in Gallipoli was in Allied hands.

The aftermath was black despair for Hamilton and his men. In three days of fighting at Suvla and Anzac, the Allies had sustained 18,000 casualties. Between August 6 and August 18, 22,000 sick and wounded men had to be evacuated from the peninsula. These were unprecedented numbers even for the sanguinary Dardanelles campaign. If the Suvla Bay landing had been exploited with even the smallest fraction of additional speed, the Ottoman shore batteries would have been raked silent from above. The mine fields in the Straits would have been removed, and the fleet brought into the Dardanelles as effortlessly as at a yachting regatta. Very probably all would then have been over for Turkey and the lifeline between the Western Allies and Russia would have been pulsing once more with traffic. The dream, though fading, still tantalized Hamilton. On August 21, he attempted a renewed offensive at Suvla, his men crossing again toward the hills. The Turks smashed the drive, inflicting five thousand casualties on the British. In the heat of the Middle Eastern sun, the earth steamed with tens of thousands of cadavers piled high from Cape Helles to the Anafarta Valley. For the living, it was an inferno beyond even the most Gothic imagination. Wounded troops, crawling with flies and lice, waited in hoarse agony for the moment of evacuation. Stopford's replacement, Mahon, found an exhausted and dispirited army strewn across the Suvla plain, apparently too feeble to do more than cling to the fragment of ground it occupied.

Evaluation and Evacuation

THE TENUOUSNESS of the Allied situation was not fully appreciated in Constantinople. Rather, the Ottoman government had become quite frantically preoccupied with the intentions of Bulgaria. The Sofia regime was capable of mustering an army of 500,000 men. The city of Constantinople, only twenty miles from the Turco-Bulgar frontier, was all but helpless against an offensive threat of that magnitude. On the other hand, if the Sofia government should declare for the Central Powers, the principal supply route from Berlin to Constantinople would substantially be opened; the small portion of the artery which ran through Serbian territory could easily be overrun. Throughout 1915, therefore, Bulgaria became the object of a rapidly escalating series of offers and counteroffers from both sides. In these negotiations the Entente powers were at a disadvantage. Their proposals of territorial compensation could be offered only at the expense of their Serbian ally, and thus were suspect. In late August, King Ferdinand's government, still nurturing bitter memories of its defeat in the Serbo-Bulgarian War of 1913, decided to accept the German-Turkish offer: of Macedonia at the expense of Serbia, and eastern Thrace at the expense of Turkey. It was a heavy price for the Turks, but well worth it. On October 11, the Bulgars formally entered the war against the Entente. A sizable Ottoman army was thus released from its immobility in guarding the capital. A month later, the railway between Berlin and Constantinople was open, and vast quantities of munitions began pouring into Turkey. The equipment included winter uniforms against the freezing rain and snow now beginning to descend in the Straits area. The fate of the Allied effort in the Dardanelles was sealed.

Toward the end of August, even before the Bulgarian regime made its move, General Hamilton sensed the desperation of his position in Gallipoli, and somewhat forlornly entreated Kitchener for another 95,000 men. The request came at a black moment in the war, for 1915 had been a year of Allied disasters on the Russian, Italian, and Western fronts. Many hundreds of thousands of men had been lost. Moreover, rumors of Hamilton's alleged ineptitude were being widely circulated in British government circles; they were based upon a published report of an Australian journalist who had briefly visited Gallipoli several weeks earlier and had been appalled by the carnage and despair he encountered there. In the resultant uproar, the war secretary was compelled to dismiss Hamilton outright and to replace him with General Sir Charles Munro, a veteran of the Western front. Upon his arrival in Gallipoli, Munro spent the sum total of twenty-four hours furiously cross-examining operations officers, then rushing like a bull along the beaches at Helles and Anzac. The flying tour was evidently all the general needed to confirm his intentions. He cabled London immediately that the only solution was to make the best of a bad bargain, to evacuate the peninsula forthwith. The recommendation profoundly shocked Kitchener; but upon paying a visit to Gallipoli himself in mid-November, the war secretary reluctantly endorsed it. The Cabinet in turn agonized for several weeks before making a decision.

If there was any doubt by then of the steps that had to be taken, they were dispelled by a blizzard of snow and sleet, the worst in forty years, which on November 27 suddenly descended upon the Straits area with roaring, primeval fury. Allied troops were still lightly clad, and hundreds of them froze to death; thousands of others succumbed to influenza and dysentery. By the end of the month, British and Anzac forces in Gallipoli had lost fully a tenth of their remaining effective strength. Physically and psychologically, the blizzard was the *coup de grâce*. On December 8 the Cabinet finally approved evacuation. The problem now was to remove some 100,000 men, 5,000 animals, 2,000 vehicles, and enormous quantities of miscellaneous stores, under the eyes of the enemy. Secrecy again was crucial. This time, however, secrecy was combined with expert and detailed advance planning. The withdrawal was carried out each night under cover of darkness, as flotillas of small boats crept into Suvla and Anzac bays, steadily loading men and equipment. Tents were kept standing, and guns maintained their normal rate of fire. By December 17, the number of Allied soldiers still remaining on the western coast had been drastically reduced, to forty thousand. The Turks suspected nothing. During the ensuing two nights the last troops were carried off safely from Anzac and Suvla. Inevitably, vast quantities of matériel were left behind. Some of the equipment was destroyed, but more was left intact, including tools, telephones, vast pyramids of ammunition, stocks of food and fuel. The men, at least, were gone.

On December 19 an Ottoman patrol was sent out in the direction of Anzac by Colonel Kannengiesser, who noted a diminution of enemy artillery fire. It was then that the Turks discovered the withdrawal. The news was instantly relayed to Liman, who was astonished and mortified, hardly knowing whether the evacuation should be regarded as a victory or defeat. Wasting no time on post-mortems, however, the German marshal immediately switched all his remaining divisions to Cape Helles at the southern front, and on January 17, 1916, ordered them to attack. Although the British garrison at the tip of the peninsula had already been reduced to 19,000 men, its defensive position was still quite formidable, and the naval bombardment from offshore proved effective beyond anything in the previous experience of the campaign. The Turkish assault was shattered hundreds of yards before reaching British lines. The British thereupon completed their evacuation successfully. Was it a victory for the Allies? Critics of the expedition insisted that it was probably the only victory of the entire campaign. Liman and the Turks preferred to regard it as an Allied disaster, and pointed out that it required fully two years to carry off the booty the British left behind. Victory celebrations were held in Constantinople and Berlin: Sultan Mehmed V assumed the title of "Gazi" (Conqueror of Christians); in Germany, Liman was fondly described as "the Hindenburg of the Orient."

The Gallipoli campaign, in Alan Moorehead's words, had been "a mighty destroyer of reputations." It undermined Kitchener's position and temporarily ruined Churchill. It ended Asquith's leadership, as well as Hamilton's. Within a few months of the evacuation the inquests began, and in 1917 a royal commission report, notable for its candor, decided that the operation had been poorly organized and ineptly executed. It condemned Kitchener for delaying the shipment of troops for three weeks without consulting the admiralty, and thus compromising the possibility of a successful amphibious operation. It was the report's conclusion, too, that a joint naval and military occupation should have been pushed through vigorously and immediately. The evaluation was a fair one. Without question the price of failure was almost insupportably high for the Allies. Of the 500,000 troops they had sent to Gallipoli, fully half had ended as casualties. All hope of practical access to Russia was now lost, with disastrous results for the chronically undersupplied Russian army. By December 1915, with the Straits closed, sixty-six British freighters were icebound in Archangel and

Alexandrova. The Trans-Siberian Railway was inoperative for lack of rolling stock. It was of importance, too, that within days following the Allied evacuation, the largest part of Liman's Gallipoli army was taken off the peninsula and dispatched in an almost endless succession of troop trains to the eastern Taurus Mountains, there to meet the Russian advance threatening Armenia.

But this was only part of the story. The Turks had suffered 300,000 casualties, losses they could afford far less than the Western Allies. Even Russian Foreign Minister Sazanov, a sharp critic of the Gallipoli campaign, admitted that the immobilization of some two thirds of the Ottoman army in the Straits-Constantinople region during 1915 "drew a part of the Turkish forces away from our frontier, thus contributing to our successes in Asia Minor, which eventually secured for us the whole of its North-Eastern district." It was possible, moreover, that if no attack had been launched against the Turks in 1915, Bulgaria, and perhaps Greece and Rumania as well, might have declared for Germany even earlier in the war. Had that occurred, Italy probably would have accepted the offer of the Central Powers. Weighed in the balance, therefore, the unsuccessful effort to force the Straits was not an unmitigated disaster for Britain. By the 1960's, a rough consensus had developed that the basic concept of the Gallipoli campaign was sound, even brilliant, and that its failure was caused rather by hasty organization, absence of central leadership, and a fatal lack of coordination between land and naval forces. The trauma of the Gallipoli campaign had an equally salutary effect upon Allied diplomacy. It emancipated Britain and France from the lockstep of an outworn nineteenth-century tradition. For generations, as we recall, it had been axiomatic that the Western maritime powers were obliged to thwart every Russian move to assure free passage through the Straits. But the events of 1915 now made it plain that closure of this historic waterway actually presented a much graver threat to Entente, and especially to British, security. Britain's lifeline evidently flowed north, toward the Black Sea, no less than south through the Red Sea. Indeed, for a mighty naval power like Britain, freedom of access to all the seven seas for every nation—not excluding Russia—was the best ultimate guarantee of imperial security. Her statesmen would learn the lesson well and apply it diligently in the critical negotiations of the postwar era.

Debacle in Mesopotamia

THE IMPASSE OF GALLIPOLI in the summer of 1915 largely determined the fate of the Mesopotamian campaign. The somnolent little river community of Amara had been an ideal stopping point for General Townshend. It was a drier and healthier site than Basra, from which it was separated by nearly two hundred miles, and it possessed excellent communications. British prestige and British oil fields in the Persian Gulf were now equally well secured. There appeared no logical reason to press on. On the other hand, Nixon's ambitions had been whetted by the deceptive ease of the campaign, and he decided to seek New Delhi's permission for an additional and even more far-reaching offensive. This one would push yet another 150 miles up the Tigris to the city of Kut, at the juncture of the Tigris and Hai rivers. Once captured, Nixon argued, Kut would serve as a logical base for a future expedition against Baghdad. In his view, the town might even function as the southern axis of a pincers movement; General Baratov's small Russian force near Lake Van in eastern Turkey would serve as the northern prong. The offensive unquestionably would stretch British supply lines to the breaking point. But the psychological advantages of possible success appeared to outweigh this danger. Nixon's confidence was infectious, and again he won over the Government of India. On August 23, 1915, General Townshend received orders to prepare his Sixth Indian Division for the expedition against Kut.

Townshend brought impressive credentials to the assignment. A cool-headed, tenacious professional, he had served a long and distinguished career in the Sudan and in the Indian Northwest Frontier region, and had once successfully withstood a forty-six-day Pathan siege of the fortress of Chitral. Despite his experience and more than ordinary courage, however, Townshend had serious misgivings about pushing upriver without communications or extensive supplies. Yet, upon inquiry, he received warm reassurances from New Delhi that Kut was the last stop. The promise was in fact conveyed personally by Sir Beauchamps Duff, commander in chief of the Indian Army: "Not one inch, Townshend, shall you go beyond Kut-al-Amara unless I make you up to adequate strength." Although far from convinced, Townshend dutifully started out on September 1, marching his force of 12,000 Indian and British troops along the sandbanks of the river. Except for a brief, sharp clash with the Turks on September 27, the Anglo-Indian force encountered little serious opposition. On October 5 it entered Kut. The odoriferous little garrison town had been deserted by the enemy; the Turks had retired to Ctesiphon, eighty miles upriver. Townshend was uninterested in pursuing them. His troops were exhausted, and his supply lines were strung back a full 380 miles to Basra. It would be wiser to settle in for the time being.

Nixon had other ideas. Euphoric over the ease with which Kut had been occupied, and quite certain that destiny had tapped him as a strategist of Napoleonic dimensions, the commander of the Tigris Army now entertained visions of capturing Baghdad as well. As he explained it to the Indian government, the occupation of Baghdad would effectively restore Britian's moral reputation in Arab eyes after the disaster of Gallipoli. Lord Hardinge, viceroy of India, shared this view. So did the War Cabinet. On October 21 a special interdepartmental committee in London approved the drive on Baghdad and authorized the transfer of two divisions from France for that purpose. Speaking in the Commons on November 2, Prime Minister Asquith could boast that "General Nixon's force is now within measurable distance of Baghdad. I do not think that in the whole war there has been a series of operations more carefully contrived, more brilliantly conducted, and with a better prospect of final success."

Well before reinforcements were dispatched to Nixon, the able and experienced Ottoman commander in Mesopotamia, General Nureddin Pasha, began a significant regroupment of his forces. These consisted of elements of five new divisions brought down from the north—twenty thousand battle-hardened Turks whose fighting quality far surpassed that of the Arab units which until then had borne the brunt of defense. Alerted to these enemy preparations, and deeply agitated by the prospect of any further offensive movements, Townshend noted in his diary on October 5 that Nixon

> does not seem to realize the weakness and danger of his line of communication. We are now some 380 miles from the sea, and we have only two weak divisions, including my own, in the country! There is my division to do the fighting, and Gorringe's to hold the line of communications from Kut to the sea. There is no possible support to give me if I receive a check.

Thirty years of military service had taught Townshend the meaning of orders, however. On November 21 he resignedly led his column of troops, mules, camels, and oxen from Kut up the riverbank. The very next day his advance patrols made contact with Turkish units defending well-entrenched positions at Ctesiphon. The Englishman failed in his efforts to lure the enemy out. As the Anglo-Indian troops advanced across the open plain, they were raked with heavy artillery and machine gun fire. By late afternoon casualties had reached 4,500. The Sixth Division disengaged and backed off.

Before Townshend could regroup his men the next day, he found himself in the midst of an unexpectedly savage counterattack, launched by Nureddin's force in the dead heat of the afternoon. The battle lasted through the night; by morning when the fighting subsided, it was clear that the Anglo-Indian force had lost half its effective infantry strength. The shock of this encounter was exacerbated by the criminal inadequacy of British medical services. Wounded men were carried back to the river and stuffed like cordwood on the overcrowded decks of the small paddle steamers. Only a small proportion survived the thirteen-day journey downstream to Basra. Later, a witness before the royal commission appointed to investigate the Mesopotamian campaign described the arrival of riverboats with men writhing on their decks, their bodies caked with offal and running sores, "their limbs splinted with wood strings from 'Johnny Walker' whisky boxes, compressed hay, wire, and that sort of thing." Townshend had originally intended to hold ground near Ctesiphon. But soon the pressure of these mounting losses changed his mind. Early in the morning of December 3, the Sixth Division, by now grievously crippled and virtually immobilized by casualties and fatigue, its stragglers waylaid and knifed by prowling Arab bands, made its way back at last to the temporary safety of Kut.

The Siege of Kut

A DENSE COLLECTION of perhaps 650 mud huts and six thousand Arabs, Kut (or, more properly, Kut-al-Amara) was located on a flat oblong peninsula devoid of walls or fortifications of any kind. The town was quite filthy, possessing no drainage system, and subject to the periodic overflow of the Tigris and Hai rivers, which formed the boundaries of the peninsula. Townshend's only hope was for his men to burrow in as deeply and quickly as possible. This they did. And initially, at least, it saved them. On December 10, the vanguard of Nureddin's troops made their first attempt to overrun Kut by storm. Nerved to the assault by their dervishes, the Turks hurled themselves against the Indian positions in successive waves. Each time they were cut down by salvoes of rifle and machine gun fire. Eventually Nureddin called off the attack. Instead he ordered his men to converge slowly on both sides of the river, and to close the neck of the peninsula by digging a network of trenches. Simultaneously, an Ottoman division above the Tigris blocked the Anglo-Indian line of retreat and the river communications with Basra. By mid-December, some 25,000 Turkish soldiers had completely isolated Townshend's force, surrounding it with an iron ring of men and guns. By then, too, impatient to share public acclaim with Mustafa

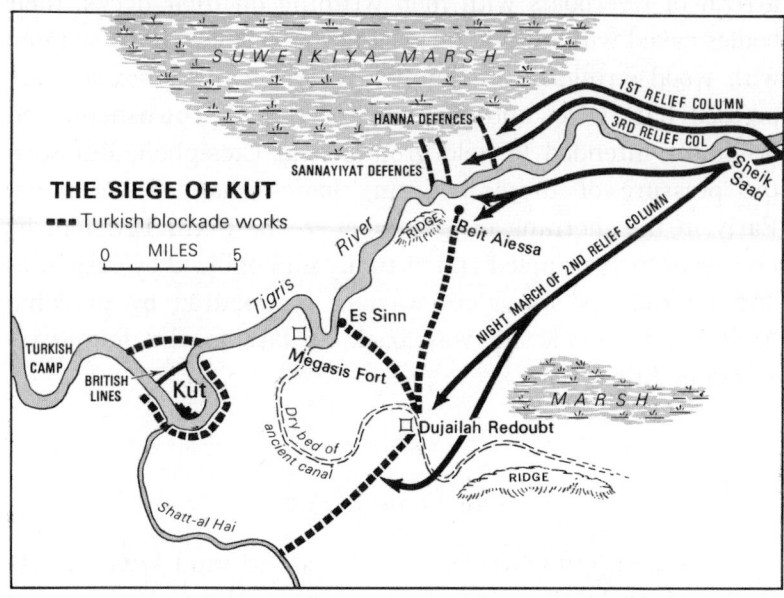

Kemal, Nureddin decided to risk yet another frontal assault against Kut. It was decisively smashed by British artillery on December 24. Thereupon the chastened and dispirited Turkish commander was removed from his command. His successor was Khalil Bey, a seasoned veteran of the Balkan Wars (and by chance an uncle of Enver), a methodical conservative who was determined to concentrate exclusively upon a siege operation.

It was a sound decision. Within Kut, Townshend possessed a force of nine thousand soldiers, three-quarters of them Indians. Although these troops were amply stocked with ammunition, their food supplies were running low even then. At the onset of the siege, therefore, Townshend imposed a strict rationing schedule on the civilian population and his own soldiers alike. From his experience in the Chitral siege of years before, the general was certain of his ability to hold out at least a month. In any case, Nixon assured him by radio that it would not be longer than a month, for by January elements of two new divisions were arriving in Basra. Nor was Nixon prepared to wait for his army to reach full strength. Rather he ordered General Sir Fenton Aylmer to move upriver toward Kut with the seventeen thousand troops already in Mesopotamia. Unfortunately for the relief effort, few river craft were available to carry these reinforcements, and Aylmer's soldiers were obliged to move on foot. By the time the column arrived at the main Turkish defensive positions, at Hannah, January 6, 1916, it had already lost four thousand men from exhaustion, disease, and Arab night raids. Nothing daunted, Aylmer flung his Seventh Division against the Ottoman trenches. The battle was fought in searing heat. The Turks were inspirited for the defense by General Khalil himself, who assumed personal command of his men in the field. By nightfall the guts had been torn out of the Army of the Tigris. Aylmer broke off contact after losing an additional four thousand troops. The shock of this defeat was the final blow for Nixon. His health broke down completely, and he relinquished his command. Nor did he appear again in public until 1917, when he was called to testify before the royal commission which had been appointed to investigate the disaster of Kut and which rightfully placed most of the blame on him. His successor was General Sir Percy Lake, until then chief of the general staff of the Indian Army.

A week and a half after the failure at Hannah, on January 18, 1916, the Third Infantry Division arrived from France, and was dispatched immediately up the Tigris. Thus reinforced, Aylmer decided immediately to attempt a second frontal attack against Hannah. It was launched across open ground on the 21st and hurled back with heavy casualties even before reaching the enemy trenches. During the battle, Townshend's soldiers in Kut could hear the distant roar of guns, even see the tantalizing flashes of cannon fire in the night sky. Ringed by successive lines of Ottoman trenches, however, they were locked in as effectively as the British relief force was blocked from entering. The winter rains now descended in torrents upon the besieged Anglo-Indian division. Fuel was growing scarce, food more so. Six weeks had passed since the original withdrawal to Kut, and the men were now on half rations. Radioed messages of encouragement continued to arrive from Sir Percy Lake, from the viceroy of India, from Russian General Baratov, even from the king, praising Townshend's courage and entreating his men to hold out. The appeals were of dwindling effect by the first week of March, as the beleaguered troops were reduced to slaughtering horses and even mules for food.

On March 12, Aylmer was replaced as commander of the relief force by General George Gorringe. Strengthened now by additional reinforcements from the Western front, Gorringe was determined to break the Turkish stranglehold on Kut, whatever the casualties. Khalil anticipated this effort, and in early April pulled his troops back to a new and stronger defensive position, at Sannayiyat, fifteen miles from Kut. And when Gorringe's men lunged forward on April 10, they were mowed down by an artillery and machine gun fusillade; fully sixty per cent of the division was put out of action. These sapping losses, together with unending rainstorms and flooded terrain, delayed any likelihood of a new attack for several weeks. When, nevertheless, on April 22, Townshend radioed that food in Kut was all but exhausted, Gorringe decided to mount yet another effort. The attack began, the British pushing forward in a quagmire up to their armpits. Again they were cut down without breaching the Ottoman lines. With that final exertion, Gorringe knew that his troops had reached the end of their resources. In April alone, 10,000 soldiers had died in three weeks of attacks, and several units had been wiped out completely. During the entire relief effort, from January to April 1916, the Tigris Army had suffered 23,000 battle casualties, and nearly that many had been debilitated by illness.

By April, too, Townshend's embattled garrison had used

up its rations. Soldiers were collapsing of starvation, and Townshend himself was continually drowsy and in a half-stupor. On the night of the 24th, the general was informed that a Basra paddle steamer, loaded to the gunwales with food and medicines, had been sent up the churning Tigris under cover of darkness. Within hours the Turks intercepted the vessel, killing its crew. Townshend by then recognized that all hope was gone. He radioed for permission to discuss terms with the enemy, and Sir Percy Lake granted the request. The ordeal by then had continued for 143 days, longer than the sieges of Plevna and Ladysmith. On April 28, Townshend received assurances from the Turkish general that all prisoners would be well treated. Accordingly, the Englishman accepted Khalil's demand for unconditional surrender. Immediately upon entering Kut, the Turks honored their promise by massacring the town's remaining four thousand Arab civilians. The fate of the Anglo-Indians troops was not much better. The haggard, starving prisoners were marched by foot more than a hundred miles to Baghdad. Those who survived that nightmare were marched in stages from Baghdad yet another five hundred miles to central Anatolia, and finally to Tarsus, where they were put to work on chain gangs blasting tunnels for the Berlin-to-Baghdad Railway. Of the troops who surrendered at Kut, seventy per cent died of this treatment. Townshend alone was handled considerately. Indeed, he was housed in his own villa on an island off Constantinople, permitted virtually free movement, even invited to attend concerts and shooting matches with his captors. The general was aware of the fate of his troops, but he did not hesitate to accept this personal hospitality. Following his return to England after the war, he lived to be elected to Parliament on the Tory ticket.

For Britain the consequences of the loss of Kut were far-reaching. Until then, the British government and nation had not fully appreciated the truly monumental incompetence of the Indian Command. After Townshend's surrender, the War Cabinet henceforth took direct and complete charge of the Tigris campaign, and the Army of India was from then on

subordinated to the imperial war office. It was London's belated decision, too, nearly two years after the initially quite
limited Persian Gulf expedition began, that the campaign in
Mesopotamia should thenceforth, and at long last, remain exclusively defensive. The Tigris Army had suffered forty thousand casualties and was exhausted by failure and sickness.
The troops were thereupon consigned to the defense-works outside Sannayiyat on the left bank of the Tigris. It was not much
of an improvement. In those furnacelike trenches the men
endured a plague of flies, the racking agony of dysentery, the
endless dull loneliness and isolation that were the desert's
authentic weapons. Not a few went mad, the victims of perhaps the most ill-conceived British military operation of the
entire war.

The Allies had been cruelly burned in the Middle East
during the eighteen months since they had embarked on the
Gallipoli offensive. Despite the losses they had inflicted on the
Ottoman enemy, it was apparent that even the immeasurable
advantages of British maritime strength and Russian land
power had not been sufficient to crack the hold of the "Sick
Man," either on his European doorstep or on his Asian hinterland. Even worse, each commitment of men and matériel
required additional infusions of troops and supplies to protect the original investment. Lethargic and dispirited as the
Turk was reputed to be, he managed somehow to put up an
astonishingly effective resistance. His ostensibly defenseless
terrain was fast becoming a bottomless quicksand for Allied
soldiery. Sobered now, the Entente governments recognized
that it was evidently not possible to depend upon their armed
forces alone to win freedom of movement in the Oriental
theater. The plain fact was that the unexpected costs of this
Middle Eastern investment would have to be supplemented by
political concessions the longer the war continued. Offers
would have to be made, bargains would have to be struck, to
mobilize the resources and manpower of the non-Turkish peoples of the Middle East. It was time for the diplomats to try
their hand.

CHAPTER IV

THE ARMENIAN GENOCIDE

The Unknown People

DURING LATE APRIL 1915, in an audacious operation that preceded by nearly a year his triumph at Kut, General Khalil Bey led a division of Ottoman troops across the plains of the lower Araxes valley in Transcaucasia. The Turkish commander's goal was the Russian oil center of Baku, on the shore of the Caspian Sea. If successful, the offensive would serve as both military and moral compensation for the disaster suffered by Enver at Sarikamish three months before (Chapter II). Even as he was en route, however, Khalil suddenly received the astonishing news that the people of Van, a normally peaceful and compliant Armenian community in southeastern Asia Minor, had apparently rebelled against Turkish authority, and even then were threatening Ottoman lines of communication in Transcaucasia. Accordingly, with typical caution, Khalil decided to pull back until the uprising could be dealt with by other units. His Russian opposite number, General Yudenich, immediately seized the opportunity opened by this retreat to launch the Russian Army of the Caucasus directly toward Van itself. On May 19, an advance Russian column entered the town and relieved the besieged Armenians. Two days later, Russian divisions encamped on the surrounding plain. The danger of a renewed Ottoman attack in the Transcaucasus had been anticipated and aborted. The Armenian revolt in Van had manifestly been a timely one for Russian purposes.

Actually, this was not the first time the Armenians had played a critical role in the military and political affairs of the Transcaucasus. Their very location at the juncture of two empires, indeed of two continents, made them, willy-nilly, the most pivotal of western Asia's numerous minority races. The sheer extent of their presence was in fact apparent the moment one entered the Ottoman realm. It was not their appearance that identified them, for they were swarthy, "Oriental," often physically indistinguishable from their Turkish neighbors. Rather, their culture was the identifying factor. Their alphabet was an offshoot of the Greek. Their religion was Christian. Their towns and villages were well developed by Asian standards, and notably more affluent than those of the Turks. Nor were any communities in the Middle East more widely flung or more densely inhabited. Thousands of Armenians lived a "European" existence in eastern Thrace; tens of thousands of others prospered mightily in Constantinople and smaller neighboring settlements. Additional constellations of Armenian towns, cities, and farms extended in linked necklaces across the northeastern highlands of Cilicia and intermingled with Turkish villages on the central Anatolian plain. Most significantly, in the highlands of Ottoman Transcaucasia an endless succession of Armenian stores, shops, and wooden churches, a forest of crosses towering over densely packed frame houses, proclaimed the final dominance of an urban Christian civilization over a Turkish and Kurdish peasant majority.

Ironically, until the turn of the century there were few races on earth about whom even educated Westerners knew less. The origins of the Armenians, their language and religion, even their precise geographic locations, were shrouded in obscurity. The limited historical evidence suggested that they may originally have been Thracians who had crossed into the Transcaucasus region about the fourth century B.C. Conquering and intermarrying there with the local Persian tribes, the newcomers evidently maintained their customs and language. During the late Roman period the Armenians embraced Byzantine Christianity, although late in the fourth century of our era, impatient with the political domination of Constantinople, they organized their own autonomous Gregorian Church.

The Seljuk sweep of Asia Minor in the eleventh and twelfth centuries accounted for the first Armenian dispersion. Tens of thousands of Christian villagers fled the Turkish *yatagan,* migrating to southern Russia, the Ukraine, and southwestern Asia Minor. The dispersion was by no means conclusive, however, for throughout succeeding centuries of Ottoman conquest, and despite continual partitions and repartitions of Transcaucasia at the hands of Turks, Russians, and Persians, the bulk of the Armenian people remained under Turkish rule. On the eve of the World War, their numbers in Ottoman territory were estimated at 1,845,000. Of this population, a quarter million were to be found in the Constantinople–eastern-Thrace region, and nearly that many in Cilicia, in southwestern Turkey. Yet by far the majority, at least one and a third million, had settled in the eastern empire, in the Transcaucasian vilayets of Erzerum, Sivas, Kharput, Diarbekir, and Van. Most were farmers; but a sizable minority of tradesmen among them fulfilled the identical mercantile role for the Turkish interior that the Greeks performed for the Ottoman import-export trade. And the truth was that the government in Constantinople, as well as the neighboring Turkish and Kurdish populations, valued the economic function carried out by this Christian people and generally left them alone.

It was the renewal of tsarist pressure on the Ottoman Empire in the second half of the nineteenth century which first undermined Armenian security. Russia's imperialist "solicitude" for the Ottoman Christian minorities was, in fact, largely responsible for the Crimean War of 1853–56 and for the Russo-Turkish War of 1877–78. At the Congress of Berlin, which followed the latter conflict, St. Petersburg exploited its avuncular interest in the Christians by insisting on assurance of reforms in the Armenian vilayets of eastern Turkey. Sultan Abdul Hamid was not unwilling to give that assurance; but the moment Russian troops evacuated Ottoman territory, his guarantee typically became a dead letter. As Djemal Pasha chose to explain the episode decades later: "The whole scheme was only a pretext on the part of Russia for snatching a very large part of Anatolia, which was inhabited exclusively by Turks and Kurds. They naturally regarded Armenia . . . as a snake let loose by Russia against them." The Armenians paid bitterly for this instrusive tsarist concern for their welfare. More than ten thousand of them were slain in pogroms that raged in the immediate aftermath of the war. Over the next few years entire Armenian villages were razed by Turkish army units and hired Kurdish irregulars.

These brutal measures evoked an immediate and far-reaching Armenian political response. During the last two decades of the nineteenth century, Armenian irredentism both in the Ottoman Empire and among the million and a quarter Armenians of Russia was powerfully stimulated by an emergent Russian-Armenian intelligentsia. The dramatists and journalists Nazarian, Nalbandian, Ardzrouni, and Soundoukian were powerful advocates of the liberal nationalism they had absorbed in their years as emigrés in Europe. So, too, were the Armenian political organizations that began springing up on Russian soil. Ultimately, the most influential of the latter were the militantly nationalist Huntchakian and Dashnaktsutiun parties. Operating from bases in Russian Transcaucasia, "Dashnak" partisans organized drilling and hiking groups, then paramilitary units, and finally conspiratorial underground cells across the Ottoman border for the distribution of propaganda, arms, and ammunition. In 1894 and 1897, the "Huntchaks" ignited a series of bloody riots against Abdul Hamid's regime in the east Anatolian provinces. Twice, in the name of autonomy, they staged daring raids on the Imperial Ottoman Bank in the very heart of Constantinople. By the mid-nineties, fierce, sanguinary clashes between Turks and Armenian revolutionaries were becoming all but uncontrollable. So was Turkish retaliation. The slaughter of Armenian men, women, and children reached perhaps fifty thousand by the end of the century.

One may therefore understand the ecstasy with which

Armenians, as well as others of the empire's millet peoples, greeted the Young Turk Revolution of 1908. Responding full-heartedly to the new vistas of freedom that appeared to be opening, the Dashnak leaders—now emerging as the most influential spokesmen of the Armenian cause—eagerly pledged their funds and their lives to the revolutionary effort. Not less intense was the shock of their disillusionment upon encountering the virulent Turkish nationalism that lurked behind the CUP's egalitarian façade. The process of Turkification gained momentum rapidly. As we recall, it was exacerbated between 1908 and 1913 by further Western incursions into Ottoman territory. Constantinople's response was to restrict drastically the cultural activities of the minority races, even the public use of non-Turkish languages. In 1913, a chain reaction of pogroms again swept through the Armenian vilayets. Kurdish irregulars were given free reign to slaughter and pillage. These were the circumstances to which St. Petersburg alluded, a year before the World War, as it decided to raise the question of Armenian reform once again, and to its own advantage.

No gesture could have been more cynical, in view of the tsarist regime's treatment of its own Armenian minority. To be sure, the Armenians of Russian Transcaucasia had enjoyed a reasonable degree of security and equality during the earlier part of the nineteenth century. But the official attitude changed radically during the Slavophile Reaction of the 1880's. The Armenians suffered equally with Russia's other minorities in the ensuing repression. The use of their language was severely curtailed. Scores of Russian-Armenian writers and publicists were imprisoned. Eventually the Dashnak Party was outlawed, and its leaders hunted down and exiled or killed. In the years preceding the World War, therefore, Dashnak hatred, festering beneath the surface of political life, was directed with equal intensity against the Russian and Ottoman governments alike. Russian officials in the Transcaucasus were assassinated, as were Armenians who collaborated with the tsarist regime. Pitched battles with government troops occurred. It was therefore for the purpose both of diverting local Armenian unrest and of probing yet another opportunity for intrusion into Turkish affairs that Foreign Minister Sazanov focused his attention once again on the Armenian provinces of the Ottoman Empire. His ultimate purpose was to acquire a sphere of Russian influence there, particularly in the region of the heavily defended Turkish fortress of Erzerum. With the Porte gravitating all but irretrievably into the German orbit, it appeared vital for the Russians to forestall its European rival in this crucial border area.

The essence of Sazanov's plan for "reform" was to combine the six Armenian vilayets into a single province under an Armenian governor invested with full administrative and police powers. As the Russian foreign minister conceived it, this administrative alienation of Ottoman Armenia from the Porte was the vital first step toward ultimate tsarist control of eastern Turkey. It was not to be that easy, of course; the Constantinople government understood immediately what Sazanov was after. So did Berlin. Both capitals rejected the plan emphatically. Sazanov persisted. Britain and France supported the Russian plan. Eventually, after a year and a half of intensive and frequently acrimonious discussion, a compromise formula was produced and accepted by the Young Turk Cabinet on January 26, 1914. By its provisions, the vilayets of eastern Anatolia would be divided into two general inspectorates, each of these posts to be held by a European, who would be nominated by the European powers and would possess full authority to supervise the local civil administrations. "The outstanding role of Russia in the Armenian Question is thus officially emphasized," Gulkievich, the Russian minister plenipotentiary who negotiated the agreement, wired to Sazanov on the day of its signing. ". . . This circumstance will certainly not fail to exert a most favorable influence on the international status of Russia and to place a halo on the head of her sovereign in the eyes of the Christians in the Near East." The danger implicit in this achievement was not lost on the embittered Young Turk regime.

Prelude to Genocide

NOR, AFTER THE OUTBREAK of war, were the Turks unaware of Armenian participation in the Russian military effort.
With the active encouragement of the Catholicos of the Armenian Orthodox Church (who resided in Etchmiadzin, in
Russian Transcaucasia), tens of thousands of Russian Armenians volunteered for the tsarist armies. Their hatred of the
Turks would have been reason enough for this upsurge of
martial spirit. But there were other inducements. Count Varantzov-Dashkov, viceroy of the Caucasus, privately informed the
Dashnak leadership that his government was prepared to grant
the Ottoman Armenian vilayets full autonomy after the war
in return for Armenian support of the Russian military effort.
It was significant that the Dashnaks themselves did not insist
upon the incorporation of these provinces into the Russian
Empire; with their experience of tsarist justice, this would
surely have been small incentive. On the contrary, later in the
war the Russian Armenian press vigorously opposed such a
plan. "The Armenians are interested, for their national problem, in conserving the sovereignty of Turkey," declared Ad-
jemov, an Armenian deputy in the Duma. Nor, initially, was
St. Petersburg willing to alienate Armenians on either side of
the border by proposing Russian domination of these Ottoman
provinces.

On the other hand, the tsarist government was hardly
prepared to forego indefinitely its well-cultivated imperialist
ambitions for this territory. Rather, a way soon would have
to be found to reconcile those ambitions with the cause of
Armenian liberation. The Armenian Catholicos first anticipated
this difficulty. To resolve it, the primate asked Count Varantzov-
Dashkov, early in December 1914, to publish an official declaration to the Armenians modeled on one recently issued to the
Poles. The latter document had rather factitiously promised
"the resurrection of the Polish nation and its fraternal union
with Russia." A similar proclamation now hopefully would

93

assure "fraternal" Armenian cooperation both during and after the war. The idea aroused misgivings among certain officials in the foreign ministry, who noted that the Armenians historically were far from brotherly in their attitude toward the Russians. These objections were rejected a week later by Gulkievich. Some sort of proclamation on Armenian autonomy would have to be made, the minister insisted, if only to undermine a similar expected announcement by the Turks and Germans. Whether under Ottoman or Russian sovereignty, "Armenia must be in the sphere of our direct influence and this completely independently of the desires of our Allies."

And, in fact, not long thereafter the promise was dutifully made—by Foreign Minister Sazanov himself. In a major address before the Duma on February 9, 1915, Sazanov endorsed the public demand for postwar Russian domination of the Straits and Constantinople. After the fulfillment of this objective, the foreign minister disclosed, one of Russia's most important war aims was "the complete liberation of Armenia from the Turkish yoke." Sazanov noted that General Yudenich's recent victories on the Transcaucasian front had brought near "the moment of the decision of the economic and political tasks connected with the exit of Russia to the open sea." This was a meaningful reference to control over Armenian Cilicia. Allowing several minutes for the Duma's thunderous applause to abate, the foreign minister then reminded the deputies that before the war he had ceaselessly advocated reforms in Ottoman Armenia in "the disinterested traditions of Russian policy, and our state interests." The Agreement of February 8, 1914, he concluded, had successfully assured Russia's "exclusive position" in resolving the Armenian question, and at the peace conference this leverage would be used "in a direction benevolent for the Armenian population."

Sazanov's was the only public statement on this issue made by the government. Notwithstanding its ambiguous and veiled reference to Russian territorial ambitions in Ottoman Armenia, the speech almost immediately aroused the Russian Dashnaks to renewed and strenuous efforts on behalf of the

94

tsar's armies. Calls for additional volunteers went out and evoked a warm and spirited response. Some 20,000 newcomers joined the ranks of the 160,000 Armenians already serving in the regular army. Refugees from Turkey would considerably swell this figure later. Their role in the war was vital from the very outset. An Armenian unit, for example, provided invaluable support in hurling back Enver's army at Sarikamish, and on several occasions in 1915 Armenian tenacity was decisive in blunting other Turkish offensives—a fact to which General Kalistin, commander of the First Russian Army Corps of the Caucasus, enthusiastically attested. The provocation was maddening to the Ottoman government. Yet it was doubtful by then if the Turks needed additional inducement for taking "preventive measures."

Ideologically, the stage had been set for reprisals during the transitional period following the Young Turk Revolution of 1908, when the CUP intelligentsia gradually made its decision to reject a policy of liberalism for one of aggressive Turkish nationalism. Ziya Gökalp, leader of the prewar Turkish renaissance (see Chapter II), was the most influential spokesman for this aroused chauvinism. Decrying the "betrayal" of the empire by the non-Turkish races of the Balkans, Ziya insisted that the state's survival depended exclusively upon a single monolithic nation, the Turks alone. The time for Ottoman heterogeneity was past, he argued, past for the "corruption" of Turkish speech and literature by non-Turkish elements, past for the "domination" of the empire's economy by Armenians, Greeks, and Jews. Ominously, Ziya suggested that the influence of non-Turkish communities, as "foreign bodies," ought to be purged ruthlessly from public and political affairs. This polemic struck an especially responsive chord in the government after November 1914. By then, the Cabinet's wartime effort to "de-Ottomanize" the empire had assumed several forms. One was the abrogation of the Capitulations, the extraterritorial privileges traditionally enjoyed by foreign nationals and corporations. Other measures required that Turkish-owed businesses discharge all non-Turkish employees and that all business activities be conducted exclusively in the Turkish language. One of the ugliest manifestations of the new xenophobia was the sudden forced uprooting of thousand of Greek villagers in Thrace and western Anatolia shortly after the outbreak of the war, the burning of dozens of Greek towns, the mass looting of Greek homes and shops (see Chapter X). But no millet people suffered as cruelly as the Armenians.

In August 1914, shortly before Turkey's entry into the war, the Ottoman branch of the Armenian Dashnaktsutiun Party convened its annual national congress in Erzerum. One of the items of the congress's agenda was an address by Otto-man government representatives who had been dispatched especially from Constantinople to meet with the assembled Dashnaks. After transmitting the Cabinet's effusive assurances of goodwill toward the Armenians, the Turkish visitors issued a formal appeal for "solidarity" in the event of war with Russia. The Dashnaks willingly gave that assurance. But the government emissaries asked for more. They proposed a scheme for the conquest of Russian Armenia and the joining of that territory to the Turkish-Armenian vilayets as a single autonomous province of the Ottoman Empire. To fulfill the plan, the government spokesmen "invited" the Dashnaks to form special legions for the purpose of infiltrating Russian Transcaucasian territory and propagandizing among their kinsmen there. In this fashion, presumably, the inhabitants of Russian Armenia would be incited to revolt against tsarist rule.

The Dashnak representatives listened courteously, if in silent incredulity, as the project was outlined. Then, with equal courtesy, they rejected it. For one thing, they were quite certain that the Turks could never carry out so extravagant and farfetched a scheme. They suspected, too, that the CUP cabinet intended to colonize Transcaucasia not with Armenians, but with Moslems transplanted from Macedonia and Thrace; the local Christian inhabitants would probably be carried off to the desert wastes of Mesopotamia. Moreover, the Armenian population of Russia had already rallied enthusiastically to the tsarist cause. Any inducement offered by the despised

Turkish regime would hardly undermine that loyalty, especially when the Reform Agreement of February 1914 was known to be a dead letter in Ottoman territory. The Dashnaks were unwilling to assure the Porte of more than their own loyalty, under these circumstances; rather, they implored the Ottoman government not to become involved in the European war. The Turkish emissaries thereupon left Erzerum and returned to Constantinople empty-handed. Learning of the equivocal Dashnak response, the CUP leaders made little effort to disguise their chagrin and outrage. Their reaction, in turn, immediately had its impact on the anxious and distraught Armenian population.

To preclude Turkish reprisals, the Dashnak leaders labored unrelentingly, after the war began, to demonstrate their loyalty to the Ottoman regime. Their communal recruiting efforts were extensive and successful. With well-publicized indignation, they spurned the overtures of Kurdish chieftains eager to revolt against the Turks. Their response to the appeals of Russian Armenian spokesmen across the frontier was one of ostentatious indignation. In large measure, to be sure, this official reaction was embellished in inverse ratio to private Armenian sympathy for the Russian cause; for the community of interest between Armenians on the two sides of the frontier was hardly dissipated by the outbreak of war. A Russian Armenian deputy, one Papadzanov, indiscreetly alluded to this bond: "The Armenian population of Turkish Armenia joyously greeted our victorious [Russian] army," he stated in the Duma on January 28, 1915. "Armenians helped wherever and however they could, and prepared a hearty welcome for the Russians." The episodes to which Papadzanov referred constituted a response not to Russian promises, but rather to years of Turkish and Kurdish mistreatment. Armenian feelings were intensified by the Ottoman terror campaign that had been steadily unfolding since the earliest days of the war, up to and including the moment when CUP and Dashnak representatives in Erzerum were solemnly conducting their discussions on "mutual solidarity."

At the opening of the war, some 250,000 Armenians were immediately conscripted into the Ottoman army together with other Moslem and non-Moslem citizens of the empire. Two and a half months later, however, conscious of the vital role played by Russian-Armenian troops in the recent disaster at Sarikamish, Enver Pasha ordered the immediate transfer of all Ottoman Armenian soldiers to "labor battalions." The phrase was a crude euphemism. General Pomiankowski, the Austrian military attaché in Constantinople, was reliably informed that "the ministry of war had issued orders to the army commanders on February 18, 1915, to isolate [the Armenian labor battalions] and decimate them company by company." And, in fact, that was precisely their fate. They were murdered silently in hidden ravines, in groups of tens and hundreds. Overhead, within sight of the villages, flocks of vultures swooped into the mountain defiles. To the families of the victims, this was the first intimation of what actually was happening. Even as the Armenian communities were stripped of the armed protection of their husbands and sons, their local food supplies were confiscated and their pack animals sequestered. It was the merest beginning. As early as February 1915, rumors of a "plan of general massacre" were circulated, then rapidly verified. In March the entire Armenian population of Zeitoun, approximately fifteen thousand people, was deported to the marshlands of Konia. Another two thousand Cilician Armenians were deported to Aleppo, ostensibly to perform forced labor on the roads. Outlying villages elsewhere were repeatedly attacked by Kurdish "irregulars." The death toll soon rose into the thousands. An ominous pattern of mass murder began to unfold steadily and rapidly.

These were the circumstances that precipitated the "uprising" at Van. American and German missionaries there furnished eyewitness accounts of the episode. The governor of the province of Van was Djevdet Bey, the brother-in-law of Enver Pasha, and as fanatical a xenophobe as the war minister himself. In March 1915, Djevdet issued secret orders to begin "clearing" Armenians from the province. The governor's associates later testified at their own trials, after the war, that the technique of "de-Armeniazation" was to allow Kurdish troops a free hand in launching massacres in the densely congested villages. In this manner fully ten thousand civilians were killed between January and April. Those who survived fled in terror to the city of Van. Consequently, on April 17, the provincial governor prepared to deal with that community directly. Its population numbered forty thousand, of whom nearly half were Armenians. Since the outbreak of the war, the behavior of these Armenian townsmen had been scrupulously correct. More than ten thousand of the local youths had volunteered for the Ottoman armed forces; the Armenian merchants had contributed generously to the Ottoman Red Crescent. Unfortunately, their record of loyalty was of no avail. Without warning, Djevdet Bey stationed a cordon of Kurdish troops around Van and ordered the city's Dashnak leaders without delay to surrender three thousand men for the "army." The announcement sent a wave of horror through the civilian population. No one doubted the intended fate of the conscripts. Spokesmen for the community offered money instead. The offer was rejected. Immediately the Dashnak committee rushed to fortify the area and prepare additional measures of self-defense.

The attack began simultaneously. Djevdet instructed his troops to shell the Armenian section of town. Soon a large part of Van was in flames. The battle appeared hopelessly one-sided: the entire Armenian fighting force consisted of less than 1,500 armed men, against 5,000 Kurdish irregulars. But the defenders were not without advantages. The city was well elevated as a natural defense promontory. In addition, the Armenian leadership consisted of army veterans. Under their disciplined command, the men fought in orderly and scientific fashion and managed repeatedly to hurl back the frontal attacks launched on their fortifications. A curious exhilaration appeared to sweep the city's defenders. Volunteers flocked to serve as front-line troops or as medical aides or engineers. Through occasional counterattacks, too, the Armenians succeeded in replenishing their armory with captured weapons. Workshops were set up to manufacture bullets. Householders donated their plate and samovars to be melted down into nickel and brass for cartridges. A homemade cannon was fashioned from plumbing parts. As the days passed, the Turks recognized that the city was not likely to capitulate. In the interval, therefore, they ravaged the countryside, massacring civilians. Some villages were unprepared; others defended themselves furiously. By the account of Dr. Samuel Ussher, an American missionary, not less than 55,000 Armenian bodies were later found strewn throughout the province. The defenders of Van, nevertheless, continued to hold out, their city a powerfully barricaded fortress. Then, on May 16, nearly a month after the onset of the siege, the ordeal unexpectedly ended. The Turks retired as a Russian army approached; the population was saved. The Russian troops were compelled to withdraw from the city only two months later, but the majority of Van's inhabitants escaped in the wake of the departing Russians, together with perhaps 200,00 Armenians who had survived the terror in other parts of the vilayet. Their sanctuary was Russian Armenia, of course. The ill and aged who remained in Van were butchered to the last soul when the Turks and Kurds entered, and the Armenian quarter was entirely demolished.

The Death of a People

AT MIDNIGHT ON APRIL 25–6, 1915, approximately a week after the onset of the siege of Van, the police in Constantinople suddenly converged upon the homes of 235 of the city's most prominent Armenian citizens. The unfortunate householders were peremptorily dragged away from their families and hustled off in manacles to a central collecting station for deportation to the Turkish interior. Two Armenian members of Parliament, Vartkes and Zohrab, were spared this fate by virtue of their official position. Accordingly, both men rushed to the office of Talaat Pasha, the minister of the interior, and demanded a personal explanation for this outrage. They got it, indeed an explanation for everything that would follow. "Your people have come down from the mountains and have occupied Van, with the help of the Armenian population of the city," the minister declared. Now, he insisted, it was necessary "to take precautionary measures" against the Armenians living in "security areas." In a later interview with the deputies on May 12, Talaat elaborated on this point: "In the days of our weakness, after the reoccupation of Adrianople [1913], you forced us to the brink by raising the question of Armenian reforms. Now we shall profit from the favorable situation in which we find ourselves . . . to disperse your people so that, for the next fifty years, no questions about reforms will enter your heads again." Shortly afterward, Vartkes and Zohrab themselves were arrested at night and spirited away to Konia; Vartkes died of a heart attack en route. It was plain that the Young Turk Cabinet had found its rationale for solving the Armenian Question. In later years, Talaat perfected it:

> The responsibility of these acts falls first of all upon the deported people themselves. Russia, in order to lay hands on our eastern provinces, had armed and equipped the Armenian inhabitants of this district [Van], and had organized strong Armenian bandit forces in the said area. When we entered the great war, these bandits began their destructive activities in the rear of the Turkish Army on the Caucasus front, blowing up bridges, setting fire to the Turkish towns and villages and killing the innocent Mohammedan inhabitants, regardless of age and sex, they spread death and terror over the eastern provinces, and endangered the Turkish Army's line of retreat.

The official version of these allegations was eventually published in a governmental blue book, *Vérité sur le mouvement révolutionnaire arménien et les mesures gouvernementales* (Constantinople, 1916). It was a fabrication from beginning to end.

The unfolding evidence of Armenian genocide was too palpable to be subject to Ottoman distortion. For now, indeed, in the spring of 1915, the storm of Turanian xenophobia which had been gathering for decades over this vulnerable minority people was released with lethal and climactic savagery. Cilicia was the first region to be "cleared," in April. Next, in June and July, came the zone bordering on Van, extending from the Black Sea to the Persian frontier. The other eastern Anatolian vilayets of Erzerum, Erzindjan, Kharput, Trebizond, and Sivas, the heartland of Ottoman Armenia, followed in July, August, and September. In November the sanjaq of Caesaria was evacuated; several of the outlying southeastern communities were reserved for the very last, the winter of 1915–16. The announced destination of this uprooted population was the desert area linking Mesopotamia and Syria. But the terms "relocation" and "deportation" were manifestly intended only for public consumption. The technique of full-scale extermination had been devised as early as April. Public criers appeared in towns and villages ordering male Armenians to present themselves at the local government building. The men came immediately, leaving their shops or farms. They were promptly detained and ordered to "make ready" for a journey to Mosul or Baghdad. Within hours the prisoners were roped and marched out of town in groups of tens and twenties. They did not get far. At the first lonely place on the road the men were shot and bayoneted by gendarmes or Kurdish frontier police. Several days later the remaining Armenian inhabitants—the women, children, and older people—were similarly ordered to prepare for departure.

Here the process of liquidation was barely prolonged. Driven out at bayonet point in convoys of several hundred, the exiles were obliged to trudge through a mountainous wilderness entirely devoid of water. The weather was generally hot. The dying began almost immediately. Those who survived the first twenty or thirty miles were frequently plundered and slaughtered by Kurds. A few thousand of the deportees somehow endured the gauntlet of terror and managed to cross the Taurus Mountains to the first way station, Aleppo. They were human skeletons by then, all but incapable of further movement. Nevertheless, they were hounded and whipped steadily onward toward Mesopotamia. Few remained alive that long.

From June through August 1915, these processions of death wound ther way endlessly from eastern and central Turkey toward the desert. Along the route of march, German, American, and other neutral witnesses saw the patented Turkish method of liquidating an entire people. On June 10, for example, the German consul at Mosul telegraphed Ambassador von Wangenheim news of the slaughter of 614 Armenian men, women, and children who had been floated down the Tigris by raft from Diarbekir; the river was clogged with human bodies and parts of bodies. On June 18, the German consul at Erzerum witnessed the massacre of no less than 25,000 women and children in the Kemekh gorge near Erzinjan. On October 8, 1915, four members of the German Mission staff at Erzinjan reported the mass deaths of women and children by starvation and thirst; local Moslems were forbidden to succor the dying. There were other reports of cannibalism, of mass torture, of sexual mutilation. A few of these descriptions were provided by the Turks themselves. Others, the most damning, came from American missionaries in the interior. Henry Morgenthau was indefatigable in transmitting to Washington detailed accounts of torture and massacre, by drowning, axing, bayoneting, by bullet and fire. A compendium of this American testimony, appearing in the Bryce Report of 1916, described mutilated corpses tied in batches and cast into the sea, women and children thrown alive into wells and fire, mass rapes, drawing and quartering, and victims, still alive, being gnawed by dogs and jackals.

Opportunities for Armenians to fight back were rare and isolated. The besieged inhabitants of Ourfa, in Cilicia, held off a Turkish regular army unit for six weeks, until the last defenders were slain. Cilicia, too, was the arena of perhaps the most renowned episode of Armenian resistance, this one in the Jibal Mousa region, where the 4,058 men, women, and children of seven villages defied the Turkish deportation edict Retreating instead to the mountain of El Musa, the beleaguered Christians kept fifteen thousand Turkish soldiers at bay, fighting continually for fifty-three days. The Reverend Dikran

Adreasian, spiritual leader of the revolt, issued an appeal to the Allies which Armenian youths bore with them as they swam along the coast, frantically attempting to draw the attention of passing European vessels:

> Sir, we appeal to you in the name of Christ. Transport us, we pray you, to Cyprus or any other free land. Our people are not indolent; we shall earn our own bread if we are employed. If this is too much to grant, transport at least our women, old people, and children, equip us with sufficient arms, ammunition, and food, and we will work with you with all our might against the Turkish forces. Please sir, do not wait until it is too late!

In this single instance, it was not too late. A French cruiser rescued the survivors and transported them to Port Saïd. The episode was the subject of Franz Werfel's novel *The Forty Days of Musa Dagh*. The rescue was atypical. By the winter of 1916 the "deportations" had largely been completed.

The immolation of the Armenian people did not take place entirely without protest. Several members of the liberal Turkish Opposition expressed their outrage both in the press and in parliament. Talaat Bey coldly refused to acknowledge this criticism, however, insisting that public discussion would be "inimical to the interest of the Empire." Ambassador Morgenthau was not easily put off: the firsthand reports from American missionaries and consuls had shaken him to his depths. "For hours they would sit in my office," he recalled, "and, with tears streaming down their faces, they would tell me of the horrors through which they had passed. Many of these . . . were almost broken in health from the scenes they had witnessed. . . . It was not only American and Canadian missionaries who made this personal appeal. Several of their German associates begged me to intercede." This he did willingly and continually. But in the minister of the interior he encountered an immovable force.

Talaat was an extraordinary personality. A tough political infighter, he had begun his career as chief clerk in the Salonica directorate of posts and telegraphy, then had continued as a strong-arm man during the early years of the Young Turk movement. By a shrewd use of influence-peddling and personal blackmail, he eventually reached the summit of governmental power as party boss of the Committee of Union and Progress. Although he was a heavy-set, muscular, coarse-featured man, Talaat was not unattractive in his very grossness, his earthy unpretentiousness. By the unremitting use of guile and political leverage, he ensured that his authority over the internal affairs of the empire should continue virtually absolute. That control extended to the millet peoples, and the liquidation of the Armenians thereupon became his private project. Rebuffing Morgenthau's appeals with his customary easy geniality, the minister of the interior based his case for the deportations on the, by then, familiar allegations of Armenian treachery, of the "inevitability of the historical process."

In his implacability on the Armenian Question, moreover, Talaat knew that he could depend upon the tacit support of the German ambassador. Wangenheim was hardly less aware than Morgenthau of what was happening. The reports he received from German consuls and missionaries in the interior were minute and detailed. But his reaction was studiously noncommittal. "I think we ought to mitigate the form [the hardships] take," the ambassador cabled Berlin on May 31, 1915, "but not to attempt to prevent them in principle. The work of the Armenian undermining, nourished by Russia, has assumed dimensions which menace the existence of Turkey." Morgenthau's appeals to his German colleague were as unavailing as with Talaat. "[Wangenheim's] antipathy to the Armenians became immediately apparent," he wrote later. ". . . In his eyes (as in Talaat's and Enver's), the Armenians were simply traitorous vermin." The American ambassador was seconded in his efforts by a number of German correspondents, who attempted on their own to intercede with Wangenheim. They were similarly rebuffed. "I think that . . . [the Turks] are entirely justified," Wangenheim emphasized to Harry Stuermer, of the *Kölnische Zeitung*. "The weaker nation must succumb."

Eventually, belatedly, the conscience of Berlin was reached. It was not Wangenheim who reached it, however, but rather the veteran and respected chief of the Protestant Mission in the Ottoman Empire, Dr. Johannes Lepsius. A middle-aged Evangelical cleric who had spent most of his life in the Middle East, Lepsius had witnessed the atrocities at first hand and, like Morgenthau, had pleaded vainly with Talaat for their mitigation. Eventually his exertions made him *persona non grata* in Turkey. Returning to Germany, Lepsius described the Armenian horrors in a series of impassioned lectures, pastoral newsletters, and, finally, two lengthy and detailed volumes of documented eyewitness accounts. At first the German government "persuaded" the eminent clergyman to depart for the Netherlands, lest he embarrass relations between Berlin and Constantinople. But unrest grew in German religious and official circles. It was reflected, after Wangenheim's death late in 1915, by the new ambassador to the Porte, Count Wolff-Metternich, a kindly old gentleman of less Pan-Germanic disposition. Unfortunately, Wolff-Metternich's circumspect protests came too late. By the end of the year the largest part of the Armenian population of Turkey had been wiped out, and yet another sixty thousands victims were disposed of in the early months of 1916.

ESTIMATES DIFFERED of the number of Armenians murdered between 1915 and the end of the war. Of the most thoroughly documented, Lepsius's survey calculated the total of Armenians slain or deported as 1,396,000. This figure included virtually the entire Armenian population of Transcaucasia, another 238,000 Armenians from Cilicia and Syria, and perhaps 30,000 from Constantinople and Adrianople. Lepsius estimated, as well, that a billion German marks' worth of Armenian property had been confiscated by the Ottoman government. Somewhat more conservatively, the British scholar and foreign office expert Arnold Toynbee concluded that 182,000 Armenians had escaped to the Russian Transcaucasus, that the Armenian populations of Smyrna and Constantinople were essentially untouched, and that the number of those killed was more accurately placed between 800,000 and 1,000,000. In either case, not more than a third of the Armenian population of 1914 remained in Turkey when the war ended. By any standards this was surely the most unprecedented, indeed the most unimaginable racial annihilation, until then, in modern history. Nevertheless, apparently unconcerned by the enormity of their affront to civilization, the members of the Young Turk regime continued to view the "deportations" as nothing more than effective diplomacy, the realization of Abdul Hamid's injunction that "the best way to finish with the Armenian Question is to finish with the Armenians."

The Russians Launch an Offensive

IN LARGE DEGREE, the Armenian massacres of 1915 were facilitated by the Turkish recapture of the city of Van on August 4 and the subsequent withdrawal of Russian troops toward their own territory. But the tsarist reverse in the eastern vilayets proved temporary, essentially a strategic regrouping of lines. The Dardanelles campaign, too, in conjunction with the British expedition in Mesopotamia, took much of the pressure off the Russians in the Transcaucasus. Thus, by the end of 1915, the Russian Caucasus Army had grown to 170,000 troops, some 50,000 more than the Ottoman force across the lines. General Yudenich was determined to exploit this numerical advantage. His plan was nothing less than the destruction of the Ottoman Third Army, possibly even the capture of Erzerum. The exertion would undoubtedly be costly, but seemed to be justified by the goal. A Carcassonne-like entrenchment of fortresses, Erzerum was the single key to the entire Ottoman frontier region in the east. Its conquest would not merely deprive Turkey of the communications routes that had long menaced Russian Transcaucasia, but, conceivably, also would open the way to the entire hinterland of eastern Asia Minor.

Yudenich, the victor of Sarikamish, was eminently suited for the job. A British observer who visited his headquarters described the Russian general as "a short, bullet-headed man with long mustaches . . . [continually surrounded] by the statue-like forms of two staff officers. His voice was short and abrupt, his manner that of one who is accustomed to command. The atmosphere was thoroughly military. It suggested that the human mind was manufactured to order and turned out according to specified pattern." It is entirely possible, indeed, that Yudenich was the ablest commander produced by the Russian army during the World War. Now, at Kars, working at his usual electric pace with a small, taut staff, he brought organization and hard-driving enthusiasm to his task. Supplies were quietly accumulated, a network of field telephone wires was laid, soldiers were fully dressed and equipped for winter. None except the senior officers knew what was afoot, and a façade of normalcy was scrupulously maintained. Russian troop reinforcements were deployed under cover of darkness. The Turks were completely unsuspecting. During the Christmas period, Mahmut Kamil Pasha, commander of the Ottoman Third Army, was on leave in Constantinople, and his German chief of staff, Major Guse, had gone to Germany to recover from typhus.

The tsarist forces began their advance on January 13, 1916. After an initial feint against the well-entrenched Turkish positions north of Erzerum, Yudenich launched his major offensive on the Passan plain to the south. So savage and unexpected was the Russian blow that the main Ottoman line cracked within six hours, and the acting Turkish commander had no alternative but to order a general retreat to the inner complex of Erzerum forts. By the 18th the Russians had invested the entire east Passan plain and the basin of the Araxes. Yudenich was convinced now that the time was ripe for a final stroke. His aviation observers informed him that Erzerum seemed unprepared to meet an attack. Large stores of munitions and supplies had been abandoned during the Turkish retreat, and no reinforcements appeared to be arriving for the fortress area. The Turks evidently considered the ridge of Karagapazar—ten thousand feet high and dividing the Araxes basin from the depression of the western Euphrates—too formidable an obstacle for the Russians to cross; its defenses were so light as to be merely perfunctory. Yudenich knew what had to be done. Immediately he began widening his communications lines and laying plans to move on Erzerum via the ridge.

It was a fearful undertaking. In the numbing cold of the Transcaucasian winter, Russian troops were compelled not only to scale the trackless, saw-toothed height, but also to pull their heavy equipment with them. These supplies included large-caliber artillery that the soldiers dismantled and carried on their backs. The combination of knifelike wind and physical exertion very nearly proved lethal to the Russian peasant conscripts. One entire battalion froze to death in a blizzard. Most of the men, however, successfully reached the crest. On February 11, the assault began. While diversionary attacks were carried out against the perimeter of the main forts, the soldiers on the ridge slowly and painfully descended. The Turkish advance guard, anticipating nothing, had burrowed deeply into their trenches to avoid the freezing wind. Shortly after dawn on February 13, they were dumfounded to see apparently endless ranks of dark figures closing in on them through the snow flurries. It seemed impossible that human beings with full equipment could have traversed that hellish ridge. The unfortunate Turks had little time to reflect on this phenomenon; they were overwhelmed. A day of bitter fighting ensued at the outlying forts, but Russian artillery, reassembled now, turned the tide. The last outer forts were evacuated on orders of the commander, and by the 16th, Yudenich's army had swept into the plain of Erzerum.

The moment the Russians breached the outer ring and entered the open plateau, the huge inner fortress of Erzerum itself, some 6,250 feet above sea level—the highest citadel in the world—was no longer defensible. In truth, Erzerum was hardly more than a vast recruiting base and ammunition magazine. Its guns were of 1878 vintage, its stone barracks a death trap for any besieged garrison. Yudenich ordered his troops to advance on this anomaly without further delay, and they did this on the late afternoon of the 16th, against negligible resistance. The Turkish defenders withdrew at the first exchange of fire; they had lost ten thousand men in the fighting of the preceding four days. The fall of the historic base supplied the Russians with over three hundred guns and tons of other captured equipment. It was an impressive victory for Yudenich. Indeed, the conquest of Erzerum was a turning point, the first major offensive success for the Allies in Asia. It was evident now that Russia would dominate the great land junction from central Europe to central Asia. Germany's Berlin-to-Baghdad plan appeared doomed.

And so it was. Once the Russians were in possession of the historic routes that converged at Erzerum from Mesopotamia, Anatolia, Persia, and the Caucasus, the conquest of the rest of the Armenian plateau—Mush, Bitlis, and Erzinjan—followed as a matter of course. During the late winter and spring of 1916, the tsarist offensive unfolded with apparently irresistible speed and power. Enver's frantic efforts to rush the Ottoman Second Army to the Transcaucasus were paralyzed by the single-track railway crossing Anatolia. Reinforcements failed to arrive at their positions until the following August. In the interval, the redoubtable Yudenich systematically hounded down and decimated the fleeing Third Army. The moment, too, that his troops had invested Mush and Bitlis, the Russian general decided to launch an immediate offensive against Trebizond. Control of this Black Sea harbor, the only usable Ottoman port on the northern shore of Anatolia, would make possible the extension of operations against the Turkish interior. It happened that way precisely. A combined military and naval bombardment smashed Trebizond's defenses on April 14, and Yudenich was now able to reprovision his army by sea. On July 25 the well-equipped Russian troops

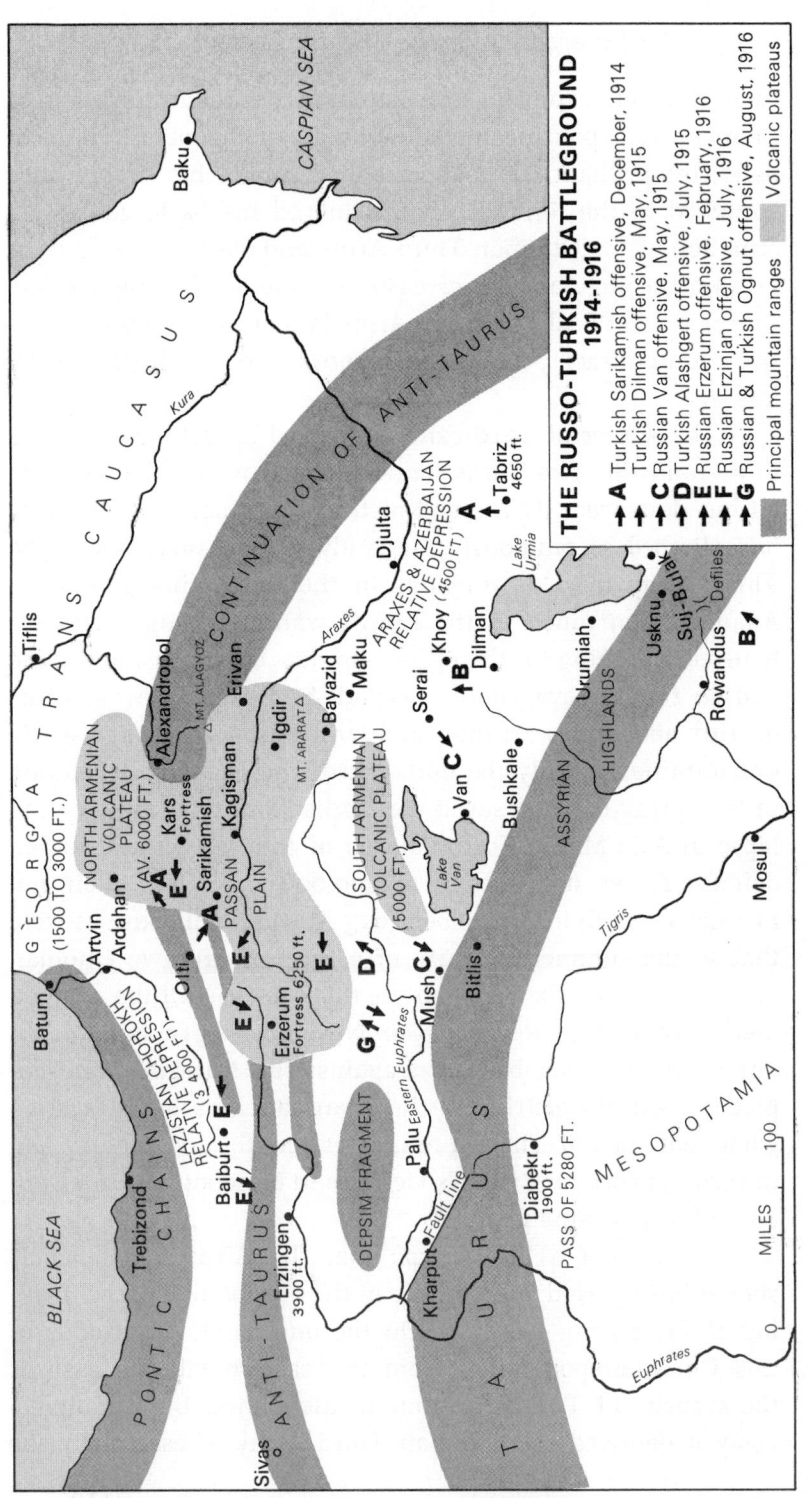

THE RUSSO-TURKISH BATTLEGROUND
1914-1916

A↑ Turkish Sarikamish offensive, December, 1914
B↑ Turkish Dilman offensive, May, 1915
C↑ Russian Van offensive. May, 1915
D↑ Turkish Alashgert offensive. July, 1915
E↑ Russian Erzerum offensive. February, 1916
F↑ Russian Erzinjan offensive, July, 1916
G↑ Russian & Turkish Ognut offensive. August, 1916

▨ Principal mountain ranges
▨ Volcanic plateaus

forged ahead, capturing the Ottoman headquarters town of Erzincan and pouring into the vast Erzincan plain. Here, finally, the brilliant commander called a halt, his supply lines stretched to the limit. He had achieved his basic goals: destruction of the Ottoman Third Army and assurance of a tight grip on the jugular vein of eastern Anatolia. During the late summer, Izzet Pasha's Second Army launched a series of tentative counterattacks, all of which were thrown back with heavy losses.

The winter of 1916 came early and brought the fighting to a standstill. The Turks had been bled white, their morale all but destroyed. By the end of the year, their desertion rate had climbed so ominously that fully 60,000 survivors of the Third Army lived as brigands in the mountains of eastern Anatolia, and much of the army's waning strength was exhausted searching for them. By then, too, exposure and disease had so fatally ravaged the Second Army that it was subsequently abolished as a unit, and Izzet Pasha was sent back to Constantinople. Only the outbreak of the Russian Revolution in the spring of 1917 saved the Turks from total military collapse in Asia Minor. For by March of that year, the Ottoman defense forces had shrunk to 400,000 men, half their numerical strength in November 1915. It was significant, as well, that in the summer of 1916, of a total of fifty-two Ottoman divisions, twenty-six were fighting the Russians. Of the 400,000 men permanently lost between November 1915 and March 1917, 300,000 had been lost against the Russians. The unprecedented bloodletting in the Transcaucasus had destroyed what remained of Turkish military strength, and thereby laid the groundwork for Britain's victories in Mesopotamia in 1917–18 and in Palestine in 1918.

It was not a little ironic that the Armenian genocide should have played a major role in the erosion of Turkish fighting ability during 1915–16. On the one hand, the exodus of this Christian population from the eastern vilayets assured the security of Turkish communication lines. But simultaneously it deprived the Ottoman Third Army of essentially the only noncommissioned officers capable of serving as interpreters, secretaries, paymasters, and technicians. (Liman had recognized the vital functions of the Armenians in these specialized services by insisting that at least the Armenian military units at his own headquarters be maintained intact.) There were other, even more invidious, consequences of the genocide. Transcaucasia and eastern Anatolia, depopulated of Armenians, were incapable of supporting the Ottoman Second Army, for the fields remained untilled, the urban centers deserted. Nor were adequate supply sources available elsewhere. Thousands of Turkish soldiers died at the front from starvation and illness as a result. So extensive was the general atrophy that German physicians were helpless to cope with the sick and dying. "It is remarkable how little power of resistance these debilitated men have even for slight operations," reported a German surgeon, Dr. Liebert. "If we do not operate on them, they die. If we do operate, they die also." The soaring death rate from malnutrition and disease was not characteristic of any other Turkish front. The ravaged countryside, the lack of fuel, food, and medicines accounted for it. "It is almost like a nemesis of fate," observed Liman, "that the expulsion of the Armenians had such repercussions for the Turkish army."

If Armenians in these eastern vilayets defected to the Russians by the hundreds before the extermination of their people, those who escaped Moslem hands now volunteered by the thousands. Maddened by grief and hatred, they carried their fight to the Turks with great savagery, attacking convoys, shooting down stragglers, and serving as indispensable scouts and spies for Yudenich's army. In the autumn of 1915 a British military observer attached to tsarist headquarters near Lake Van wrote of these Armenian collaborators:

> [One of them] knew where water and pasture were to be found, and what mountain-tracks led to them; what sort of food could be obtained in each district, and whether barley grew there. Best of all, he could speak like a Turk, and dress like one; he knew the workings of their minds, and could guess what a Turkish commander would do in

a given situation. . . . None but native Asiatics could have performed such a feat. . . . Yeghishey [the Armenian] described how the Turks had advanced their outposts from the Bitlis region, and had occupied some rocky heights, a movement which he considered was threatening the left wing of the Russian force, and might have become serious if they received reinforcements. The news was at once sent to the General commanding at Van, and a council held to decide what measures to take.

Hundreds of such episodes occurred.

And there was a final penalty for the deportations of 1915. As Yudenich's troops pushed forward, investing Van, Bitlis, Mush, Erzerum, Erzinjan, and later Trebizond, it soon became the turn of the Moslem population to taste Armenian vengeance. In a panic, the Turkish inhabitants of the region streamed westward in the winter of 1916, many of them dying in the fearful desolation of the mountains. Although the magnitude of their ordeal was hardly comparable to the primordial horror visited upon the Armenians, thousands of these civilians were slaughtered by Armenian volunteer companies. The retaliatory atrocities were extensively described in Turkish literature. Nor did they go unmentioned in Russian accounts. The memoirs of a Lieutenant Colonel Tverdokhlebov graphically described the fate of Turks in Erzerum in 1916, the torture, rape, and mutilation they suffered at Armenian hands. Russian occupation troops witnessed entire Moslem villages destroyed by Armenian irregulars, hacking, torturing, burning women and children alive, hundreds at a time. In Erzerum the carnage became too sickening even for the battle-hardened Russian officers; they threatened to use artillery unless the Armenians stopped. As always in war, it was the helpless civilians who paid the final price for military and quasi-military barbarism.

This fleeting spasm of retaliation was, in any case, the last and only revenge the Armenians would ever achieve for their crucifixion. Talaat Pasha's "solution" for the Armenian Question was a legacy destined to outlast the empire's death, and his own. That was the classic simplicity of genocide. It resolved the complex political problem of a troublesome minority people by the ingenious device of eradicating the people itself. In Europe this technique had not occurred even to the Slavophilist rulers of tsarist Russia. It was surely not surprising that a brutish Asian regime, presiding over a quasi-primitive agricultural population, should have been the first government in modern times to discover and execute the scheme of mass extermination. Nor was there anything re-markable in the ferocity of the conception itself. Indeed, Turanian history was steeped in conquest and slaughter, the predatory exploitation and more than occasional enslavement of conquered peoples. The agony of Christian women and chil-dren touched no strain of conscience in this central Asian war-rior race.

What was astonishing, rather, was the efficiency and speed with which the notoriously inept Turkish bureaucracy engineered a liquidation of these dimensions. But perhaps here at least there were corroborating circumstances. One was the camouflage afforded by a state of general warfare. Another was the tacit complicity of a European partner. German equipment, after all, German-built roads and administrative methods, and not least important, the meaningful silence of the German government, proved all but indispensable weapons for the accomplishment of the task. Moreover, it is of interest that the genocide was cited approvingly twenty-five years later by the *Führer* of the identical European nation, who found the Ar-menian "solution" an instructive precedent for a campaign of even broader scope and finality against another people.

CHAPTER V

THE ARAB REVOLT

Prelude to a Battlefield

However grievous their setbacks in the Dardanelles and Mesopotamian campaigns, the British ultimately measured the fate of their commitments and interests in the Middle East by a single immutable criterion: the security of the eighty-mile jugular, the Suez Canal. The imperial general staff in London presumably should have been breathing easily on this issue. Protracted and sanguinary warfare on three separate fronts had taken a heavy toll of the enemy. By late 1915, Djemal Pasha, commander of the Ottoman Fourth Army, was left with barely 25,000 men to hold the Gaza-Beersheba line guarding Palestine, and most of them were underfed and ill-equipped. Yet Allied Intelligence remained curiously uninformed on the straitened condition of Djemal's army. Although reports from Greek and Arab informers hinted at the parlous circumstances in Syria, neither General Maxwell nor his successor (after January 1916), General Sir Archibald Murray, found these accounts credible. Indeed, on the personal orders of Kitchener himself, no less than 300,000 British and imperial troops were garrisoned in the Suez delta, guarding every mile of the approaches to the Canal. Not since Gallipoli had so huge a concentration of soldiery been packed into so limited an area and for so sterile a purpose.

Ironically, while Murray exaggerated enemy strength, he had actually anticipated Djemal's intentions, although for all the wrong reasons. The Turkish commander was stubbornly unwilling to relinquish his cherished dream of invading Egypt. He recognized by 1916, of course, that the Egyptian people were not about to career through the streets in open revolt against the British and that Suez itself was all but invulnerable to capture. But perhaps, Djemal speculated, if several artillery pieces were even momentarily emplaced on the Canal's eastern bank, their initial barrages might sink a few passing vessels; by itself this obstruction could block the waterway for months. The idea, however, was more farfetched than it sounded. As Liman von Sanders patiently explained to Djemal, Suez could not be put out of extended operation except by vast and systematic destruction; anything less would represent only a momentary annoyance to the British. The Turkish commander was unconvinced. Moreover, he continued to win support from General von Frankenberg, chief of the Ottoman general staff, and from Colonel Kress von Kressenstein, Djemal's own chief of staff, the man who had planned the original invasion attempt. Kressenstein, like Djemal himself, had developed a kind of monomania on the question of Suez, and he was certain a second attempt could be made to work. His confidence was strengthened on April 23, 1916, when a Turkish probing column surprised and wiped out an entire English cavalry battalion in the Qatiya Oasis, the buffer zone on the eastern bank of the Canal.

With full approval from Constantinople, therefore, Djemal and Kressenstein organized a specially trained "Sinai" division of ten thousand men, and on July 27 dispatched this force along the old coastal route from El Arish to Kantara. It was the hottest season of the year in the Middle East, and all marches during the seven-day trek had to be restricted to the nighttime, with water supplies rigorously conserved. Notwithstanding these precautions, by the time the main body of Turkish infantry reached the entrenched camp of Romani, twenty-four miles east of the Canal, the men were seriously dehydrated and altogether incapable of facing prolonged battle. Even the element of surprise was forfeited. British air patrols had followed the expedition from the first day. On August 4, as Kressenstein launched his assault on the outposts just beyond Romani, the British were waiting. The massed Ottoman troops were etched with diamond clarity against the tawny backdrop of the desert and offered excellent targets. The outcome was never in doubt: the Turkish attack soon dissipated itself against the fortified line. Whereupon General Lawrence, the senior British field officer, ordered his men forward out of the screen of the dunes. Within a few hours, waves of British and Anzac troops were pouring through the shattered Turkish ranks. The pursuit continued for three days. Four thousand of the enemy were killed or captured, and vast supplies of booty were taken. In this manner, the second invasion of the desert collapsed even more disastrously than the first. From the British point of view, to be sure, the security of the Canal probably could never be guaranteed so long as a Turkish army remained stationed across the Sinai frontier in Palestine. Yet by the same token, the ease with which Kressenstein's expedition had been repelled suggested to the staff officers in Cairo that a more active defense of Suez might be distinctly feasible. From the summer of 1916 onward, therefore, Sinai and Palestine were to serve increasingly as Britain's chosen battlefield against the Turks.

The Arabs Bestir Themselves

IT WAS ON THAT BATTLEFIELD, too, that the English discovered the presence of an entirely unanticipated ally. Several months before the outbreak of the war, in February 1914, a fragile, doe-eyed little Arab had arrived in Cairo from Constantinople to pay a goodwill visit to General Kitchener, then serving as British agent general for Egypt. The visitor was the Emir Abdullah ibn Hussein al-Hashimi, second son of the sherif of Mecca and Medina. As the scion of a distinguished family and as a deputy to the Ottoman parliament, Abdullah had been closely associated with the various ideological and nationalist currents sweeping through the Arab world. In those days the Turkish capital was the entrepôt for officers, merchants, scholars, and parliamentary deputies from Arab lands as far-flung as Mesopotamia and Yemen. Abdullah had come to know many of these men. He informed Kitchener that they were

restive under Turkish rule, chafing for the opportunity to emancipate their people from the leaden grip of the sultan. Abdullah's own father, moreover, the Sherif Hussein, was eager to
lead this revolt, for he had been reliably informed that the
Young Turk Cabinet was scheming to depose him. It was for
this reason that Abdullah had traveled to Cairo, to determine
whether the British government would be inclined to help his
father in the event such a revolt took place. The question
startled Kitchener. The Arabs had long been known as the Ottoman Empire's most passive, even lethargic subjects. It seemed
profoundly unlikely that they would now be induced to col-
laborate actively with the Christian enemies of their Turkish
overlords. Kitchener therefore felt it wiser to give a noncommittal reply. But privately he instructed Sir Ronald Storrs,
Oriental Secretary of the British Agency in Cairo, to remain
in contact with Abdullah, and through him to appraise Arab
sentiment.

How widespread was disaffection among the Arabs
on the eve of the war? Evidently not so widespread as
Abdullah claimed. Indeed, nationalism developed later in
the Arab communities than among any of the other subject peoples in the empire, with the possible exception of
the Albanians. Whatever serious Arab discontent existed
during the era of Abdul Hamid was confined primarily to the
Christian Lebanese. Even the anti-Turkish strictures of al-
Afghani, Muhammed Abdu, Rashid Rida, and other Moslem
ideologues had not been directed primarily against the cruelty
or intolerance of the government. Their resentment had been
aroused, rather, by the Porte's manifest inability to protect
the empire from the incursions of the Christian West.
Actually, this bruised Moslem pride, far more than any other
factor, accounted for Arab unrest during the last years of
the Hamidian regime. Nor, apparently, was the Young Turk
Cabinet better equipped to stem the chronic hemorrhage of
Ottoman territory and peoples. Between 1908 and 1914 the
last of the Balkans were lost, as were Tripoli and the Dodecanese Islands. For the first time, too, Arab advisers, who had

enjoyed an influential role in the pre-revolutionary period, were dropped from the regime, and their places increasingly taken by ardent Turanian reactionaries. Unlike the Greeks and Armenians, moreover, who as Christians enjoyed near-total cultural autonomy, the Arab Moslems for the first time were compelled to attend Turkish-language schools. Their total population in the empire was twice that of the Turks; but they were restricted to a third of the delegates in parliament.

It was this combination of Ottoman ineptitude and Turanian arrogance which first evoked anti-Turkish feelings among a small but articulate group of Arab writers, students, and businessmen. In the last half decade before the war, the al-Fatat and al-Ahd parties, recently established under the leadership of Syrian and Mesopotamian army officers, also began tentatively to express upper-middle-class Arab demands for cultural and political autonomy. The appeal was echoed by a collection of Syrian and Egyptian journalists living in Cairo, most of them former members of the (by then) defunct Ottoman "Decentralization" Party. There were other, smaller groups. But as late as 1914, the specific grievances and complaints of Arab politicians and soldiers had not coalesced into an organized movement for autonomy. Of the perhaps twenty million Arabs under direct Ottoman rule, most were backward to the level of primitivism. Only a few hundred thousand were literate, and even they were well aware that, after all, their overlord was still a Moslem power. It would require the impact of a totally alien civilization—that of France, for example, and later Britain—or Europeanized Jewry, to kindle in the Arab world the sort of rabid nationalism that had long been a fact of life in the Christian Balkans.

Yet restiveness was far from uncommon by 1914, particularly in the half-Christian, half-bourgeois enclave of Syria known as the Lebanon. When the war began, the official responsible for governing Syria, with its mercurial Levantine agglomeration of peoples, was Ahmed Djemal Pasha, the minister of marine and commander of the Ottoman Fourth Army.

Like Talaat and Enver, his colleagues in the Young Turk triumvirate, Djemal had sprung from humble origins, and as a young officer had thrust his way into the center of the Ottoman political arena by sharing in the overthrow of Abdul Hamid's government. In his mid-forties now, he was a pale, undersized, altogether unimpressive-looking man of seemingly questionable vitality. Morgenthau recalled that it was only when Djemal arose and moved that his energy revealed itself, for he uncoiled like a spring and his eyes suddenly glittered in acute, near-feverish concentration. In military as in political matters, too, his ambition and decisiveness were nothing less than awesome. Interestingly enough, Djemal was not pro-German. Neither was he a Turanian xenophobe. Although personally he entertained little regard for the Arab race, he evinced a genuine restraint in dealing with the local population once he assumed his command in Damascus, and exerted himself to befriend Arab notables of all religious faiths, to distribute baksheesh among them, to attend their literary festivals and praise their language. "I myself am not one of those," he told them, "who think it a harmful or dangerous thing that the two races, Arab and Turkish, should secure their unity while remaining separate nations, subject to the same Caliph." Thus, in the early months of the war, Djemal scrupulously avoided confiscating the food or chattels of the Arab civil population and exercised the same care in protecting the rights of the Christian minorities. By and large, the Moslems reciprocated this toleration. Apparently their motives were in part Islamic veneration of the sultan as caliph, in part fear of Djemal and his Turkish garrisons, and in part, as well, a historic and well-nourished Moslem suspicion of French penetration and domination (see Chapter VI).

The Fourth Army commander maintained his policy of forbearance until the summer of 1915. By then, however, the evidence of underground Christian-Lebanese negotiations with the French was too flagrant to be ignored. The threads of the conspiracy to disembark French troops at Alexandretta eluded Djemal, and he remained unaware that a number of Syrian officers in the Ottoman army were the authentic leaders of the plot. Instead, he arrested several known Arab nationalists, some Christian, some Moslem, and ordered them hanged in August. Other hangings followed in May 1916. The unexpected ruthlessness of these measures stunned the local population. Their anguish was intensified, too, by the sapping famine that even then was descending on the Levant. Nearly a third of the inhabitants of the Lebanon, perhaps 100,000 people, died of starvation in 1917 and 1918. The Allied blockade was principally responsible for choking off food supplies; but Djemal exacerbated the creeping hunger as a punitive measure by refusing to allow the free movement of wheat and other crucial grains. Nor were these restrictions ineffective. Enfeebled and intimidated, the population of Syria remained quiet through the largest part of the war. The al-Fatat and al-Ahd cabals continued secretly active, but were almost entirely impotent.

Britain's Search for an Ally

THE STATE of national feeling in the Levant was hardly of less importance to London than to Constantinople, for British imperial commitments in Arab-inhabited territory were always vulnerable to the potential appeal of jihad. British oil and maritime interests along the Persian Gulf were crucial enough to warrant the initial Indian landing at Basra, and later the expedition up the Tigris. Britain's investments were carefully guarded, too, along the Gulf's southwestern shoreline by a series of Arab buffer principalities—Kuwait, Oman, Hadramaut, Asir, Nejd, among others—associated with the Government of India by treaty since the nineteenth century. By the eve of the war, there could be little doubt that Britain exerted the dominating influence along the entire eastern coast of Arabia. But this control demanded uninterrupted reinforcement. Although the Arabian Peninsula was a veritable sea of Arab sheikdoms, not all these tribal suzerainties lay within range of British naval guns. The more thoroughly Turkish rule elsewhere in the peninsula was undermined, therefore, the safer the British would rest.

In fact, several of the Ottoman dependencies in Arabia were strategically quite pivotal. One of the most important of these was the Hejaz, a bleak, sun-scorched domain extending from Mecca and Medina up the coast of the Red Sea to the Gulf of Suez. The Hejazi population consisted of about 600,000 Harb tribesmen, most of them Bedouin who subsisted on the camel and pilgrimage trade. The ruler of Hejaz, the Emir Hussein ibn Ali al-Hashimi, bore the honorific title of Sherif of the Holy Cities of Mecca and Medina by virtue of a blood connection which his Hashimite dynasty traced back to the Prophet Muhammed himself. The status of Hussein's wartime loyalties was of more than incidental consequence to the British. His Red Sea coast was a likely site for German submarine bases. As keeper of the Prophet's birthplace and tomb, the sherif was capable of mobilizing hundreds of thousands of Arabs throughout the peninsula against British interests there. London would have settled for his passive benevolence. His active friendship was entirely unanticipated.

Hussein was sixty years old when the war began, a diminutive, energetic, hot-tempered man, half-Arab, half-Circassian, learned in Arabic literature, and remarkably *au courant* on world affairs for one who had been kept in enforced residence in Constantinople for the last sixteen years of Abdul Hamid's reign. After the Young Turk uprising in 1908, he had been selected to take over the sherifate of the Holy Places from Abdul Hamid's former incumbent. As it turned out, Hussein's administrative abilities were not less impressive than his genealogical qualifications. Swiftly bringing peace and order out of the anarchy he found in the Hejaz, he managed, as well, to subdue the Harb tribes and principalities abutting his eastern and southern frontiers. From the point of view of the government in Constantinople, he was perhaps too successful. For it became increasingly apparent that the sherif was intent on exploiting his office, with its immense revenue potential from the pilgrim trade, rather more for himself and his dynasty than for the power and glory of the Ottoman sultan. Initially, to be sure, in the first months after the Porte's entrance into the war in 1914, Hussein found it necessary to play a deferential and circumspect role. The Turks had more direct access to the Hejaz than to any other region of the peninsula; a branch of the Berlin-to-Baghdad Railway connected Damascus and Medina—although, to Hussein's relief, the line had not yet been extended from Medina to Mecca. The sherif was aware, too, that the government had stationed four divisions in western Arabia, including one and a half divisions in the Hejaz itself. It would not have been politic for him to assert his ambitions too flagrantly in this Turkish military presence.

Yet Hussein was not without advantages of his own in resisting the authority of Constantinople. His exalted office made him incomparably the most influential Arab in the Ottoman Empire. The Young Turk regime itself recognized this fact when the war began by soliciting him repeatedly for a *fatwa,* a sherifal pronouncement sanctifying the holy war in the name of the Prophet. Hussein craftily extended his private assurances of support, even removed the original Standard of the Prophet from its ossuary and sent it on to Djemal's headquarters as a token of goodwill. But he stopped short of issuing a *fatwa.* His shoreline was too vulnerable to naval bombardment, he explained. Actually it was not the sherif's purpose, if he could help it, to place his influence at the disposal of the hated Turkish overlord. He was not unaware that the Hejaz was located at the nerve-center of Ottoman communications in the peninsula. Without his cooperation, the Turks could not govern the Hejaz; their garrisons were hardly more than prisoners within their forts. Conversely, Hussein was in a position to sever the Ottoman railway connecting to the north, in this fashion isolating Turkish military units not only in the Hejaz, but also in Asir and Yemen. When, therefore, the sherif's son Abdullah paid his first visit to Cairo in February 1914, he took with him the offer of an alliance based on these factors of dynastic jealousy, political prestige, and strategic location. The British, as we have seen, were unable to accept the offer at the time. Nevertheless, it was already apparent to Storrs, the Oriental Secretary, that the friendship of the sherif of Mecca was potentially more important than that of any other Arab chieftain.

It was Kitchener who later conceived the idea of approaching Hussein directly. During his prewar incumbency in Cairo, the general had met a number of prominent Arabs from various parts of the Ottoman Empire. He fancied that he understood their grievances under Turkish rule, although he had never credited them with revolutionary zeal. While he had been noncommittal on the occasion of Abdullah's visit, the idea of an autonomous Arab government under British tutelage began to interest him. "He marvelled how seldom people remembered the greatness of England not only as a Christian but as a Mohammedan Power," wrote Kitchener's biographer. "He would immerse himself agreeably in such subjects as the interplay between the Sunni and Shiah sects, or the place of the Sultan of Turkey vis-à-vis the Sherif of Mecca as religious hierarch of Islam." On the eve of hostilities with the Turks, Kitchener, then war secretary, cabled Storrs from London on September 24, 1914, to probe Hussein's attitude in the event Turkey joined the Central Powers. The message was carried by Arab messenger to Mecca, where the sherif discussed it with his sons. Feisal, the third son, favored standing by Constantinople and earning the regime's gratitude. Abdullah took an opposing position, for he had traveled extensively throughout the Levant and was confident of widespread Arab support. Hussein himself, torn between these views, procrastinated. His response to Storrs intimated that he would need assurances of effective support from Britain before taking any drastic step on behalf of the Entente. Kitchener in turn dropped a meaningful hint of his own: "It may be that an Arab of truth will assume the Khalifate at Mecca and Medina," he wrote on October 31, "and so good may come by the help of God out of all the evil that is now occurring." Tantalized by this veiled offer, the sherif asked for time to reflect upon it.

Thereupon, immediately after the Porte's entrance into

the war, Hussein began systematically investigating the depth of Arab sentiment for an uprising and weighing this likelihood against the possibility of increased Turkish largesse. To that end, he dispatched Feisal to Constantinople via Damascus. The third son encountered a discouraging response in both cities. In Damascus, Feisal discovered that the leading Arab opponents of the Ottoman regime, even the most articulate members of al-Ahd and al-Fatat, were quite reluctant to embark on hostile action against the government. In a formal protocol, they notified Feisal that only the most hard-and-fast British guarantees of complete Arab independence would persuade them to risk an uprising under the sherif's banner. Anyway, not a single Ottoman Arab division was stationed in the Levant to provide trained manpower for a revolt. In Constantinople, on the other hand, the Young Turk leaders disdained to offer so much as a single inducement of their own. On the contrary, they brutally implied that even Hussein's continued tenure as sherif would depend upon his willingness to issue a *fatwa* of holy war. It was surely this threat and Kitchener's offer, rather than the equivocal Arab response, that determined Hussein's course of action.

On July 14, 1915, the sherif dispatched his first personal letter to Cairo, stating his terms for leading an insurrection. It was the beginning of a historic and controversial exchange that Arab politicians, not all of them followers of the Hashemites, would later invoke as the legal foundation for their sweeping claims to postwar Arab nationhood and independence. Hussein's conditions in this initial message were those of the "Damascus Protocol"—i.e., a British guarantee of Arab independence—with the additional proviso that he personally be awarded public recognition as caliph. Sir Henry McMahon, the new British high commissioner in Egypt, who received the note, was frankly taken aback by the magnitude of the demand. It seemed a great deal from a tribal chieftain who earlier had spoken only of protection for his dynasty. Hussein's insistence, too, upon full independence manifestly conflicted with British and French plans for Syria and Mesopotamia (see Chapter

VI). After discussing the message with Storrs and (by cable) Kitchener and Grey in London, the high commissioner dispatched a somewhat evasive reply to Mecca on August 30. He reiterated Kitchener's earlier promise of the caliphate and the liberation of the Arabs from Turkish rule, but offered nothing more.

McMahon must have sensed that the sherif could not be won over with generalities, and indeed that was the case. On September 9, Hussein testily demanded a precise definition of future Arab boundaries. Thereupon additional telegraphic correspondence followed between Cairo and London. At this juncture, too, a foreign office specialist, Sir Mark Sykes, arrived in Egypt from England to help mastermind the negotiations. Until shortly before then, Sykes had not been an advocate for the Ottoman minority peoples, whom he considered a "Levantine melange" with little evident potential for self-government. But Constantinople's "betrayal" of its British patron and Hussein's sudden manifestation of dynastic ambition and pro-Allied sentiment now changed his mind. He recommended acceptance of the sherif's conditions. Thus, on October 24, 1915, McMahon sent the letter destined to become the most significant in the extensive correspondence. The high commissioner announced that he was now prepared "to recognize and support the independence of the Arabs in all the regions within the limits demanded by the sherif [namely, the entire Arab rectangle, including Syria, Arabia, and Mesopotamia], with the exception of those portions of Syria lying to the west of the districts of Damascus, Homs, Hama and Aleppo," which "cannot be said to be purely Arab, and should be excluded from the limits demanded. . . ." In addition, Britain would guarantee the security of the Holy Places and assist the Arabs in establishing a government, with the understanding that the Arabs would "seek the advice and guidance of Great Britain only, and that such European advisers and officials as may be required for the formation of a sound form of administration will be British."

These were major concessions. Hussein accepted them

gratefully on November 5. At the same time, he continued to hold firm on Arab rights in western Syria. McMahon would not budge on that issue, however. In his reply of December 13, the high commissioner forcefully emphasized that prior "French interests" in the Syrian littoral excluded that area from Arab rule. The language was plain, and it registered on Hussein. In his reply of January 1, 1916, the sherif disclaimed any intention of disrupting the Anglo-French alliance. He would not abandon his claim to the territory, he warned, but he agreed to postpone the question until after the war. McMahon appreciated this conciliatory response, and indicated as much in his final note, on January 30. But he also reiterated his government's commitment to Anglo-French solidarity. In view of the bitterness of the Arab-French confrontation at the end of the war (Chapter IX), it is worth noting that the priority of French claims in western Syria was clearly delineated, and not merely in this celebrated eight-letter exchange between Mecca and Cairo. It also was well articulated in Cairo itself, in repeated interviews between Sir Ronald Storrs and Mohammed Sherif al-Faruqi, Sherif Hussein's appointed representative to the British high commissioner. Through Faruqi, in turn, during the entire war Hussein was kept fully informed of the Middle East concessions that Britain had agreed to make on behalf of France. Indeed, on November 20, 1915, the sherif's emissary agreed that France should be granted the monopoly of all concessionary enterprise, special recognition of all French educational establishments, and absolute priority as European advisers and functionaries everywhere in Syria and Palestine. Testifying before the Peace Conference in 1919, D. H. Hogarth, research director of the Arab Bureau in Cairo, insisted that the Arabs had been apprised of almost every square mile of territory which would be reserved for the French, and that a climate of perfect candor had always been maintained between Arab and British spokesmen. This avowal of unqualified frankness was similarly confirmed in 1921 by the prominent nationalist ideologue, Mohammed Rashid Rida, who admitted outright that Hussein had been kept thoroughly informed on Anglo-French plans for Syria and Mesopotamia. Without doubt, then, the revelations in 1917 of the Sykes-Picot Agreement (Chapter VI) could not have taken Hussein or his sons by surprise. Those who later professed themselves duped were rather the British Middle East specialists, men like Storrs and even Kitchener himself, who were appalled at the extensive concessions they had been maneuvered into offering a Bedouin chieftain, still quaking in his shoes for the protection of his dynasty. Storrs wrote later:

> It was at the time and still is my opinion that the Sharif opened his mouth and the British Government their purse a good deal too wide. It seemed to me that having been little more than a sort of Erastian Administrator for the Turks, the Sharif and his people would be well treated and amply rewarded if they were gratuitously enabled to defeat and evict their traditional enemy, and were guaranteed immunity from external aggression in their permanent possession of the two Holy Cities, together with the independent sovereignty of their country of origin, the Hejaz. If to this a sufficient majority of Moslems chose to add the Khalifate, that was their business, not ours.

Nevertheless, with this coup accomplished, Hussein was at last prepared to emancipate himself from Ottoman authority. It is of significance, moreover, that the sherif had not merely haggled the best possible bargain with the English. During the seven months of his negotiations with Cairo in 1915–16, this minor Bedouin potentate, who in later years would have much to say about Arab self-sacrifice, whose sons after the war would repeatedly denounce the British and the French for betraying their Arab partners, simultaneously carried on parallel discussions with the Turks in the expectation and hope that, even at the last moment, it would still be possible to assure the hereditary authority of his dynasty in the Hejaz. Anything else would represent a windfall. Thus, in September 1915, Feisal, the third son, returned once more to Constantinople and warmly, effusively protested his father's loyalty to the sultan. In Damascus, later, where he was received with great honor by Djemal, Feisal solemnly promised the Turkish minister an Arab volunteer corps of 1,500 camelry for the renewed invasion of Egypt. Shortly before leaving Syria, the young emir went so far as to deliver an emotional speech to Djemal's entourage, swearing "by the glorious soul of the Prophet to return at an early date at the head of his warriors" and help "fight the infidels to the death."

And then, in February 1916, Hussein dropped his bombshell. He telegraphed Constantinople demanding immediate recognition of the hereditary claims of his dynasty. To emphasize the demand, the sherif's Bedouin warriors took up positions around Medina, blocking the further movement of Turkish soldiers there. Enver suspected what was coming, and temporized. So did Feisal. Acutely embarrassed, the sherif's son repeatedly implored Djemal's pardon for his father's "impetuousness." His family were not traitors, the emir declaimed. "How could we be traitors, members of a family descended from the Prophet, a family whose greatest honor it is to be the most devoted and loyal followers of the Khalif?" Then Feisal somewhat querulously begged permission to depart for Mecca. He explained that his purpose was to escort the Arab "expeditionary force" to Jerusalem. Djemal allowed him to go. It was the last the two men ever saw of each other.

On June 5, 1916, Hussein formally proclaimed the independence of his Hashemite dynasty and the existence of a "state of revolt" against Ottoman authority. A fortnight later, in a lengthy pronunciamento, the sherif listed ten reasons for his action. He cited the loss of influence and territory suffered by the empire since 1908, the ineptitude of the Young Turk regime in domestic as well as foreign matters, Constantinople's unfair treatment, specifically, of the Hejaz, and the brutal hangings of certain eminent Arabs. Yet the largest part of the manifesto was devoted to religious grievances; e.g., laws of Islam had been disregarded, the Sharia (Moslem sacred law) had been flouted, the Koran had been breached, fast days had not been observed. Apparently Hussein preferred to base his case on the alleged atheism and impiety of the Young Turks, the coarse and heretical politicians who had bungled away the sultan's domain and laid sacrilegious hands on the sultan's prerogatives. The sherif was not trusting to Arab nationalism in those days. Nor did he in the months that followed. Rather, in his exhortations to his followers, the inducements Hussein offered were openly and palpably material.

The Revolt Begins

WITHIN DAYS AFTER RAISING the standard of revolt, the sherif's followers achieved their first successes. One was painless: the dispersal of the Stotzingen Mission. The Mission—a picked collection of forty German communications and propaganda experts, led by Major Freiherr Othmar von Stotzingen—had been attached to a column of Turkish reservists en route to Yemen via Medina. Its purpose was to install a radio station near the Red Sea port of Yanbo in western Arabia, and from there to transmit propaganda broadcasts to Somaliland, Ethiopia, and possibly India. The Germans had just arrived in Yanbo when the revolt began. Their reaction was not in the most austere Prussian tradition; throwing most of their equipment into the sea, they immediately fled for their lives. Within a few days, too, other successes were achieved. The tiny Turkish-Circassian garrison at Mecca was besieged by an Arab mounted force and compelled to surrender after three days of wild shooting. The captives were slaughtered instantly. On June 9, another 4,000 Arabs attacked the port of Jidda. Initially they were beaten off; but two days later a squadron of British gunboats and seaplanes bombarded the town, and the Turks promptly capitulated to the Arabs. Rabegh, 100 miles north of Jidda, defended by less than 30 Turks, was captured with similar ease. So, on July 27, was Yanbo, fully 200 miles northwest of Jidda. Taif, 70 miles southwest of Mecca itself, was besieged by 5,000 tribesmen and eventually surrendered on September 22. In this fashion, within the period of one summer, virtually the entire Arabian Red Sea coast had been cleared of Turks. For the British, the significance of this feat

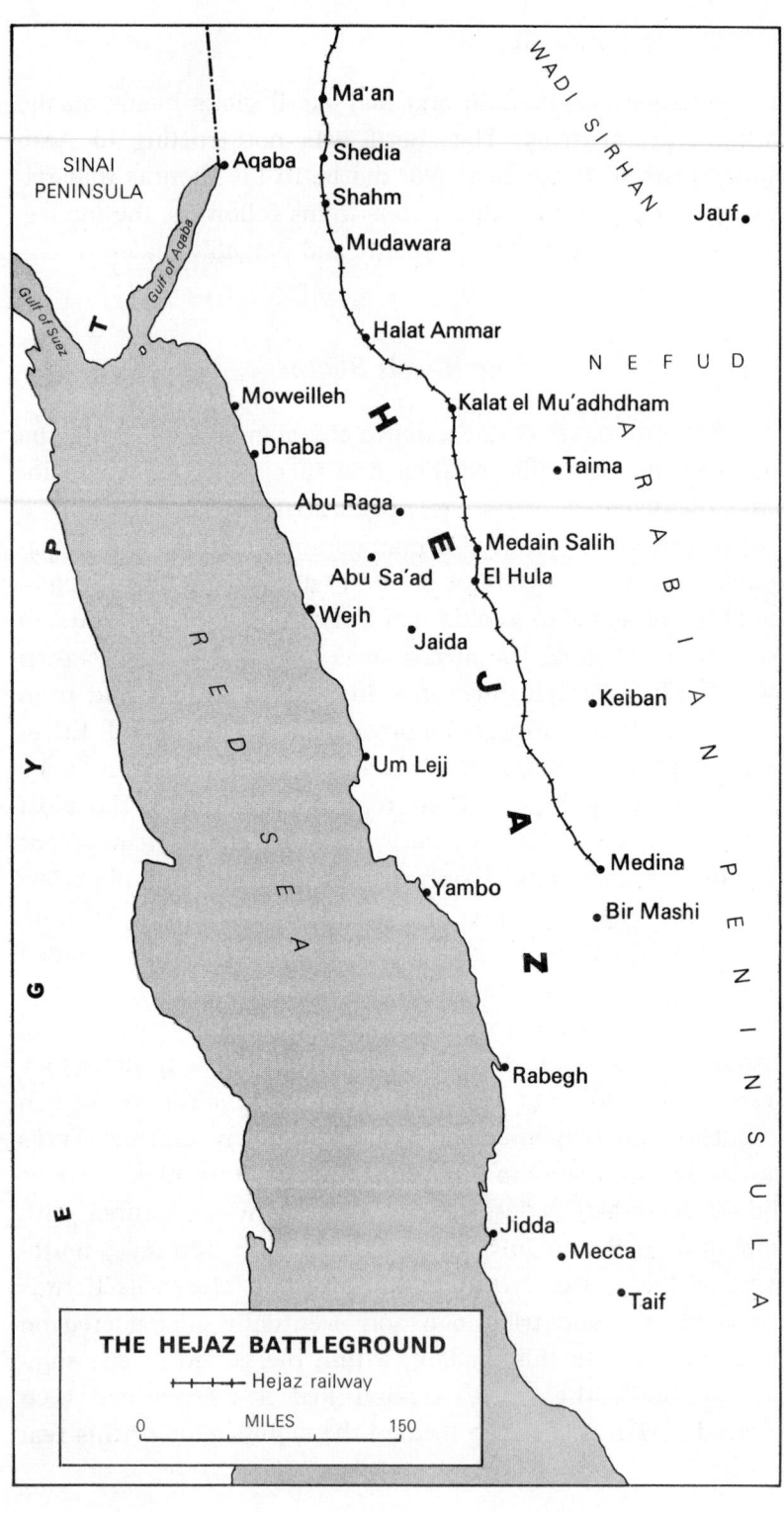

THE HEJAZ BATTLEGROUND

+−+−+−+ Hejaz railway

0   MILES   150

was its elimination of potential refueling bases for German submarines.

After these initial victories, however, the revolt soon lost its momentum. Hussein's men failed to overrun other Turkish strongholds in the Hejaz. Some 15,000 Ottoman troops protected Medina and its surrounding villages and easily and decisively crushed a series of Arab frontal attacks. Significantly, only three weeks after the revolt began, the troops at Medina were able to issue forth from their stockade to drive the Arabs back twenty miles from the city. They threatened to push even farther, for the Bedouin scattered whenever a Turkish artillery shell was lobbed their way. The sherif's undisciplined bands hardly formed an army in the modern sense. Led by Hussein's sons, the Arabs were concentrated in three principal groups: one of about 5,000 men under Ali, based on Rabegh; another of 4,000 under Abdullah, near Mecca; and another of 7,000 under Feisal, based on Yanbo, and operating against the railway. The number of men available to this combined force fluctuated between 10,000 and 40,000. There was little organization. Officers were a mixed collection of Ottoman Army veterans, native sheiks, and tribal chieftains. Among the army veterans was the tactical commander, Ja'far Pasha al-Askari, a leader of the Senussi uprising in Egypt who had been a British prisoner of war in Cairo until released specifically to join the revolt. Ja'far was a capable man, but without a reserve of experienced NCO's he was obliged to forgo a major offensive.

Even the sherif's original hope of igniting a series of uprisings throughout the Arab world was swiftly dashed. Although the revolt deprived the Ottoman government of tribal support in the Arabian Peninsula itself, none of the sheiks outside the Harb Confederation was prepared to supply men for the Hashemite cause. Some of the Harb leaders, particularly those around Medina, chose to remain loyal to the empire until the end of the war. Nor was there any visible response to the insurrection in other Arab communities. Except for British-occupied territory, Mesopotamia remained tightly linked to the Ottoman regime, most of its somnolent population content to endure the familiar, lethargic rule of a Moslem administration. Occasional Mesopotamian nationalists existed, to be sure, but these were essentially army officers whom Constantinople had prudently stationed in other parts of the Turkish empire. As deserters, they ultimately furnished the best commanders of the Arab uprising—in the Hejaz. From Syria there was hardly a ripple of unrest; until Hussein's men reached Palestine, the fighting could have been going on in another world. The Ottoman government was in fact so confident of its ability to recapture Mecca that in the autumn of 1916 it laid plans for the formal installation of Ali Haidar as successor to Hussein, whom it had "deposed." For that purpose, a Turkish column set off for Mecca, and soon closed on the way station of Rabegh in a pincers movement. The Hashemite forces were separated. The revolt had begun with a series of brilliant surprises. But the Turks had regained their composure, and within six months after Hussein's declaration of independence, they were threatening to win back all they had lost.

The sherif's appeals to the British mounted in frequency and intensity. Conferring with Storrs at Jidda in October 1916, Hussein implored the Englishman to provide additional "material" support, although by then the British had supplied more than fifty thousand rifles and corresponding stores of ammunition. Indeed, by the end of 1916 the British were providing the Arab revolt with its central direction altogether. Control of military activities in the Red Sea area, for example, devolved on the governor-general of the Sudan, Sir Reginald Wingate. The governor-general, for his part, was increasingly dependent upon two men who soon exerted decisive influence in the emergent Anglo-Arab relationship. The first of these was Wingate's personal deputy, Lieutenant Colonel C. E. Wilson, commander of the military mission stationed in the Hejaz. It was Wilson, one of the most underrated figures of the Arab uprising, who served as the crucial liaison between the sherif's Bedouin troops and British military forces in Egypt. Brigadier General Gilbert Clayton, chief of military Intelligence in Cairo, played an equally dynamic role. Under Clayton's astute leadership, a group of experts on Arab affairs—the "Arab Bureau"—was gathered together in February 1916 under the working direction of the brilliant Oxford orientalist Dr. (by then Commander) D. G. Hogarth. Most of Hogarth's associates were archaeologists and philologists, and included such erudite minds as Aubrey Herbert, Leonard Wooley, Philip Graves, and T. E. Lawrence. Their task was to investigate political unrest in the Arabian Peninsula and to make recommendations for British policy there.

Ironically, the Bureau's preliminary efforts to mobilize the rest of the Arab world were heatedly resisted by the sherif, who insisted on placing his trust exclusively in the Harb confederation of his native Hejaz. Nor, as a devout Moslem, would Hussein permit the landing of British troops on Hejazi soil. Confronted with this implacable parochialism, therefore, the Bureau and Wilson finally arranged for a limited number of Moslem instructors to be admitted into the Arab ranks. Small groups of Egyptian specialists were brought over. Their cadres gradually increased to four hundred as the revolt progressed. During the spring, another two hundred officers and NCO's were added. By then, Hussein had finally decided to turn a blind eye to the Allied presence as long as none of the foreign personnel set foot in Mecca. Led by Lieutenant Colonel P. C. Joyce, Wilson's chief of staff, these British military advisers were actually the unsung heroes of the Arab uprising. Their accomplishments and names have been obscured by the more dramatic accounts of T. E. Lawrence's career. But such officers as Captain H. S. Hornby and Lieutenant Henry Garland initially taught the Arabs the art of demolition, the planting of mines, the daring guerrilla foray. The French, too, were ably represented. Under the brilliant leadership of Lieutenant Colonel Edouard Brémond, 17 Moroccan and Algerian officers and some 356 Berber troops established their headquarters at Yanbo, cheek by jowl with Joyce's Anglo-Egyptian forces. Although this French mission was essentially a political effort to deny Britain an exclusive foothold in the Middle East, its military value in the revolt was crucial. By 1918, in fact, the largest number of officers and noncommissioned officers in the sherif's army were Allied personnel from Egypt and North Africa.

Even Hussein's "irregular forces," the troops used for garrison duty in captured towns, were replenished increasingly with Arab prisoners of war who had been serving their time in Egyptian and Indian camps. They were by no means good material. Of four thousand taken to Aqaba after the capture of that port in 1918, all but three hundred refused to serve. A few proved to be useful officers, most particularly Mahmud Mukhlia and Nuri es-Saïd, both Mesopotamian veterans of the al-Ahd society. The rotund and jovial Ja'far al-Askari was perhaps the ablest. Their work would have been useless, however, without British subsidies. Hussein and his sons were unceasing in their requests, the British in their generosity. The funds were shipped across the Red Sea, packed in bags of gold sovereigns, and paid *en bloc* to the sherif or Feisal. The latter, in turn, devised an effective wage scale for their followers: two pounds a month per man, or four pounds for a man and his camel. Additionally, there was the not unappealing inducement of all the loot an Arab could strip from dead or captured Turks. Without this "remuneration," it was highly problematical that the revolt could have been sustained.

A Stuttering Offensive

WILSON, WHO PLANNED the Arab strategy, recognized that a bold stroke was necessary to abort an Ottoman drive on the port of Rabegh, 150 miles southwest of Medina. As he conceived it, there was no alternative to a daring advance up the coast from Yanbo and the establishment of a new front at Wejh capable of threatening the enemy flank along the railway. If the move proved successful, the Turks would fall back. Feisal was unwilling at first to contemplate an offensive so far afield from Yanbo, his base of power and prestige. He was by nature a timorous man. The truth was that, like T. E. Lawrence himself, Feisal emerged in the hands of journalists as one of the most highly embellished personalities of the war. There was little doubt of his sophistication, achieved during his career as a deputy in the Ottoman parliament, nor of his striking personality, his grave courtesy, his charming smile and sudden, erratic moods of uncontrollable anger. Physically, he looked the aristocrat, small-boned, delicate-featured, his eyes black wells in the taut parchment of his face. Lawrence, who met Feisal when the emir was thirty-one, offered a memorable description in *Seven Pillars of Wisdom* of a "white figure waiting tensely," the man "I had come to Arabia to seek—the leader who would bring the Arab Revolt to full glory." The Englishman's private accounts were somewhat more restrained. Years later, Lawrence confided to Liddell Hart that "Feisal [was] a timid man, hated running into danger," and admitted that he had magnified him primarily "to get the British to support the Arabs." Feisal was unquestionably a charismatic personality who inspired fierce loyalty among his troops and nurtured and projected exalted political ambitions for his people. As a military leader, he was quite ineffective.

Not until the beginning of 1917 could Wilson finally persuade the young Emir to abandon the comparative security of Yanbo. The plan was for the older brother, Abdullah, to lead his forces astride the Hejaz railway north of Medina. Hopefully, the Turks would be drawn off to counter this move, and thus leave the way open for Feisal's offensive against Wejh. The scheme worked perfectly. The Turks were successfully diverted to the railway, and on January 18, 1917, Feisal led ten thousand Arab horsemen on a march of nearly two hundred miles toward Wejh. The operation was never in any serious danger, for the mounted force remained well within the protective range of the British Red Sea Fleet. In fact, by the time this column reached Wejh on January 24, the town was in Allied hands; Feisal learned that five hundred Arabs, landed from British ships two days before, had easily wrested the town from its minuscule Ottoman garrison. The long trek had nevertheless served its purpose. The area under Hashemite control had been widened. From then on there was never any question of an Ottoman drive on Mecca. The Turkish garrison at Medina was thrown permanently on the defensive. Not least of all, for the first time, a major threat was now presented to Ottoman communications in the Hejaz.

An integral branch of the Berlin-to-Baghdad Railway, the Hejaz line had been extended successfully after 1904 from Damascus to Ma'an to Medina, the latter fully 820 miles from Damascus. It was the Porte's single route of supply into the Arabian Peninsula, and it was accordingly guarded by garrisons posted at each station in blockhouses along the route between Ma'an and Medina (see map); in the Medina fortress seven thousand troops guarded the terminus of the line. Even before the march on Wejh, Arab marauders had carried out isolated and generally ineffectual raids against the track. After Wejh, British officers transformed these attacks into an objective strategy. It was entirely a subsidiary effort to the wider goal of extending the revolt to Syria; but it was not ineffective. The technique was perfected by the British engineer Hornby and put to immediate and dramatic use by Newcombe and Garland, and later by the Frenchman Brémond. Under cover of darkness, the Allied officers and their small parties of Arabs laid charges of gelignite under bridges and culverts, waited behind sand dunes until the Ottoman trains pulled into view, then detonated the explosives by electric wire. For the Bedouin irregulars, the raids proved a useful method of destroying enemy supplies with trifling losses to themselves. Yet the ultimate value of a sporadic guerrilla campaign was, in itself, inevitably very limited. In Medina a Turkish railway repair battalion expertly replaced many hundreds of damaged rails from an ample stockpile of reserves. Inadequate as it was, therefore, this pathetic artery managed to survive almost uninterrupted Arab attack, enabling the city of Medina to hold out for the entire war and actually beyond it, until January 1919, when it was eventually captured by British troops. On the other hand, there was little doubt that Newcombe's train-blowing, and later

Lawrence's, had much to do with dispersing Turkish forces, perhaps fifteen thousand troops in the entire Arabian Peninsula by 1917, at a time when Ottoman manpower was already strained to the limit.

Of greater significance was the primary effort to extend the revolt itself. The port of Aqaba was the next likely goal. Its capture would project the Hashemite cause well beyond the Hejaz for the first time, indeed some eight hundred miles north of Mecca, and deny the Turks their last outlet to the Red Sea. The town was by no means impregnable. Twice earlier during the war, Allied naval raiders had occupied it briefly; but without adequate land communication, the marines had been unable to maintain their occupation. It was Brémond who first suggested a landward seizure of the port by a fast-striking party of Bedouin. The initial and most imposing task was to win the support of the Transjordanian desert tribes who inhabited the hinterland route of march. Fortunately for the Hashemite cause, the loyalty of the most important of the tribes—the Tawayha branch of the Huwaitat Confederation—was secured at the very outset. Auda Abu Tayeh, the colorful fifty-five-year-old Tawayha chieftain, was the most renowned desert warrior of his generation and exerted an absolute mastery over his tribesmen. It was Auda who now assured Feisal that, with the help of the Tawayha fighters, a landward assault on Aqaba was entirely feasible. His view was endorsed by a British liaison officer, T. E. Lawrence, who eagerly volunteered to accompany the expedition.

No personality of the First World War has been the subject of more extensive or heated biographical controversy than Thomas Edward Lawrence. The illegitimate son of an Anglo-Irish baronet, as a youth a brilliant student of modern history at Oxford, Lawrence spent his summers traveling extensively in the Levant, where he acquired a fluent knowledge of conversational Arabic and of Arab customs and traditions. At the outset of the war he was billeted to Cairo as a temporary second lieutenant in the map department of the Arab Bureau, working under Hogarth. There, for the next two years, his personal assignment was routine Intelligence, considerably removed from the politics or strategy of British-Arab relations. While Lawrence's own memoirs imply that Hogarth had singled him out for top-secret assignments from the beginning, Storrs wrote later that "[Lawrence's] enduring world-fame makes it difficult to replace him now in his original perspective, and I must confess . . . that my sentiments in applying for him were mainly gratitude for his assistance in the Hejaz stamp issue. . . ." In October 1916, fascinated by the budding revolt, Lawrence wangled a free trip with Storrs to the Hejaz, where he met Feisal and Abdullah. Upon his return, his incisive analysis of the potentialities of guerrilla warfare in the Hejaz impressed Wingate, who assigned him to the Hashemite forces as liaison officer.

Lawrence's acute grasp of the Arab idiom and mentality also made him an increasing favorite of the Hejazi leaders. In anticipation of the Aqaba campaign, for example, Feisal decided to appoint the Englishman as his secret envoy to Arab nationalist groups in Syria. Thereupon Lawrence made an extraordinary journey north in May 1917, riding with his small group of Bedouin camelmen nearly five hundred miles behind Turkish lines to the very outskirts of Damascus. Despite his fair skin and blond hair, he managed to avoid detection (although once, according to a highly colored account in his later writings, he was misused by a homosexual aga). In his interviews with Syrian sheiks, and with various leaders of the al-Ahd society, Lawrence appealed for a mass uprising in support of Feisal's impending offensive on Aqaba. Yet for all his charm and eloquence, he was unable to win more from the nationalist leaders than assurances of their goodwill; they would not commit themselves to fight. The appeal of Arab nationalism evidently was not worth the risk of punitive action by the Ottoman Fourth Army, which was ensconced throughout Syria. Lawrence did rather better among the Transjordanian tribes, for the danger of Turkish retaliation was considerably less in the Edomite uplands. On June 28, the march toward Aqaba began from the railway south of Ma'an. It was led by Auda, accompanied by Lawrence, and comprised an initial force of three hundred tribesmen. Although modest in size, the Bedouin group proved large enough for its purpose. At the very outset of the trek, it shot up an isolated Turkish battalion at Abu el-Lissal, on the Ma'an-Aqaba road, and immediately thereafter news of this victory attracted many hundreds of new adherents from surrounding tribes. The clash had its unnerving effect on the enemy, too. The tiny Ottoman garrisons on the landward side of Aqaba either surrendered after a nominal defense or retreated to Khadra, the last fortified position covering Aqaba against a landing from the sea.

At Khadra, the Turks were well provisioned. Yet they had never anticipated attack from the interior, and of all their imposing defense lines not a trench or pillbox faced inland. By then, too, the defenders were heavily outnumbered by the attacking Arabs. The issue was decided when Auda grimly threatened to butcher all prisoners unless they surrendered instantly. The threat was well timed; the Ottoman commander panicked, ran up the white flag, and allowed his men to be disarmed. Thereupon, in Lawrence's exultant recollection, Auda's men quenched their thirst from Turkish canteens, then "raced through a driving sandstorm down to Aqaba, four miles further, and splashed into the sea on July the sixth, just two months after our setting out from Wejh." In those two months the little raiding party had killed some 1,200 Turks and had traversed fully 800 miles of desert to attack a fortress only 250 miles away from its starting point. They had taken the defenders completely by surprise. The longest way had proved the easiest way.

The victory provided immediate and dramatic inspiration for the Hashemite cause, for the capture of Aqaba was clearly an accomplishment of high strategic value: it placed the Arabs close to Sinai and threatened the Ottoman invasion route against Suez. At this point, too, with a well-cultivated instinct for the romantic, Lawrence decided to notify the British of the feat personally by leading a small party of Arabs on a camel dash to Suez, 150 miles across the desert. It was a fitting climax to the sherifian odyssey. After riding nearly fifty hours with hardly a pause, Lawrence turned up in Ismailia, aching and exhausted, bearing the totally unexpected news of Aqaba's capture. The information was flashed to Wingate, who immediately dispatched a supply ship and several naval vessels to the port. Wejh was now replaced by Aqaba as the principal British Red Sea harbor. Moreover, at imperial staff headquarters in London, it was swiftly appreciated that the ragamuffin band of Arab mercenaries had galloped and raided all the way from Mecca in little more than a year, and had now suddenly become a factor in the war. Lawrence, too, was thrust into the limelight for the first time, wined, dined, honored, and publicized in Cairo. The Frenchman Brémond, swallowing his pride, awarded Lawrence the *croix de guerre*. Allenby, the new commander of the Egyptian Expeditionary Force, promoted Lawrence to major on the spot and recommended him for the Order of the Bath. The young officer luxuriated in this new acclaim. One observer described him as a "shy show-off," another as a "tin-pot exhibitionist." No longer, in any case, the obscure subaltern in Hogarth's map-room, Lawrence henceforth was recognized as the influential and respected spokesman for the entire theater of war in the Arabian Peninsula and the Arab Levant. He would not be diffident in exploiting this newly won eminence.

The "Right Wing" of Allenby's Army

THE POTENTIAL VALUE of Britain's alliance with the Arabs was now thoroughly reappraised in Cairo, and for the first time taken with full seriousness. The Egyptian Expeditionary Force needed all the help it could find in Syria to protect its right flank; for on the left flank, the British campaign against Palestine had ground to a halt. After having decisively repulsed the Turks in the Sinai confrontation of August 1916, General Murray, commander of the EEF, had decided to undertake a more aggressive defense of the Canal, indeed to push to the gates of Palestine, and perhaps beyond. Murray's notion of "aggressiveness" was profoundly conservative, however. By the end of 1916 he had established an elaborate military apparatus in Sinai: hundreds of miles of railway, roads and piping, scores of reservoirs, workshops, camps, and airdromes. He secured the dispatch of troops from other fronts until his army reached the impressive proportions of twelve divisons. Only upon completing the organization of this extraordinary superstructure of manpower and matériel, on December 22, 1916, did Murray venture to advance against the Ottoman border post of El Arish, an enemy garrison of 1,600 soldiers. The Turks then discreetly withdrew the remainder of their posts from Sinai. On January 9, 1917, Murray invested Rafah; there he stopped, refusing to continue until his railhead had been moved forward. At last, in March 1917, the Expeditionary Force encamped outside Gaza, a town of forty thousand guarding the frontier-entrance of Palestine. And there, ironically, Murray decided that the moment had come to strike quickly. It was an unfortunate decision, as precipitous as his earlier advance had been cautious. The general's Intelligence had shortsightedly concluded that the Turks were ready for the knockout and that an unparalleled opportunity now existed for the British to take Syria on their own, thus pre-empting the French, to whom it had been assigned by treaty (see Chapter VI).

Ottoman strength in Palestine actually was much greater than Murray appreciated. Enver and Kressenstein were determined to make a vigorous stand along the Beersheba-Gaza line, and to that end called down reinforcements from Anatolia and the Caucasus. By March the Turks numbered 33,000. They manned an excellent defense line: the sea on one side, the spine-cactused desert on the other. Gaza served as a natural barrier between the two, and Kressenstein converted the placid little coastal town into an ingenious fortress of earthworks, barbed wire, and trenches. Secondary defenses extended as far as Beersheba, nearly thirty miles from the sea. Behind the lines a first-rate road network had been created by German engineers. The defense was in depth. Murray found it so on March 26 when he launched a frontal assault on Gaza in a thick, rolling fog. The moment news of the attack reached him, Kressenstein called down his reserves and hurled them against the British flank. The battle raged for two days, until Murray issued orders to break off contact. His troops had sustained 2,700 casualties, the Turks only half that number. Shaken by this reverse, the British general summoned a fresh division from the Canal zone. On April 19, rather more cautiously, he ordered a new offensive against Gaza. This time the Turks not only defended their positions tenaciously but also launched a slashing infantry counterattack against British supply lines just below the town. After thirty hours of chaotic fighting, the British withdrew again, this time having sustained 7,000 casualties. Turkish losses were a third that number. Murray was incapable of renewing the assault. His men were spent and demoralized. Nor was London willing to send him new troops. Rather, several of the EEF divisions were shipped off to Macedonia. A few weeks later, Murray himself was relieved of his command and ordered home to England.

Under these painful circumstances, Murray's successor, General Edmund Allenby, was understandably grateful for any sort of diversion that could be mounted across the Red Sea. Lawrence's unexpected appearence in Cairo gave him his chance. When the young lieutenant, bedecked in his Arab robes, arrived in the Egyptian capital with news of the fall of Aqaba, Allenby received him with grave respect and courtesy. Although the general could never decide how much of Lawrence was genuine performer and how much poseur, he was willing to gamble on a more active support of the Arab revolt. He agreed, therefore, to bring Feisal's Arab troops directly under the control of his own headquarters in Cairo, styling them now the "right wing" of his own army. For Aqaba was a mere 150 miles from the British advance post at Rafah, and within easy communication of EEF headquarters. Allenby decided also to pour vast quantites of matériel into the Red Sea port. Whereupon the little coastal village was transformed almost overnight into a major supply center, with British officers arriving by the scores to supervise the construction of a radio station, jetties for the landing of equipment, even a small airport. Only Hussein in Mecca remained unenthusiastic about the new relationship with Cairo. The old sherif, "an obstinate, narrow-minded, suspicious character," as Lawrence described him, was deeply agitated about becoming a mere cog in the strategic plans of the British. His son Feisal, on the other hand, could not have been happier. During the winter and spring of 1917 the emir concentrated on augmenting his forces and extending the range of his Arab alliances. By the end of 1917 he had won the allegiance of every major tribe in the Transjordanian wastes, and his "army" had grown from barely two thousand men to a well-equipped infantry brigade and two mounted battalions, totaling nearly twelve thousand.

Simultaneously, Auda and Lawrence, together with French and Algerian experts, launched a new series of expeditions against the railroad, demolishing tracks, bridges, and culverts. The raiders soon achieved a high degree of refinement in gunning down Turkish escort units. The guerrilla forays gained momentum in the autumn of 1917 in conjunction with Allenby's drive on Jerusalem (see Chapter VII) and reached an intensity unknown during the earlier period, when the revolt had been confined to the Hejaz. Under Brémond's direction, the Algerians proved especially adept at train-blowing. Lawrence, too, now perfected his dynamiting skills. In one of his memorable autobiographical accounts of this period, the English liaison officer recalled the destruction of a train near the wilderness of Petra:

> There followed a terrific roar, and the line vanished from sight behind a sprouting column of black dust and smoke a hundred feet high and wide. Out of the darkness came shattering crashes and long, loud metallic clangings of ripped steel, with many lumps of iron and plate; while one entire wheel of a locomotive whirled up suddenly black out of the cloud against the sky, and sailed musically over our heads to fall slowly and heavily into the desert behind. . . . As I watched, our machine-guns chattered out over my head, and the long rows of Turks

on the carriage roofs rolled over, and were swept off the top like bales of cotton before the furious shower of bullets which stormed along the roofs and splashed clouds of yellow chips from the planking. . . . The Arabs, gone raving mad, were rushing about at top speed bareheaded and half-naked, screaming, shooting into the air, clawing one another nail and fist, while they burst open trucks and staggered back and forward with immense bales, which they ripped by the railside, and tossed through, smashing what they did not want. . . . [Finally] the Arabs, sated with spoils, were escaping one by one towards the hills, driving tottering camels before them into safety.

In their cumulative attrition of Ottoman troops and matériel, these raids undermined Turkish strength at a time when the Porte needed every available man and gun to oppose the British advance on Jerusalem. By the spring of 1918, the Turks had lost 5,000 men killed and 8,000 captured to a succession of Arab ambushes. It was not an insignificant number, although hardly the 20,000 killed and 40,000 prisoners claimed by Feisal at the Paris Peace Conference. Both Germans and Turks considered the uprising a painful harassment. The political consequences of these guerrilla tactics were even more alarming. Arab conscripts were now deserting the Ottoman ranks in large numbers. Few of them joined the sherif's forces; but they ensured that British troops advancing into Palestine no longer risked partisan attacks from a hostile citizenry.

The Arabs Shoot Their Bolt

NOTWITHSTANDING these accomplishments, the Arab offensive was far from crystallizing into an effective "right wing" for Allenby's campaign. Well in advance, the British commander had divulged to Lawrence his plans for launching a renewed drive against the Gaza-Beersheba line in October 1917, hopefully to break through to Jerusalem in the winter. Allenby emphasized that in this offensive he expected the

Arabs to lay siege to Deraa, the junction of the Jerusalem-Haifa and Damascus-Medina railways, the nexus of the Turkish defense system in Syria. Lawrence had twelve thousand Bedouin at his disposal, theoretically enough for the task. At first he was confident of success. "We knew, better than Allenby, the enemy hollowness, and the magnitude of British resources," he wrote. Then, unexpectedly, Lawrence aborted the operation before it began. He explained later: "Deraa's sudden capture, followed by a retreat, would have involved the massacre . . . of all the splendid peasantry of the districts." Uncertain of the ability of Feisal's men to sustain a major offensive, "I decided to postpone the hazard for the Arabs' sake." Instead, Lawrence suggested to Allenby a more limited operation. This one would blow the railway bridge across the River Yarmuk, thus blocking the Ottoman line of retreat through Palestine at the moment of the British advance. Somewhat resignedly, the general agreed.

Accompanied by Ali, one of Hussein's younger sons, Lawrence departed for his mission on October 24, 1917. His raiding party consisted of a handful of English and Algerian officers and about forty Arabs. En route to the river, they could hear the thunder of British artillery as Allenby's long-awaited offensive began. The group pressed on. After four days of marching, it reached the Jordan. There Lawrence and his party discovered to their dismay that none of the local tribes was willing to help. After a momentary pause, they decided to continue the mission on their own, by stealth. Yet the attempt to plant dynamite under the bridge at Tel al-Shehab failed; the Arabs panicked under sentry fire. With the Turks alerted to their presence, moreover, Lawrence and his men were obliged to beat a hasty retreat to Aqaba. This second failure was a source of deep mortification to Lawrence. But for the second time Allenby was willing to be tolerant. The offensive had succeeded anyway, although at much higher cost than if the bridge had been destroyed. The general accordingly offered Lawrence another chance, suggesting that the Arabs occupy and ravage the Jordan Valley, choking off

Turkish supplies from the farms and villages there. The task did not seem beyond Arab capabilities, and Lawrence agreed to it enthusiastically. Recruiting new troops for this operation, he offered the munificent payment of six pounds monthly per man. A group of two thousand raiders was soon assembled. This time, in their initial efforts of January and February 1918, the Arabs enjoyed a limited success; they harassed the Turks out of the cluster of small market towns leading to the Dead Sea. But achievement of the larger objective—the occupation of the entire "corn belt" in the eastern Jordan Valley—was prevented by the cold weather. In February, to compound Lawrence's frustration, most of his troops threatened to desert him; they were held in line only by the timely arrival of thirty thousand pounds in gold.

Late that month, Allenby offered Lawrence a final chance. With the coming of spring, plans were being laid for a renewed British offensive toward Damascus. This time it was vital that the Arabs seize and hold Ma'an. If they were successful, enemy pressure on the Egyptian Expeditionary Force would be relieved by the diversion toward Ma'an of thousands of Turkish soldiers. To ensure success this time, Allenby turned over large quantities of equipment to the Arab force, including many new machine guns, seven hundred baggage camels, and no less than £300,000, for Lawrence to distribute in payments. The gift occasioned great joy among the Bedouin. On April 13, four thousand of them gathered under Feisal's banner to launch the new drive. Allenby, in turn, anticipating a powerful Hashemite offensive, captured Amman in a secondary thrust and held it far beyond his lines of communication. But in the end the Arabs left him hanging there. When Feisal's troops charged Ma'an, they were driven back with heavy losses. Shamed and infuriated by this setback, Lawrence promptly hand-picked a smaller, mixed unit of British, Egyptian, and Bedouin soldiers, and led them toward Shem, one of the important stations on the railway. There, at last, the Arabs captured the town, and afterward destroyed eighty miles of track from Ma'an to Mudowwara. The effort was not sufficient to extricate Allenby's forward units. They remained overextended in the Jordan Valley, and ultimately were obliged to abandon Amman altogether. From May to July 1918, the Arabs marked time, ignoring Allenby's pleas for renewed offensive action. Nor would they move again until the last month of the Middle Eastern war, when they set off for Damascus virtually unopposed in the wake of the Egyptian Expeditionary Force.

By the summer of 1918, too, Lawrence accepted the fact that Hussein's forces had lost interest in the campaign from the moment the capture of Aqaba had ensured the security of the Hejaz. Actually, he had sensed this indifference even earlier. As far back as December 1916, when the Turks seemed likely to recapture Rabegh on their route to Medina, Arab desertions had begun to mount almost uncontrollably. Lawrence disembarked at Yanbo in the midst of the crisis, and was met by Feisal's quite explicit threat to enter into peace negotiations with Constantinople. The Englishman managed to retrieve the situation at the last moment by increasing the subsidy. But again, in August 1917, six weeks after the fall of Aqaba, Lawrence discovered to his horror that even the redoubtable Auda had been corresponding with the Turks. When confronted with the evidence, the desert chieftain somewhat blusteringly threatened to hand the port back to the enemy unless he received a larger share of the booty. The subsidy was enlarged once more. Then, in February 1918, the sherif's youngest son, Zeid, discouraged by the failure of the Jordan Valley campaign, stubbornly refused to continue unless more money was forthcoming. At this point Lawrence himself decided to offer his resignation to Allenby. Wilson talked him out of it. In the summer of 1918 Lawrence reacted with cold bemusement to another choice revelation: Feisal had again entered into conversations with an emissary of Djemal, and was offering to forsake the British if the Turks would evacuate Amman and turn the province over to the Arabs. The Englishman this time restricted himself to a single telegram of warning to Mecca. It was sufficient. Hussein wired back, vehemently repudiating the clandestine negotiations. Feisal immediately let the matter drop. By then Lawrence had long since abandoned any lingering illusions about Arab loyalty or fixity of purpose.

Moreover, from the very outset of the revolt, Lawrence had entertained no illusions whatever about the authenticity of Arab nationalism. "Their idea of nationality," he wrote Cairo in a report of November 1916, "is the independence of tribes and parishes and their idea of national union is episodic, combined resistance to an intruder. Constructive politics, an organized state, and an extensive empire are not only beyond their capacity, but anathema to their instincts. . . . Unless we, or our Allies, make an efficient Arab empire, there will never be more than a discordant mosaic of provisional administrations." This unblinking judgment was shared by Hogarth and Storrs, who were never really certain that Hussein and his sons were preferable to the Turks as governors of the Arab people—a doubt fully shared by the Arabs themselves. In the end, as matters turned out (Chapters IX, XII), it was the intrusion of the alien West which awakened and mobilized Arab national ardor. Manifestly, the limited exigencies of war alone had briefly and cynically linked Briton and Arab. One may therefore wonder that, at the Peace Conference, it was of such importance for Lawrence and his colleagues in the Arab Bureau to dramatize, even to magnify, the wartime achievements of the Hashemite troops, whom they secretly held in contempt as quixotic and unreliable guerrilla mercenaries. Actually there were precedents for this stylized hypocrisy. As in the case of Russian solicitude for the Armenians, British solicitude for the Jews (and Arabs), French solicitude for the Lebanese Christians (see Chapters VI, VII), or, indeed, German solicitude for the Turks, far-reaching political aspirations transcended even the momentary demands of war. It was still an era when nations could take the long view of their political interests and of the special role to be fulfilled on their behalf by grateful client-peoples. By the summer of 1916, the British and French governments had reached tentative agreement on their respective future spheres of influence in the Arab world. Yet, considering the abrasiveness that historically had characterized imperial relations between the two Western nations, the projected equilibrium was by no means certain. "The success or failure of the Sharifian invasion of Syria," Lawrence wrote, ". . . is going to affect the other phase of European rivalry in the Levant, by determining whose candidate is going to gain control of the trade routes and commercial centres of Western Asia." Long before the firing ceased in the Middle East, Lawrence and his colleagues in the Arab Bureau had clearly fixed the image of their adversary, and that enemy was not the Turk.

CHAPTER VI

═══════════

INDUCEMENTS
FOR EACH OTHER:
THE SECRET TREATIES

Sazanov's Dream

THEY WOULD COME HOME to roost after the war, the promises made to Armenians and Arabs, to Jews and Greeks—even to Turks. But no commitments were destined to haunt the Allies with more nagging persistence than the ones entered into between themselves. For the Secret Treaties dealt in large measure with the eastern Mediterranean, precisely that corner of the world which in decades past had envenomed relations not merely between Russia and Britain, but equally between France and Britain, and, peripherally, between France and Italy. As maritime nations, to be sure, neither of the two major Western partners had ever aspired to the metropolitan possessions of the other; that kind of rivalry was confined to the land powers. For London and Paris, imperial competition was projected logically outward, to the unraveling trade routes of North Africa and the Levant. Historians traditionally described this Anglo-French rivalry as a matter simply of "pinpricks," the abradant proximity of neighbors with graver preoccupations elsewhere (Germany, in the case of France; Russia, in the case of England). But if "pinpricks" they were, they had inflamed Anglo-French relations seriously enough to threaten war during the Mehemet Ali episode of 1839–40 and the Fashoda confrontation of 1898.

When at last, in 1904, the two colonial powers agreed to resolve their differences and present a common front to the

German danger, it was significant that the disposition of Egypt and Morocco was their first item of priority. Additional understandings were similarly reached between the Western Allies in 1912, when Sir Edward Grey formally stated his nation's disinterest in Syria (traditionally a French sphere of influence); and again in 1914, on the very eve of hostilities, when an exchange of letters assured France a monopoly of railroad concessions in Syria, and Britain predominance in the communications of the Persian Gulf area (see Chapter I). But these loose and general agreements on spheres of influence became outdated the moment Turkey entered the war. The opportunity for actual territorial spoliation at Ottoman expense opened a new and entirely unanticipated phase of imperial aggrandizement in the Mediterranean. By the same token, an old and dangerous chasm of rivalry and mutual suspicion was widened again among the Entente nations. As in decades past, too, neither the formulation of treaties nor the end of the war itself would succeed in bridging that gulf.

Ironically, the question of allocating the spoils was first reopened not in the Western capitals, but in St. Petersburg. Count Sergei Dimitrievich Sazanov took the initiative. Aristocrat, linguist, career diplomat, and Russian foreign minister since 1910, Sazanov was obsessed by the conviction that the Armaggedon of the World War offered that providential moment when the tsarist empire must at last fulfill its historic drive for access to the warm waters of the Mediterranean. The Russian people had earned that right. Their offensive in Poland and eastern Prussia had cost their armies 1,350,000 casualties by the end of 1914, and had probably saved the Western Entente at the moment of Germany's near-triumphant offensive against Paris. If further sacrifice was to be made, the foreign minister suggested to General Yanushkevich, the chief of staff, let it be for something tangible; let it be for nothing less than Constantinople, for "Tsargrad," home of the Mother Church, and for the Bosporus and the Dardanelles. The proposal met a cold response. The general found it necessary to explain to Sazanov that the entire question of a Straits offensive had been thoroughly discussed, and rejected, several months before the war. The plain truth was that Russia lacked the fleet and essential supply facilities to support an amphibious operation of such magnitude. Moreover, Russian troops were already dispersed far too widely in Europe and the Caucasus to embark on further adventures. The enemy must be defeated in Europe and Europe alone, Yanushkevich emphasized.

Sazanov and his colleagues in the foreign ministry thereupon determined that other, diplomatic steps would have to be taken. They knew precisely how much the Straits were worth to Russia in trade and access to Western munitions, and how grievously their closure had crippled the Russian war effort. "The war will have no meaning for us," Paléologue, the French ambassador in St. Petersburg, quoted the insistent refrain in court circles, "if it does not bring us Constantinople and the Straits. . . . Tsargrad must be ours, ours alone." No more obliquely, the tsar issued a manifesto calling for the fulfillment of "Russia's historic mission on the shores of the Black Sea." For their part, the British saw the handwriting on the wall. Facing the exigencies of war and Russian pressure, they appreciated that the time had come at last to reverse the diplomatic stance of more than a century. Under no circumstances could the tsarist empire be exposed to the temptations of a separate peace with the Central Powers. On November 9, 1914, therefore, the foreign secretary, Sir Edward Grey, dropped the hint to Russian Ambassador Benckendorff: if Russia would respect Persia's frontiers and limit herself to an attack on Turkey from the Caucasus, the fate of the Straits and Constantinople would be decided "in conformity with [Russian] interests." These same general assurances were repeated by Buchanan, the British ambassador in St. Petersburg, and by King George V, who had no authority to promise anything. Nor did the French government demur at the proposal. On December 14, 1914, Paléologue ventured only to raise the question of compensation in Syria. "Yes, certainly," the tsar eagerly replied. With that consensus, Sazanov could let matters rest for the time being.

But as the Allied invasion of the Dardanelles became increasingly imminent, in February 1915, generalities were no longer sufficient for St. Petersburg. "When the Gallipoli expedition was finally decided upon by our Allies . . ." the Russian foreign minister recalled, "I had difficulty in concealing from [the Allied ambassadors] how painfully the news had affected me." Accordingly, on March 7, determined to offer the Russian people "the realization of their secular dream," Sazanov presented Buchanan and Paléologue with an official demand, the celebrated "Great Memorandum," in which the Russian government formally listed its claims. These included Constantinople, the western shore of the Bosporus, the Sea of Marmora, the Dardanelles, southern Thrace to the Enos-Midia line, part of the Asiatic shore, the islands of the Sea or Marmora, and Imbros and Tenedos, the islands flanking the Dardanelles. It was a formidable catalogue, but Britain's acquiescence was virtually a foregone conclusion. Indeed, at a special war committee meeting in Downing Street on March 10, the notion of rejecting Sazanov's territorial claims hardly seemed worth discussing. The principal question, in Prime Minister Asquith's words, "was what we are to demand in return for the recognition of Russia's ultimate claim to Constantinople and the Straits." In the course of intensive conversations between March 10 and March 19, Sir Edward Grey raised the issues of possible territorial acquisition in the Middle East, and of the feasibility of granting Islam political as well as religious status. The former question remained undecided. At the urgent recommendation of Kitchener, however, the committee members agreed that full consideration should henceforth be given the preservation of a Moslem political entity under British auspices and the maintenance of the Moslem holy places.

Britain's counterclaims were submitted during two personal meetings between the tsar and Ambassador Buchanan on March 14 and March 20. The ambassador explained candidly that London wished to incorporate the Persian Neutral Zone into the British sphere of influence. Additionally, to guarantee the security of the "emergent Moslem nation in Arabia," Britain would expect free access to the Straits, a free port in Constantinople, and Russian cooperation in persuading Rumania and Bulgaria to enter the war. These terms seemed a not unreasonable *quid pro quo* to ensure support for Russian territorial demands. Tsar Nicholas smilingly accepted them. Initially, however, the French proved somewhat more reluctant than the British. To his associates in the Cabinet, Foreign Minister Delcassé admitted that the "Great Memorandum" had absolutely "stupefied" him. After all, French prewar investments in the Ottoman Empire had exceeded even those of Germany. French citizens held the largest blocks of shares in the Ottoman Public Debt and in the Ottoman National Bank, and they also controlled a wide variety of Ottoman public utilities. Nevertheless, it soon became evident that the French government would achieve more for itself by insisting on appropriate compensations. "Everything is linked," President Poincaré sagely observed; "we can only second Russian desires in proportion to the satisfaction that we ourselves receive." Paléologue revealed his country's terms in an interview with the Russian foreign minister on March 14. They were nothing less than Syria, including the Gulf of Alexandretta and Cilicia to the Taurus range. The demand left Sazanov and the tsar unfazed. They had some reservations about Cilicia, the Armenian population of which had always been the special objects of Russian "solicitude." The question of Palestine, too, important to the Orthodox no less than to the Catholics, was held in abeyance. Otherwise, the Russian government unofficially gave its approval on March 18.

Significantly, at the height of the negotiations in mid-March, Allied willingness to accommodate Russia was increasingly influenced by fear of a parallel offer mooted by the Central Powers. It happened that the day after the opening of the British naval attack on the Dardanelles forts, conversations dealing with the Straits were initiated with the Porte by the

German embassy in Constantinople. Discussions continued through the ensuing weeks of March and April 1915, as the threat mounted of a decisive Allied breakthrough into the Marmora. Eventually, on April 18, a joint proposal was officially formulated for luring Russia out of the war; but in fact the basic outlines of the plan had already reached the tsarist government via Switzerland as early as mid-March. It was nothing less than an offer for joint Russian-Turkish economic and naval access to the Straits. As a major concession for entering into peace negotiations with the Central Powers, Russia would be assured absolute freedom of the Bosporus and Dardanelles for its commercial shipping. A special understanding could then be worked out for the passage of Russian warships through the Straits—although the terms of this understanding were left deliberately vague. In fact, the entire offer made little impression at all on the St. Petersburg regime, and Sazanov coldly rebuffed it. Even so, Sazanov did not hesitate to divulge the enemy overtures to his Allied partners.

Notwithstanding the confluence of these pressures, the Western Allies came off well in the "Agreements on Constantinople and the Straits," as the sum of these tripartite exchanges was known. They assured their own access to the Straits. They left purposely vague the claims they would later make on Ottoman territory, and this assured them extensive diplomatic latitude. Every inducement seemingly existed for continued and vigorous military effort. And yet, notwithstanding these ironclad guarantees, when the British liquidated their Gallipoli campaign during the late winter of 1915, suspicion mounted in St. Petersburg that the Western Allies had lost their desire to break through to the Turkish capital once they had signed away "Tsargrad" and the Straits to Russia. Indeed, within the Russian imperial general staff the advocates of a separate peace became increasingly vocal. Everywhere Paléologue moved in government circles, he heard the same lament: "The question is settled now; we shall never get Constantinople . . . Then what's the good of going on with war?" So bleak was the mood in St. Petersburg that Prime Minister Trepov's formal announcement of the Straits Agreement to the Duma on December 2, 1916, elicited only indifference. "Several months ago," Paléologue wrote, "I was already observing the progressive disappearance of the Byzantine dream. The charm has been broken."

The Formulation of
the Sykes-Picot Agreement

HOWEVER REMOTE from fulfillment, the decision on Constantinople and the Straits nevertheless opened up the whole question of postwar settlement in the Ottoman Empire and led directly to further negotiations and allocations among the Allies. The British and French had unquestionably achieved an understanding with the Russian government in the spring of 1915; but they had yet to reach a meeting of minds among themselves. The need for an early agreement was particularly clear to France. As early as March 1915, Sir Edward Grey had first intimated to the French ambassador the existence of special British "arrangements" in the Arab world. Later, in October and mid-November, the foreign secretary went further and decided to reveal the basic substance of the Hussein-McMahon correspondence. "[Grey] has hinted that the Arabs would probably claim certain areas which we consider as dependencies of Syria," Poincaré noted. "He said he would leave it to us to decide what concessions to make." Finally, on March 23, 1916, the French were specifically informed that those "certain areas" were Damascus, Homs, Hama, and Aleppo. To the Quai d'Orsay it seemed perfectly certain by then that London intended to use an "independent" Arab empire as a façade for British supremacy in the Middle East. Evidently this was Kitchener's ulterior purpose in recommending an amphibious landing at Alexandretta, a scheme that Paris vetoed out of hand.

The need for an Anglo-French understanding on the Middle East became more acute when the Russians, riding the wave of their spectacular victories over the Turks in the autumn of 1915, began to encourage a recently discovered antigovernment plot in Constantinople. In December of that year, Sazanov informed the Allied ambassadors that a Russian Armenian physician, one Zavriev, had succeeded in opening circuitous and clandestine negotiations with Djemal Pasha. Apparently Djemal had been in touch with a secret, disaffected cabal of army officers and bureaucrats in the Turkish capital. For whatever reasons of chargrin or individual ambition, the Fourth Army commander had offered to lead a revolt against the government and declare himself sultan—if the Allies supplied him with arms. Djemal further informed Dr. Zavriev that he personally was reconciled to the loss of Constantinople and the Straits, and indeed even reconciled to the need of compensating the Armenians for their sufferings. He asked only that the Allies be prepared to establish autonomous states in Syria, Palestine, Mesopotamia, Arabia, Armenia, Cilicia, and Kurdistan. The offer appeared plausible. In fact, Foreign Minister Sazanov was willing to negotiate on that basis. So was Sonnino, the Italian foreign minister, once the scheme reached the Western capitals. But not the French and British governments; they had well-nourished and carefully formulated plans of their own for the Middle East. Their veto immediately doomed the Djemal-Zavriev negotiations. On the other hand, the discussions between British and French diplomats were significantly hastened thereby.

In London, to be sure, Asquith and Grey, Liberals of the old school, were at first hesitant to speak in imperialist terms on the question of partitioning Ottoman territory. But in any case, British policy in the Middle East was not within their sole province to decide. The Cabinet had appointed an interdepartmental committee under the chairmanship of a foreign-office expert, Sir Maurice de Bunsen, to lay plans for the future disposition of the Ottoman Empire, and this committee decided in favor of Anglo-French talks. The French government promptly agreed to the suggestion without any qualms of conscience whatever, and dispatched its representaive to London in November 1915. He was Charles François Georges-Picot, the former consul general in Beirut, and now special adviser to the Quai d'Orsay on Middle Eastern affairs. Sir Arthur Nicolson, the permanent undersecretary, had originally been selected as Britain's delegate, and, indeed, had met twice with Georges-Picot. Clashing almost immediately, however, both men soon became inflexible in their positions; accordingly the Cabinet decided to substitute Sir Mark Sykes for Nicolson. The choice appeared a rather surprising one, initially, for Sykes was not a professional diplomat. Although well born, the scion of an affluent Catholic family of Yorkshire, Sykes had abandoned his studies at Cambridge for a free-ranging career as traveler through the Middle East and had written several rather erratic volumes of observations on the area. He spoke Arabic easily, if not grammatically, and in 1911, elected to the Commons on the Tory ticket, he became his party's acknowledged authority on Islam and the Middle East. Most recently he had been serving as a consultant on Kitchener's staff in Cairo, and it was from this post that he was now called to the Foreign Office to negotiate a Middle East settlement with Georges-Picot. Sykes was unfazed by the responsibility. His guidelines had been generally laid down by the De Bunsen committee; while as a Catholic and Francophile, he demonstrated a marked sympathy for traditional French interests in the Levant.

The committee had met repeatedly during the spring and early summer of 1915, and on June 30 had submitted to the Cabinet a twenty-nine-page report on Britain's desiderata in the Middle East. The political department even then had considered Turkey in Asia expendable and a strong Arabia a more likely bulwark of future British strength. Yet, at the insistence of the military department, which was fearful, as always, of an overweening Russian presence in the area, the extreme solution of a partitioned Turkey was temporarily shelved in favor of merely decentralizing the Ottoman Empire. This comparatively moderate approach to the enemy was, of course, projected before the full cost of the Gallipoli and Tigris campaigns had been felt. Eventually, by the autumn of 1915, nearly all the members of the De Bunsen committee had recognized the need of taking a much harder line toward the Turks. Even in the June report, however, the territories guaranteeing Britain's fundamental security requirements in the Middle East had been outlined. These remained unchanged in ensuing months, and were accepted by Sykes as the fixed limits of his negotiations. The areas, logically, were the Red Sea and the Persian Gulf, the crucial termini of the imperial lifeline to India.

As matters developed, Sykes and his French counterpart reached basic agreement in less than a week. British interests were in fact so deeply anchored and well defined that Georges-Picot did not dream of contesting them. Without the slightest difficulty, therefore, Sykes was able to assert his country's direct supervision over the projected Arab State in a "Red Zone" encompassing the north Persian Gulf, the Tigris-Euphrates crescent up to and including Baghdad, and the Kirkuk oil region. Elsewhere, the British staked out for themselves an area of indirect influence: "Zone B," covering southwestern Mesopotamia and most of Transjordan and southern Palestine to Sinai, flanking both the Mediterranean and the Red seas. There London would enjoy "a right of priority in enterprises and local loans" among the Arab chieftains, and would "alone supply foreign advisers or officials on the request of the Arab State or Confederation of Arab States." This area of indirect control was rather akin to the "sphere of influence" that Britain had obtained in Persia by the terms of the Anglo-Russian Agreement of 1907. Its geographic range was considerably greater, however. By functioning as a corridor between the Mediterranean and the Persian Gulf, "Zone B" would protect imperial communications for the entire distance from India to Egypt.

Well before the Sykes-Picot meeting, French priorities in in the Middle East were as sharply defined as those of Britain. Some of them had had their origins during the Crusades, in the kingdoms and principalities established by French knights in Palestine, Syria, Asia Minor, and Cyprus. In the sixteenth century, the Capitulations had forged rather tighter links. In fact, these commercial and juridical conventions represented the authentic beginning of French material ascendancy in the Ottoman Empire, a pre-eminence that lasted almost uninterruptedly until the late nineteenth century. By their provisions, French nationals in the Ottoman Empire were exempted from the jurisdiction of Ottoman courts, from Ottoman taxes and tariffs; French ambassadors and consuls in the Levant became the official protectors of all Middle Eastern Catholics; French vessels and diplomats were assured priority over the ships and ambassadors of other European powers. Well into the age of imperialism, in sum, France enjoyed favored diplomatic status over all her rivals in the Turkish Empire.

That influence faded somewhat in the nineteenth century, when France adopted as her protégés such rebellious Ottoman vassals as Mehemet Ali and the Christians of the Lebanon. French political strength and prestige were further undermined in Moslem eyes by Britain's entry into Egypt and later by Britain's diplomatic triumph at Fashoda in 1898. By way of reaction, however, the French intensified their cultural and economic activities in the Levant. In the two decades before the World War, French religious orders—Marians, Dominicans, Lazarists, Franciscans, Trappists, Benedictines, and many others—established vast complexes of schools, colleges, and hospices throughout Syria, the Lebanon, and Cilicia. Although it was the heyday of anticlericalism within the French Republic itself, Gambetta summarized the nation's imperialist policy in his oft-quoted remark that "anticlericalism is not an export article." Thus, the Jesuits, expelled from France, were encouraged in 1875 to open the first medical school in the Ottoman Empire, in Beirut, and were the recipients of generous subsidies from the French government. Indeed, well before the opening of the twentieth century, Paris was channeling 800,000 francs a year into these Roman Catholic institutions. By 1914, the effort, costly as it was, had ensured the triumph of French culture and the French language among the educated classes of the Levant. On the eve of the war, for example, 120,000 children, from Egypt to Cilicia, were receiving their education in French schools.

Nor were French economic interests in the Middle East less impressive than French educational and cultural influence. They totaled some 200,000,000 francs in value by the outbreak of hostilities. Perhaps a quarter of this amount was invested in Syrian silk production financed by French banks and transported in ships owned by French financiers in Lyon. There were other investments: tobacco factories, municipal utilities, ports, harbors, dry-docks. By far the largest economic commitment, however, was in railroads, not less than 100,-000,000 francs on the eve of the war. Actually, the division of the Ottoman realm into financial spheres of influence in 1914 at the hands of Britain, France, and Germany (see Chapter I) was based almost entirely upon the railroad ambitions of the Great Powers. The rail interests of France were concentrated in the Levant. On the eve of the war, French capitalists owned 472 miles of tracks and equipment in Syria, a rail net extending from Aleppo in the north via Homs to Tripoli and from Beirut to Rayak, and later from Jerusalem to Jaffa.

With the proliferation of these holdings in mind, the Lyon Chamber of Commerce exhorted Foreign Minister Delcassé in June 1915 not to stint in his claims for the Levant or to be satisfied with anything less than full possession of integral Syria. "The ports of Jaffa, Haifa, Beirut," they warned, "are insufficient to develop our maritime commerce [or] . . . the riches of the interior." The appeal was reiterated even more emphatically by the Marseille Chamber of Commerce the same month. It was given all but official force that summer by a special report of a Senate committee—"the Flandin Report" —which delineated precisely the limits of the territory France coveted. These projected boundaries were: in the north, the regions of Aleppo, Urfa, and Cilicia; in the east, the desert; in the south, a line running from Aqaba on the Red Sea to Rafah on the Mediterranean; in the west, the entire coastal littoral (see map). It was a vast patchwork quilt of deserts, mountains, and arid wadis, perhaps too extensive an administrative burden for its comparatively limited economic resources. But Paris was influenced no less by military considerations. Once in possession of the Syrian littoral, the French army and navy could achieve domination of the entire eastern Mediterranean. As Flandin noted in his report, the augmentation of French strength in the Levant would "complete in the east the defenses of Toulon which guard us to the north and of Bizerte to the south." Georges Leyguès put it even more trenchantly to the Chamber of Deputies on May 10, 1915: "The axis of French policy is in the Mediterranean. One of its poles is in the west, through Algeria, Tunisia, and Morocco. It is necessary that the other pole be in the east with Syria, Lebanon, and Palestine." Later Cyprus was added to this list, although the claim was never strongly pressed by the Briand government.

Sir Mark Sykes knew better than to confront this virile accession of French imperialism head-on. His principal concern was to reconcile the interests not of Britain and France, but rather of the Sherif Hussein and France. And here Whitehall's earlier revelations to Paris of the Hussein-McMahon correspondence proved imaginative statecraft; for Georges-Picot was persuaded to reciprocate the spirit of mutual confidence. The inducement was buttressed when Sykes shrewdly undermined Georges-Picot's more extremist advisers by playing on French Catholic fears of a Turkish terror campaign against Lebanese Christians. As he explained to the De Bunsen committee: "We require diplomacy which would be able to show great sympathy with clerical feeling in France, and to point out that if matters are allowed to drift they will lose their real anchorage in Syria, owing to anticipated massacres of the Syrian Christians in the same way that the Armenians were massacred." These tactics were successful. After consultations in Paris, the French emissary agreed to "sacrifice" Aleppo, Hams, Hama, and Damascus to the Arab area, in accordance with McMahon's promise. In return, however, France laid claim not merely to direct authority over the Syrian lit-

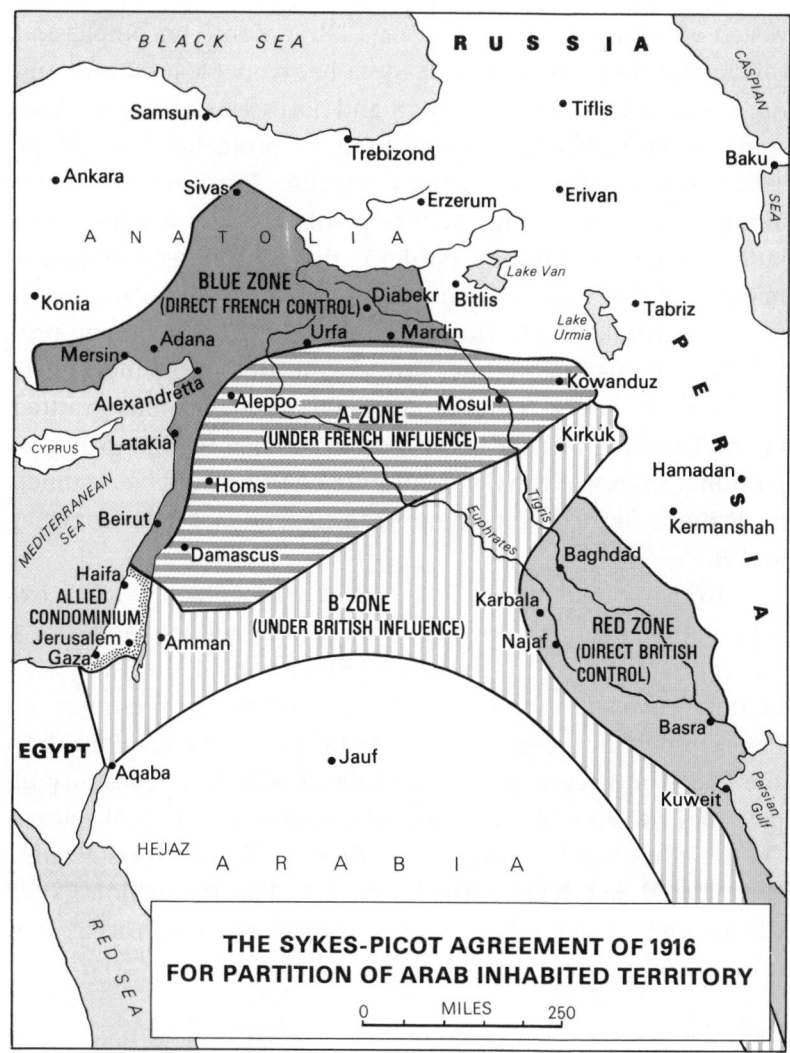

THE SYKES-PICOT AGREEMENT OF 1916
FOR PARTITION OF ARAB INHABITED TERRITORY

0   MILES   250

toral, but equally over Alexandretta and the Cilician hinterland. Actually the Armenian population of Cilicia was far less tinctured by French culture than the Levantine Syrians and Lebanese, and French investments there were minimal. But Sykes was not constrained to argue the point. With London's approval, he acquiesced less than two days after discussions began.

By the terms of the final agreement, France would be invested with direct authority over a "Blue Zone" encompassing Cilicia and the coastal strip of Syria between Alexandretta and Acre, and including the Lebanon and northern Galilee. An Arab state under rather less direct French "protection" would be established in "Zone A," embracing the Mosul area of upper Mesopotamia (from the British point of view, a convenient buffer along the Russian border), the central section of the main Baghdad Railroad, and the Syrian interior to the north of the Yarmuk River. Other features of the agreement provided for a customs union between the Red and Blue Zones, and between Zones A and B. All previous concessions granted by the Ottoman regime would be maintained unchanged; proportional shares of the Ottoman Public Debt would be assumed by Britain, France, and their Arab dependencies in Zones A and B.

In many respects the Sykes-Picot arrangement was an exceptionally gratifying one for France. She had acquired direct and indirect control not merely of Syria, a land she had traditionally coveted, but also of Cilicia to the very borders of Persia, where her connections were far more tenuous. Similarly she had won access to the oil fields of Mosul, a repository of potential wealth which had not been among her original claims. On the other hand, it was certain that the French foreign ministry would not have settled for less. For the windfalls of Cilicia and Mosul represented the *quid pro quo* for a very serious concession, that of Palestine.

The Sykes-Picot Agreement: Qualification and Evaluation

IF, THROUGH THE YEARS, France had carved out for herself certain pre-emptive rights in Syria, it was the not illogical view of the government in Paris that those rights applied to Palestine as well. "Why Palestine?" rhetorically queried the Flandin Report. "Because it forms with the rest of the territory an indivisible unity . . . Palestine in reality is only the south of Syria. . . . No more from the geographic than the ethnic point of view can Palestine be differentiated from Syria." That much was true; the country was an integral part of the Ottoman-Syrian administration. But unfortunately for Paris, other, non-administrative factors obtruded. Palestine was unique precisely because it was the Holy Land, the cynosure of the most highly imperialized religious rivalries in Christendom. For this reason, in January 1915, the tsarist government began having second thoughts about ceding to Catholic France supremacy over a country in which Russian Orthodox interests were hardly less extensive or jealously guarded than those of the Roman Catholics. Eventually, in late March, Foreign Minister Sazanov warned Paris bluntly that St. Petersburg would not under any circumstances countenance exclusive French rule over the Holy Places. Sazanov insisted, too, that more than the fate of Jerusalem was in question. Orthodox interests extended throughout the Holy Land, including Galilee, the Jordan, and Lake Tiberias, and the religious shrines in those areas were inseparable from the surrounding terrain.

It soon became evident, moreover, that London was hardly less adamant than St. Petersburg on the question of Palestine. The motives were less religious than military. From the British point of view, territory of such strategic proximity to Suez could not be allowed to fall into the hands of another power. Of course, Foreign Secretary Grey was too astute a statesman to demand unilateral control for Britain. Instead, at a Cabinet meeting on March 14, 1915, he asked his colleagues' support for the internationalization of Palestine. The formula seemed a promising one, and in July, on the recommendation of the de Bunsen committee, the Cabinet endorsed it. Confronted with the opposition of both their allies, the French recognized by December 1915 that some form of internationalization would have to be accepted. Accordingly, Sykes and Georges-Picot produced a compromise by which a Franco-Russian-British condominium would be established in a "Brown Zone" embracing central Palestine—an area bounded by one line drawn from Acre to the Sea of Galilee and another from the Jordan River and the Dead Sea to Gaza. Under these terms, neither France nor England fully relinquished its special interests in Palestine. Skirting this central zone, for example, Britain would control Acre and Haifa Bay; a British railroad would connect Haifa and Baghdad, with the right of easement, if necessary, through French Syria. Additionally, Britain's Zone B embraced Transjordan and southern Palestine, thus assuring Britain priority of influence over the Negev, Aqaba, and the Red Sea. In this fashion, the international area of Palestine would be surrounded on three sides by territory under British control or influence (see map). As compensation, the French would enjoy the right of using the British railroad to connect their Zone A with Haifa Port; northwestern Palestine, including all of upper Galilee, with its fertile wheat fields, its water sources, and its venerated religious shrines, was included in the French Blue Zone.

Which nation, then, had won the lion's share in the Sykes-Picot negotiations? Immediately after the agreement was signed, Grey complained that British interests had been sacrificed. Sykes agreed. "Poor Mark Sykes!" lamented Lord Bertie, Britain's ambassador in Paris. "He was considered by the war cabinet as the expert par excellence on affairs in the Near East, but he was tricked by the French diplomat, Picot." The French did not see it that way. In their view, integral Syria had been fractured except for a single connecting railroad moving west to east, and central Palestine had been taken from them. It was true that France had been allocated the area of German influence between Alexandretta and Mosul. Britain, on the other hand, had been awarded Baghdad and the Kirkuk oil region of Upper Mesopotamia and had won permission to build the Haifa-Baghdad railroad, originally vetoed, in 1914, by the Germans and French. Not least of all, Britain had been allowed a major share in determining the future of Palestine. The arrangement was not unfavorable for either nation; but Britain had unquestionably achieved the more dramatic advance as compared with 1912, when London had committed itself to a policy of noninterference in the Levant. The Sykes-Picot Agreement was signed on February 4, 1916, in Paris, in London four days later.

But the diplomatic impasse in the Middle East had by no means been resolved conclusively. The Anglo-French Agreement represented a meeting of minds only between the governments of the two Western Allies. Russian approval would still be necessary. This approval was particularly indispensable where French claims happened to impinge on the Russian sphere of influence: in Cilicia. For it was in Cilicia, or "Little Armenia," that the French were determined to find their compensation for Palestine. In his speech to the Duma of February 1915, Russian Foreign Minister Sazanov had rather generally alluded to a plan for the autonomy of Ottoman Armenia (see Chapter IV). By the spring of 1916, however, the Ottoman army in the Transcaucasus had been virtually obliterated, and Russian troops were in occupation of the larger part of "Greater Armenia." It was now possible, therefore, for the tsarist government to re-evaluate the foreign minister's original scheme. Indeed, Sazanov himself had never been reconciled to the tsar's concession of Cilicia to France on March 14, 1915, as part of the *quid pro quo* for Constantinople and the Straits. Only a month later, on April 17, the foreign minister had dispatched his favorite Armenian emissary, Dr. Zavriev, to plead the cause of "Armenian nationalism" in the Allied capitals. Zavriev took with him a rather devious plan by which an autonomous Armenia, including Cilicia, would be placed under the joint "protection" of Russia, Britain, and France. The blueprint was a transparently Russian device; as the single adjacent land power, the tsarist empire clearly would exert the dominating influence in this protectorate. The idea was of course not even faintly palatable to the French, who rejected it without hesitation. For the time being, Sazanov allowed the matter to rest.

But now, on March 9, 1916, nearly a year later, Sykes and

Georges-Picot arrived in St. Petersburg with their own agreement in hand. They were not unaware that General Yudenich's pulverizing victories in the Transcaucasus had strengthened Sazanov's bargaining position. Under these circumstances, the first Russian exploratory probe naturally demanded that France abandon its claims to Cilicia altogether. Georges-Picot courteously held firm. The Frenchman recognized, on the other hand, that concessions could not be entirely one-sided. In fact, the tsar himself offered the first hint of a solution, on March 13. "Personally, I am not contemplating any conquests in Armenia," he observed to Paléologue, "with the exception of Erzerum and Trebizond, possession of which is a strategic necessity for the Caucasus." Sykes, apprised of the interview as he was dressing for a royal banquet at the Winter Palace, became so excited that he dropped his cuff link, for he instantly detected the seed of an agreement. He nurtured it by offering a compromise of his own to Georges-Picot and Sazanov after the evening's festivities had ended. France, he suggested, would be viewed as the "protector" of Cilicia, whereas Russia, for its part, would be ceded eastern Anatolia outright, without bothering with an Armenian autonomous region. The proposal was discussed at length by the Allied representatives and their advisers. Negotiations on boundaries were detailed and intensive. But eventually the main contours of Sykes's compromise proved acceptable to both the Russians and the French. The agreement became official in an exchange of notes among the three Allied capitals on April 26 and May 23, 1916. Under the provisions of this addendum to the Sykes-Picot Agreement—or the Sykes-Picot-Sazanov Agreement, as it was now to be known—the Russian government accepted both the terms of the original Anglo-French treaty and the additional rights of France in Cilicia. The Western Allies, in turn, reaffirmed their earlier understanding on Constantinople and the Straits, but endorsed the additional allocation to Russia of the Armenian provinces of eastern Turkey.

The agreement, like the earlier Sykes-Picot understanding, was secret. Yet even before the Bolshevists revealed it, in the autumn of 1917, the Armenians sensed a shift in Russian policy toward them. They inquired of Varantzov-Dashkov, viceroy of the Caucasus. The viceroy queried St. Petersburg. In his confidential reply of June 27, 1916, Sazanov noted that so few Armenians were left in eastern Turkey that a grant of autonomy to the area would "lead to the subjugation of a [Moslem] majority by a minority." It would therefore be best, Sazanov observed, to incorporate the occupied regions directly into the Russian Empire. The foreign minister pointed out that the Armenians would of course be assured full religious and cultural rights, the right to use their own language and govern their own villages; but nothing more would be practicable. With this glib and sanctimonious response, Sazanov conveniently buried the implied promise of autonomy in his Duma speech of March 1915. On more than one occasion, the Young Turk regime had warned the Armenians that Russian promises were worthless. Now those warnings were vindicated. Unlike British and French pretensions to benevolence in the Arab world, the Russian approach was straightforward, frank and brutal. It was conquest.

Between May and September 1916, minor territorial modifications in the Sykes-Picot-Sazanov Agreement were routinely negotiated in an exchange of notes among the Allied foreign ministers and their ambassadors. Perhaps the unruffled calm of these negotiations, no less than their secrecy, help to account for the opprobrium with which historians later viewed the tripartite understandings. In their bland indifference to public awareness or reaction, their cool allocation of Arab and Armenian populations soon to be "liberated," the treaties came to be regarded as a particularly choice example of diplomatic machiavellianism, the epitome of deceitful policy and language. Even Lloyd George afterward described the Anglo-French agreement as "a foolish document. . . . It is inexplicable that a man of Sir Mark Sykes' fine intelligence should never have resented the constant and indelible reminder that his name was and always would be associated with a pact . . . of which he thoroughly disapproved." On the other hand, the foreign office strenuously denied this charge in later years. After Sykes's death, a Whitehall spokesman noted that "the late Sir Mark Sykes himself was fully conscious of the short-comings of the arrangement . . . [yet] he regarded it as containing the best solution of the Arab questions which cir-cumstances at the time permitted."

That is probably closer to the truth. Much has been written, for example, about discrepancies between the Hussein-McMahon correspondence and the Sykes-Picot Agreement, but less has been said about where they coincided. Actually, both provided for unilateral British control in southern Mesopotamia and unilateral French control of the Syrian littoral. Both pro-vided for the independence of the Arab peoples. They differed on two main points. First, the Sherif Hussein had been led to believe that the Syrian interior would be wholly independ-ent; there is in truth some evidence, from inter-Entente cor-respondence of 1916, that the British government shared this view. The French, on the other hand, appointed exclusive supplier of "advisers or foreign functionaries," conceived of their role as a supervisory one. There was confusion, secondly, about the precise status of Palestine, whether the Holy Land fell within or outside the area reserved for Arab self-govern-ment. As the British historian Elizabeth Monroe has observed, however, the difference between the McMahon letter and the Sykes-Picot Agreement was mainly one of spirit. When they were signed, the area of uncertainty hardly seemed important. Indeed, the one eventuality that never occurred either to McMahon or to Sykes and Georges-Picot was that the peoples liberated from the Turks would expect to govern themselves. "The Sykes-Picot Agreement," wrote one knowledgeable scholar, Elie Kedourie, "was the last responsible attempt on the part of Europe to cope with the dissolution of the Ottoman Empire, and to prevent the dissolution from bringing disaster."

The alleged secrecy of the agreement has similarly been misunderstood. It was not openly publicized, of course, but less out of concern for antagonizing the Arabs than for fear of stiffening Turkish resistance. In fact, as we have seen (pp. 127–9), the Sherif Hussein was well aware of British and French claims in the Middle East; Arab leaders stated later that the Bolshevist revelations were no shock to him. Sykes and Georges-Picot jointly visited Hussein at Jidda in May 1917. Lloyd George recounted later:

> In the course of the conversations the King [Hussein] admitted the necessity for European advisers to heads of departments and referred to Syria and Iraq. . . . In an interview on the second day, a declaration by the King, in answer to a message from the French Government which had been delivered to him by M. Picot, was read aloud, to the following effect: "H. M. the King of Hedjaz learned with satisfaction that the French Government approved of Arab national aspirations; and that, as he had confidence in Great Britain, he would be content if the French Government pursued the same policy towards Arab aspirations on the Moslem-Syrian littoral as the British did in Baghdad."

Evidently Hussein's secret hope was to play the Allies against each other, for in conversations with Lawrence and Storrs he made several jovial and meaningful allusions to Fashoda.

The basic divergence, then, was not primarily between the Hussein-McMahon and Sykes-Picot agreements. It was rather between the Sykes-Picot understanding and later British promises to the Arabs. On December 6, 1917, shortly after the Bolshevist revelations, Djemal Pasha had the provisions of the Anglo-French agreements circulated throughout the Moslem world as proof of Allied duplicity toward the Arabs. "I have recently addressed a letter to the Sherif," Djemal announced proudly, "in which I depicted the facts in their true light and represented to him the gravity and dangers of the present situation. If he is a true Moslem and has the qualities and sentiments of a real Arab, he will turn against the British and return to the fold of the Caliph and of Islam." At that point Hussein, who earlier had been informed of the agreements by his agent, al-Faruqi (see Chapter V), sent Djemal's letter on to Cairo as proof of his good faith.

In their answer of February 8, 1918, the British in turn thanked the sherif for his loyalty. They denigrated Ottoman propaganda and assured Hussein that the Allies would "stand by the Arab peoples in their struggle for the establishment of an Arab world in which law shall replace Ottoman injustice, and in which unity shall prevail over the rivalries artificially provoked by the policy of Turkish officials." Nevertheless, increasingly concerned lest enemy propaganda exploit the newly revealed documents, British officials in Cairo and London decided to amplify their promises to the Arabs. In May 1918, Clayton, chief of Intelligence in Cairo, intimated to Feisal that the Sykes-Picot Agreement would probably not be fully implemented by the "surviving parties." (By then, Russia was *hors de combat.*) A month later, on June 8, Wingate telegraphed Hussein to reassure him that the Allied understandings "do not constitute an actually concluded agreement but consist of records of provisional exchanges and conversations between Great Britain, France and Russia." Wingate noted that Djemal, in publicizing the documents, "has . . . ignored the fact that the subsequent outbreak and the striking success of the Arab revolt, as well as the withdrawal of Russia, has long since created an altogether different situation."

About a week after that, seven prominent Syrians living in Cairo expressed a very different fear: of Hussein's boastful claim to the overlordship of Syria, Mesopotamia, and the Arabian Peninsula, a Bedouin presumption that these sophisticated Levantine emigrés angrily repudiated. The foreign office felt constrained to answer these misgivings, too. On June 16, in the so-called "Declaration to the Seven," Whitehall reassured the correspondents that "it is the wish and desire of His Majesty's Government that the future government of these regions should be based upon the principle of the consent of the governed, and this policy has and will continue to have the support of His Majesty's Government." It was an innocuous assurance. Even so, when publicized, the declaration was seized out of context by Hussein's followers as proof of Britain's further retreat from the provisions of the Sykes-Picot Agreement. Hussein and his sons entered the last days of the war in eager expectation of territorial and dynastic aggrandizement, convinced now that a new understanding existed between them and London, that the British government had decided to support their claims against the aspirations of France. As it later developed, the perils of contextual interpretation, of semantic and administrative definition, were destined for years afterward to haunt both the Allied peacemakers in Paris and their Arab and (as we shall see) Jewish protégés.

An Italian Foot in the Door

INITIALLY, HOWEVER, the revelation of the Sykes-Picot-Sazanov Agreement had a more unsettling effect upon one of the partners of the Western Alliance than upon the Arabs. Italy had played an active, if irascible, role in Middle East negotiations from the outset of hostilities, and it was, in fact, the promise of aggrandizement at Ottoman expense which had helped to induce the Italians to enter the war at the side of the Entente. The nation's imperialist ambitions were dictated by its social and economic structure. Poor, backward, heavily dependent on imports even for the most basic staples, Italy during the nineteenth and early twentieth centuries had sought to carve out markets for herself and ensure her sources of raw materials by military adventures in Eritrea, Somalia, Ethiopia, and Tripoli. For the most part, these efforts had proved sterile. By 1914, humiliated and embittered, the Italian government was already well in the process of re-evaluating its alliance with the Central Powers; it seemed increasingly apparent that the choicest future gains might best be acquired at the expense of Italy's current partners. Although Rome had in mind especially the irredentist territories of Habsburg, Dalmatia and the Trentino, the tempting prospect of a share in the Ottoman inheritance was also worth consideration.

For several years before the war, the Italian ministry of trade had followed with close interest the nation's rising commerce with Asia Minor. In 1913, Italian creditors of the Ottoman Public Debt managed to extract concessions for railroads in Adalia and Makri and to increase their investments in the Heraclea coal mines east of Constantinople. Other business opportunities were forthcoming a year later in the province of Adalia, including preferential trading rights in rice, tobacco, cotton, opium, and fruit, and access to the lignite, chromium, and manganese resources of that area. Additionally, the Dodecanese Islands, wrested from Turkey during the Tripolitanian War of 1911–12, became for Italy a convenient chain of steppingstones extending directly to the Adalian hinterland. Limited and meager as these holdings were, they represented the full extent of Italian interests in the Middle East. The investment surely was not as crucial a factor as Adriatic irredentism in persuading the Italians to remain neutral when war began. But neither was Rome prepared to neglect its east Mediterranean ambitions as it embarked upon its cynical and protracted negotiations with the Allies.

The Marquis Imperiali, Italian ambassador to London, made his first bid for a share of Asia Minor on August 12, 1914. Among his other terms for allegiance to the Entente, the ambassador insisted upon recognition of Italian claims to Adalia and the Dodecanese. Sir Edward Grey reacted coldly to this proposal. Although unfazed by Rome's ambitions in the Adriatic, the foreign office was not interested in encouraging a new challenge to Britain's naval and military predominance in the east Mediterranean. For his part, Baron Sidney Sonnino, Italy's shrewd and aggressive foreign minister, was willing to be patient, confident that his nation's alliance value would rise as hostilities continued. As it turned out, the Italian government was obliged to wait only half a year. Under the pressure of the Gallipoli campaign, Grey decided to reconsider his options. Accordingly, at a meeting in London in mid-April 1915, Imperiali, Grey, French Ambassador Cambon, and Russian Ambassador Benckendorff sat down to formulate the official agreement that would bring Italy into the war. Even then, however, much to Italian discomfiture, the Entente representatives were unwilling to define precisely Italy's territorial allocations in the Ottoman Empire. As Grey explained by letter to

Italian Prime Minister Salandra, "no discussion has taken place on this thorny subject with France and Russia, and to start one now would be inopportune. . . ." That much was true. Except for the accord on Constantinople and the Straits, the Sykes-Picot-Sazanov agreements were themselves still a year away. "The reasons he then advanced were probably given in good faith," Salandra admitted later, "though one cannot be sure that this was so, as he subsequently made agreements with Russia and France without our knowledge. . . ." On April 25, 1915, following two weeks of secret discussions (which of course embraced much more than the partition of Turkey), the Treaty of London was completed and signed. Its Article Nine provided simply that if Turkey in Asia were dismembered, Italy "must obtain an appropriate share of the Mediterranean region adjacent to the province of Adalia. . . ." The portion was not specified, and due account had to be taken "of existing interests of France and Great Britain."

Notwithstanding the treaty's promise of impressive territorial gains, the Italians still refrained from entering the war outright; several months passed before Rome finally persuaded itself that the Central Powers were unable to match the Entente terms. In the light of this opportunism, it was hardly surprising later that the Allies did not feel constrained to inform the Italian government of the Sykes-Picot-Sazanov agreements. On the other hand, the anger of the Italians was not entirely without justification when their ambassador to Russia, the Marquis Carlotti, ferreted out the information on his own, on May 18, 1916. Astounded and indignant, Foreign Minister Sonnino immediately dunned Paris and London. Whereupon French Premier Briand rather embarrassedly promised to discuss the agreement with Rome and to make every provision to protect fully the rights and interests of Italy. Several days later, Grey similarly admitted the existence of the agreements and gave the same pledge. But Sonnino was not one to be placated by bland assurances. He demanded an immediate meeting with representatives of the Allied governments to guarantee "the equality of Italian rights in the Middle

East." The request had to be honored. On April 19, 1917, therefore, after five months of preliminary negotiations, the chiefs of government and their advisers met at St.-Jean-de-Maurienne, a small Alpine mountain village on the Franco-Italian border. By then the tsarist regime had given way to a new provisional government, and Russia was not represented.

Neither St.-Jean-de-Maurienne's soaring Alpine heights and placid blue waters nor even the sumptuous, overheated luxury of the conference railroad car managed to dispel the formal chilliness of these Allied discussions. Although Lloyd George and the French premier, Ribot (Briand's successor), were willing to consider modifications in the Treaty of London, they expressed frank exasperation at the niggardliness of the Italian contribution to the Middle Eastern war. Sonnino, in turn, bridling at this "slur," refused to accept an Italian military commitment as a *quid pro quo* for his demands. Rather, he chose the less costly method of wearing down the British and French statesmen by sheer force of stubbornness and acrimony. The technique proved successful. Lloyd George and Ribot eventually agreed to offer the Italians a much larger sphere of influence in southern Anatolia, including territory densely settled with Greek communities. The Athens government had not yet entered the war; it was felt safe to include Smyrna in the Italian zone. The Treaty of St.-Jean-de-Maurienne was confirmed by a governmental exchange of notes between August 10 and September 27, 1917. By its terms, Italy accepted the provisions of the Sykes-Picot Agreement; the French and British governments, using the same agreement as their model, allocated to Italy the "Green" and "C" zones as indicated on Map IX (see pp. 180–1). The "Green Zone" of direct Italian administration included the southern half of Asia Minor from the top of the Gulf of Smyrna east to Erjies Dagh. The Dodecanese Islands also fell within this area of primary control. The "C Zone," an enclave of indirect administration extending to Brousa and encompassing Itaya and Ak Sheh, represented a significant augmentation of influence for Italy, for it included the Smyrna, Adalia, and Konia districts. Italy was permitted, as well, to share fully in the condominium of the "Brown Zone"; i.e., central Palestine. Finally, Sonnino managed to extract an assurance of parity for Italy in the event of alterations in the territories ultimately to be occupied by Britain and France. The statement appeared to be the very model of an ironclad contractual guarantee.

And yet Italy's partners insisted on a clause of their own, seemingly innocuous at the time, which later all but doomed the "parity" addendum. "It has been agreed," the closing statement declared, "that the present memorandum shall be communicated to the Russian Government, in order to permit it to make its views known." On the face of it, the sentence represented an act of simple courtesy toward an absent ally. But Russia's preoccupation with its own revolution, and its failure, therefore, to "make its views known," indeed its failure even to sign this agreement, undermined the legality of the Treaty of St.-Jean-de-Maurienne altogether. At the Paris Peace Conference (see Chapter X), the Italians ventilated their outrage at the willingness of Britain and France to implement their own Sykes-Picot Agreement and simultaneously to exploit a "legal" loophole at Rome's expense. Unfortunately for Rome, the Secret Treaties were representative less of "legalities" than of deep-rooted historic interests. Whatever the Italian investments overseas, Rome's unimpressive little bridgehead in southern Anatolia before the war hardly ranked with the massive cultural, economic, and strategic interests that Britain and France had long since carved out for themselves in the Middle East, and that later they pre-empted for themselves by force of arms in the war itself. Precisely because the Sykes-Picot Agreement formalized these powerfully buttressed imperial commitments, the treaty survived both Russia's defection and Wilsonian opprobrium at the Peace Conference. By the same token, as we shall see, it was for the lack of similarly anchored claims and not of a Russian signature that the Treaty of St.-Jean-de-Maurienne would fail.

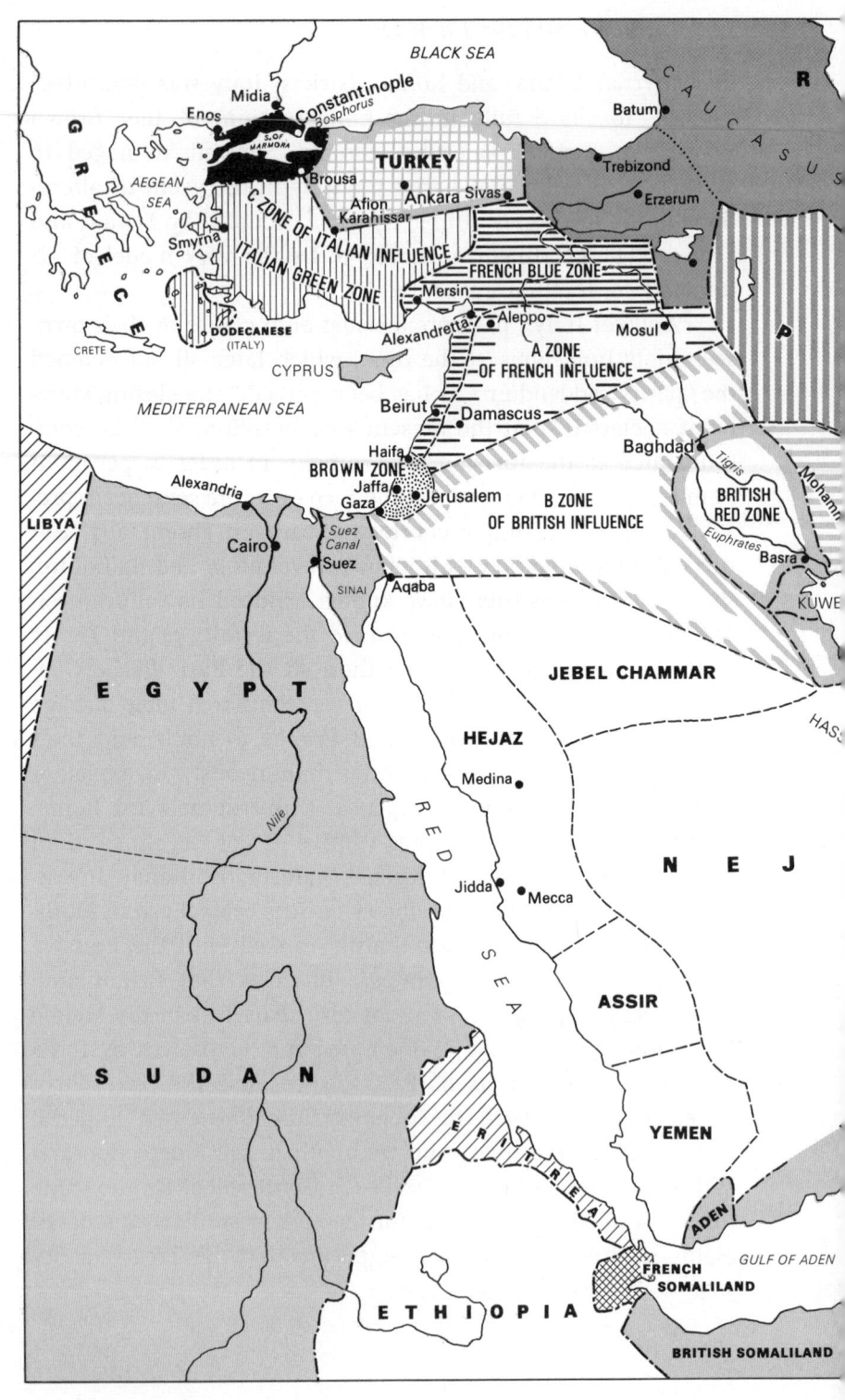

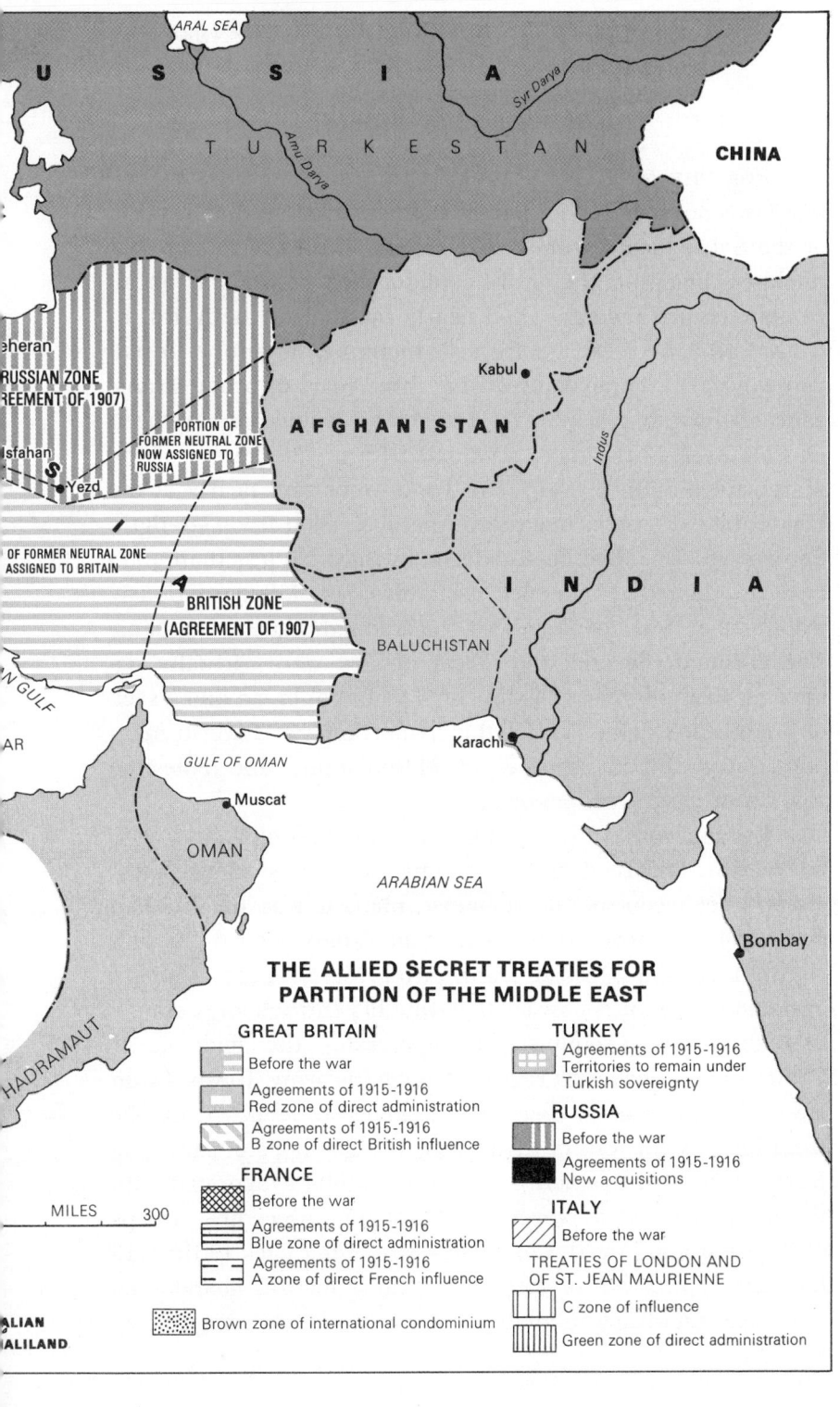

ARAL SEA

U S S I A

S I A

CHINA

T U R K E S T A N

Amu Darya

Syr Darya

eheran

RUSSIAN ZONE
REEMENT OF 1907)

Kabul •

Isfahan

S

PORTION OF
FORMER NEUTRAL ZONE
NOW ASSIGNED TO
RUSSIA

A F G H A N I S T A N

• Yezd

Indus

OF FORMER NEUTRAL ZONE
ASSIGNED TO BRITAIN

I N D I A

BRITISH ZONE
(AGREEMENT OF 1907)

BALUCHISTAN

N GULF

Karachi

AR

GULF OF OMAN

• Muscat

OMAN

ARABIAN SEA

Bombay

THE ALLIED SECRET TREATIES FOR
PARTITION OF THE MIDDLE EAST

GREAT BRITAIN

Before the war

Agreements of 1915-1916
Red zone of direct administration

Agreements of 1915-1916
B zone of direct British influence

FRANCE

Before the war

Agreements of 1915-1916
Blue zone of direct administration

Agreements of 1915-1916
A zone of direct French influence

Brown zone of international condominium

TURKEY

Agreements of 1915-1916
Territories to remain under
Turkish sovereignty

RUSSIA

Before the war

Agreements of 1915-1916
New acquisitions

ITALY

Before the war

TREATIES OF LONDON AND
OF ST. JEAN MAURIENNE

C zone of influence

Green zone of direct administration

MILES   300

HADRAMAUT

ALIAN
ALILAND

The Demise of Russia

FOR THE MIDDLE EAST, the significance of Russia's collapse was not merely the shadow suddenly cast on the "legality" of the Sykes-Picot-Sazanov agreements. With the fall of that mighty belligerent, the entire configuration of the war on all fronts changed radically, and nearly fatally, for the Allies. In truth, had it not been for Russia's monumental efforts in pulverizing the Ottoman army during three years of brutal Transcaucasian warfare, the Secret Agreements would not have been effected even in the most attenuated form. On the eve of the March Revolution in 1917, the Turks were very nearly at the end of their resources in eastern Anatolia. Their troop strength, 800,000 in 1915, had been reduced by half. No less than 300,-000 of their "permanent" casualties, in killed, seriously wounded, or deserted, had been suffered fighting the Russians. The Ottoman Second and Third armies were virtually destroyed, their survivors existing on a pound of bread and a sack of dried beans daily. But for this hemorrhage in Turkish manpower, the British victories in Mesopotamia and Palestine would not have been possible.

Russian losses in the Transcaucasus had obviously been heavy, too, and food and munitions were in continual short supply. Yet troop morale remained high. It was the Russian and Bolshevist revolutions alone that fatally eroded Russian strength on the Turkish front. After March 1917, General Yudenich found it necessary to devote his entire energy simply to maintaining discipline and suppressing the epidemic of Communist propaganda raging through his army. It was a vain effort. By summer of that year, soldiers were deserting the front lines by the tens of thousands. The last hope of salvaging Russia's forward position in eastern Anatolia evaporated with the Bolshevist *coup* in November. Throughout December, troops of the First and Fourth Corps were streaming back to Russian territory at the rate of forty thousand a month, abandoning immense quantities of matériel. Clearly, all the magnificent accomplishments and heroic sacrifices of the 1916 Transcaucasian campaign had been wasted. By the end of 1917, hardly a Russian soldier remained on Turkish soil. The steady deterioration of Russian military power was reflected, as well, in the increasingly pacific declarations of Russian statesmen. During the republican interregnum, Prime Minister Kerensky hinted at an abandonment of Russian territorial ambitions and spoke of "a peace without annexations, without indemnities, and on the basis of the self-determination of peoples." Lenin went much farther, on December 7, simultaneously revealing and flatly repudiating the Secret Treaties, with their designs on Constantinople, the Straits, and Armenia. "We declare that the division of Turkey and the subduction from it of Armenia, is null and void," he announced. "Immediately after the cessation of military activities, the Armenians will be guaranteed the right of free self-determination of their political fate."

Unfortunately for the Armenians and other Transcaucasian nations, the Bolshevist regime was in no position to confer self-determination on the Ottoman millet peoples. Rather, by the terms of the Treaty of Brest-Litovsk, the Soviets were obliged to cede back to Constantinople territory that had been painfully won in the Russo-Turkish War of 1877–78: the provinces of Kars and Ardahan in Russian Armenia and Batum in Georgia. This retrocession signified a fresh disaster for the Armenians. It cut away a third of the area in which native Russian Armenians and Ottoman Armenian refugees alike depended upon Russian protection. As it developed, most of the Georgian, Azerbaijani, and Armenian inhabitants of Russian Transcaucasia were strongly anti-Bolshevist. Indeed, almost immediately after the November revolution, the leaders of the three peoples organized their own "Transcaucasian Federation" and embarked on a somewhat disjointed effort to repel Ottoman invasion. The attempt to organize a new defense force out of the bedraggled, essentially Armenian, military units of the former tsarist army was a pitiable affair. The Transcaucasian minority peoples did not really trust each other, and the Armenian militia of sixteen thousand men, serving under the command of General Nazarbekian, a former tsarist officer, was hardly capable of resisting a serious Ottoman offensive.

When news of the Brest-Litovsk concessions reached the Transcaucasian Sejm (parliament) in March 1918, it frantically set about negotiating separate terms with Vehib Bey, the Ottoman Third Army commander. Thereupon began a comic opera of stuttering diplomacy. Somewhat tremulously, the Sejm presented an offer to cede back a small fraction of the original Brest-Litovsk award. This was contemptuously rejected on April 7 by Vehib, who countered with the tough, unequivocal demand that Ardahan and Batum be evacuated immediately. The unnerved Transcaucasian delegation accepted this brutal ultimatum on April 10. A week later, however, the Sejm experienced an unaccountable revival of confidence and repudiated the agreement, "formally" declaring war on Turkey. Thoroughly exasperated by then, Vehib Bey launched his troops across the old Russo-Turkish border. On April 15 the Black Sea port of Batum surrendered after feeble resistance. Two days later, the Turks impulsively launched a frontal attack against the citadel of Kars. It was thrown back. At this point, Vehib Bey, still hoping to avoid an unnecessary expenditure of men, offered on April 22 to resume negotiations with the Transcaucasian Federation. Almost hysterically grateful for the new lease on life, the Sejm promptly sent a delegation to Batum to reopen discussions with the invaders.

This time it was the enemy who proved devious. No sooner had the conference begun than the Ottoman representatives declared the Brest-Litovsk Treaty outdated. New and even more drastic concessions would have to be forthcoming from Russian Transcaucasia, they insisted, and these were nothing less than the regions of Akhaltzkikhe, Akhalkalaki, and Alexandropol, the Trans-Georgian Railway, and free use by the Turks of all Transcaucasian railroads as long as the war against the Entente continued. It was plain now that Enver hoped to achieve his original Pan-Turanian goal of conquering the entire

Tatar hinterland of central Russia up to the northwestern borders of Persia and Afghanistan. There remained nothing further to discuss; negotiations were broken off. The Turks subsequently used the language of force. Thirty thousand of their troops plunged deeper into Russian Armenia, overrunning and sacking the city of Alexandropol on May 16 and then careening off along the southern frontiers of Georgia, toward Azerbaijan and the vital Caspian oil city of Baku. Enver was convinced that the Tatar inhabitants of Azerbaijan were certain to give their invading blood brothers full support. It happened that way exactly. With the green banners of the Prophet fluttering on their lances, six thousand Turkish regulars and twelve thousand Tatar volunteers galloped their horses swiftly across the Azerbaijani highlands, reaching the vicinity of Baku in late August 1918.

Baku, a highly industrialized city of 300,000 inhabitants, half of them Russians and Armenians, the rest Moslems, was entirely isolated by the surrounding Tatar hinterland and suffering from an acute shortage of food and weapons. As the "Army of Islam" drew near, the city government renewed its urgent appeals to the English forces in southern Persia. Actually, it was a matter of considerable importance to Britain that the inland approaches to India remain well protected by a Caspian buffer zone. That protection was seemingly assured by ninety thousand British and Indian troops garrisoned in Mesopotamia, simply marking time after the fall of Baghdad (see Chapter VIII). The dispatch of even one of these six divisions would probably have been enough to redress the entire balance of power in Transcaucasia. The British were aware of that fact. And yet their headquarters in Baghdad proved unaccountably grudging. Refusing to "weaken" the Army of the Tigris, the Anglo-Indian staff officers decided instead to dispatch a much smaller force, a token relief column under the routine command of one Brigadier General Dunsterville. This turned out to be an unimpressive collection of six hundred Anzac and Afrikaner commissioned and noncommissioned officers, a group of machine-gunners, and a line of truckers, cooks, and various service personnel. The "Dunsterforce," as the motley company was known, reached Baku by the Caspian route on August 17, sailing in on a small fleet of gunboats. Its arrival was hardly the occasion for wild rejoicing in the city. The local inhabitants had expected massive reinforcements, not a pathetic column of fifteen hundred men. Yet the civilian population might still have made a fight of it if the "Dunsterforce" had not insisted on shattering the last of their illusions. On September 14, under heavy Turkish shelling, the British and Indian newcomers abandoned their positions, embarked in their gunboats at nightfall, and sailed off amid the curses and expletives of the infuriated citizenry. The Turks entered the city the next day, and for the next forty-eight hours the Tatar irregulars indulged in their favorite pastime of slaughter and pillage.

The capture of Baku was the apogee of Ottoman military fortunes in the war—and indeed in all of Turkey's wars in modern times. However precarious the strategic position on other fronts, the Turkish people were electrified by news that advance units of the Army of Islam were already strung out along the shores of the Caspian as far as Petrovsk. Surely a final, supreme offensive would realize Enver's colossal vision of a Turco-Tatar federation extending from the Volga to the Urals. Ironically, only a year earlier, with their armies reeling under Yudenich's hammer blows, no responsible Turkish official, least of all Enver himself, would have dared even give public utterance to that fading imperial dream. But the truth was that nothing was the same after Russia left the war. The Middle East had been turned upside down. The absence of one of the "signatories" to the Secret Treaties had totally altered that west Asian hinterland the Great Powers had intended to partition. Whichever of the Allied nations lacked strength to repair the damage, or to lay claim by force of arms to a well-developed complex of earlier commitments and investments, would find painfully meager solace in legal assurances at the peace conference.

CHAPTER VII

AN INDUCEMENT
FOR THE JEWS

Palestine and the Jews

EVEN AS THEIR TROOPS were marching toward an "internationalized" Palestine, British foreign-office and military officials shared growing misgivings about the prize their diplomacy had forfeited: the opportunity for total and unilateral control of the Holy Land. As early as March 22, 1915, months before the Sykes-Picot Agreement was even mooted, T. E. Lawrence had expressed Cairo's well-nourished hope "that we can rush up to Damascus, and biff the French out of all hope of Syria." He recalled later: "For my part, I did not tell Brémond (but he knew) that I meant to defeat his efforts and to take the Arabs soon into Damascus." The ambition to exert the dominating influence in the Levant became all but obsessive when, in the spring of 1917, the British were marshaling tens of thousands of their own men for the offensive against Palestine. For that reason the War Cabinet flatly vetoed repeated French demands to participate in the enterprise. Indeed, Britain's intention to reverse the Sykes-Picot Agreement hardened after her realization that the treaty permitted France to maintain its competitive prewar railroad concession in southern Palestine. On April 19 a special "Committee on Territorial Terms of Peace" under the chairmanship of Curzon re-evaluated the stragetic vulnerability of the Suez Canal, and all but unanimously emphasized the importance of unilateral British control in Palestine after the war. Two days later, Lloyd George informed Lord Bertie, his ambassador in Paris, that "the French will have to accept our Protectorate over Palestine." The prime minister noted later that an international regime in the Holy Land "would be quite intolerable to ourselves. . . . Palestine is really the strategic buffer of Egypt." A foreign-office memorandum stated the issue succinctly: "The presence of a foreign Power in Palestine might seriously affect the position of Great Britain both in the Suez Canal and in adjacent Arab areas."

That was the essence of the issue. For several decades, in truth, London had been acutely sensitive to Palestine's strategic importance. Beginning in the 1890's, the British agent-general in Cairo had conducted a resolute, if oblique, political campaign to get a foothold in the Holy Land. His approach (not altogether successful) was to redefine Egypt's Sinai boundaries at the expense of Ottoman Palestine. Similarly, in the Anglo-French-German agreements of 1914 that allocated areas for railroad construction in the Ottoman Empire, the British had insisted on the privilege of a rail link between the Persian Gulf and Suez via Palestine's Negev. Most conclusively of all, Djemal's two Sinai expeditions appeared to confirm Palestine's importance as a staging base for offensives against the Canal. In the hands of a major European power, such military value would unquestionably be compounded many times. Nevertheless, even with this consideration in mind, Whitehall had been prepared as late as 1916 to settle for a "condominium" in the Holy Land. Perhaps the compromise was inevitable at a time when the British had been thrust back onto the defensive in the Middle East, licking their wounds after Gallipoli and Kut. It was also the period when the French were carrying the heaviest burden of the struggle on the Western front. In any case, by the terms of the Sykes-Picot Agreement, the British had taken care to guard their crucial rail interests in southern Palestine and Haifa Bay, and thus to preclude the threat of direct French access to the Sinai Peninsula.

As the months passed, however, the prospect of a French military enclave in Palestine, even as an integral part of an Allied condominium, became increasingly unpalatable to London. The idea was to become altogether unacceptable when Allenby launched his full-scale invasion of the Holy Land and planted his troops on the country's soil. Unfortunately for Great Britain, the old equation of possession with nine points of the law was hardly an appropriate basis for dealings between wartime partners. A more impressively "idealistic" rationale would still have been preferred at a time when Sir Mark Sykes's signature was barely dry on the 1916 agreement with Georges-Picot. Initially Whitehall failed to appreciate that such a rationale already existed. It had been supplied by a rather unlikely source, the Jews, ostensibly the most internationalist of all Europe's peoples. Actually the Jews had provided an interesting opportunity for a foothold in Palestine as early as 1902. In October of that year, Theodor Herzl, founder of the modern Zionist movement, first approached British Colonial Secretary Chamberlain with a proposal for a charter of Jewish settlement in El Arish in the eastern Sinai Peninsula. An astute diplomat, Herzl suggested to Chamberlain that once the Jews were in El Arish under the Union Jack, Palestine, too, would be drawn into the British sphere of influence. Nothing came of the plan, since it was rejected by Lord Cromer, the British agent-general in Cairo. But the episode offered the British their first momentary glimpse of a volatile, highly charged nationalism which even then was sweeping with increasing passion and momentum through a large part of the Jewish world. This folk movement was particularly vigorous in the densely packed Jewish hinterland of Eastern Europe, where some five million Jews lived entirely to themselves, speaking their own language, nurturing their own religion and folk mores, and responding to gentile contempt and persecution with a reciprocal ethnic clannishness of their own.

In its literary and polemical origins, Jewish nationalism bore a close similarity to the romantic awakening of Balkan and other Ottoman millet peoples in the nineteenth century. Even in its physical urgency, the Jewish response to Alexander III's pogroms resembled the dynamic Bulgarian and Armenian reaction to Abdul Hamid's massacres. The uniqueness of Zionism was to be found, rather, in the homeland on which it focused. Like the Greeks and Armenians, the Jews did not distinguish between the ancestral religion and the ancestral soil. In their case, however, physical connection with the ancestral homeland of Palestine had been extremely tenuous since the destruction of Jewish statehood in 70 A.D. To be sure, there had been episodes of revival in Galilee under Roman and early Arab rule; but, more frequently, these were interspersed with malevolent epochs of persecution and virtual annihilation at the hands of Byzantines and Crusaders. The land was ravaged and deforested. Any possibility of growth or progress under the Turks was all but aborted by Ottoman indolence and corruption. To compound the difficulties of national restoration, the Jews who traveled back to Palestine in the eighteenth and nineteenth centuries were essentially otherworldly pietists, content to spend their days in prayer within the shadows of Jerusalem's ancient Temple wall and to subsist on the charity sent by kinsmen from abroad. They numbered perhaps twenty thousand by 1876, and of these two thirds were Oriental Jews from the Arabic-speaking domains of the Ottoman Empire, and were hardly less backward than the Moslem neighbors they had left behind. This was unlikely material on which to build a folk renaissance.

But the fact of the connection itself provided a crucial opening wedge for the Zionists. They were East European Jews, most of them—secular, alert, intensely motivated by the ideological appeals of such romantic nationalist writers as Smolenskin and Ahad Ha'Am, and later of the Socialist Zionists Syrkin and Borochow. Their dream was the establishment of a viable Jewish enclave in Palestine and the transformation there of the insecure urban Jew of the Exile into the rooted and self-assured inhabitant of his own homeland. With single-mindedness bordering on fanaticism, the Jewish nationalists by the end of the century had succeeded in establishing a network of Zionist agricultural outposts throughout Palestine's coastal plain, and in Judea and Galilee. If their beachhead in the wilderness of Zin remained a precarious one, it was not for absence of physical resourcefulness, but rather for uncertainty of juridical status. As non-Ottoman immigrants, the

Zionist settlers enjoyed no rights before the law, not even the right to be in Palestine, still less the right to own land there. They bought their way in by baksheesh and were obliged to engage in endless legal fictions for every farm or shop they opened. It seemed an extraordinarily involuted way to establish a homeland.

Theodor Herzl, in fact, denounced this technique of bribery and illegal infiltration as altogether fruitless and self-defeating. A Central European Jew, a distinguished journalist totally immersed in European culture, Herzl had arrived at the idea of Zionism exclusively as a panacea for anti-Semitism. Jewish cultural revival meant little to him. As he saw it, the issue was simple: his people were homeless and rightless; accordingly, his people needed a state. The book he published in 1896 to document this thesis bore the symbolic and unequivocal title *Der Judenstaat.* The following year, Herzl convened an international Zionist Congress in Basel to support his efforts to extract a charter of Jewish settlement in Palestine from the Ottoman sultan. Although the Congress failed initially to raise the vast sums needed for immediate mass settlement in the Holy Land, it supplied Herzl with plenty of moral encouragement; for the very dazzling simplicity of his approach kindled the imagination of Jews everywhere. He failed in his quest for a charter, however, despite elaborate and time-consuming negotiations with the sultan himself, with the kaiser, and with other royalty and diplomats. It was a measure of the man's desperation that he was finally willing to explore alternatives such as El Arish, and later Uganda, with Colonial Secretary Chamberlain—neither possibility ever materializing. Herzl died in 1904, certain that his Zionist quest had been a failure.

The opposite was the case. The Zionist movement had been profoundly stimulated. Indeed, by the first decade of the twentieth century it had become a major force in both the Eastern and the Central European Jewish world, although it remained a minority movement among the Jews of the emancipated West. The institutions of the World Zionist Organization—a bank, a national fund, an agricultural agency with branch offices in Constantinople and the major European capitals—all were instrumental in helping to underwrite a steadily growing stream of Jewish migration to Palestine. By 1914, some 85,000 Jews lived in the Holy Land. Admittedly, they still lacked juridicial status. In the 1908 and 1914 elections to the Ottoman Parliament, for example, not one Jew was returned as a delegate. Few Jews could so much as vote. But if the Zionists enjoyed little standing in Turkish eyes, in their own eyes they had taken great strides toward national regeneration. Their rural settlements numbered forty-three. On the coastal plain their citrus groves were earning profits for the first time. So were their shops, foundries, and printing presses in the cities. They spoke Hebrew as their daily vernacular by then, and guarded their own farms. Even the nucleus of self-government was dimly perceptible by 1914 in the grass-roots democracy of collective settlements, the federation of Judean colonies in the south, and the organization of lower Galilee in the north. The official Zionist Office in Palestine already was printing its own stamps and its own scrip. When, therefore, a Zionist leader like Chaim Weizmann (see below) spoke to British statesmen of a Jewish national home, he was not speculating about the future alone. He also had in mind the tangible accomplishments of the present.

Yet the war, which opened new vistas for Zionist diplomacy on the world scene, very nearly throttled the Jewish settlement in Palestine itself. Most of the Jews settled there by 1914 were still not Ottoman subjects, and had come to depend upon the European consuls to ensure their elementary physical security. With the abolition of the Capitulations, that assurance was now gone. On December 17, 1914, Beha-a-Din, the Turkish governor of Jaffa, ordered the six thousand Russian Jews who lived in his port city to be immediately expelled from the country. In terror of future deportations, Jewish communal leaders urged all Jews then domiciled in Palestine to apply immediately for Ottoman citizenship. Offices for that purpose were opened throughout the country, even at the home of the chief rabbi of Jerusalem. Within several weeks an effective naturalization campaign had avoided at least the physical danger of mass expulsion. A number of Jewish officials, including the Zionist Labor spokesman David Ben-Gurion and Yitzhak Ben-Zvi, sought to go further and petitioned the Ottoman authorities for the right to establish a Jewish militia to share in the defense of the country. The appeal was curtly rejected, an omen of things to come.

Early in 1915, Beha-a-Din was appointed to the staff of Djemal Pasha, as "secretary of Jewish affairs." A remorseless enemy of Zionism and Arab nationalism alike, the former governor of Jaffa launched a systematic attack on the entire Jewish redemptive effort in the Holy Land. Zionist newspapers, clubhouses, and schools were closed down. Hebrew posters and stamps were forbidden, Zionist flags confiscated. All Zionist public activities were banned. The Anglo-Palestine Bank was closed. Even more ominously, Jewish land titles were called into question, and Arabs were encouraged to pillage Jewish colonies. When Ben-Gurion and Ben-Zvi ventured to protest these measures, they and other Zionist leaders were summarily exiled.

It was not the hostility of the Ottoman authorities alone that threatened the security of Palestine Jewry. The "normal" hardships of war were bad enough. The British naval blockade choked off philanthropic remittances and food imports from abroad. The citrus crop withered and died on the trees, and with it the basis of the Jewish agricultural economy. Ruthless and arbitrary Turkish requisitions of animals and foodstuffs intensified the suffering, reducing many formerly prosperous Jewish and Arab families to maize grits as their basic staple and to flint and steel for fire. By the end of 1915, the Jews of Palestine, no less than the Arabs of the entire Levant area, were critically debilitated by hunger and disease. Still, remarkably, widespread starvation was avoided. The intervention of two influential Western Jews proved especially timely. One was Dr. Arthur Ruppin, director of the Zionist office in Jaffa, a German citizen who was permitted by the Ottoman authorities to distribute funds received from German Jewish sources.

Far more important was the intercession of the American ambassador to Turkey, Henry Morgenthau. As a Jew, Morgenthau felt it necessary to lean far over backward in the studied impartiality and mildness of his protests. On the other hand, as the representative of a powerful neutral country, enjoying the full personal support of President Wilson, Morgenthau was bound to be taken seriously in his concern for the fate of the Jewish minority. It was principally at Morgenthau's request that Djemal gradually eased his repressive measures during the spring of 1915 and ended the wave of expulsions and arrests. The American ambassador even secured permission for American cruisers to bring occasional relief shipments of food and money to Palestine. This uncertain trickle of supplies and funds from abroad enabled the Palestine Jewish community to survive the war, however precariously.

Yet the fundamental brutality of Ottoman officials was neither forgotten nor forgiven by many hundreds of younger Jews who had been driven into exile during the early months of war. Interned in Alexandria, they petitioned the British authorities for the right to serve as a Jewish legion in an offensive against the Turks in Palestine. Sir Henry McMahon, the high commissioner in Cairo, approved the idea. The emigrés were promptly organized into a special transportation unit, the Zion Mule Corps. Their assignment was not Palestine, however, but the impending Dardanelles campaign. Although a British officer, Lieutenant Colonel John Patterson, was placed in charge of this unit, its animating spirit was Patterson's deputy, Captain Joseph Trumpeldor. A seasoned veteran of the Russian army, decorated for his heroism in the Russo-Japanese War, in which he lost an arm, Trumpeldor in recent years had been serving as a farmer-pioneer on a collective settlement in northern Palestine. When the World War began, he departed for Alexandria and volunteered his services to the British army. Patterson found him indispensable now in organizing the new Jewish force.

Its numbers were not large. By the end of August 1915, about five hundred Palestinian and Egyptian Jews had joined the Zion Mule Corps. The recruits took the military oath in the presence of the chief rabbi of Alexandria, who enjoined them to be loyal and devoted soldiers of the "exalted British Government." The men were not informed until the last moment that they were going to Gallipoli. Upon being landed at Helles beach, the Corps performed creditably enough, the men leading their supply mules to the front trenches through heavy fire. Trumpeldor himself was wounded. Many other casualties were suffered, but were immediately replaced by new Jewish volunteers. The effort was apparently unavailing either for the Jews or the British. With the end of the Gallipoli campaign, the order came on December 28, 1915, for the Zion Mule Corps to be disbanded. Unrealized at the time, however, the first tentative step in Anglo-Zionist collaboration had already been taken.

The Origins of the Anglo-Zionist Alliance

FOLLOWING THE OUTBREAK of the war, the leadership of the World Zionist Organization painstakingly avoided suspicion of collaboration with any of the belligerent nations. A special "Bureau for Zionist Affairs" was established in neutral Copenhagen to maintain contact with Jewish communities among both the Central Powers and the Entente. Within individual countries, too, local Zionist federations patriotically identified themselves with the respective national war efforts. Thus, the German Zionists courted officials in Berlin, urging the government to take the initiative in establishing a Jewish homeland in Palestine—which then would surely form a "bastion" of German influence in that part of the world. The Wilhelmstrasse rejected these overtures; it was not prepared to alienate its Turkish ally by making a public statement of support for Jewish nationalism. Elsewhere, the government of France was aware that Herzl, Wolffsohn, and other early Zionist leaders were Central European Jews by training and culture, if not by birth, and Paris therefore suspected Jewish nationalism as "the advance guard of German influence." In Russia, in whose

Jewish community Zionism was a considerably more powerful movement than in any other, the tsarist government was hardly likely to evince any sympathy for Jewish nationalism at a time when it was driving half a million Jews like cattle into the Russian interior. England appeared an even less likely source of help for the Zionist cause. Its Jewish community of a quarter million consisted largely of Russian immigrants. Although their sympathies were Zionist, most of the newcomers were far too poor and inchoate to exert any influence in public or communal affairs. Conversely, the older, acculturated, and well-established Jewish families were largely unsympathetic to Jewish nationalism. As a consequence, the British government was perhaps less aware of the Zionist renaissance in Palestine than that of any other major power.

Ironically enough, nevertheless, within two years after the outbreak of the war, the Zionist connection with official circles was stronger in England than in any other nation. One reason, although not the exclusive one, was the extraordinarily persuasive group of Zionist leaders who happened to be living in England at the time. Their acknowledged spokesman was Chaim Weizmann, then in his early forties, a reader in chemistry at the University of Manchester. Russian-born, and university-trained in Switzerland, Weizmann was an extraordinarily lucid and convincing propagandist. He soon won a loyal following for the Zionist cause among a number of distinguished personalities in the Anglo-Jewish community. Perhaps the most influential of these after Weizmann himself was Herbert Samuel, a president of the local government board and later home secretary in the Asquith government. Samuel's concept was not simply of a Jewish homeland, but of a Jewish homeland under a British protectorate in Palestine, an arrangement that would conveniently forestall occupation of Palestine by any other power. He was the first to moot this idea to Asquith and Sir Edward Grey, both of whom viewed it with some reserve. "I confess," Asquith wrote later, "I am not attracted by the proposed addition to our responsibilities, but it is a curious illustration of Dizzy's [Disraeli's] favorite maxim that 'race is everything' to find this almost lyrical outburst proceeding from the well-ordered and methodical brain of H. S."

Samuel persisted, however, and, with others, introduced Weizmann to several luminaries of the Establishment. These included Charles P. Scott, editor of the Manchester *Guardian*, and Henry Wickham Steed, editor of the London *Times*, both of whom became devoted advocates of the Zionist cause. Through them, too, Weizmann met several of the key political figures of the day: Lloyd George, Winston Churchill, Lord Robert Cecil. Indeed, Weizmann's relationship with these men was strengthened by a vital service that he performed for the British Admiralty. In March 1916, he was summoned to London to help solve the shortage of acetone, the solvent used in making the naval explosive, cordite. It required two years of experimentation, but Weizmann eventually accomplished the task by devising an ingenious process of fermentation. During those two years, moreover, the friendships Weizmann had made earlier were cemented on the highest level. As always, the force of the man's personality was almost irresistible. He was physically imposing, for one thing, the brow of his massive bald head finely etched with veins, his eyes shrewd and piercing, his mustache and goatee elegant, his clothing always superbly tailored. A slight Russian accent lent a touch of exoticism to Weizmann's perfect command of the English language. "As a speaker," wrote Sir Ronald Storrs later, "[he] was almost frighteningly convincing. . . ." Mark Sykes recalled: "I sometimes wonder whether his fellow Jews realise how deeply he impressed us Gentiles by his heroic, his Maccabean quality."

Weizmann's efforts were buttressed by other advantages. One was the almost mystical veneration with which many devout Anglo-Saxon (or Welsh or Scottish) Protestants regarded the Old Testament traditions, the Children of Israel, and particularly the Holy Land itself. Lloyd George recalled that in his first meeting with Weizmann, in December 1914, place names of Palestine were mentioned that were "more familiar to me than those of the Western front." Balfour, too, had evinced a lifelong interest in the Holy Land and its history; like Lloyd George and Smuts, he felt deeply Christianity's debt to the Jews. That debt was compounded not merely by Weizmann's personal services to the Allied war effort, but also by his uncompromising devotion to Britain, his public and repeated insistence that the fate of Zionism was inexorably linked to that of the Allies. Thus, Weizmann's letter severing relations with the "neutralist" Zionist Bureau in Copenhagen was kept by Scotland Yard (unknown to Weizmann) and certainly influenced the authorities as much in his favor as did his scientific research for the admiralty.

Against this background of Anglo-Zionist cordiality, Weizmann's allusions to a "British protectorate over a Jewish homeland" struck an increasingly responsive chord among government officials. The basic moment of reappraisal in Middle Eastern policy came in December 1916, when Lloyd George and Balfour succeeded Asquith and Grey as prime minister and foreign secretary. If, as the new government recognized, the Sykes-Picot Agreement was no longer a sufficiently watertight safeguard for British interests in Palestine, then perhaps the Jews as a client people might be as useful an opening wedge for England as the Lebanese Christians for France or the Armenians for Russia. The proposal was forthrightly advocated by Lord Milner, Lloyd George's closest friend and collaborator in the War Cabinet, by Lord Robert Cecil, undersecretary for foreign affairs, by Philip Kerr, the prime minister's personal adviser on foreign policy (later ambassador to the United States), and, perhaps most importantly, by the three young men who served as the Middle East specialists of the War Cabinet secretariat: Sir Mark Sykes, Leopold Amery, and David Ormsby-Gore (Lord Harlech). Sykes was the most influential of this group, the man who served as "marriage broker" in the progressively intimate relationship between the British government and the Zionist leadership.

This was a strange role for Sykes, who really never cared much for Jews at all. His Zionism stemmed in part from personal snobbery, a dislike of the "hyphenated" and "diluted"

Jews who were beginning to make their way in English society. In truth, Sykes was unshakably convinced that the Jews were incapable of becoming a "normal" people until they produced "a virtuous and simple agrarian population" rather than, as he saw it, financiers, cosmopolitans, and radicals (in some degree, this was also a Zionist argument). During his travels in Palestine, Sykes had come to admire the Zionist colonies and to recognize their potential value as a rejuvenating force among the Jewish people. Plainly, however, more than concern for the future of the Jews animated Sykes's emerging Zionism. Although initially reluctant to upset the 1915 agreement with France, by autumn of the following year he had reluctantly come to share his colleagues' ambitions for a revisionist imperial policy in the Middle East. Thus, the chain of liberated national groups (Armenians, Arabs, Greeks) whom Sykes envisioned as Britain's logical Middle Eastern allies against the Turks would necessarily include the Zionist Jews. The idea did not spring full-blown from his own mind. Rather, it was suggested to him in October 1916 by one James Malcolm, a Persian-born Armenian who had been raised in England, and whose family maintained intimate connections with Jews. Malcolm attached himself to the Zionist cause early, partly out of genuine conviction, and partly in the hope, too, "that Jewish haute finance will help the Armenians. . . ." Through Malcolm, Sykes met Weizmann. After that, it became Sykes's mission in life to wed Zionist and British interests.

Time now became a crucial factor, for by the opening days of 1917 the British military offensive in Palestine was approaching its planned fulfillment. On February 7, Sykes met with the key Jewish leaders and hinted that the government was prepared to view favorably a Zionist solution to the Palestine question. Obviously, Sykes was not in a position to reveal the existence of the Sykes-Picot Agreement and the inhibition that this treaty placed on the Cabinet's freedom of action. He observed simply that the Zionists themselves would have to take the initiative in persuading the Allied governments of the need for a Jewish homeland and in making evident to them the Zionist preference for a British protectorate. Weizmann and the others agreed. They set about immediately presenting their case in Paris and Rome. The effort was not unsuccessful. Both the French and the Italians expressed a friendly interest in the Jewish homeland, although they remained noncommittal on the question of British patronage. All the while Sykes, in the background, carefully stage-managed the negotiations. Nahum Sokolow, Weizmann's most intimate collaborator and the Zionist representative in these Allied discussions, wrote later:

> ... As I was crossing the Quai d'Orsay on my return from the Foreign Ministry I came across Sykes. He had not had the patience to wait. We walked on together, and I gave him an outline of the proceedings. This did not satisfy him; he studied every detail; I had to give him full notes and he drew up a minute report. "That's a good day's work," he said with shining eyes. The second [meeting] was a day in April, 1917, in Rome. Sykes had been there before me and could not wait my arrival. He had gone to the East. I put up at the hotel; Sykes had ordered rooms for me. I went to the British Embassy; letters and instructions from Sykes were waiting for me there. I went to the Italian Government Offices; Sykes had been there, too; then to the Vatican, where Sykes again prepared my way.

The other Allies were hardly unaware of what Britain was up to. On April 6, 1918, Sykes actually informed Georges-Picot point-blank that Britain's military efforts in Palestine would have to be taken into account at the peace conference. "[Picot] is convinced," Poincaré wrote in his diary on April 17, "that in London our agreements are now considered null and void. British troops will enter Syria from the south and disperse our supporters." Neither were the Zionists ignorant of their function as an extension of British policy. Indeed, they welcomed the role, for the support and friendship of this mighty imperial power was now all but official. Precisely for that reason, Weizmann and the others, impatient for a public statement from the War Cabinet, were mystified that support continually fell just short of a public commitment. They knew nothing of the prior understanding with France, of course. "It was *not* from [Sykes] that we learned of the existence of the agreement," Weizmann recalled, "and months passed . . . before we understood what it was that blocked our progress." Charles P. Scott of the Manchester *Guardian* was the first to uncover the details of the Sykes-Picot understanding, and he immediately informed Weizmann. The Zionists were appalled. Evidently the disposition of Palestine was to have been a joint one between France and Britain all along. When Weizmann confronted Lord Robert Cecil with this information, the under-secretary neither confirmed nor denied it, although he warmly reiterated the government's sympathy for Zionism. And then, for the first time, Cecil suggested that perhaps more yet could be done in persuading the Cabinet officially to declare the identity of British and Zionist goals, in this fashion under-mining objections to a revision of the Sykes-Picot Agreement. It would be helpful, the undersecretary observed, if Zionists not simply in England but throughout the world should openly express themselves in favor of a British protectorate in the Holy Land. The implication was clear, too, that it would be no less useful if Jews throughout the world would use their influence generally on behalf of the Allied cause.

The Quid Pro Quo *of Jewish Friendship*

THE HOARY AND TENACIOUS MYTH of the power and wealth of world Jewry extended back to the Baroque Era, when Jewish court bankers functioned as dependable supporters of the absolutist dynasties. It was regarded with equal solemnity in the nineteenth century, when as astute a statesman as Palmerston could importune the Ottoman government to allow large-scale Jewish settlement in Palestine "because the wealth they would bring with them would increase the resources of the Sultan's dominions, and . . . would be a check upon any future evil designs of Mehemet Ali or his successor. . . ." It was taken no less seriously in the twentieth century. In February

1916, Sykes could write Georges-Picot: "If the great force of Judaism feels that its aspirations are not only considered but in a fair way to realisation, then there is hope of an ordered and developed Arabia and Middle East." Nearly all the major belligerent governments shared this awe for the—essentially legendary—power of world Jewry. It was significant that both Germany and France included Jewish "advisers" among their wartime missions to the United States, men ostensibly with special connections to help mobilize American Jewish support for their respective causes.

Lloyd George, too, expressed the prevailing conviction of Jewish "influence" in other lands, notably in the United States, where several powerful Jewish leaders were alleged to be inhibiting the American government from pulling its weight in the war. The notion was entirely spurious; but that was less important than what the prime minister believed. And Lloyd George's beliefs in 1917 were conditioned by the worst crisis of the war: Russia virtually out of action, France exhausted, Italy demoralized after Caporetto, German submarines taking a fearful toll of Allied shipping, not a single American division yet in the trenches. The need to exploit America's resources many times over, to keep Russia in the war, was all but overpowering. "In the solution of these two problems," Lloyd George wrote, "public opinion in Russia and America played a great part, and we had every reason . . . to believe that in both countries the friendliness or hostility of the Jewish race might make a considerable difference." Actually, the attitude of Jews was a negligible factor in both Russia and the United States. Weizmann must have suspected this; but he was willing at least to cultivate Jewish support in other lands for the much more limited cause of a British protectorate over a Zionist homeland. Even here his efforts were largely wasted. In the case of the United States, he was kicking at an open door. The country had already entered the war, the nationalist passions against the kaiser were by then well inflamed; Jewish influence, or lack of it, was no longer relevant. Until very shortly before, too, the Russian Zionist leadership's attitude toward the Entente had been poisoned by a grim and uncompromising hatred of the tsarist regime and all that tsarism meant in terms of Russian-Jewish suffering.

Vladimir Jabotinsky discovered this opposition the hard way. A brilliant Russian-Jewish poet and linguist, still in his twenties when the war began, he served as correspondent to the Western front for the liberal Russian newspaper *Russkiya Vyedomosti.* The moment the Ottoman Empire joined the Central Powers, Jabotinsky sensed the mighty opportunity that would accrue to Zionism if the Turks could be driven out of Palestine. To emphasize the Zionist commitment to the Allied cause, therefore, Jabotinsky hurled himself into the effort to organize a Jewish legion for "the liberation of the Holy Land." In this task he collaborated with the Russian-Jewish engineer Pinhas Rutenberg, who recruited principally in the United States. Joseph Trumpeldor, too, was an early advocate of a Jewish legion, and for that purpose helped organize émigré Palestinians into a fighting unit under the British flag. But as we have seen, this original group, the Zion Mule Corps, was sent to Gallipoli instead and afterward was disbanded. Early in 1916, Jabotinsky accordingly moved on alone to London, where he set about recruiting Jewish volunteers for still another Palestine liberation force. This time his efforts nearly met disaster. Whenever he ventured to address Russian-Jewish audiences in the ghetto of London's East End, he was furiously hooted and shouted off the platform. At times he needed police protection. The truth was that the immigrants wanted no part of a Jewish legion or any other unit dedicated to fighting the enemies of the tsar. It was of interest, too, that most of the leaders of British Zionism (except for Weizmann) were equally cold to Jabotinsky's scheme, although for different reasons. They pointed out that the Jewish settlement in Palestine was a hostage of the Ottoman government; if it became known that Jews abroad were mobilizing specifically to drive the Turk from Palestine, the Zionist enclave in the Holy Land would conceivably suffer the fate of the Armenians.

This analogy was by no means farfetched. In 1916 very nearly the same tragic result was provoked by a small group of Palestinian Jews engaged in transmitting military data to the British. A certain Aaron Aaronsohn was the driving force behind this clandestine organization. The son of a Zionist farmer, Aaronsohn was an agronomist of authentic genius; at the age of twenty, he carried out the explorations upon which most of the knowledge of the flora and fauna of Palestine is based to this day. Two years later, he won international recognition for discovering a weather- and disease-resistant wild wheat. In 1910, the United States department of agriculture, which found this primeval "mother of wheat" ideal for the arid lands of the American West, endowed a special research station for Aaronsohn in Athlit, a coastal village at the foot of the Carmel range. There, in succeeding years, the renowned agronomist carried out the most fundamental research on dry farming techniques ever undertaken in modern times. Even as he explored methods of reviving Palestine's wasted soil, however, Aaronsohn was driven reluctantly to the conclusion that the land of Palestine, and indeed the Jewish settlement there, had no permanent future under the slothful, brutish Ottoman regime. The outbreak of the war, the expulsions and sequestrations carried out in Palestine against Jew and Arab alike, the horror visited upon the Armenians, whose pathetic refugees straggled in small bands through the countryside, seemed to confirm this premonition. The Jews' best hope, Aaronsohn was convinced, was simply to wrest Palestine away for themselves. His view was shared by a small band of associates, including his brother, Alexander, his sisters, Sarah and Rebecca, and a group of other young Palestinians who worked for him in the research station.

Aaronsohn and his companions had anticipated a British invasion once the war began. When the landings occurred at Gallipoli instead, the Athlit group decided to take the initiative in establishing communication with the British and in offering to provide the Allies systematic information on Ottoman troop movements in Palestine. Aaronsohn and his workers were in a unique position to supply this data. They were veteran settlers of the country, known and respected for their work in improving and cultivating the land, and generally permitted freedom of movement throughout Palestine for planning antilocust campaigns. A young member of the conspiracy, Avshalom Feinberg, managed to pass through the Turkish lines and reach Port Saïd with the help of an American vessel bringing relief supplies, the destroyer *Des Moines*. Arriving in Egypt, Feinberg delivered his message to Lieutenant Leonard Woolley, one of the Arab Bureau's team of experts. Woolley was impressed with the Jewish proposal. He agreed to use the little Athlit group for Intelligence purposes. A plan was devised for a British frigate to drop anchor periodically several miles down the coast from the agricultural station. There Aaronsohn and his associates would turn over dispatch pouches containing information on Turkish bases, equipment, troops and supply movements. The scheme was impressive. Yet at the beginning the frigate visited only intermittently; British headquarters did not entirely share Woolley's enthusiasm for dealing with the Jewish spies, and the connection was, in fact, nearly abandoned. In the winter of 1916, however, Aaronsohn received the ominous information that the Turks were concentrating large numbers of troops for a second invasion attempt against the Suez Canal. Somehow the British had to be apprised of the urgency of this threat. It was vital, too, that they appreciate another danger: unless Palestine were swiftly liberated from the Turks, the population of the country might not survive the famine that was reaching into every corner of the land. Aaronsohn's problem was to find a way of leaving the country and meeting personally with key British military officials.

An impending invasion of another kind—of locusts—gave him his opportunity. In a personal meeting with Djemal, he persuaded the Fourth Army commander to let him depart for Germany in order to carry out "research on a new variety of sesame rich in oil." And, in fact, once in Germany, Aaronsohn diligently performed his research and sent the results back to Athlit. But he also traveled on to neutral Copenhagen, and through the Zionist Bureau there worked out a plan to reach England without appearing to defect. He set sail for America. En route, by prearrangement, a British patrol vessel intercepted the ship, "arrested" Aaronsohn as an Ottoman citizen, and carried him back to England. Within hours of his arrival in London, Aaronsohn was pouring out his information to Sir Basil Thomson, chief of British Intelligence. The agronomist offered compelling evidence of Turkish vulnerability to an invasion through Palestine. Thomson was impressed, and sent Aaronsohn on to Egypt for conferences with the military authorities there. General Murray, Clayton, and Hogarth (see Chapter V) were as intrigued by the information as Thomson had been, and promised active collaboration with the Jewish spy ring. They were deeply impressed, too, by Aaronsohn as a man. He remained in Cairo as liaison between the British and the Athlit group, and his vision of a restored Jewish Palestine helped make Zionists of Ormsby-Gore, Sykes, James Malcolm (the Armenian), and others who came to know him there.

The NILI organization, as the spy network was called (from the initials of its Hebrew password, *Netzach Yisrael Lo Yishaker*—"The Eternal One of Israel shall not lie") worked for the next eight months under the very noses of the Turks and Germans. Aaronsohn's sister Sarah directed the effort, collecting detailed information on Ottoman military bases and army movements and transmitting it to the British frigate every two weeks at nightfall. The intelligence was of critical importance to the British. When Allenby assumed command of the Egyptian Expeditionary Force in the spring of 1917, he asked the NILI spies for information on Turkish defenses around Beersheba, the site of his contemplated offensive. Sarah Aaronsohn and her associates at once set about fufilling the assignment. Their dispatches included vital data on the weather, on the location of water sources and malaria swamps, on the precise condition of every known route to Beersheba from the Negev. The response was considerably more than

Allenby had hoped for. "It was very largely the daring work of the young spies . . ." wrote Captain Raymond Savage, Allenby's deputy military secretary, "which enabled the brilliant Field-Marshal to accomplish his undertaking so effectively."

The espionage, intensely precarious at all times, came to an end in September 1917, when one of the NILI carrier pigeons fell into the hands of the Turks. Investigations followed. Eventually, by threats and the intimidation of neighbors, the police traced the spy network back to Athlit. Most of the group's members were caught. Their fate was predictable. Sarah Aaronsohn herself was tortured in an effort to extract information from her. On the third day of her ordeal, aware that her resistance was failing, she seized a pistol from a Turkish guard and shot herself. Other members of the organization were similarly tortured, and most of them were eventually hanged. Although the merest handful of Palestinian Jews knew of the NILI plot, the imminent capture of Jerusalem by Allenby's army in the winter of 1917 alone saved the Zionist settlement from mass arrests and possibly mass hangings and deportations. Under these conditions, most of Palestine's Jewish settlers took an ambiguous, even hostile, attitude toward the espionage and refused to give aid or comfort to the survivors of the NILI ring. There were few enough survivors, in any case. Aaron Aaronsohn himself, living in Cairo, was the only member of the inner group to live out the war. With a certain classic inexorability, the NILI story ended in December 1918, when Aaronsohn's plane crashed into the English Channel en route from London to the Paris Peace Conference.

The Issuance of the Balfour Declaration

WITHOUT QUESTION, the fate of the NILI spies was one of the dangers the British Zionist leadership had in mind when it refused initially to endorse Jabotinsky's plans for a Jewish legion. Indeed, this identical fear of transforming Palestine into another Armenia restrained the Russian Zionists from endorsing a British protectorate over Palestine. Significantly, their decision was taken at the Zionist convention in St. Petersburg in June 1917, well after the fall of Nicholas II, when hatred of the tsarist regime was no longer a decisive factor. Faced with this equivocation at home and abroad, Weizmann and his colleagues might have proceeded far more cautiously in their effort to extract a pro-Zionist declaration from the British government. But changing circumstances were a relentless prod. Weizmann's knowledge of the Sykes-Picot Agreement convinced him that any danger had to be risked to avoid the dismemberment of Palestine and its Jewish settlement into disjointed and unwieldy zones of conflicting sovereignties. "This arrangement embodies all the faults of an Anglo-French and an international settlement," he protested angrily to Cecil on April 25, "and is aggravated by the fact that Palestine is cut up into two halves and the Jewish colonizing effort, which has been going on before the war for more than thirty years, is thus annihilated. . . ." Moreover, Allenby's Palestine offensive was imminent, and Weizmann sensed the urgent need for a government declaration strongly implying unilateral British control over the Holy Land. The Zionist leader's impatience was intensified by another factor. On May 24, 1917, several eminent Jewish communal leaders published a statement in the London *Times* violently attacking the Zionist position. These men were in turn repudiated by their own constituents, and by the *Times* itself, in subsequent published correspondence. But the exposure of an apparent schism within the Jewish community made it imperative for the Zionists and the government alike that the issue be resolved quickly.

The remote possibility existed, too, that the Turks still would prefer to extricate themselves from the war, and thus avoid the partition of their empire. Henry Morgenthau was convinced that such a possibility might usefully be explored with his own "reliable" Ottoman sources. When the former ambassador proposed to his government in May 1917 that he embark upon negotiations with certain "intermediaries" in Switzerland, Secretary of State Robert Lansing approved. Lansing suggested, however, that the mission ought to have a "cover." Eventually a ruse was devised by which Morgenthau would sail for Europe in June 1917 ostensibly to discuss the fate of Palestine Jewry with his "fellow Zionists." The British government, informed of the mission's real purpose, reacted coldly; the eve of Allenby's invasion was hardly the moment to give the Turks a way out of the war. The Zionists shared these misgivings. Thus, at the request of the foreign office, Weizmann agreed to intercept Morgenthau in Gibraltar. The extraordinary meeting took place. In a lengthy and occasionally heated interview, the Zionist leader bluntly warned Morgenthau that the chances of actual peace with the Turks were nil, and that indeed the British government wanted no part of the scheme and would do its best to scuttle it. Morgenthau was chagrined, but finally convinced. He passed another six weeks in aimless discussions with his "contacts" in Switzerland and then returned to the United States.

Weizmann, meanwhile, visiting Balfour on July 17, warned the foreign secretary that the risks of delay were mounting, and that an official declaration of governmental support for a Jewish homeland could no longer safely be delayed. Balfour did not have to be convinced. As early as 1906, during the closing months of his incumbency as Conservative prime minister, he had been perhaps the first of England's public figures to meet and respond to Weizmann. "It was from that talk with Weizmann that I saw that the Jewish form of patriotism was unique," he stated later. "Their love of country refused to be satisfied by the Uganda scheme [for an alternative Jewish homeland in Africa]. It was Weizmann's absolute refusal even to look at it that impressed me." With the memory of that original conversation still alive, Balfour received Weizmann in 1914, and the earlier cordiality between the two men was instantly revived. Weizmann's eloquence on behalf of a Jewish homeland literally stirred Balfour to tears. The

Zionist leader wrote later: "In bidding me good-bye, he said with warmth: 'Mind you come again to see me. I am deeply moved and interested. It is not a dream. It is a great cause, and I understand it.' " Balfour's sympathy and encouragement did not flag after he became foreign secretary in Lloyd George's Cabinet. There were those who considered him cold and emotionless, a rather forbidding man, reticent and impassive. But he was far from unfeeling, and particularly on the Jewish question. Like Smuts and Lloyd George, Balfour had been nurtured on the Old Testament, and his lifelong study of Jewish history had filled him with inner remorse about Christendom's treatment of the Jews. "The Jews are the most gifted race that mankind has seen since the Greeks of the Fifth Century," he told Harold Nicolson in 1917. "They have been exiled, scattered and oppressed. . . . If we can find them an asylum, a safe home, in their native land, then the full flowering of their genius will burst forth and propagate." Of course, imperial considerations were paramount in the government's calculations, together with the desire to mobilize "world Jewry" on behalf of the Allies. Yet, in Balfour's case, a genuine vein of Zionist mysticism unquestionably strengthened commitment to the Jewish national home. In response to Weizmann's pleas of June 17, the foreign secretary urged the Zionists themselves to draft an appropriate statement for presentation to the War Cabinet. He would stand behind it.

Weizmann and his closest associates labored intensively to prepare a suitable declaration, modifying and remodifying the text after numerous consultations with Balfour himself. The final statement was ready on July 18. It did not lack forthrightness. "His Majesty's Government," it declared, "accepts the principle that Palestine should be reconstituted as the National Home of the Jewish People. His Majesty's Government will use its best endeavours to secure achievement of this object and will discuss the necessary methods and means with the Zionist Organization." The letter, submitted to the ministers on September 3, elicited the warm approval of the Cabinet majority. "It would affect Jewish national opinion,"

Smuts observed enthusiastically, "and nationally they are a great people." Ironically, the most forceful opposition came from the one Jew in the Cabinet, Sir Edwin Montagu, secretary of state for India. Born and raised in London's East End, Montagu had fought an uphill battle to escape his ghetto origins and win acceptance in the privileged circles of government, as he himself once admitted to John Morley. In this case, a "national home" for the Jewish people seemed to raise for him embarrassing questions of Jewish dual loyalty. Now, on September 3, Montagu insisted that the proposed government statement would both alarm the Moslems of India and place the Jews of England in an untenable position." Balfour's niece, Lady Dugdale, acidly noted later: "Mr. Montagu could not extend to his own people the sympathy he evinced later for nationalism in India." In any case, the vehemence with which Montagu opposed a pro-Zionist declaration persuaded the Cabinet to drop the matter from the agenda.

Neither the Zionists nor their supporters in the government accepted this setback as more than temporary. Indeed, Lloyd George confidently put the question of the declaration on the agenda for the next Cabinet meeting. And when the meeting took place, on October 4, Balfour himself emphatically presented the Zionist case, this time consulting a detailed personal memorandum from Weizmann which lay on the table before him. Once again, Montagu opposed the draft, with more intensity even than before. "I understand the man almost wept," Weizmann wrote. "When he had ended, Balfour and Lloyd George suggested that I be called in, and messengers were sent for me. They looked for me high and low—and I happened to be a few doors away in the office of Ormsby-Gore. I missed a great opportunity." Montagu's opposition had the effect not of changing the minds of Balfour, Smuts, Lloyd George, and other Zionist sympathizers, but of convincing them of the need for a compromise text simply to get the question resolved without endless delay. While Weizmann and his colleagues urgently maintained their pressure on the government, Amery and Milner labored over a compromise formula that became the essential draft of the Balfour Declaration. The earlier phrase, "that Palestine should be reconstituted as the national home" of the Jews, was dropped in favor of a somewhat more equivocal statement (see p. 214). The Zionists were deeply chagrined by the alteration. Nevertheless, they were fearful of tampering with the modified resolution lest they jeopardize it altogether.

Lloyd George was prepared at last to force the issue through. Before making his final move, however, the prime minister was determined to win a firm commitment of diplomatic support for Zionist aspirations. It was by then open knowledge in Western government circles that the very notion of a Jewish national home was wedded to the corollary of British protectorate. Lloyd George therefore required assurance that a declaration implying such a protectorate would not encounter serious opposition at the peace conference later. At this point Sykes's tactics in dispatching Sokolow on the round of Western capitals finally began to pay dividends. Received at the Vatican in April 1917, Sokolow described the Zionist ideal to Pius X and elicited from the pontiff a cordial statement of goodwill: "I believe that we shall be good neighbors," Pius assured his Jewish visitor. Equally friendly, if innocuous, statements were issued by the Italian ambassadors in Paris and London, and by Paul Cambon, the highly esteemed French ambassador in London. However much Cambon may have resented a British-Zionist alliance, he, no more than the English, dared ignore the alleged power of world Jewry.

Ultimately, the prestige and influence of the American government proved decisive in resolving the issue for the British Cabinet. Washington had never declared war on the Ottoman Empire. But the United States, then mobilizing its immense strength for the Allied military effort in Europe, would unquestionably exert a crucial impact on all phases of the future peace settlement. An emphatic pro-Zionist statement from the American president would accordingly insure Britain against diplomatic isolation on the Palestine issue. At Weizmann's suggestion, the task of interceding with Woodrow Wilson was undertaken by Louis Brandeis, a distinguished member of the American supreme court and the most influential Zionist in the United States. On September 23, Brandeis discussed the matter of a Jewish national home with Colonel Edward House, the president's intimate adviser. Exposed to the jurist's celebrated eloqence and persuasive powers, House dropped his own earlier misgivings about Zionism. When Brandeis was received by Wilson that same day, therefore, he was able to confirm the president's support. "I find in my pocket the memorandum you gave me about the Zionist movement," Wilson wrote House a few days later. "I am afraid I did not say to you that I concurred in the formula suggested from the other side. I do, and would be obliged if you would let them know it." Actually, the formula Wilson thought he was endorsing was outdated. The text of the original Zionist draft had since been altered in favor of the more pallid Milner-Amery version. But the president probably did not know or care much what he was approving, for the question was of marginal interest to him. The fact of his endorsement, on the other hand, was all that mattered to the delighted pro-Zionist faction in the British government. The moment House's message arrived on October 16, they had what they needed.

The War Cabinet voted for the declaration on November 2—over Montagu's last dispirited objections. Significantly, the principal rationale by then was no longer the evident need to preclude French occupation of the Holy Land. Allenby's army was already on the verge of conquering Palestine, and the issue undoubtedly would be resolved by the substantial presence of the Egyptian Expeditionary Force. It was rather the vaunted power of world Jewry which influenced the War Cabinet's discussions of October 4 and 31, the obsessive desire to win the friendship of the Jewish community in both Russia and America. Lloyd George was counting on this support. "The Zionist leaders," he wrote later, "gave us a definite promise that, if the Allies committed themselves to . . . a National Home for the Jews in Palestine, they would do their best to rally to the Allied cause Jewish sentiment and support throughout the world. They kept their word in the letter and the spirit. . . ." Other factors determined the Cabinet's vote, too. One was surely the genuine personal feeling of Balfour (and Smuts and Lloyd George) for the Holy Land and the Jewish people. "Near the end of his days," Balfour's niece wrote, "he said to me that on the whole he felt that what he had been able to do for the Jews had been the thing he looked back upon as the most worth doing." Others in the Cabinet may have been animated by even more complex motives: Protestant millenarianism, an uneasy conscience about Christendom's treatment of the Jews, conceivably the need to endorse a humane and constructive act in the midst of the holocaust.

The declaration itself seemed curiously bland, however, and quite devoid of religious or mystical overtones of any kind. It took the form of a letter from Balfour to Lord Rothschild, president of the British Zionist Federation:

> Dear Lord Rothschild, I have much pleasure in conveying to you, on behalf of His Majesty's Government, the following declaration of sympathy with Jewish Zionist aspirations which has been submitted to, and approved by, the Cabinet: "His Majesty's Government view with favour the establishment in Palestine of a national home for the Jewish people, and will use their best endeavours to facilitate the achievement of this object, it being clearly understood that nothing shall be done which may prejudice the civil and religious rights of existing non-Jewish communities in Palestine, or the rights and political status enjoyed by Jews in any other country." I should be grateful if you would bring this declaration to the knowledge of the Zionist Federation.

The original Zionist draft of the declaration had called for "the reconstruction *of* Palestine [italics the author's] as the national home for the Jewish people." The phase "national home," employed in both versions, actually was unknown in international law and usage. The Zionists had coined the expression in 1897, at their first congress, to avoid the term "Jewish state," which the Ottoman government might have found provocative. Now, however, the Balfour version dispensed with the need of defining the boundaries of the Jewish settlement *in* Palestine. The "national home" might be no more than a small enclave within the country. Only five years later, the broad uplands of Transjordan were cut away, and fifteen years after that yet a further amputation would be proposed by the Peel Commission—all without violating the letter of this declaration. Moreover, the need to protect "the civil and religious rights of existing non-Jewish communities in Palestine" could and would ultimately be interpreted as justification for limiting, even foreclosing, Jewish immigration in order to placate Arab nationalism.

Yet the eventual fate of the declaration was not necessarily consonant with the original intention of its authors. Colonel Meinertzhagen, General Allenby's political officer, recorded a conversation in which Balfour stated: "My personal hope is that the Jews will make good in Palestine and eventually found a Jewish State." Lloyd George was quite explicit in his description of the Cabinet's intentions:

> It was not their idea that a Jewish State should be set up immediately by the Peace Treaty without reference to the wishes of the majority of the inhabitants. On the other hand, it was contemplated that when the time arrived for according representative institutions in Palestine, if the Jews had meanwhile responded to the opportunity afforded them by the idea of a National Home and had become a definite majority of the inhabitants, then Palestine would thus become a Jewish Commonwealth. The notion that Jewish immigration would have to be artificially restricted in order to ensure that the Jews should be a permanent minority never entered into the heads of anyone engaged in framing the policy. That would have been regarded as unjust and as a fraud on the people to whom we were appealing.

It is worth assessing the effectiveness of the appeal to "world Jewry." The Jews of England were thrilled and grateful, as their public meetings throughout the country and their innumerable resolutions of thanks made evident. Heartened by this response, in turn, and intent upon duplicating it in other countries, the government organized a special Jewish section within the department of information, staffing it primarily with Zionists. The task of these functionaries was to prepare literature for distribution through local Zionist societies and other intermediaries to virtually every known Jewish community in the world. Copies of the Balfour Declaration were circulated by the millions, including leaflets dropped from the air over German and Austrian towns. In Russia, news of the declaration evoked wild rejoicing. In the larger cities, huge, cheering crowds gathered outside the British consulates. In Odessa, a two-mile procession of Jews acclaimed the British consul on his balcony, their bands alternately playing *God Save the King* and *Hatikvah,* the Zionist anthem.

Meanwhile, embarking on a redoubled effort to mobilize Jewish support against the Central Powers, Weizmann and Brandeis cabled friends in Russia, entreating them to intercede with the new Communist government on behalf of the common Entente war effort. This, in the end, was wasted effort. The War Cabinet's notion that the Jews of Russia could somehow exert pressure on the Soviet regime was totally naïve. The fifteen or twenty Jewish Bolshevists possessed of any real influence in the country were hostile to Jewish nationalism, and indeed were generally indifferent to the fate of their people altogether. On the other hand, the Jews of Germany and the Dual Monarchy remained steadfastly loyal to the cause of their governments. American Jewry, to be sure, was hardly less exhilarated by the news of the Balfour Declaration than were the Jews of Britain and Russia. Among them, too, public expressions and demonstrations of gratitude were evoked in the same full measure. But the United States was already at war. The hated Russian tsar had already fallen. Nothing remained to inhibit the enthusiastic participation of American Jews in their national war effort, and nothing further was required to stimulate it. "The American Loan [to Britain] went much as had been anyhow expected," wrote Sir Ronald Storrs in 1937, "no sympathies for Britain accrued from the Soviet (which shortly denounced Zionism as a capitalistic contrivance); and the loyalty of German Jewry remained unshaken

—with the subsequent reward that the world is now contemplating."

Perhaps the one tangible military result of the Declaration was Jabotinsky's belated success in organizing a Jewish legion. With the overthrow of the tsar in March 1917, Jewish opposition to the plan largely evaporated. Moreover, by late spring, the imminence of a British offensive on Palestine all but dispelled fears of Turkish reprisals. For their part, Lloyd George and Balfour recognized that Zionist and British interests would equally be served by a Jewish legion entrenched in Palestine. Accordingly, after repeated appeals by Jabotinsky and Weizmann, the war ministry made the decision in August to establish a special Jewish infantry regiment. The unit would be awarded its own name and badge, the "Thirty-eighth Battalion of Royal Fusiliers," and its own privileged destination: i.e., Palestine. At this juncture, Colonel Patterson, former commander of the Zion Mule Corps, was summoned to London with orders to begin organizing the new group immediately. Not surprisingly, his first recruits were veterans of the original Zion Mule Corps. This time, too, their numbers were significantly augmented from the immigrant Jewry of London's East End. Nor was the recruitment effort limited to England. Patterson and Jabotinsky ordered the distribution of circulars to Jewish communities in America, Canada, and Argentina. The Balfour Declaration had been issued by then, and in the United States volunteers soon began registering at British consular offices. Among the first to enlist were Ben-Gurion and Ben-Zvi, whom Djemal Pasha had exiled from Palestine in 1915. They and other recruits were sent on to a military camp in Windsor, Nova Scotia, and by July of 1918 were on their way to England as members of the Thirty-ninth and Fortieth battalions of the Royal Fusiliers.

The initial vanguard of this legion disembarked at Alexandria as early as March 1918 and received advanced training outside Cairo. Whereupon Jabotinsky, serving as Patterson's aide, urgently set about recruiting among the Jews of southern Palestine and Jerusalem, the area already liberated by Allenby's army. "The anticipation [of Jabotinsky's arrival] was almost hysterical," wrote Eliahu Golomb, a founder of the original Palestine-Jewish self-defense force. "We had been waiting for the man with whose name was connected our greatest drama—the Jewish Army. We expected him to come and fulfill our vision." Thousands of Palestinian youth volunteered for service, although only several hundred of them could be accepted. Within a month the Thirty-ninth Battalion and units of the Fortieth arrived in Egypt. They were quickly sent to join the Thirty-eighth in patrolling the Jordan Valley against a threatened Turkish counterattack from across the river. For five weeks, the Jewish troops remained in the valley, the lowest spot on the earth's surface, suffering acutely from sunstroke and dysentery. When it became evident that the British staff officers, most of them anti-Zionist (see p. 221 below), intended to consign the Jews to this ordeal indefinitely, Patterson threatened to resign. The protest was effective, and the legion, now reduced by a third, was allowed to participate in Allenby's climactic autumn offensive. The Thirty-eighth Battalion was one of the first to enter Transjordan. By then the legion numbered five thousand men, a sixth of the British army of occupation and half the size of Feisal's Arab force at its median strength in 1918. The legion did not remain in that sector long. Allenby soon transferred its men to the area west of the Jordan, while Arab troops to the south of the Dead Sea and east of the river continued to occupy the highlands. By then friction between the two peoples had to be avoided at all costs.

The Arabs and the Jews

THE QUESTION of Arab-Jewish relations had not really been taken seriously earlier by either the Jews or the British. Before 1914, Zionist spokesmen had rarely considered the inchoate, largely illiterate Arab community in Palestine as a political factor. They were largely indifferent to the heated press campaign that Arab nationalists, most of them Syrians, were mounting against Jewish settlement and land purchases in the Holy Land during the immediate prewar era. In 1913, Nahum Sokolow arranged several conciliatory parleys with a group of Egyptian and Syrian notables. These conversations did little to alleviate Arab misgivings, however, which most of the Zionist leadership in any case still preferred to ignore. Neither, during the war, did the British government sense any inconsistencies between its patronage of an Arab revolt and its encouragement of Zionist aspirations, or between the terms of its original promise to Hussein and its subsequent declaration in favor of a Jewish national home in Palestine. It will be recalled that in McMahon's crucial letter to the sherif, on October 24, 1915, the British high commissioner excluded from the area of Arab independence the land west of the "districts" of Damascus, Homs, Hama, and Aleppo. A dispute erupted at war's end and raged bitterly for years afterward on the question of Britain's intention to exclude Palestine from the area of Arab independence. The wording in the correspondence was hardly precise, for "district" was not a Turkish administrative term. Was McMahon actually referring to "vilayets"? That was the Arab contention. Had it been accepted, the strip of territory excluded from Arab rule would have been far too narrow to embrace Palestine. The Jews took the opposite position, arguing that exclusion of only a nominal territorial enclave was something the French unquestionably would not have accepted. If the high commissioner had intended to exclude all the land west of the vilayet of Aleppo, for example, no land would then have been left to exclude; the vilayet extended to the sea. For their part, the British always insisted that the term "district" was being used simply in a loose sense, meaning vicinity; and thus a line drawn west of the vicinities of Damascus, Homs, Hama, and Aleppo, separating this territory from the coastal region, apparently excluded Palestine.

McMahon did not content himself with excluding a specific area. He informed the Arabs that British promises, even within the territory conceded to Hussein and his followers, applied only to "those regions . . . wherein Great Britain is free to act without detriment to the interests of her ally, France" (see Chapter V). It was accepted both in Mecca and in London that France was committed to the acquisition of a major sphere of influence in western Syria and Palestine. Years later, in a letter to the London *Times* of July 23, 1937, McMahon restated the British case, emphasizing that "it was not intended by me in giving this pledge [to Hussein] to include Palestine in the area in which Arab independence was promised. . . ." Lloyd George took this qualification for granted in his discussion with Sykes on the eve of the latter's departure for the Middle East in April 1917. He cautioned Sykes to say and do nothing that might prejudice the Zionist cause, and, indeed, to refrain from making even the most general commitments to the Arabs on the subject of Palestine. The Arabs were aware that there was no likelihood of their being allowed even partial control over Palestine, the prime minister observed.

In January 1918, after the issuance of the Balfour Declaration, Commander Hogarth was dispatched from Cairo to Jidda to clarify for Hussein the implications of the Zionist program. After assuring the sherif that Arab freedom would be safeguarded in every way, Hogarth added, significantly: "In this connection, the friendship of world Jewry to the Arab cause is equivalent to support in all states where Jews have political influence. The leaders of the movement are determined to bring about the success of Zionism by friendship and cooperation with the Arabs, and such an offer is not one to be lightly thrown aside." The hint—perhaps it was too explicit an inducement to be called that—was received with alacrity by the Arab leader. Hogarth noted later: "[Hussein] probably knows little or nothing of the . . . economy of Palestine and his ready assent to Jewish settlement there is not worth very much. But I think he appreciates the financial advantage of Arab cooperation with the Jews." Initially, Hogarth's optimism did not seem misplaced, for the sherif issued several cordial invitations to the Jews to return to their "sacred and beloved homeland."

Immediately following Allenby's conquest of Palestine, however, the political future of the Holy Land was increasingly shaped by the British occupying authorities, many of whom shared the anti-Zionist sentiments of the Arab Bureau in Cairo. Clayton had opposed the Balfour Declaration. So had Wingate. Sykes himself apparently experienced misgivings about the direction Arab nationalism might take, for he cautioned a Jewish gathering on December 2, 1917, to deal generously with the Arabs and to recall that the Holy Land would have to be shared fully by both poeples. "You want to know the Arab is free," Sykes reminded his audience, "because he is, and always will be, your neighbor." The Zionist leadership was not oblivious by then to the need for manageable relations with the Arabs. In the summer of 1918, Weizmann met with a group of Syrian emigrés living in Cairo and used the full resources of his charm and persuasiveness to reassure them of Zionist intentions. Arab rights and sensibilities would be fully respected, he promised. The Arab representatives were neither charmed nor persuaded. They countered, rather, with a suggestion for the proportional representation of the Arab majority in any future Palestine government. This reaction so unsettled Weizmann that he decided that there was no further time to be lost before meeting personally with Feisal. To that end he and Ormsby-Gore departed on a ten-day journey to Amman, in Transjordan. The two men were greeted cordially, even lavishly, in the traditional Arab manner; a sumptuous banquet was prepared in their honor. Weizmann was eager to settle matters. He wrote later:

> I explained to [Feisal] . . . our desire to do everything in our power to allay Arab fears and susceptibilities, and our hope that he would lend us his powerful moral support. He asked me a great many questions about the Zionist program and I found him by no means uninformed. . . . I stressed the fact that there was a great deal of room in the country if intensive

development were applied, and that the lot of the Arabs would be greatly improved through our work there. With all this I found the Emir in full agreement, as Lawrence confirmed to me by letter.

Feisal promised to convey the gist of the talk to his father. "The first meeting in the desert," Weizmann recalled, "laid the foundations of a lifelong friendship."

However warm the understanding between the two leaders, cooperation between their peoples was not destined to come that easily. Moslem-Christian societies were even then springing up throughout Palestine, not infrequently with the private encouragement of British military officials (see Chapter XII). The Arab slogan *Falastin biladna*—"Palestine is our country" —was first uttered in the summer of 1918, at the very moment when Allenby's army was thrusting deep into Galilee. Even as the War Cabinet and the Zionist leadership in London exulted in the evident fulfillment of their joint ambitions for the Holy Land, the sound of the Arab challenge gained in intensity. It had its Hebrew counterpart, too—*Eretz Yisrael Shelanu*— as Jewish legionaries and veteran Zionist farmers greeted each other ecstatically in growing numbers of liberated Palestinian villages. In the not distant future both credos would sear themselves indelibly into the British conscience.

CHAPTER VIII

THE DEATH
OF THE SICK MAN

The Fall of Baghdad

By 1916 THE ANGLO-INDIAN CAMPAIGN in Mesopotamia had turned into a bleeding ulcer for the Allies. Undertaken originally as a limited defensive move to insure Britain's prestige and oil at the head of the Persian Gulf, the commitment of men and matériel had burgeoned almost uncontrollably into a full-scale drive on Baghdad and had failed disastrously at Kut. Even following that debacle, however, the Government of India found it difficult to accept the logic of a withdrawal to Basra, its principal base of supply. Rather, it ordered the Army of the Tigris to maintain a "bold" front just below Sannayiyat, a mere sixteen miles from Kut. The expeditionary force did so, in scorching heat, plagued by clouds of flies, all but overcome by sapping fatigue and loneliness. Eventually, in July 1916, a major attempt was begun to improve the logistics of the unfortunate Indian and British infantrymen dug in along the riverbanks. New roads were constructed; transport was repaired. The Basra port was enlarged, and heavy equipment began arriving in significant quantities. So did an army of civilian labor from all parts of the empire: Negroes from the West Indies, Chinese from Hong Kong, mechanics from India and Burma, bricklayers and riveters from Scotland, boatmen from Goa, stokers from Egypt and Zanzibar. The effects of this vast human orchestration were soon manifest. Assured of decent communications, the troops at the Sannayiyat front enjoyed fresh meat and vegetables for the first time since arriving in the country. Morale in the ranks began to steady, and then, tentatively, to rise.

So did the ambitions of the Tigris Army's new commander, Lieutenant General Sir S. G. Maude. A keen, well-read tactician in his early fifties, Maude had replaced the aging and discredited Sir Percy Lake after the Kut failure. In the ensuing months he moved deliberately to avoid Lake's mistake of outrunning his lines of supply. By late autumn of 1916, Maude was satisfied that he had solved the logistics problem. Accordingly, with cool disregard for the fate of his predecessors, he asked London for permission to resume the drive on Baghdad. The proposal nearly caused an explosion among the imperial general staff; they, at least, had learned the lesson of Kut. Nevertheless, the War Cabinet was somewhat more receptive. Asquith and most of his colleagues were political animals, after all. As in the original Baghdad offensive, they remained sensitive to the need for a dramatic achievement on the Tigris to counterbalance military setbacks on other fronts. Unwittingly, too, the ministers found it necessary to justify the prodigious cost of equipping the Tigris Army by an additional, even more expensive operation. Ultimately a compromise was reached, and on September 27 the government informed Maude that he might push his troops "as far forward" as was consonant with safety. The general was determined to make the most of this rather ambiguous mandate. By October he could boast a sizable expeditionary force under his command—no less than 48,000 front-line soldiers, plus 100,000 supporting troops, a concentration of men four times larger than the Turkish army guarding the Tigris and Hai defenses. It was a tempting ratio for an offensive, and Maude decided to move forward on December 10.

The sheer weight of British and Indian numbers made itself felt almost immediately. By December 15, the Turks had been driven back into Sannayiyat proper, only seven miles west of Kut. Grinding on slowly and methodically, the Tigris Army scourged the retreating enemy with its massive firepower. Finally, on February 22, 1917, the Ottoman commander, Khalil Bey, ordered the evacuation of Kut. From then on, organized resistance on the banks of the river ceased entirely. With the Turkish army streaming in retreat to Baghdad, the road to the city was open. Indeed, by then it was hardly necessary to capture Baghdad in order to guarantee the headwaters of the Gulf. But strategic considerations alone were no longer paramount. Lloyd George recalled that even "the War Office could not ignore the fact that [the capture of Baghdad] would be a very valuable success, wiping out the shame of our defeat at Kut a year before, and encouraging both our own people and our friends in the East." On March 2, Maude received permission to continue his offensive.

The general saw no reason to alter his tactics. He maintained his steady, methodical, unspectacular advance, using his four-to-one numerical superiority to pulverize enemy defenses. On both sides of the river the columns of the Tigris Army converged inexorably on Baghdad. The Turks put up a last, brief resistance on March 10, and then fled north. On the afternoon of March 11, the Anglo-Indian force entered Baghdad. Presumably Townshend and those who fell at Kut were avenged. The city had beckoned tantalizingly from a distance, with its palm and orange groves, and shimmering gold domes and minarets. Once occupied, however, it proved to be an unimpressive prize. An observer wrote:

> The outskirts were covered with corpses and bones of dead animals, and within the mud embankment that encircled it were crowded thousands of Mohammedan graves presenting a mournful and unkept appearance; while, in the city itself, the miserable-looking and rather dilapidated houses of mud-brown brick, and the narrow filthy streets completed the disillusion. The one broad thoroughfare, named (in memory of his capture of Kut) Halil Pasha Street, was of recent construction, and was still fringed in places by partly demolished buildings. There were no sanitary and scavenging arrangements, noxious smells abounded and hundreds of diseased and half-starved dogs roamed everywhere.

Baghdad's population of 150,000 Arabs was starving and ravaged by plague. Maude's first task was immediately to distribute food, and to inaugurate widespread sanitary improvements. Antimalarial and drainage measures were instituted, hospitals were cleaned out, water was chlorinated. Within a few weeks the danger of famine was averted. The city began to function again.

But the truth was that Maude had gained little for his efforts. Separated from its port of supply in Basra by five hundred miles, Baghdad possessed little tactical value as a staging base for an additional major offensive. The remote possibility existed, to be sure, of joining forces with Baratov's Russian army in Persia. To that end, Maude began a cautious, probing advance another two hundred miles upland in March and April. With the deterioration of the internal situation in Russia, however, Baratov's army simply melted away. From the summer of 1917 on, neither the British nor the Turks felt constrained to exert themselves further in the purgatorium of the desert, and fighting in Mesopotamia came to a halt. Maude himself died suddenly of cholera on November 19, and was interred in Baghdad, England's first national hero of the war. With his death, the military effort along the river was paralyzed altogether. Some critics observed that the halt was long past due. By then the supreme command had committed no less than 447,000 men to the Tigris offensive, and had mobilized half a million tons of ocean shipping, innumerable river craft, and hundreds of miles of railroad track. It was an extraordinary exertion for a single campaign removed by nearly the entire breadth of the Middle East from the enemy's major political and economic centers. The so-called "defensive" Mesopotamian campaign, in fact, had accomplished little more than to siphon away trained soldiers and munitions from India, and thus to impose a serious drain on the Allied armies in Europe.

Easterners and Westerners

INDEED, THE UNRESOLVED QUESTION of priority of military effort between Europe and the Middle East had become highly inflamed by mid-1917. Field Marshal Sir William Robertson, chief of the imperial general staff, continued to be obsessed by the Western front. In Europe, as he saw it, the incomparable German army remained the single most ominous threat to the integrity of the Allied positions—and, for that matter, to the very survival of France. In Roberston's view and that of his associates, the entire Middle Eastern war effort was an appalling diversion of vital manpower. The Turkish army would take care of itself, these staff officers insisted; but the Germans had driven alarmingly close to Paris in 1914, and were capable of trying it again at any moment. This orthodox approach was strenuously contested by Lloyd George. As minister of munitions in the Asquith government, the fiery Welshman had been one of the most vigorous advocates of turning the German flank by "knocking the props" from beneath her enfeebled allies, Bulgaria and Turkey. Thus, from the beginning, he had supported the Salonica expedition (see pp. 244–5). Later, as prime minister, he was to raise Britain's commitment in the Balkans. His contempt for the traditional Western-front mentality of the general staff was total and scathing. In his memoirs he recalled his interview with Robertson in November 1916, shortly after the frightful bloodletting of the Somme offensive:

> I then asked him whether he would mind telling me whether he had formed any views as to how this sanguinary conflict was to be brought to a successful end. For the time being the question took him aback, and he looked like a general in full dress who thought to himself "This is one of those fool questions that ignorant civilians always fire at you, and they must not be encouraged." He just mumbled something about "Attrition."

In December 1916, Lloyd George succeeded Asquith as head of government, and determined to waste little time translating his views into action. On the basis of Intelligence reports, he was convinced that the Ottoman armies were demoralized and probably vulnerable to annihilation in a single sustained offensive. He was not wrong. By the opening of 1917 the Turks were reeling under the pressures of a multifront war. The dreadful toll of the Transcaucasian campaign had exerted its impact on every other front. In Syria, for example, troops were subsisting on half-rations, and their livestock were dying of starvation. In Palestine, soldiers received hardly enough bread to maintain their sedentary defensive positions. Medical equipment existed in such limited quantities that even major surgical operations were performed without anesthesia. Not least of all, the evidence of army corruption and graft had finally become too overwhelming even for the traditionally stoic Turkish peasant-conscripts. By the beginning of 1917, 300,000 of them had deserted. In the ensuing year that number would double.

By the spring of 1917, too, the German high command, no less than the British, sensed the very real likelihood of a general Ottoman collapse. On several earlier occasions, Ludendorff's advisers had discussed the possibility of shoring up the Turks by infusions of German manpower. The field marshal, like his Allied counterparts, had remained unalterably opposed to the diversion of troops from the European theater. But now, with the fall of the historic Moslem citadel of Baghdad, the Porte felt obliged to remind the Germans of their obligations under Article 4 of the Turco-German treaty: ". . . in case of need to protect with force of arms Ottoman territory, in the event that the latter should be seriously menaced." It was irrefutably clear that nothing less than an impressive military victory was capable of salvaging Turkish morale. In August, therefore, general staff headquarters in Berlin agreed to supply all possible help for a major Ottoman counteroffensive against Baghdad. *Yildirim*—"Lightning"—was the title selected for the projected operation. The plan envisaged a deployment of 120,000 Turkish soldiers, virtually an entire army. Selected formations of German and Austrian artillerymen, engineers, and medical specialists, 6,500 in all, were assigned to this force. Berlin's choice for commander of the Yildirim army was General von Falkenhayn, former chief of the German general staff. A talented if obstinate strategist, Falkenhayn had only recently been displaced from his high office after the unprecedented hemorrhage of Verdun and the defection of Rumania to the Allies. The Yildirim assignment seemed a convenient way for Berlin to get him out of Europe and at the same time continue to make use of his unquestioned military ability. The general swallowed the humiliation. He conceived the assignment as a supreme opportunity to regain his prestige by a swift, devastating victory in a hitherto neglected military area.

Unfortunately for Yildirim, Falkenhayn went about his assignment with a notable lack of sensitivity to Ottoman military tradition. He delegated operating command of the army to a top-heavy retinue of German officers, few of whom knew anything of the peculiar circumstances of Turkish military life or of the psychology of Turkish soldiers. Liman von Sanders and his mission staff, with their painfully accumulated years of experience in Turkey, were not so much as consulted. To Falkenhayn, the Turkish officer corps appeared woefully, almost deliberately, sluggish in carrying out his orders. For example, the transfer of the Yildirim army to Aleppo, the staging base for the reconquest of Baghdad, was incredibly laggard and inept. The unfortunate troops were billeted in open camps under the blazing sun; almost immediately the older men began dying of exhaustion and typhus. By September, 1917, the death and desertion rate among the wretched conscripts had climbed alarmingly. Despite elaborate security precautions, too, the Yildirim plan came to the knowledge of British Intelligence at an early stage. Both the condition and the destination of the Ottoman troops were known in some detail.

This time Lloyd George was determined not merely to smash the Turks once and for all, but also to smash them on ground of his own choosing. Rather than await the arrival of the Yildirim force in Mesopotamia and confront it there, he would anticipate and abort Falkenhayn's drive by a counteroffensive of his own in Palestine, far closer to Britain's main lines of supply. The prime minister submitted the plan with such unshakable conviction that even Robertson, albeit grudgingly, had to accept the inevitable. The two men agreed, however, that an offensive in Palestine would require new leadership. Murray had been discredited by his second failure at Gaza, in April 1917. After some hesitation, Lloyd George offered the command to Jan Christian Smuts, the Boer military hero, and South Africa's representative in the War Cabinet. Here Robertson took his revenge on the prime minister. Hoping to restrict the scope of the campaign by limiting the prestige of its leadership, the chief of staff successfully talked Smuts out of accepting the offer. In the end, the command was given to General Sir Edmund Allenby, an officer of indeterminate reputation who had served on the Western front, and whose new assignment was at least partially the result of his abrasive relations with Haig, the chief of the British Expeditionary Force in France. The prime minister's instructions to Allenby were unambiguous: the Cabinet expected him to hand them "Jerusalem before Christmas."

Perhaps Robertson expected the new commander to quail under this responsibility. But once Allenby learned that he would be answerable to the War Cabinet alone for his actions, bypassing even the chief of staff, his enthusiasm for the task grew rapidly. Indeed, upon arriving in Egypt in June 1917 and studying the flat expanse of Sinai and southern Palestine, the new commander's self-assurance positively brimmed over. For Allenby's military background was in the cavalry, a branch in which he had distinguished himself during the South African War; while his long, all but immobilized, stint in the trenches with the Third Army in France made him a fanatic on the subject of speed and movement. Now, in the Middle East, he found ideal terrain for implementing his tactics. He communicated this assurance to all around him. A powerfully built, imposing man well over six feet tall, with a roaring temper that had earned him the nickname of "the bull," Allenby promptly set off on a whirlwind tour of the front to communicate his intentions to every senior officer of the line. "My word, he is a different man to Murray," Meinertzhagen noted in his diary. ". . . His manner is brusk, almost to rudeness, but I prefer it to the oil and butter of the society soldier. Allenby breathes success, and . . . [the] Egyptian Expeditionary Force is already awakening from its lethargic sleep under Murray. . . ." The Australian *Official History* confirms this reaction:

> Troops who caught only one fleeting glimpse of him felt that here at last was a man with the natural qualities of a great driving commander. . . . At last they had a commander who would live among them and lead them. Within a week of his arrival Allenby had stamped his personality on the mind of every trooper of the horse and every infantryman in the line.

In fact, the essential outlines of Allenby's offensive had been prepared for him by Brigadier General Guy Dawnay, one of the most brilliant, if subsequently underrated, strategists of the war. The plan recognized that the obvious line of advance into Palestine was through Gaza, hugging the seacoast, thus securing the full advantages of naval cooperation and adequate water supply. Unfortunately for the British, the Gaza defenses were far too solid to be breached except by slow and costly siege. The interior, on the other hand, ten miles northwest of Beersheba, was almost a natural gateway to the north. Turkish defenses were weaker in that region, and ample room existed for cavalry maneuver. Dawnay's idea was to attack there. Admittedly, the inland route presented its own formidable challenge. Vast and extensive transport improvements were required to enable a column to thrust out on the high ground between Beersheba and Hareira. And preliminary to everything was the capture of Beersheba itself, with its valuable wells for men and horses. Yet awesome as the challenge was, Dawnay and Allenby accepted it eagerly. Lloyd George had promised full support, and it was forthcoming—one division from Salonica and four other divisions consisting of Anzac and territorial battalions training in Egypt. Thirty thousand camels were assembled to carry initial supplies of water for the troops attacking Beersheba. Thousands of Egyptians were set to work laying roads behind the front line. Suez became an enormous base of workshops and supply depots, of ships coming and going. Allenby personally supervised every detail of the immense operation. It served in the nature of therapy. On July 29, word arrived from France of the death in action of his only son, at the age of twenty.

Secrecy remained the vital element in the forthcoming offensive. During the summer, thousands of Allied troops were concentrated opposite Gaza. It was only at the last possible moment, in late October 1917, that most of them were quickly and stealthily shifted across toward Beersheba. Other ruses were devised to mislead the enemy. In one of the most effective military deceptions in modern history, the young Intelligence officer, Richard Meinertzhagen, drafted a mock agenda for a staff conference. It described a major attack on Gaza to be preceded by a "feint" against Beersheba. Riding into no man's land on October 10, Meinertzhagen drew the fire of a Turkish cavalry patrol, then "dropped" a haversack (stained with horse's blood) containing the fake agenda. The documents were found by the Turks and believed.

By then, in any event, responding to the concentration of British forces in Palestine, Falkenhayn had abandoned his Yildirim drive against Baghdad. Yet the German's new defensive plans were hopelessly undermined by the almost unbelievable lassitude with which one of Yildirim's two component armies, the Seventh, was transferred from Aleppo back to Palestine. Not until September 28 did this military force actually receive its orders to proceed southward. For weeks afterward, Ottoman divisions newly arrived from Cilicia and Rumania were immobilized for lack of rolling stock and were compelled to loll around idly at Syrian rail sidings awaiting transportation. As a final irony, Falkenhayn himself did not reach his headquarters in Jerusalem until November 1, after the battle had already begun. Meanwhile, the battle-hardened Ottoman Eighth Army, stationed on the Gaza line, where the heaviest British offensive was expected, consisted of no more than 25,000 men on a thirty-mile front, and the troops were short of ammunition and rations. "Thus even before a shot was fired," wrote Archibald Wavell, one of Allenby's staff officers, "the danger to Baghdad had vanished. And the opening of the British offensive caught the enemy commander-in-chief with his plans incomplete, his organization in the process of change and himself and his staff on the railway between Aleppo and Jerusalem."

Allenby's luck failed in only one respect. He had intended to divert Falkenhayn's Seventh Army before launching his major offensive. For this he counted on Lawrence and the Arabs to provide a distraction by capturing Deraa, the junction of the Jerusalem-Haifa-Damascus railroads—"the navel of the Turkish armies in Syria, the common point of all their fronts." But, as we recall (Chapter V), Lawrence's nerve failed at the last moment, and he declined to attack. His assault on the Yarmuk Valley bridge ended as a fiasco. Undeterred by this lapse on his right flank, Allenby moved his principal divisions stealthily eastward. Zero day was fixed for October 31. During the last forty-eight hours before the attack, all the vacated camps behind Gaza were left standing, and were well lighted at night. The ruse was marvelously effective. The bulk of the Ottoman Seventh and Eighth armies remained dug in expectantly along the Gaza line. The battle was decided before it began.

Breakthrough at Beersheba

BEERSHEBA WAS a large, rather drab Arab village, notable only for its reasonably abundant water supplies and the extensive lines of trenchworks surrounding it. The British, in their numerical superiority, were determined to overrun these trenches with instant, paralyzing power and to seize the wells before the Turks could destroy them. They accomplished both objectives. The attack, launched at dawn on October 31, achieved total surprise. In endless waves of savagely pounding hooves and flashing lances, the magnificent Anzac cavalry swept in through Beersheba's northern, least-defended side and invested the town and its wells by mid-morning. An entire Ottoman division, the Twenty-seventh, was rounded up by the invaders and marched off to the rear, stunned and disbelieving. In one of the most heroic exploits of the campaign, Colonel Newcombe and a camel corps of a mere seventy troops moved down to the Beersheba-Hebron road, deep in the enemy's rear, and galloped recklessly along the Turkish flank, blocking communications between Hebron and Beersheba and creating havoc behind the Ottoman lines. Steuber, the regimental chief surgeon, described the panic at Turkish headquarters in Hebron as the army staff members hurriedly packed and saddled, readying for flight before the expected arrival of the British main force. He recalled that a fey touch was given to the affair by an old Arab procuress, who in the midst of the pandemonium was calmly preparing to meet the enemy "with a band of scantily clad dancing girls wearing colored transparent veils."

Allenby's plan had encompassed not merely the capture of Beersheba, but also the encirclement and destruction of the entire Yildirim army. In this latter goal he was less successful, notwithstanding the disruption of Ottoman communications and the failure of the Turks to counterattack at Beersheba. The heat of the desert sirocco was murderous and Beersheba's water sources less ample than had been anticipated, while the defenses north of Beersheba proved unexpectedly strong. Eventually the British resigned themselves to a more deliberate advance up the coastal plain and the grinding, methodical conquest of Ramle and Ludd against tough enemy resistance. Despite the anticlimactic pace of the offensive, the Turkish armies were hopelessly disorganized, all the more so as their rear guards were harassed continually by the Royal Flying Corps. Falkenhayn eventually managed to extricate the bulk of his forces from the British trap, but only after two weeks of fighting and the loss of many thousands of soldiers.

Determined to exploit the enemy's confusion before the winter rains began, the English commander began an immediate advance against the Seventh Army in the hills around Jerusalem. It was an audacious decision, for Jerusalem historically was an all but impregnable fortress. Even Lloyd George and other members of the War Cabinet, for all their eagerness to take the Holy City "before Christmas," felt it necessary to caution Allenby against undue haste. The weather added its own warning. On the day on which British troops entered the Judean hills, the winter rains began and turned the main road into a quagmire. With supply lines disrupted, it soon became impossible to equip the advance columns with vehicular transportation or adequate winter clothing. Still, Allenby's forces pushed on. One division of mountain-wise Gurkhas actually battled halfway to Jerusalem, to the head of the Bab el Wad defile; on November 21 these remarkable troops stormed the height of Nebi Samwil, eight miles closer to the city. There, at last, Turkish resistance hardened. Allenby permitted his exhausted troops to rest.

During the ensuing two weeks, the British and Anzac forces reorganized their supply lines and brought up the equivalent of three fresh divisions. On December 8, in a pouring rainstorm, Allenby renewed the offensive. Although Turkish defenses around Jerusalem were quite impressive, the strength of the remnant Ottoman Seventh Army was by then reduced to a pitiful sixteen thousand men facing three times that many British. Turkish morale had been eroded by the succession of defeats and the likelihood of facing still more British reinforcements. The unnerved Falkenhayn hardly improved matters by closing down his headquarters in Jerusalem on November 14 and racing for Nablus; by this precipitous departure, he all but destroyed his influence. By then the Turkish rearguard had abandoned hope altogether and during the night of December 8 began to evacuate its positions. The next morning, the mayor of Jerusalem, a somewhat befuddled Arab in striped trousers and frock coat, walked out to surrender the keys of the city to a group of British mess cooks who wandered by.

Two days later, Allenby himself made his formal entry into Jerusalem, thereby becoming the first victorious Christian soldier to set foot in the city since the Crusades. In a moving ceremony at the foot of the Tower of David, the English general assured a gathering of local dignitaries that he had arrived as a liberator, not a conqueror, and that Jerusalem's Holy Places would be scrupulously protected, as would freedom of worship for all religions. The deliverance from Turkish oppression was received with overflowing gratitude by the distraught, half-starved Arab and Jewish populations. Sir Ronald Storrs, newly appointed as military governor of the city, recalled both the joy and the agony of liberation:

> For those were the days when the trace of a great fear was yet in men's eyes, and the gulf of relief still at their throats; when for friendship with the Allies, true or suspected, whole families of Christians had been exiled, at an hour's notice, into the interior of Asia Minor, a Moslem Kadi hanged at the Jaffa Gate, and a young Jewish girl tortured to suicide. . . . Throughout those early days in Jerusalem my chief, my nightmare anxiety, was the scarcity of food amounting almost to famine. One morning early in January I became aware of a crying and a screaming beneath my office window. I looked out on a crowd of veiled Arab women, some of whom tore their garments apart to reveal the bones almost piercing their skin. And the sight in the hospital of the children's limbs swollen with emptiness was not good; nor was the dread that we should have delivered Jerusalem only to starve her to death.

That was not to be the case. Allenby gave first priority to food supplies, which were imported directly from Egypt. The American Near East Relief soon followed with large shipments of clothing and medicines for the Christian and Moslem populations; the Zionist Organization matched these efforts for the Jewish inhabitants of the city. Elsewhere, news of the capture of Jerusalem was greeted with a rapture far transcending the city's strategic importance. It was no mere Ottoman fortress that had fallen, after all, but rather the Holy City itself, the cynosure of Christian religious hopes and dreams for a millennium and a half. Thus, in London the great bell of Westminster Cathedral rang for the first time in three years.

236

The bells of every church in Rome rang for an hour. In Paris a special Mass was conducted in Notre Dame Cathedral.

Conversely, the impact of Britain's victory at Jerusalem sent shock waves through the entire upper echelon of the Central Power command structure. Djemal "resigned" as governor of Syria. In a move long overdue, Falkenhayn was replaced by Liman von Sanders, who used his detailed knowledge of Turkish mentality and temperament to shift defensive efforts from mobility to a static, foot-by-foot resistance. Indeed, mobility would hardly have been possible when Ottoman supply animals each day were falling dead by the hundreds for lack of forage and the troops themselves were reduced to a state of near-starvation. This information was known to British Intelligence, and it convinced the War Cabinet that a single renewed offensive could administer the death blow to the Ottoman war effort. Allenby agreed, but insisted upon a delay of several months to reorganize his army and his communications and supply facilities. During the winter interval of 1917–18, meanwhile, the English commander made plans to occupy the Jordan Valley, thus securing his right flank, and depriving the Turks of the area's abundant grain supplies. He depended on the Arabs to carry out this limited operation. As we have seen (Chapter V), all the efforts of Lawrence and Feisal in that direction—the assault on Ma'an, on Tafila, the joint Arab-British drive on Amman—were failures. By then, Allenby was finally convinced that Feisal's troops were a guerrilla force, to be deployed simply for harassing the enemy. Even that function was not without its advantages, of course; the British general would know how to use the Arabs as irregulars in his impending offensive. But on March 21, even as Allenby entered the final stages of his preparations, the Germans suddenly launched their long-awaited drive in France. A week later, orders arrived from London to ship several divisions back to the Western front, and for the moment to adopt a defensive posture. Throughout the spring and summer of 1918, therefore, Allenby slowly filled the gaps in his manpower with

Indian brigades from the Persian Gulf command and painstakingly refined the strategy for his long-delayed offensive.

The Conquest of the Levant

ALLENBY'S BLUEPRINT for smashing the Turkish armies in northern Palestine was masterful in its simplicity and logic. It was the Gaza-Beersheba movement in reverse. He would begin with a feint toward Transjordan. The Turks probably would be expecting an attack there on the basis of the Beersheba operation. Immediately afterward, however, the General would thrust forward with the bulk of his armed strength straight through the Jaffa line, then on across the Carmel range into the Vale of Esdraelon and Galilee. With nearly 100,000 combat troops and 500 guns at his disposal, outnumbering the enemy four to one, Allenby expected this time to outflank successfully the entire Yildirim force. As always, speed, momentum, and secrecy were the key elements in his conception. He therefore ordered all moves to be carried out by night, and artfully camouflaged his vast concentration of troops in the olive wood and orange groves north of Jaffa. In fact, the British striking force in the coastal area was doubled without being spotted from the air. Simultaneously, fake camps were thrown up in the Jordan Valley, and the deserted horselanes there were filled with some 15,000 canvas horses. Small troop units were marched back and forth, raising great dust clouds. Agents east of the Jordan bargained for large quantities of forage around Amman, suggesting the imminence of an attack in that region. Actually, no more than 25,000 British troops ever were deployed inland, against the same number of Turks, while 45,000 men were packed into the coastal strip, against a mere 8,000 of the unsuspecting enemy.

On September 16, Feisal's Arabs began their guerrilla forays against the railroad to the south, cutting the line between Deraa and Amman, cutting it again a day later between Deraa and Damascus, and then between Deraa and Afula.

238

Liman reacted predictably, swiftly transferring a large quantity of his reserves from Haifa inland to Deraa. On September 18, in a blocking maneuver, Allenby sent his Australians into Nablus, thus sealing the eastern exits from the hill country around Nablus to the Jordan Valley (see map). He was ready now to drive the Turks into the pocket. On September 19 the sudden earth-shaking roar of 385 cannon announced the opening of the great offensive in the coastal plain. Even before the smoke of the bombardment had cleared, nine thousand Australian horsemen galloped through the shattered Ottoman lines. In ten minutes the van of the attackers was well behind the enemy rear and racing up the coast. By mid-morning two divisions had ridden through, heading eastward in two columns toward Caesarea on the coast and Jenin and Megiddo inland. The Turks were aghast at the speed and power of the onslaught. Isolated from its headquarters, its communications smashed, the Ottoman Eighth Army soon broke into hopeless confusion, its remnants streaming up the plain. By nightfall British infantry had reached and captured Tulkarem, closing the vise on the Turks.

Meanwhile, the hard-riding Anzacs fanned out through the Vale of Esdraelon, reaching Nazareth on the evening of the 20th and overrunning Turkish headquarters there. Because of the rupture of communications, Liman himself had remained unaware of the breakthrough. Now, dressed in pajamas, a flashlight in one hand and his personal papers in the other, the startled field marshal escaped by automobile to Tiberias in the nick of time. Within hours, Afula fell to the onrushing Anzac horsemen, then Beisan, then Jenin on the 21st. In thirty-four hours the Anzacs had covered eight-five miles, a feat that would have been remarkable even in the later era of mechanized warfare. Liman's efforts to rescue his forces were much too late. The Ottoman Seventh and Eighth armies were caught in the Allied pincers, their natural avenue of retreat through the Jordan Valley sealed off, most of their elite European troops already prisoners of General Chetwode's Australian XX Corps. The planes of the Royal Flying Corps bombed and strafed the survivors mercilessly as they crowded into the Wasi Fara gorge near Nablus.

> For four hours [wrote Lawrence, who watched in fascination from a distance] our aeroplanes replaced one another in series above the doomed columns: nine tons of small bombs or grenades and fifty thousand rounds of [small arms ammunition] were rained upon them. When the smoke cleared it was seen that the organization of the enemy had melted away. They were a dispersed horde of trembling individuals, hiding for their lives in every fold of the vast hills.

On the 22nd the British captured Haifa. By then, most of the Turkish force had been effectively destroyed, with seventy thousand men captured or killed. This time, too, sensing the irreversible tide of battle, the entire Arab rural population rose at last against its Ottoman masters and joined with the Hashemite forces in mercilessly harrying and killing the exhausted Turkish stragglers. "In a madness born of the horror of Tafas we killed and killed," wrote Lawrence, "even blowing in the heads of the fallen and of the animals. . . . Every field and valley had its Turks stumbling blindly northward. Our men were clinging on." Feisal's Arab column, riding through the Jordan Valley in tandem with Allenby's advancing army in Palestine, swiftly occupied a chain of abandoned towns, gutted the rail line, slaughtered and looted prisoners, all with such efficiency that Allenby proposed to leave to the Arabs alone the task of rounding up additional Turkish stragglers in the eastern Jordan Valley. But here Feisal protested, as did Lawrence. The Hashemite leaders intended to hang closely on the flank of Allenby's expeditionary force, for they would not be denied participation in the capture of Damascus, queen city of the Levant.

The British commander had already issued his orders for the advance on Damascus on September 25, the day news arrived of the capture of Tiberias. It represented yet another tough challenge for the hard-riding Anzac cavalry; the Syrian capital was still a good 140 miles away. So complete was the demoralization of the Ottoman forces, however, that the assign-

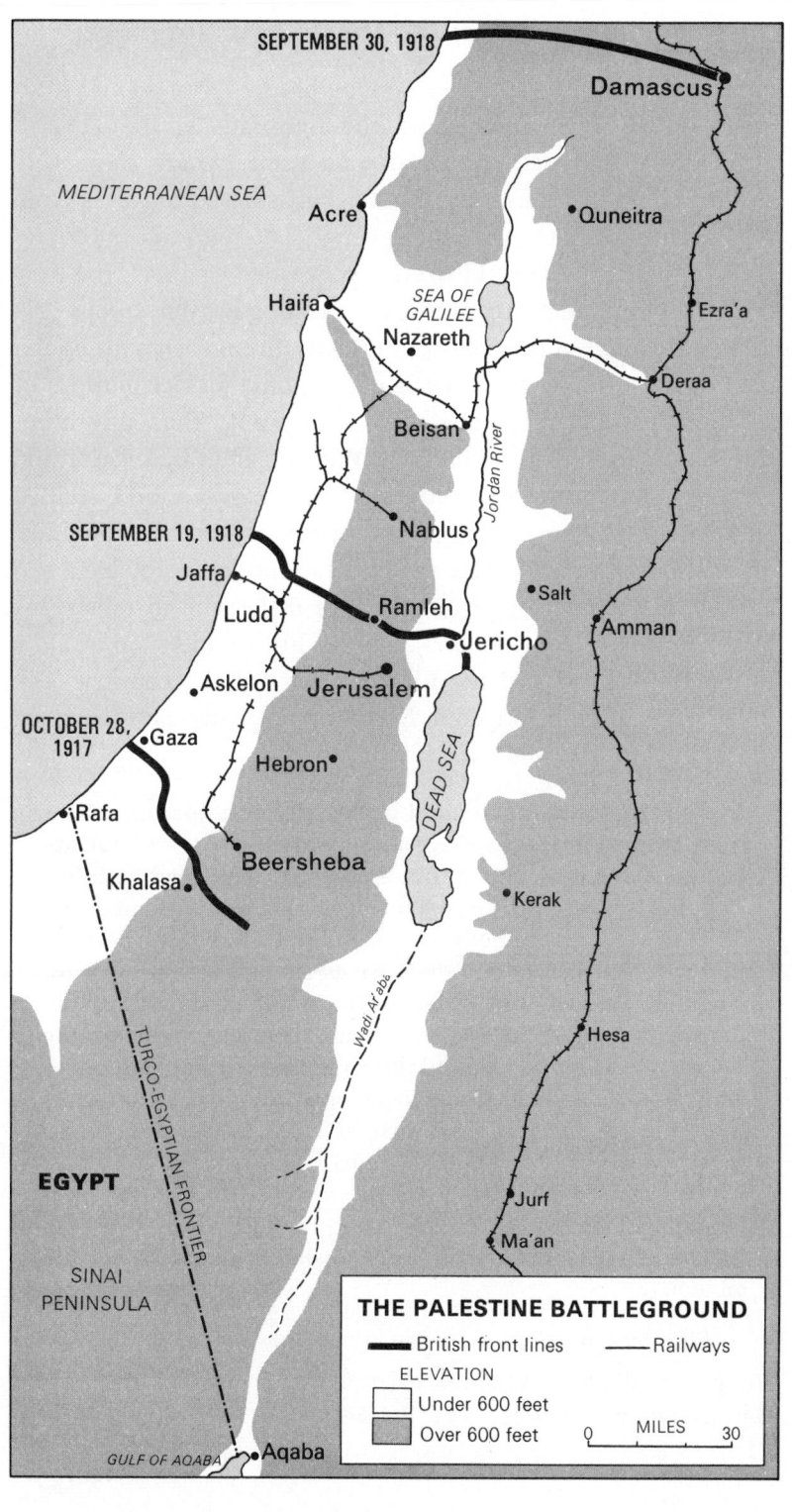

SEPTEMBER 30, 1918

Damascus

MEDITERRANEAN SEA

Acre

Quneitra

Haifa

SEA OF GALILEE

Ezra'a

Nazareth

Deraa

Beisan

Jordan River

Nablus

SEPTEMBER 19, 1918

Jaffa

Salt

Ludd

Ramleh

Jericho

Amman

Askelon

Jerusalem

OCTOBER 28, 1917

Gaza

Hebron

DEAD SEA

Rafa

Khalasa

Beersheba

Kerak

Wadi Ar'aba

Hesa

EGYPT

TURCO-EGYPTIAN FRONTIER

Jurf

Ma'an

SINAI PENINSULA

THE PALESTINE BATTLEGROUND

━━━ British front lines ——— Railways

ELEVATION

☐ Under 600 feet

▨ Over 600 feet

MILES

0   30

GULF OF AQABA

Aqaba

ment was fulfilled without a serious battle. After a final rear-guard stand on September 28, the remnants of the Turkish army broke and fled for Damascus itself, where they were swallowed up by thousands of other half-starved fugitives from the Palestine disaster. On September 30, Ottoman rule in the city ended. At that moment Lawrence persuaded Chauvel, the Australian commander, to allow the Arab guerrilla troops the first ceremonial entry. Passing quickly through Damascus the next day, therefore, the Anzacs caught only a brief glimpse of an incomparably more attractive community than any other they had seen in the Middle East. With its abundant water and greenery, its courts and fountains, the mosaics and stained glass of its mosques, Damascus seemed a veritable paradise of wealth and luxury after the endless succession of bleached and shabby Arab villages. There was little time to relish this prize, however, for Chauvel pushed his troopers on rapidly to the Homs road and the northern part of the country. The joy of occupation belonged to Feisal's men. Lawrence described the arrival of the main Arab column:

> Every man, woman and child in this city of a quarter-million souls seemed in the streets, waiting only the spark of our appearance to ignite their spirits. Damascus went mad with joy. The men tossed up their tarbushes to cheer, and women tore off their veils. House-holders threw flowers, hangings, carpets, into the road before us: their wives leaned, screaming with laughter, through the lattices and splashed us with bath-dippers of scent. Poor dervishes made themselves our running footmen in front and behind, howling and cutting themselves with frenzy; and over the local cries and the shrilling of women came the measured roar of men's voices and chanting, "Feisal, Nasir, Shukri, Urens (Lawrence)" in waves which began here, rolled along the squares, through the market, down along streets to East gate, round the wall, back up the Meian; and grew to a wall of shouts round us by the citadel.

Allenby's men were deprived of this vision of liberation as they galloped ahead to seize Aleppo, 200 miles beyond Damascus, on October 22. Between the two cities, French warships had already anchored off Beirut and disembarked companies of French marines. Indeed, at Lawrence's suggestion, a token force of Feisel's Arabs had actually occupied the Lebanese capital several days earlier, but were ordered withdrawn forthwith by Allenby on October 15 and 16. Elsewhere, however, Feisal's troops occupied Baalbek and Homs without opposition. By then the fighting was all but over. In five and a half weeks the Egyptian Expeditionary Force had advanced the front 340 miles in the most dramatically successful offensive of the war, and had captured 75,000 prisoners, against a loss of 5,000 casualties. But even this unprecedented final drive represented only the most spectacular phase of the war effort in the Levant. That effort had engaged no less than 1,192,000 Allied troops in the Sinai, Palestine, and Syrian campaigns during the entire four years of conflict, with a total of 58,000 battle casualties.

Conceivably, much of this human and material expenditure was wasted. Some military critics insisted that the identical result could have been achieved more economically by an earlier landing at the Gulf of Alexandretta or by a more determined naval effort to force the Straits. Thus, Wavell wrote later:

> The conduct of our war against Turkey shows how objectives originally clear and simple may become clouded, and even lost to sight, in the turbid atmosphere of war councils. Our only real interest in the direction of Palestine was the safety of the Suez Canal, and in Iraq the protection of the Persian oil fields. Yet in 1918 two great armies, based on Egypt and Basra respectively, almost the furthest points from the heart of Turkey that it would have been possible to select, were invading the Turkish Empire in uncoordinated fashion.

There were political overtones to these operations, however, which soldiers like Robertson or Wavell may not have grasped. In Europe the principal beneficiaries of victory over the Central Powers would be the former subject peoples of the Austrian and German empires. In Africa and Asia, on the other hand, the imperial possessions of the Central Powers were insignificant. The plain truth was that the Middle East was virtually the only battlefield available for major territorial aggrandizement by the Western Allies. The British War Cabinet was well aware of this fact as it shipped hundreds of thousands of troops to Mesopotamia and Palestine. Lloyd George, particularly, knew exactly where he wanted his armies to be when the shooting stopped. So did the French whose naval vessels floated at anchor in Beirut harbor well in advance of the British arrival. For both of the Western Allies, the Secret Treaties represented the merest opening point of departure. In the end, priority of imperial influence in the Middle East depended upon priority of military strength in the conquered territories themselves.

Open Road to Constantinople

ALLENBY'S CAMPAIGN was in many respects the most brilliantly executed Allied operation of the entire war. It decisively smashed Constantinople's grip on the Levant and all but fatally drained away Turkish manpower and morale. Ironically, it was not Allenby's breakthrough in Palestine that gave the Turks the *coup de grâce*. That was the achievement, rather, of General Franchet d'Esperey's offensive in Macedonia —against the Bulgarians. For more than three years an army of 200,000 Allied troops had remained entrenched in Salonica, the port of Macedonia, in a condition of military and diplomatic limbo. Ostensibly the army served as a barrier against Bulgarian and German penetration to the east Mediterranean coast. But in fact this huge agglomeration of soldiery simply vegetated in the encampments around the port until the Allied Supreme Command could make up its mind to provide the necessary support for an offensive through the Varder Valley. The decision to mount that offensive was not taken until the last year of the war (see Chapter XI). Typically, the issue was resolved by Lloyd George, for it represented yet another of the prime minister's cherished maneuvers to "knock the props" from under Germany's allies, in this case Bulgaria. By September 1918, the supreme command had poured enough reinforcements into the mixed Allied army at Salonica to raise its troop strength to 570,000 men. Under the leadership of the dashing, aggressive French commander, Franchet d'Esperey, this powerful force was unleashed on the morning of September 14 along the mountainous Serbo-Greek border east of the Crna River. The Bulgars by then could no longer depend upon German support, for Ludendorff had hurled all his reserves into the breach opened by the mighty Allied offensive in France. Within a fortnight, three of the five Bulgarian-dominated mountain ranges were in Allied hands, and on September 25 Bulgarian troops began deserting en masse. A week later, recognizing its inability to fight on without sizable infusions of German troops and matériel, the Sofia government decided to accept Allied terms. On October 3, King Ferdinand I abdicated in favor of his son.

The defection of Bulgaria was the beginning of the end for the Central Powers. It opened a direct route through southern Europe to the Habsburg Empire and cut the vital communications line between Turkey and Germany. German economic and military aid thenceforth was blocked from reaching Constantinople, and German political pressure could no longer be exerted on the Turkish regime. By then, hardly more than 100,000 Ottoman troops were capable of front-line service. The CUP regime had avoided recognizing the semimoribund state of its army as long as possible. Indeed, the disintegration of the Russian military effort in the Transcaucasus and the near-fulfillment there of the Pan-Turanian dream partially disguised the true state of affairs during the early summer of 1918. By July the failure of Ludendorff's spring offensive in France began to have its ramifications in Constantinople. The Young Turk leaders saw the handwriting on the wall even before the Allied victories in Palestine and Bulgaria. On October 7, as a result, the CUP Cabinet resigned, and a new government was formed under the leadership of a respected nonpolitical figure, Marshal Izzet Pasha. Within two weeks the Committee of Union Progress was dissolved altogether.

Actually, Constantinople had begun to send out peace overtures as early as October 5. The response from London was immediate. Vice-Admiral Sir S. A. Gough-Calthorpe, British naval commander in the Mediterranean, was dispatched to Mudros, on the island of Lemnos, to meet with the Turkish plenipotentiaries. It was hardly surprising that London should have assumed this authority by itself without bothering to consult the other Allies, for the British considered the Middle East entirely their own sphere. No less than 2,551,000 of their men had passed through the various Ottoman fronts, and 262,000 had been killed or wounded there. The French, by contrast, had suffered only 30,000 casualties in the Middle East, nearly all at Gallipoli. Now, too, the British deployed 900,000 men on the spot: in Egypt, Mesopotamia, Palestine, and Syria, in the Mediterranean and Indian Ocean fleets. At first, the French had angrily attempted to send an admiral of their own to take part in the talks at Mudros. Calthorpe categorically refused to deal with him. Three days later, Clemenceau submitted an agitated protest to the Supreme Council. The French had no choice, however, no more indeed than the Turks, but to allow direct Anglo-Turkish negotiations. It was in simple recognition of this British predominance that the Izzet Pasha government conceived the interesting idea of using an Englishman as their intermediary. He was Major General Charles Townshend, who had been a privileged "guest" of the Turks since his surrender at Kut (see Chapter III), and who was known to be well disposed toward his captors. The Porte's confidence in Townshend was not misplaced. The general cooperated fully in the effort to secure lenient peace terms for the Ottoman realm. The proposal he brought with him to Mudros would have assured the independence of Turkey and the "autonomy" of the rest of the empire under Turkish sovereignty. "Let England do things quietly and trust Turkey as a gentleman," was the ingratiating suggestion of a prominent

Turkish official, quoted with approval by Townshend later. "That is what Turkey will appreciate." But the strategy failed. The offer was flatly and contemptuously rejected.

Instead, the British presented their own terms on October 26, in a meeting with the Turkish envoys on the battleship *Agamemnon* in Mudros harbor. After four days of intensive and frequently acrimonious discussions, in which the British refused to relinquish a single one of their demands, the armistice was eventually signed on October 30. Calthorpe affixed his signature "in the name of the Allies." The provisions of the agreement were straightforward and uncompromising. The Straits were to be opened immediately to the Allies, who would occupy the forts along the waterway. The Allies were to have the right to occupy any vantage point in Ottoman territory, including all six Armenian vilayets, necessary to ensure their strategic advantage. The Ottoman army was to be demobilized immediately except for a small caretaker force sufficient to maintain internal order. Other terms required the evacuation of Cilicia; the surrender of all war vessels (including the *Goeben*) in Ottoman waters; the evacuation from Ottoman soil of all German and Austrian personnel; and the suspension of Ottoman relations with the Central Powers. The armistice went into effect the next day. During the ensuing two weeks, units of the Army of the Tigris moved from their strongholds in the Baghdad vilayet to occupy Mosul, while regiments of the Egyptian Expeditionary Force disembarked on the islands of the Turkish straits. On November 13—four and a quarter years after the *Goeben* and the *Breslau* had steamed into the Bosporus and trained their guns on Constantinople—a majestic procession of British, French, and Italian warships, led by Calthorpe on the *Agamemnon*, sailed the identical route, dropping anchor in the Golden Horn.

It had been an expensive war for all the participants. Their combined losses in manpower and wealth reached 1,400,-000 casualties and the equivalent of nearly three billion dollars. The cost was bitterest for the Turks, whose casualties in dead and wounded exceeded 1,400,000. The number of seriously ill, or those who simply "disappeared," swelled this figure to an incredible 2,290,000. Of the able-bodied men who saw active service at the front, not more than twenty per cent returned to their villages. The number of fatherless children left behind reached 400,000, and only a small fraction of these could be taken in by orphanages. There was apparently no end to the ramifications of the tragedy. Hardly any social welfare payments existed for the bereaved mothers, many of whom perished of destitution. Dr. Riza Nour Bey, an economist who later analyzed the statistics compiled by the postwar Turkish government, asserted that Anatolia had lost no less than a fifth of its inhabitants as a conseqence of the war, reducing the base population from 12,000,000 to approximately 9,500,000. The figure was exclusive of the Armenian deportations. This was perhaps the most fateful irony of the Middle East War: that even after the virtual annihilation of the Ottoman Armenian minority, and the depredations similarly inflicted on Greeks, Jews, and Arabs, no millet people in the empire should have suffered quite the demographic losses endured by the ruling Turkish nation itself.

There were other yardsticks for measuring the consequences of defeat. The terms of the Mudros Armistice (later confirmed by the peace treaties) pared away from the empire 770,000 miles of territory and 10,000,000 inhabitants, or about fifty per cent of its prewar terrain and population. The nation was ruined financially. By 1918, its public debt of 1914 had quadrupled—officially—to 454,163,925 Turkish pounds, if indeed the obligation could be measured at all in the light of requisitions, war damage, the general despoliation and misery of the land, the raging inflation. The Taurus tunnels, the supreme engineering achievement of the Baghdad Railway project, had only just been completed in September 1918. They were destroyed in the last days of the way to cover the Turkish retreat from Syria, together with German war matériel worth perhaps fifty million Turkish pounds. In fact, nearly all German industrial construction in the Ottoman Empire was either sacrificed or left in ruins. So, too, were the CUP's ambitious

Pan-Islamic and Pan-Turanian programs for territorial aggrandizement. The mighty Osmanli, in ages past the very incarnation of militant Islam on the march, whose armies once had terrorized Vienna, Budapest, Cairo, Baghdad, and Isfahan, now returned home at last to a ravaged Anatolian village, its emaciated widows trembling in neglected, leaking huts, its dogs and children scavenging in refuse bins or rooting in weed-strewn fields.

Turkey's patrons and wartime allies were no longer present to contemplate this scene of desolation. By November 4, in compliance with the Mudros Armistice arrangements, most of the German troops in Turkey had been shipped to Odessa via the Black Sea, and from there sent on by train through the Ukraine to the Polish-German frontier. At the railroad siding at Adana, Liman von Sanders bade good-bye to the Turkish officers on his staff. He thanked them for their services, praised them for their courage. "I trust that God may grant to the Osmanic people and its allies for the future, peace, tranquillity, and recovery from the wounds inflicted by the long war." Then he entrained for Constantinople. On January 29, 1919, Liman traveled on by British ship from Malta to Venice, and subsequently by rail to Verona and Innsbruck. The *Drang nach Osten* had flowed back to its source.

In a personal epilogue to the national tragedy, there were Turks, too, who found it necessary to beat a hasty departure. On orders of the new Ottoman government, the former strong men, Enver, Djemal, and Talaat, were hustled out of the Golden Horn on German torpedo boats hours before Allied marines landed at Constantinople. Had they not moved quickly, it was certain that they would have been among the 150 political leaders immediately arrested by the Allied command. They found refuge, instead, on German territory. Thus, Djemal survived for about a year as a penurious fugitive in Berlin. In 1920 he departed for Afghanistan, where he served as a military adviser. Two years later, under political pressure from the Kemalist government in Turkey, the Afghans declared Djemal *persona non grata*. He returned to Europe, and finally wangled a job as adviser on Transcaucasian affairs to the Soviet administration in Georgia. Late in 1922 he was shot and killed by an unknown assassin in the Georgian capital of Tiflis.

Enver's fate was not much happier. Like Djemal and Talaat, the former War Minister was condemned to death *in absentia* by the Turkish government in 1919. He, too, maintained a precarious refugee existence in postwar Berlin, then journeyed to Russia to try his luck with the Bolshevists. Always the opportunist, Enver played both sides during the Russian civil wars, serving first as an officer in General Denikin's White Army, and then, after the dissolution of this force, as director of the Asiatic department of the Soviet regime in Azerbaijan. At this point, he faded from view. Once he turned up briefly at a conference in Baku as ostensible leader of the Russian Asian Communist movement. At other times, glimpses were caught of him at party meetings in various parts of Transcaucasia. In the end, however, it was rumored that he turned against the Bolshevists, and ultimately met his death leading a cavalry charge against Soviet forces in the mountains of Russian Turkestan in 1922. He was then in his early forties.

Talaat was the only member of the original triumvirate who remained in western Europe and did not slip into total obscurity. In February 1921, Sir Basil Thomson, chief of Scotland Yard, and the noted writer Aubrey Herbert traveled to Berlin to interview a celebrated fugitive. The refugee was Talaat. "He had grown much thinner, and his good looks were sinister," Herbert wrote. "His black hair was turning grey; his eyes were very bright, glittering while he talked like the eyes of a wild animal in the dusk. The urbanity of his manner remained the same." So, apparently, did his unquenchable Turkish patriotism. Herbert reported that, for all the harsh treatment meted out to Talaat by the nationalist Turkish government in Ankara (Kemal, like Izzet Pasha, upheld the death sentence against the CUP leaders), the former minister exulted in the resurgence of Turkish independence. Indeed, he begged Herbert to interpret the authentic meaning of the Turkish revival to England and the West.

The Death of the Sick Man

It was the last interview Talaat would ever grant. A few days later, he was accosted in a public boulevard by a prosperously dressed young man. The stranger was one Solomon Teilirian, an Armenian who, as a child, had seen his father stripped and murdered by the Turks, his mother and sister set on the road for the Mesopotamian desert, only to be raped and butchered by their guards. Someone had found the youngster lying nearly unconscious, and later had him sent on to Russian Armenia, where he survived as a ward of the Near East Relief (see Chapter XI). In his adolescence, Teilirian had somehow made his way through Russia to Berlin. There, he said later, he had experienced a vision. His mother was standing over him saying: "You know Talaat is here. But you seem quite heartless and are not my son." Driven by this vision, the young man sought Talaat out. Finding him at last, he pulled a revolver from his briefcase and emptied it into the Turk's body. At the murder trial on June 2 and 3, 1921, Teilirian's attorney based his case on Talaat's responsibility for the Armenian genocide. Whereupon an endless succession of former German consuls and missionaries took the witness stand to offer eyewitness information on the 1915–16 horrors. Dr. Johannes Lepsius was one of those who provided eloquent and moving testimony for the defense; Liman von Sanders was another. Among the documents presented in evidence were signed instructions from Talaat to Ottoman officials in eastern Anatolia, in plain and unequivocal language ordering the mass deportation of the Armenian people. German newspapers for the first time printed full and detailed accounts of the behavior of the nation's wartime ally. The members of the Berlin jury required less than two hours to determine their verdict: they acquitted Teilirian. It seemed no less appropriate a judgment on the Sick Man.

CHAPTER IX

THE PARTITION OF THE LEVANT

Britain at the Apogee of Power

RARELY HAD THE FRUITS of military victory been as palpable as those savored by Britain when the fighting stopped. By December 1918 her imperial legions had planted the Union Jack in Palestine, Syria, southern Turkey, Mesopotamia, and lower Persia, a vast swath of territory encompassing all the historic land routes between the Mediterranean and the Indian Ocean. It was an imperialist dream fulfilled, a solution of the historic Eastern Question by force of British arms. Nor was there any significant pretense of indirection or obliqueness in the exercise of that power. By the terms of the Sykes-Picot Agreement, for example, direct British control in Mesopotamia was not to be extended to the interior, where the Arabs were to enjoy virtual independence. By the summer of 1918, however, the Government of India was treating occupied Mesopotamia as a single unit under a single administration directed by a British civil commissioner, staffed with British and Indian personnel, and financed by Indian currency in place of Ottoman currency. "The world at large," Sir Arnold Wilson, the acting civil commissioner, rather complacently explained, "recognized that it is our duty and our high privilege to establish an effective protectorate and to introduce a form of Government which shall make possible the development of this country. . . . " And that settled the matter. For the next year and a half all official British discussions relating to Mesopotamia envisaged the country as essentially another Egypt.

In Syria, it was only by sufferance of General Allenby that

the French established a civil administration in the coastal littoral (occupied Enemy Territory North), and that the Hashemite Arabs managed their own political affairs in the interior (Occupied Enemy Territory East). The British restricted the area of their own major occupation to Palestine (Occupied Enemy Territory South). With several exceptions—a corner of northeast Palestine held by the British, a strip of the "Blue" Zone assigned to the Arabs—the arrangement seemed a rough approximation of the provisions of the Sykes-Picot Agreement. There was one important difference, however. Each of the OET zones was under the ultimate authority of the British army. Allenby's officers were his vice-regents in every major city in the Levant, even Beirut in the Lebanon. For this was the central reality in the Middle East at war's end: 200,000 British troops, visibly and impressively ensconced at every major strategic site in the Arab world. And, by contrast, a poorly equipped, ragtag French army of 6,000 men (half of them Armenian refugee conscripts), hopefully representing the French "presence" in the eastern Mediterranean. The gesture impressed neither the Arabs nor the British military authorities.

Nor did it impress Lloyd George in London. For him, Britain's incomparable bargaining position in the Middle East dictated an immediate revision of the Sykes-Picot Agreement. "When Clemenceau came to London after the War [in December 1918]," Lloyd George wrote later, "I drove with him to the French Embassy through cheering crowds. After we reached the Embassy he asked me what it was I specially wanted from the French. I instantly replied that I wanted Mosul attached to Irak, and Palestine from Dan to Beersheba under British control. Without any hesitation he agreed." Indeed, the French premier had little choice. Defending these concessions before the Chamber of Deputies the following summer, André Tardieu astutely reminded his colleagues: "It was a question . . . of coming to an agreement with England on certain points. We had to obtain from her what she opposed at any price: the occupation of the left bank of the Rhine. We had to obtain coal from the Saar and many other things besides. These are the conditions under which M. Clemenceau went to London." Anyway, there were other Middle Eastern compensations for Paris. These included Cilicia, potentially a richer and more fertile region than Palestine, and its harbor, Alexandretta, an ideal terminus for an oil pipeline from Mosul. The supply of oil was similarly assured. Lloyd George agreed to hand over to France twenty-five per cent of the shares of the Turkish Petroleum Company, the portion that formerly had belonged to Germany. In later months Clemenceau would similarly allude to a third concession, namely tacit British approval for administration by France of the whole of Syria. The implication, as we shall note, was categorically rejected.

For their part, Feisal and his Arab supporters were convinced that Britain's opportunity in the Middle East was no less their own. The very presence of their guerrilla army in Damascus was a British gift—proof, as the Hashemites saw it, that the might of the British Empire supported their cause. Elie Kedourie has written astutely: "The abandonment of Damascus to the Sherifians, and the version of the Arab Revolt spread by [Lawrence's] *Seven Pillars of Wisdom*, are perhaps the two most important influences on Middle Eastern events in the years after 1918." Feisal's assurance of British support was in fact solidly reinforced by a joint Anglo-French declaration on November 4, 1918, stating that "France and Great Britain are at one in encouraging and assisting the establishment of indigenous Governments and administrations in Syria and Mesopotamia . . . and recognizing these as soon as they are actually established." The British seemingly had made the promise in good faith, for in ensuing months Allenby voiced no objection to the establishment of an "Arab Military Government" in Damascus. Nor did British officers protest when, in the course of a flying visit to the Lebanon on November 17, Feisal enjoined his followers to resist strenuously any "outside" rule. The French retaliated to this provocation with cold finesse. Later that month, when Feisal stopped off unexpectedly in France en route to England, the Quai d'Orsay instructed its officials to "treat the Emir Feisal as a person of distinction," but not to "accord him any diplomatic recognition." Lawrence, who accompanied Feisal, was all but invited to leave the country. The message was not lost on the emir. By the time he departed for London he had been made keenly aware of the hostility of the French government and of the likelihood that Arab independence could be realized only with the active and apparently exclusive support of London. The events of the Peace Conference bore out this conviction.

Surely no issue was more bedeviling to the statesmen assembled at Paris than the formulation of a new territorial order for the Middle East. Russia, originally slated to occupy eastern Anatolia, was now *hors de combat*, and President Wilson was ambiguous about filling the vacuum by assuming a mandate for the Armenian vilayets. The Italians and Greeks presented conflicting claims to western Asia Minor (see Chapter X). Thus obstructed and delayed, the final peace treaty with the Turks would not be signed until every other moribund empire had long since been disposed of. At first, nevertheless, it appeared that the future at least of the Arab territory could speedily be determined. Whatever uncertainty shrouded the fate of Turkey proper, the diplomats at Paris were unanimously agreed that the non-Turkish portions of the Ottoman Empire should be permanently sheared away from Turkish control. Allied commitments on this point included: a public assurance by Lloyd George on January 5, 1918; Point Twelve of Wilson's celebrated Fourteen Points, issued three days later; specific assurances to the Arabs (the Hussein-McMahon correspondence, the Anglo-French declaration of November 1918); and to the Jews (the Balfour Declaration); and finally, on January 30, 1919, a formal Peace Conference Resolution stating that "Armenia, Syria, Mesopotamia and Kurdistan, Palestine and Arabia must be completely severed from the Turkish Empire." Even the problem of reconciling the promises of Arab independence with the Secret Treaties was disposed of without serious difficulty. On December 16, 1918, Jan Christian Smuts, the South African representative, devised an ingenious juridical formula by which "people and territories formerly belonging to Russia, Austria and Turkey [would be] placed under the mandate of the League of Nations." Although this mandate formula precluded direct territorial annexation by the Powers, it allowed for a period of Allied "tutelage" under the supervision of the League Council itself. The compromise was a happy one. It appealed particularly to Wilson, and was formally adopted by the Peace Conference on April 28, 1919, as Article Twenty-two of the League of Nations Covenant.

The problem of non-Turkish territories, therefore, did not center on the principle of self-determination. The Western Allies had accepted that principle in the mandatory scheme, and indeed were quite willing to repeat it in the most amiable and general terms to Feisal and his entourage. It was rather the application of the principle that created serious difficulties. Feisal was a maximalist. Appearing formally before the Council of Ten on February 6, 1919, a slim, exotic figure in his white gold-filigreed robes, the young emir made it plain that he was insisting upon the complete and undivided freedom of the entire Arab rectangle. Nor did Feisal err on the side of understatement. The Arab world was a single unit, he declared, a uniquely civilized people, endowed with a common language and natural frontiers. As a faithful ally during the war, having contributed no less than "100,000 men" to the common war effort, the Arab nation now unequivocally demanded that its sacrifices be recognized and sanctified by full independence, nothing less. Under questioning by the delegates, Feisal agreed that Palestine fell outside the area of Arab claims, and could be left for the "mutual consideration of the interested parties." But at the same time he insisted that "[the] Arabs asked for freedom only and will take nothing less. . . . The Arabs are an ancient people, civilized and organized at a time when the nations represented in this room were unformed."

When Feisal ended his testimony, Clemenceau countered by presenting to the Council a Lebanese Christian delegation that emphatically rejected any plan to impose a "nomadic" Hashemite dynasty on the "advanced" races of Syria. Wilson suspected that the delegation was merely a puppet of French imperial ambitions, but it was more than that. Its appearance at the Conference represented a basic fact of life in the Middle East. Far from comprising a single monolithic entity, the Arab world was a vast congeries of peoples and cultures. The country of Syria alone, two thirds the size of England, seven times larger than Switzerland, allowed ample scope for regional differences. Its peoples were variously Mediterranean, Amorite, Hittite, Turkish, Arab, and Jewish. Two thirds of the population were Sunni Moslems; but the Shiite population of 200,000 was hardly an insignificant minority. Neither were 100,000 Druses or 40,000 Jews. Neither, surely, were some 300,000 Maronite Christians, 100,000 Greek Orthodox, 50,000 Greek Catholics, and 60,000 Armenians. Most of these latter groups were impacted in the coastal littoral along the Lebanese mountain range, and by and large were considerably more advanced, culturally and economically, than their Moslem neighbors. Since 1860, these half-million Christians had enjoyed an autonomous status in Mount Lebanon. They were altogether terrified now by the prospect of being returned to Moslem rule. Nor were the statesmen at Paris eager to return them against their will. Even the American delegation, not privy to the Sykes-Picot arrangement which had assured the establishment of French authority over Lebanon, recognized that Feisal's claims to all of Syria would require ample qualification.

The Anglo-French Impasse

IN FACT, BOTH the Sykes-Picot Agreement and the Hussein-McMahon correspondence had alluded to a special regime for the Christian minorities in the Levant (the intimation of their advanced status was barely disguised) under direct French supervision. The problem arose when it became evident that Paris would not be satisfied with a mere advisory function in the Syrian interior. Rather, the French government was quite plainly intent upon extending its authority from the littoral to the entire country. In the eyes of the Quai d'Orsay, the alternative to French influence in Syria was not simply Arab independence; it was British influence, and this was intolerable. After all, the right of naked occupation surely worked two ways. "If the British were dealing with Mesopotamia as they saw fit," explained Robert de Caix, a French foreign-ministry official, "why should the French not claim the same right in Syria?" Following a less than amicable conversation with French Middle East officials on March 8, 1919, Lord Milner, Britain's Colonial Secretary, warned Lloyd George that the French position was becoming increasingly rigid.

London's misgivings were confirmed at the private conference of the Big Four that convened at Lloyd George's flat on the Rue Nitot in Paris on the afternoon of March 20. While Clemenceau remained silent, glowering out the window, his foreign minister, Pichon, launched into an extended disquisition on France's historic connections with Syria and the political and economic logic of a unitary French mandate in that country. Lloyd George's response to this opening bid was equable at first. He reminded Pichon of the limitations imposed on French occupation not only by the Sykes-Picot Agreement, but also by promises made to the Arabs. Thereupon Pichon somewhat waspishly remarked that it was not France which had contracted the agreement with the Arabs; on the contrary, Paris had known nothing of the Hussein-McMahon agreement until much later. Lloyd George's own temper rose at this "legalism." The agreement with Hussein may have been contracted by England alone, he shot back, but there would have been no Syrian Question at all had it not been for Britain and her Arab allies; nearly a million British and colonial troops had entered the battlefield against Turkey, and Arab help had been essential in that campaign. Allenby, sitting beside the prime minister, dutifully added that the Arab Revolt had indeed been "invaluable."

The issue was joined on moral, legal, and military grounds. It was destined to be kept alive throughout the spring and early summer of 1919. For his part, Clemenceau was determined not to yield his demand for control of the Syrian interior. On one occasion he actually threatened to resign if his claims were not met. At a meeting of the Council of Four on May 21, for example, the premier bitterly complained that Lloyd George had not kept his promise to evacuate British troops from Syria and let them be replaced with French units. The following day, Lloyd George, no less unyielding, repeated his earlier arguments: the legal one, based on the Sykes-Picot and Hussein-McMahon agreements; the military one, based upon the "125,000 white casualties" sustained by the empire in carrying the burden of the Turkish campaign, as against France's "negligible" contribution. Here Clemenceau hotly interjected that he had ceded Mosul and Palestine to Britain on the assumption of a *quid pro quo* in Damascus and Aleppo. It was evident by then that both men had strayed far from their earlier, official stance on the Sykes-Picot Agreement.

The somewhat neurotic intensity of French demands for Syria reflected a constellation of institutional pressures on the government in Paris. One was the formidable influence of those vested Catholic interests that were determined to ensure the historic French "presence" in the Middle East. Another was the brusque, centralized authoritarianism with which the French had traditionally governed their Moslem protectorates in North Africa, and which they were determined to apply in equal measure to the Moslem Levant. Perhaps most important of all, the pressure reflected the French nation's wartime discovery that the colonies, however expensive, were of crucial, even life-and-death, value to the mother country. The empire had supplied France with 1,918,000 troops, 680,000 of whom had actually fought on Europe's battlefields. Most of these soldiers had passed through metropolitan France at some time during the war, and the extent of their numbers, the sheer variety of their races, had made a profound impact on the local population. An observer, Stephen Roberts, wrote:

> Arabs and Berbers and Tunisians, Negroes and Moors and Somalis, Hovas and Sakalavas and Betsileos, Annamites and Pacific-Islanders and Creoles of the Old Colonies were all

there, and the Empire at one stroke had been vitalized. The dimly realized abstractions had become realities of flesh and blood, and a France, overwrought with war emotions, was thrilled with the interest of it all. It is difficult to reconstruct this emotional intensity, or to feel how France gasped and quivered at this sight of her new-felt colonies.

In the light both of this discovery and of the unprecedented hemorrhage of French manpower on the Western front, it was perhaps logical that the most crucial issue to the French government, in its interpretation of the mandatory articles of the League Covenant, was the right to conscript native troops for defense of the home country.

France had acquired more from the colonies than soldiers, however. The empire had also supplied nearly a billion francs in money and two and a half million tons of products, including grains, oils, and other vital foodstuffs. Syria was not deficient in these resources, as centuries of trade and decades of French investment had proved (see Chapter VI). Much of the country was arid, to be sure. But it did not lack for palm, cedar, olive, and mulberry trees, or for banana and citrus fruits. Through the years, French industrialists had cultivated Syria's vineyards, its wheat, barley, cotton, hemp, and silk. Manifestly, it was a country worth having. All the more so as the English, with a kind of Palmerstonian arrogance, were even then occupying territory in Palestine and Mosul which had not even been promised them in the Secret Treaties. It was unthinkable that British imperialism, behind the façade of promises to the Hashemites, should attempt to cheat France of this prize.

Even as British statesmen contested French demands for Syria, it was unquestionably true that they were animated by a less than romantic view of their Arab protégés. Evaluating the Arab Revolt, for example, Lloyd George admitted that

no help came from Syria. The Turks, having been made aware of the conspiracy in that province, had taken stern measures to suppress it. The Arabs of Palestine, who might have been helpful in many ways, were quiescent and cowering. Right through the War and up to the end there were masses of Arab soldiers from Mesopotamia, Syria and Palestine in the Turkish armies fighting against the liberation of their own race. . . . The Arabs . . . of Lower Mesopotamia [were indifferent] to the general cause of Arab freedom [and this] was symptomatic of the lack of national cohesion in the race.

By 1919, too, the Arab Bureau, with its ex-Oxonians Lawrence and Hogarth, had given way to Lloyd George's "garden suburb." This was an interdepartmental committee under the chairmanship of Lord Curzon, the acting foreign secretary. Both he and Lord Milner, Lloyd George's foreign affairs adviser, shared the prime minister's coldly rational view of the Arab military effort and Arab nationalism, and were not about to be set dancing in the streets by Britain's "moral" obligations to Feisal and his father. Rather, the aim of Curzon and Milner was quite simply to guard Britain's imperial interests in Egypt, Mesopotamia, and Persia. To that end, the Arabs and Jews were both seen as useful agents of British policy.

But it was equally certain that the French exaggerated British deviousness. Notwithstanding the anti-Gallicism of the Arab Bureau in Cairo, the government in London never seriously entertained the notion of repudiating its wartime commitments to France in the Middle East. Milner was speaking for the entire Cabinet when he insisted, in a memorandum to Lloyd George of March 8, 1919, that "I am totally opposed to the idea of trying to diddle the French out of Syria." Indeed, Milner fully endorsed the original provisions of the Sykes-Picot Agreement by which France would control the Syrian littoral, and Feisal and his Arab colleagues would govern the interior with the help of French money and guidance. In this vein, at a private conference on March 25 in the Paris apartment of Wickham Steed, editor of the London *Times*, even Lawrence voiced his agreement that "the movement for Arab unity possesses no serious political value for the present or, indeed, for the future," and that the best thing would be for Feisel to attempt to work out matters with the French directly. Accordingly, on June 12, when Allenby suggested to London that

Britain support Arab national aspirations by assuming the Syrian mandate herself, Curzon wired back immediately to scotch the proposal. In a separate cable, Lloyd George sternly warned Allenby to refrain from encouraging Feisal's agitation against the French. A month later, nevertheless, Balfour learned that some British military men in the Middle East still refused to abandon hope of "diddling" the French out of Syria. "General Allenby's serious attention ought to be called to this," the foreign secretary noted in a memorandum to Curzon, "and steps taken to ensure that our policy of *désintéressement* in regard to Syria is as widely known as possible."

But if London entertained no serious intention of evicting the French from Syria, whether through direct means (by assuming a mandate), or indirectly (by significantly enlarging Arab sovereignty beyond the limits of the Sykes-Picot Agreement), the military administration in Cairo did maintain a consistently anti-French policy. Perhaps some of the difficulties were the inevitable result of French weakness in the Middle East. French troop strength in the Syrian littoral, as we have seen, numbered barely six thousand men, an altogether negligible sum when measured against the vast reservoir of British military power. It was not a simple matter for officers of the Egyptian Expeditionary Force to disguise their contempt for this French "presence." Allenby himself set the tone by openly encouraging Arab communal leaders in the French zone to bypass Georges-Picot, who had arrived in Beirut as France's chief political adviser, and to negotiate their problems directly with British military officials. There were other grievances: French officers were stationed in the rear echelons of Allied military parades; French banks were refused licenses in Beirut; the circulation of French currency was prohibited; instruction in the French language was not permitted even within the area of direct French occupation.

Occasionally Cairo's bureaucratic officiousness became particularly gratuitous and vindictive. As an example, from the moment of its arrival in the Middle East, France's skeletal task force of soldiers and priests had labored with selfless, even heroic, dedication to relieve the hunger of the local Arab population. Allenby, however, flatly refused to cooperate in this effort, and denied transportation facilities to the French beyond the limits of OET West, the technical boundaries of the Blue Zone. The port of Beirut was closed to French relief vessels. The British insisted even upon administering and tightly controlling the French-owned railroad system. An editorial in *Le Temps* of July 26, 1919, voiced the embittered reaction of the French government. "The brutal fact remains," it commented, "that, outside the Government, British agents are trying to apply in the Levant a policy that aims at the exclusion of France."

Galling as British obstructionism was, a middle-level policy of pinpricks and arrogance, it might have been endurable if Feisal's Arab supporters had not also continually and openly assailed the French position in the littoral. Paris was convinced that the British at least tacitly encouraged this campaign. From the first week of the armistice, the Hashemite press in Damascus furiously attacked French colonial policy, excoriating the French regime in Algeria and Tunisia, scoring alleged French immorality and licentiousness and the blatant proselytizing activities of French Catholic orders. In many cases the Arab press simply reissued, without so much as changing a syllable, anti-French propaganda that had been circulated by the Turks during the war. Directly outside the French zone of administration, too, Feisal's agents crudely intimidated Arab *mukhtars* suspected of being lukewarm to the Damascus regime. Nor did it escape French observers that the leaders of the propaganda campaign were frequently emigré Syrians who had lived in Egypt, and who had served there as British functionaries; that British agents in the interior were continually emphasizing France's historic role as the patron and protector of the local Christian communities, and thus, by implication, as the enemy of the Moslems. In 1919, Paris shared with London a monthly four million franc subsidy of Feisal's government, and insisted, therefore, on its right to examine the Hashemite accounts to determine how much of this sum was being spent on anti-French propaganda and on arms acquisition. Allenby vetoed the request.

Faced with these successive humiliations, the Quai d'Orsay found it difficult to maintain diplomatic restraint in its negotiations with the British foreign office. Occasionally, too, the French foreign ministry used semiofficial organs such as the *Bulletin de l'Asie française*, and such eminent public figures as Marshal Lyautey, former proconsul of Morocco, and André Bruneau, statesman and unofficial spokesman for the foreign ministry, to accuse London of "perfidious machiavellism," of hiding behind the "façade" of Arab nationalism to undermine French influence in Syria. The charges were too baldly stated, and revealed more of France's historic anxieties in the east Mediterranean than the actual intentions or directives of British government policy. But it was true beyond question that London not infrequently turned a blind eye to the provocations and indiscretions of its officials in the Levant. Thus, Curzon's pious explanation of August 8 to Sir Ronald Graham, British minister in Paris:

> The French Government could not pretend to have any cause of complaint against Field Marshal Allenby or against His Majesty's Government. Their whole position in Syria was dependent upon our support. . . . We had categorically, repeatedly, and publicly disclaimed any intention of accepting a mandate for Syria, and had, insofar as was possible, supported French claims. If the French position in Syria was bad they owed it to their extreme unpopularity and the want of confidence which they inspired.

Feisal in Search of Allies

IF CURZON WAS GLIBLY RATIONALIZING AWAY French "cause of complaint" against Allenby and his staff, he was entirely accurate in his appraisal of French "unpopularity." Feisal made plain the reason for Arab distrust in an exceptionally frank conversation with Clemenceau in May 1919: "You know that many Frenchmen nourish the hope that Syria will

be a new France," he told the premier, "and cherish colonization plans to that end. In Paris men of affairs have told me:
'We cannot admit Syrian independence, because of the possible repercussions this may have in Algeria and Tunisia.'
You see the gulf that divides us; for myself, I favorably
regard your help, but I shall never accept slavery." These
were brave words. Yet Feisal was not so politically naïve
that he failed to appreciate the importance of allies in the
struggle against French imperialism. The British had done
much for the Arabs, to be sure; but the British had commitments of their own to their wartime partner. Other friends
and connections were urgently needed. Feisal sought them
out. The Zionists seemed one likely choice (see Chapter
XII). The Americans were another.

The Americans, it is recalled, had brought their well-
advertised idealism to the Peace Conference. They were inhibited neither by secret treaties nor by private pressures.
Quite the contrary, Point Twelve of Wilson's Fourteen Points,
issued in January 1918, was the president's means of serving
notice that he would not be bound by the Sykes-Picot Agreement. "The Turkish portions of the Ottoman Empire should
be assured a secure sovereignty," it declared, "but the other
nationalities which are now under Turkish rule should be
assured an undoubted security of life, and an absolutely
unmolested opportunity of autonomous development. . . ."
Arriving in Paris, Wilson made it clear from the outset that
he expected to be taken literally. When, in February 1919,
the issue of the Middle East was first raised in an official
conference of the Big Four, the American president insisted
upon learning whether the inhabitants of Syria and Mesopotamia actually desired France and Britain as their manda-
tors. He suspected the answer, for his Intelligence section had
already warned him of Arab unrest in Syria. Now, before
the Council of Four, the testimony of Feisal, of Allenby and
other British military officials, and of American Protestant
missionaries with experience in the Middle East (which
included experience, among other matters, of competition

with the French Catholic orders) all appeared to confirm a genuine Syrian terror of French domination.

On March 20, therefore, at the celebrated meeting in Lloyd George's flat on the Rue Nitot, Wilson formally requested that the Supreme Council send an inter-Allied investigating commission to the Middle East to determine the explicit wishes of the Arab peoples. The idea, conceived by the American Intelligence section, was acutely embarrassing to both Clemenceau and Lloyd George. Whatever their differences, the two prime ministers were mortified at the very notion of basing their military occupation upon Arab "goodwill." Neither Allied leader could find any plausible way of rejecting the plan, however, and it was approved by the Supreme Council on March 25. It is related that when news of this decision reached Feisal, he drank champagne for the first time in his life, then went for a drive past the headquarters of the Allied delegations and threw cushions at the Crillon, the Majestic, and the Quai d'Orsay, explaining that, lacking bombs, this was his only method of expressing his feelings.

Wilson, meanwhile, appointed the commission's two American members. They were Henry C. King, president of Oberlin College, a former Protestant religious director of the American Expeditionary Force in Europe; and Charles Crane, a Chicago valve manufacturer and influential contributor to the Democratic Party, a man who in later years would become an ardent Arabophile and anti-Zionist. Their staff, borrowed from the Intelligence section, included Professor William Lybyer, an eminent orientalist; the Reverend George Montgomery, a Protestant missionary who had lived in the Middle East for years; and Captain William Yale, a veteran trouble shooter for the Standard Oil Company. Throughout April and May, the little group dutifully collected all relevant Middle East data, which it filed, studied, and discussed. Then, on May 20, almost at the last moment before departure, the Americans were officially informed that Clemenceau would not appoint delegates to the commission unless Syria was garrisoned by French instead of British troops. Lloyd George rejected the demand without qualification; he was not prepared to abandon Feisal altogether. Whereupon Clemenceau, again losing his temper, threatened that if the prime minister persisted in sending his commissioners, and did not withdraw his troops, "he would no longer associate with the British in this part of the world because the harm done to his country was too great." At this point Lloyd George decided to meet his rival half way: with the French withdrawing from the commission, the British decided that they had no recourse but to do the same. In the end, after some indecision, but prompted by an anguished appeal from Feisal, Wilson informed the Council that he was sending the American commissioners to the Middle East anyway. Crane departed for Constantinople on May 25, to be followed by the rest of the group four days later. The Americans remained in the Turkish capital only a few days, then left by steamer for Palestine, arriving in Jaffa on June 10, 1919.

The excitement the commission's arrival generated among the Arabs was all but indescribable. On June 7, Feisal convened a Syrian "Congress" specifically for the purpose of presenting a solid Arab front to the visiting Americans. It was hardly a representative body, having been selected by the old Ottoman electorate that had sent delegates to the Constantinople parliament of 1909. Only sixty-six of eighty-eight representatives were able to meet in Damascus, and most of those absent were from the French-dominated west and north zones. King, Crane, and their advisers were taking their own soundings well before then, however. During their six weeks in Palestine and Syria (Mesopotamia had been dropped from the itinerary), the commissioners visited 36 important towns and received 1,863 petitions, as well as individual delegations from some 1,500 villages. The Arab demands were overwhelmingly and often violently anti-French, although most of the petitions were carefully phrased in the language of Wilsonian idealism. The methods by which this consensus was obtained were not always as idealistic. As a direct result of Moslem intimidation, for example, very few Lebanese Christian representatives managed to see the commissioners at all. One who did, and who testified against the sherifians, the Emir Saïd of Aleppo, was immediately removed by British troops to Haifa and finally locked up in Cairo "for his own protection." The episode had a disastrous effect on pro-French elements in Syria, who afterward were fearful of opening their mouths. Lybyer admitted later

> that often much pressure was put upon individuals and groups; that sometimes delegations were prevented from reaching the Commission; and that the representative authority of many petitions was questionable. But the Commission believes that these anomalous elements in the petitions tend to cancel one another when the whole country is taken into account, and that, as in the composite photograph, certain great, common emphases are unmistakable.

Indeed, to King and Crane these common emphases were so unmistakable that the two commissioners began wiring back their impressions to the American delegation in Paris even before completing their journey through the rest of the Arab world. To illustrate: in a dispatch from Jaffa on June 12, they warned that Zionist aspirations could not be implemented "except through the support of a large army." They repeated this warning from Beirut on July 11, and then noted that Feisal

> has become unique outstanding figure capable of rendering greatest service for world peace. He is heart of Moslem world, with enormous prestige and popularity, confirmed believer in Anglo-Saxon race, and great lover of Christians. Could do more than any other to reconcile Christians and Islam and longs to do so. Even talks seriously of American College for women at Mecca.

The official report, completed on August 21, fully amplified these earlier observations. It recommended that the unity of Syria be preserved, although with autonomy for

Palestine (stripped of an "extreme" Zionist program) and Lebanon, and that it be placed under a single mandatory power. The commissioners did not regard France as an appropriate choice for this role in view of the intense opposition of the Moslem Arabs and of the allegedly "inferior" quality of French education (no Scripture reading, no ball games, a tendency to immorality). Instead, they suggested, the responsibility ought first to be offered to the United States, a nation whose "humanitarian" disinterest and philanthropic institutions in the Middle East were already world-renowned. Failing the United States, however, Britain was evisaged as the next most likely mandator. Several of the commission's advisers found it difficult to concur in this recommendation. Montgomery and Yale appended two lengthy memoranda to the report, questioning both the authenticity of Arab nationalism and Feisal's ability as a ruler. It was their recommendation that Palestine, incorporating the Jewish national home, be placed under a separate British mandate, that the Lebanon be placed under a French mandate, and Syria proper under a joint Anglo-French mandate.

It is doubtful that Wilson ever read this document. By the time it reached the White House, on September 27, the president was already heavily preoccupied with the League of Nations and was campaigning through the American West on its behalf. At that late date, too, the United States delegation at Paris was hardly less eager than the British and French to have done with an Ottoman settlement. The American government, in fact, had lost much of its brief influence in Middle Eastern affairs by its evident unwillingness to accept an Armenian mandate (see Chapter XI). When, therefore, Lloyd George and Clemenceau finally reached their own meeting of minds on the Syrian impasse, the United States delegation was not in a position to contest it. Grateful, rather, that the Middle East imbroglio was at least being resolved, the Americans decided against releasing the King-Crane report to the Peace Conference. The British and French accordingly proceeded to do what they had agreed to do in 1916:

i.e., partition the Arab world between them. Feisal's gamble on the Americans had failed.

The Anglo-French Settlement

IT WAS SIGNIFICANT that Allied agreement was achieved not by mutual concessions, but rather by calculated, if grudging, retreat on the part of Lloyd George. Burdened with mounting unrest in Ireland, Egypt, and Mesopotamia, the prime minister had decided that the expense of maintaining 200,000 troops in the Middle East was fast becoming intolerable. Curzon, too, was heartily weary of having Anglo-French relations continually envenomed by fancied obligations to the Hashemite dynasty. It was to him now that Lloyd George assigned the task of resolving the impasse in any way possible. "This morning at the end of our third Cabinet . . ." Curzon wrote to his wife, "the Cabinet led by the P.M. unanimously asked me to go out to Paris and take in hand the Eastern Question, and gave me authority for any settlement that I might like to effect." The main basis of settlement was actually prepared jointly by Curzon and Lloyd George. It was a simple and unequivocal acquiescence to the key French demand: the British would pull out in favor of the French, leaving the Syrian interior at the mercy of French troops. Balfour entirely concurred in this agreement, and had already devised his rationalization: "It will be difficult," he wrote from Paris on September 9, "to show reason why Feisal should have a larger measure of independence in Damascus and Eastern Syria than we are prepared to accord to him or other Arab rulers in Mesopotamia."

Clemenceau was of course delighted to accept a solution he had advocated from the beginning. On September 13, the two prime ministers met and agreed that the British army would evacuate the Syrian littoral west of the Sykes-Picot line. Its garrison camps would be taken over by French troops. This understanding represented more than the substitution of one army for another. It signified that the British no longer would stand between the French and the Hashemite regime in Damascus. Thenceforth, after November 1, 1919, the Arab government would function on borrowed time. There remained only the painful matter of breaking the news to Feisal, and this was done by cable the same day. The emir was shattered. In a feverish series of letters to Lloyd George, he alternately accused the British of treachery, entreated them for understanding, and warned them of bloodshed throughout the Arab world. But by then neither Lloyd George nor Curzon would be moved. When Feisal arrived in London in late September, Curzon bluntly informed him that the Arabs would now have to turn to Paris for funds and advisers. Would it not be better, the acting foreign secretary asked, for the emir to meet Clemenceau personally and work out the best possible terms man-to-man? And in the end, Feisal was obliged to accept this counsel. In late October he crossed the Channel to France. A conscience-stricken letter from Lloyd George to Clemenceau preceded him, entreating the premier to receive Feisal as the "heroic ally" and "prince of the blood" that he was.

Actually, this was not the first time that Feisal had attempted to strike a bargain with the French government. Throughout the spring of 1919 he had intermittently discussed the Syrian question with Robert de Caix, the French liaison officer in Damascus, and had even expressed interest in a limited French mandate, provided that Arab independence would be maintained and that the French would restrict themselves to a purely advisory role. Feisal had informed Clayton privately on May 12 that he "never had any intention of carrying out the arrangement." Certainly the French, for their part, would not have accepted Feisal's condition that they dismiss their administration in the littoral. By the end of May, these fitful overtures had been abandoned altogether. Now, however, in the autumn of 1919, Feisal was constrained to reopen negotiations on his own, this time with Clemenceau, in an effort to extract the most liberal possible interpretation of the French "presence" in the Lebanese coastal area. The emir's earlier deviousness weighed against him. From the outset of their meeting on October 22 the old premier was courteously evasive on French intentions in Syria. On November 2, he assured Feisal that French troops would remain on the coast only to "keep peace and order," and emphasized that France was willing to allow the Arabs to perform the same administrative function in the interior. But he added: "I am entirely ready to answer your first appeal to help you maintain order, if trouble is caused by agitators who can only compromise Arab interests and diminish the confidence that the Conference is prepared to accord them." Fending off the emir's inquiries, Clemenceau stubbornly refused to commit himself on the question of permanent boundaries or of political authority. These matters, he insisted, must be reserved for the Peace Conference. Subsequently, Feisal's succession of piteous and despairing appeals to Lloyd George evoked only embarrassed silence.

Then, remarkably, even as it appeared that he would leave Paris altogether empty-handed, the Arab leader apparently worked out a last-minute compromise with Clemenceau. The circumstances of the agreement were obscure, and to this day the discussions between the two men have not come to light. The essential provisions of the agreement were nevertheless outlined to Feisal on December 17 in a letter from Philippe Berthelot, secretary-general of the foreign ministry. The entire land of Syria was to become a *de facto* French mandate. France offered "to guarantee the independence and boundaries of all Syria against external aggression" and to provide Feisal with all the counselors necessary to operate the Syrian government, including personnel who would "reorganize" Syrian finances and police. In return, Paris asked that its diplomatic and economic predominance in Syria be recognized as against other powers, that France represent Syria abroad diplomatically, that Syria, "adjust" its foreign policy to that of France and permit France to market its goods abroad, and that Feisal recognize the independence of Lebanon under a French mandate. Subject to these not unimportant qualifications, the Arab government of the interior would be "independent." The arrangement took the form of an exchange of letters expressing a "harmony of views" founded on a "mutual feeling of confidence"; presumably Feisal would later sign a formal document for ratification by his government in Damascus. One may imagine the chagrin and frustration with which the emir finally accepted these painfully rigid French conditions. Maintaining a brave front, he admitted to Colonel Waters-Taylor later that "this agreement was largely distasteful to him, and would be unpopular with his people, but that the attitude of British authorities gave him no choice and that he had been [bound over], tied by his feet and hands to the French."

Feisal demonstrated an inept sense of timing in his capitulation, no less than in his earlier intransigence. The agreement was doomed even in the very limited political advantages it secured the Hashemite regime. During the four months of the emir's sojourn in Europe, the extreme nationalists had gained the upper hand in Damascus. When Feisal returned to Syria on January 16, 1920, he was appalled to learn that his closest friends had turned away from him, and that demonstrations against him were actually taking place in the streets. (The leading spirit in this movement was Yasin Pasha al-Hashimi, an ambitious Iraqi-born former Turkish general.) Moving quickly to retrieve the situation, therefore, the emir assured a group of notables in a speech before the Arab Club on January 22 that he had not altered his position during his visit in France, and that his fixed aim remained the independence of all the Arab lands. He asked only for confidence and restraint in devising an acceptable solution with the French. The notables acknowledged this plea with the barest courtesy. In the streets the demonstrations continued. Bands of tribesmen and villagers already were raiding and pillaging in the western coastal zone, combining looting with patriotism. Gradually, Feisal, too, began to succumb to the extremist pressures around him, although, in a final effort to establish a moderate consensus, he reconvened the dissolved National Congress on March 6. It was the assembly that had been called originally to present its views to the King-Crane commission. The lawyers, sheiks, cadis, and other notables who filled its ranks also included representatives from Palestine who had gathered in a special "Palestine Conference" on February 27 to reject the claims of the Zionists in the Holy Land, and who now joined forces with Syrian nationalists in the larger conclave.

The "General Syrian Congress" established more than a consensus. Within twenty-four hours it repudiated the Feisal-Clemenceau agreement and proclaimed the full and undivided independence of Syria, including Palestine. The delegates simultaneously announced the election of Feisal as their constitutional king, and "the termination of the present occupying military governments in the three Zones." The Lebanon was promised autonomy, "provided it keeps away from any foreign influence." The following day, March 8, the declaration was read to a cheering crowd from the balcony of the Damascus town hall. Feisal himself was greeted with ecstatic huzzahs as 101 artillery salvoes announced the birth of the new kingdom. A few minutes later, yet another proclamation declared the "complete independence of Iraq" under the kingship of Feisal's older brother, Abdullah. Somewhat shaken by his new monarchical status, Feisal nevertheless proceeded to establish a cabinet and to promise a reign of law, order, and equality and the protection of all foreign interests. A committee was appointed to draft a Syrian constitution, and after ten weeks did in fact produce a text, loosely modeled on European lines, but discreetly silent on the question of the new kingdom's boundaries. Feisal meanwhile sent telegrams of friendship to the major Allied capitals, not excluding France. Paris ignored the communication. From London, an angered Curzon warned Feisal that Britain would not recognize the self-appointed regime, and assuredly would not countenance the right of any group of people in Damascus to speak on behalf of Palestine and Mesopotamia. The Maronite patriarch received a flood of protests from Christians in all parts of the Lebanon, rejecting the sovereignty of the Hashemites even more forcefully and indignantly. With French encouragement and protection, moreover, a group of Lebanese Christian notables met at Be'abda on March 22 and formally proclaimed the independence of the Lebanon, hoisting the first Lebanese flag on the staff of government house.

Undaunted by the manifest hostility of these responses, Feisal continued to reign for four months after his coronation as if his kingdom were assured of security and permanence. It was in fact perilously close to anarchy, despite Lawrence's subsequent claims that a viable regime had been established in Damascus. Major Desmond McCallum, a British liaison officer assigned to the Hashemite court, wrote later that "Damascus and the surrounding country, between January 1 and January 24, 1920, was in a state of anarchy and chaos too extraordinary to describe. There were often occasions when the entire population of the Christian quarter of the city was forced to remain in its houses for fear of a general massacre by the Moslems; trade was at a standstill and public security nil." A few Arab officials were themselves so confused and uncertain about the status of the kingdom, and so fearful of French retaliation, that they urged Feisal to make common cause with Mustafa Kemal, the Turkish nationalist leader. The Turks, at least, were fellow Moslems, they argued, and even under the sultan there had existed a certain lethargic mutual rapport; a new understanding between Moslem equals was surely preferable to the danger of rule by a centralist Catholic power. In quest of such an understanding, two prominent Syrians actually journeyed to Ankara and even worked out a tentative arrangement with Kemal's representatives by which Turks and Arabs would unite along the same lines as Austria and Hungary in the prewar Dual Monarchy, thus presenting a united front to the West. But when the emissaries returned to Damascus in April, Feisal had already moved too far along extreme nationalist lines for this kind of partnership. Later, in July 1920, confronted with an imminent French invasion, the emir changed his mind; but by then it was too late.

The possibility of compromise was not doomed by Syrian extremism alone. Actually, the issue was decided as early as September 15, 1919, by the Lloyd George-Clemenceau agreement for British withdrawal in favor of the French. Seven weeks later, the British began pulling out of the littoral. Their place was immediately taken by French African troops arriving in large numbers, swelling the original garrison force of six thousand to twenty thousand by March 20, 1920. French self-confidence mounted in direct proportion to this burgeoning military strength and was given focus by the appointment of General Maurice Gouraud as French high commissioner in Syria and commander of the Army of the Levant. A one-armed veteran of the Gallipoli campaign, later an energetic commander on the European front, Gouraud was a man of high prestige, with a long and distinguished record as a forceful administrator in Mauretania and Morocco. In French Catholic circles, where interest in Syrian matters was particularly keen, the appointment was received enthusiastically, for Gouraud was known as much for his devotion to the Church as for his uncompromising firmness in dealing with Moslems. He was accompanied, in the capacity of secretary-general, by the scholar and Middle East expert Robert de Caix, an ardent, single-minded imperialist. The very announcement of these appointments convinced French rightists of the imminent achievement of French ambitions in Syria. "The Emir Feisal has no right to be in Damascus, Homs, Hama, or Aleppo," insisted Maurice Barrès, the royalist deputy and poet, in the *Echo de Paris* of December 11, 1919. "France knows how to give these towns a Syrian Government. What is Feisal to us or to the Syrians? A man of straw set up by England, without a title, without influence. . . . If England wishes to give a kingdom to this emir, let her set him up in Baghdad." In a letter to the acting foreign secretary in London, Colonel Meinertzhagen confirmed the growing belligerence of French officers in the Lebanon, the arrogant boast of their ability to march into the interior at any time and place of their choosing. By early 1920, ominous reports were arriving in London that the French already had occupied communities well beyond the line of the Lloyd George-Clemenceau agreement of the previous September 15. In response to Whitehall's inquiries, however, the Quai d'Orsay insisted that these maneuvers were intended exclusively to "restore order" in one town, Beka'a. It seemed increasingly obvious, nevertheless, that the French would not long delay in expanding eastward, once they had augmented their power in the coastal cities of the Levant.

Lloyd George sensed the impending crisis. "The French," he recalled, "had managed to impress upon the Arabs and the British that they had no intention of quitting Syria once they were in control, and that their real purpose was to annex the country and constitute it an integral part of the Empire." That impression became even more distinct after January 18, 1920, when Alexandre Millerand succeeded Clemenceau as premier. The new government was a coalition of right-wing parties, and its Middle East policy was largely shaped by Philippe Berthelot, the foreign ministry's staunchly imperialist secretary-general. In a letter to Lloyd George of early February, Berthelot left no doubt where he stood on the Syrian issue:

> He [Berthelot], personally, placed the greatest confidence in [Feisal's] good faith. [But] he fully realized that the Emir possessed a weak character and that his position would be a difficult one, on account of his being surrounded in Damascus by a group of enemies, who entertained anti-French sentiments. But, should the Emir Feisal lose authority owing to his weakness, it was understood that all agreements entered into with him (i.e. the Clemenceau-Feisal agreement) would, *ipso facto*, lapse.

Accordingly, in March, when the Syrian Congress proclaimed the independence of Syria and Feisal decided to accept the proffered crown, both French and British statesmen recognized the compelling need for a final *de jure* settlement of Middle East problems. To that end, the Supreme Council swiftly reassembled in the Italian resort community of San Remo on April 19. In six key sessions, from the 19th to the 24th, the basic provisions of the Turkish treaty were formulated. There was little pretense to idealism this time, nor any further attendance upon the moral approval of the United States (the American ambassador, Robert Underwood Johnson, spent his

277

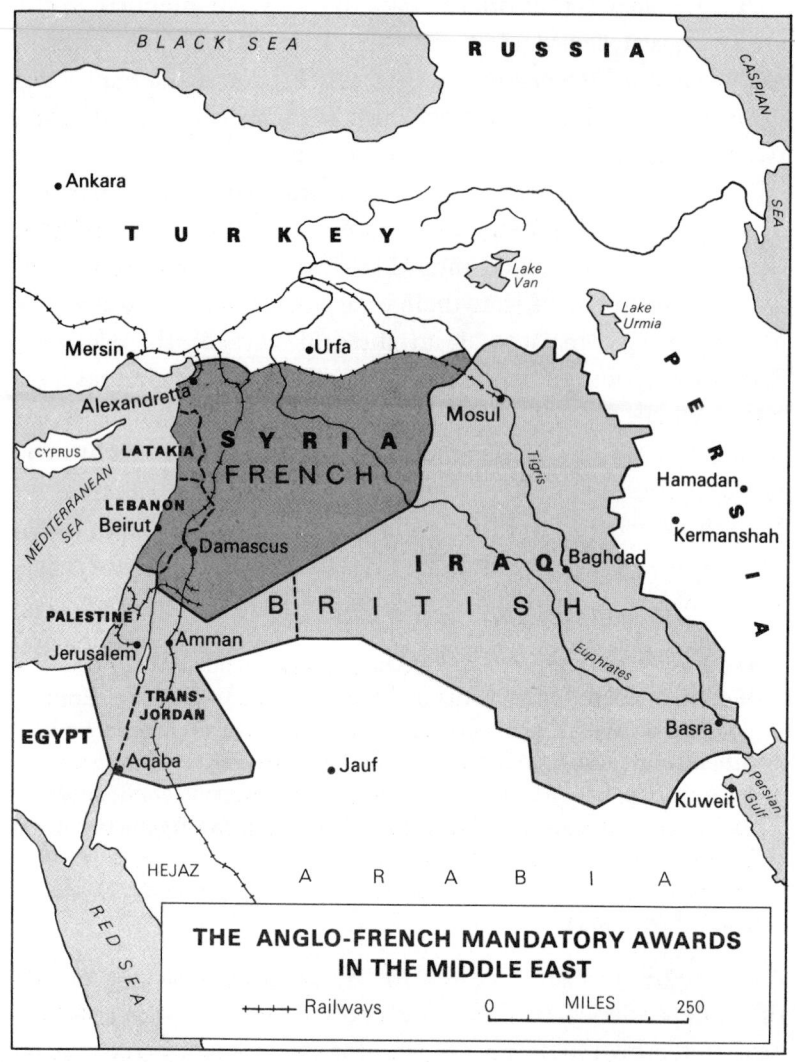

THE ANGLO-FRENCH MANDATORY AWARDS
IN THE MIDDLE EAST

┼┼┼┼ Railways   0   MILES   250

time reading newspapers in the hotel garden while the British
and French settled the most important matters). Article
Ninety-four of the treaty severed Mesopotamia and Syria from
Turkey and arranged for their provisional independence as
mandated territories. The actual allocation of the mandates, in
turn, was covered by separate agreement among the powers
during the same conference.

To no one's surprise, Berthelot remained immovable in his demand for a unified French mandate in Syria. All arrangements with the Hashemites, he insisted, would have to be worked out directly between Damascus and Paris. Lloyd George had of course conceded the essence of this demand to Clemenceau the previous September. The Millerand government simply wanted its final legal recognition. Moreover, the French now placed Britain under additional pressure to abandon the Arabs altogether, refusing to endorse Britain's mandate for Mesopotamia and Palestine or to confirm the Anglo-French oil agreement. The latter was a particularly sensitive matter for London. Fully a year earlier an understanding had been reached between Walter Long, British minister for petroleum affairs, and Senator Alphonse Berenger, commissioner-general of petroleum products in France, for the allocation to France of a twenty-five per cent share of the Mosul oil fields, and to Britain of port and pipeline rights in the (French) Blue and A zones of Syria. Several months after signing the original agreement, the British presented an additional request for a railroad easement across Syrian territory. The French took the appeal under advisement; Berthelot let it be known that his *quid pro quo* was assurance that Lloyd George would drop his objections to the Syrian mandate—objections that, in any case, were hardly more than lip service to Feisal by then. The prime ministers agreed. The final version of the oil pact was then formally signed by Sir John Cadman and Berthelot on April 25. On the following day the Supreme Council unanimously awarded the mandates for Palestine and Mesopotamia to Britain, and for Syria to France.

The Legacy of Palestine

BY THE TERMS of the mandatory awards at San Remo, Syria and Mesopotamia were to be recognized as "provisionally independent" states, subject to mandatory control and tutelage. Special treatment was reserved for Palestine. Actually, until the last month of the war Balfour himself had remained somewhat equivocal on the subject of the Holy Land. While certain in his own mind that a Jewish national home must be encouraged at all costs, and that participation by France in the Palestine mandate was out of the question, the foreign secretary was by no means insistent on unilateral British control. Neither was Lloyd George, who gave occasional consideration to the concept of an American protectorate over Palestine. It was Curzon and the military who finally put a stop to these fantasies. Indeed, Curzon himself formulated the draft that provided for the *verbatim* incorporation of the Balfour Declaration into the mandatory document. It was a provision which the Zionists regarded as of prime importance, he explained. And, as he did not have to explain, it was the Balfour Declaration, with its endorsement of a Jewish national home in the Holy Land, that served as Britain's moral and political case for revising in its own favor the Palestine clauses of the Sykes-Picot Agreement. By the time of the San Remo meeting, the other powers had accepted that reality, as evidenced by Clemenceau's concession on Palestine during the London meeting with Lloyd George in December 1918. Nevertheless, the Allied statesmen could not resist a last-minute temptation to hedge and qualify British priority in this mandated territory. Italy's Foreign Minister Sonnino, for example, still favored a discredited Vatican plan to internationalize Palestine and toyed with a hare-brained scheme of establishing a "Mediterranean Sephardic Union" whose loyalties would be directed toward Rome rather than London. Berthelot, on the other hand, objected to the inclusion of the Balfour Declaration, a mere "semiofficial" document (which the French had never taken seriously), in the text of the mandate award. In its place he submitted a draft maintaining France's prewar prerogatives as guardian of the Roman Catholics and their Holy Places in Palestine. Lloyd George's single concession to these demands was a plan by which a League commission could undertake investigations concerning the status of minority groups; London would abide by its subsequent decisions. After a good deal of tedious haggling, Millerand and Berthelot accepted the compromise, although both statesmen insisted upon putting their reservations and qualifications into the record. Eventually, with the inclusion of the Balfour Declaration in the mandatory text, the Holy Land was placed in a unique category, quite distinct from the other A mandates. As we shall see (Chapter XII), the development of self-government alone would not be the principal criterion of British success in Palestine. Rather, the establishment of a "viable" Jewish national home was also imposed as an obligation of the mandatory power.

On the basis of exhaustive geographic and geologic surveys, the Zionists in the last year of the war had formulated a statement of what they conceived to be the indispensable territorial requirements of a "viable" Palestine. Obviously the historic frontiers of the first and second Jewish commonwealths of antiquity—"from Dan to Beersheba," the term used by Lloyd George in his December 1918 conversation with Clemenceau—were somewhat ill-defined. Instead, modern security considerations required that Palestine control the historic routes of invasion. In the Zionist version, these routes included the desert areas to the south and west; the Beka'a Valley between the slopes of the Lebanon and Mount Hermon on the north; and, finally, the Hejaz Railroad between Dera'a and Ma'an. Economically, too, water resources were vital. Irrigation plans were largely based on the area to the north and northwest, encompassing the Litani River and the snows of Mount Hermon (the headwaters of the Jordan) and the Yarmuk River and its tributaries. Lacking fuel, Palestine was entirely dependent for its future industrialization on the exploitation of hydroelectric power, and this also could best be supplied by the falls of the Litani and the Yarmuk. Gilead, in the region east of the Jordan, was valuable as the site of the only remaining wooded heights outside the Lebanon. On the plateau of Transjordan, moreover, and in the arid Negev in the south, were to be found the last remaining stretches of unoccupied land avaliable for large-scale Jewish settlement. In sum, the Zionist Organization asked the Supreme Council for a Palestine bounded in the north by the slopes of the Lebanon, the headwaters of the Jordan, and the crest of Mount Hermon; in the east by Transjordan to the Hejaz Railroad; and in the south by the Gulf of Aqaba.

It was significant that Feisal raised no objections to these maximal frontiers. The Zionists, after all, had promised him the use of Haifa and Aqaba, and had left to him exclusive use of the Hejaz Railroad. Meanwhile, the British could only view with favor a proposal to enlarge and enrich their future mandate. In a memorandum of February 19, 1919, the general staff stressed the importance of extending the northern frontiers of Palestine northeastward to protect the railway routes from the Mediterranean to Mesopotamia. A straight line through the Haurand and the Jezirah would have been economically more feasible than a diverted railway through the southern desert. In response to a Zionist appeal, Balfour sent off two memoranda to Lloyd George, one on June 26, the other on August 11, 1919, supporting Zionist claims to the water resources of the upper Jordan and the Litani and to an eastern frontier running just west of the Hejaz Railroad. Yet it was not to be expected that the French would amiably accept these claims. As far back as February 1919, a Lebanese delegation, manifestly speaking for France on the Palestine issue, warned the Peace Conference that the "historic and natural frontiers" of Greater Lebanon included the sources of the Jordan. Foreign Minister Pichon endorsed this position in the crucial March 20 meeting in Lloyd George's apartment on the Rue Nitot. Indeed, the foreign minister rejected a British appeal even to revise the Sykes-Picot boundaries, and insisted that northern Galilee, with its complex of Jewish settlements, must remain within the Syrian enclave. Clearly, the British could not accept this literalist interpretation of the Sykes-Picot border, for their troops were even then garrisoned throughout all of Galilee as part of Occupied

Enemy Territory South. Allenby and Gouraud had already smoothly worked out the military lines of demarcation on that understanding. It was also the agreement that had originally been reached (Palestine "from Dan to Beersheba") between Lloyd George and Clemenceau in their London meeting of December 1918. Despite this understanding, in ensuing months, as the Zionists watched in alarm, Allied negotiations on Palestine remained hopelessly stalled. At one point, on May 21, disagreement on the Syrian–Palestinian frontier became so heated that Clemenceau and Lloyd George almost came to blows. Far from compromising on British—and Zionist—demands, Pichon seemed intent on carving away a vital northern area already under British occupation. It was his sweet revenge for London's support of the Arabs.

The impasse continued until February 1910. Then, at last, in response to Britain's tacit abandonment of the Syrian interior, the new Millerand government agreed to resume discussions on Palestine. This sudden show of magnanimity actually represented little more than acceptance of the existing military boundaries. The maximalist frontiers requested by the Zionists were simply ignored. Lloyd George, no less eager than the Millerand regime to finish with the Middle East, seemed prepared to accept the status quo. He had not forgotten that Britain required control of Palestine for reasons largely associated with the defense of Egypt, including the use of Haifa as a Mediterranean naval base and the construction of a railroad and pipeline from Mesopotamia to the sea. These requirements could be met within the existing frontiers. The Jews had been useful in achieving these objectives, to be sure. But the kind of utopian Zionist borders that would assure Palestine complete economic viability represented merely a secondary imperial objective for the British, and apparently could be achieved only at the price of alienating the French altogether. Subsequent negotiations were interrupted by the fall of the Millerand government and the establishment of the Leygues regime in its place. But eventually, on December 4, the British and French prime ministers reached final agreement on the boundary issue. The formal treaty was signed at Paris three weeks later. By its terms, Palestine's northern frontier included the Jordan up to a point just south of Banias-Dan (see map), then ran northeastward along the watershed of rivers flowing into the Jordan, and finally dropped southward just to the east of the Jordan and Lake Hula. These were essentially the Sykes-Picot boundaries. France's single concession to Britain was the right to use the Hejaz Railroad between Lake Galilee and the Syrian Desert and to lay a pipeline across French territory in this area. Leyguès additionally promised the Jewish settlements in the north free use of the waters of the upper Jordan and the Yarmuk—which were, however, to remain in French hands.

The arrangement was a painful setback for the Zionists. To the east, the assigned boundaries cut the Jews off from vast areas of cultivable land. To the north and northeast, the country was deprived of almost all the major water resources—the Litani River, the northernmost sources of the Jordan, the spring of the Hermon, and the greater part of the Yarmuk—needed for the power and irrigation plans that were even then being formulated. Leyguès's promise to allow Jewish settlements free use of the waters of the Yarmuk and of the northern Jordan springs was never honored. The frontiers similarly ignored the historical entity of Palestine as described in the Bible and as envisaged in the original negotiations leading to the Balfour Declaration. Moreover, by failing to approximate any natural geographic boundaries, the borders left the country all but indefensible militarily. As it turned out, this legacy of economic and military vulnerablity was to curse the Palestine mandate, and later the entire Middle East, for decades to come.

But in the short run, Britain had little reason for complaint in the disposition of mandates and concessions. She had been awarded Palestine and Mesopotamia, and had been allocated a seventy-five-per-cent share in the petroleum holdings of Mosul. Indeed, the agreements permitted the English to transport the oil to the sea through Syria by railroad and pipeline; to connect their railroad system in Mesopotamia with that of the Hejaz; and thus to forge still another link in their Cape-to-Cairo-to-India chain of imperial communications. In sum, the Anglo-French agreements represented the culmination of Britain's policy in the Levant, the apogee of her influence in the Middle East. She had obtained all her cherished goals in the partition of the Ottoman Empire: enlarged mandates, formal recognition by the Treaty of Sèvres (see Chapter X) of her position in Cyprus and Egypt, assurance of free naval passage through the Turkish straits.

As it happened, the Treaty of Sèvres, by which Constantinople renounced its Arab possessions in favor of the Allies, was stalled because of the Turkish nationalist movement. The Council of the League of Nations was therefore obliged to postpone its ratification of the mandatory awards. But the San Remo provisions were carried out in spite of these difficulties. Britain and France agreed tacitly to consider the Sèvres Treaty valid in their relations with one another. So did the Council of the League of Nations, which on September 29, 1922, finally approved the mandates for Palestine and Syria (the mandate for Mesopotamia was delayed as a result of special arrangements with Britain). With the signing of the new peace treaty in Lausanne on July 24, 1923, the Turks were simply called upon to recognize a *fait accompli*.

The French Keep an Appointment

INSTINCTIVELY MODERATE, Feisal was unwilling at first to regard the San Remo agreements as a direct provocation to war against France. On the other hand, he was unable to restrain his officers and bands of irregulars from acts of violence against the French zone of occupation. Arab guerrillas, many of them plain and simple bandits, launched a reign of terror against Lebanese Maronite settlements on the coastal littoral. Villages were looted and burned and their inhabitants murdered; traffic between towns was all but paralyzed. These attacks were directed with growing frequency against Frenchmen as well. The nation's martial ardor, somnolent during the Arab Revolt against the Turks, apparently was more easily aroused against the infidel Europeans. French officers and troops were trapped in Lebanese mountain passes, arrested, stripped, occasionally killed. But it was Feisal himself who precipitated hostilities in late June 1920 by suddenly denying the French army the right to use the Rayak-Aleppo railroad. At this time most of the French garrisons in the Middle East were located in Cilicia, and were heavily dependent upon the Rayak-Aleppo line for their supplies. The Arab leader's decision immediately undermined their security.

For General Gouraud, Feisal's impulsive act represented a final, intolerable provocation. On Bastille Day, July 14, 1920, the high commissioner sent Damascus a sharply worded ultimatum. He accused the Hashemite government, by its mounting campaign of violence against France and the Arab Christian communities, of betraying the Clemenceau-Feisal agreement of December 1919 (actually never ratified), and the trust that the Peace Conference had bestowed upon France to "ensure peace and order in Syria." Whereupon Gouraud laid down five conditions for immediate acceptance by the Arab government. These included France's "absolute" right to use the Rayak-Aleppo railroad and to occupy Aleppo as a "guarantee"; the abolition of compulsory military service within the Arab zone; full recognition of the French mandate by the Hashemite regime; acceptance by the Arabs of French currency as the national currency of Syria; and punishment of the "criminals" responsible for hostile acts against the French and Lebanese. These conditions were presented *en bloc* and had to be accepted *en bloc* within three days, by midnight of July 17. Otherwise Gouraud would take all "necessary action." In a personal letter accompanying the ultimatum, the general appealed to "His Royal Highness the Emir Feisal" to listen to the voice of reason and to dissociate himself from the extremists in his government.

When the note reached Damascus, it created panic.

Yasin al-Hashimi, the Syrian military chief of staff, warned Feisal that his army possessed barely two hours worth of ammunition. The emir hardly required the warning. On July 18 he telegraphed Gouraud, accepting the high commissioner's conditions "personally and in principle." The general was gratified by this conciliatory response, and in turn conceded Feisal's request for an extension until midnight of the 21st, provided that the emir would immediately "execute the conditions" of the ultimatum. Without a moment's hesitation, Feisal dispatched a second, concurring telegram. And then, on the morning of July 21, French troops unaccountably began an advance into the interior. Horrified, Feisal rushed a trusted adviser to Beirut to protest the violation of the agreement. At the French headquarters, the emissary, Sati al-Husri, was calmly informed by Gouraud that Feisal's telegram had arrived a half-hour beyond the deadline; evidently Arab irregulars had cut the wires. Husri was almost beside himself with frustration. He implored the high commissioner at least to order a withdrawal now that he had the facts of the emir's intentions. Gouraud's glacial response was that it was "too late." At this point the general read off his demands for eight new "guarantees." In essence, by requiring that French troops now be stationed freely throughout the Syrian interior, the guarantees signified nothing less than an ultimatum for Arab surrender. Upon receiving these new terms, the shaken Feisal called an emergency Cabinet meeting. Yet it was plain by then that there was no way of accepting the conditions without igniting a civil war; the Moslem population had been driven into an anti-French hysteria.

On July 22, the Third Division of the Army of the Levant advanced toward Damascus in three columns. The largest column, ten thousand Senegalese troops under General Goybet, pushed along the main Beirut-Damascus road. No resistance was encountered during the whole of that day, and at night the soldiers encamped just outside Quneitra, blocking the Arab retreat from Damascus into Palestine. On the 23rd the advance continued through the twisting, rocky gorges of the Anti-

Lebanon range. Again, through the whole of this day, the Arabs offered no resistance. The column deployed at nightfall at the western entrance of a narrow gorge, some five miles long, flanked on each side by precipitous cliffs. Although the defile was a natural ambush, Goybet ordered his troops into it on the morning of the 24th. Perhaps he had decided on a calculated gamble. The tropical heat necessitated the consumption of great quantities of water, and the general was determined to reach the wells at the exit of the ravine by nightfall. Otherwise, retreat was inevitable, with a possibly disastrous loss of face.

The Arab commander, Azme Bey, was a not incapable soldier. Trained in France and Germany, he had earned considerable distinction in the Ottoman army during the war. He was, therefore, hardly less aware than Goybet that a few steadfast Arab troops, armed with machine guns and bombs, would have been capable of immolating virtually the whole of the Third Division in that gorge. Nevertheless, almost incredibly, Azme Bey permitted the French column to begin its evacuation from the defile in marching order before opening fire with his howitzers and machine guns. The French suffered a considerable number of dead and wounded, but maintained their discipline. Goybet, who quickly appraised the situation, ordered his cavalry regiment to gallop back to the western entrance of the ravine, then to enter the mountains farther south and attack the Arabs from the rear. Even as this maneuver was being precisely carried out, a French air squadron flew over to bomb and strafe. Within a few minutes the Arab army of twenty thousand became a rabble fleeing in terror toward Damascus. Azme Bey, gallantly attempting to rally his demoralized troops, was himself blown to pieces by a tank shell. The next day the Hashemite capital was a scene of pandemonium as returning Arab soldiers galloped through the streets and bazaars of the city looting shops, firing indiscriminately at passer-by. Upon learning the results of the battle, Feisal and his advisers hurriedly left by train for the south. Their departure was the death knell of the Arab kingdom.

The French arrived in Damascus on July 26 and immediately restored order, much to the relief of the civilian population. General Goybet's terms were exceptionally firm, and were put into effect without compromise. The Syrian army was disarmed and disbanded. An indemnity of ten million francs was imposed on the Hashemite government to recompense Arab citizens who had suffered from nationalist depredations. Leading offenders were brought to trial before French courts-martial. The use of the Arab flag was forbidden. A puppet cabinet was appointed, and on August 8 General Gouraud arrived in Damascus to establish a taut, centralized French regime for the entire country. Twelve days earlier, on July 27, Gouraud had addressed a letter to Feisal on behalf of the French government, requesting the emir to leave Damascus as soon as possible. "A special train will be at the disposal of Your Royal Highness and suite," the note stated curtly. "The train will leave the Hejaz Station at 0500 hours tomorrow, July 28, 1920." Administrative complications postponed departure for several days. But on August 1, trembling and silent in his affronted dignity, Feisal boarded the train, accompanied by his brother Zeid and 114 members of his official retinue.

It was an uncomfortable moment for the British. With some feeling, Churchill wrote Lloyd George that

> the operations had been conducted very largely by black African troops, and it was extremely painful to British opinion, and to British officers particularly who had served the Arabs, to see those who had been our comrades such a little time before and our Allies, and who looked to us for protection and to see their wrongs righted, to look on while they were thrashed and trampled down and their cities taken against the spirit of the treaties, if not against the letter, by the French. . . . However, we have these strong ties with the French and they have to prevail, and we were not able to do anything to help the Arabs in the matter. . . .

Only the formalities could be observed. Sir Herbert Samuel, British high commissioner in Palestine, prepared a guard of honor for the Arab leader as the train passed through Lydda. Feisal's eyes brimmed with tears, for he had believed at first that the troops were there to arrest him. From Haifa the emir boarded a second train for Egypt, en route to Italy. His royal titles were not recognized by the sultanate of Egypt, and when he changed trains again in El Qantara at the Suez Canal, he was obliged to wait on the platform for his connection, seated ignominiously upon his luggage.

It was small consolation for Feisal at the time, but the Western Allies were not in occupation of Syria, or of any other Arab territory for that matter, by virtue of their own authority or military power alone. They governed rather in the name of the League of Nations and the local populations. This may have been a matter of form, but not empty form. The native inhabitants were left with a meaningful, tangible hope. Although their promised freedom had been indefinitely postponed, their right to independence had nevertheless been recognized under international law. This was a fact of more than academic importance. It meant that the mandate system could not be used as a cover to establish new Algerias in the Middle East. France, for example, was precluded from colonizing Syria or integrating Syria politically into the metropolitan homeland. By the same token, efforts to achieve national independence could never be declared wholly illegal by the mandatory powers. In the name of peace and order, the French or British might suppress popular movements to that end, but at least the principle of national independence could not be denied. It was a principle which in future years the Arabs, the Turks, and later the Jews would assert by legal and political appeal, by public demonstration, and ultimately, with conclusive if sanguinary effect, by mass unrest and the brute and indiscriminate force of arms.

CHAPTER X

===

THE PARTITION OF TURKEY AND THE RISE OF THE GREEK EMPIRE

The Shock of Conquest

WITHIN FORTY-EIGHT HOURS of the signing of the Mudros Armistice, a powerful Allied naval flotilla cruised through the Dardanelles into the Sea of Marmora, and steamed majestically toward Constantinople. The convoy was strung so far that observers in its middle could see neither its beginning nor its end. The British dreadnoughts led the way, followed by the French, then the Italians, then the Greeks. The armada's entrance into the Bosporus was a moment of unutterable jubilation for the Christian inhabitants of Turkey; the hour of their long-awaited deliverance had finally arrived. They packed the shores by the tens of thousands, cheering ecstatically and waving Allied flags. The Turks, conversely, remained in the background, watching in silence from their windows, shaken and subdued before this awesome display of Allied might. Nothing must be done to provoke the victors, they knew. Their country was totally dependent upon Allied goodwill for sheer sustenance; food and fuel were in desperately short supply; a raging inflation had all but destroyed the value of the Turkish currency. It was, accordingly, for plain and dire reasons of economic self-interest that the new government had been hand-picked to ingratiate itself with the Allies. And to that end, the new regime faithfully carried out

Allied orders to demobilize. Indeed, within two months of the Mudros Armistice, barely forty thousand Turkish soldiers remained under arms. Even these were employed merely as a kind of supernumerary police guarding the military arsenals on behalf of the victors. Otherwise, as Winston Churchill wrote of the small but mobile British occupation force:

> . . . Our officers in twos and threes were all over Asia Minor supervising the surrender of arms and munitions as prescribed in the Armistice. They rode about freely and unarmed from place to place, and with their finger indicated what should be done. They were almost mechanically obeyed. Important "dumps" of rifles, machine guns, cannon and shells were being submissively piled up; Turkey was under the spell of defeat, and of deserved defeat. "Let us be punished by our old friend England."

The Turks had a sure instinct for where the power was, and everywhere they turned that power was in British hands. The Straits, for example, were under the firm and exclusive authority of Admiral Calthorpe, commander of Allied naval forces in the eastern Mediterranean and British high commissioner for Turkey. Constantinople, too, as well as all the railroads of the Anatolian interior and the entire Black and Caspian Sea coasts, were occupied by detachments of British colonial soldiers. Even the six thousand French troops stationed in Cilicia answered to the orders of General Allenby in Cairo. If the Turks misjudged the new state of affairs, it was not in their evaluation of British strength, but only in their sanguine expectation of English benevolence. British public opinion had been outraged by the Ottoman government's desertion of its former patron and protector, and even more by the gratuitously cruel treatment of British prisoners of war and the massacres of the Armenians. Members of Parliament vied with each other in denouncing the Turk as the "bane of civilization" or the "pariah among nations." When, on June 17, 1919, an Ottoman delegation entreated the Supreme Council not to visit the crimes of the CUP on the Turkish people, it was the mild and tolerant Balfour who coldly rejected the appeal. "Every nation must be judged by the Government which rules it," he warned.

As the master arbiter of Turkish destinies at the Peace Conference, however, the British delegation was severely handicapped in formulating an early or effective settlement. For one thing, a curious lacuna existed in the administration of British diplomatic affairs. Foreign Secretary Balfour and his retinue of experts sat with Lloyd George at the Peace Conference in Paris. Curzon, the acting foreign secretary in London, depended upon transcribed minutes of each day's proceedings at the Conference, which had to be brought by airplane across the Channel the following morning. "A. J. B. [Balfour] is in Paris pursuing one policy," wrote Curzon irritably to his wife on August 19, "I am here pursuing another." This absence of coordination became especially apparent on the issue of Constantinople, "the international city of the Eastern world." Curzon, an avowed imperialist, was determined to amputate the great metropolis permanently from its Turkish hinterland, and in its place revive the Anatolian town of Brousa as the Ottoman capital. On the other hand, Lloyd George and Balfour were impressed by the warnings of Montagu and the India Office that expulsion of the sultan-caliph from Constantinople might seriously inflame the British Empire's vast and far-flung Moslem populations. The arguments continued throughout 1919, with the experts divided, and Lloyd George, Balfour, and Cecil vacillating between the positions of Curzon and Montagu.

It was not merely a divided adminstrative approach which bedeviled efforts to cope with the Turkish problem, but also the sheer complexity of the problem itself. As Lloyd George summarized it:

> In some respects the settlement of the Turkish Empire presented greater difficulties than that of any other enemy country. . . . The racial problems defied any satisfactory solution. In European Turkey, Turks, Greeks, Bulgars, Serbs, Jews and Armenians were hopelessly mixed up in the same towns and villages. Statistics alone conveyed no clear notion of the

desperate tangle. The position in Anatolia was equally confined. There was a hard core of Turks in the centre of Anatolia. But outside, the further from the centre, the greater the jumble and jostle of races and religions.

From the very outset it was evident that the collapse of Russia had left an immense gap in Allied plans not only for Constantinople, but also for the interior of Asia Minor, and particularly for the mountainous, inaccessible Armenian provinces. The Western members of the Entente were entirely capable of imposing a severe armistice on Turkey, even of garrisoning and administering the Arab communities of the Middle East. But their resources and manpower were hardly extensive enough for an indefinite occupation of the Anatolian and Armenian hinterlands. Nor was Clemenceau or Lloyd George eager to assume so formidable and thankless a task. Rather, skirting the issue, the Allied statesmen concentrated alternately upon the German, the Italian, and the Syrian Question. For most of the winter and early spring of 1919 the Supreme Council did not deal with Turkish matters at all.

The Supreme Council's rather unsystematic and lethargic discussions on Turkey were deceptive, however. For one thing, the Western diplomats cherished the hope of persuading the United States to fill the vacuum in the Turkish interior (see Chapter XI). As early as December 2, 1918, Lord Eustace Percy of the Foreign Office first hinted to American representatives that the United States was Britain's first choice as mandator in Constantinople and the Straits. It was the merest overture to a far more extensive proposal. By the opening days of 1919, the Allies were envisaging America as mandator for nothing less than the entire hinterland of northeast Turkey. Indeed, on May 5, Lloyd George officially submitted this recommendation to the Supreme Council. When President Wilson's response was not initially encouraging, the prime minister suggested postponing the final allocation of Turkish territories until the attitude of the United States was known more definitely. As shall be seen, no single factor was more responsible for delaying the Turkish peace treaty than this indecision about America's role. Ironically, it was the very decisiveness with which the president rejected the Secret Treaties—his moralistic intention to "completely ignore" them—which blocked a compelling alternative for filling the Turkish vacuum. The other alternative was naked imperialism. For there was yet an additional factor to complicate a swift resolution of the Turkish Question. It was the determination of Italy and Greece to claim payment on their promissory notes for the Turkish interior.

If the Italians had proved obstreperous allies during the war, their behavior at the Peace Conference was even more disconcerting. Their territorial claims in Dalmatia conflicted head on with those of the newly established Yugoslavian kingdom. And when the other Western statesmen brusquely rejected Italy's demands, Italian Prime Minister Orlando pressed with mounting insistence and irascibility for acceptance of his nation's "rights" in Turkey. His ambitions there were based on two agreements. The first, the Treaty of London of 1915, had promised Rome "a just share of the Mediterranean region adjacent to the province of Adalia." The second, the Treaty of St.-Jean-de-Maurienne of 1917, was considerably more detailed and extensive: it offered the Italians Smyrna, the sanjaks of Menteshe, Adalia, and Itchili, the largest part of the vilayet of Konia, and a zone of influence extending over most of the southern and southwestern coastline. This prospective allocation represented a combined area of 42,000 square miles, and Italy wanted it all—under both treaties. "If it is a question of a protectorate or a zone of influence," ex-Foreign Minister Tittoni insisted before the Italian Senate on December 14, 1918, "we must be treated equally; if there are commercial and economic advantages, we must obtain the same."

The other Allied powers did not see it that way. They accepted Italy's claims to a not unrespectable strip of Turkey along the southern littoral. But the notion of awarding Rome all of Adalia and the entire Smyrna region seemed unthinkable. Moreover, the Allied objection was not simply a legal one, the fact that one of the partners to the St.-Jean-de-Maurienne agreement—i.e., Russia—had been unavailable to sign the final document. It was rather the entirely practical objection, voiced by both Lloyd George and Clemenceau, that Italy had contributed literally nothing to military operations against the Ottoman Empire. If the Italians had made a serious effort to pull their weight in the Middle Eastern theater, even Wilson might have been constrained to alter his rigidly moralistic position, as indeed he did when the Arab world was partitioned between Britain and France. But the president chose now to stand forthrightly on the twelfth of his Fourteen Points, assuring "a secure sovereignty" to the Turkish portions of the Ottoman Empire. Finally, on April 24, 1919, exasperated by Allied rigidity on both the Dalmatian and the Turkish Question. Orlando and his foreign minister, Sonnino, left the Peace Conference and departed for Rome. They had already begun to make it clear, however, that they did not intend passively to base their Middle East policy on the sufferance of the Supreme Council. As early as March 29, individual units of Italian troops had stealthily begun to occupy the coastal areas of Adalia. By the first week in April, other landing parties had moved into Konia and installed a garrison in the Bay of Ismidt, across the terminus of the Taurus railroad.

The first Allied statesman outside Italy to receive word of these landings, on April 12, was Prime Minister Venizelos of Greece, whose extensive private network of Greek agents kept him well informed on significant developments in the eastern Mediterranean. Venizelos immediately notified the Supreme Council. Investigation by French and British naval units confirmed the information. The Allies discovered, as well, that additional Italian troops were in the vicinity of Smyrna, and were evidently preparing a drive on the city itself. On May 6, therefore, Clemenceau and Lloyd George urgently requested President Wilson, the only "disinterested" statesman present, to block the invasion of Smyrna by rushing American troops to the Turkish interior. To be sure, the president was hardly less outraged than his colleagues by Italian "duplicity."

Nevertheless, he was obliged to decline action on legal grounds; his country had not been a belligerent in the Middle East. Thereupon Lloyd George came up with an ingenious proposal. Venizelos, he suggested, should be invited to land several Greek divisions in Smyrna to "protect his fellow-countrymen in Turkey." The idea was mooted almost as an afterthought. Yet it was destined to be one of the most fateful proposals in the recent annals of the Middle East, and surely one of the most disastrous in the modern political history of Greece and Britain alike. Its effect, as we shall see, was in large measure to reverse the consequences of the Turkish surrender at Mudros and of the Turkish peace treaty yet to be written.

Venizelos's Good Intentions

RARELY DID THE CONFLUENCE of national fulfillment and personal career blend as dramatically as in the case of Greece and her charismatic prime minister, Eleutherios Venizelos. The country's history in modern times was an odyssey of raging irredentism and painfully achieved national consolidation. The Greek boundaries of 1832 had encompassed the barest threshold of the Attic peninsula. In successive wars with the Turks, those frontiers were steadily enlarged to include, by 1881, the Ionian Islands, Thessaly, and part of Epirus. Even then, however, the majority of Greeks lived outside the nation's borders. In his own lifetime, Venizelos brought them into the kingdom. He was a Cretan, son of an impoverished lower-middle-class family and heir to the irredentist's burning passion for union with the Homeland. Trained in the law, he moved rapidly into politics, where his driving energy and not undeveloped talent for demagoguery played a central role in igniting the Cretan insurrection of 1896. The political (if not military) success of the uprising won Venizelos a reputation as the most uncompromising of all Greek nationalists. Soon thereafter he was elected to the Greek parliament and began his rise to the premiership, which he achieved in 1911. Armed with governmental authority for the first time, Venizelos moved audaciously to fulfill his vision of a Greece restored to her ancient boundaries. His imaginative leadership in 1912 engineered the alliance of Greece, Bulgaria, and Serbia against Turkish rule in Thrace and Macedonia. The war began that same year. Within six weeks the armies of the three Balkan allies succeeded in driving the Turks entirely out of Europe except for Constantinople and its immediate environs.

For the victors there remained only the division of the spoils. The Bulgars, who had done the lion's share of the fighting, expected in return the vital Macedonian port of Salonica. But Greece and Serbia were not willing to cede it, particularly when the Western powers blocked Serbian access to the Adriatic. As a result, in 1913, war again erupted, this time with Bulgaria pitted against Greece, Serbia, and Rumania. The Bulgars were decisively beaten and were stripped of all their earlier conquests with the single exception of western Thrace. Venizelos, on the other hand, emerged as the authentic legatee of the southern Balkans. Within two years he had added to the Kingdom of the Hellenes southern and eastern Macedonia, the unclaimed remnant of Thessaly, southern Epirus, all the crucial Aegean islands except the Dodecanese, and the islands of Imbros and Tenedos, which guard the entrance to the Turkish straits. Some three million new kinsmen had thereby been incorporated into the "Old Kingdom," the territory of which was nearly doubled. For a while the prime minister was content to digest these gains and to reinforce his country's alliance with Serbia against the possibility of a future Bulgarian attack. The outbreak of the World War brought no initial change in Venizelos's position. Personally, he was strongly pro-Entente. Yet so long as his country's two archenemies, Bulgaria and Turkey, remained neutral, Greece too would remain defensively neutral.

It was the likelihood of Turkey's entrance into the war that first shifted Venizelos to a more actively pro-Entente position. As the prime minister conceived his nation's interests, it appeared far shrewder to anticipate Turkish vengeance by collaborating militarily at the side of the Allies from the very outset. Much to his chagrin, however, the suggestion was vetoed by King Constantine.

> It is obvious [Venizelos protested to Constantine] that Turkey will want to settle her accounts with us before she demobilizes. When we have before us the prospect of prosecuting the war against Turkey with the help of powerful and numerous allies, are we to throw away such an opportunity in order to find ourselves someday compelled to fight the same war without allies and without friends?

There is little evidence that the monarch's neutrality was animated by either moral weakness or pro-German sentiment. Handsome, cultivated, and charming, Constantine was adored by his subjects as the first Greek prince to be born on Greek soil since the fall of Byzantium. During the Second Balkan War he had demonstrated an outstanding capacity for military leadership, decisively smashing the Bulgars on the field of Kilkich. It was true that the king was related to the German royal house; his wife, Sophie, was the kaiser's sister. He had been trained in Prussian military academies, bore the title of Marshal of the German Army, and spoke German fluently. Yet this close relationship counted for little in his foreign policy, as his brother-in-law, the kaiser, ruefully discovered when the World War began. Wilhelm continually and urgently entreated Greek help, offering as his inducement generous territorial gains at the expense of Serbia. Nor did the kaiser hesitate to issue ominous and heavy-handed warnings—e.g., "Let Athens know that I have concluded an alliance with Bulgaria and Turkey to fight the Russians, and I shall treat Greece as an enemy if she does not join us immediately." Constantine remained politely noncommittal.

His ostensible reason was the legitimate danger of Bulgarian counteraction. But in fact, at the outset of the war, the king was hardly less pro-Serbian than his prime minister. As early as August 1914, Constantine permitted the Serbs to open a base and a huge revictualing center at Salonica, in Greek-occupied Macedonia. The National Bank of Greece was instructed to make foreign credits available to Serbia. When the Austrians launched their first offensive in November, the king went so far as to "lend" Serbia his nation's entire reserve of artillery ammunition, a loan that saved the embattled defenders. It was with Constantine's approval, too, that Greek Intelligence information on the Straits was turned over to the British naval attaché in Athens, a service that helped lay the groundwork for the Gallipoli campaign. The issue between Venizelos and Constantine, therefore, was never one of either basic sympathies or ultimate purpose. It was rather one of strategy and timing. For with the entrance of Turkey into the war, the prime minister was determined to gamble everything on pro-Allied intervention, and in this decision he refused to be limited by constitutional obstacles.

Venizelos was motivated by more than a vague hope of Allied benevolence. Once the Turks had cast their lot with Germany, the British were prepared to offer important territorial incentives at Ottoman expense. In response to Venizelos's rather explicit hint of his interests in that direction, the British foreign secretary, Sir Edward Grey, assured the Athens government on January 15, 1915, that "both France and Russia will readily admit most important territorial compensations for Greece on the coast of Asia Minor, and if M. Venizelos wishes for a definite promise, I believe there will be no difficulty in obtaining it." Grey attached an important condition to this general assurance. The friendship of Bulgaria, a state whose neutrality thwarted the Central Powers' desire for direct access to Turkey, still remained the pivot of London's policy in the Balkans. Accordingly, it was vital to placate the Sofia regime with territorial concessions, and those concessions could be offered solely in Cavalla, a border region in Macedonia recently occupied by the Greeks in the Second Balkan War. For his part, Venizelos was quite prepared to make this sacrifice in exchange for a foothold in Asia Minor. Immediately after receiving Grey's note, the prime minister drew up a secret memorandum for Constantine in which he formulated for the first time his goal of Asian expansion, the establishment of a Greece beyond the seas in the ancient territories of Ionia and Aeolia, two of the wellsprings of Hellenic civilization.

Colonel Metaxas, acting chief of the Greek general staff, was not impressed by this chimerical vision. Neither was the king, who regarded Allied promises for Asia Minor as much too vague, and the cession of Cavalla as unpalatable to the Greek people. Venizelos was undeterred by these reservations. Even then, in March 1915, an Allied fleet was gathering for the assault on the Dardanelles. The prime minister was convinced that this armada represented his nation's golden opportunity; as he told his colleagues later, he "could almost hear the bells of Santa Sofia [the former Greek Orthodox Church in Constantinople]." With some excitement, he drew up a plan and submitted it to the Crown Council on March 3. It offered the Entente the Greek fleet and 35,000 men for the Straits expedition. The prime minister insisted that, in making this contribution, Athens would simultaneously buttress its claims in Asia Minor and mobilize the nation for a holy crusade to liberate the historic Byzantine capital. Unfortunately for Venizelos, his plan was vetoed not only by the king and Crown Council, but, unknown to him, by the Russian government as well. The last thing Foreign Minister Sazanov wanted was an army of Greeks challenging Russian claims to "Tsargrad" (see Chapter III). Rebuffed and humiliated, Venizelos promptly resigned on March 5. Until that moment the Royal Hellenic Navy had actually been under steam for battle action at the side of the Allies.

Although the departure of Venizelos was a severe blow to Allied diplomacy in the Balkans, France and Britain persisted in their determination to lure the Greeks into the war. If the Dardanelles expedition was too sensitive a joint venture for Russian approval, four or five Greek divisions could still be of inestimable value in Serbia. So could a Greek territorial concession to the Bulgars. The inducement was not withdrawn, "the territorial acquisitions already promised in the Aidin Vilayet," Grey cabled Sir Francis Elliott, the British minister in Athens, on April 7. Two days later, the foreign secretary fattened the offer. "We are prepared to promise Smyrna and a substantial portion of the Hinterland to be hereafter defined," he declared. Nor were pro-Allied sympathies in Athens dissipated simply because Venizelos had resigned. On April 14, the new prime minister, Gounaris, stated his willingness to enter the war immediately, provided the Entente would guarantee Greek territorial integrity both during and after the war. It was the one condition the Allies could not accept; for them, Greece was still valuable principally as a source of concessions to Bulgaria. The policy was cynical: by the secret Treaty of London of April 26, 1915, the Allies made a similar promise of concessions in Asia Minor to Italy (see Chapter VI). The policy was also bankrupt. After carefully weighing all offers, the Sofia government eventually opted for the tangible reward of vengeance and territorial aggrandizement at Serbian expense. On October 12, 1915, the Bulgarian army launched its much-feared drive into Serbia, and thereby entered the war at the side of the Central Powers. The gallant little Serbian kingdom, which earlier had withstood the full weight of the Habsburg army, now finally succumbed to the overwhelming power of two invading forces. If it was a time for mourning and despair in Belgrade, it was no less an occasion for shame and humiliation in Athens.

Salonica and Revolution

IN FACT, IT WAS Bulgarian aggression that gave Venizelos a second, and apparently ideal, opportunity for intervention at the side of the Allies. He had been returned to the premiership in a national election some five weeks earlier, but had waited in angry frustration as his monarch rigorously guarded the country's neutrality. Now, on September 22, with the first announcement of Bulgarian mobilization, the resourceful Cretan immediately devised his own scheme to circumvent the King.

THE EASTERN MEDITERRANEAN AND THE BALKANS
AT THE OUTBREAK OF THE WORLD WAR

Allied Powers

Central Powers

Neutral states

Under British occupation

0   MILES   250

He secretly invited the Allies to land their troops at the Macedonian port of Salonica, from which vantage point they would gain access to the beleaguered Serbs. The operation would probably not be approved by Constantine, Venizelos warned, and he, the prime minister, would be obliged officially to protest; but that protest would be entirely *pro forma*. The ruse worked. Battalions of French troops disembarked at Salonica on October 3 and encountered no opposition. Venizelos dutifully protested, then implored Constantine to exploit the Allied presence by declaring war on Bulgaria. Understandably outraged by this duplicity, the monarch forthwith dismissed both his prime minister and the pro-Allied Chamber of Deputies. Venizelos thereupon left office a martyr, in the eyes of the Entente powers a noble victim of their cause—and the repository of Greek postwar claims.

In other, purely military respects, however, the operation failed ignominiously. The Allied expeditionary force advanced rapidly to the Macedonian-Serbian frontier, where it was immediately repulsed by a larger, well-entrenched Bulgarian army. Confounded by this unexpected resistance, General Maurice Sarrail, the Allied commander, hurriedly led his divisions back to Salonica and ordered them to dig in at the outskirts of the city until "reinforcements" arrived. The wait stretched out to nearly three years. During 1916, meanwhile, even as the Allied force vegetated in Macedonia, the Greek government and people were subjected to intensive pressure from both sets of belligerents. The notoriously corrupt Greek press was all but purchased outright by the German embassy, which used it to mount a virulent propaganda campaign against the Allies. The French embassy, through its own bribed agents, organized demonstrations against the royalist government. At the same time, General Sarrail was confiscating Greek supplies at will for his troops, while the Allied fleets blockaded the Greek coasts, ostensibly to stop pro-German "smuggling," but in effect reducing the country's population to near-starvation. The object of these Allied measures was quite plainly to topple the Greek monarchy. If the Western powers took Constantine's pro-German bias for granted, however, their policy all but assured it in the summer of 1916. On May 27, the king succumbed to a German ultimatum and turned over a border fortress to the Bulgars. This unfortunate act, in turn, gave the French and British the official excuse they needed.

With the timely help of Allied funds and weapons, Venizelos on August 30 launched an antiroyalist uprising in Salonica. Establishing a revolutionary government in the coastal city, the former prime minister issued an urgent appeal for national support from the Hellenic people. That support was forthcoming mainly in the islands. By the end of 1916, Venizelos had raised a "national defense" army of sixty thousand men. As the revolt gained momentum through the month of December, Queen Sophie frantically dispatched a series of letters to her brother, the kaiser, imploring him to send military help before it was "too late." Indeed, it was already too late. The Allies had impounded the entire royalist navy in the harbor of Piraeus. On December 31, the Western ambassadors demanded that Athens immediately liberate all imprisoned Venizelists and demobilize the royalist army. By spring, Greece was Allied-occupied territory both in name and fact. The nation's fast-waning independence was extinguished altogether in June 1917, when the British and French representatives ordered Constantine to leave the country immediately. The king had no choice but to comply, and departed for Switzerland amid the frenzied lamentations of tens of thousands of his loyal subjects. The throne thenceforth was occupied by Constantine's second son, Alexander (Crown Prince Nicholas was known for his pro-German sentiments). The premiership was once again assumed by Venizelos, whose first act was to reconvene the suspended pro-Allied parliament. On June 29, the chamber of deputies formally declared war against the Central Powers. Notwithstanding the speed and efficiency of these moves, the Greek people in later years would not forget that Venizelos had returned to office with the support and encouragement of French bayonets. Neither would the savagery of Venizelos's retaliation against the royalists be forgotten. Executions were not uncommon, barren islands were transformed into mass concentation camps, mutinies of army reservists and royalist officers were pitilessly suppressed.

In the midst of these tumultuous changes, General Sarrail's staff began enlarging and reorganizing the Greek army for modern warfare. It took time. The schisms of the revolution ran deep; the tradition of oriental indolence was inbred. By the spring of 1918, however, nearly a year later, 200,000 Greek soldiers had finally been trained, re-equipped, and made available for service on the Macedonian front. There, too, remarkably, under the new French commander, General Franchet d'Esperey, they distinguished themselves on the battlefield. On May 30, four Greek regiments took the heights of Skra-Di-Legen, a powerful Bulgarian defensive citadel. In the climactic offensive of September and October, fully 300,000 Greek troops fought hard and well across the Bulgarian frontier, in the process suffering 26,000 casualties. Venizelos cherished and meticulously recorded every tribute from the Allied general staff. Moreover, like the nineteenth-century Italian statesman Cavour, the prime minister found yet another way to stake a claim to Allied gratitude. In the early postwar period a French expeditionary force undertook to block a Soviet offensive in the Ukraine. Venizelos unhesitatingly placed two Greek divisions at this army's disposal. Five hundred additional Greek casualties were sustained in this disastrous venture, for no conceivable strategic advantage to Greece itself, but manifestly for the vital political objective of imposing yet another lien on the statesmen at Paris.

Venizelos Presents His Claims

BY THE OPENING of the Peace Conference, therefore, Venizelos could remind the Allied leaders that his nation had made as significant a contribution to the war effort as had the Czechs, the Poles, or the Serbs. The parallel ended there. Unlike the Czechs, the Poles, and other successor nations, the Greeks were not popular. They conveyed the faint aroma of treachery, the legacy of Constantine and his ample following. Venizelos admitted it. "I fully understand," he wrote Lloyd George on November 2, 1918, "that the promise of the Entente Powers in regard to the concessions to Greece in Asia Minor is not now binding on those Powers, as the promise was made under conditions that Greece has not carried out." But in the same letter, and at the Peace Conference, Venizelos recalled and emphasized his own exertions on behalf of the Allies, and the sizable Greek contribution to the Entente cause after 1917. The prime minister's claim to reward was additionally strengthened, too, by the density of Greek settlement in Turkish and Bulgarian territories, and he based that claim squarely on the Wilsonian ideal of self-determination. In his testimony before the Supreme Council on February 3, 1919, Venizelos informed the assembled delegates that no less than 120,000 Greeks lived in northern Epirus, together with 100,000 in the Dodecanese, 395,000 in eastern Thrace, and 44,000 in western Thrace. These Greek enclaves deserved to be attached to the Kingdom of the Hellenes, the prime minister insisted. On the other hand, Venizelos did not press his demands for Constantinople, despite the city's historic Byzantine associations and the 300,000 Greeks who lived there; he was not interested in provoking a conflict with the Russians in the event Moscow later revived its claim to "Tsargrad." Anyway, once the Thracian hinterland was transferred to integral Greece, the huge Greek minority within Constantinople would probably dominate the city.

But the prime minister reserved his most far-reaching and controversial proposals for the territory east of the Straits. Never more than a breath away from Wilson's Point Twelve, Venizelos launched into an extensive and erudite historical survey of Greek settlement in Asia Minor. As he explained it to the Supreme Council, Greeks had lived along the Aegean and Black Sea coasts as seafarers and traders for centuries even before Alexander the Great, and had actually penetrated

307

as far inland as central Anatolia. Ultimately it was Alexander's conquests, his Hellenization of the East, that stimulated the principal Greek colonization effort. The Hellenistic influence was enlarged and broadened, if not deepened, by the successor Byzantine emperors. The Ottoman conquest of Constantinople in 1453 did not eradicate that influence. On the contrary, the Greeks were entrusted with a wider degree of personal liberty and freedom of movement than any other millet people in the Ottoman realm, for their largest population centers were mercifully distant from the sensitive frontier zone. Maintaining both their cultural vitality and their commercial acquisitiveness, therefore, the Hellenes prospered, becoming the wealthiest merchants and most dependable civil servants in the empire, the privileged governors of the Balkans. Venizelos was not about to minimize the extent or impact of their settlement. He had enlisted the help of an American journalist, Stephen Bonsal, in translating a German travel book rich in descriptions of Greek villages in Asia Minor. Now, before the Supreme Council, the prime minister traced the volume's route from the Mediterranean to the Persian Gulf, dwelling eloquently on the ruins of imperial cities that once had been the densely populated and fecund Hellenic communities of the Kingdom of Ionia, and that currently gave every promise, Venizelos insisted, of a "glorious renaissance." In truth, even then western Asia Minor pulsated with a Greek religious and economic life fully as rich and vital as that in the Old Kingdom itself.

As Venizelos saw it, this modern-day "Kingdom of Ionia" comprised Asia Minor west of a line drawn between Kaszoirzo and the Straits, and included all the Greek islands along the shore. Exclusive of Constantinople, the prime minister declared, no less than 1,132,000 Greeks lived within this compact southwestern enclave. His figure was probably not exaggerated, for even Turkish handbooks admitted a Greek population there of 1,300,000 (including Constantinople), and later an Allied commission of experts placed 509,000 Greeks in the sanjak of Smyrna alone. Yet it was not entirely irrelevant that at least a million Turks lived in the immediate vicinity of Smyrna, and that the territory of western Asia Minor was far from geographically or ethnically contiguous. Just beyond the coastal area a central plateau extended five valleys like fingers from a hand; and in those valleys the Greeks were by no means a majority. Economically, it was hardly possible or feasible to separate the Anatolian plateau and the valleys. Nevertheless, Venizelos proposed to do so.

In his disquisition before the Supreme Council, the prime minister was too astute to minimize the difficulties of Greek separatism. But he observed that the risk of dividing the two peoples was more than counterbalanced by the danger of leaving these Greek communities under Turkish rule. And there he had a point. He documented it by cataloguing the full list of Turkish persecutions since the days of the CUP Revolution of 1908. It was a melancholy account: of cultural strangulation and physical oppression, which, even before the war, had driven tens of thousands of Thracian Greeks into the Old Kingdom for refuge; and then, during the war, the brutal and systematic deportations from the littoral area, the wanton destruction of Greek community life in Gallipoli, on the Hellespont and the coast of the Straits, in the mixed Greek-Armenian vilayets of the northeast. Between 240,000 and 300,000 of these people were herded like animals into the interior, where a fourth of them died of hunger and expossure. The death rate was unquestionably far smaller than that of the Armenians; yet it provided Venizelos with some of his most compelling testimony at the Peace Conference. Even Orlando and Clemenceau, who were not particularly sympathetic to Greek territorial claims, were visibly moved as the recital of grievances was presented.

Venizelos's impact on the statesmen owed no less to his own exceptionally keen intellect and radiant personality. He was fifty-four years old in 1919, a stocky, square-jawed, blue-eyed man, endowed with an almost hypnotic charm (a widower, he kept a string of devoted mistresses throughout Europe), and an unfailing ability to present a case with sweet reason and sensitivity to the mood of his listeners. Nicolson recalled the Cretan's appearance on February 3:

To the Supreme Council in the morning to hear Venizelos deliver his oral statement on his claims. This is a different sort of thing from Bratianu's performance. He begins by bringing with him some fine photographic albums showing the sponge fisheries in the Dodecanese. He says that as they all had his written statement he will not repeat it but merely tell them some stories to illustrate his argument. He talks gaily and simply and they look at his photograph albums which put them in a good temper. He begins by paying a deft compliment to the Italians, which gives a good *stimmung*. He then goes on to Northern Epirus and says that the language test is of little significance. "For instance," he says, "many prominent Greeks . . . speak Albanian in their homes, even as Mr. Lloyd George would speak Welsh to his own grandchildren." L. G. beams at this.

Lloyd George had been impressed by the Greek prime minister's "velocity of mind" long before this particular display of diplomatic adroitness, and he had declared on several occasions that "[Venizelos] was the greatest statesman Greece has thrown up since the days of Pericles." Even Francesco Nitti, the Italian foreign minister during the latter half of the Peace Conference, admitted having "met few men in my career who united to an exalted patriotism such a profound ability as Venizelos. . . . In asking he always had the air of offering, and, obtaining, he appeared to be conceding something."

Notwithstanding these genial initial exchanges between Nitti and the Greek Prime Minister, the Italian delegation took the lead in emphatically and vigorously contesting Venizelos's demands. In regard to eastern and western Thrace, where Britain, France, and the United States enthusiastically favored Greek claims, the Italians expressed their reservations on "ethnic" grounds. And in regard to western Asia Minor, where the other Allies were more equally divided on the region's ethnic predominance, Orlando's and Sonnino's refusal to concede Smyrna to the Greeks was based not on Turkish population statistics, but on Italy's own prior claim to the territory by right of the St.-Jean-de-Maurienne Treaty. To emphasize the point, the Italian fleet maintained an implacable blockade around the Dodecanese; and in northern Epirus, Italian officers organized

Albanian resistance against a possible Greek occupation. The United States delegation shared this opposition to Greek demands in Asia Minor. There was some irony in this stand when contrasted with Wilson's unbudging anti-Italian position on the Fiume issue. Yet Professor William L. Westermann, the American representative on the Greek territorial claims committee, was persuaded that the demography of western Anatolia was essentially Turkish, and that the region therefore ought to remain in Turkish hands. Wilson himself firmly supported this recommendation. Accordingly, the report of March 7 was a standoff: Britain and France supporting Greek claims, the United States and Italy rejecting them. For all his eloquence and charm, Venizelos appeared initially to have obtained little satisfaction for his nation in Asia Minor.

The Smyrna Landing

THE SERIES OF FURTIVE ITALIAN LANDINGS in western Turkey, occurring precisely during the Italo-Allied impasse on the Dalmatian issue, suddenly offered the Greek prime minister his golden opportunity. The ensuing diplomatic developments provided some shockers. On May 6, 1919, when Lloyd George proposed that Venizelos be allowed "to protect his fellow countrymen in Turkey," Wilson astounded his own delegation no less than the Allied statesmen by emphatically concurring. Indeed, the president went so far as to urge that Greek troops be disembarked at once, observing that "the men did not keep in good condition on board ship." Clemenceau raised no objections. The Italian delegation was, of course, not available to protest; it had stormed out of the Peace Conference and entrained for Rome during the Fiume debate. Moreover, legal justification for the measure was swiftly invoked on the basis of Article Seven of the Mudros Armistice, which permitted the Allies "to occupy any strategic points in the event of any situation arising which threatens the security of the Allies." Now, ostensibly, the "threatening" situation had arisen as a consequence of Turkish "unrest" in Greek-inhabited areas. If Venizelos could be persuaded to ship one of his divisions to Asia Minor, the troops would constitute an official Allied force serving under Greek command.

Venizelos required no persuasion. Rather, during the ensuing week, the prime minister was in a near-delirium of excitement, cabling elaborate and interminable orders for the dispatch of the First Greek Division to "Ionia," the appointment of a high commissioner for Smyrna and the recruitment of gendarmes, and sending other, even more extensive and detailed instructions. The landing was scheduled for May 14, and the preparations were carried out in absolute secrecy. It was the Council's intention that the Italians and Turks alike should be presented virtually with a *fait accompli*; although, in the end, Rome and Constantinople were given a bare thirty-six-hours notice. Upon receipt of this Allied pronouncement, Orlando rushed back to the Peace Conference in a state of high dudgeon. But by then matters were out of his hands. On May 14, transports bearing the First Greek Division arrived off the coast of Smyrna, escorted by a sizable flotilla of British, French, and American warships.

In May 1919 the port city of Smyrna and its surrounding hinterland encompassed a mixed Greek and Turkish population of approximately a million. Although neither people represented an absolute majority, the Greeks manifestly dominated the commercial life of the region, and during the centuries of their settlement in southern Turkey they had transformed Smyrna into the most important city in Asia Minor, the natural entrepôt for the agricultural produce of the Anatolian interior. To the north and south of the city, a ridge of hills rose 2,500 feet above the serrated Aegean coast. Within the metropolitan area, Konak, the congested business center, extended to the very limits of the wharves. On the forenoon of May 14, as Admiral Calthorpe led the Allied convoy into the bay, Smyrna's stone houses and shops gleamed whitely in the mild spring sunshine. The local Turkish population watched sullenly as British marines disembarked and occupied the public buildings. Twenty-four hours passed without incident. Then, on the morning of the 15th, the entire Greek division marched down the gangplanks. It was met by a jubilant, uproarious ovation from the awaiting Greek population. Flowers and Hellenic banners waved through the assembled crowds like a field of poppies. Bells chimed in the churches. The local metropolitan and clergy blessed the troops, then fell on their knees weeping before their "liberators."

The mood of rejoicing lasted a bare quarter-hour. As the fifteen thousand Greek troops paraded through the Konak district, a volley of rifle fire from adjoining doors and windows suddenly tore through their ranks. After a moment's initial shock, the soldiers redeployed. A brief, sharp exchange of fire followed. Turkish resistance then ended almost as quickly as it began. At this point, and for the next sixteen hours, the infuriated Greek population took its revenge by looting and pillaging in Turkish neighborhoods. Over four hundred Turkish civilians were killed and wounded, and two thousand other Turks were arrested. The savagery with which the Greek mob killed and destroyed represented, of course, more than a momentary reaction to a sudden provocation. It signified, rather, an explosion of long and painfully repressed ethnocentrism, of anguish finally seething over for generations of humiliating *dhimmi*-status, and for even more gratuitous and brutal persecution at the hands of the CUP during the Balkan and World Wars. Yet even the vengeance exacted at Smyrna was the merest beginning.

In the next three weeks, the Greek division was heavily reinforced by seven additional battalions. Most of the new units were garrisoned in Smyrna, but several cautiously began moving into neighboring communities in the vilayet of Aidin. There they encountered stiff resistance from a number of Turkish nationalist units. Whereupon, on June 5,

Venizelos submitted a formal memorandum to Clemenceau, then president of the Council, describing the ominous situation in southwestern Turkey and requesting permission to extend Greek occupation beyond the Meander River for the purpose of controlling the railroads. Clemenceau did not reply. Nor did he respond to two subsequent appeals in the next week. Finally, on June 23, Venizelos decided to act on his own. He issued the order to Sterghiades, the Greek high commissioner in Smyrna, for an offensive across the river.

The assault in force began immediately. It was completely successful. The Nationalist guerrillas were driven out of Aidin. In addition, with their numbers augmented by the recent arrival of two new divisions, the Greeks were able to push vigorously after the retreating Turks. By mid-July the expeditionary force had invested the entire valley of the Meander and the neighboring valleys of the Kaiston and the Hermon, a much broader occupation than had been envisaged by the Peace Conference. On July 19, therefore, the Supreme Council issued an urgent resolution prohibiting any further advances. By then, too, the Allied statesmen had been strongly influenced by the investigations of an inter-Allied commission which, in mid-July, had tentatively concluded that "the Greek occupation, far from presenting itself as the execution of a *mission civilisatrice,* immediately took on the aspect of a conquest and of a crusade." Indeed, by midsummer the Allies recognized that Venizelos had plainly abused his blank check to "keep order" in the vicinity of Smyrna.

Allied Reconsiderations

ALTHOUGH CURZON and Churchill had warned Lloyd George not to permit the Greek landing, the prime minister had not acted impulsively. It had never been his intention that the new Greek domain should remain an isolated colony on the lip of Asia. Ultimately, he was certain, the French and Italians would be awarded zones abutting, and thereby reinforcing, Smyrna; while the government of the future Turkey would surely be under the direct supervision of the great powers. In any event, if the Armenians, the French, and the Italians were to be granted autonomy or spheres of influence in Turkey (without any "ethnic" justification, in the case of the latter two), how was it possible to refuse the Hellenic communities on the southwestern coast the privilege of self-determination? In the prime minister's mind, it was hardly less than obscene to equate the sensibilities of the Turks— "that human cancer . . . that marauding herd"—with the moral claims of the Greeks, and particularly of Venizelos himself, "one of the greatest modern statemen [who] . . . never promised what he could not perform. Upon that rock could the new Ionia, the new Aegean be triumphantly based." Not least of all, Lloyd George was sure in his own mind that Greece would continue to be largely dependent upon the friendship and support of the strongest naval power in the Mediterranean. He wrote later:

> We could not invariably rely upon the Dardanelles remaining closed to a future Russian fleet. It would thus be of direct British advantage to safeguard our communications with India by placing at the point of immense naval advantage . . . a country whose benevolent neutrality, or even alliance, would, in time of war, be certainly assured to us.

That was the crux of it. The Greek archipelago, with its involuted necklace of vulnerable coastlines, would unquestionably continue to be as dependent upon British naval protection in the twentieth century as it had been in the nineteenth. In fact, with the Turks *hors de combat,* the enlarged Hellenic Kingdom would probably acquire renewed and enhanced importance as a client of British imperial policy in the eastern Mediterranean. Whatever the excesses of the Greek army in the Smyrna region, therefore, Lloyd George was determined not to falter in his support of Venizelos's basic claims.

At the outset, too, Rome managed unwillingly to ensure British support by clumsily undermining the Greek occupation at every chance. Within the city of Smyrna itself, the Italians secured control of the local maritime offices, opened up branches of the Banco di Roma, established dispensaries and a series of newspapers, even subsidized an Italian boy scout organization to compete with the Greek boy scouts. Outside the area of Greek occupation, Italian agents vigorously encouraged the Turkish Nationalist movement. Moreover, as early as May 17, two and a half days after the Greek landing, the Italians disembarked additional troop units on the southwestern coast of Turkey and were soon in possession of the Asia Minor littoral from Scala Nuova to Adalia. Whereupon Lloyd George, provoked by such "insolence," acidly contrasted this Italian aggressiveness with the marked lack of Italian initiative in the war against Turkey. He bluntly warned Orlando that if Italian troops were not removed at once, he would "disinterest" himself entirely in Italian claims in Asia Minor. These views were fully shared by Wilson, who on June 26 suggested that the Italians "should be asked clearly to state whether they remained in the Entente."

Much as he deplored Italian acquisitiveness, Lloyd George was shrewd and compassionate enough to understand the sense of inferiority that motivated Italian behavior: Rome's feeling of "not being treated quite as a great first-class Power." On the very day of the original Greek landing at Smyrna, the British prime minister had proposed a scheme by which Italy might accept a mandate over the Adalia region, the area first outlined in the Treaty of London, but without the elaborate additions of the St.-Jean-de-Maurienne accord. At first, the other statesmen were noncommittal, and Lloyd George was not constrained to press the issue. But in July, reports of Greek abuses in Smyrna persuaded the Supreme Council to reconsider the plan. This new spirit of tentative rapprochement was encouraged by the sudden fall of the Orlando Cabinet in Rome and its replacement by the comparatively moderate Nitti government. Indeed, on July 7, Tittoni, the new Italian foreign minister, intimated his willingness to consider a territorial compromise in Turkey if the Supreme Council did not insist upon the total withdrawal of Italian troops from Asia Minor.

Grateful for a chance to resolve the impasse, the Allied statesmen did not insist. Rather, on July 8, Balfour and Clemenceau instructed General Milne, the British senior officer in Asia Minor, to seek agreement between the Greek and Italian commanders in Turkey on lines beyond which neither would move. Hopefully, the Italians and Greeks would manage to resolve by direct means their unseemly rivalry in the Turkish interior.

It was a not unrealistic hope. For ten days, Tittoni and Venizelos engaged in intensive negotiations, and on July 18 finally announced a meeting of the minds on their "respective zones of demarcation" in Turkey. Italy, they declared, would support Greek claims in eastern and western Thrace, in northern Epirus (southern Albania) and the Dodecanese. Greece, for its part, would recognize an Italian mandate over the rest of Albania. In Asia Minor, the principal area of confrontation, Italy agreed to renounce its claims to Smyrna put forward under the St.-Jean-de-Maurienne agreement; Greece renounced its own maximalist claims in the sanjaks of the Meander Valley. As a guarantee, it was understood that if either of the two nations did not obtain full political endorsement of these demands at the Peace Conference, both would reassume complete "liberty of action." The likelihood that the Western Allies would reject the agreement was quite remote, however. While the Supreme Council dutifully noted on July 21 that "this occupation has only a provisional character corresponding to the actual state of affairs," it was tacitly understood that the Greco-Italian spheres in Asia Minor had been settled in the best possible way, by the protagonists themselves. Only Wilson, who had since returned to the United States, protested this apparently cynical reversion to *Realpolitik*, on August 3. Yet by this time even Balfour had lost patience with the president's moralizing. So had the other members of the Supreme Council. On September 5, they warned the American government that postponement of agreement merely exacerbated the danger of continuing racial strife between Greeks and Turks. No further complaints were heard from Washington.

Turkish Resistance Mounts

IN THEIR ADMONITION to Wilson, the Allies had not exaggerated the perils of mounting violence. The Greek occupation had lashed a wasted, dispirited nation, semicomatose within its ring of enemy bayonets, into a state of outraged wakefulness. The Mudros Armistice, after all, permitted the occupation of integral Turkish soil only under conditions threatening "the security of the Allies," and no Allied officer or diplomat had ever seriously accused the Turks (as distinguished from the Italians) of provoking that kind of situation. Conceivably the Turks might have endured occupation, even illegal occupation, by a powerful and victorious British army; but hardly the ignominy of territorial violation by the Greeks, a former subject people. When the news reached Constantinople on May 16, 1919, the shocked Cabinet immediately submitted its resignation to the sultan. Mass demonstrations and riots occurred throughout the city. Black flags were hung from windows. Women draped themselves in mourning veils; men wore black armbands. Many of the demonstrations and speeches carried strong pietistic overtones; natonality and religion seemed equally affronted by the *dhimmi* invasion.

Mustafa Kemal, hero of Gallipoli, was in the central Anatolian city of Sivas when details of the landing reached him. Although he had been ordered to the interior to supervise the demobilization of the Ottoman army, the general had in fact secretly altered his orders, empowering himself to assume "full military authority" in the event of an emergency. Now the emergency had evidently arisen. Instinctively, Kemal reacted to Greek occupation by ordering an immediate halt to the surrender of arms and ammunition to the Allies. His instructions were carried out with a vengeance. British control officers along the Anatolian Railroad were henceforth ignored, then insulted, and finally chased for their lives or captured and flung into jails. Within a week the weapons dumps passed from British to Turkish control. Kemal meanwhile hurriedly extemporized a fighting front against the Armenians, whose armed forces were gathering under French protection in Cilicia. Indeed, just nine days after his arrival in Anatolia, Kemal had succeeded in initiating a program of general resistance to Greek and Armenian incursions, in issuing an appeal for national solidarity, and simultaneously engineering the establishment of a shadow government in the Anatolian interior.

The response was sluggish at first. The Turks were desperately war-weary. The last exhausted remnants of their army were far off in the eastern part of the country. Many otherwise sympathetic Turkish provincial officials frankly doubted Kemal's abilities as a political leader. These obstacles notwithstanding, the young general was soon joined by other military and civilian associates from Constantinople. Together, on June 19, the dedicated little group issued an appeal for a national "congress" to assemble in Sivas the following September. The purpose of this gathering, it was announced, would be nothing less than the organization of nationwide resistance to the Western invaders, and most particularly to the Greeks. The appeal evoked an astonishingly emotional reaction. By midsummer, despite the forebodings of provincial and local authorities, national defense committees were springing up throughout Anatolia, and during late July and August, province after province in central and eastern Asia Minor fell under the control of Kemal's "Nationalist Party." The military objective, to repel foreign troops, was not as easily achieved, but at least a beginning was made. Weapons and ammunition were unearthed from old army caches. New breechblocks and rangefinders for artillery were constructed out of scrap metal. Other weapons were smuggled in from the Russian Caucasus. Demobilized troops, in rags and frequently barefoot, began to straggle back to their former units.

Meanwhile, Kemal and his close associate Rauf Bey assembled a caucus of supporters in the ruined fortress-city of Erzerum and drew up a party platform there. The Arab portions of the Ottoman Empire would be relinquished, the statement declared, together with unilateral Turkish control over the Straits. But elsewhere Turkish sovereignty would remain inviolate. Thus, integral Turkey would not suffer the amputation of the Armenian vilayets, or of Smyrna, or of Constantinople, or of eastern Thrace. The Capitulations, which for years had provided extralegal status for Western nationals and businesses, would not be restored. It was precisely this "declaration of independence" which was later reaffirmed at the Sivas Congress on September 4, and which was known thenceforth as the National Pact. In addition, the delegates assembled at Sivas repudiated the authority of the Constantinople government. Establishing instead a rival National Assembly, the Congress authorized a permanent executive to sit continuously in the provincial railroad town of Ankara (Angora).

By the autumn of 1919, control of the Anatolian countryside was so manifestly in the hands of Kemal's Nationalist followers that the position of the Damad Farid Cabinet in Constantinople became untenable. It fell on October 5 and was replaced by the pro-Nationalist regime of Ali Riza. The Allies were by then well aware of the ferment in the interior. Nationalist strength and self-assurance were growing in direct proportion to the withdrawal of British military forces. By December, General Milne's "Army of the Black Sea" totaled a paltry 9,836 men, of whom nearly half were garrisoned in the Constantinople area. In Cilicia, the French commanded 13,000 soldiers, and of these the majority were Armenians. Italian troop strength in Adalia did not exceed 7,000 Otherwise, the one sizable "Allied" force in Asia Minor consisted of the 75,000 Greek troops in Smyrna and the Aidin vilayet. "It would be more difficult today than it would have been eight months ago to impose on Turkey a distasteful Peace Treaty," the British high commissioner wrote to Curzon. ". . . Every week that the peace terms are delayed sees further acquisition to the power of resistance which Turkey means to oppose to any 'humiliation' which such terms may impose." Admiral Calthorpe's observation was, if anything, an understatement. The "official" parliament in Constanti-

nople echoed the new mood of national belligerence by overwhelmingly adopting the program of the National Pact on
January 28, 1920.

Meanwhile, in the interior, Kemal was making preparations to translate that mood into action. He struck first in
Cilicia, on January 21. The French had established a humane
and competent administration in this region. Taking over
amid near-famine conditions, they had energetically restored
the economic life of Cilicia's 400,000 inhabitants. Unfortunately for the Christian population, General Dufieux's tatterdemalion defense force of 13,000 men, like the population
of "Little Armenia" itself, consisted for the most part of
refugees. It was pitiably weak. Kemal knew it. Accordingly,
he aimed his two divisions of hard-bitten army veterans
straight for Marash, the capital city of the district, with its
vital granary. The attack was devastatingly effective. In less
than thirty-six hours half of General Dufieux's force was
wiped out, Marash was captured, and its population of 20,000
was slaughtered almost to the last soul. For the Allies, the
shock of this disaster was compounded by the attitude of the
Constantinople government. A large number of regular Turkish army troops had participated in Kemal's attack. When the
Allied high commissioners urgently brought this "treachery"
to the attention of Ali Riza, the prime minister coldly declined
responsibility and insisted instead that it was the Greek
landing that had provoked Turkish military resistance. The
reply seemed unprecedented arrogance on the part of a
defeated nation. Even as the commissioners debated an ap-
propiate response, however, units of Kemal's army raided a
munitions depot on the Gallipoli Peninsula and other troops
crept to the outskirts of Constantinople. On February 6, Admiral de Robeck, Calthorpe's successor as high commissioner,
wired London for permission to take immediate, drastic measures.

The representatives of the Supreme Council, meeting in
London on March 3, agreed that a strong line had to be taken
quickly. "The Turks, like all Orientals, if treated leniently grow

insolent," declared Cambon, the French ambassador. Lloyd George added that "the Allies must make up their minds once and for all either to show the Turk that they could enforce the terms of the Treaty of Peace or decide not to send [forces] in at all." Until 1920 the Turkish capital had been spared more than a token military occupation; Allied forces had been concentrated instead in the vital Straits area. Now, by the unanimous decision of the Supreme Council, more forceful measures were taken. On the night of March 15, General Milne's troops suddenly occupied the telegraph offices in Constantinople, then deployed into the immediate hinterland to isolate the capital from Asia Minor. Simultaneously, brigades of infantry executed a series of lightning raids within the capital, arresting every Nationalist parliamentary deputy they could lay their hands on. By dawn of March 16, most of these legislators were aboard British ships en route to barbed-wire compounds on Malta. The sultan and the rump government learned their lesson well as a consequence of this decisive, if belated, Allied action. They would not give trouble again. Only the population of the Anatolian interior, beyond the grasp of the meager Allied detachments in the capital, remained to be convinced.

The Formulation of the Sèvres Treaty

IN DEALING WITH the newly intransigent Turks, Lloyd George found his task complicated by the uncontrollable fractiousness of his Italian and French allies. It was perhaps not surprising that the virulent Anglo-British dispute over Syria should have affected relations farther north. From the moment when Admiral Calthorpe submitted his armistice ultimatum at Mudros, Paris had bitterly resented the predominance of British influence in Constantinople. In subsequent months, repeated efforts by the French to share General Milne's military authority in Turkey, or at least in the Turkish capital, proved fruitless. The British remained adamant. In the end, the position of the French commander in Constantinople, General

Franchet d'Esperey, became untenable, and he was relieved. The loss of face rankled in Paris. The French by then were quite certain that Britain intended to rule Asia Minor no less single-handedly than it dominated the Arab rectangle. French journalists were continually speculating on an alleged secret "understanding" between London and Constantinople. According to this theory, Britain would enjoy "priority of influence" in Turkey in return for her willingness to guarantee the territorial integrity of the country. No such agreement ever existed, although the Turkish government had occasionally made veiled overtures to London in that direction. With a powerful fleet cruising the Straits at will and a protégé Greek expeditionary force solidly implanted in Asia Minor, the British government hardly required additional clandestine arrangements behind the backs of the other Allies.

Once kindled, however, suspicion of British duplicity was not easily extinguished. It accounted for the opening of exploratory French contacts with the Turkish Nationalists in the autumn of 1919. The initial discussions between Kemal and Georges-Picot took place at Sivas in November, which not significantly productive then, the talks nevertheless represented the Quai d'Orsay's first shift from a harshly punitive approach to the defeated enemy. In January 1920, Millerand shocked Lloyd George by suggesting that the sultan be allowed to remain in Constantinople. "The important thing was to defer to the sensibilities of the Turks," Lloyd George recalled the premier's remark, "who were a most sensitive people and whose prejudices it was desirable to respect." Unspoken, too, in this solicitude was Millerand's awareness of the preponderance of French investments in Constantinople and Asia Minor. French bondholders alone held eighty per cent of the Ottoman debt, and the need for establishing communication with a possible future Nationalist regime was becoming more evident every week. This reappraisal was shared by the new Nitti-Tittoni administration in Italy. The brutal efficiency with which Kemal had conquered Marash raised grave doubts in Rome whether any territorial concession in Turkey could really be protected.

The Italian army was in a state of near-mutiny as it was. Also, once Tittoni had renounced Smyrna to Venizelos, he found his interest in Adalia fading rapidly. Perhaps a commercial zone of influence would be more feasible than a zone of occupation, he speculated, provided it was accessible to Italian military "assistance." If so, the goodwill of the Turkish government, in either Constantinople or Ankara, would be increasingly important.

Lloyd George sensed the growing vulnerability of Britain's position both in Turkey and in the Allied capitals. By mid-winter of 1920 it was as plain to him as to the other Western statesmen that the American government was unwilling to assume responsibilities in Asia Minor (see Chapter XI), and that a Turkish peace treaty could not safely be postponed much longer. The cost of maintaining even a skeletal force in Turkey was becoming insupportable. On February 12, therefore, the Supreme Council (actually the representatives of Britain, France, Italy, and Japan) reconvened, this time in London. The entire conference lasted barely a month, until March 12, and during that period the essential decisions on a Turkish settlement were reached with comparative dispatch. The issue of Constantinople had been resolved even earlier, over the vehement, tearful objections of Curzon. Lloyd George and Balfour, persuaded at last by the arguments of the India Office, had decided in favor of keeping the sultan in Constantinople, although under tight Allied supervision. The decision was unanimously endorsed by the other Allied statesmen. Both the French and the Italians formally renounced any intention of annexing territory in the Turkish interior. In addition, under relentless needling by Lloyd George, Berthelot abandoned the effort to establish a *de facto* French mandate in Cilicia. Instead, the French diplomat accepted a compromise which had first been proposed by Italian Foreign Minister Nitti. In their respective spheres of Cilicia and Adalia, France and Italy would simply enjoy first option for economic investment and priority in supplying advisers for the Turkish police system. The term "advisers" was admittedly flexible; it could and did permit a sizable military or quasi-military force to remain. A final decision was also reached on the smoldering question of Greek territorial acquisitions. By February 20 a rough draft of Greco-Italian spheres of influence was accepted by the Council, essentially on the lines of the original Tittoni-Venizelos agreement.

Within these basic guidelines, six commissions set to work elaborating details of the treaty. Their sessions were long and exhaustive. The completed version was a mosaic of such painstakingly defined items as Turkish navigation and currency rights, the rotation of chairmen on the Straits commission, and the precise angles of a boundary along a river bank. On March 3 the job was completed. The instrument had only to be submitted to the Supreme Council. By chance, the Allied diplomats had scheduled the next Council meeting for mid-April with the purpose of deciding the final allocation of mandates for Arab territories. It was agreed that the Turkish peace treaty would be considered at the same time. The Western diplomats consequently gathered at the Italian resort of San Remo on April 18. During the ensuing eight days, the assignment of the mandates was intensively discussed and successfully consummated (see Chapter IX). So, almost immediately afterward, was the Turkish peace treaty. To be sure, there was the inevitable minor quibbling, mostly by the Italians, on such fine points as the configuration of the Thracian border and the composition of the financial commission. But the basic provisions worked out in London were ratified in San Remo, almost by default. On May 11, in the Parisian suburb of Sèvres, the Supreme Council formally presented the completed document to two melancholy, frock-coated representatives of the Constantinople government.

By the terms of the Sèvres agreement the Turks were obliged to renounce permanently their entire empire, including eastern Thrace, all their former Arab territories, their island possessions in the Aegean, and the territory of Armenia— although the precise boundaries of Armenia were to be left to delimitation by President Wilson. As shall be seen, the Smyrna area was virtually delivered over to the Greeks. Constantinople remained nominally in Turkish hands, but under the strictest Allied control. Turkey's western boundary barely extended beyond the suburbs of the capital, and thus Constantinople was left well within Greek artillery range. Indeed, once the Greeks were assured sovereignty over Gallipoli and western Asia Minor (see p. 327), Constantinople was almost completely isolated from both Europe and Asia, and purposefully transformed into an Allied hostage for Turkish good behavior. The freedom of the historic city was rendered even more palpably fictitious by the internationalization of the Straits. A commission of ten powers was invested with full authority over the entire length of the famous waterway, and this authority included the commission's right to direct shipping, to collect tolls, to operate its own Straits budget, and above all, to ensure that the Straits remained open "in peace and war to all merchant and naval ships and planes without distinction of flag." Finally, Britain, France, and Italy alone possessed the right of maintaining armed forces within and along the shores of the Straits. This last provision was in essence a victory for British sea power, and thus a source of irritation to France and Italy. Nevertheless, the articles relating to the Straits, Constantinople, and eastern Thrace were, by and large, the least unsatisfactory part of the Sèvres Treaty. They represented an honest and intelligent attempt to dispose of a chronically festering international sore spot.

The lengthiest tractate of the Sèvres Treaty dealt with the remainder of integral Turkey, and it imposed so elaborate a grillwork of restrictions and servitudes on the country as to extinguish its sovereign independence in fact if not in name. As in the case of the other defeated enemy states, the size of the Turkish armed forces was severely limited. In this instance, however, the financial and juridical clauses of the treaty were much tougher than those imposed on Germany, Austria, Hungary, and Bulgaria. An Allied commission now supervised the annual Turkish budget and exercised absolute veto power over all public expenditures. The Capitulations were restored in their entirety. Still another Allied commission ensured that members of millet peoples (i.e., Greeks, Armenians, and Arabs) still remaining in Turkish territory, as well as nationals of other countries, were exempted from the jurisdiction of Turkish courts. Thus, in Smyrna, Adalia, and Cilicia the minority races actually could opt for Greek, Italian, or French citizenship, and thereby presumably enjoy full extraterritorial privileges. Two of these three regions were parceled out in a separate but associated Tripartite Pact among Britain, France, and Italy. By its terms, a sphere of "special interest" was allocated to Italy in, roughly, the southwestern part of Asia Minor outside the Smyrna area, and to France in Cilicia. The "special interest," as has been seen, allowed priority of investment and advisers in these zones, and administrative and police "assistance." The latter measure presumably did not exclude the maintenance of limited French and Italian military forces on Turkish soil; in any event, French and Italian troops did not initially withdraw following the conclusion of the tripartite agreement. The pact represented a half-hearted attempt on the part of France and Italy to acquire the benefits promised them in the Secret Treaties, crossed with a British effort to secure additional protection for minorities as a *quid pro quo*. Actually, this humiliating instrument was of dubious legality, for Turkey was neither consulted nor asked to sign it; she was simply ignored.

It was reserved for Greece, a nation that had not dispatched a single soldier to fight the Turks in the World War, to emerge as the principal territorial legatee of the Turkish partition. The augmentation was impressive: western Thrace (transferred by Bulgaria to the Allies, and by the Allies to Greece); eastern Thrace to the very limits of Constantinople itself; the Gallipoli Peninsula; the islands of Imbros and Tenedos, guarding the entrance to the Straits, and other neighboring islands; the Dodecanese chain of islands (by special arrangement with Italy), steppingstones to Smyrna. Finally, there was the Smyrna zone itself, surely the most vital accession, embracing both the city and its immediate hinterland,

and thus nearly the entire vilayet of Aidin. The frontiers, observing the limits of the Venizelos-Tittoni agreement, were artificial, cutting across river valleys and railroads at right angles and bearing little relation to the distribution of nationalities. The legal terms of the grant were no less artificial. Formally, Turkish sovereignty in the Smyrna area was not abolished, but merely "suspended." The Athens government would simply be "responsible" for the administration of the enclave, and Turks living there would be "treated as" Greek nationals, with their rights ostensibly protected by a minorities treaty signed both by Greece and the Allies. This terminology, of course, was simply a euphemism for Greek sovereignty. The Smyrna region unquestionably encompassed several hundred thousand Greeks, but the Turkish inhabitants were no less numerous. Moreover, of all the Greeks resident in Anatolia in 1920, two thirds lived outside the Smyrna zone altogether, and many of them resided in areas, such as Trebizond, far less integrally intertwined with the surrounding Turkish economy. The sanjak of Smyrna represented nothing less than the authentic wealth of Asian Turkey. It was the second largest manufacturing community in the nation, and Anatolia's major outlet on the Mediterranean, accounting for forty-five per cent of the imports of the Ottoman Empire. The ultimate consequences of its amputation from the Turkish hinterland were incalculable.

Venizelos was perfectly aware of the magnitude of his accomplishment; but he also appreciated the debt he owed Lloyd George. "The British prime minister declared to me that he was happy having succeeded in winning for Greece Smyrna," Venizelos wrote to his colleagues in Athens on February 16, 1920, "and he added that on this question he had to fight not only against the French premier [Millerand], who favored only a sphere of economic influence, but also against his own foreign secretary [Curzon]." At the close of the San Remo Conference, Venizelos opened his heart to his patron: "I feel . . . that I am quite unable to give adequate support to my feelings, for indeed, all that Greece has now realised of her legitimate claims,

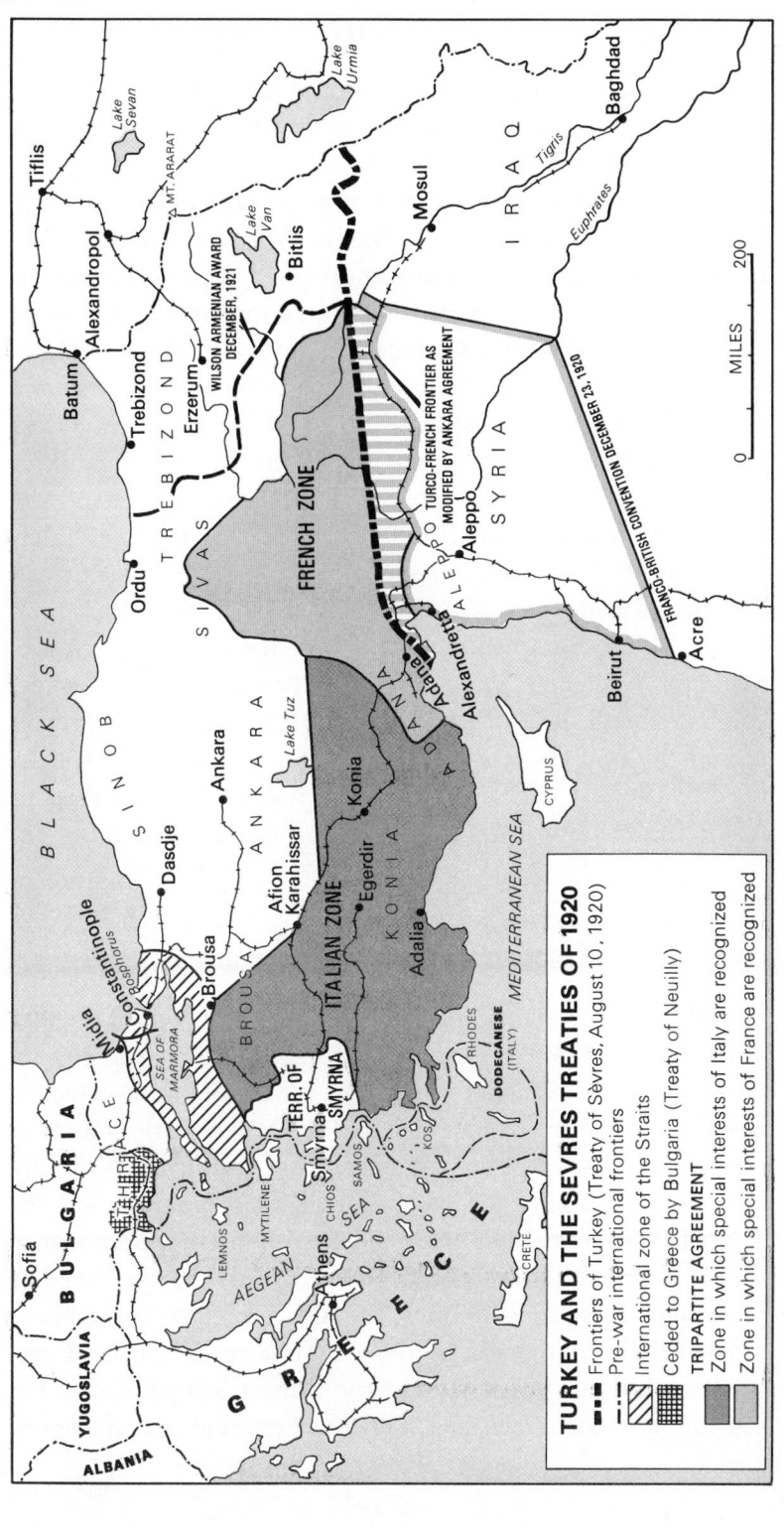

TURKEY AND THE SEVRES TREATIES OF 1920

━━━ Frontiers of Turkey (Treaty of Sèvres, August 10, 1920)
━·━·━ Pre-war international frontiers

▨ International zone of the Straits

▦ Ceded to Greece by Bulgaria (Treaty of Neuilly)

TRIPARTITE AGREEMENT

▨ Zone in which special interests of Italy are recognized

▨ Zone in which special interests of France are recognized

MILES

0   200

Baghdad

IRAQ

Tigris

Euphrates

Mosul

Tiflis

Lake Sevan

Alexandropol

MT. ARARAT

Lake Urmia

Batum

Lake Van

Bitlis

WILSON ARMENIAN AWARD DECEMBER, 1921

Trebizond

Erzerum

TURCO-FRENCH FRONTIER AS MODIFIED BY ANKARA AGREEMENT

SYRIA

T R E B I Z O N D

Ordu

S I V A S

FRENCH ZONE

Aleppo

A L E P P O

FRANCO-BRITISH CONVENTION DECEMBER 23, 1920

Acre

Beirut

B L A C K   S E A

S I N O B

Ankara

A N K A R A

Lake Tuz

Dasdje

A
D
A
N
A

Adana

Alexandretta

CYPRUS

Konia

Afion Karahissar

Egerdir

K O N I A

Adalia

MEDITERRANEAN SEA

Constantinople

BOSPHORUS

Brousa

B R O U S A

ITALIAN ZONE

SEA OF MARMORA

Midia

BULGARIA

Sofia

T H R A C E

TERR. OF SMYRNA

Smyrna

RHODES

DODECANESE (ITALY)

KOS

SAMOS

CHIOS

MYTILENE

LEMNOS

A E G E A N   S E A

CRETE

Athens

G R E E C E

YUGOSLAVIA

ALBANIA

is due in major part to your powerful and effective support, and no words of mine can efficiently express my country's deep sense of thankfulness to you."

But of course Lloyd George was no philanthropist. With Gallipoli and Thrace in Greek hands, Britain possessed a European land approach to Constantinople. Greek occupation of Imbros and Tenedos assured Britain control of the mouth of the Dardanelles. With a dependent client state all but dominating the Turkish capital, London hardly required a Straits commission to ensure that the British fleet would enjoy free access to the Black Sea, and consequently to the vulnerable flank of the Russian southwestern coast. From their base in Persia, too, the British enjoyed the right of transit through the "internationalized" port of Batum to Soviet Russia's other, southeastern flank. Plainly, Russia not less than Turkey had been victimized by the Allied peace treaties. It was an exalted moment for Whitehall. The Sèvres partition of integral Turkey, combined with the San Remo award of Arab mandates, represented the impressive high-water mark of Britain's power in the Middle East. Hers was now the magisterial influence in Asian affairs from Constantinople to the gates of China.

Venizelos Enforces a Signature

WHEN, AT SÈVRES, the Turkish delegates received the text of the treaty, on May 11, 1920, they had their first opportunity to examine its contents carefully. What they saw shocked them mute. It was a reaction shared by Damad Farid, returned not long before as prime minister, who obtained the text by telegram. Regaining his composure several hours later, the Turkish statesman met with the British high commissioner to plead humbly for modification of the treaty's harsher provisions. After consultations, the Allied foreign ministers expressed their willingness to allow a Turk on the Straits Commission. It was a concession of the utmost insignificance. On the fundamental provisions, Lloyd George and his colleagues held firm. Whereupon Damad Farid bitterly denounced the treaty and refused to sign it. Curzon's reaction was swift and remorseless. Unless the Turkish government quickly signed the document, he warned, the Supreme Council would reconsider its decision to leave the sultan in Constantinople.

This Allied self-assurance was severely tested less than three weeks later. The moment the terms of the peace treaty were revealed, the commander of Turkish regular forces in eastern Thrace declared his army's independence of Constantinople and his allegiance thenceforth to the Nationalist cause. Tens of thousands of other Turkish soldiers and civilans rushed to join the Nationalist forces. Emboldened by this support, Kemal decided to risk his makeshift army in an audacious stroke. Early in June he sent ten thousand men in two columns marching directly on Constantinople. The regiments converged first on the Ismidt area of the Bosporus. In Pera and Galata, the Greek quarters of the capital, news of Kemal's sudden advance struck horror through the entire population. Instead, the panic soon became uncontrollable, as many of the inhabitants interpreted the slightest noise in the night as an "intense cannonade" or an "extraordinary fusillade," and conjured up visions of a new Hamidian massacre. There was ample reason for terror. In the Ismidt peninsula less than two thousand British marines faced a concentration of at least five times as many Turks; it was evident that the British could not defend this crucial point of access alone. Additional Allied troops were stationed in Constantinople, but barely enough to maintain order in the city itself.

These were the circumstances that impelled Lloyd George once again to send for Venizelos. For twenty months the Greek premier had kept the equivalent of fifteen divisions in readiness on the Thracian frontier. In February 1920, the general headquarters of the entire Hellenic army were shifted from Salonica to Smyrna. Venizelos did not disguise his impatience to use this force. On January 22, in a private dinner with Wilsons' adviser, Colonel House, he had expressed himself vigorously:

Flesh and blood, not even Greek flesh and blood, can stand further delay in the approach toward a settlement of our problems. For six months now we have had two hundred and fifty thousand men mobilized and in the field at the request, I might even say at the order, of the Allies. This has cost us millions upon millions of drachmas which we haven't got, which we have borrowed and shall have to repay. Mobilized, yes; but mobilized for what? We are not told. . . .

Venizelos envisaged more for this army than its use as an occupation force in the Smyrna area. On a number of occasions he stated frankly to Lloyd George his hope and expectation that Greece would obtain new and extensive advantages. He had in mind, for example, a Federal State of Pontic-Armenia, as an extension of the Smyrna frontier north from the Gulf of Endremid, and perhaps ultimately *de facto* possession of Constantinople itself.

But in the summer of 1920, Lloyd George contemplated a rather more limited objective for the Hellenic forces. Summoning the Greek prime minister to the French resort village of Hythe, on June 20, he desired to know only if Greek troops were available to block the Turkish threat to Ismidt. As always, Venizelos was reasonable, precise, and helpful. "I take the responsibility," he confidently assured Lloyd George, "not only of sending a division to the English at Ismidt, but of wiping out the Kemalist army which faces us on our front [near Smyrna], and of guaranteeing the entire coast of Marmora against Kemal's incursion. . . ." The military advisers of the Supreme Council, however, did not share Venizelos's confidence. Both Marshal Foch and General Sir Henry Wilson warned that punitive expeditions against the dedicated Kemalist army, with its interior lines of communication, risked disaster; the memory of Cilicia was still fresh in their minds. Winston Churchill echoed these misgivings to Lloyd George. But the prime minister would not be dissuaded. "You must decide whom you are going to back," he explained to Lord Riddell. "The Turks nearly brought about our defeat in the war. . . . You cannot trust them and they are a decadent race. The

Greeks, on the other hand, are our friends, and they are a rising people. . . . Of course the military are against the Greeks. . . . The military are confirmed Tories. It is the Tory policy to support the Turks. They hate the Greeks." Thereupon, on June 21, the other Allied statesmen rather hesitantly endorsed the invitation for Venizelos to unleash his soldiers. It was not, after all, entirely in French and Italian interests that the Nationalists should take possesion of Constantinople, slaughtering Christians again and seriously endangering foreign investments.

Accordingly, on June 23, an entire Greek army, well equipped and well trained, suddenly emerged from its entrenched camp dominating the Smyrna enclave. Its success was electrifying. General Nider, commanding the Greek First Corps, thrust straight down the Valley of the Meander with two divisions. There his troops encircled and virtually annihilated a large Kemalist force at Philadelphia on June 23–4, inflicting fully ten thousand casualties on the Turks. Between July 2 and July 8 three Greek divisions encircled a combined force of twenty thousand Turkish regulars and Nationalists in the Panderma-Brousa region, cut them to pieces, then drove on to Panderma, and finally to Brousa itself, the Turkish capital in medieval times. In Thrace, another Greek army corps, pushing forward toward Adrianople, engaged a regular Turkish army division, led by General Djafer Tayar. The Turks conducted a resistance of exceptional gallantry, contesting the Greek advance house by house, yard by yard. The city did not fall until Djafer Tayar himself was wounded and captured. Afterward, on July 24, the Greeks launched savage reprisals that did not exclude the gutting of Adrianople's historic mosques. In his imaginative, precisely executed campaign of hardly more than three weeks, General Paraskevopoulos, the Greek chief of staff, had apparently smashed the hard core of Turkish resistance and vindicated the fondest hopes of Lloyd George and Venizelos. On July 26, King Alexander and his ministers made a ceremonal entry into Adrianople.

News of the Greek victories, the capture of Adrianople

333

and Brousa, were joyously welcomed in Athens. Flags were hung from every window and balcony. *Te Deums* were sung in churches. "I do not think there is now a single paper which does not claim Constantinople for Greece," the British ambassador wrote, "and most of them are already talking of the move from Athens to Constantinople." Rendered almost euphoric by these triumphs, Lloyd George addressed the Commons on July 29, paying a highly emotional tribute to the "superb *élan* and courage of the Greek race. Even the chagrined and embittered Turkish Grand Vizier, Damad Farid, could see the handwriting on the wall. Less than a week after the capture of Adrianople, he summoned eighty prominent deputies to the Yildiz Kiosk and asked them to ratify the Allied peace terms (the Ottoman parliament was not in ession). The deputies remained silent. Cursing them furiously, Farid then and there declared the terms duly accepted on his own authority. On August 10, he dispatched three representatives to sign the Treaty of Sèvres. Actually it was a cluster of treaties, negotiated variously among Turkey, the Allies collectively, Britain, Bulgaria, Greece, Italy, and Armenia, and covering all phases of territorial concessions and minority guarantees. As far as Athens, London, and Constantinople were concerned, however, the major provisions were those that established the Greek Empire. Venizelos had good reason to be satisfied with his ten years of strenuous diplomacy. In the course of that decade, four million Greeks had been liberated and the territory of Greece had been doubled, with the promise of yet additional territory to come. Far from resuming its earlier role as a constricted little Balkan state, the Kingdom of the Hellenes was hardly less now than a front-rank Middle Eastern power, its domains extending from the Adriatic to the Black Sea.

It was a political triumph well timed for home consumption, as well. Venizelos had been absent from Greece for nearly two years, and under the oppressive administration of his deputy, Emanuel Repoulis, royalist sentiment among the traditionally mercurial Greek population had threatened to boil over once more. Much of that opposition was now dissipated by the spectacular military and diplomatic victories of recent weeks. It was as a measure of desperation, therefore, two days after the signing of the Sèvres Treaty, that a band of Greek naval officers attempted to shoot Venizelos down as he entered Paris's Gare du Lyon on his way back to Athens. The prime minister's bullet wounds were not serious, however, and within a fortnight he was able to board the cruiser *Averov* at Marseille for his return home. As the vessel docked in Piraeus harbor—the port of Athens—two days later, Venizelos looked out on a sea of humanity: cheering, flag-waving, leaping, surging forward in joy and adulation. A crowd of 400,000 adoring followers escorted him in his open landau through the central thoroughfare of the capital. A 101-gun salute announced his entrance into Parliament Square. And when Venizelos entered the Chamber itself, he was mobbed by hundreds of weeping deputies, grappling furiously for the honor of kissing his hand. The hoarse, roaring crescendo did not stop for forty minutes. It was a moment of supreme vindication for a once impoverished, provincial Cretan lawyer who, in the course of a generation of unremitting and impassioned Hellenic patriotism, had all but single-handedly revived a forgotten empire for his people.

CHAPTER XI

ARMENIA
AND AMERICA

"Independent" Armenia

OF ALL THE SUBJECT NATIONALITIES in the Middle East, —Arabs, Jews, Greeks—none evoked as heartfelt a moral commitment from the West as the Armenians, for none had been as pitiably ravaged, nor the object of more frustrated Christian compassion. To be sure, the Mudros Armistice had liberated the territory of Russian Armenia from the invading Ottoman armies. At the same time the Allied nations, shaken to their depths by the well-publicized accounts of the massacres (see pp. 103–6 above), supplied vast quantities of charitable funds to help revive the Armenian Republic's near-moribund economy and sustain its ramshackle parliamentary government. But in the immediate postwar era, even this massive infusion of philanthropy from abroad could not protect the self-proclaimed nation, glutted with nearly half a million refugees from the Turkish provinces, from the incursions of famine and epidemic. Under these circumstances of unparalleled physical desperation, it was all the more remarkable that this unstable, isolated little Transcaucasian successor state, bordered by hostile Georgian and Azerbaijani neighbors, should have had the temerity to lay claim to a vast stretch of land beyond its own borders. Nevertheless, the country's redoubtable president, a physician and veteran Dashnak politician named Khatissian, conceived of Erivan as the Piedmont of a Greater Armenia, the homeland not only of its own Russian Armenian citizens, but the nucleus, as well, of a state embracing the entire desolated Armenian people on both sides of the Russo-Turkish frontier.

At the Paris Peace Conference this not immodest demand was articulated by representatives of Ottoman and Russian Armenia alike. Their joint spokesman, the distinguished Erivan poet, Avetis Aharonian, formally presented his people's case before the Supreme Council on February 26. Citing the figures of the (maximal) prewar Armenian population and the bald statistics of the nation's genocide, Aharonian emphasized that his people were not asking for vengeance, but for the simple right to a home of their own which should be both independent and viable; the "martyred" corpses of the Armenian people "cried out from the very earth" for this assurance to their survivors. The Allied statesmen were visibly moved. They listened, too, without dissent as the full spectrum of Armenian territorial claims was submitted. It included the seven eastern Ottoman vilayets of Van, Bitlis, Diarbekir, Kharput, Sivas, Erzerum, and Trebizond, and the four Cilician sanjaks of Narash, Sis, Djebel-Bereket, and Adana, including Alexandretta. With the joinder of these provinces to the Erivan state, the new Greater Armenia would extend from the Russian Caucasus to the Straits of Alexandretta in the Mediterranean Sea, and from the Caspian to the Black Sea.

It was a formidable demand, rather in the nature of a quest for ancient, semimythic imperial boundaries. A man like Venizelos, soliciting Allied approval for a revived "Kingdom of Ionia," could appreciate both the imagination and the realism of Aharonnian's claims. Indeed, the two men warmly supported each other's positions, each cherishing the prospect of a friendly neighbor in Asia Minor. The Turks, of course, viewed with unmitigated horror the possible amputation of a third of their homeland. To forestall this move, Constantinople made the Dashnak government a flat offer of autonomy for the Ottoman Armenian vilayets. The proposal was rejected out of hand. To counteract rumors of a possible future compromise, moreover, the Dashnak parliament, on May 28, 1919, proclaimed the "indissoluble" unity of Russian and Turkish Armenia under the republican government in Erivan. By implication, it remained only for the Supreme Council to confirm this union and to delineate the Armenian boundaries more specifically.

There was never any doubt of Allied goodwill. As early as January 30, 1919, the Peace Conference had resolved unanimously that both the Armenian and the Arab territories "must be completely severed from the Turkish Empire." Even with the boundaries of Armenia still in limbo, therefore, the Supreme Council decided on January 19, 1920, to recognize the *de facto* independence of the united Armenian Republic "on the clear understanding [in Curzon's words] that this does not prejudice the ultimate delimitation of Armenia. . . ." For here was the crux of the difficulty. Where and how could those boundaries realistically be set? The most extreme of Armenian demands could not be recognized, if only because Cilicia had been allocated as a French sphere of influence. Elsewhere, in the former Armenian vilayets of eastern Turkey, only small, isolated communities of Armenians remained alive. The tragic paradox was that Armenia's claim to this territory was based on the virtual extinction of the region's former inhabitants. Of the approximately 845,000 Ottoman Armenians still alive, fully half a million were refugees in Erivan; the rest survived as fugitives in the Arab world or under French protection in Cilicia. Eastern Anatolia itself was little more than a wasteland. The area was swarming with discharged Turkish soldiers by the spring of 1919, and later with Kemalist troops who, largely by default, occupied and exploited thousands of abandoned Armenian homesteads.

The European Allies were at least partly responsible for Turkish reoccupation of these lands. None of the Western powers evinced the slightest desire to guard a territory of such forbidding inaccessibility and destitution. Rather, they had cordially acquiesced in 1915–16 when the Russians had insisted on attaching eastern Anatolia to the tsarist empire (see Chapter VI). The region possessed few natural resources and did not

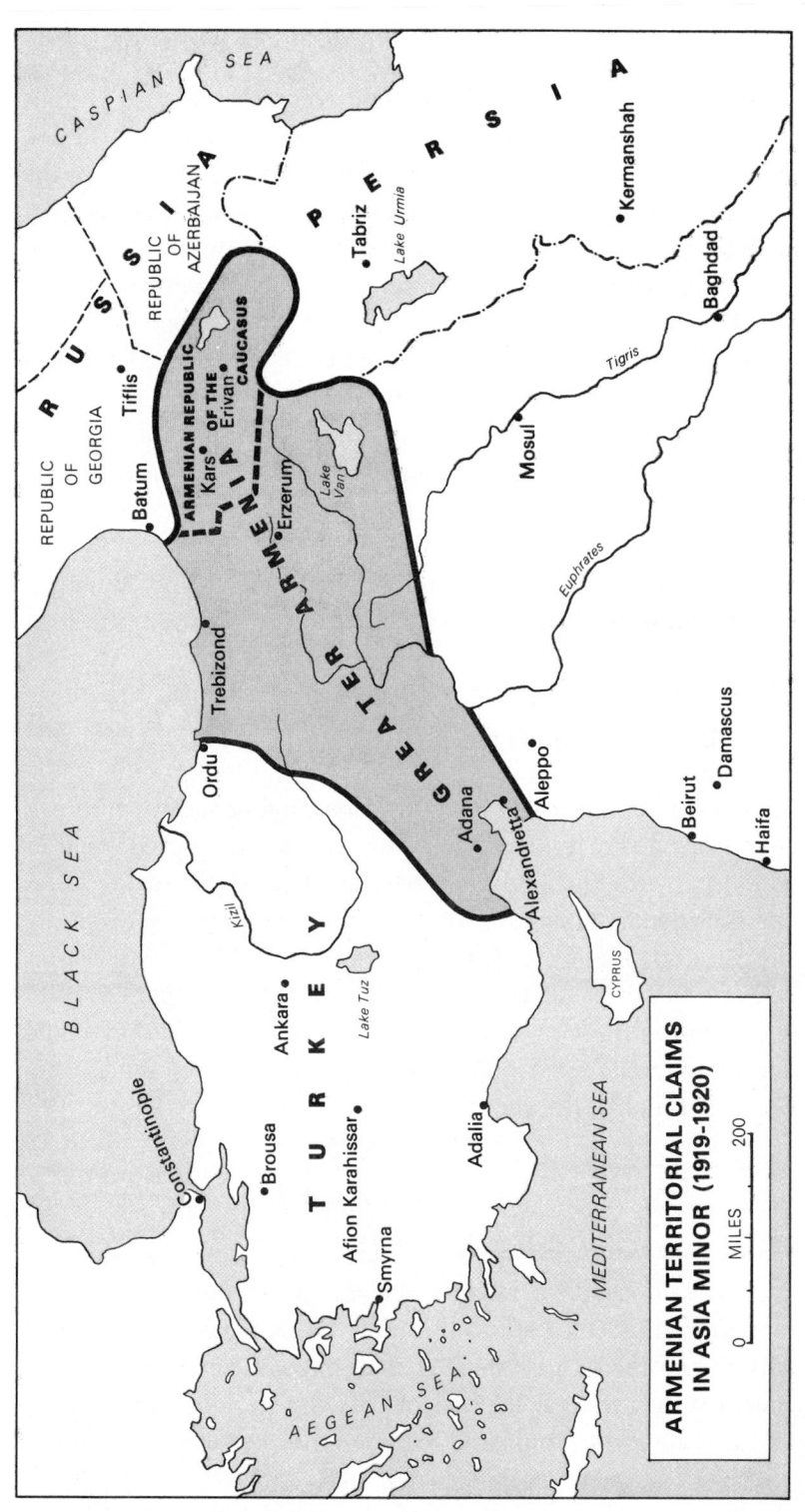

RUSSIA

CASPIAN SEA

REPUBLIC OF GEORGIA

Tiflis

Batum

REPUBLIC OF AZERBAIJAN

PERSIA

Tabriz

Lake Urmia

Kermanshah

Baghdad

Tigris

ARMENIAN REPUBLIC OF THE CAUCASUS

Kars

Erivan

GREATER ARMENIA

Erzerum

Lake Van

Mosul

Euphrates

Aleppo

Damascus

Beirut

Haifa

Trebizond

Ordu

Adana

Alexandretta

BLACK SEA

Kizil

TURKEY

Ankara

Lake Tuz

CYPRUS

MEDITERRANEAN SEA

Constantinople

Brousa

Afion Karahissar

Smyrna

Adalia

AEGEAN SEA

**ARMENIAN TERRITORIAL CLAIMS
IN ASIA MINOR (1919-1920)**

0   MILES   200

impinge on any historic Western interest. Britain and France had staked out their own claims in the Arab world and Cilicia; the Italians and Greeks had won promises of acquisitions in the Turkish littoral area. If, then, the region was to be garrisoned, revived, and somehow transformed into an autonomous Armenian homeland, the Allies were far more intent upon persuading the United States to accept this task than upon carrying it out themselves. From their own point of view, what safer buffer could possibly be found between Russia and their own mandated territories than an American protectorate? The invitation to assume this responsibility, addressed to Wilson officially by the Supreme Council on January 30, 1919, and privately by Lloyd George throughout February and March, referred loftily to America's unique "disinterest" and "prestige" in the Middle East; or else, in Lloyd George's warning of June 26, to the danger that Armenia might fall into the "wrong hands" (Turkish? Russian? Italian?). At the outset, the President appeared unimpressed by the offer (see Chapter X) and disinclined to accept it. On the other hand, the Supreme Council was equally unimpressed by Wilson's public lack of interest; they were aware that privately he was discussing the matter seriously with his advisers (see pp. 352–3). The day after the President's departure for America, therefore, on June 29, the Western statesmen formally notified Turkey's emissaries at Paris that a peace treaty would have to be postponed "until such time as the United States could state whether they could accept a mandate for a portion of the territory of the former Turkish Empire."

The Origins of American Interests
in the Middle East

In choosing to ignore Wilson's disclaimers of interest in Turkey, the Allied statesmen were by no means preoccupied with the national interests of their own countries alone. On the contrary, they were well aware of the existence of certain important and long-standing American commitments in Asia Minor.

Those commitments, interestingly enough, bore no relationship whatever to *Realpolitik*. For example, neither Turks nor Armenians appeared likely agents for American penetration of the Middle East, as Maronites, Jews, and Arabs fulfilled a similar purpose for the French and British. By the same token, American trade with the Ottoman Empire had been less than negligible during the nineteenth and early twentieth centuries. American political interests in the region were equally nonexistent. Far from reflecting self-interest, American commitments in southwestern Asia were exclusively those of religious public service and philanthropy. Since the latter part of the nineteenth century, the missionary activities of the Congregational Church had exerted a more far-reaching influence on American-Turkish relations than any other single factor. From its headquarters in Boston, the American Board of Commissioners for Foreign Missions subsidized an extensive network of philanthropic institutions throughout the Ottoman Empire. These included nine hospitals, forty-two out-patient clinics, and over six hundred primary and secondary schools attended by 25,000 students (in 1914) in Turkey, Syria, and Palestine. Additionally, two leading institutions of higher learning in Turkey, Robert College and Constantinople College for Women, were directed and staffed by Congregationalist missionaries, as were six junior colleges in Asia Minor. To be sure, the schools were attended primarily by the children of Christian millet peoples, the Armenians and Greeks, but the Americans maintained excellent rapport with the Moslem population as well. Their clinics and hospitals were open to all. Their station treasuries served as free banks of deposit for Turkish farmers. By any standards, then, American interests in Turkey were almost self-consciously altruisic. "I gave my chief attention to encouraging the work of the Christian missionaries," Henry Morgenthau wrote of his tenure as ambassador, "and spreading the gospel of Americanism."

This amiable and mutually tolerant relationship between Americans and Turks, as exemplified in the benign efforts of a Jewish ambassador to encourage Christian missionary work, was jeopardized within months after the outbreak of the war by the systematic Turkish murder of the Armenian people. We recall (Chapter IV) that American missionaries were the first to document the massacres in 1915. Their accounts, widely publicized both in the American press and in the later Bryce Report, set off a chain reaction of mass-sympathy meetings in some of the largest cities of the United States. President Wilson was deluged by tens of thousands of letters from individuals and religious organizations, imploring his intervention on behalf of the victims. It was a not unnatural reaction. In the entire contemporary Western experience no precedent existed for a martyrdom of this scope and brutality. To the Christian citizens of the United States, the ordeal of the Armenians revived historical memories of catacomb and gladiatorial arena. It was a twentieth-century Passion. As a result, the American response owed less to traditional generosity than to religious consecration. It was in that spirit, too, that the president repeatedly interceded with the Ottoman government to end the killing. The effort was in vain. "It makes me sick at heart," Wilson wrote Cleveland Dodge, "and yet, unfortunately . . . there is apparently nothing that it is possible for us to do." There was much the United States could do unofficially, however. At Morgenthau's instigation in August 1915, and with the president's ardent support, a charitable fund, the Near East Relief (originally the Armenian and Syrian Relief), was organized for the victims of Turkish persecution. Within months the charity's list of sponsors included the most respected names in American religious and political life.

Rarely in history did an appeal for voluntary contributions evoke so instantaneous and heartfelt an outpouring of public generosity. Rallies for the Near East Relief packed New York's Amsterdam Opera House, the Philadelphia Stadium, Detroit's Billy Sunday Tabernacle, and other arenas in some of the nation's largest cities. Telegrams from President Wilson and Theodore Roosevelt, impassioned speeches delivered by Morgenthau, by Rabbi Stephen Wise, Bishop Greer, Secretary of State Bryan, senators, mayors, and congressmen exhorted huge audiences to give of themselves without stint or mercy. Broadway and film actors marched down Fifth Avenue in the vanguard of giant Near East Relief parades. The entire proceeds of the Harvard-Yale football game of 1916 were donated to the fund. A Congressional Resolution of October 22, 1916, officially designated one Sunday of every year as Near East Relief Day, and fifty thousand churches throughout the United States took up collections. By then the cause of the "starving Armenians" had become the talisman of American compassion. Some of the contributions came in blocks of unprecedented size for those days: $150,000 from the Rockefeller Foundation, $30,000 from the Guggenheim Fund, $75,000 from a rally at the New York Hippodrome, gifts of $10,000 and $5,000 each from several hundred wealthy families; and other, modest donations from hundreds of thousands of private citizens. In 1915, $6,000,000 was raised, in 1916, $20,-000,000.

The funds were promptly transmitted to the U.S. embassy in Constantinople, which, in turn, ensured their distribution through the various consuls and missionaries in the interior. The Turkish government did not obstruct the effort; the money, averaging better than $100,000 a month by 1917, was a valuable stimulus to the nation's sagging economy. By that year, too, some half-million Armenians, Syrians, and Jews had managed to remain alive on the Near East Relief's primitive staples. Even larger numbers of refugees would have been saved if American-Turkish diplomatic relations had not been severed on April 20, 1917, following the U.S. declaration of war on Germany. The American government was soon under heavy pressure to declare war on Turkey, as well. It is significant that Wilson resisted this popular demand largely out of concern for the missionaries and their relief work. But American forbearance by then made little practical difference in the rescue effort. The Turks, quite hostile now, choked off all funds to the interior. During 1918, and particularly in the final months of the war, the tiny skeletal group of thirty-six missionaries was itself reduced to near-starvation.

It was nevertheless the survival of this little caretaker force which soon after the Mudros Armistice made possible a dramatic revival of the rescue effort. On January 2, 1919, three ocean liners chartered by the Near East Relief and packed with food and medical supplies departed New York for Constantinople. The ships were forerunners of a philanthropic campaign which, in scope and generosity, would dwarf even the prodigious fund-raising drives of 1915–17. The methods were essentially the same: mass meetings, public parades, endorsements by political figures, clergymen, and film actors. This time, too, the Near East Relief's quota for the year, $30,000,-000, was oversubscribed in less than three months. As before, the well-experienced missionaries of the American Board were responsible for distributing the relief supplies. In the course of 1919 and 1920, however, it became increasingly evident that the rescue effort would no longer be concentrated in Turkey proper, but would be focused rather on Erivan, in former Russian Armenia. There the largest numbers of refugees were gathered, a half-million of them still hanging on, ragged, starving, exposed to the elements. Thousands of these pathetic victims died in the first winter (1919), notwithstanding the most strenuous and heroic efforts by workers of the NER. The majority barely managed to survive. At the blackest period of the crisis, in 1919, supplementary food and medical supplies were also forthcoming from the American Relief Administration, a U.S. government agency, directed in Russian Armenia by Colonel William Haskell. Even then, however, the money and most of the staff continued to be provided by the Near East Relief. By 1921, the Soviet authorities were cooperating fully in the rescue effort. In Russian Armenia between 1920 and 1929, the Near East Relief was permitted to operate 63 hospitals with 6,552 beds, 11 rescue homes, and 229 orphanages accommodating 54,000 children. The period of acute emergency eased only in the late 1920's, with the gradual integration of the refugees into the surrounding economy. Not until 1929 was the Near East Relief officially terminated. During its fourteen-year existence it had raised and

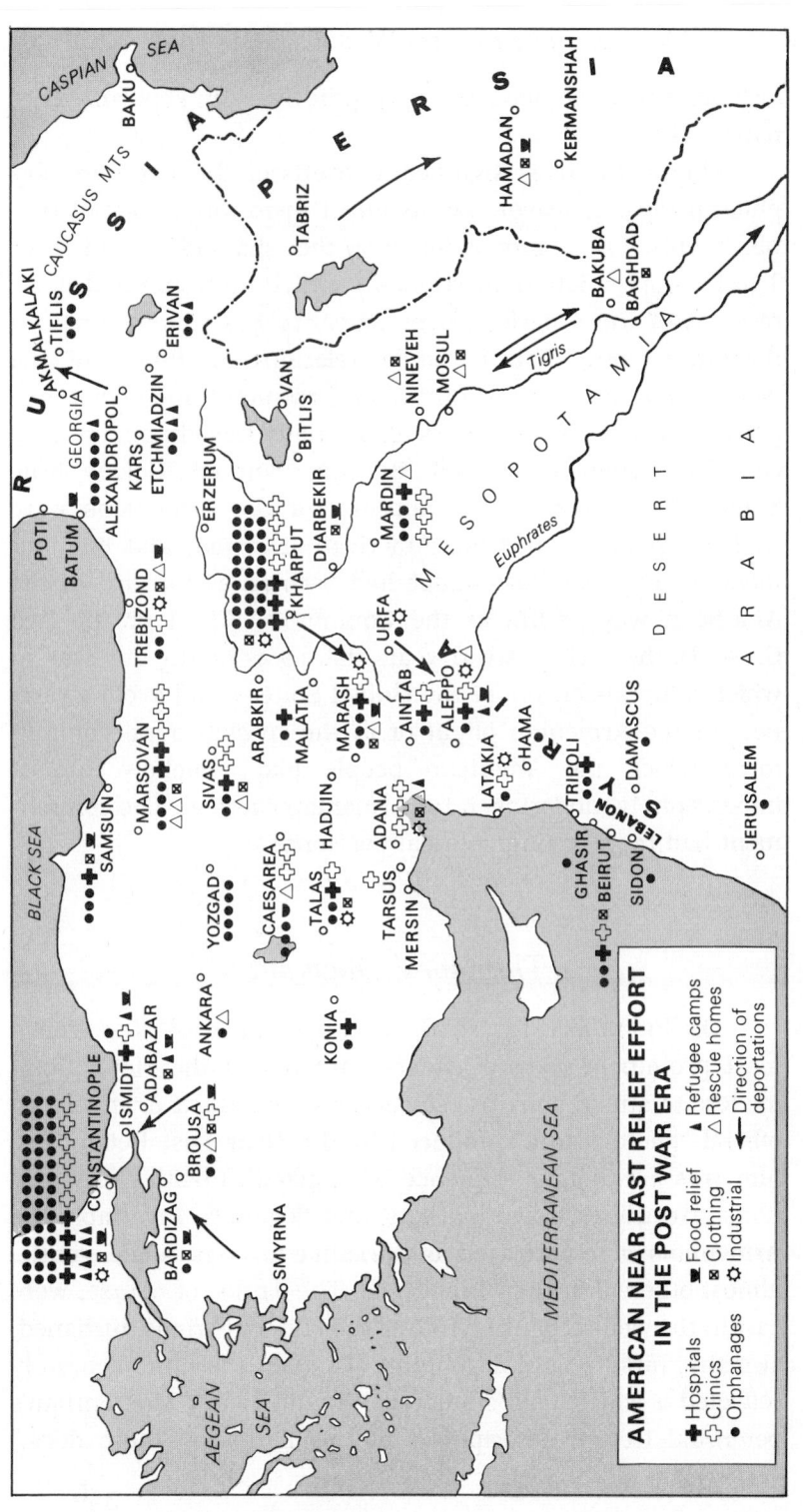

CASPIAN SEA

BAKU

CAUCASUS MTS

AKMALKALAKI
TIFLIS
GEORGIA
ALEXANDROPOL
KARS
ETCHMIADZIN
ERIVAN

TABRIZ

PERSIA

HAMADAN
KERMANSHAH

BAKUBA
BAGHDAD

Tigris

NINEVEH
MOSUL

VAN
BITLIS

MESOPOTAMIA

Euphrates

DESERT

ARABIA

ERZERUM

KHARPUT
DIARBEKIR

MARDIN

POTI
BATUM

TREBIZOND

ARABKIR

MARSOVAN

SAMSUN

SIVAS

YOZGAD

CAESAREA

MALATIA
MARASH

URFA

AINTAB
ALEPPO

HAMA

DAMASCUS

JERUSALEM

LATAKIA
TRIPOLI

LEBANON

GHASIR
BEIRUT
SIDON

SYRIA

BLACK SEA

TALAS
HADJIN

ADANA

TARSUS

MERSIN

ANKARA

KONIA

CONSTANTINOPLE
ISMIDT
ADABAZAR
BROUSA
BARDIZAG

SMYRNA

MEDITERRANEAN SEA

AEGEAN SEA

RUSSIA

AMERICAN NEAR EAST RELIEF EFFORT
IN THE POST WAR ERA

✚ Hospitals	▲ Refugee camps
✚ Clinics	△ Rescue homes
● Orphanages	→ Direction of deportations
▰ Food relief	
⊠ Clothing	
✿ Industrial	

expended $85,000,000, and had quite literally kept an entire nation alive.

One of the most significant results of this extraordinary philanthropic endeavor was its effect upon the American people themselves. Compassion for the shattered victims of Turkish oppression unquestionably welled up from the deepest recesses of the American conscience. It was equally true, on the other hand, that the public-relations machinery of the Near East Relief, with its official endorsements and elaborately publicized fund-raising drives, continually fueled national concern for Armenian survival. By 1921, annual "Golden Rule Sundays" and presidential appeals for the Armenians were well incorporated into the American tradition, and commitment to the Near East Relief had become as integral to the American way of life as the Community Chest or the Red Cross. In the early postwar years there was hardly any way in which a literate citizen of the United States could avoid awareness of the Armenian plight or of the special moral commitment which the American people had somehow, almost imperceptibly, undertaken for Armenian survival. The commitment had far-reaching political overtones.

The Moral Dilemma

ON FEBRUARY 14, 1918, several hundred of New York's most prominent society leaders gathered at the Hotel Commodore to attend a private screening of *Ravished Armenia,* an official "photo-drama" produced by the Near East Relief. The film was a two-hour sequence of enacted atrocities, deportations, executions, slave markets, and floggings. Invariably the Armenians were portrayed as Christlike martyrs—pale, gentle, almost ethereal in their innocence. The Turks, of course, were cast in the well-recognized role of sadistic barbarians, turbaned, swarthy, hirsute, and degenerate. By then the film accurately reflected a widespread stereotype. So did Henry Morgenthau's perennial lecture descriptions of the Turks as "those dogs," "those vermin," "the pariahs of the world," all of whom were guilty of a "people's crime." There was indeed complete unanimity in the United States that the Armenian people must never again be returned to Turkish rule, that their independent nationhood ought permanently to be guaranteed. It was a position fully endorsed by the lay and professional leadership of the American Board and the Near East Relief (an identical group, for the most part). Throughout the country, church federations and political leaders of both parties flooded the president with telegrams and petitions on behalf of Armenian independence. One especially formidable appeal, of March 5, 1919, carried the signatures of no less than 20,000 clergymen, 36 governors, and 250 university presidents. Their support, in turn, had been mobilized by one Vahan Cardashian, the resourceful Armenian lobbyist who conceived and organized the American Committee for Independence for Armenia and persuaded James Gerard, former U.S. ambassador to Germany, to accept the committee's chairmanship. By mid-1919 such eminent public figures as Morgenthau, Stephen Wise, and William Howard Taft were addressing overflow audiences under the auspices of this organization. Soon, in fact, Armenian rescue and Armenian independence blended into a virtually indisinguishable ideal for the American conscience.

Public opinion had evidently not outpaced government policy. Wilson's Point Twelve, with its assurance of Armenian liberation, was unequivocal enough. Moreover, it reflected the expert advice of the Inquiry, the team of scholars assembled by the White House to investigate the possibilities for a postwar settlement in advance of the Peace Conference. Under the direction of professors David Munro and W. L. Westermann, both eminent authorities on the Middle East, the specialists of the Inquiry devoted more than a year to an intensive examination of the Ottoman Question. Their ensuing monographs, lengthy, detailed, and knowledgeable, unanimously branded the Turks as unfit to govern non-Turkish peoples and totally unqualified to rule the Armenians. It was surely the influence of these reports, no less than the impact of American public opinion, which persuaded Wilson to grant *de facto* recognition to the Armenian Republic on January 23, 1920. Yet, initially, the president was unwilling to accept Dashnak territorial claims to all the former Ottoman Armenian vilayets and Cilicia. His reluctance was perhaps curious for a man whose government had been more devoted to the cause of Armenian survival than that of any of the Western Allies. The truth was, however, that Wilson's moralistic position on the Secret Treaties inhibited him from going further. As early as December 1, 1917, he had sent off a cable to Colonel House in Paris, warning that "our people and Congress will not fight for any selfish aim on the part of any belligerent . . . least of all for divisions of territory such as have been contemplated in Asia Minor." Indeed, Point Twelve served notice that the United States would insist upon the principle of self-determination for the Turks no less than for non-Turkish peoples.

Once in Paris, Wilson found it rather more difficult to apply this principle to the Arab rectangle; British and French troops were already in occupation there. Accordingly, the president simply expressed his reservations about the Sykes-Picot Agreement and afterward dispatched the King-Crane commission for a study tour of the Levant (see Chapter IX). Ultimately, he accepted Smuts's mandates plan as an acceptable compromise toward Arab independence. The problem of Asia Minor, unfortunately, was far more complicated. There an Arab-style mandate for Armenia would correspondingly undermine Turkish self-government. Much as the president supported Armenian aspirations, he was hardly unaware that even before the deportations of 1915–16, Turks and Armenians were well diffused through each other's principal areas of settlement; while after the deportations it was manifestly impossible any longer to describe a specifically "Armenian" vilayet. If the surviving Armenians were to be assured any autonomous development at all, therefore, foreign occupation of the very heartland of Turkish Anatolia would surely have been necessary. But Wilson had committed himself to the integrity of Turkish Asia Minor. During the Supreme Council meetings of February

348

and March 1919, he surpassed even Lloyd George in his zeal to block Greek and Italian efforts to amputate this territory.

Then, quite unexpectedly, Wilson found himself in the position of having to choose between rival claimants. In late April, as will be recalled, he received news of the Italian landings in the Adalia region of southwest Turkey. Already thoroughly exasperated by Orlando's stand on Fiume and the Trentino, the president now decided on the spot to endorse Lloyd George's appeal for a Greek "protective force" at Smyrna (see Chapter X). To the staff of the Inquiry, Wilson's move came as more than a complete surprise; it was a profound and unnerving shock. In the first flush of his amazement, Westermann, chief of the Middle East section, actually took the president to task for abandoning his well-advertised moralistic principles. Professor Albert Lybyer went further. Noting that a precedent had now been established for even more far-reaching Greek or Italian partition of Asia Minor, Lybyer argued that the United States was left with no alternative but to act quickly to accept a mandate for the Turkish-Armenian hinterland; no other power could be trusted to supply disinterested protection for the peoples of Turkey. And the truth was that, from the very outset of the Peace Conference, the Turks and Armenians had themselves advocated this solution, although with differing emphases. On March 13, 1919, Lewis Heck, the senior United States diplomat in Constantinople, wired the president that "there is a fairly overwhelming turning to America by all classes of the Ottoman population," and that it was all he could do to prevent Turkish public demonstrations on behalf of an American mandate. Western journalists in Turkey confirmed this impression. Several weeks earlier, in fact, the Ottoman government had shrewdly dispatched Chaim Nahoum, Grand Rabbi of Constantinople, on a "goodwill" trip to the United States. The journey's transparent purpose was to win the support of Morgenthau and American Jewry (whose influence was exaggerated, as always) for the mandatory idea.

Not surprisingly, the most impassioned advocates of an American protectorate were the Armenians themselves, al-

349

though they hardly conceived of it in the form of an undivided mandate for Asia Minor. Vahan Cardashian and Miran Sivasly, spokesmen for the Dashnak republic in the United States, ventured to assure Secretary of State Lansing on March 5 that fifty thousand Armenian troops would serve unreservedly under the command of United States officers; but a standing army probably would not be necessary, they added, for "the American eagle soaring over Mount Ararat" would accomplish even more than an army to assure peace and order in Asia Minor. Aharonian made his nation's request official several days later, formally appealing to Wilson to assume the mandate for "integral Armenia, which would be in full accord with the decision already taken in principle by the Peace Conference." Throughout the ensuing spring, the Armenian delegation at the Peace Conference clung tenaciously to the American commissioners, inundating them with memoranda, buttonholing them in every corridor and foyer, anxiously studying their daily schedules and gauging their daily moods. On April 26, the Armenian Catholicos even telegraphed Wilson premature thanks for the President's "acceptance of a mandate."

But the notion of an American protectorate in Asia Minor did not originate among the European Allies, the Turks, or even the Armenians. During the last two years of the war, in the horrified aftermath of the massacres, the protectorate idea was already the subject of discussion by thoughtful and influential Americans. The *New York Times* of May 13, 1917, printed a column on the subject by Jackson Fleming, a respected specialist on Middle East affairs, and followed later with a series of articles by Henry Morgenthau on the American role in Turkey. Both men envisaged a United States protectorate in Asia Minor as a logical extension of their country's renowned humanitarian tradition in the Middle East. Morgenthau found an additional precedent in America's successful *mission civilisatrice* in the Philippines. He assured his readers that the United States would accept an identical responsibility in Turkey "merely as a work of altruism, looking for no reward except the satisfaction of . . . helping to set on their feet certain unfortunate peoples who for centuries have been subjected to unimagined sufferings." This uniquely benevolent approach was not restricted to journalists or eccentric former ambassadors. It was endorsed, in a report to the Inquiry, by James T. Shotwell, a renowned authority on international law. It was repeated during the winter and spring of 1919 by Stephen Wise, Cleveland Dodge, James Barton, by clergymen and congressmen, by most of the interchangeable stalwarts of the American Board, the Near East Relief, and the American Committee for the Independence of Armenia. "But what would the United States get out of the Armenian enterprise?" the rhetorical question invariably was posed—and answered: "A consciousness of a job well done, of a nation saved in the first place. And in the second place, a material reduction in the risk of disorder in the world." Understandably, Cardashian and the Armenian lobbyists, speaking through Gerard, worked overtime to popularize the idea. So did Barton and the veterans of the American Board. For them, even the remote possibility of conducting missionary activity in Asia Minor under the protective shadow of the American flag was a vision of paradise.

By the spring of 1919, the conception of a United States mandate in the Middle East, whether restricted to Armenia or embracing the entire breadth of Asia Minor, had become a choice subject of discussion among the American commissioners in Paris. Most of them favored the proposal. Writing to Senator Henry Cabot Lodge on April 14, Henry White noted than an American presence offered the likeliest method of sparing Turkey "from becoming a looting ground on the basis of the secret treaties." Six days later, Westermann and his colleagues endorsed the scheme. In a bulky ninety-six-page memorandum, they observed that the one feasible method for ensuring the security of the Christian minorities was for the United States to assume a protectorate over Anatolia, Armenia, and all Transcaucasia—nothing less than the entire hinterland of western Asia. The memorandum's supplementary reports dealt with such purely technical matters as rolling-stock requirements, barracks facilities, and sanitation measures. The mandate idea clearly was growing beyond the limits of mere theoretical debate.

Actually it was Wilson himself who allowed objective speculation to be translated almost imperceptibly into the practical preparation of working blueprints. He still refused to commit himself overtly, to be sure, even after approving the precedent of the Smyrna landing. By late May, however, the president evidently accepted the Inquiry view that an American mandate was the only alternative to cynical *Realpolitik* in Asia Minor. He first tipped his hand to Westermann in a conversation on May. 22. "The President began by saying [Westermann wrote afterward] that . . . he was prepared to propose to the American people that the United States take mandates for Armenia and the State of Constantinople. . . . The President said that the United States, if he [*sic*] held mandates over Armenia and Constantinople would be in a strategic position to control that portion of the world. . . ." The moment Wilson intimated his interest in the undertaking, his representatives in Paris, Constantinople, and Washington barraged him with their pet theories for putting the mandate into effect. The flurry of activity was hardly a secret to the Supreme Council. Lloyd George was delighted.

> The prospect of a mandate for Armenia and Constantinople appealed to President Wilson's idealism [he recalled]. There was no need for persuasion. . . . The President had already sounded his leading supporters and found them favorable to the idea. . . . When he finally left Paris, his Allied colleagues in the Conference were under the impression that a personal appeal from him to the American people might override any possible opposition, and their subsequent discussions on the Turkish Treaty were based on this assurance.

Thus, on June 29, as will be recalled, the Supreme Council notified the Ottoman delegation of its decision to postpone a final settlement of the Turkish Question "until such time as the United States could state whether they could accept a mandate for a portion of the territory of the former Turkish Empire."

352

The Commissions

FOLLOWING THEIR SIX-WEEK TOUR through Palestine and Syria, the members of the King-Crane commission (see Chapter IX) returned to Constantinople fatigued and short-tempered, and decided against embarking on a similar journey throughout integral Turkey. Instead, they chose to receive the various Turkish, Greek, and Armenian delegations in the comfort of their hotel suite. The hearings lasted approximately ten days. The commission issued its report to Wilson in mid-September 1919. The six participants were unanimous in their conception of America's role in the Middle East. Their recommendation was for the United States to accept no less than three mandates: for Constantinople, for Armenia, and for the rest of Anatolia. No sordid considerations of self-interest tainted their judgment. Their premises were the by then familiar ones of American idealism, American indifference to territorial gain, American experience in Cuba and the Philippines. The approach evoked an appreciative response from the president. Well before the King-Crane report was formulated, he had already intimated to Allied statesmen his willingness in principle to consider a Middle East mandate. What he required were tangible facts and details, the kind of cost estimates and supply data that could hardly be accumulated in a series of hotel-suite hearings. As early as mid-July, therefore, Wilson issued orders for still another study group to be organized, this one to undertake a systematic and thorough survey of conditions in Asia Minor and of the purely technical feasibility of establishing an American mandate there. At Morgenthau's recommendation, the president on August 13, 1919, appointed Lieutenant General James G. Harbord, Pershing's astute and widely respected chief of staff, chairman of the new investigating body. The Mission was given a deadline of two months for completing the journey and preparing its report.

Harbord, a tall, powerful, energetic man, set about organizing a staff with his characteristic enthusiasm and resourcefulness. Within two weeks he recruited a team of thirty specialists, two-thirds of them army officers, most of them engineers, geographers, economists, or political scientists. Accompanying the group was the brilliant Armenian-born interpreter, Lieutenant Harry Khachadoorian, whose papers comprise the principal record of the Mission. For a week and a half the members intensively studied the vast compendium of information in the files of the Inquiry, until "we literally dreamed Armenia and the massacres," Harbord wrote later. Subsequently, on August 24, the Mission departed for Constantinople by ship. There followed three and a half days of consultations with American diplomatic and missionary personnel in the Turkish capital. The members then entrained for the interior. As they crossed Asia Minor, they could see for themselves the fearful desolation wrought by the wartime massacres. Wherever the train stopped, Armenian delegations, ragged, emaciated, and frequently mutilated, greeted the Mission at the sidings to present gruesome testimony of their ordeal. The Americans solemnly recorded it all. In contrast, Harbord was less impressed by the effusive courtesy of the Turkish Nationalists, their elaborate banquets and public receptions, their casual dismissal of the 1915–16 atrocities as mere "incidents." Nevertheless, a five-hour interview with Kemal at Sivas convinced Harbord that the Nationalist leader was "no cheap political adventurer." It was obvious that the man and his movement would have to be reckoned with seriously.

On September 21, the Mission crossed the prewar Russian frontier and entered the Dashnak Armenian Republic. There it was greeted by a full-dress military parade. From the border the American motor caravan was accompanied by an armed, if somewhat bedraggled, escort across the mountainous terrain to the capital city of Erivan itself. The reception awaiting the Mission in this drab little government town was almost unbearably poignant. In Harbord's honor, the government had proclaimed a national holiday. Floral arches covered the city gates. Dense crowds of lean, ardent refugees cheered the visitors ecstatically as modern messiashs. "We knew that much depended upon [Harbord's] report," President Khatissian remarked later, "and we made serious preparations to receive his Mission." Those preparations included the formulation of detailed answers to questions the Americans had sent on in advance, including vital political and economic data. During the next five days of intensive joint discussions, carried on under flickering gas lamps in the shabby presidential office, Khatissian and his associates effectively documented the Armenian case. Their conclusions were baldly stated: the country was starving, congested with half a million refugees; the Kemalists were systematically infiltrating both sides of the border; an American mandate was now a matter of life or death. Harbord and his staff were quite shaken by this testimony. On October 4, taciturn and dispirited, they departed for Constantinople. After a final interview there with Admiral Mark Bristol, the United States high commissioner in Turkey (who disliked Armenians, but favored an undivided American mandate), the group left for Paris and then for the United States to prepare its report.

The document was finished in the second week of November. It was a weighty compendium of specialized monographs, each dealing with one or another of the purely technical problems an American mandatory administration would encounter. Nevertheless, as Harbord completed his own summation, he could not resist polling his senior colleagues on their personal attitude toward the mandatory idea. Significantly, only one of these ostensibly hard-bitten professionals rejected the challenge; for most of them, the "moral" obligation was overwhelming. Harbord's own evaluation, despite its rather florid literary style, was initially somewhat more restrained. He accepted the Inquiry's, and Bristol's, proposition that only an undivided mandate for Asia Minor was politically and economically feasible, for either Turks or Armenians. With his staff members, the general was similarly persuaded that the cost of even this extensive a protectorate would not be unbearable and that a maximum of sixty thousand American troops would suffice to keep peace and order. But at the close of his twenty-two-page summation, venturing an opinion on America's "objective" responsibility for the mandate, the general apparently chose to remain impartial—indeed, mathematically so, for he concisely listed thirteen points in favor of a mandate and thirteen against. The antimandate position reduced itself to self-interest: Asia Minor was a desolated, inaccessible area, a burden that the European Allies had shrewdly avoided; the United States would be well advised to follow their example. The pro-mandate approach had been thoroughly ventilated in the press and Congress. It rested essentially on America's unique tradition of humanitarianism in Armenia, on the exemplary precedent that a clear and simple act of altruism—"as in the case of Mexico, Cuba and the Philippines"—presumably would set for the rest of the Allies. The arguments were submitted without adornment or commentary. Not so in the *New York Times*, however. There, in a full-page interview on February 22, 1920, Harbord finally left no doubt at all where he stood:

> If we are to take no part in the settlement of the Near East question [he warned], our material interests in that region might as well be abandoned. If we hope for an open door in that land of undeveloped but tremendous possibilities we must hold it open. Meanwhile 500,000 destitute people . . . have been left on our national doorstep.

Actually as far back as October 1919, the essential tenor of the Harboard Report, its cumulative emphasis in favor of the mandate, had been known to the press. Sensing that the Administration was fast approaching its moment of decision, therefore, advocates of the mandate intensified their efforts. They were aware, too, that isolationist sentiment in the United States was far more deeply entrenched than was apparent in discussions on the Armenian issue alone. The intensity with which the polemical campaign against the League of Nations was being conducted served as a warning: apparently the nation's pro-Armenian sympathies could not necessarily be equated with willingness to accept a mandatory commitment in western Asia. Often, in fact, the warmest protagonists of Armenian freedom were the most implacable critics of the League. It was becoming increasingly evident that the mandate idea was in for hard sledding. Thus, to overcome the anticipated opposition, the *New York Times* during the opening months of 1920 put its full editorial resources behind the concept of an undivided United States mandate in Asia Minor. It was supported in this endeavor by hundreds of other American newspapers and journals, ranging from the liberal *New Republic* to the influential, scholarly monthly *Asia*, which devoted its entire January issue to the mandate question; and, too, by virtually the entire Protestant church press in the United States. In Congress, the cascade of pro-mandate petitions and resolutions mounted steadily, including a document of support from the Federal Council of Churches of Christ in America. Sixteen state legislatures passed resolutions in favor of the proposal.

Impressed by what appeared to be a rising crescendo of pro-mandate sentiment, the Allied governments accordingly decided that the time was opportune to renew their pressure on Washington. On April 27, 1920, Curzon drafted a note on behalf of the Western powers assembled at San Remo, formally and officially requesting the United States to accept an Armenian mandate. Significantly, the note also expressed the hope that, whatever the American decision, President Wilson would at least see fit to arbitrate the Armenian boundaries and to provide Armenia with several contingents of U.S. troops "on an interim basis," together with sufficient credits to help the Armenian Republic survive its difficult transitional period.

The Last Act

CURZON ACTUALLY HAD UNDERSTATED the magnitude of the danger confronting the Armenian nation. When, on May 28, 1919, the Dashnak government in Erivan announced the "incorporation" into its territory of former Ottoman Armenia, the incitement to the Turks was not less flagrant than the Greek landing at Smyrna two weeks earlier had been. At first, the Russian Armenian regime was curiously laggard in appreciating the Nationalist danger. But the moment of awakening was Kemal's sudden, pulverizing conquest of Marash in Cilicia, in late January 1920 (see Chapter X). Another Cicilian city, Adana, was also very nearly overrun; only the last-minute arrival of sizable French reinforcements lifted the Turkish siege. The Erivan republic, meanwhile, was confronting another kind of danger from within: the escalating strike and sabotage activity of local Communists. Under Moscow's direction, these Red agents succeeded effectively in disrupting an already precarious economy. During the early months of 1919, the Armenian Communists were not strong enough to move against the Dashnak government openly. But with the bolshevization of neighboring Azerbaijan in late spring, the "revolutionary committee" of the industrialized Armenian railroad town of Alexandropol decided boldly to proclaim a national Communist uprising on May 10. The insurrectionists, however, picked a bad moment for their gamble. Soviet Russia was still preoccupied with the Polish war and with General Wrangel's counterrevolutionary offensive. Spared from outside interference by the Red Army, the local Dashnak forces managed to suppress the revolt. The Communist ringleaders fled to nearby Azerbaijan. Yet the episode was a costly one. It all but paralyzed the national economy, and the pathetic weakness of the Armenian army revealed the little country's obvious vulnerability to aggression, whether from north or south.

To American partisans of the mandatory idea, watching the course of events in Cilicia and Erivan during the spring of 1920, it was evident that protection for the remnant Armenian nation could no longer be delayed if it was to be offered at all. Accordingly, on May 8, Wilson sent a memorandum to Acting Secretary of State Frank Polk, noting that "it is our clear duty to assume that mandate and I want to be left as free as possible to urge such an assumption of responsibility at the opportune time." The president overcame his final inhibitions within a matter of days. On May 11 he informed the State Department that he was preparing a message to Congress asking for authority to accept a mandate for both Armenia and Constantinople. And on May 24 the "opportune time" arrived. In a message to the Senate, the president formally requested that he be empowered to accept the mandate. Even at this last moment, however, Wilson evidently was animated by the curious impulsiveness with which he had approved the Smyrna landing a year before. "In response to the invitation of the Council at San Remo," he declared, "I urgently advise and request that the Congress grant the Executive power to accept for the United States a mandate over Armenia." Over Armenia—not over an undivided Asia Minor, as Harbord, King, Crane, Bristol, Westermann, Munro, and virtually every other American adviser on the Middle East had suggested; not even over Constantinople, as Wilson himself had proposed to Secretary of State Colby less than two weeks before. Nowhere, in fact, as the president's critics observed with some asperity, did this remarkable appeal to Congress betray even the faintest scintilla of national self-interest or concern for administrative manageability. Wilson's idealism was unashamed and evidently unalloyed. "The sympathy with Armenia," his message declared, "has . . . come with extraordinary spontaneity from the whole of the great body of Christian men and women in this country by whose free-will offerings Armenia has practically been saved at the most critical juncture of its existence." The United States was now honor bound to finish the task of salvation. "I am conscious," he stated, "that I am urging upon the Congress a very critical choice, but I make the suggestion in the confidence that I am speaking in the spirit and in accordance with the wishes of the greatest of the Christian peoples."

The legislators heard out the president's message in frigid silence. Seven months earlier, they had rejected a far milder appeal for international commitment: the Versailles Treaty, incorporating in its text the Covenant of the League of Nations. A *New York Times* editorial of May 26 rather forlornly summarized the president's dilemma:

If the Armenian mandate had been offered to the United States on the day after the armistice was signed, there can hardly by any doubt that both Congress and people would have responded with a ready acceptance. . . . But in the last eighteen months many things have happened both at home and abroad. It is a different task which is set, and a different people to which it is offered. A majority of Americans, we fear, would regard the acceptance of the mandate as hardly possible. The economic and political disorganization of Transcaucasia has increased since the armistice; thousands of Armenians have died of disease and starvation, and the remnant is surrounded by enemies. The Allied Powers have withdrawn their military forces, and the vigorous Turkish revival under Mustapha Kemal has made it evident that a mandatory for Armenia will have to do some fighting.

That was the nub of it. During the first months of 1920, in the period between the issuance of the Harbord Report and Wilson's message to Congress, the situation in Armenia had deteriorated from tragedy to all but certain disaster. The crisis evoked anguished appeals from supporters of the Armenian cause. Their voices in the church press and in the legislative resolutions of Southern and Western states continued to rise in passion and intensity. It was simply the majority of the American people, those articulate or silent opponents of the League months earlier, whose fears the Senate once again probably divined.

In the course of the five days of debate following the president's message, opposition to the mandate was by no means confined to the Republican majority in the Senate. A significant number of Democrats also voiced their misgivings. These included a few, like Senator Hitchcock of Nebraska, who had led the Administration forces in the Treaty fight. It included others, like Smith of Georgia, whose state legislatures had earlier passed resolutions in favor of the mandate, but who sensed now that those pronouncements were intended simply as generalized expressions of sympathy for a martyred Christian people. At one point in the debate, when several liberal Democrats ventured to equate the mandate with a "mere" governor-general and a "few" advisers, they were derisively howled down by their Republican colleagues. Here, as on the issue of the League, Henry Cabot Lodge expressed the mood of his party. He proposed a formal resolution to deny the president authority to accept a mandate, at the same time insisting upon his own very deep personal sympathy for the Armenian people. The Massachusetts senator was in fact quite willing to raise funds for the Armenians by private subscription, and even to approve the dispatch to the Transcaucasus of "a number" of Americans to help reorganize the Armenian armed forces. But a full-blown mandatory scheme, involving sixty thousand American troops and an estimated expenditure of $250,000,000, was anathema to Lodge. It was the sentiment of his colleagues, and probably of the nation. The Lodge Resolution passed easily on June 1, by a vote of fifty-two to twenty-three.

Somewhat gratuitously, the House of Representatives four days later passed a resolution of its own, similarly rejecting the president's appeal. On June 10 the Republican national convention in Chicago approved an anti-mandate plank, and even went so far as to "condemn President Wilson for asking Congress to empower him to accept a mandate for Armenia." Ten days after that, Warren Harding, the Republican presidential nominee, publicly challenged his Democratic counterpart on the issue: if elected, would Cox renew Wilson's appeal for an Armenian mandate? Cox did not commit himself. Neither by then did any other candidate for public office. The issue was dead.

A Paper Award

WELL BEFORE THE PRESIDENT submitted his request to the Senate, the Allied leaders at San Remo, uncertain whether a United States mandate in Armenia would ever materialize, prudently formulated an alternative arrangement. It was for Wilson simply to arbitrate the Armenian boundaries in Asia

Minor. When the suggestion was communicated to him on May 11, 1920, the President was receptive. "I shall be glad," he informed Colby, "of an opportunity to do justice to the poor people there who have had a rather raw deal so far." The Allied governments thereupon incorporated the assurance of Wilson's good offices into the actual text of the Sèvres Treaty. Article Eighty-nine declared:

> Turkey and Armenia as well as the other High Contracting Parties agree to submit to the arbitration of the President of the United States the frontier to be fixed between Turkey and Armenia in the vilayets of Erzeroum, Trebizond, Van and Bitlis, and to accept his decision thereupon, as well as any stipulations he may prescribe as to access for Armenia to the sea, and as to the demilitarization of any portion of Turkish territory adjacent to the said frontier.

In the subsequent provision, Article Ninety, Turkey agreed to renounce its rights and title to Armenian territory once the frontiers were officially arbitrated. Wilson dutifully fulfilled his assignment. He turned the boundary problem over to Westermann, whose committee worked through the summer delineating a set of borders. The report was submitted to the president early in November. Wilson transmitted the proposals to the Supreme Council on November 22, 1920, "having examined the question in the light of the most trustworthy information available, and with a mind to the higher interests of justice." To no one's surprise, the decision conferred on the Erivan republic some forty thousand miles of Ottoman soil extending from the Black Sea to the Caspian Sea, an augmentation of territory encompassing the entire northeastern third of Asia Minor.

The award was hardly less surrealistic than Wilson's original request for an Armenian mandate. By autumn of 1920 the Turkish Nationalists were in firm occupation of nearly every square mile of the allocated territory. Moreover, on several occasions before the ratification of the Sèvres Treaty, Kemal had issued veiled warnings of direct military action against the Erivan government if it persisted in its claims to

Turkish soil. The Dashnaks persisted, and the Turks moved. In late September, General Kiazim Karabekir led three Nationalist divisions across the Armenian frontier and pushed rapidly toward the fortress city of Kars. Although the Turkish forces were still inadequately equipped, the Armenian troops in their turn were quite dispirited, their morale eroded by Bolshevist propaganda, their officers ill trained. After a single pitched battle, on October 14, the Armenian army melted away. The civilian inhabitants of Kars manned their fortifications a few weeks longer. But on October 30, they too finally collapsed before a Turkish frontal attack. The pattern of ensuing slaughter and pillage was by then all too familiar. On November 7 the Turks occupied Alexandropol.

At the end of its resources, the Dashnak regime was now frantic to terminate the disastrous conflict. Simultaneously, on November 29, a Bolshevist "Military Revolutionary Committee" crossed into the Erivan republic from Azerbaijan and announced the establishment of a Soviet government. Detachments of the Red Army occupied the northern part of the country the same day. Crushed in this Turco-Soviet nutcracker, the demoralized Erivan government accepted Turkish peace terms on December 2. The ensuing Treaty of Alexandropol annulled the Armenian provisions of the Treaty of Sèvres and stripped the Armenian Republic of every mite of territory its troops had wrested from the Turks, including Ardahan and Alexandropol, in the weeks immediately following the defeat of the Ottoman Empire. The country was disarmed and demilitarized, as well, and laid open to the free movement of the Turkish army. A day later, the Bolshevist "military committee" occupied the city of Erivan, where it accepted the reins of authority from the Dashnak administration and proclaimed a Soviet republic. One of the new regime's first acts was to round up the various Dashnak leaders for imprisonment, exile, or, frequently, execution.

The Allies watched the final denouement of this tragedy in dismay and embarrassment. On November 17, 1920, Lord Cecil, the British foreign undersecretary, somewhat plaintively

requested the League Council to intervene on Armenia's behalf. It was a hollow and meaningless gesture; clearly, the
League was no stronger than the resolution of its Allied members. Rather, on December 1, the Council preferred to solicit
the intervention of the United States, a nonmember. President
Wilson, for his part, expressed a willingness to send a "medi-
ator," but plainly could no nothing more. The Kemalists disdained even to acknowledge the offer of mediation.

One last Dashnak hope was realized, however. The new
Bolshevist regime in Erivan, speaking with the full endorsement of Soviet Russia, insisted upon a more equitable revision
of the Treaty of Alexandropol. The Turks, eager for good
relations with their powerful Russian neighbor, soon agreed
on terms for a compromise. The latest Russo-Turkish understanding was embodied in the Treaty of Moscow of March 7,
1921. By its provisions Alexandropol was returned to Soviet
Armenia, while Batum was placed under a Soviet-Turkish
condominium. This agreement, in turn, was reaffirmed between
the Armenians and the Turks directly in the Treaty of Kars
on October 13 of the same year. It was meager consolation for
the Armenians who remained under Communist rule. The
country was sovietized, its private property sequestered, and
much of its depleted food supply requisitioned for Soviet military needs. Worse was to come. The famine of 1921 cut like
a scythe across the entire Russian mainland; but the Armenians, already thoroughly debilitated by their earlier ordeals,
were among its first and most vulnerable casualties.

Pitiable as these circumstances were, the fate of the last
Armenian enclaves on the Turkish side of the line was even
more reminiscent of the 1915–16 genocide. As French occupation troops withdrew from Cilicia, fulfilling the terms of the
Franco-Turkish agreement of October 20, 1921 (see Chapter
XIII), a mass, instantaneous exodus of some 100,000 Armenian civilians followed in their wake. The refugees inundated
the port of Alexandretta or crossed the Syrian frontier. During
succeeding weeks, vessels bearing these distraught wretches
roamed like phantoms across the Mediterranean. The after-

math of the Armenian tragedy, therefore, was not merely the ordeal of the Soviet Armenians; nor of the scattered handfuls of Armenian communities barely surviving in isolated Anatolian and Transcaucasian towns and villages; nor even of the 40,000 Armenians maintaining a tremulous, self-effacing existence in Constantinople. It was the climactic agony of approximately 300,000 stray Armenian derelicts, veterans of both the original deportations of 1915–16 and the flight of 1919–21, who during the 1920's wandered the Middle East singly or in bands, scavenging, begging, thieving, even murdering in a half-crazed animal struggle to remain alive.

On December 14, 1920, Kevork Pasdermadjian, the Dashnak government's emissary in Washington, formally communicated his thanks to Wilson for being "the one true champion" of the Armenian people, who now were "entering their darkest hour." Wilson was touched. On December 16 he sent a memo to Secretary of State Colby: "I do not know what is the proper way to reply to the very delightful and moving message conveyed by you for Doctor Pasdermadjian. . . . I have been deeply moved by the message and would like to have him and those for whom he speaks know it." Pasdermadjian's communication was the last his nation would ever transmit to the government of the United States. Subsequently the various Armenian representatives abroad—Aharonian, Boghos Nubar, Cardashian, Pasdermadjian himself—all became self-styled spokesmen for the "Provisional Government of the Republic of Armenia in Exile." For his part, Woodrow Wilson chose never to refer to the Armenian Question again. Two years later, he had a portrait of an Armenian refugee girl hung over the living room mantel of his private Washington residence. It hangs there today, the child's luminous, orb-like eyes reproachfully evoking a faded and guileless interlude in American diplomacy.

CHAPTER XII

THE SECOND ARAB REVOLT: IRAQ

Iraq Under Military Occupation

As the British tightened their grip on Mesopotamia in the last year of the war, they found themselves in occupation of a ruinously neglected semi-desert, semi-swamp of 171,599 square miles. Its population of some three million inhabitants was a festering agglomeration of sectarian and social rivalries. The Arab Moslem majority was divided almost equally between the Sunni and Shi'a sects, the one oriented toward Mecca, the other toward Persia, and then infinitely fractured into tribes and clans, each nurturing its private fealties and blood feuds. The fellahin, blending almost indistinguishably with their animals into the sun-scorched landscape, despised the wealthy sheiks and city merchants, a corrupt and narcissistic aristocracy. Peasant and townsman alike reciprocated the hatred of the 700,000 Kurds, half-Moslem, half-animist, who glowered down on them from the mountain fastnesses of the northeast. Baghdad, a rather unimpressive collection of gaudy bazaars and twisting residential side streets, depended almost entirely upon its powerful, literate Jewish minority for commercial and administrative leadership. Only the British Cabinet, its lines to the Middle East tangled among the war office, the home government, the Government of India, and the Arab Bureau in Cairo, nurtured the sanguine conception of a single Arab nation "to be administered [in the vilayet of Baghdad] behind the Arab façade as far as possible as an Arab province by indigenous agency and in accordance with existing laws and institutions." The guideline was issued by London on

March 29, 1918, and presumably was an honest effort to carry
out the Sykes-Picot Agreement, to restrict direct British administration to the coastal Basra vilayet, and to encourage
Arab self-government in the interior.

Sir Percy Cox, the veteran agent-in-chief for the Persian
Gulf, and now civil high commissioner (under the Indian
Army) for occupied Mesopotamia, made short shrift of the
suggestion. In a curt telegram of April 7, he warned that the
establishment of an Arab government would merely exacer-
bate the chaos of Turkish withdrawal. Cox intended to run
the country his way, the only "practical" way, under tight
military rule and with the Indian forces who had conquered
the land. And so he did. Indeed, there was no one to say him
nay. The Cabinet was incapable of interfering. When the
war ended, Curzon presided over an "Interdepartmental Committee on the Middle East" almost completely immobilized
by the conflicting viewpoints of its members. The French
could hardly protest by then; during Clemenceau's visit to
London in December 1918, he had accepted Lloyd George's
demand for a clear field in Mesopotamia, including Mosul.

Most significantly, Cox's methods seemed to work. Well
before the Mudros Armistice, his Anglo-Indian administration had provided the land with a reasonable degree of peace
and security. Normalcy slowly returned to the villages and countryside. In Mosul, Baghdad, and Basra, streets were widened,
market places enlarged, and schools opened. Interurban
traffic began to flow once again, and trade among the communities gradually resumed and then surpassed its pre-1914
level. "By the end of the war," Cox could write later with some
pride, "the people of Mesopotamia had come to accept the fact
of our occupation and were resigned to the prospect of a
permanent British administration; some, especially in Basrah
and the neighborhood, even looked forward with satisfaction
to a future in which they would be able to pursue their commerce and agriculture with a strong central authority to preserve peace and order." Curzon, too, had to admit that things
were working well. He informed the House of Lords in February

1919 that "more has been done in two years for those places than has been done in the five previous centuries. . . . There are no shadows in the picture."

The administrators of Mesopotamia were determined to keep it that way. When Sir Percy Cox departed for Teheran in May 1918 to serve as British minister to Persia, he delegated his responsibilities to his assistant, Lieutenant Colonel Arnold Wilson, a thirty-four-year-old career officer in the Indian political department. The new acting civil commissioner made no secret of his derision for London's occasional qualms of conscience toward the Arab world. The Anglo-French declaration of November 7, 1918, for example, assuring the Arabs freedom and self-government, frankly horrified him. So did a fleeting proposal of Montagu's and Lawrence's, twelve days later, that Abdullah and his brother Zeid be placed on the thrones of "Lower" and "Upper" Mesopotamia, respectively. Gertrude Bell, the Administration's adviser on Arab affairs, succinctly phrased the Government of India's viewpoint in a letter to her father on December 27, 1918. "In Mesopotamia [the Arabs] want us and no one else because they know we'll govern in accordance with the custom of the country," she stated flatly. To prove this assertion, on November 21, 1918, the acting commissioner expressed his willingness to conduct a "plebiscite" of Arab opinion. This offer was accepted nine days later by Curzon's interdepartmental committee in London. Thereupon Wilson instructed his political officers throughout the country to conduct the poll "when opinion is favourable" and to ensure that the "right" answers were forthcoming from the most dependable sheiks. Carried out in January 1919, the "plebiscite" of course supplied the "right" answers; it rejected a Hejazi ruler in favor of the British. The vote delighted Curzon, who now heartily endorsed the policy of firm control in Mesopotamia. During the ensuing year, therefore, a tight, centralized, Indian-style government was officially reinforced and heavily staffed with Indian civil servants under the direction of British senior officials. The very titles carried by the bureaucracy in New Delhi—civil commissioner, political officer, revenue officer, judicial officer—were precisely reproduced in this miniature Indian administration. So was the Indian legal code and even the Indian currency, based on the rupee. London was placid. Wilson later recalled with satisfaction that "no word of criticism, benevolent or otherwise, reached me from the Foreign Office during 1919. . . ."

The Winds of Revolt

THE ARABS HAD a few reservations. The Anglo-Indian regime was alien to them in a way Ottoman rule had never been: non-Arabic-speaking, its top officials non-Moslem, its taxes collected with relentless efficiency and impartiality, its public projects disrupting the normal tempo of daily life. The popular reaction was initially somewhat more lethargic than in Syria, however. For Arab nationalism in sectarian, torpid Iraq (as we, like the Arab nationalists, shall now call Mesopotamia) had developed rather more slowly than in the urbanized Syrian littoral; Ottoman rule had been less heavy-handed in those eastern vilayets than in the regions nearer Constantinople. In the prewar era, to be sure, Saïd Talib Pasha and a few other well-born Iraqis had made a discreet and mild case for Arab autonomy in the Ottoman Chamber of Deputies, and several Iraqi army officers, including Nuri es-Saïd, had joined underground nationalist cells in Constantinople. Their numbers increased once hostilities were joined and the Anglo-Indian force had successfully invested the vilayet of Basra (Chapter III). Nevertheless, as its troops witnessed the predatory looting and killing by Iraqi scavengers on both sides of the battlefield, the Government of India was reinforced in its scorn for the Arabs as a race and coldly disdained the services of occasional potential Arab allies. Faced with this quite explicit contempt, many of the Iraqi officers ended up in Feisal's Hejazi army, where for the first time they imbibed the emotionally charged slogans of the Hashemite revolt. Their fervor was additionally inflamed, at war's end, by the painful discovery that the best posts in Feisal's Syrian government were reserved for Syrians.

Returning to Iraq during the course of 1919, therefore, the embittered nationalist officers cast about for allies, some of whom they had failed earlier to recognize, but whom now, belatedly, they hurried to cultivate. These included the religious hierarchy of the Shi'a Ulema, an exceptionally xenophobic group of itinerant cadis whose sermonical oratory aroused the backward and credulous Shi'ite tribes of the middle Euphrates Valley; the urban lower-middle class, increasingly sullen and restive under alien Christian rule; the Kemalist Turks, who shared their grievances against the British and were therefore prepared to channel a certain number of weapons through the Mosul border community of Daïr al-Zor. An additional ingredient in the nationalist ferment was the declaration by the Syrian Congress of Feisal's kingship on March 8, 1920, and its simultaneous proclamation of Abdullah as King of Iraq. Rumors of Feisal's intention to attack Mosul had in fact circulated throughout the Tigris and Euphrates valleys as far back as the late spring of 1919. The British were not altogether oblivious to the mounting unrest. In August 1919 a Baghdad police report hinted at imminent violence. "It was clear," wrote Major Hubert Young, a veteran of the 1916 Arab Revolt, and now an adviser to the foreign office, "that events were moving very fast in the Middle East, and I warned Lord Curzon . . . that we should certainly have trouble in Mesopotamia if we are not very careful."

With a remarkable lack of urgency, however, Curzon delayed calling a meeting of the interdepartmental committee until November 1919, and it was fully a month and a half after that before he cabled Wilson, suggesting that the Anglo-Indian regime be liberalized, and that at least partial Arab self-government be inaugurated. The reply of the acting civil commissioner was a classic of Kiplingese. He predicted chaos and anarchy if an "amateur" Arab government were established. "We must therefore go slowly," he insisted. "Effective British administration is vital to the continued existence of

Mesopotamia as an independent State or administrative entity." But Curzon was increasingly alarmed by the warning of Major Young and of other returning members of the Arab Bureau, and his correspondence with Baghdad accordingly grew more insistent. Bowing to this mounting pressure from the foreign office, Wilson instructed his judicial officer, Sir Edgar Bonham-Carter, to draw up a compromise blueprint for Arab participation in the British administration. As it was finally completed and sent on to London in May 1920, the scheme provided for nothing more than a consultative Arab assembly under the direction of a predominantly British council of state. The members of the interdepartmental committee greeted the plan with open guffaws. This time there was no further temporizing. On June 16, Wilson received explicit instructions to lay the groundwork for an Arab council of state and an Arab general elective assembly. This was London's first concrete policy directive on Iraq since the Mudros Armistice twenty months earlier. Even so, it came too late. In the coffee shops and tribal councils of Iraq, exasperation with the Westernized administration was reaching the boiling point. The arrival in Baghdad of a contingent of Britsh officers' wives appeared to confirm Anglo-Indian intentions to remain in the country indefinitely. "There's a lot of semi-religious and semi-political preaching and reciting of poems," Gertrude Bell noted in a letter to her father on June 1, "and the underlying thought is *out with the infidel*." The thought was stated openly and wrathfully during mass gatherings in the courtyards of Shi'ite mosques in Diyala and Kirkuk.

At precisely this moment of seething disquietude, Winston Churchill, now war secretary, chose to issue a public warning that the expense of military occupation in the Middle East was no longer supportable. The army commander in Iraq, a somewhat unimaginative infantry general named Haldane, decided in turn to take Churchill literally. He reduced his mobile forces to a paltry 3,500 troops and deployed them selectively to guard 170,000 square miles of territory.

It was a blank check for trouble. Hostilities began at Daïr al-Zor, on the northwestern frontier. Under the leadership of Jamal al-Midafi, one of Feisal's lieutenants in the 1916 revolt, a band of three hundred Arabs equipped with Turkish weapons swept down on a group of neighboring British frontier outposts and captured them without difficulty. The defenders were slain to the last man. This sudden, ferocious cavalry attack set the pattern of the emergent rebellion. The surrounded and outnumbered Anglo-Indian garrisons were systematically liquidated. During the early weeks of the uprising, the army was unable to supply reinforcements to so much as one of the beleaguered outposts; no effective communications whatever existed outside the immediate area of Baghdad. Ironically, Arnold Wilson's personal qualities of courage and steadfastness never showed to better advantage than in the wreckage of his imperial policy. A rock of calm strength, the acting civil commissioner made repeated flying trips to the isolated garrisons (his plane occasionally dropping bombs on Arab marauders en route), entreating the outnumbered defenders to hold on. Each time he returned heavy-hearted in the virtual certainty that his British and Indian troops were doomed to unspeakable deaths.

With the tribal population of the entire lower Euphrates inflamed, fresh uprisings broke out north and west of Baghdad. Diltawa fell to the rebels on August 13, then Ba'quba, then Shahraban. At that point the insurgents felt confident enough to declare a provisional Arab government, although the loose collection of tribal sheiks hardly compared in organization or discipline with its earlier Syrian counterpart. Soon bands of picked nationlist guerrillas began to infiltrate the Kirkuk region. One of their first acts was to cut the throat of the chief British political officer of the northwest area, the highly capable and admired Colonel George Leachman. This brutal deed in turn became the signal for a new series of risings. By mid-August 1920, the entire Iraqi countryside, except for the Tigris Valley in the south, was the scene of Arab cavalry raids and of the remorseless slaughter and mutilation of Anglo-Indian garrisons and of suspected pro-British collaborators among the native population. Baghdad itself, on the other hand, remained quiet, under heavy military occupation. Indeed, the capital's moderate nationalist leaders, men like Saïd Talib Pasha, deplored the uprising. They were the exceptions.

The Government of India was not idle during the hostilities. Throughout the summer months it poured a continual stream of men and supplies into Iraq. By the end of September, Haldane's forces had been augmented by 25,000 Indian and 5,000 British troops, plus an air squadron. These reinforcements gradually stabilized the British position in the densely inhabited southeastern part of the country. With new mobile columns at his disposal, the British commander began tentatively to reoccupy captured outposts and towns. By the opening days of 1921, the tribal invaders of Kifri and Khaniqin were reduced to hunted outlaws. The countryside surrounding Diyala and Baghdad was also slowly pacified. In the late winter, Haldane felt strong enough to embark upon a series of harsh punitive expeditions throughout the lower Euphrates Valley. Entire villages were demolished by British artillery and armored cars. Suspected ringleaders were shot down without trial; livestock was sequestered or destroyed on the spot. By late March, the Arab rebel government had simply evaporated, and the revolt began guttering out. The cumulative toll it had taken in British lives was perhaps not large when measured by the losses even of earlier British frontier campaigns. Some 426 British soldiers had been killed, 615 were missing as prisoners and presumed dead, and 1,228 had been wounded. It was estimated that the rebels themselves had suffered between 8,000 and 9,000 killed and wounded. But vast quantities of military stores had been destroyed, and the sheer extent of territory to be reoccupied and secured raised the total cost of the uprising to some forty million pounds, a rather larger sum than had been spent on the entire Hashemite revolt during the World War. The fact of the rebellion itself, moreover, its duration and wanton cruelty, aroused serious doubts in

Britain about the responsibility the government had undertaken in "liberating" Iraq from Ottoman rule.

The Aftermath

BY THE AUTUMN OF 1920, Englishmen were beginning to wonder, as they had never wondered about Egypt, whether Iraq was worth the cost. What strategic interests, they asked, could justify the expense and bloodshed of a frontier war less than two years after Britain had irretrievably smashed Ottoman power in the Middle East? Suez was safe. India was safe. The oil reserves of Mosul were as yet untested; the Abadan refineries in the Persian Gulf supplied England with more than enough fuel for its internal needs. What conceivable threat, then, did Iraqi nationalism pose to British imperial communications or British economic development? Sharing these misgivings, and sensitive to the darkening mood of British public opinion, the Cabinet swiftly embarked on a number of basic administrative changes. Arnold Wilson, exhausted and expendable, was sent off on permanent "leave." His predecessor, Sir Percy Cox, was summoned from Teheran for urgent conferences in London, then dispatched to Iraq in October with unequivocal orders not merely to terminate the rebellion, but swiftly and firmly to inaugurate a new regime. Cox was fifty-six at the time, a tall, courtly, ascetic man, by far the most experienced Middle East hand in the British diplomatic service, not excluding Curzon himself. Gertrude Bell, at the Baghdad railroad station to greet her former chief, suddenly experienced an upsurge of spirit as he stepped from the train:

> I thought as he stood there in his white and gold lace, with his air of fine and simple dignity, that there had never been an arrival more momentous—never anyone on whom more conflicting emotions were centered, hopes and doubts and fears, but all confidence in his personal integrity and wisdom. It was all I could do not to cry.

374

For his part, Cox rose to the expectations of the moment by declaring, in fluent and graceful Arabic, that he had come to take counsel with the people of Iraq in order to establish an Arab government under British supervision. From that moment, military government in the country was for all practical purposes terminated.

It soon became evident that Gertrude Bell's faith in the high commissioner was to be dramatically vindicated. While she served as his "Oriental Secretary," his closest adviser on Arab affairs, and thus, virtually, his alter ego in Baghdad, he in turn flew off to various areas of Iraq, meeting with notables, reasurring them of his determination to modify radically the Bonham-Carter proposals. The council of state would be Arab, Cox explained in these meetings, assisted by British advisers; and a comprehensive Iraqi—not Indian —civil service would assume control of the Administration. It was admittedly difficult at first to convince the Arab nationalists that London was sincere in endorsing these changes, for the proposed new regime signified a fundamental departure in British imperial policy among non-European races. Notwithstanding those initial misgivings, one of the high commissioner's earliest successes was to persuade the venerable *naqib* (Moslem communal leader) of Baghdad, Saïd Abd al-Rahaman al-Gaylani, to accept the presidency of the council, thus investing the new regime with respectability in native eyes. Soon other moderate Arab leaders, equally convinced that Cox meant what he said, agreed to join the council of state as Cabinet ministers. They now became the effective national government, although subject to the ultimate authority of the high commissioner. True to his word, moreover, Cox substituted many hundreds of Iraqi civil servants for the imported British and Indian officials. The latter were sent home shortly afterward, complaining bitterly that the "wogs" would never succeed in managing their own affairs. Undeterred by this criticism, the high commissioner even arranged for the transfer into Iraqi hands of local military authority, a power never before delegated in British imperial experience. The British troops themselves were slowly withdrawn in favor of a national militia.

But these were palliatives. A long-term solution for the problem of the country remained to be formulated. From All Souls College, Oxford, to which he had retreated in despair after Britain's abandonment of Feisal at the Peace Conference, T. E. Lawrence issued a steady barrage of letters to the press throughout 1920, angrily denouncing the entire concept of overseas mandates. "How long will we permit millions of pounds," he wrote in the Sunday *Times* of August 12, "thousands of Imperial troops, and tens of thousands of Arabs to be sacrificed on behalf of a form of colonial administration which can benefit nobody but its administrators." Lawrence's polemic was ardently supported by his Labor and Liberal friends in Parliament. Increasingly disillusioned with the chimera of national grandeur, faced with ugly syndicalist riots among the unemployed, and with the suppurating chancre of Irish terrorism within the borders of the United Kingdom, the government's critics wondered what dubious prestige or additional security the empire would achieve by holding the wastelands of Iraq at the risk of future and sporadic warfare, with all its human and financial cost. By the early spring of 1921 the force of this rising criticism had shaken the Cabinet and persuaded it that at least the system of divided administrative authority on Arab policy ought to be ended. Moving quickly, the government efficiently transferred Middle East affairs *in toto* to the colonial office, now under the direction of the ubiquitous Winston Churchill. It was the opinion of Churchill's collection of experts, moreover, that a full assembly of senior military and civilian officials should be summoned from throughout the empire to help devise a method for immediately and safely reducing Britain's expenditures in the Middle East.

The choice of site fell on Cairo, the halfway house between East and West. The meeting, convened in the second week of March 1921, was attended by no less than thirty-eight participants. These included such eminent service personalities as Lawrence himself, together with Hubert Young, chief of the Middle East department under Churchill; Colonel Richard Meinertzhagen, Young's military adviser; Air Marshal Sir Hugh Trenchard; Lieutenant General Sir Walter Congreve, commander in chief in Egypt and Palestine; Sir Herbert Samuel, high commissioner of Palestine; Wyndham Deedes, civil secretary of the Palestine government; and Sir Percy Cox and Gertrude Bell from Iraq. Even Sir Arnold Wilson turned up, in his new capacity as adviser for the Anglo-Persian Oil Company. Churchill presided loosely over the group, frequently breaking away from committee sessions in the Mena House Hotel to paint oils of the Pyramids. The conference was a remarkable success, as it turned out; the guidelines it laid down proved to be of enduring importance in the future evolution of Middle East policy. Agreement was reached, to begin with, that the Arabs of Iraq should be granted more extensive self-government and should be allowed to accept permanently the major responsibility for their own defense and budget. Of course, the corollary of this proposal was for the mandate scheme to be revised in favor of a treaty relationship similar to the one in effect between Britain and Egypt. The idea appealed to Churchill, who endorsed it warmly. The other participants shared the colonial secretary's enthusiasm. It was evident to all of them that the heaviest imperial expenses could be pared down almost automatically when the plan was put into effect. In this fashion, Britain's huge standing army in Iraq could be reduced to ten or twelve battalions by the end of the year, while the heavy bombers of the Royal Flying Corps at Habbaniyah Air Base could assume the major burden of ensuring security.

Iraq would need a ruler—an Arab ruler, of course, not a British high commissioner. By then, Cox and Gertrude Bell were persuaded that only a member of the Hashemite dynasty would command a national following. Feisal was without question the likeliest choice. For one thing, a number of influential Iraqi officers had served under him during the war and had remained his active and vocal partisans. The emir had been "at liberty," too, residing in a villa on Lake Maggiore, since his exile from Syria in August 1920. Indeed, with Churchill's blessing, Lawrence and Sir Kinahan Cornwallis of the colonial office had actually approached Feisal on the subject of the Iraqi throne several weeks before the Cairo conference began. The emigré king was not initially receptive. Embittered by what he construed to be England's betrayal of his Syrian monarchy, Feisal was unwilling to be used elsewhere as a tool of British imperial policy. Anyway, he argued, his older brother Abdullah deserved the right of first refusal in Iraq. At this point, Lawrence took it upon himself to visit Abdullah in the Red Sea port of Jedda. During the course of a single afternoon's conversation, he won the Arab chieftain's promise not to oppose Feisal's candidature. Accordingly, on March 1, 1921, after successive luncheons with Lawrence and Cornwallis at the Shipp Inn at Whitehall, Feisal was tempted at last by the prospect of an alternative throne, and decided to accept the offer.

When Churchill arrived in Cairo, therefore, he brought with him a ready-made solution that he hoped the conference would support. It did, unanimously. Cox's single reservation was also accepted: that Feisal ought not to be presented to the Iraqi people as a *fait accompli*, but rather as their own freely selected choice. Thus, the emir would announce his availability to the leaders of Iraq; if they accepted him upon his arrival in that country, he would assume the crown. It seemed an intelligent and logical solution. Churchill, exhilarated by the success of his diplomacy, hurried back to London to report to the government. As he outlined to the House of Commons the military and economic advantages of the proposed treaty relationship with Iraq, the colonial secretary clearly implied, as well, that by offering the throne to Feisal, the government was purging its conscience for having originally abandoned the emir to the French. The speech was received with prolonged and enthusiastic applause. With what mathematical tidiness the entire Middle East imbroglio was being resolved! All that remained now was for Feisal to play out his role.

The Iraqis Find a Monarch

COX WAS THE FIRST to return to Iraq, on April 12, to lay the groundwork for Feisal's impending arrival. He wasted little effort on the trappings of democratic procedure. When Saïd Talib Pasha and the *naqib* expressed their reservations about an alien Hejazi ruler in a Persian Gulf nation, Cox had Saïd arrested forthwith and deported to Ceylon. The *naqib* and others immediately hastened to affirm their support of Feisal. With the high commissioner's benevolent approval, too, a Hashemite party was formed, while the government-controlled press began publishing articles in lavish praise of Feisal. Gertrude Bell made preparations of her own. It was now, in fact, following the Cairo conference, that this extraordinary woman finally came into her element, carrying out her work with such dazzling imagination that her name suddenly evoked general recognition among the British public at large.

She was the daughter of a wealthy North Country steelmonger, the recipient of an excellent classical education at Oxford's Lady Margaret Hall. Traveling widely upon graduation, she had become particularly enamored of the Middle East. With characteristic single-mindedness, she studied and mastered Persian and Arabic, then prepared to settle in Teheran with her fiancé, a foreign-service officer. The young man, however, died of cholera shortly before the scheduled marriage. From that moment, Gertrude Bell turned her back on Europe and resumed her Middle East travels with almost fanatical intensity, churning out a brilliant series of volumes on the mores and politics of the region. Her reputation secured her an influential billet in the Arab Bureau in Cairo when the war began, and afterward an assignment as Cox's assistant during the Mesopotamian campaign. Now, in 1921, at the age of fifty-two, serving the high commissioner as Oriental Secretary, she was a slim, fragile, patrician-featured woman, whose crisp, authoritative manner fell somewhat short of complete femininity and belied the uncertain state of her health. With her un-

379

paralleled connections among the local Arab tribes, Gertrude Bell envisaged herself by then as champion of the Iraqi national cause, and preferred to overlook her more orthodox imperialist approach of only a year before.

As she hurried to make suitable arrangements for Feisal's arrival, no detail escaped her attention. She it was who organized the reception committee, arranged the emir's travel itinerary, picked the royal servants, designed a temporary flag for Iraq and had it sewn, even superintended the drilling of the guard of honor. As a result of these efforts, Feisal's ceremonial entry into Baghdad on June 23 went reasonably smoothly, although the assembled dignitaries had to wait two hours in the midafternoon sun for the royal train, which had broken down en route. During the next fortnight, Miss Bell whisked the thirty-six-year-old Arab leader from one tribal reception to another, sitting through innumerable banquets, winning pledges of allegiance to the Hashemite standard. Few difficulties were encountered. Deprived of the opportunity to vote for an alternate candidate, the council of ministers and "ninety-six per cent of the population" (Cox's figures) predictably approved Feisal as the country's monarch. Early on the morning of August 23, 1921, the Hejazi prince was enthroned as King of Iraq in the courtyard of the government building in Baghdad. He wore a plain khaki uniform and spiked helmet. His speech was equally unadorned, a moving pledge to his new compatriots of a constitutional regime, which he supplemented with assurances of friendship for Britain and of his determination to cooperate with Britain's emissaries. It was enough.

Within a few months the royal figure became the unquestioned center of all Iraqi political and social life. His relations with Cox were friendly, as the Englishman continued on as high commissioner in his office across the Tigris. Nevertheless, the precise relationship between the British and Iraqi governments had yet to be formalized. Even before his arrival in Baghdad, Feisal had approved the suggestion to regularize the Anglo-Iraqi connection by treaty rather than by mandatory supervision. The arrangement was subject, as well, to the approval of the Council of the League of Nations. In fact, the British had already submitted a draft mandate instrument to the League, and had asked the Council to accept a treaty incorporating the document's terms as the equivalent of the mandate. "It is not intended as a substitute for the mandate," explained H. A. L. Fisher, the British representative, on November 17, 1921, ". . . [for the mandate] will remain the operating document defining the obligations undertaken by His Majesty's Government on behalf of the League of Nations."

The man charged with overseeing the preparation of this ingenious, all-purpose treaty was Hubert Young, dispatched to Baghdad by Churchill that month to help Cox formulate the agreement. The essential provisions were those of the original mandatory draft, i.e., Britain's obligations to frame an Organic Law, to ensure religious and educational freedom, and to perform other "supervisory" responsibilities. But new terminology had to be found to clarify Iraqi sovereignty and satisfy nationalist *amour-propre*. Here Young and Cox drew upon British experience in Egypt. The high commissioner would serve as "adviser" to the King. The latter, in turn, would pledge to be "guided" by the high commissioner's advice. Other subsidiary agreements provided for the use of British legal experts by the Iraqi regime, for the maintenance of the Capitulations, for British command and instruction of the Iraqi army, and for Britain's right to utilize Iraqi communications at will. The main lines of the treaty were settled by the opening of 1922. Young flew back to Cairo euphoric in his accomplishment. "Difficulties there would certainly be," he surmised, "but as the aeroplane bore me on its strong wings over the desert I felt that a new era had dawned."

Difficulties there undoubtedly were, more than Young had envisaged. On February 19, 1922, the treaty was placed before the Iraqi council of ministers. It remained there for eight months. To the British, the document seemed a clever method of obtaining a *de facto* Iraqi mandate, without the trouble and expense entailed in a formal mandatory assignment. The Arab nationalists conceived of the treaty otherwise. To them it was

381

a substitute for the mandate, a way of securing British advice on foreign, military, and political matters without the obligation of necessarily accepting it. Feisal shared this view. Although he voiced it discreetly and moderately, not all his followers were as restrained. Several of them undertook to whip up unrest among the Shi'ite community. But this time Cox would not be caught unprepared. He demanded and secured the dismissal of the extremists in the royal entourage. In late August and early September, following an emergency appendectomy performed on the king, the high commissioner used Feisal's long period of convalescence to assume personal direction of the government. Immediately the Englishman closed the offices of the extremist parties, suppressed two opposition newspapers, and exiled several leading agitators. The speed and uncompromising rigor of these measures thoroughly intimidated the Arab opposition. Shaken and chastened, the Iraqi Cabinet signed the treaty on October 10.

Additional months of tedious negotiations passed, however, and an additional British ultimatum was required before the document was finally ratified by the Iraqi constituent assembly on June 10, 1924. Thereupon the treaty was at long last submitted to the Council of the League, which adopted it on September 27 of the same year. The instrument became a kind of prototype of all future Anglo-Arab treaties: formulated painfully, negotiated bitterly, the subject of endless recriminations, protests, and resignations, each step of the way tracing the gestation of Arab nationalism, the slow corrosion of Arab gratitude for Britain's imperial patronage. In their mutual exhaustion, nevertheless, the Arabs and British appeared at least to have accepted a grudging *modus vivendi*. For the immediate future a kind of lethargic quietude settled on Iraq. It was destined to endure for nearly a generation. By the standards of the volatile Middle East, the respite was not the least successful to be achieved by the Western imperial powers.

CHAPTER XIII

THE SECOND ARAB REVOLT (Continued): PALESTINE

High and Early Hopes in the Holy Land

WHEN GENERAL ALLENBY'S TROOPS occupied Palestine in 1917–18, they took possession of the single most desolated and backward province of the Ottoman Levant. Arid, malarial, sparsely inhabited by a depleted population of perhaps 560,000 Arabs and 55,000 Jews near the war's end, the country had been starved by Allied blockade, ravaged and ruined by Turkish depredations. Entire villages had been razed, trees and orange groves laid waste, public security all but extinguished. Allenby's first order of priority, therefore, was somehow to reorganize the administration and revive the economy of this prostrated land. The country was promptly divided into districts, each under a British military governor, with central departments of finance, justice, health, agriculture, education, and public works established in Jerusalem. British officers and civil servants generally held the senior administrative posts; native Palestinian Arabs and Jews served in the lower-echelon positions. The system worked well enough to become the basic pattern of the later mandatory regime. Vigorous measures were taken to improve the health and sanitation of Palestine, as sewage canals were dug and hospitals and clinics opened. The purchasing power of a large British army effectively stimulated local trade; substantial material benefits soon accrued to the country's inhabitants. The atmosphere in Palestine for the time being was tranquil, even hopeful.

So, initially, were the prospects for the Zionists. They had received not merely the "official" recognition embodied in the Balfour Declaration, but, as well, assurance of cordial goodwill and support from statesmen on the highest level of government. By the end of the war, Lloyd George and Balfour had accepted the Zionist cause as an unshakable one on its own merits, no less than as *raison d'être* for a British mandate. Balfour, in his celebrated memorandum of August 11, 1919, to Curzon's interdepartmental committee, emphasized that "Zionism, be it right or wrong, good or bad, is rooted in age-long traditions, in present needs, in future hopes, of far profounder import than the desires and prejudices of the 700,000 [sic] Arabs who now inhabit that ancient land. In my opinion that is right. . . . It is not enough, moreover, that the Jews should have access to Palestine, but that their homeland be a viable one." Nor were serious objections to the Zionist homeland expressed in other quarters. Clemenceau had ceded Britain the Palestine mandate during his visit to London in December 1918. His successor in office, the more intransigent Millerand, insisted upon denying Britain—and the Zionists—the headwaters of the Jordan, but even he did not challenge the concept of a Jewish national home. Rome, too, was satisfied merely to place two Italian Jews on the Zionist commission serving in Palestine. The American secretary of state, Robert Lansing, remained firmly anti-Zionist; but President Wilson himself reassured Weizmann of his own warm, personal support. In a note of May 16, 1919, to Felix Frankfurter, then a member of the American Zionist delegation, Wilson again sought to allay Jewish misgivings: "I never dreamed that it was necessary to give you any renewed assurance of my adhesion to the Balfour Declaration, and so far I have found no one who is seriously opposing the purpose which it embodies." In entrusting Palestine to Britain, moreover, the Allied statesmen at San Remo incorporated the entire Balfour Declaration into their statement of allocation. The essential moral support of the Allied governments seemed firmly established.

For a long while, too, the friendship of the Hashemite Arab

leadership appeared equally beyond question. Embroiled in his diplomatic struggle with the French (see Chapter X), and convinced that the Zionists possessed alliance value in that battle, Feisal was prepared to affirm his active, if expedient, sympathy with the Zionist movement. In fact, nothing could have been more pleasing to Mark Sykes than a solid front among his favorite client nations. It was accordingly under Sykes's auspices that Feisal and his retinue were brought together again with Weizmann and other Jewish leaders, this time in London early in December 1918. With Lawrence serving as translator, each group expressed mutual understanding and support for the other's position. Feisal emphasized the danger both to Arab and Jewish aspirations implicit in French policy. Weizmann outlined Zionist claims in some detail and asserted his respect for Arab communal rights. It was thereupon agreed that all water and farm boundary questions should be settled directly between the two parties. The atmosphere was cordial. Interviewed by a Reuters correspondent soon afterward, Feisal emphasized that "Arabs are not jealous of Zionist Jews, and intend to give them fair play; and the Zionist Jews have assured the Nationalist Arabs of their intention to see that they too have fair play in their respective areas." Again, at a banquet given in his honor by Lord Rothschild, the emir expressed himself in similarly equable terms: "No true Arab can be suspicious or afraid of Jewish nationalism," he assured his listeners. ". . . We are demanding Arab freedom, and we would show ourselves unworthy of it, if we did not now, as I do, say to the Jews—welcome back home—and cooperate with them to the limit of the Arab State."

These discussions and exchanges of courtesies eventually were formalized in a document signed by Weizmann and Feisal, an agreement envisaging a common policy at the Peace Conference. It stated:

> His Royal Highness the Amir Feisal, representing and acting on behalf of the Arab Kingdom of Hejaz, and Dr. Chaim Weizmann, representing and acting on behalf of the Zionist Organization, mindful of the racial kinship and ancient bonds

existing between the Arabs and the Jewish people, and real-
ising that the surest means of working out the consummation
of their national aspirations is through the closest possible
collaboration in the development of the Arab State and Palestine, and being desirous further of confirming the good understanding which exists between them, have agreed upon the
following Articles. . . .

And the most important of those articles offered the Jews
assurance of their right to free immigration into Palestine and
settlement on the land. It was accompanied by a reciprocal
assurance that Arab tenant farmers would be protected in their
rights and assisted in their economic development. Significantly, one of the final clauses provided for British arbitration
of all disputes between the two peoples, clear evidence of
Whitehall's role in stage-managing the agreement. The "treaty"
was signed on January 4, 1919. Unknown to the Jews, however, Feisal unilaterally attached an addendum below the
signatures on the Arabic version: "Provided the Arabs obtain
their independence as demanded in my Memorandum dated
the 4th of January, 1919, to the Foreign Office of the Government of Great Britain, I shall concur in the above article."
Otherwise, the codicil declared, the agreement would be null
and void.

A week later, the Zionist leaders offered the Arabs a number of vital concessions, including a free zone at Haifa port,
and a joint Arab-Jewish free harbor in the Aqaba area. When
Feisal, in turn, appeared before the Peace Conference on February 6 to demand independence for the Arab countries, he
agreed that Palestine should be given separate status as the
prescribed area of the "Zionist Jews." But Feisal expected more
than a territorial *quid pro quo* from the Jews. He expected
Zionist diplomatic support against the French. On January
24, two of the emir's key advisers approached the Zionist leaders with a proposal for an Arab-Jewish entente, a "Semitic"
understanding in preference to the Western mandates. Together the two peoples would oppose French claims to the
Syrian interior, so the suggestion went. The initial Zionist

reaction to this overture was not clear. Nevertheless, Feisal's advisers returned to it continually. On one occasion Weizmann tentatively promised to explore the proposal favorably, but asked Feisal at least not to interfere with the French regime in the Syrian littoral "for tactical reasons." Whereupon the Arab leader, suspecting Jewish equivocation, hinted that he might be compelled to reappraise his attitude to Zionism. Feisal was not ready to press the issue, however. In response to an urgent inquiry from Felix Frankfurter, the emir was still prepared to offer reassurances that "we will do our best . . . to help [the Zionists] through; we will wish the Jews a hearty welcome home."

It was a difficult tightrope for Feisal to walk, resisting Arab nationalist pressure against the Jews in the hope of eliciting active Zionist cooperation against the French. In fact, it was a doomed hope. Weizmann was unwilling to embarrass his British patrons. By mid-1919, as a result, Feisal terminated his public meetings with the Zionists and politely requested them to desist from issuing statements invoking his name. Even his January 4 "treaty" with Weizmann was not revealed at this time, and the Zionists, respecting Feisal's wishes, withheld mention of it until 1936, when a Palestinian Jewish journalist first published an authenticated version of the document. By the summer of 1919, in any event, it was becoming virtually impossible for the emir to withstand the pressure of Arab extremists. Colonel French, an Intelligence officer in Egypt, wrote Curzon on August 26:

> In my opinion, Dr. Weizmann's agreement with Emir Feisal is not worth the paper it is written on or the energy wasted in the conversation to make it. On the other hand, if it becomes sufficiently known among the Arabs, it will be somewhat in the nature of a noose about Feisal's neck, for he will be regarded by the Arab population as a traitor. No greater mistake could be made than to regard Feisal as a representative of Palestinian Arabs.

By September, Feisal had reached a state of complete disillusionment with the Zionist connection. He chose increasingly now to envisage the Jewish national home merely as a sub-province within the Arab kingdom. "But when some Zionist speak about Palestine becoming as Jewish as England is English . . . they are really talking unreasonably," he declared. In the late autumn of 1919, the emir expressed the wish, through intermediaries, to cease all public and private communication with the Zionist leadership. His policy of invoking Jewish co-operation for Arab diplomatic purposes manifestly had failed.

The Stirring of Arab Palestine

COLONEL FRENCH'S VIEW, that the Feisal-Weizmann agreement was "not worth the paper it is written on," was fully shared by the majority of British civilian and military officials in Palestine. It strongly influenced their policy toward Arab and Jew alike. Hurriedly assembled from the army and the Egyptian civil service, the military administration was a somewhat undistinguished collection of lower-middle-class functionaries, few of whom were noted for imagination or sensitivity. Because their principal connections were with the Arabs, whom they considered picturesque and appropriately servile, many of these officials undoubtedly were convinced that Moslem friendship alone should be the central preoccupation of British policy. The Jews sensed—indeed, exaggerated—this combination of mediocrity and philo-Arabism and bitterly resented it. Not infrequently, too, they provoked British animosity by aggressive insistence upon what they conceived to be their rights. This was particularly true of the ardent East European immigrants. Activists like Menahem Ussishkin, for example, Weizmann's hard-driving and somewhat pugnacious deputy on the Zionist commission, pressed the British administration relentlessly to assure immediate employment for Jews in the public services and to abolish restrictions on Jewish immigration and on land transfers to Jews. Eventually the British adopted a stiffly formal approach to the Zionists. Ronald Storrs commented ruefully later that "a people can be at once bitterly wronged and yet withal so maddeningly tiresome as sometimes

to annihilate surprise, though never regret, for their suffering."
By the end of 1919, useful communication between the Zionists and the military regime had all but stopped. Sir Louis
Bols, chief administrator of the country, repeatedly complained to London of Zionist aggressiveness, of "intolerable"
Zionist accusations against the British administration. As early
as June 8, 1919, Sir Arthur Money, Bols's predecessor, had
warned that "fear and distrust of Zionist aims grow daily
[among the Arabs]. . . . A British mandate for Palestine on the
lines of the Zionist programme will mean the indefinite reten-
tion in the country of a military force considerably greater
than that now in Palestine." Each month the unrest, the barbed
Arab newspaper editorials, and the warnings mounted ominously.

However sincere the concern of the British authorities, it
was the view of Philip Graves, the *Times* correspondent in the
Middle East, that local officials erred in permitting Arabs to
conduct anti-Zionist parades and demonstrations. Under Turkish rule, he pointed out, it was tacitly understood that demonstrations were allowed only when the government actually
intended to incite violence. The argument made little impression on the military administration, which preferred to believe
that the best policy was to allow the Arabs to "let off steam."
The Jews insisted, on the other hand, that failure to suppress
unrest encouraged Arab extremism. In February 1920, a strong
party of Arab raiders attacked the Jewish colonies of Metullah
and Tel Hai in the extreme north of Palestine. Among those
who fell defending the outposts was Joseph Trumpeldor, wartime leader of the Zion Mule Corps (see Chapter VII). Shocked
and alarmed by this loss, the Palestinian Jewish population
immediately set about enlarging their communal defense
force, the Haganah. The Arab nationalists, in turn, had already organized a series of militant liberation societies—Al
Nadi al-Arabi, Al Akha w'al-Arab, Al Fedaiyeh—in various
parts of the country. On August 29, Colonel French transmitted to London a detailed Intelligence report from a political
officer in Palestine:

In brief [it warned], practically all Moslems and Christians of any importance in Palestine are anti-Zionist, and bitterly so. . . . In other words, if we mean to carry out any sort of Zionist policy we must do so with military force and adopt a strong policy against all the agitators in the country. . . . We must also be ready to risk disorders in the Moslem world at large and be prepared for the propaganda that is certain to be made with regard to Jews taking possession of the Holy Places and the Holy Land.

The allusion to the Holy Places may have been specious, for Jewish religionists were interested exclusively in their own Temple site. But the Arabs were well aware that Zionist ambitions for Palestine were hardly limited to this single ancient shrine. Colonel French's evaluation of Arab hostility was therefore by no means farfetched.

From the seventh century until the British conquest, Palestine had been a peripheral and altogether neglected province of the Islamic Empire, a backwater of the Arab and Ottoman realms alike. Its soil, ruined under Turkish domination, as late as 1882 barely supported perhaps 260,000 Arab inhabitants. It was essentially Jewish immigration and economic development that stimulated the growth of the Arab population to 515,000 by 1914, and to 600,000 by 1920. Except for a small Christian minority in the cities, most of these inhabitants were Moslem peasantry, economically and culturally backward to the level of primitivism. Under the Turks, their political activities had been equally rudimentary, consisting for the most part of maneuvers for civil office among rival families of the upper effendi class. The change came after the war, with the replacement of the indolent, Moslem Ottoman overlord by a Christian British administration—and under the British, the introduction into Palestine of a seemingly alien foreign minority. Even then the Arab political reaction manifested itself quite lethargically. Indeed, the local *mukhtars* were initially grateful for the infusion of British and Jewish capital into the country. At the outset, moreover, Arab nationalism was somewhat vaguely focused on French rule in Syria, and its leadership emanated primarily from Damascus; in those days

The Second Arab Revolt: Palestine

Palestine was meaningfully described as "southern Syria." In January 1919, at an "all-Arab Palestine Conference," the local notables issued a resolution that simultaneously demanded repudiation of the Balfour Declaration, the rejection of French claims on Syria, and the "establishment of a united independent Syrian government."

During the course of 1919, an authentically Palestinian Arab nationalism began to develop slowly among the younger elements in the towns and cities. Religious emotionalism played a role. So did the example of the Hashemite regime in Damascus. But so did outrage—at the dynamic, secularized, "insolent" Zionist youth, with their Western clothing, their higher wages, their free and cocksure assumption that someday they would govern their own Jewish state in Palestine. The Zionists and their supporters did not take Arab unrest, or even Arab sensitivities, quite seriously at first. "I do not pay much attention to this . . . normal state of affairs," Colonel Meinertzhagen wrote in his diary, "although it produces a feeling of insecurity among the community who regard Zionism as the spark which may light a general Palestine conflagration, an opinion which I do not share." The death of Trumpeldor was the Zionist moment of recognition. In March 1920, in a curious reversal of roles, Weizmann cautioned Allenby that trouble was brewing among the Arab population of Jerusalem. This time the British minimized the danger. "There *can* be no trouble," Bols assured Weizmann, "the town is stiff with troops!" The Zionist leader was not as sanguine. That month the Syrian National Congress offered Feisal the throne of a united Syria. More portentously yet, it was the season of Nebi Musa.

The Nebi Musa festival, which fell that year on April 4, was essentially a local holiday, a traditional counterpart to Easter or Passover, when pious Moslems of the Jerusalem-Hebron area undertook a pilgrimage on the Jericho road to the tomb of Moses (an Islamic no less than a Hebrew patriarch). Sir Ronald Storrs, governor of Jerusalem, wrote later:

Nebi Musa was normally a blameless (if rather pointless) event, consisting of a week's hot sticky holiday by the Dead

391

Sea, with mild feasting, both of fruit and sweets, and shows ranging from an indelicate variant of Punch and Judy to the circumcision of anxious little boys before a gaping assembly of proud relations. No untoward incident had hitherto occurred, but in 1920 the air was full of rumours of that nervous quality to which the altitude of Jerusalem undoubtedly contributed. We made what were then considered adequate dispositions, though I had more than once represented that the placing of the Jerusalem police force in charge of a young Lieutenant was hardly fair to the City, to me, or to himself. The pilgrims not being expected to arrive at the Jaffa Gate until after midday, I went with my father and mother to Easter Matins at St. George's Cathedral, ordering a member of the staff to warn me there as previously, as soon as the procession was within an hour of Jerusalem. He forgot.

The revelers arrived, a colorful procession of fluttering banners and prancing dervishes. Out of respect for Moslem religious sensibilities, the Administration had assigned Jewish policemen elsewhere for the day. Unfortunately, the Arab police were listless and poorly trained. Outside the municipal building the Arab mayor of Jerusalem greeted the crowd with a fervently patriotic speech. Immediately afterward, Moslem agitators, not all of them local, began to harangue the mob and extol the name of Feisal. It was evident that their purpose was to influence the Allied powers, scheduled to dispose of the mandates in San Remo within the next fortnight. The crowd became unruly, the Arab police joined in the applause, and the violence began. Stones, sticks, and knives were used indiscriminately. During the next three hours, 160 Jews were wounded. Eventually British troops arrived and quelled the disturbances. The next morning, however, the British released the Arab instigators who had been detained overnight, and attacks on the Jews promptly commenced again. Order was not restored until the third day. A number of Jews and Arabs had been killed by then, and several hundred wounded.

The aftermath of the bloodletting was hardly less unnerving to the Zionists than the violence itself. The Arab mayor of Jerusalem was sacked forthwith, and two leading Arab instigators, Haj Amin al-Husseini and Aref al-Aref, were given stiff prison terms. But the majority of Moslem rioters received only light jail sentences, whereas Vladimir Jabotinsky (see Chapter VII), who had sought to organize a Jewish self-defense group in Palestine during the turmoil, was sentenced to fifteen years imprisonment by a military court. Immediately, in England, as in the Jewish world, the reaction both to the violence and to the disparity of the sentences afterward was so uproarious that Whitehall promptly agreed to convene an official court of inquiry. During the hearings in Jerusalem, the officers of the military government defended their administration, insisting that Zionist provocation alone had inflamed the Arabs. The Zionists, in turn, boldly accused the mandatory government of complicity, of sanctioning Moslem nationalist activity despite urgent and fully documented warnings. At this point, moreover, to the astonishment and indignation of the British authorities, Colonel Richard Meinertzhagen, chief Intelligence officer in Cairo, took the witness stand in order to endorse fully the Zionist accusations. Summarizing his testimony years later in his published diaries (the proceedings of the inquiry were never made public), Meinertzhagen wrote:

> I had ample warning that these riots might occur and I warned General Bols and Waters-Taylor [the financial officer]. I warned both Bols and Allenby, neither of whom paid much attention; no precautionary measures were taken in Jerusalem, Waters-Taylor absenting himself in Jericho for the day. I regarded the rioting as a deliberate attempt by the Administration to show H. M. G. the futility of trying to [impose] Zionism on Palestine. On April 14, I addressed a dispatch to Lord Curzon. . . . I criticized the British Administration centred in Jerusalem, I recorded that the officers of the Administration are, almost without exception, anti-Zionist in their views and are encouraging the Arabs.

It was a sensational indictment. Meinertzhagen went so far as to incorporate it in a document that he sent off to the Cabinet in London. By his "disloyalty" to his immediate superiors, of course, the Intelligence officer had ended his usefulness to Allenby. He was dismissed out of hand. Nevertheless, he had accomplished his purpose. The Palestine military administration was now hopelessly compromised in the eyes of the government. British public opinion, as well, had been unsettled by the riots and outraged by the palpable ineptitude of the army bureaucrats in Jerusalem. A radical change in the Palestine government clearly was overdue. On April 29, 1920, four days after the Supreme Council at San Remo allocated the Palestine mandate to Britain, London announced the imminent dismantling of the military regime in the Holy Land in favor of a provisional civil administration.

Herbert Samuel and the Regime of Sweet Reason

IT WAS IN SAN REMO, a day before the assignment of the mandates, that Herbert Samuel first learned of his selection by Curzon and Lloyd George as civil high commissioner for Palestine. The choice was not illogical in view of Samuel's record as a Liberal Party leader and former Cabinet minister. He was known, too, as an observant Jew and a Zionist sympathizer, and seemingly this reputation emphasized the government's commitment to the Jewish national home, its refusal to be intimidated by violence. The appointment obviously was not without its dangers. Allenby direly predicted "outrages against Jews, murders, raids on Jewish villages, and raids into our territory from East if no wider movement." Feisal warned that "the Arabs would inevitably regard such an appointment as being made at their expense." Ironically, even the eminent Anglo-Jewish novelist Israel Zangwill, an active Zionist, viewed Samuel's appointment as "a mere cover for the practical repudiation of the Balfour promise"; the new high commissioner unquestionably would favor the Arabs to prove his impartiality, Zangwill insisted. In the light of these rather ominous prophecies, when Samuel arived in Palestine on June 30, 1920, it was deemed expedient to escort him from the railroad station in Jerusalem to government house on the Mount of Olives with a sizable contingent of armored cars, and to have him accompanied everywhere by detectives.

Many of these precautions and misgivings appeared to be unjustified. Samuel's initial appointments aroused warm enthusiasm in both England and Palestine. They included the able and progressive Wyndham Deedes as chief secretary of the Administration; Norman Bentwich, a distinguished barrister and avowed Zionist, as attorney general; Sir Ronald Storrs, retained as governor of Jerusalem as a symbol of impartiality; and experienced senior army officers brought over from Egypt as governors of the Jaffa and Haifa districts. Neither Jews nor Arabs seemingly had reason for complaint. Samuel's opening speech before the assembled notables of Jerusalem, promising absolute impartiality and fairness to all Palestine's citizens, was convincing and generally well received. So were the commissioner's earliest executive decisions: to determine landholdings by a cadastral survey, to establish credit banks, and to undertake a large program of public works, including road and railroad construction, telegraphic and telephonic communications, and swamp drainage. The high commissioner's intimate connections in the government also were Palestine's good fortune. He got what he wanted from London. His budgets were always passed. Personally, the man all but radiated fairness and patient courtesy. Norman Bentwich recalled that even Arab extremists respected Samuel: "'Nafsu Sharif!' they would say, 'his self is honourable.'"

But this very impartiality, as Zangwill had feared, proved to be the high commissioner's Achilles' heel. "All my life a convinced Liberal," Samuel wrote later, ". . . I was the last man to take a hand in any policy of oppression. . . . Nothing could be worse than if it were to appear that the one thing the Jewish people had learnt from the centuries of their own oppression was the way to oppress others." It was conceivably this preoccupation with fairness that influenced the high commissioner to appoint E. T. Richmond, an ardent anti-Zionist, director of the political department of the secretariat, in that capacity the *de facto* planner of the Administration's Arab policy. The same concern for objectivity was probably responsible for Samuel's decision to withhold a large block of public land from Jewish purchase in the Beisan area and to establish an annual quota for Jewish immigrants. Far from placating Arab nationalism, however, these conciliatory gestures apparently encouraged it. As an example, the commissioner's advisory council was scheduled to include twelve British officials, three Jews, and seven Arabs. Yet the Arab leadership contemptuously boycotted the council rather than acknowledge Jewish participation in it. In the long run, to be sure, the boycott may have proved self-defeating. For whereas the Jews managed to develop their own quasi-government for internal Jewish communal affairs, the Arabs evolved very little political experience and only the most rudimentary kind of national leadership. But that leadership compensated in extremism for what it lacked in sophistication.

Indeed, the entire representation of the Moslem population was embodied in the Grand Mufti of Jerusalem, a jurisconsul empowered to issue decrees on koranical law. As it happened, this key religious office became vacant shortly after Samuel arrived in Palestine, and to the high commissioner fell the governmental prerogative of appointing a new incumbent. Rivalry for the post, as for almost every other public or quasi-public office in the country, had traditionally been contested between the two wealthy clans of Nashashibi and Husseini. The most recent mufti had been Kemal Effendi Husseini; the mayor of Jerusalem was now Ragheb Bey Nashashibi. The Nashashibis very nearly captured the muftiship, as well, until Samuel intervened. Determined to keep the honors balanced between the two factions, the high commissioner, on April 27, 1921, was persuaded to approve the dubiously honest election of Haj Mohammed Amin al-Husseini, a younger brother of Kemal, to the post for life. It was not the happiest choice. Although disarming in appearance and demeanor, with mild blue eyes, gentle, well-modulated voice, and courtly, ingratiating manner, Amin al-Husseini was in fact a notorious

Arab xenophobe, a preacher of venom and destruction against his nation's—and his family's—enemies. Only the year before, he had been sentenced to ten years imprisonment for his role in the Nebi Musa riots, and had but recently been pardoned. Upon learning of this appointment now, Meinertzhagen was almost beside himself with outrage. He had cautioned Samuel of the possible consequences, and now warned Churchill "without mincing words of the harm we must expect from such a scoundrel." Actually, the danger resided less in the office of mufti than in the much more influential presidency of the Supreme Moslem Council, a post the mufti of Jerusalem traditionally occupied. The Council exercised full authority over the *waqfs*, the Moslem charitable and educational investment funds, most of them in landholdings; over the Islamic religious courts of Palestine; and over the appointment of all other provincial and regional muftis. Its powers of patronage were enormous, and the sheer prestige of its office exerted a formidable psychological effect on the devout and illiterate Arab peasantry of the country. The Zionists knew what to expect from a firebrand like Haj Amin al-Husseini in that post, if Samuel did not.

Anti-Zionist agitation was indeed renewed during the summer of 1920, immediately after the expulsion of Feisal from Damascus. It was led this time by Palestinian Arabs, officials in the former Syrian kingdom who suddenly found themselves without employment in the aftermath of the French occupation. For them and their followers, Palestine was the last remaining focus of nationalist discontent. Yet, as always, the "official" spokesmen of the Palestine Moslem community were the Husseinis and Nashashibis. Moreover, at a special Palestine Arab Congress that met in Haifa in December 1920, the two clans united under the chairmanship of Musa Kazem al-Husseini, the recently dismissed mayor of Jerusalem. The resolutions issued by this gathering left no room whatever for compromise; they insisted upon an end to the Balfour Declaration, to Jewish immigration, to all restraints on full and free Arab self-government in Palestine. As it happened, the Palestine mandate was not officially issued by the League of Nations until July 1922 (see p. 406). In the interval, therefore, Arab political intrigue gained momentum in the shadows of public coffeehouses and private divans. Large sums of money for underground activity arrived from Beirut. Without specific information, but continually on the alert, the British kept Jerusalem under heavy military occupation.

The renewed troubles began in Jaffa. On May 1, 1921, a ragtag group of Jewish Communists brashly conducted an unlicensed march through the center of town in the wake of a Jewish labor parade. The incident incensed the Arabs. They rioted, then looted Jewish stores and workshops. Finally, when nationalist instigators reached the scene, the rioters began to murder. One of their principal targets was the Zionist immigration depot, where they promptly hacked to pieces thirteen Jews newly arrived from Europe, including several women. By the end of the first day the mobs had killed thirty-five Jews. The violence then spread rapidly to the countryside. On May 5, the Jewish orange-growing colony of Petach Tikvah was attacked by nearly a thousand Arabs from nearby villages. The defenders would have been annihilated had it not been for the unexpected arrival of a detachment of Indian cavalry on a training march. In the next few days other Jewish farm colonies were besieged. By the end of the week, when the British finally suppressed the last attack, forty-seven Jews and forty-eight Arabs had been killed and several hundred Jews and Arabs wounded.

As the Administration surveyed the apparent wreckage of Samuel's policy of benign restraint, it contemplated at first taking drastic and forceful punitive measures against the Arabs. But eventually the high commissioner, influenced by Storrs, decided to maintain his earlier approach of even-handed conciliation. Most of the arrested Arabs were released. Another commission of inquiry was organized, this one directed by Sir Thomas Haycroft, chief justice of Palestine. For the next seven weeks the little group of civil servants urgently conducted their investigation, and a fortnight after that, submitted their report.

In the riots themselves the Arabs were unquestionably the aggressors, the document stated. Yet the fundamental causes went much deeper, "the feeling against the Jews was too genuine, too widespread and too intense to be accounted for in [a] . . . superficial manner." The report declared that the Arabs were convinced that Britain was favoring the Jews, that the Zionist commissioners had been invested with far too much authority, that disproportionate numbers of Jews were employed in the public service, that Jewish labor was displacing Arab workers, and that the immigrants displayed arrogance and contempt for Arab social ideas. Although specific recommendations did not appear in the conclusion, they were implicit in the commission's thinly veiled sympathy for Arab resentment. Worse, from the Zionist viewpoint, was Samuel's decision to placate the Arab nationalists by temporarily conceding their demands to stop Jewish immigration. The ban was shortly lifted, in July 1921, but under more rigid controls, including a guarantee of available employment. The very notion of "artificial" restrictions bitterly rankled the Zionists; during the summer the leaders of the major Palestinian Jewish organization resigned in protest. Samuel held firm, however. The key to his policy was revealed in his Jerusalem speech of June 3, 1921, assuring a group of Arab notables that their interests would not be sacrificed in favor of the Jews and that Jewish immigration would continue to be limited by the "economic absorptive capacity" of the country. The Zionists, hardly less concerned by this statement than by the original inquiry report, were certain that it foreshadowed a policy of retrenchment in the implementation of the Balfour Declaration. They were not wrong.

Reformulating the Jewish National Home

DURING MOST OF 1920, the community of interest between the Zionists and the British Cabinet remained essentially intact. At London's insistence, the very text of the Balfour

Declaration was incorporated *verbatim* both into the San Remo award, and later into Article Ninety-five of the Treaty of Sèvres. Britain's treaty obligation to establish a Jewish national home clearly placed the Holy Land in a unique category among the mandates. This obligation was made even more explicit as the Zionist leadership and the foreign office worked in virtual partnership to draft the mandatory instrument for submission to the League. Whatever difficulties arose in preparing the draft arose elsewhere, not initially in London. One was the purely mechanical failure of the Peace Conference to ratify the Turkish peace treaty. Kemal was blocking that. Another was the continual, niggling obstruction raised by the Italian government on behalf of the Vatican, demanding that the Holy Places commission be invested with extraterritorial powers. By 1921, this difficulty was successfully resolved in a compromise formula giving the commission direct access to the League Council. The United States, for its part, insisted upon unreserved assurance of an Open Door in the mandates, and this agreement was not formulated until 1922.

By late 1921, misgivings about the government's pro-Zionist policy were also expressed with increasing frequency in England. Returning officials of the former Palestine military government, including Waters-Taylor and a number of recently cashiered army personnel, were in the vanguard of the attack. In a gesture of long-awaited revenge, they took it upon themselves to serve as advisers to the Arab delegation that had arrived in London to protest the Balfour Declaration. Their most useful weapon was the desperate anxiety of the British people to demobilize their far-flung military units, to minimize areas of abrasion abroad, and under all circumstances to reduce imperial expenditures. The Iraqi uprising of 1920 had aroused misgivings that the riots in Palestine seriously exacerbated. Additionally, in late January 1922, Lord Northcliffe, publisher of the London *Times,* stopped off in Palestine during a world tour and was both offended by the churlishness of the Jewish farmers he met there and alarmed by the evidence he saw all around him of heavy military precautions. Convinced that Palestine was on its way to becoming a "second Ireland," Northcliffe and his chain of newspapers embarked upon an editorial campaign against this particular mandatory responsibility, urging the government to drop it like a hot potato. The issue was raised in Parliament. On June 21, 1922, several Tory members of the House of Lords actually slipped an anti-mandatory resolution through a sixty-member quorum. The gesture may have been purely symbolic; but it came in tandem with an attack launched in the House of Commons by Sir William Joynson-Hicks, who warned that a Palestine mandate was a financial albatross. To the Lloyd George government it was plain—indeed, it had been evident as far back as the spring of 1921—that peace and order would have to be restored swiftly in the Holy Land lest Parliament reject the mandate altogether.

In the spring of 1921, it will be recalled, Churchill summoned his Cairo conference. While the central purpose of his Middle East visit was to devise a solution for the Iraqi question, it also provided the logical occasion to explore a Palestine settlement. Thus, finishing with the conference, the colonial secretary in late March journeyed on to Palestine. As he motored from Jaffa up to Jerusalem, escorted by Samuel and Lawrence, he bowed and smiled to the large Arab crowds shouting at him excitedly until Lawrence whispered in his ear that they were demanding the murder of the Jews. In Jerusalem, leaders of the Palestine Arab Congress presented the nationalist viewpoint rather less violently, but with equal intransigence. Churchill was no less unbudging, however, and firmly reiterated his support of the Jewish national home. As he ceremonially planted a tree in the garden of the future Hebrew University on Mount Scopus, he assured the attending Jewish dignitaries that "my heart is full of sympathy with Zionism. . . . I believe that the building of a Jewish National Home in Palestine will be a blessing to the whole world, a blessing to the Jewish race . . . a blessing to Great Britain."

These reassurances notwithstanding, Churchill's visit to the Middle East was not all moonlight and roses for the

Zionists. It resulted in the separation of Transjordan from Palestine and the issuance of the "Churchill" White Paper. Nominally within the boundaries of the Palestine mandate, Transjordan was a high plateau-land, fertile in many districts, inhabited by some 300,000 Arab peasants and seminomads. With the end of the war, this entire region east of the Jordan was included within OETA East, i.e., in the Arab sphere, for there was a vague understanding that it might have been reserved to the Arabs by the Hussein-McMahon correspondence. No attempt was made by Feisal to administer the area, however, and individual sheiks were laws unto themselves. Then, following the emir's enforced departure from Syria in the summer of 1920, Transjordan was reduced entirely to a no man's land, and Bedouin attacks on the settled Jewish areas west of the Jordan River soon threatened to get out of hand. On August 7, 1920, Samuel cabled the foreign secretary in London requesting permission to include Transjordan directly in the Palestine administration lest the situation "result in anarchy or French control across the border." In his reply, Curzon proposed instead that a few "suitable" officials be dispatched across the river to guide the Arabs to eventual self-government. The high commissioner thereupon sent off two junior officers to the eastern highlands. In Kerak, under the direction of Alec Kirkbride, a "National Government of Moab" was organized. In Amman, an "Ammonite Government" was established under Kirkbride's younger brother, Alan. Despite the cooperation of a few local sheiks, however, these little tin-pot regimes were ineffectual in restoring order and security beyond their town limits.

It was at this juncture, in the late summer of 1920, that Emir Abdullah appeared on the fringes of Transjordan with his retinue. He was en route to Syria via the Hejaz Railroad, to help "restore" his brother Feisal to power. In fact, Abdullah's arrival seemed an almost providential coincidence. Of the entire Hashemite family, he was the only member for whom a domain was not yet provided. Feisal was the candidate for the kingship of Iraq. The Sherif Hussein was back in Mecca with

Ali, his heir apparent to the Hejaz. And now here was Abdullah, without a throne in sight, materializing in the countryside in his wheezing little train, stopping every few miles along the Hejaz line to chop down telegraph poles for the locomotive firebox, and detraining finally in Amman to ask all "true Arabs" to rally to his banner. The response was not encouraging. The Arabs expected to be paid. Undaunted, Abdullah continued on with some two thousand men toward Kerak, where he was cordially, if circumspectly, greeted by Alec Kirkbride. Finally the Hashemite chieftain pushed on toward Amman in March 1921. By chance, at this very moment Churchill's Middle East Conference was underway in Cairo and news of Abdullah's mission at first aroused consternation among the assembled officials. Clearly the little emir had to be stopped lest he provoke a crisis between France and England. And then it occurred to Lawrence and Churchill that the problem might be resolved by asking Abdullah to remain in Transjordan. There he would reign (although not rule) as Britain's protégé. In return for a British subsidy, the emir could easily be persuaded to renounce all claims to Iraq, in that fashion clearing the way for his brother Feisal. Entranced by the sheer symmetry and logic of the plan, Churchill immediately cabled London and obtained Whitehall's permission to meet with Abdullah. The invitation for discussions in Jerusalem was tendered on March 24, and Abdullah somewhat cautiously accepted.

On May 26, the two men met and conferred for a day and a half in government house, in the presence of Samuel and Lawrence. Unlike his younger brother, Feisal, Abdullah was short and stocky, a "cheery-faced, shrewd, genial little man," as Churchill described him, "aristocratic though not of great distinction." He listened intently as the colonial secretary outlined the proposals recently formulated in Cairo. By their terms, Abdullah would abjure any further action against the French. He would additionally renounce his claims to Iraq, maintain order in Transjordan, and recognize Transjordan as an integral part of the Palestine mandate. Finally, the emir would establish an Arab government in Amman and administer the territory in the name of the British mandate. In return, Britain would undertake to provide Abdullah with a monthly subsidy, with trained advisers, and with the assurance of Transjordanian independence at some future date. It seemed a large dose to swallow at once. Nevertheless, Abdullah discussed the proposition with his advisers overnight, and on the morning of the 27th he accepted the offer without qualification.

Churchill thereupon departed for home glowing with self-satisfaction, confident that he had accomplished nothing less than the restoration of tranquillity in the Middle East. He had avoided embroilment with France, for one thing. No less important, he had managed to reduce the imperial burden on the British taxpayer. Abdullah, for his part, promptly established his capital in Amman, a shabby, overgrown village in the Edomite hills, and built a couple of modest palaces. With the counsel of T. E. Lawrence, and later of H. St. John Philby, he organized a patriarchal Hashemite government and thereby guaranteed the rule of law and order in his "realm." For London it was a cheap and ingenious scheme for maintaining peace and British supremacy beyond the Jordan.

The arrangement had to be sold to the Jews, however. The creation of an Arab government east of the Jordan River was Britain's first explicit admission that Transjordan was included in the area of Arab autonomy, as promised by McMahon to Hussein in 1915, rather than in integral Palestine. It followed logically that the Balfour Declaration could not be applied to that territory. Interestingly enough, Balfour himself never had made that assumption. In a memorandum to Lloyd George on August 11, 1919, the foreign secretary emphasized the importance to the Jews of drawing the frontier well east of the Jordan for the development of Zionist agricultural interests. Even Abdullah must have experienced some astonishment at the shift in Britain's position, for later he declared: "He [God] granted me success in creating the Government of Transjordan by having it separated from the Balfour Declaration which had included it since the Sykes-Picot Agreement assigned it to the British zone of influence." This major concession to the Arabs evidently did not register at first on the Zionists, and they did not press the issue. Nowhere in their earlier correspondence either with the British or among themselves had they expressed any serious interest in Transjordanian territory; their colonies were all west of the river. Only later, when the mandate officially excluded the Jewish national home from Transjordan (see p. 406), did awareness of the lost bargaining point suddenly dawn on the Zionist leaders, to their mounting and increasingly vocal dismay.

Still other restrictions were imposed on the Jewish national home. In May 1922, Herbert Samuel returned to London to impress on the colonial office the need for dispelling Arab fears on the Palestine Question. Only by painstakingly reinterpreting the Balfour Declaration, he insisted, was it possible to assure the support of Arab moderates in putting the mandate into effect. His recommendation was accepted. A statement of policy was drafted for issuance over Churchill's signature. The document, henceforth to be known as the "Churchill White Paper," restricted the application of the Balfour Declaration to the region west of the Jordan River. Even in this limited area, the British government made it clear that it had no intention of creating a predominantly Jewish state. Although the White Paper upheld the ideal of a Jewish national home, it rejected the notion that the Palestine Zionist Executive should have any part in the administration of the country. Similarly, Jewish immigration was to be limited strictly to the "economic capacity of the country." The statement read in part:

> Phrases have been used such as that Palestine is to become "as Jewish as England is English." His Majesty's Government regard any such expectation as impracticable and have no such aim in view. . . . When it is asked what is meant by the development of a Jewish National Home in Palestine, it may be answered that it is not the imposition of a Jewish nationality upon the inhabitants of Palestine as a whole but the further development of the existing Jewish community . . . in order that it may become a center in which the Jewish people as a whole may take . . . an interest and a pride. But

in order that this community should have the best prospect of free development . . . it is essential that it should know that it is in Palestine as of right and not on sufferance.

The document was submitted to the Zionist Organization in June. Under intense pressure from the colonial office, and in fear of losing British support for the Jewish national home altogether, Weizmann and the Zionist Executive reluctantly, even bitterly, agreed to accept it, on June 19. The Arab delegation, on the other hand, flatly rejected it. Notwithstanding this mixed reception, the government published the Churchill White Paper on July 1, 1922, as the official interpretation of the British mandate in Palestine. On that basis the mandate won easy acceptance by the House of Commons five days later. The League Council's approval followed very quickly, on July 24. Britain's authority in Palestine was formalized at last.

The Pattern of the Future

THE ZIONISTS HAD SUFFERED a reverse of sorts, but by no means a fatal one. After all, in the preamble of its award the League Council recited the Balfour Declaration almost *verbatim* and imposed on the British the obligation not simply to permit, but to "secure" the Jewish national home, to "use their best endeavors to facilitate" Jewish immigration and encourage settlement on the land. Hebrew was recognized as an official language. A Jewish Agency (provisionally the Zionist Organization itself) was authorized to cooperate with the mandatory power in the development of natural resources and in the operation of public works and utilities. From beginning to end, the document manifestly was framed to protect the Zionist redemptive effort. It was significant, for example, that the word "Arab" did not once appear in the mandatory award, and that the Arab and other peoples in Palestine were repeatedly described merely as "non-Jews." Nor was there any doubt, once the mandate was duly ratified, that the British government intended to stand behind it. The Bonar Law

Cabinet, which succeeded the Lloyd George coalition in October 1922, firmly rejected every Arab effort to alter Britain's support of the Zionists. In Palestine itself, Samuel also now seemed committed to making the national home viable, if on the more moderate format of the Churchill White Paper. Even Meinertzhagen revised his earlier misgivings about the high commissioner. "What I mistook for weakness," he wrote, "was in reality a determination to be just and impartial." A steady flow of immigration had increased the Jewish population to nearly 85,000 by the end of 1922, and new Zionist farm communities and urban settlements were springing up along the coast and in the Galilee.

But if Zionist achievement was the pattern of the future for the Holy Land, so was Arab hostility, keenly felt and increasingly envenomed. The executive of the Palestine Arab Congress, under the presidency of Musa Kazem Pasha al-Husseini, was operating in close association with the Supreme Moslem Council under the presidency of the mufti, Haj Amin al-Husseini. Indeed, as early as 1921 it was clear that the Husseinis were rapidly becoming Britain's most formidable and resourceful enemies in Palestine or, for that matter, in the entire Middle East. Under their leadership, the Arab nationalists continued to boycott Samuel's efforts to establish an advisory council. In May 1921, the fourth Palestine Arab Congress dispatched a team of representatives to England to lobby against the Balfour Declaration. Setting up their headquarters in the Hotel Cecil, the Arabs buttonholed colonial- and foreign-office personnel at every opportunity. To no avail, however; they found the government unbending on the subject of the Jewish national home.

The Husseinis claimed a revenge of sorts shortly after the League mandate was issued. A month later, in August 1922, London promulgated a "constitution" for Palestine in the form of an Order in Council. One of its provisions was for a mixed legislative council of elected and appointed members. The arrangement would not have permitted an Arab majority. Accordingly, the fifth Palestine Arab Congress unanimously rejected participation in the elections for this body. With the Arab population boycotting the whole scheme, the elections were a fiasco. In 1923, Whitehall tentatively formulated another plan, this one for a revived advisory council with an Arab Moslem majority. But the Congress leadership rejected the new overture, as well, and the idea was scrapped. Other proposals were mooted in following weeks, but also got nowhere. Completely disenchanted by then, Samuel recommended that the colonial office terminate all negotiations with the Arabs, and his suggestion was approved. Henceforth Palestine was administered by British officials alone. Participation in the mandatory regime, the evolution of self-government, Arab-Jewish cooperation—all evidently were utopian visions for the Holy Land.

Nevertheless, the Zionists were still hopeful that some form of *modus vivendi* could be worked out with the Arabs. In the spring of 1922 a series of unofficial Arab-Zionist meetings took place in Cairo. They were attended by several leading Syrian nationalists, although by no delegates from the Palestine Arab community. At each discussion the usual amenities were exchanged, the pious references to a common Semitic revival in the Middle East. In the initial meeting on March 18, however, the Arabs renewed their far-reaching proposals of January 1919. One was for the Jews to cooperate with the Arabs in evicting the French from Syria and the Lebanon. Another suggestion, even more pregnant in its implications, was for the Zionists to repudiate the Balfour Declaration and deal directly with the Arabs "nation to nation." Acceptance of the first offer clearly would have been a serious embarrassment to London. Acceptance of the second would have made the Jewish enclave in Palestine dependent upon an Arab agreement rather than upon British protection. Weizmann and his associates obliquely rejected the proposals, although asking for time to consider them. The Zionists owed too much to His Majesty's Government to be willing to negotiate behind its back or to undermine the British mandate. Two subsequent meetings, on April 2 and April 4, were equally cordial and equally inconclusive. The Arabs were unwilling to countenance the Balfour Declaration. The Jews refused to act independently of London; they had come too far working in collaboration with their British patrons to risk a move now without Whitehall's approval.

Perhaps it is naïve to speculate that if Weizmann had authorized a direct understanding with the Arabs independently of Britain, or even of the Balfour Declaration, much of the acrimony of the Palestine Question might have been avoided. Little assurance existed that any responsible Palestine Arab faction would have agreed to the unlimited continuation of Jewish immigration. Rather, it appeared more likely that the pattern of hostility had been frozen by then. The Arab nationalists evidently were convinced that their best hope of seizing Palestine for themselves was to maintain a posture of flat intransigence. Ultimately that hope failed, of course. But in the generation that followed, it became equally plain that Zionist reliance upon British protection and benevolence was no less bankrupt a position. London's policy was shifting rapidly and inexorably in favor of the Arabs. The fate of Palestine was eventually resolved, therefore, when the Jews decided to re-examine their traditional stance and were the first to repudiate it without concern for the shibboleths and fixations of the past.

This emergent hostility between their two protégé peoples in the Holy Land was a bitter legacy for the English. But the promises made in the heat of war, whatever their undetected time bomb of future conflict, had by no means been issued in vain. Notwithstanding the burden equally of Jewish and Arab ingratitude, Britain had nevertheless won a foothold in Palestine which ensured the security of the Suez Canal during two wars and the years between. The furor and outraged recriminations of the client nations whose support had helped achieve that foothold may have been a high price for strategic advantage, but the cost was hardly prohibitive for the role the Palestine military complex fulfilled in assuring the survival of the British Empire. Generations later, as it turned out, the price of rising and malignant hatred was to weigh less heavily on London than on the Palestine successor states themselves, and no less on all the Middle Eastern peoples from the Nile to the Persian Gulf.

CHAPTER XIV

THE RISE OF TURKEY

Constantine Inherits an Empire

O N OCTOBER 2, 1920, King Alexander of Greece, who three
years before had succeeded his exiled father, Constantine, was
taking a leisurely stroll through the palace zoo in Athens, accompanied by his spaniel. The youthful monarch stopped for
a moment to watch the antics of a pair of rhesus monkeys.
Suddenly the dog attacked the female monkey, and the male
in retaliation sank his teeth into Alexander's thigh. An infection
developed in the king's leg and spread rapidly through his
body, and after three weeks of agony he died. The accident was
destined to alter radically the course of modern Greek history,
for the problem of succession immediately became acute.
Alexander's infant son was hardly an appropriate heir, having
been born of the king's morganatic marriage to a commoner.
On the other hand, there was apparently no question of permitting the return of Constantine, whom the government and
pro-Allied elements despised. After some indecision, therefore,
Venizelos eventually persuaded the Cabinet to offer the throne
to the late king's brother, Prince Paul. But the problem was
not to be resolved that easily. Paul, living in exile, was unwilling to accept the invitation without first allowing the Greek
people a chance to vote for or against his father's return. Admittedly, Venizelos could have declined this challenge to a
national election; by launching a revolution in 1917, he had
placed the issue of Constantine beyond the bounds of normal
political intercourse. The incense of triumph was still in the
prime minister's nostrils, however. Oblivious to the partisan nature of his original triumphant reception three months earlier,
he was convinced that a national election would provide just

the massive vote of confidence necessary to buttress his political ambitions for the 1920's.

It was a disastrous miscalculation, one of the few of Venizelos's career. In allowing the election campaign to become a popularity contest between Constantine and himself, he profoundly underestimated the depth of royalist sentiment among the nation's traditionally conservative peasantry. The sons of this silent majority had carried the brunt of the fighting in Macedonia, and even now were crouched again in the trenches of Asia Minor. Farmers and city-dwellers alike were desperately weary of war, taxes, and government oppression. Their moment of revenge came at last on election day, November 14, 1920. Despite flagrant and brutal acts of intimidation by Venizelist partisans, the people of Greece voted overwhelmingly in favor of the royalist party. Indeed, Venizelos himself was personally unseated. It was an astounding, shattering humiliation for the prime minister. He resigned his office immediately and quit Greece for Italy three days later on a friend's yacht. Whereupon the new anti-Venizelist government, hardly believing its good fortune, promptly made arrangements for a plebiscite to decide the issue of Constantine's return. And in spite of warnings from Paris and London that restoration of the "pro-German" monarch would mean the end of Allied financial assistance, the Greek nation voted decisively to invite Constantine back. The exiled king gratefully accepted this mandate. On December 19, he returned amid demonstrations of tearful rejoicing that dwarfed even Venizelos's reception three months earlier. Outraged, but manifestly helpless before this royalist avalanche, the Allies decided officially to continue diplomatic relations with the Hellenic government without at the same time acknowledging Constantine's return. The Western ambassadors in Athens accordingly made it their practice to ignore the king's very existence and declined to attend court functions.

Presumably the vote for Constantine offered the royalists an ideal opportunity to repudiate Venizelos's imperialist adventures of the past three years, or at least to limit Greek commitments in Asia Minor. At first, to be sure, the need for this limitation might not have appeared compelling. The dramatic military victories over the Turkish Nationalists in the summer of 1920 had convinced Lloyd George that "the Turks are broken beyond repair." Sterghiades, the energetic and imaginative Greek high commissioner in Smyrna, was effectively asserting his civil authority in the occupied area and was repatriating and employing some 120,000 Greek refugees there. Nor was there any doubt that the Smyrna occupation had dramatically revived national feeling among the Greek-speaking inhabitants of Asia Minor. Traveling through western Turkey, Arnold Toynbee reported that the Hellenic renaissance by 1920 had actually driven out the Turkish piaster in favor of the Greek drachma. Many thousands of local Greeks were opting for citizenship in the Old Kingdom. "Even isolated Greek communities have cast their lot with the Old Kingdom," Toynbee reported, "as nationalism has welled up strong and compelling."

These accomplishments notwithstanding, the Greek enclave in Asia Minor continued to remain an island in a Turkish sea, isolated commercially from the Turkish hinterland and surrounded by an overwhelmingly Turkish population. Deprived of economic help from Athens, the Greek high commissioner barely managed to finance his regime. By the winter of 1920–21, too, the palpable hostility of the local Turkish citizenry kept Sterghiades's gendarmes confined to their stockades after nightfall, while an efficient Kemalist civil administration extended its authority to the very gates of Smyrna. Meanwhile, the Nationalist army was training and re-equipping with impressive speed. In contrast, the Greek Smyrniot population remained almost pathologically averse to military service. It was a matter of brutal clarity to Sterghiades that a local conscript army would be useless in the event of a renewed Greek drive from Smyrna to Ankara, a distance of 360 miles.

Yet the new royalist government was contemplating precisely such an offensive. Rather than consolidate the army's gains in Smyrna, Constantine and his followers were fascinated by the temptation to push farther inland and destroy the Kemalist movement once and for all. By now, indeed, court circles were fairly bursting with eagerness to prove how little Venizelos himself had been responsible for Greek military successes. The ex-chief of staff, General Metaxas, vainly warned the new government, as he had warned Venizelos before, that it was futile to continue the expedition. Allied experts added their note of caution. As far back as March 1920, Marshal Foch had insisted that a minimum of twenty-seven divisions would be required to pacify Anatolia. The Greeks had stationed barely a third that number—110,000 men—in western Asia Minor. But Constantine would not be deterred. If Venizelos had disregarded this "expert" advice in July and smashed the Turks at Brousa and Adrianople, the king, a military leader of proven distinction in the Balkan Wars, could hardly be less audacious. On the contrary, his accomplishments should be such as to make Venizelos's earlier triumphs appear puny by comparison. His goal was nothing less than the capture of the Nationalist capital of Ankara itself. Constantine was certain, too, that it was still possible to rely on British support. Only recently, on December 22, 1920, Lloyd George had declared that "the friendship of the Greek people [is] vital to us in that part of the world [Asia Minor], a part of the world which [is] vital to Great Britain, more vital than to any other country in the world." The implication could not have been plainer. In January 1921, Constantine ordered his military staff to prepare for the move eastward into the very heartland of central Anatolia.

Mustafa Kemal and the Emergence of a Government

HE WAS AWAITED THERE by a man who knew his Greeks well. Mustafa Kemal had been born and raised among them in Salonica. Still vivid in his memory was the flight of his mother and sisters from the city in 1912, the abandonment of their modest home to the invading Greek army. The recollection blended with others: with the pulsating nationalism of his classmates at the War College in Constantinople, the liberal dreams he had shared with other young officers in underground meetings of the Committee of Union and Progress, the example of Western secularism and parliamentarianism he had studied and cherished during his years as military attaché in France and Germany. Moreover, the chance to translate those ideals into action was the direct consequence of Kemal's reputation as the nation's most celebrated war hero. In the aftermath of the Mudros Armistice, as will be recalled (Chapter X), he exploited that reputation to block the demobilization of Turkey's armed forces. Instead he undertook the opposite, the recruitment of a national revolutionary army. The Greek occupation of Smyrna was the only spur he needed: "I felt," he said afterward, "as if a cage had been opened, and as if I were a bird ready to open my wings and fly through the sky." Kemal flew high. Within the space of a year he had called the Erzerum and Sivas congresses, engineered the proclamation of the National Pact in September 1919 and ultimately the convocation of a "Grand National Assembly" in March 1920, with himself as president of the council of ministers.

Ankara, the capital of this self-proclaimed regime, was separated from Constantinople by two hundred miles of harsh mountainous terrain. A fire had raged through its business section early in the war and reduced its population to less than twenty thousand. Nestled into a hill some three thousand feet above sea level, the city looked down on an antiquated railroad station that served as the last depot in the rail network of central Turkey. In fact, it was the rail connection, as well as Ankara's inaccessibility as a mountain fortress, that had induced Kemal to select the town as his headquarters. Otherwise, with its meager population, the community was at best a squalid collection of ruined mud-brick houses and twisting alleyways. The leadership operating from this highland citadel could hardly have been excelled, however. Kemal's ablest commanders, Fevzi Pasha, who also served as defense minister, and Nuri Ismet Pasha, chief of the Nationalist army general staff, were both experienced veterans of the Balkan and World wars. They kept tight reins on the lines of authority extending through the two thirds of Turkey that lay beyond Constantinople, Adana, and the Smyrna enclave.

But more than any other factor, Kemal's own personality animated the entire Turkish resistance. He was thirty-nine at the time, a soldier with fifteen years of hard service. The ravages of hard drinking and wenching were already beginning to thicken the poised angularity of his jaw and chin. Yet the tenacity of character, the lionlike courage, the elemental drive and energy that seemed to well up in the man from inexhaustible reservoirs, all struck with near-physical force those who met him. He radiated self-confidence and authority. With his blond hair, moreover, his steely blue eyes penetrating from a massive head, and his mouth a thin slit, Kemal remained the incarnation of feline power and ruthlessness, and the very antithesis of that Levantine caricature of the Turk so dear to the West. Halidé Edib Adivar, a distinguished woman journalist who had joined the Nationalist movement in the Ankara retreat, described Kemal in this period:

> He was by turns cynical, suspicious, unscrupulous, and satanically shrewd. He bullied, he indulged in cheap street-corner heroics. Possessing considerable though quite undistinguished histrionic ability, one moment he could pass as the perfect demagogue—a second George Washington [sic] —and the next moment fall into some Napoleonic attitude. . . . Of course, one knew all the time that there were men around him who were greatly his superior in intellect, moral backbone, and far above him in culture and education. But though he excelled them in neither refinement nor originality, not one of them could possibly cope with his vitality. Whatever their qualities, they were made on a more or less normal scale. In terms of vitality, he wasn't.

These resources of will and strength were applied not only to the Allies and Greeks, nor even only to the quarrelsome semi-rabble that constituted the Grand National Assembly. For much of 1920 and part of 1921, Kemal was obliged to fight a war within a war, a sapping guerrilla campaign against Circassian irredentists and religious fundamentalists, most of them tribal fanatics who revered the sultan-caliph and accepted royal subsidies. These individual risings had to be suppressed one by one, and the task was not completed until January 1921. Little mercy was shown the captives. Pity was a luxury Kemal could not afford when he was seeking to galvanize his entire people into an awareness of its nationhood, to assure them that they were not simply relics of a semi-Byzantinized empire or carriers of the Islamic faith, but rather children of the Hearth, the penultimate homeland of the Turkish race and nation. Ziya Gökalp had preached this message (see Chapter IV) before and during the war. But Kemal's followers were concerned lest its impact had been dissipated by the Allied victory, by the dissolution of the CUP, and perhaps by the arrest of Ziya himself at the hands of the British in 1919. They need not have been concerned. The pride that had been awakened during Enver's offensive in the Transcaucasus in 1917 and 1918 and by the assiduous propaganda of the war period was fanned to a blaze after May 1919 by the ultimate indignity of Greek occupation. Newspaper plants in Ankara, operating on linotype machinery and news-type smuggled out of Constantinople, began grinding out tens of thousands of daily copies exhorting the Turkish population to renewed efforts of resistance. By 1921 the Nationalist regime had succeeded both in conquering its internal enemies and tightening its grip on the Anatolian hinterland, as well as in mobilizing the loyalty and devotion of the overwhelming majority of the nation's common people.

Not the least of the Ankara government's feats was its success in guaranteeing Turkey's northern frontiers by productive diplomatic negotiations with the former Russian enemy. Kemal and his associates were convinced that a mutually helpful arrangement could be worked out with the new Soviet regime. Badly shaken by its own civil wars, the Russian government shared the Turks' fear of Western imperialism in the Middle East, in this case, along the Soviet Union's southern borders. In Moscow's view, an independent Turkey would serve as an ideal buffer, protecting Russia's exposed flank in the Caucasus. In the summer of 1920, therefore, Gregory Zinoviev, president of the Communist International, issued a public message of sympathy with the Nationalist government in Turkey. The hint was clear. Kemal accepted it immediately by sending his foreign minister off to Moscow to seek a possible alliance. The subsequent negotiations proved cordial and fruitful. On August 24, a Turko-Soviet draft treaty was initialed.

A final political understanding was not reached so easily, however. Official ratification of the agreement was delayed fully seven months, as both Moscow and Ankara maneuvered to increase their control in the Transcaucasus area. Eventually it was the Turks who strengthened their position by invading Erivan and forcing the Armenian Dashnak government to return the fortress-city of Kars (see Chapter XI). As it happened, the Treaty of Alexandropol of December 2, 1920, represented Ankara's first international agreement as a sovereign government. Operating from this new position of strength, Kemal was able, early in 1921, more effectively to resume his negotiations with the Bolshevist regime. The ensuing Treaty of Moscow (March 12, 1921) represented a major victory for the Turks. By its terms, Kars and Ardahan were officially recognized as Turkish. The Soviets accepted the National Pact in its totality. Each government agreed to ignore any treaty imposed on the other by force, to suppress the activities of any group whose purpose was the overthrow of the other government (Communist subversion in Turkey continued nonetheless), and to repudiate any decision on the Turkish straits reached by nations other than themselves.

Perhaps the most far-reaching consequence of the negotiations was one that never explicitly appeared in the treaty at all. It was the provision for Soviet aid. The actual amount has never been established conclusively. The Russians tended later to exaggerate the quantities, and Kemal was always reticent on the subject. But in subsequent years General Ali

Fuat Cebesoy, Ankara's first ambassador to Moscow, stated that the Soviet government provided a cash gift of a million rubles and enough weaponary to equip three Turkish divisions. Hardly less significant was the guarantee of security along Turkey's northern borders, the assurance of Russian moral support and encouragement, the knowledge that Turkey was no longer alone in the world. These factors proved of crucial importance as the Nationalists braced themselves for a renewed and potentially decisive Greek offensive.

Constantine's Supreme Effort

IN DECEMBER 1920, General Papoulas, the recently appointed Greek commander in Asia Minor, was ordered to attack and capture the Turkish bastions of Afion-Karahissar and Eskishehir. Once these two anchors of the Turkish interior rail net were separated by the desert, the Greek front would be reunited and served by a continuous chain of railroad from Smyrna to Ismidt. The odds favoring the offensive appeared good. By the end of the year the Greek "Army of Asia Minor" consisted of 110,000 men with 243 heavy guns; whereas the Turks numbered hardly 60,000 and were still unimpressively equipped for large-scale warfare. Heartened by this numerical preponderance, the Greeks began their advance on January 6, 1921, with the main thrust, from Brousa, aimed upward over steep ridges in the direction of Eskishehir. But the results of the summer offensive were not to be duplicated. Ismet Pasha, the Turkish field commander, was lying in wait with his troops in a valley at Inönü, directly before Eskishehir. And there, to the astonishment of the West, he launched a sudden and devastating attack on the Greek flank, inflicting 6,000 casualties on the invaders within twenty-four hours and driving them back to their original lines.

The First Battle of Inönü (as it was later to be known) had a traumatic effect on London and the other Allied capitals. At long last, Lloyd George awakened to the possibility that the Greeks, despite their impressive earlier accomplishments, were reaching the limits of their resources and mobility. British military authorities had long been convinced of the need for a compromise between the two antagonists. Now, grudgingly, Lloyd George began to pay heed to their views. These misgivings were fully shared by the French and Italian governments. In order to reassess the crisis in Turkey, therefore, the Supreme Council assembled again in London on February 21. The invited participants included representatives not only of the Allies and of Athens and Constantinople, but also, for the first time, of the Ankara government. Indeed, Bekir Sami, the Kemalist delegate, gave every indication of justifying this tentative recognition. As proof of his moderation, he even declared his willingness to discuss limited Hellenic control over the Smyrna area. As it turned out, this was the last chance the Greeks would ever have to maintain at least a partial foothold in Asia Minor. Fixated, however, by the tantalizing vision of imperial glory, Greek Prime Minister Gounaris intemperately rejected the opportunity, insisting on nothing less than full implementation of the Sèvres Treaty. Finally, on March 23, Athens doomed the conference altogether by suddenly launching a renewed offensive against Eskishehir and Afion-Karahissar. The move was exceptionally ill timed. Ismet was awaiting the main thrust, again at Inöuü, and this time with better fortifications and with additional troops and equipment. After nearly a week of savage fighting, a powerful Turkish counterattack once again was successful. The Greeks pulled back to their original positions at Brousa on April 4. Toynbee watched them retreating, "an interminable procession of troops, mules, ox-carts and lorries crawling along a foundered road." The Turks probably could have overrun the stragglers, if they themselves had not been exhausted. Nevertheless, General Papoulas, aware of the fragility both of military and civilian morale, congratulated his army for "attaining the objectives assigned to this first phase of the campaign." So ended the Second Battle of Inönü.

So ended, too, all hope of official Allied support for the

420

Greek cause. However much they detested Constantine, the Western governments had been unwilling to condemn the royalist adventure as long as even the remotest likelihood existed that it might succeed. But now that possibility had evidently faded, and the notion of offering the Greek king a blank check for military disaster, with all its potential diplomatic ramifications, was unthinkable to the Allied statesmen, even to Lloyd George. Accordingly, following Gounaris's withdrawal from the London conference, and his impetuous renewal of the offensive in Anatolia, the Allies on May 21 solemnly declared their neutrality in the Greco-Turkish conflict. Thenceforth the royalist government would no longer find it possible to take legal refuge in the Treaty of Sèvres, or to claim to be acting as an agent of the Allies. Four months later, nevertheless, in an effort to close out the war at almost any cost, the Supreme Council urgently renewed its offer to mediate between Athens and Ankara. Again the Greeks refused. In the midst of their preparations for an additional offensive, the royalists were certain that Lloyd George would not abandon them. "Nothing struck me more forcibly during the eight months that I was in touch with the Greek Army and public," Toynbee recalled, "than the universal belief that Great Britain . . . would see them through. It was the one point on which all Greeks . . . were in enthusiastic agreement." They were not far wrong. Regardless of his official disclaimers, the British prime minister could not bring himself to abandon a policy of pro-Hellenism that had become all but second nature to him and the very lodestar of his diplomacy in western Asia. Churchill recorded Lloyd George's panegyric:

> The Greeks are the people of the future in the Eastern Mediterranean. They are prolific and full of energy. They represent Christian civilization against Turkish barbarism. Their fighting power is grotesquely underrated by our generals. A greater Greece will be an invaluable advantage to the British Empire. . . . They are good sailors; they will develop a naval power; they will possess all the most important islands in the Eastern Mediterranean. These islands are the potential sub-

marine bases of the future; they lie on the flank of our communications through the Suez Canal with India, the Far East, and Australasia.

The Athens government sensed this unofficial continuity of British support, which, indeed, Lloyd George did little to disguise. In June 1921, proclaiming himself supreme commander of the Hellenic forces in Asia, King Constantine departed for army headquarters at Smyrna, and thereby became the first Christian monarch to set foot on Anatolian soil since the Crusades. In Athens, meanwhile, Prime Minister Gounaris ordered the military to make all necessary preparations for encircling and decisively smashing the Kemalist armies. From April to July 1921, the Greek general staff urgently re-equipped and reorganized its forces. New classes of reserves were mobilized; new ordnance was brought to the front. Under the able direction of General Dusmanis, the field commander, the Greeks this time launched their offensive not from the northern front, as expected, but from the south. Rather than attack Afion-Karahissar and Eskishehir directly, the Hellenic regiments snaked out in long encircling columns, threatening the Turkish rear. The strategy worked; the Turks had overconcentrated their strength in the north. Eskishehir was outflanked, and soon evacuated. On July 21, Ismet launched a furious counterattack against the city. He was too late. His troops were repelled.

At that moment, Kemal himself arrived on the scene. Grimly evaluating the military situation, the Nationalist leader recognized immediately that the only salvation for his forces was a general retreat. He ordered it on the spot. Sixty thousand troops thereupon began pulling back deeper into the Turkish interior. Eventually they took up new positions behind the great bend of the Sakkaria River, only fifty miles west of Ankara. Simultaneously, Prime Minister Gounaris, exultant at what appeared to be a victory of massive dimensions, rushed to Constantine's headquarters and implored his monarch to press on across the Sakkaria and occupy Ankara forthwith.

It was a typically civilian conception, and the military leaders angrily opposed it. General Papoulas observed that his army now controlled the entire rail network protecting the Smyrna enclave, and therefore was in an ideal position to consolidate its strength behind the natural frontier of the Sakkaria. The risk of further advance was totally unwarranted, he insisted. After some hesitation between these two views, the king decided to cast the die in favor of attack.

Despite the misgivings of the royalist staff, the chances for a pulverizing Greek offensive appeared quite as impressive to the Turks as to Constantine and his government. In Ankara itself the Grand National Assembly was aghast and panic-stricken at the drastic retreat of the Turkish army. It appeared an unlikely psychological moment for Kemal to demand full martial powers for himself as commander in chief. Nevertheless, after savagely browbeating the deputies, he got his way and immediately launched into feverish defensive preparations. Although ragged and badly mauled, the Turkish army was still intact. In a drastic series of nationwide requisitions, therefore, Kemal ruthlessly commandeered pack animals for the troops, as well as stocks of cloth, leather, foodstuffs, shoes, and oil. By then the civilian population, consumed with a patriotism and unity of purpose previously unknown in modern Turkish history, hardly required formal orders to turn in all household and barnyard weapons, even ancient muskets and wrought-iron fences to be melted down into bayonets. Defense Minister Fevzi Pasha performed herculean feats of re-equipping the army with adapted left-over quantities of dismantled artillery and misfit ammunition. With babies lashed to their backs, women were arriving in Ankara in oxcarts laden with the food and ammunition they had driven from places as far as Diarbekir, Sivas, and Trebizond. Men walked scores, even hundreds, of miles to enlist, and not infrequently equipped themselves with weapons taken from the dead and wounded. Again, Halidé Edib described the nightmarish scene of troops pouring through Ankara toward the front along the Sakkaria:

At each station new recruits came and took their places in the trucks; women stood on the platform and looked on with silent agony on their faces; one old woman ran after the train, her toothless mouth a black gap frozen into a voiceless groan of despair. The men held each other's hands in the truck and called out to those in other trucks, asking for any who might be from their particular place or village. "Is there a man from Castamoni?" "Is there a man from Changiri?" "Is there?" one heard them say. . . . As the train plunged into the illimitable wastes of Anatolia I knew that this was going to be the turning point in the hardest ordeal Anatolia had as yet undergone.

The Sakkaria, one of the three great rivers of Anatolia, twists and turns northward through bare, primitive plains for some fifty miles before cutting back west through rocks and gorges. It was the last natural barrier between the Greeks and Ankara. In the most equal division of strength since the war began, the Greeks had packed 50,000 combat troops into the front line along the river, the Turks 44,000. Greek Intelligence was well informed this time, and its battle plan, endorsed by the general staff, was to strike in force where the Turks least expected it, in the northern hill area. On August 10, the Greek army moved out, proceeding first along the southern desert area, then suddenly shifting northward. The plan was an imaginative one. Due to an error in reconnaissance, however, the Greeks failed to move far enough north. They launched their frontal attack in the center, where the Turks were entrenched in unexpected strength. The battle raged for twenty-two days. It was in fact the longest pitched battle, until then, in modern history. Trenches and hilltop positions changed hands repeatedly as each side attacked and counterattacked. During the first ten days the Greeks gained eleven miles, and the battle lines swiveled around from east to west rather than from north to south (see map). Kemal directed the operations of his army from a small village behind the Turkish lines, plugging each gap in the front with his dwindling reserves. The ferocity of the struggle could not have been exceeded. Men died by the thousands; entire divisions on both sides were blotted out or reduced to battalions, and then to companies. Turkish officers were mowed down with terrifying rapidity; seven division generals were killed in the close fighting. Across the lines, the Greek supply services were so thoroughly disrupted that little water remained for the men's canteens, and rations were limited to dry maize. Nevertheless, day after day under the malevolent August sun, the Greeks attacked with stoic tenacity. The Turks hung grimly on. It was a primeval contest of extermination, a city of corpses populating a blasted and ruined landscape.

Eventually the two armies fought themselves to a standstill. After three weeks of uninterrupted slaughter, the Greeks had lost eighteen thousand men, and the Turks nearly that many. At this critical moment, with both sides pausing in agonized immobility, a Greek unit slipped back despairingly on a key hill. It was the opportunity Kemal had awaited. In an inspired gamble, he hurled his entire army down the mountain, overwhelming the primary Greek defenses. The men in the Greek secondary lines began abandoning their positions. Soon Greek battalions were collapsing like rows of dominoes. When news of the break in the front reached headquarters at Smyrna, the morale of the senior staff cracked with disastrous finality. Prince Andrew watched General Papoulas retire into his tent "like a wrathful Achilles" and refuse to speak to anyone. Pulling back, then breaking into headlong retreat, the exhausted and maddened Greek troops set fire to every Turkish village they passed through until by September 12 a trail of scorched earth marked their withdrawal from Sakkaria the entire distance to the original Afion-Karahissar-Eskishehir line. Constantine and the supreme headquarters had no alternative but to evacuate Smyrna and return to Athens itself, where they were received with icy contempt. The reaction was markedly different in Ankara. The Grand National Assembly, all but delirious with relief and gratitude, unanimously conferred upon Kemal the honorific title of Gazi, conquerer of Christians. The delegates had sensed the shift of the tide. The Turkish Hearth was saved. The final expulsion of the infidel from Turkish soil was now only a matter of time.

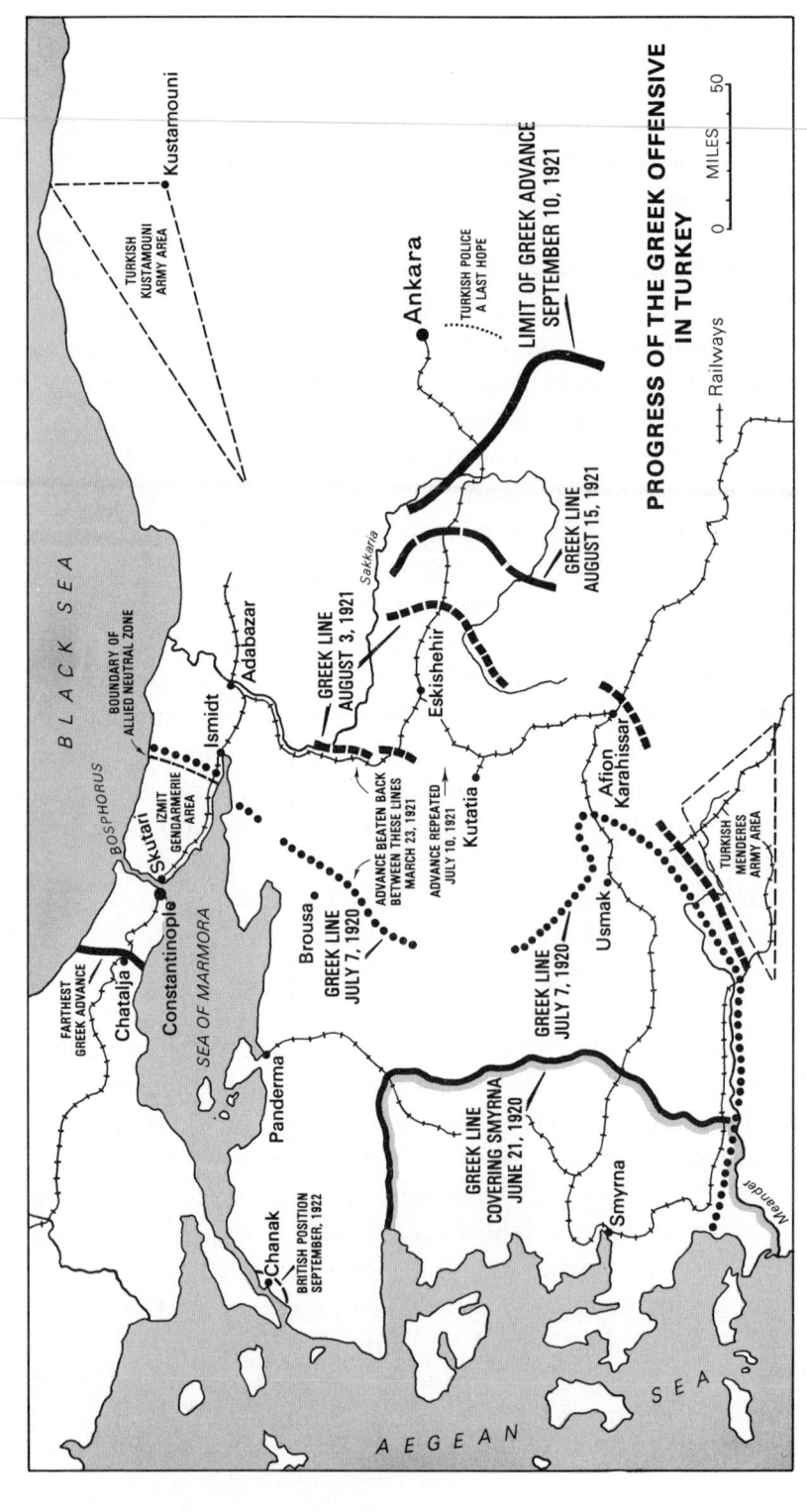

PROGRESS OF THE GREEK OFFENSIVE
IN TURKEY

0   MILES   50

Railways

BLACK SEA

Kustamouni

TURKISH
KUSTAMOUNI
ARMY AREA

Ankara

TURKISH POLICE
A LAST HOPE

LIMIT OF GREEK ADVANCE
SEPTEMBER 10, 1921

Sakkaria

GREEK LINE
AUGUST 15, 1921

GREEK LINE
AUGUST 3, 1921

BOUNDARY OF
ALLIED NEUTRAL ZONE

Adabazar

Eskishehir

BOSPHORUS

Ismidt

IZMIT
GENDARMERIE
AREA

Skutari

ADVANCE BEATEN BACK
BETWEEN THESE LINES
MARCH 23, 1921

ADVANCE REPEATED
JULY 10, 1921

Kutatia

Afion
Karahissar

TURKISH
MENDERES
ARMY AREA

Constantinople

SEA OF MARMORA

Brousa

GREEK LINE
JULY 7, 1920

GREEK LINE
JULY 7, 1920

Usmak

FARTHEST
GREEK ADVANCE

Chatalja

Panderma

GREEK LINE
COVERING SMYRNA
JUNE 21, 1920

Smyrna

Meander

Chanak

BRITISH POSITION
SEPTEMBER, 1922

AEGEAN   SEA

The Dissolution of the Western Alliance

ONE OF THE MOST SIGNIFICANT CONSEQUENCES of the Turkish victory at Sakkaria was the dramatic *volte-face* it revealed in French and Italian policy toward the Kemalist regime. It was a change Lloyd George later chose to describe as "the treachery of some of the Allied Governments, who surreptitiously encouraged the Turks and helped to arm their forces." From the outset, in fact, both the Italian and the French government had expressed serious misgivings about encouraging the Greeks in their campaign. The Italians, for example, lost interest in enforcing the Sèvres Treaty once that agreement had deprived them of the potential outlet of southern Anatolia, and flouted the St.-Jean-de-Maurienne Treaty of 1917 by turning Smyrna over to Greece. Indeed, the new Italian foreign minister, Count Carlo Sforza, was frankly intent upon undermining the position of his Greek rivals. At his instructions, Italian military and police "advisers" south of the Meander River harbored and supplied the Turkish guerrilla bands that penetrated their zone. Following the collapse of the London conference of June 1921, moreover, Sforza entered into a private agreement with Bekir Sami, the Nationalist emissary, whereby Italian forces would be evacuated from Adalia altogether. Actually the gesture merely accepted the *fait accompli* of Kemalist authority throughout Asia Minor, but it was Rome's first explicit renunciation of solidarity with Britain and Greece.

Yet it was the reorientation of French policy that sent the most extensive diplomatic shock waves resounding throughout Europe. Ironically, of all the Entente powers, none had been more ardent than France to bring Greece into the war on the Allied side (see Chapter X). This ardor had waned drastically in late 1919 and early 1920. One reason was the rapidly escalating cost of maintaining a French buffer regime against the Turkish Nationalists. "Neither financially nor militarily," Poincaré warned in an article in the *Revue des deux mondes* of March 1921, "can we support indefinitely the burdens that weigh upon us in the Levant." Even earlier, Constantine's return to power had allowed the French government to state its reservations explicitly. Briand had warned Athens then that Paris could not indefinitely maintain a large army in Asia Minor. Concerned with safeguarding their position in Syria, the French badly needed peace on Syria's northern border. Besides, French businessmen possessed important financial investments in Turkey; before the war, these had included the majority shares of the Ottoman Public Debt. Powerful Catholic religious interests, too, resented the growing penetration of Asia Minor by the Greek Orthodox Church. Not least of all, bitterness toward England unquestionably influenced French policy. Paris had long been convinced of the existence of a British plot to expel the French from the Levant and to transform Feisal into the puppet-king of a pro-British Arab confederation (see Chapter IX). Feisal's enthronement as King of Iraq in 1921, barely a year after the French had expelled him from Syria, appeared further to prove this intention. So did the conclusion of an Anglo-Soviet trade pact on March 16, 1921, at a time when the French investing public had not yet overcome its horror and outrage at Moscow's cancellation of the tsarist bond issue.

Responding to the confluence of these pressures, therefore, the French government as early as December 1919 instructed Georges-Picot to meet with Kemal in an effort to achieve a truce in Cilicia. The discussions gained momentum following the royalist triumph in Greece in late 1920. Soon thereafter, Foreign Minister Briand used the occasion of the London conference to arrange a separate agreement with the Kemalist representative, Bekir Sami. In return for economic concessions from the Ankara regime, the French would evacuate their military "advisers" (i.e., troops) from Cilicia. Sforza worked out an identical arrangement for Italian evacuation of Adalia. These economic concessions were later repudiated by the Grand National Assembly, as it happened (although the Italians withdrew anyway in June 1921); but the thread of negotiations between Paris and the Turkish capital was not dropped. Rather, in the early summer of 1921, Paris dispatched a semiofficial emissary to Ankara. He was Henri Franklin-Bouillon, a corpulent, jovial ex-deputy who had once served as chairman of the Chamber's foreign affairs committee. Plying Kemal with vintage cognac, effusive in his sympathy for the Nationalist cause, Franklin-Bouillon soon won the Gazi's confidence and friendship. After the Battle of Sakkaria, the Frenchman was rushed back to Ankara to exploit this personal camaraderie. In London, Curzon followed the reports of these visits with anxiety. Suspecting a private deal, he began making discreet but urgent inquiries of Paris. Briand's replies were cordial and reassuring. The discussions were entirely personal, he stated; under no circumstances would any new policy departure take place without previous agreement with Britain. Then, on October 20, 1921, the premier belied this assurance with a policy departure of the most fundamental and far-reaching consequences imaginable.

It took the form of the Treaty of Ankara, an agreement signed between Franklin-Bouillon and Yusuf Kemal Bey, the Kemalist foreign minister, which represented the most significant triumph of Turkish diplomacy since the inception of the Nationalist movement. In return for certain—nonexclusive—investment opportunities in Asia Minor, Paris agreed to terminate its state of war with Turkey, and to cede the Turks some ten thousand square miles of Syrian territory, including all the strategic positions essential for the defense of Syria toward the north (i.e., the Amanus Tunnel, the Euphrates railroad bridge). Presumably, Turkish goodwill would now serve France as her best security guarantee in the Middle East. Thus, Paris agreed formally to recognize the Ankara regime as the official government of Turkey and to support the Nationalists' efforts to ensure Turkish sovereignty and independence. For the Quai d'Orsay, the treaty's importance lay not merely in its economic concessions and its promise of Turkish friendship, but also in the opportunity it provided France to retrench in Asia Minor and concentrate her forces in Syria. For the Turks, the treaty's enduring value lay in official recognition of their new government by a major Western power, and a bilateral revision of the Sèvres agreement which was virtually a separate peace behind Britain's back, one that freed thousands of Turkish troops from the Cilicia area.

When Curzon learned the terms of this agreement, his initial reactions were utter disbelief followed by trembling indignation. In a note to Paris on November 5, the foreign secretary abandoned diplomatic amenities altogether. He bluntly charged France with a naked and flagrant breach of the joint wartime agreement against separate peace negotiations with the common enemy. The evacuation of Cilicia, Curzon insisted, was a gross violation both of this tripartite agreement and of the Treaty of Sèvres; the surrender of northern Syria betrayed the mandate system and undermined Britain's strategic position in Iraq, thus seriously threatening Allied relations. It was a thunderbolt of an indictment. In his response, Briand could offer nothing more than a platitudinous serving of mild and general disclaimers. Indeed, the reply was swiftly exposed as a fabrication, for the evacuating French garrisons in Cilicia were even then turning over large quantities of their military equipment to Kemal's army. In the next few months, Curzon's diplomacy was a symphony of frustration. Throughout the final weeks of 1921 and the early part of 1922 he conducted urgent diplomatic *pour-parlers* with Paris and Rome. Eventually, to be sure, the French and Italian governments were persuaded to consider a "compromise" peace plan that in effect was a reversal of Britain's stance of the past two years in the Middle East. By the terms of the new proposal, the Greek army would be allowed to evacuate Asia Minor zone by zone under inter-Allied supervision, with full protection for the minorities left behind. The Western powers reached tentative agreement on this formula. Their next task was to exert strenuous pressure on the Greek Cabinet to accept the compromise in principle. Athens ultimately agreed. It was the Turks, rather, who proved adamant, insisting upon a full and complete Greek evacuation of Anatolia even before the signing of a peace treaty. The demand was so palpably arrogant that it was rejected by the Allies and Greeks alike.

Actually the Turks had grounds for their self-assurance. Each day they gained in strength, as French and Italian weapons supplemented the matériel arriving from Russia. In December 1921, a new Ukrainian Soviet mission arrived in Ankara to provide for the further dispatch of Soviet military supplies and, for the first time, of Soviet military advisers. Mobilizing extensively, therefore, winning tangible diplomatic and military support in many quarters, the Nationalist regime was confident that a single telling thrust on the battlefield would render its bargaining position impregnable. It was evident by then, too, that the Greek army was no longer an offensive threat. The most experienced and battle-tested Hellenic divisions had fallen back on entrenched positions covering the Smyrna-Aidin enclave, where they remained disconsolately month after month. Many of the 110,000 Greek soldiers had been under arms for over three years, and had not seen their families at all during that period. Their best officers had been replaced because of real or suspected Venizelist sympathies. These included General Papoulas, the commander in chief, who was discharged in favor of the aging General Hadjianestes, a veteran royalist. Simultaneously, Bolshevist agents, under the secret direction of Colonel Skyros of the Thirteenth Division, were circulating among the units, systematically eroding their fighting spirit, urging them to lay down their weapons and desert. When King Constantine unwisely paid a visit to the troops at the front early in 1922, he was taken aback by the impassioned cries for peace and demobilization that greeted him. Political and financial circumstances in Greece itself were hardly better. The country was riddled with dissension. Uncompromising in their mutual hatred, royalists and Venizelists endlessly conspired against one another. Executions and assassinations were common. Gounaris and foreign minister Baltazzi made the rounds of the Allied capitals early in 1922, desperately attempting to raise loans, but failing everywhere.

By late spring of 1922, the new commander, General Hadjianestes, had privately decided to wipe off Asia Minor as a bad debt and concentrate upon holding the frontier at Thrace. The methods by which he sought to accomplish this aim, however, were far from orthodox. Brooding in the cafés of Smyrna, Hadjianestes somehow conceived the notion of intimidating the Turks into a quick settlement by occupying Constantinople—a city off limits to the Greeks since the end of the war. On July 22, as the Allied governments followed events in astonishment and mounting alarm, twenty thousand Greek troops were suddenly transferred from their lines guarding Smyrna and eastern Thrace and marched in the direction of the Turkish capital. So unexpected was this move that the Allied commander in Constantinople, General Harington, had no time to communicate with London. On his own responsibility, therefore, he warned the Greeks that he would resist their entrance into the capital, if necessary by force. Informed afterward of Harington's threat, Lloyd George reluctantly decided not to veto it; he could hardly support a violation of the Sèvres Treaty, after all. At this point Hadjianestes lost his nerve. Rather than face a clash with the British, he withdrew his forces to their original positions, although (as shall be seen) with fatal tardiness. Ironically, soon afterward Lloyd George experienced a sudden twinge of conscience, and resolved once again not to be found wanting in his support of the Greeks. On August 4, in a bizarre lapse, the distraught and harassed prime minister appeared in the House of Commons to announce his decision:

> Peace the Kemalists will not accept [he declared] because they say we will not give them satisfactory armistice terms; but we are not allowing the Greeks to wage the war with their full strength. We cannot allow that sort of thing to go on indefinitely in the hope that the Kemalists entertain that they will at last exhaust the little country. . . .

Six days later, both Lloyd George and Curzon refused to meet with the Kemalist emissary, Fethi Bey, who had arrived in

London to discuss peace terms. The message was clear to Ankara.

The Fall of the Greek Empire

FOR KEMAL, the hour had struck for unleashing his long-delayed offensive. It was plain that London would have to be convinced decisively that the Greek cause was lost. From the tactical viewpoint, General Hadjianestes's ill-conceived drive on Constantinople, with its transfer of two experienced Greek divisions from the Smyrna front, left Turkish and Greek forces in Anatolia on numerically equal terms for the first time. Determined to exploit this chance for all it was worth, Kemal left immediately for his headquarters at Eskishehir. Secrecy was crucial. At his orders, reports that the Turkish army was not yet prepared for an offensive were selectively planted among known foreign agents. The rumors seemed credible. The Greek front stretched over three hundred miles from the Sea of Marmora to the Meander Valley. Its strong points remained Eskishehir in the north and Afion-Karahissar in the south; both were heavily fortified with double lines of trenches and amply supplied by rail and motor roads. Indeed, the powerful mountain citadel of Afion-Karahissar appeared all but invulnerable. For this reason, it was precisely at Afion-Karahissar that Kemal decided to attack. Aware that the Greeks expected the main assault in the flatter terrain to the north, the Turkish leader shifted his forces to the south by night marches. In daylight hours their presence was well camouflaged. By the last week in August, 80,000 men were concentrated on the Afion-Karahissar front against a Greek force of 75,000. Kemal was ready. On August 24, his adjutant issued hundreds of invitations to a ball scheduled for the evening of the 26th. The next day, however, all communications between Anatolia and the outside world were abruptly severed. In the dark of night Kemal moved his headquarters to a point only three hundred yards behind the crest of Koja Tepe, the Greek de-

433

fense bastion. And there he issued his battle order: "Soldiers, your goal is the Mediterranean."

The attack began at dawn on August 26 with a thunderous artillery barrage, then a massive frontal charge by Turkish infantry. Surprise was complete. Although the assault was entirely uphill against successive terraces of Greek fortifications, all the ridges were in Turkish hands by midmorning. The Greeks were stupefied. Still convinced, nevertheless, that this was not the main offensive, they fatally held their reserves in readiness to the north. During the next two days of furious attacks, the hard-driving Turkish infantry bridged the last crest in the south and reached the valley that led toward Smyrna. Afion-Karahissar itself fell without a shot. It was a total breakthrough. The Nationalist cavalry and mobile infantry, covering thirty-five miles a day, wheeled farther to the west in an effort to close the Greek line of retreat. Although several Greek divisions managed to evade the Turks and eventually reached the Sea of Marmora, by August 30 Kemal's First and Second armies had trapped the largest number of these wretched conscripts in the Kiziljidere Valley. The ensuing slaughter was of armageddonic proportions. Within the next four days the entire Hellenic Army of Asia Minor was either destroyed or driven back to the sea.

The distance from Ushak to Smyrna was more than 160 miles, but the few surviving members of the Greek Southern Corps traversed that distance in a week, living off the countryside and, in crazed revenge, indiscriminately burning Turkish communities along their route. The pursuing Kemalist troops found nothing but heaps of ashes, and beside them maddened Greek villagers shrilly anathematizing Lloyd George. Smyrna hopelessly awaited its fate. A week passed before the Turks reached the city. Some fifty thousand terrified Christian civilians remained there. In ensuing days this number was increased by tens of thousands of refugees from the outlying villages. A deathlike silence greeted the arrival of the invading Nationalist cavalry. Although exhausted, the Turks were apparently still well disciplined. Kemal himself entered the city in the wake of the cavalry division. Earlier he had assured Allied representatives that the local population would not be harmed. Shooting and pillaging began within hours of the occupation, however. Virtually all Armenian homes and property were looted, and soon the rumor circulated of an impending massacre of Christians. Perhaps inevitably, therefore, within forty-eight hours of the Turkish capture, a panic-stricken exodus clogged the streets and alleyways as men, women, and children frantically elbowed their way toward the wharves and the awaiting Allied warships. In one day alone, forty thousand Greeks were taken off by eleven ships, working in relays. And still refugees continued to pour into the city, thrusting toward the quay in the pitiless heat of the Mediterranean sun. The American correspondent Clare Sheridan described the scene:

> Those who fought their way through, having been whipped and trampled on and systematically robbed at each barrier, arrived on the gangway in a state of collapse. The women were crying or fainting, some of them had lost their reason; it was necessary to take their babies from them and help them on board. I handled babies until my arms ached, dirty half-dead babies covered with scurvy, sucking at their mothers' empty breasts. There were cases of childbirth on the quay. . . . A young boy dreadfully overburdened with the family's belongings stumbled on the gangway and fell between the ship's side and the quay and was drowned before he could be recovered. A frenzied woman beat her breasts and screamed— it was her son—but there was no time for sympathy, others came crowding on, she was lost in their midst. There were dead and dying everywhere. When the piergates were closed after the departure of a ship, people who seemed to be asleep were really corpses.

Smyrna's ordeal was not yet over. On September 12, a Turkish mob besieged a family of Armenians in a house and decided to burn them out. To divert the Turks, a group of neighbors lit other fires nearby. The flames leaped out of control, and by nightfall the entire city was ablaze. Additional thousands of townspeople began fleeing toward the quay. Suddenly the entire waterfront exploded in a deafening roar of

435

yellow steam. For the next day and a half, as the inferno burned itself out, the crews of Allied warships picked survivors out of the sea. Nothing could be done for the city: two thirds of *Gâvur Ismir* ("Infidel Smyrna"), the last remaining Christian enclave in Asia Minor, had been destroyed. Kemal was not through. His troops had rounded up nearly 150,000 Greek and Armenian males in western Turkey to serve as "labor battalions" in the Anatolian interior. All other Christian refugees—mainly Greek now—were ordered evacuated within thirty days. The Gazi had obviously decided to solve the minority problem in his own way. Throughout late September and October, under the experienced direction of the Near East Relief, a combined flotilla of Greek, Allied, and American warships evacuated approximately 400,000 more Greeks who had descended on Smyrna from all corners of the Anatolian hinterland.

The magnitude of this combined disaster, from the Nationalist military triumph to the destruction of Smyrna and the later eviction of the surviving Greek community, all but paralyzed the Athens government. In the space of ten days it had lost a domain which the Greek army had required three years to conquer, and on which innumerable dreams of glory had rested. On September 8, the Gounaris Cabinet resigned. The army would not let the unnerved ministers off that easily, however. On September 24, Colonel Nicholas Plastiras engineered a successful revolt of the armed services against the royalist government. Three days later, Constantine abdicated in favor of his son, Prince George, and left the country, sailing from the port of Oropos, the site of his departure in 1917. This time he did not return. Broken in health and spirit, the king died of heart failure in Palermo, Sicily, the following January. Meanwhile, the new revolutionary committee, determined at any cost to save the Greek population of Thrace from Turkish invasion, took draconian measures to strengthen the army. One of the committee's first acts, too, was to telegraph Venizelos, living in exile in Paris, entrusting the foreign policy of Greece to his hands.

Chanak and the End of the Sultanate

KEMAL WAS AWARE that more than half the Greek army in Asia Minor had managed to reach eastern Thrace and was reorganizing there and digging in at the frontier of the Dardanelles. This arid, rock-strewn wedge of territory possessed more than symbolic importance as Turkey's last remaining foothold in Europe before the World War. It served also as a vital buffer protecting the western approaches to Constantinople. Accordingly, Kemal's intention was to cross the Straits into Thrace and if possible overwhelm the Greek defenses before they were completed. But it was precisely here that the Turkish commander encountered the firm and unbudging opposition of Britain. The Sèvres Treaty had delineated the entire Straits area as a neutral zone, and on September 11, 1922, the three Allied high commissioners in Constantinople sternly warned Kemal against any violation of this restricted area. To lend emphasis to the warning, the British reinforced their meager detachments on the Ismidt Peninsula and at Chanak on the Asian shore of the Dardanelles. Whatever the cost, London intended to stand firm. Churchill recalled: "The Government might break up and we might be relieved of our burden. The nation might not support us: they could find others to advise them. The Press might howl, the Allies might fold. We intended to force the Turk to a negotiated peace before he should set foot in Europe." Nor was this ultimatum a gesture of desperation. The British fleet lay in the Marmora, and its flotillas effectively blocked the passage of any army from Asia into Europe. The British Cabinet, meeting in prolonged session, was no less confident of its ability to enlist the help of the rest of the empire. To that end, Churchill cabled the various dominion governments on September 16. "The announcement of an offer from all or any of the Dominions to send a contingent even of moderate size," he stated, "would undoubtedly exercise in itself a most favourable influence on the situation."

437

Within three days, replies to the cables began arriving from the imperial capitals. They proved a shocking disappointment. Each government wanted to "know more." New Zealand alone unhesitatingly agreed to send a contingent. South Africa and Newfoundland offered moral support, but nothing else. Prime Minister Hughes of Australia, in what Lord Beaverbrook later termed a "complaining, hectoring and bullying dispatch" of nearly two thousand words, refused to risk the life even of one soldier. Mackenzie King, prime minister of Canada, rejected the appeal with equal firmness. By the time the last reply was in, the Cabinet suddenly faced the appalling realization that Britain was isolated diplomatically. Lord Beaverbrook, meeting with Lloyd George on September 17, found the prime minister in a condition of stunned incoherence.

The debacle was compounded by an imprudent public communiqué issued by Churchill—who had failed to consult either Curzon or the other Allied governments—announcing that Britain would resist all danger to the Straits by force of arms. Indeed, the release touched off the worst crisis in Anglo-French relations, until then, in the twentieth century. The French and Italian press furiously castigated London for issuing a unilateral ultimatum on a matter of such incalculable potential danger. The official reaction from the Allied capitals was even more splenetic. On September 18, Paris ordered the French contingent withdrawn from Chanak. The Italians followed two days later. Curzon therupon raced to Dover and boarded the Channel steamer to France in a last-minute effort to remonstrate with Poincaré, who had returned to office as premier. The meeting, on September 21, soon degenerated into violent mutual recriminations. At one point Curzon actually staggered from the room to weep on the arm of Lord Hardinge, the British ambassador (afterward, nerving himself with swigs of brandy from a hip-flask, the foreign secretary finally managed to resume the discussion). A compromise was eventually reached. General Harington, the British commander in Constantinople, would meet Kemal at Mudania and fix a line beyond which the Turks should not advance. The understanding was clear that after a brief period of Allied supervision the Turks would be allowed into eastern Thrace, but would preserve the neutrality of the Straits.

Precisely at this moment the army revolution in Athens drove Constantine into exile. Kemal, fearing a revival of pro-Greek feeling among the Allies, ordered his troops to advance forthwith to Chanak. This they did, until only twenty yards of barbed wire separated them from the British contingent. Both sides immediately began strengthening their forces. The Turks soon reached forty thousand men. The British numbered less than three and a half battalions, but augmented these with three more by September 28, and by several score of heavy guns and fighter planes. As always, too, General Harington was assured of the limitless power of the navy behind him. For a terrible moment the Anglo-Turkish confrontation seemed to raise the specter of Gallipoli. Actually, there was little real danger of a clash. In the front lines, both the Turks and the British evinced good humor, and occasionally even fraternized with each other. Meanwhile, the ubiquitous Franklin-Bouillon had returned to Kemal's headquarters, this time at Smyrna, to urge restraint. The appeal was hardly necessary. Kemal was aware that he had already been promised eastern Thrace without a shot being fired. His maneuvers were intended essentially to gain political advantage for the negotiations to follow. Shortly before midnight of September 29, the Turkish leader agreed to a military conference.

The gathering took place, as previously agreed, in the town of Mudania, a shabby, mosquito-ridden port serving the Turkish interior from the southern shore of the Marmora. The Turkish and British delegates met in a small house formerly belonging to the Russian consul. Kemal's representative there was General Ismet Pasha, victor of the two battles of Inönü. He opened the proceedings on October 3 with the expected demand for Turkish right of passage across the Straits and the occupation of eastern Thrace. Harington coldly refused. Whereupon General Charpy, the French representative, accepted Ismet's terms on the spot. This second "betrayal" by the French

439

immediately provoked yet another round of anguished negotiations between Curzon and Poincaré in Paris. Finally, on October 5, the premier returned to the original compromise of September 20: the Greeks would withdraw to western Thrace at the line of the Maritza; Allied detachments would occupy eastern Thrace and operate the civil administration of the territory pending its final restoration to the Turks. On this basis, negotiations were resumed at Mudania. After a last-minute show of intransigence, Ismet accepted the proposal. Obviously the Turks did not require Chanak any longer; they had the ultimate assurance they wanted. On October 11, the armistice papers were formally signed. "Everyone showed signs of strain," Clare Sheridan wrote. "The beards of the men had grown visibly during the night. At that moment there was a strange noise from the Greek ship in the harbor. 'A groan from the Greeks,' said someone. It was a reminder of their existence." Two days after the agreement was reached, Kemal appointed Refet Pasha military governor for eastern Thrace, with his headquarters provisionally in Constantinople. Refet left immediately for the historic capital, there to assert the authority of the Nationalist government and all that it implied in the way of Turkish independence.

> As [Refet's] steamer approached the Golden Horn [wrote Lord Kinross], thousands of small boats sailed out from either bank to greet her, all decked with flags—red and white for Turkey, green for Islam—and with fluttering streamers. The Galata Bridge itself was festooned with garlands. The Turkish flag flew from each roof, each dome, each minaret. . . . The people themselves, in tens of thousands, expectantly thronged the streets. . . . Spectators clustered on the roofs of the houses, on the domes and minarets of the mosques, even on the masts of the boats in the harbour. As Refet's ship drew alongside the air was rent by a deafening chorus of sirens from every ship at anchor in the Bosporus and the Golden Horn, and a full-throated roar from every man, woman and child on shore.

Even as the Turkish official embarked upon his new responsibilities, the Allied governments took a maladroit step that gave the Kemalists a long-awaited opportunity. Still adhering to protocol, the Western powers extended invitations for the impending peace conference at Lausanne both to the government of the Sublime Porte in Constantinople and to the Nationalist regime of Ankara. This insult sent the delegates of the Grand National Assembly into a paroxysm of rage. They retaliated immediately by voting the formal abolition of the sultanate, a step which in any case was probably inevitable, but which otherwise might have required months of cautious debate. On November 4, 1922, Sultan Vahd-ed-Din was ordered to resign. A few days later, the old man secretly left the country on a British warship, which carried him off to Malta. Prince Abd al-Mejid, the sultan's cousin, accepted the residual position of caliph. But the Ottoman dynasty itself, the very symbol and embodiment of the Sick Man, now expired ingloriously with the shattered hulk of its empire.

Vahd-ed-Din had been preceded into poltical obscurity by a statesman of rather larger dimensions. Eight days after the signature of the Mudania Armistice, Lloyd George was out of office. Criticism throughout England had become so heated as a result of the Chanak crisis that the impetuous Welshman was persuaded to dissolve Parliament and go to the country at once. Otherwise, he knew, he faced the danger of being repudiated by the Conservatives, the principal support of his coalition government; his own Liberal Party was by when in the minority. He was outmaneuvered, however. Learning of the prime minister's intentions, the Conservatives shrewdly advanced the date of their scheduled conference a full month. On October 19, the assembled politicians declared that they would henceforth campaign as Conservative Party members, not as members of the coalition. Thereupon Lloyd George resigned in favor of Bonar Law. Parliament was dissolved on October 27, and in the general elections that followed, the Conservatives won a smashing victory. Indeed, it was a blow from which the Liberal Party never recovered. Nor did Lloyd George. Until the end of his days he brooded over the inconstancy of the public that had turned him out, and the perverse sympathy shown the Turk—"he plunders, he slays, and outrages"—that creature of nine lives, annihilated by Lloyd George's armies as by no other armies in history, which in the end, nevertheless, survived to become the prime minister's nemesis.

The Conference of Lausanne: Curzon's Triumph

AND SO IT WAS to begin all over again, the exhaustive and apparently interminable process of disposing of Asia Minor, of resolving the Turkish Question, if not satisfactorily, at least conclusively. The diplomats gathered in Lausanne on November 21, 1922. This time, however, the Westerners among them deliberated with less than their customary arrogance, without the traditional assurance that they alone would decide the fate of Turkey, consulting the Turks themselves from time to time as the spirit graciously moved them. Yet the mood, if restrained, was hardly defeatist. On the contrary, Curzon, who remained on as foreign secretary in the Bonar Law government, was determined to make of Lausanne the triumph of his career, hopefully a steppingstone to the prime ministry. He very nearly succeeded. He was a physically imposing man, to begin with, well over six feet in height, handsome in a florid, overstuffed sort of way, and by no means unaware that his sheer bulking presence often had an intimidating effect on both his adversaries and his underlings. No one in Europe surpassed him, and few matched him, in his near-total command of the strategisms and legalisms of the diplomatic art. Self-confidence, thoroughly well justified, appeared to radiate like a halo from the man's huge, granitic bald head. As the most experienced statesman present, moreover, pre-empting for himself the chairmanship of the pivotal territorial committee, Curzon virtually was in the position of dictating the agenda of the conference. He had strengthened his hand en route to Lausanne by finally maneuvering Poincaré into a common stand on the Turkish Question; a delicate warning on the

442

subject of German reparations had reached the mark. Mussolini, new in office in Rome, willingly followed the Anglo-French lead. These were important advantages to place in the balance against Turkey's military victories. Curzon used them to brilliant effect in his debates with the fretful, inexperienced Ismet Pasha. Thrace was a case in point, Ismet began by demanding western as well as eastern Thrace, a province that Turkey had lost in the First Balkan War fully a decade earlier. This was an obvious bargaining gambit. By shrewdly mobilizing the support of the Balkan nations, including even Turkey's former ally, Bulgaria, Curzon demolished Ismet's claim and forced the Turk to abandon it.

The foreign secretary's mastery of the art of statesmanship was even more apparent when the Straits Question was taken up on December 4. The dining room of the Hôtel du Chateau was packed with the representatives of the Black Sea littoral powers, among them Georgi Chicherin, the Soviet Union's polished, multilingual commissar of foreign affairs. The Russians watched intently and approvingly as Ismet read off Article Four of the National Pact, with its demand for unqualified Turkish control of Constantinople and the Straits. Minutes later, Curzon placidly rejected Ismet's contention, insisting upon the principle of open Straits—first for "safeguarding" the Black Sea nations against Russian attack, and secondly to "protect" commercial vessels in the Black Sea. Of course, this was a euphemism. Barrère, the chief French delegate, was less oblique. Closure of the Straits and the disaster of Gallipoli had had a traumatic effect upon the Allies, he stated bluntly. "On the day of their victory the Allies resolved that the dangers of this situation must never be allowed to recur." The Turks were in control of their homeland, and no one would quarrel with that. But neither would the Allied fleets anchored in the Straits be ignored. The waterway henceforth must remain open. Ismet did not press the issue.

The Bolshevists did. For them, the Ukrainian black-earth regions and the oil fields of Baku were dangerously vulnerable to an attack from the Black Sea. Nor was the possibility of an

443

Allied naval offensive a mere abstraction in Soviet eyes. Chicherin emphasized this in his opening statement of December 4:

> One need only recall the occupation of Odessa, Nikolaev, Kherson, Sevastopol, Batum and other ports of the Black Sea by the Allies. It was only the passage of the Allied naval forces through the Straits which enabled the Powers of the *Entente* to create in our southern districts the armies of Denikin and Wrangel and to support their fight against the Governments of Russia and her allies.

Two days later, in an eloquent appeal aimed directly at Curzon, the Soviet foreign commissar implored the Allies to allow Russia to begin its new era in peace—"based on the principle of a partition wall between us and on the principle of the freedom and sovereignty of Turkey." Chicherin's invocation of Turkish "sovereignty" was too good a target for Curzon to ignore. "M. Chicherin must have mistaken his role and assumed the *kalpak* [military headgear] of Ismet Pasha," the Englishman blandly declared. "M. Chicherin has said that his views were those of both Russia and Turkey; then why did not Turkey say so?" It was a shrewd move, driving a wedge between Chicherin and Ismet. For Curzon sensed that the Straits no longer represented a crucial issue for the Kemalist government. After all, the Turks had been at war for twelve years and were clearly exhausted. They had driven out the Greeks and compelled the major European Allies to evacuate Asia Minor. By insisting now on control of an international waterway, they risked provoking the retaliation of overwhelming Allied naval power. The Nationalist movement was too Asiatic and peasant-based to arouse enthusiasm for that kind of war. Obviously the Turks did not wish to lose Constantinople; but exclusive domination of the Straits no longer represented a *sine qua non* for them. There is some evidence that Ismet hinted this to Curzon before the Lausanne Conference began.

Faced, therefore, with this combination of Turkish equivocation and Allied firmness, the Russians were backed into a corner. When the final draft convention of the Straits was presented, it contained nearly every feature Chicherin had opposed: freedom of navigation for all commercial vessels in both peacetime and wartime; freedom of passage for warships during peacetime, with the single qualification that no single foreign power could send into the Black Sea a force larger than the strongest Black Sea fleet (Russia's, of course). The qualification was obviously meaningless, for any combination of Allied fleets could easily overwhelm the Soviet Black Sea Navy. Russia's underbelly was now open to the West (no one could have imagined, then, that someday the situation would be reversed, that the Mediterranean littoral would be threatened by Soviet naval power). Finally, with the Straits demilitarized for a distance from the shore of fifteen kilometers on each side, there could never again be another Gallipoli. All transportation and navigation on the waterway would similarly be governed by a Straits Commission. In the long run, the arrangement was probably advantagous for Ankara. It spared the Kemalist government the embarrassment of being dependent on the Soviets. But it was first and foremost a stunning victory for the West, altogether Curzon's finest hour at Lausanne.

The foreign secretary's performance was not less dazzling in resolving the Mosul question in Britain's favor. It was Ismet's position that this crucial, oil-rich vilayet, claimed by Britain as part of the Iraq mandate, was in fact integrally Turkish. Curzon disagreed. When Ismet presented an elaborate ethnographic brief to support Turkish claims to this vilayet, the Englishman, in a *tour de force* of overwhelming erudition, demolished Ismet's case by proving that the territory was actually a *mélange* of races of which the Turks were only one, and a minority at that. Exploiting his advantage, the foreign secretary then warned Ismet that if negotiations remained at an impasse, he would seek a meeting of the League of Nations Council under Article Eleven of the Covenant, which dealt with "threats of war." The ultimatum worked. Ismet decided not to press the matter, and it was tabled for direct British-Turkish negotiations independent of the Lausanne Conference. Later, as a consequence of discussions that extended from

445

1923 to 1926, the Mosul territory eventually was awarded to Iraq, although the Turks were assured a ten-per-cent share of the region's oil profits for a period of twenty-five years. But the outlines of this final decision were already implicit in Ismet's compromise at Lausanne.

The last major issue of importance to Curzon was not territorial, and in fact the initiative in its resolution was taken by Venizelos, on behalf of the Athens government. It dealt with the fate of the Greek and Armenian minorities still remaining in Turkey. The Allies unanimously endorsed Venizelos's plea that these unfortunates be protected by written guarantees under League of Nations supervision, in the pattern of the minorities treaties adopted for the European successor-states. But the proposal was immediately and angrily rejected by Ismet, who declared the very notion of League supervision to be an intolerable infringement of Turkish sovereignty. Turkish law was sufficiently liberal to protect all Turkish citizens, Ismet insisted; anyway, the flight of Greeks and Armenians had rendered the question academic. He was on strong ground with this last point. The evacuation of the Greek army from eastern Thrace, occurring in several stages after the Mudania Armistice, had duplicated the earlier Greek mass exodus from Anatolia. By the opening days of 1923 the number of Greek refugees in the Old Kingdom reached the almost incredible total of 1,200,000. This represented more than a migration. It was an elemental glacier of humanity. A demographic shift of such proportions was not unwelcome to the Turks, of course. On the contrary, Ismet made a point of emphasizing that the outflow of Christians was irrevocable. Although his rationale was the swath of destruction left by the retreating Greek army, he clearly had in mind the priceless social and military advantages of a homogeneous Turkish nation.

This approach received endorsement from an unexpected source: Dr. Fridtjof Nansen, a Norwegian diplomat of international reputation whom the League had commissioned to study the Middle East refugee question. As early as December 1, 1922, Nansen had declared at Lausanne that a mass flight of refugees of such epic dimensions was not reversible. He suggested instead that the exodus be treated as a *fait accompli* and as the political basis for a mutual exchange of Greek and Turkish minorities under the supervision of the League. By the opening of 1923, Venizelos, always the realist, was prepared to accept this solution in principle. His not unimportant condition was simply that the Islamic population of Macedonia and other Greek regions—some 400,000 persons—should similarly emigrate to Turkey and abandon their lands to be occupied by the Greek newcomers. The proposal was transmitted to Ankara and accepted within hours. Only the details remained to be worked out. Venizelos was insistent that the well-integrated and affluent Greek population of Constantinople should be allowed to remain, and that the Greek patriarch should similarly be permitted to maintain his seat in the old Turkish capital. Ismet made a show of resistance, but eventually agreed to these exceptions.

On January 30, 1923, a convention was formally presented for the reciprocal migration of Greek and Turkish populations, a document that was later incorporated in the Lausanne Peace Treaty. By its provisions a mixed commission would supervise the exchange and ensure that Turks returning to Turkey would receive property there equal to the value of their abandoned property in Greece. The same terms applied to the Greeks, of course, and the balance would be paid by the debtor governments. Finally, both nations granted their remaining minorities full and complete amnesty, covering the period between August 1, 1914 and November 20, 1922. With the signing of this agreement, therefore, the irredentist question that had plagued the Ottoman Empire for centuries and all but destroyed it, was laid to final rest. The exchange represented surely the most daring and unprecedented solution of an endemic political problem ever to have been devised in modern history. The cost of the solution, in money, political turmoil, and human suffering, was hardly to be underestimated (see pp. 452–3, below). Both sides were prepared to bear it, however. Except for the Greek enclave in Constantinople and the Turkish enclave in western Thrace, Turkey and Greece would experience at last the incalculable and enduring blessings of ethnic homogeneity. In future years the lesson of this exchange would not be lost on such other peoples as the Germans, Czechs, Poles, Indians, Pakistanis, and Israelis.

The Conference of Lausanne: Ismet's Triumph

ON THE ISSUES of greatest consequence to Britain—the Thracian boundary, the Straits administration, the Mosul question, the fate of the Greek minorities—satisfactory agreement had been reached. All that now remained to be settled were questions of finance, economics, and personal status; and with these, France and Italy were more directly concerned than Britain. Curzon thereupon informed the Allied and Turkish delegations on January 24, 1923, that if the Turks could not agree to the draft treaty (then undergoing final revision) by February 4, he would insist upon the dissolution of the conference. The foreign secretary remained impervious to Allied and Turkish pleas for extension. He knew his Orientals, and was determined not to be worn down by endless Turkish haggling. As it happened, the issues still outstanding were those dealing with the status of foreigners in Turkey, the security of foreign economic concessions, the payment of the Ottoman Public Debt and of Greek "reparations." These were precisely the matters Ismet regarded as unnegotiable. And the Allies discovered that in questions the Turks regarded as vital to their sovereignty, Ismet Pasha could be fully as stubborn and unbudging as Curzon.

Ironically, the task of diplomatic negotiations was the last one Ismet had wanted. A professional soldier, a veteran of Turkey's four wars since 1912, and most recently the hero of the two battles of Inönü (from which he later, in fact, took the name Ismet Inönü), Ismet had been hand-picked for the Lausanne assignment by Kemal. Presumably the loyalty and

448

toughness of a soldier were qualities that Kemal prized above the subtlety and adroitness of a professional diplomat. Ismet was thirty-eight when the conference opened, a slight, prematurely bald, sallow-faced man, deaf in one ear, and altogether ill at ease with statesmen as polished as Curzon. Denied leeway on matters affecting Turkey's domestic freedom of action, Ismet wasted little time in elaborate technical arguments, but took refuge instead in recitations of the National Pact, mumbling embarrassedly, almost deferentially, about Turkey's absolute insistence on "sovereignty." This phlegmatic, plodding, totally "undiplomatic" approach exasperated the British foreign secretary, who attempted repeatedly to chivvy Ismet into concessions by force of erudition and ultimatum. "Ismet, you remind me of nothing so much as a music box," Curzon exploded on one occasion. "You play the same old tune day after day until we are all heartily sick of it—sovereignty, sovereignty, sovereignty."

Yet there it was. Ismet would not be moved. He rejected flatly any proposal of reviving extraterritorial judicial status for foreigners. He turned his deaf ear to suggestions of preferential treatment or guarantees for Allied economic concessions. Turkey would not shoulder the entire prewar Ottoman Public Debt alone, he warned; nor would the Ankara government abandon its right to reparations for damage inflicted by the Greek occupation. Neither was Ismet fazed by Curzon's time limit. On the contrary, when the deadline for February 4 arrived, the Turk actually was the first to leave. An American observer, Joseph Grew, recalled:

> In a moment Ismet appeared descending the stairs followed by his delegation; he took off his bowler hat, bowed right and left to the crowd in the hall, smiling broadly, and left the hotel. . . . In a moment Curzon appeared; he burst into the room like an angry bull, glared at us and began to pace up and down waving his fist in the air. He was perspiring and looked about all in. He shouted: "We have been sitting here for four mortal hours and Ismet has replied to everything we have said by the same old banalities—independence and sovereignty. We have all done our best."

449

Ninety minutes later Curzon boarded his train and left Switzerland. The conference had been suspended.

It was resumed, however, on April 23. The Ankara regime expressed its willingness to enter new discussions if the essential tenets of its position were accepted. In the interval since February 4, the Allied governments had painfully accepted the unlikelihood of any significant shift in Turkish policy. The basic priority now, it was universally agreed, was a completed, signed treaty. Indeed, the time that had already elapsed since the Mudros Armistice of October 1918 was longer than the entire four years of Turkey's participation in the World War. When negotiations were resumed, therefore, the Western delegates—this time the various Allied high commissioners in Constantinople—dropped their insistence upon Capitulations and special economic concessions. The Ottoman Public Debt was distributed equitably between Turkey and the Balkan successor-states of the former empire, the latter assuming approximately a third of the total sum of 141, 166, 199 Turkish pounds. The one issue that apparently remained frozen on dead center was the Turco-Greek dispute over reparations. Ismet remorselessly insisted upon compensation for damage the Greeks had inflicted in Asia Minor. With equal stubbornness, Venizelos rejected the demand, emphasizing that the Greeks had occupied Asia Minor at the specific request of the Allies; and that, in any case, the Turks owed compensation for the million and a quarter Ottoman Greeks hounded out of their ancestral homes. The controversy very nearly erupted into hostilities in May. Venizelos called on Ismet in the latter's hotel suite and solemnly hinted at the possibility of war if Turkish demands were not dropped. It was not an idle warning. The Greek army, reorganized and on its own territory in western Thrace, was once again a serious threat to European Turkey.

Fortunately for Venizelos, his caveat was enforced by the timely intervention of Yugoslav Foreign Minister Yovanovič, who informed Ismet bluntly that a resumption of hostilities in the Balkans would immediately range the Yugoslav army be-

450

side the Greeks. Sobered by this threat, Ismet met the following day with Venizelos and the other Allied delegates in the bridal suite of the Hôtel Château d'Ouchy. For three hours, peace again hung in the balance, while three hundred journalists besieged the hotel, awaiting the final verdict. Then, exactly at 6:00 p.m., Venizelos emerged from the suite radiant with joy. He cried out to the waiting crowd: *"Messieurs! C'est la paix!"* Grew recalled that at this point "Venizelos and Ismet, calling each other 'mon cher ami,' had their hands on each other's arms, laughed like schoolboys and appeared to be on the point of actually embracing. . . . Rumbold [the English delegate] showed his wild enthusiasm by a contraction of the facial muscles which amounted almost to a smile." The Turks had dropped their financial demands. In return, the Athens government had accepted the moral responsibility for damage inflicted by the Greek army in Anatolia, but had coupled the admission with a formal statement of its inability to pay. On this note of final compromise, the Lausanne treaty was signed on July 24, 1923, together with five conventions, one agreement, four declarations, and six protocols. By and large, it was an overwhelming, all but unimaginable victory for the Turks. Except for the Straits and certain qualifications regarding Constantinople, they obtained hardly less than the absolute sovereignty and irreducible territorial frontiers they had stipulated in their National Pact. On August 24, the Grand National Assembly ratified the agreement almost unanimously. A day later, the Allies began their evacuation of Constantinople and the Straits. Within six weeks not a foreign soldier remained on Turkish soil.

A few hours after signing the Treaty of Lausanne, Venizelos received a telegram of appreciation from King George in Athens, entreating him to return to Greece and continue his efforts for the country's welfare. The veteran statesman courteously refused. He had endured enough of civil strife for a lifetime, he emphasized in his reply; the elections of 1920 had put an end to his political career. Unstated in Venizelos's wire were the personal rewards to which he looked forward. Several years earlier he had married a wealthy woman, and he and his wife now preferred to return to Paris and the luxury of their fashionable Right Bank apartment. Nor was Venizelos's appraisal of Greek political difficulties overstated. During the first month of the Lausanne Conference, in November 1922, the revolutionary regime in Athens had appointed a commission of inquiry to fix the blame for the Asia Minor disaster. The commission decided that the archcriminals were none other than three ex-premiers (including Gounaris) and General Hadjianestes, the former commander in chief. The accused were promptly arrested, placed on trial, and within two weeks sentenced to execution. A day after sentence was announced, the prisoners were carried in trucks to a wall outside Athens and shot by a firing squad. Britain immediately severed diplomatic relations with Greece.

The executions helped prolong a blood feud that had begun with the Venizelos-Constantine rivalry in the World War, and that effectively poisoned Greek political life throughout the subsequent two decades. During the first fourteen years after the Asia Minor debacle, no less than nineteen changes of government took place in Greece, together with three changes of regime and seven military revolutions. In the short term, the Anatolian defeat of 1922 may actually have produced more disastrous repercussions than the fall of Constantinople in 1453. The original Turkish conquest, after all, had not evicted entire Greek populations from their European and Asian homesteads. The Kemalist victories did. A million and a quarter human beings were permanently uprooted from the land of their birth, from the soil and ancestral households they had known all their lives. In his well-upholstered Italian exile, Prince Andrew could poeticize:

> For the first time after many centuries, since the time of the Byzantine rulers, a Greek King and a Greek army trod the immense plains of Asia Minor. . . . Is it in vain, this last sacrifice in Asia Minor? No! For the seed sown by the Greek soldier will one day burst forth into a great and flourishing

452

tree. Meanwhile our glorious dead lie by the side of their ancestors, the Hoplites of Alexander the Great . . . and the murmur of the waves of the Aegean bears to the Greek shores the re-echoing sounds of their message: "O stranger, go, tell the Lacedaemonians that here we lie, faithful to their orders."

But as they tried to wrench a livelihood from the rock-strewn soil or the squalid marketplaces of integral Greece, the newcomers did not share this Homeric vision. Nor did they, then, appreciate the ultimate political advantages that would flow from the mass exodus, namely, avoidance of the kind of heterogeneous empire that would have duplicated the fractured political and national loyalties of its Ottoman predecessor. Instead, with the departure of 460,000 Macedonian Turks and the arrival of 1,200,000 Greek refugees, the Old Kingdom became a more compact and viable nation than ever before in its history.

In the case of the Turks, the two-way migration of peoples, the sudden phenomenon of ethnic homogeneity, was a political windfall of the first order. Irredentism had been the single most persistent curse of the moribund realm, and over the decades had played a crucial role in fatally sapping the empire's resistance. Neighboring lands and world powers had encouraged and subsidized this minority hatred of the Turkish overlord. In the eyes of the millet peoples, the Turk was barbarism incarnate, notwithstanding his occasional Western disguises, his costume of Western cut, and his Levantine flow of Western languages. This corrosive enmity, fully reciprocated in acts of savage retaliation, had taken its toll not merely of the Armenians, Greeks, Slavs, Arabs, and Jews who had suffered for generations under the Ottoman master; it had inflicted no less grievous a wound on the Turks themselves. For it was the stoic and phlegmatic Anatolian peasant who had traditionally shouldered the agonizing burden of the empire's wars. Through the years none of the subject peoples, not even the Armenians, had shed as much blood as the Turks themselves. Those days were over now. A Turkish youth called

453

from his plow in a future war would be summoned for the kind of struggle he had just fought and could best understand, the war to preserve a land and people that were his alone.

This was the heritage similarly bequeathed to the former Ottoman subject nations. With the termination of the Greco-Turkish War and the ratification of the Treaty of Lausanne, the basic configuration of the contemporary Middle East had emerged. Plainly, the Arabs were not yet sovereign in the manner of the Turks or the Greeks; nor were the Jews; nor, surely, were the surviving Armenians. Indeed, these former millet peoples understandably measured what they achieved by the yardstick of the ordeal they had endured. They remembered the Arab and Jewish martyrs hanged in Damascus and Jerusalem for loyalty to the Allied cause, the homes and crops and animals brutishly sequestered by Djemal's soldiery, the train of Armenian corpses winding from eastern Turkey to the deserts of Mesopotamia. For the survivors of that wartime inferno, quasi-independence, qualified independence, delayed or postponed independence could not represent adequate emotional solace or political fulfillment. Their leadership sought to evaluate what, precisely, was in their hands once the Turks were gone and the Allies ensconced in the former Ottoman dependencies.

The inheritance was seemingly an unimpressive one on the face of it. Paris had imposed a taut, centralized regime in Beirut and Damascus, had staffed it with French officers and bureaucrats, had sponsored a proliferating network of French schools and libraries throughout the Levant, and had aborted the development of a united Arab political or cultural identity by carving Syria into a number of smaller, disjointed administrative units. The British were less heavy-handed in Iraq, to be sure. But Iraqi extremists hardly had to labor the point that the final decision on matters affecting the nation's foreign and military policy rested with London. In Palestine, moreover, Britain ruled quite as single-handedly as it administered its most backward African or East Asian crown colonies, with no functioning institutions of national self-government whatever

454

to inhibit its mandatory officials. In Soviet Armenia, communized more effectively with every passing month, its former Dashnak activists murdered, imprisoned, or exiled, the memory of two brief, fragile years of independence was fading away now into the haze of folklore, an epic of interwoven fact and myth to be recited quietly before the family hearth.

Yet all was not gall and wormwood in the mandated territories, not even by the standards of the most ardent and uncompromising chauvinists. However extreme their programs of political liberation, the more sophisticated and knowledgeable among the nationalist leaders did not forget what the incubus of Ottoman rule had meant over the years. It had brought with it not only the gibbet and the dungeon, nor merely the predatory confiscations of crops and property, the kidnapping of children for garrison duty in distant provinces or for the secret pleasures of depraved agas. It had meant, as well, indolence and medievalism from one corner of the empire to the other, squalid and fetid bazaars, choked and refuse-strewn streets, rampant plagues, dervishes and faith-healers in the place of clinic and hospital, and justice, even for Moslems, administered with acute sensitivity to baksheesh or a discreet warning from a well-connected senior official. All that, at least, was changing now. The West had something to offer that the Turks manifestly had not been capable of providing, and that the former Ottoman subject peoples were not yet in a position to supply for themselves. This was plain and simple material progress: the innovation of sanitary engineering and clean hospitals, of paved roads and bridges and culverts, of assurance of peace and security in the countryside, of statutes and ordinances honestly administered, if necessary against the mandatory governments themselves. All this signified a departure in Middle Eastern tradition that was hardly negligible or irrelevant to the aspirations even of the nationalist intelligentsia.

Nor was this Middle Eastern educated elite oblivious to the very genuine promise implicit in the peace treaties and mandatory awards. Soviet rule in Armenia, to be sure, offered little more than cultural autonomy and a reasonable degree of administrative integrity. Yet, as we have seen, the basis upon which the British and even the French had arrived in the Middle East was legally provisional. For Arabs and Jews governed by these Western democracies, the promise of eventual independence had been articulated, the geographical boundaries defined. If not everywhere perfected, or even established, the institutions of self-government had nevertheless been tentatively proposed. The likelihood of ultimate freedom was distinctly visible in Iraq, and its possibility more than faintly discernible in Syria and the Lebanon, and even in Palestine. The task of fulfillment would belong to a new generation. But the precedents set during nine and a half years of convulsive birth trauma all but assured that the challenge would some day be met, indeed, met within the space of a single generation—a span of time that represented the merest syllabic inscription on the ageless palimpsest of the Middle East.

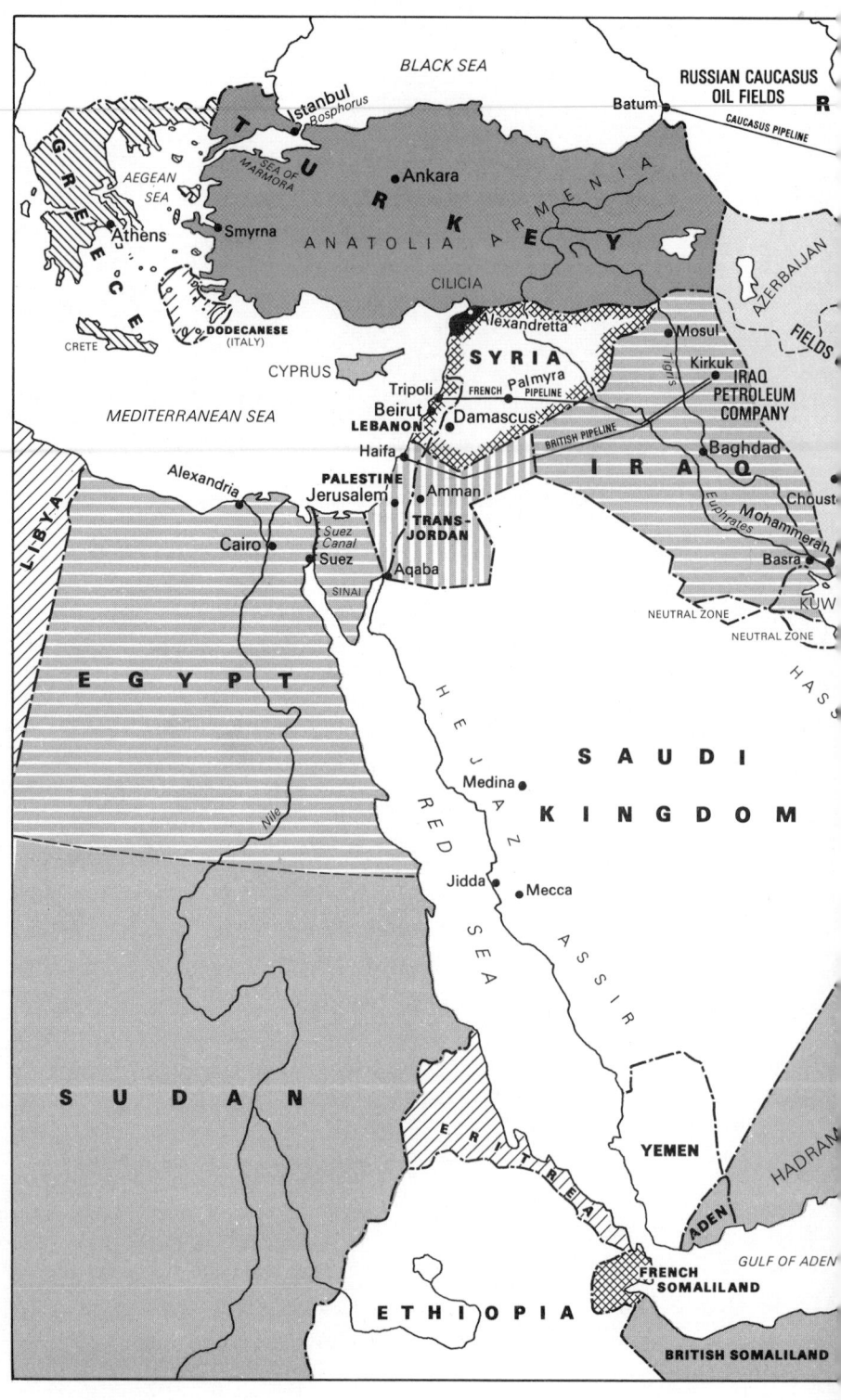

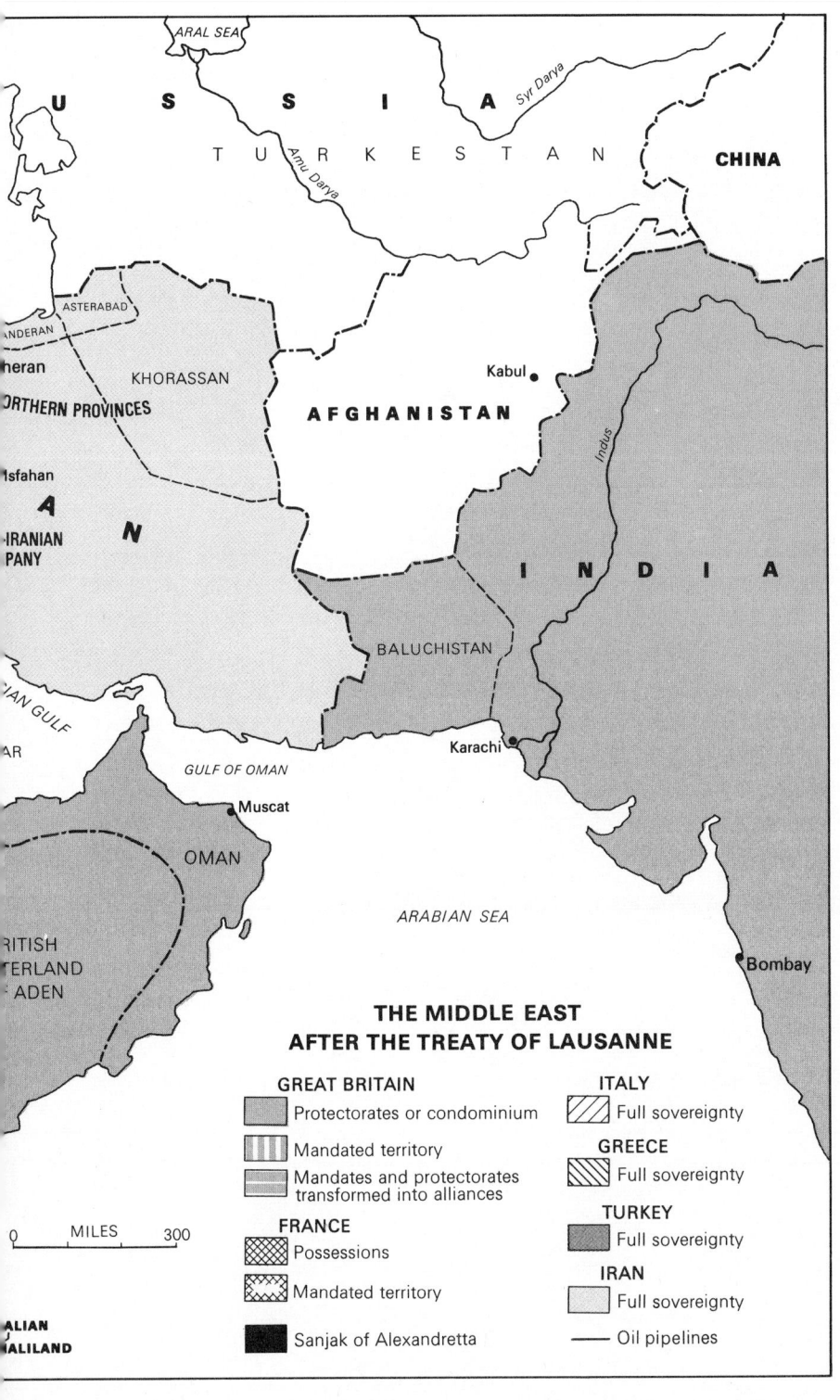

ARAL SEA

U S S I A

T U R K E S T A N

Syr Darya

Amu Darya

CHINA

ASTERABAD

ANDERAN

heran

KHORASSAN

ORTHERN PROVINCES

Isfahan

A

IRANIAN
PANY

N

Kabul •

AFGHANISTAN

Indus

I N D I A

BALUCHISTAN

Karachi •

IAN GULF

AR

GULF OF OMAN

Muscat •

OMAN

ARABIAN SEA

Bombay •

RITISH
TERLAND
ADEN

**THE MIDDLE EAST
AFTER THE TREATY OF LAUSANNE**

0   MILES   300

ALIAN
ALILAND

GREAT BRITAIN	**ITALY**
Protectorates or condominium	Full sovereignty
Mandated territory	**GREECE**
Mandates and protectorates transformed into alliances	Full sovereignty
FRANCE	**TURKEY**
Possessions	Full sovereignty
Mandated territory	**IRAN**
Sanjak of Alexandretta	Full sovereignty
	—— Oil pipelines

Notes

I. The Sick Man's Last Adventure (pages 5–31)

6. "The Germans have captured Turkey": Henry Morgenthau, *Ambassador Morgenthau's Story* (New York, 1922), pp. 80–1.

13. "To export even the droppings of dogs": Alma Wittlin, *Abdul Hamid: The Shadow of God* (London, 1940), p. 253.

15. "Mobilization and operation in a future war": O. V. K. Liman von Sanders, *Five Years in Turkey* (Annapolis, 1927), p. 27.

15. Germany . . . protecting her stake in Anatolia and Mesopotamia: R. J. Kerner, "The Mission of Liman von Sanders," *Slavonic Review*, VI (June 1927), 5.

15. Kaiser . . . personally and enthusiastically approved the Mission: Ibid., 12.

16. "Guarantee of the existence of the Ottoman Empire": Ibid., 327.

16. Mahmud Shevket rejected Entente protest: Ibid., 543–56.

17. Vocal and belligerent Pan-German press: Hugo Grothe, *Deutschland, die Türkei und der Islam* (Berlin, 1914), pp. 64–5.

17. "The Power which controls the army": R. Silbert, *Entente Diplomacy and the World War* (New York, 1921), pp. 684–7.

17. Foreign Secretary Zimmerman heartily agreed: Kerner, op. cit., p. 290.

18. "Trying to be equally good to all the European Powers": Talaat Pasha, "Posthumous Memoirs," *Current History*, XV (November 1921), 287.

19. Ottoman Empire helpless pawn of German military policy: Ulrich Trumpener, "Liman von Sanders and the German-Ottoman Alliance," *Journal of Contemporary History*, I (October 1966), 181–2.

19. "And never proposed anything else": Talaat, op. cit., p. 290.

21. "We could hardly believe": Ibid., pp. 290–1.

21. "Never, never shall I forget": Ahmed Djemal Pasha, *Memories of a Turkish Statesman, 1913–1919*, p. 116.

21. "Looking more like a parson": Lewis Einstein, *Inside Constantinople* (London, 1917), p. 255.

21. Dardanelles closed to warships since 1840: Admiral Sir Archibald Milne, *The Flight of the Goeben and the Breslau* (London, 1921), p. 83.

23. Wangenheim apostle of Pan-Germanism: Morgenthau, op. cit., p. 5.

23. Enver and Djemal approved "sale" of cruisers: Herman Lorey, *Der Krieg in den türkischen Gewässern* (Berlin, 1928–38), I, 32.

24. Blank charge warned the Englishman off: Ibid.

24. Germans serenaded the Russian ambassador: Morgenthau, op. cit., p. 79.

24. "Hadji Wilhelm": Ernst Jäckh,

The Rising Crescent (New York, 1944), p. 140.

24. "Summon Musselmans . . . to holy war": Ibid.

25. "When will you join us?": Talaat, op. cit., p. 289.

25. Their principal value lay in benevolent neutrality: Lt. General Joseph Pomiankowski, *Der Zusammenbruch des ottomanischen Reiches: Erinnerungen an die Türkei der Zeit des Weltkrieges* (Vienna, 1928), pp. 16–17.

25. View shared by Liman von Sanders: Liman von Sanders, op. cit., p. 9.

26. German boxcars unable to proceed to Constantinople: Ulrich Trumpener, "German Military Aid to Turkey in 1914: an historical re-evaluation," *Journal of Modern History*, XXXII (June 1960), 145–9.

26. Germans behaved as if masters of the city: Morgenthau, op. cit., p. 64.

28. Djemal and Talaat decided not to protest decision: Ulrich Trumpener, "Turkey's Entry into World War I: an assessment of responsibilities," *Journal of Modern History*, XXXIV (December 1962), 369–80.

28. "In a few weeks the Bosphorus": Morgenthau, op. cit., p. 111.

30. Russians had intended to mine Bosphorus, Enver insisted: Trumpener, "Turkey's Entry Into World War I," p. 376.

30. "If we had insisted": Talaat, op. cit., p. 293.

II. The Stage of Battle (pages 32–52)

32. "For the ordinary soldier": Liman von Sanders, op. cit., p. 9.

32. "The humble Turkish soldier": Maurice Larcher, *La guerre turque dans la guerre mondiale* (Paris, 1926), p. 65.

32–3. Half the artillery ammunition defective: Ibid.

34. By 1918 25,000 Germans in Ottoman armed forces: Ulrich Trumpener, *Germany and the Ottoman Empire, 1914–1918* (Princeton, 1968), pp. 104–5.

34. Ottoman armed forces never mere instrument of German policy: Ibid., p. 105.

34. Liman's relationship with Porte increasingly acrimonious: Ibid., pp. 84–104.

34–5. Enver assigned 100,000 Turkish soldiers to other fronts: Ibid., p. 66.

36. Eight Russian divisions along Transcaucasian frontier: Ibid., p. 82.

38. Barrett determined to enlarge this bridgehead: Edmund Dane, *British Campaigns in the Near East, 1914–1918* (London, 1918), p. 37.

39. "And promises to stir up": Harry Stuermer, *Two War Years in Constantinople* (New York, 1917), pp. 127–36.

43. Canal traffic suspended two nights: W. T. Massey, *The Desert Campaigns* (New York, 1918), pp. 15–16.

43. "Are you defending the Canal": Ibid., p. 20.

46. "All roads pass through Berlin": W. E. D. Allen and Paul Muratoff, *Caucasian Battlefields* (London, 1953), p. 231.

46. "Until now it was not certain": Felix Guse, *Die Kaukasusfront im Weltkrieg* (Leipzig, 1940), p. 313.

47. "It is a vast and eternal region": quoted in Uriel Heyd, *Foundations of Turkish Nationalism* (London, 1950), p. 119.

47–8. Schellendorf prepared the master plan: Guse, op. cit., p. 313.

50. Eighty thousand men lost in Third Army: Larcher, op. cit., p. 383.

50. Yudenich emerged one of ablest commanders: Allen and Muratoff, op. cit., p. 240 *et seq.*

51. Continuous Ottoman appeals for financial assistance honored: Trumpener, *Germany and the Ottoman Empire, 1914–1918,* pp. 271–84.

51. Ottoman government pressured Berlin for revision of Turco-German alliance: Ibid., pp. 130–4.

III. Allied Catastrophes in the Middle East (pages 53–86)

57. "If the Straits . . . were not permanently closed": General Erich von Falkenhayn, *General Headquarters and its Critical Decisions* (London, 1919), p. 19.

57. "Should the Dardenelles fall": Admiral P. von Tirpitz, *Memoirs* (London, 1919), II, 99.

59. Improvements made in Dardanelles' defenses: E. R. Prigge, *Der Kampf um die Dardanellen* (Weimar, 1916), p. 68.

60. Most of the shells missed: General Hans Kannengiesser, *The Campaign in Gallipoli* (London, 1928), pp. 114–15.

60. "The German General Staff": Morgenthau, op. cit., p. 181.

60. Von der Goltz and Kühlman certain the Allies would enter Marmora and Constantinople: Ibid., p. 184.

61. Turkish ammunition nearly expended: C. Mühlmann, *Der Kampf um die Dardanellen* (Oldenburg, 1927), p. 74.

61–2. "To make a passage for the Navy": General Sir Ian Hamilton, *Gallipoli Diary* (London, 1920), I, 41.

62. Military expedition probably a necessity: Robert R. James, *Gallipoli* (London, 1965), p. 65.

62. Liman hoped for eight days: · Kannengiesser, op. cit., p. 143.

65. "With pity and with pride": John Masefield, *Gallipoli* (London, 1916), p. 42.

66. "Not to attack, but to die": Larcher, op. cit., p. 218.

66–7. "At the moment from the apparently dead ground": Kannengiesser, op. cit., p. 143.

67. The shore ran red with blood: James, op. cit., p. 131.

68. Allied offensive was broken: A. P. Herbert, *Half-Hours at Hellas.*

69. Turks withstood ordeal better: Einstein, op. cit., p. 23.

70. Eighty thousand Turks evacuated: Kennengiesser, op. cit., p. 143.

70. Effort made to poison Liman: Liman von Sanders, op. cit., p. 254.

73. Mahon found army barely clinging to its fragment of ground: James, op. cit., p. 306.

76. "A mighty destroyer": Alan Moorehead, *Gallipoli* (London, 1956), p. 336.

76. Royal commission concluded occupation should have been pushed vigorously: "The Cromer Report," *Current History*, XI (March 1917), 167–70.
77. "Drew a part of the Turkish forces away": S. D. Sazanov, *Fateful Years* (London, 1928), p. 233.
79. "Not one inch": Sir Charles Townshend, *My Campaign in Mesopotamia* (London, 1920), p. 86.

79–80. "And with a better prospect": Sir Arnold T. Wilson, *Loyalties: Mesopotamia, 1914–1917* (London, 1930), I, 86.
80. "If I receive a check": Ibid., p. 124.
81. "Their limbs splinted with wood strings": E. H. S. Sherson, *Townshend of Chitral and Kut* (London, 1928), p. 290.
84. Radioed messages of encouragement: Townshend, op. cit., p. 287.

IV. The Armenian Genocide (pages 87–115)

88. Thraceans crossed into Transcaucasus: See Sarkis Atamian, *The Armenian Community* (New York, 1955), Chapter I, and Hrant Pasdermadjian, *Histoire de l'Arménie depuis les origines jusqu'au traité de Lausanne* (Paris, 1949), Chapters I, II.
89. On eve of war their numbers 1,845,000: Johannes Lepsius, *Der Todesgang des armenischen Volkes* (Potsdam, 1930), p. 35; citing registry figures of Armenian patriarch in Constantinople.
89–90. "The whole scheme": Djemal, op. cit., p. 246.
90. Nazarian and others advocated liberal nationalism: Louise Nalbandian, *The Armenian Revolutionary Movement* (Berkeley, 1963), p. 15 *ff*.
90. Fifty thousand Armenians slaughtered: M. Varandian, *Histoire de la Dashnagtzoutune* (Paris, 1932), I, 325–7.
91. Constantinople curtailed minority cultural activity: Johannes Lepsius, *Deutschland und Armenien, 1914–1918* (Potsdam, 1919), p. 17.

92. With Porte gravitating into German orbit: R. H. Davison, "The Armenian Crisis, 1912–1914," *American Historical Review*, XLIII (April 1948), 481 *ff*.
92. "In the eyes of the Christians": Djemal, op. cit., p. 274.
93. Later Russian Armenian press opposed such a plan: Lepsius, *Der Todesgang des armenischen Volkes*, pp. 262–3.
93. "The Armenians are interested": Ibid.
93. "The resurrection of the Polish nation": C. J. Smith, Jr., *The Russian Struggle for Power, 1914–1917* (New York, 1917), pp. 125–7.
94. "Armenia must be in the sphere": Ibid., pp. 126–7.
94. "In a direction benevolent": Ibid., pp. 200–1.
95. Armenian tenacity helped blunt Turkish offensives: Atamian, op. cit., pp. 199–200 *ff*.
95. Zia urged purging of non-Turkish communities: Heyd, op. cit., Chapters IV, V *passim*.
97. Dashnaks spurned Kurdish overtures: Lepsius, *Der Todes-*

gang des armenischen Volkes, p. 207.

97. "Armenians helped wherever . . . they could": Jäckh, op. cit., p. 43.

98. "The ministry of war had issued orders": Pomiankowski, op. cit., p. 93.

98. American and German missionaries eyewitnesses: Lepsius, Deutschland und Armenien, p. 17.

100. Account of Dr. Samuel Ussher: Morgenthau, op. cit., p. 299.

101. "To take precautionary measures": Lepsius, Der Todesgang des armenischen Volkes, p. 213.

101. "Will enter your heads again": Ibid., p. 220.

101. "Endangered the Turkish Army's line of retreat": Talaat, op. cit., pp. 289–90.

103. Local Moslems forbidden to succor the dying: Lepsius, Deutschland und Armenien, p. 232 ff.

103. Descriptions provided by Turks themselves: "The Memoirs of Naim Bey," in The Turkish Armenocide (Newton Square, Pennsylvania, 1965), pp. 4–5.

103. Morgenthau transmitted detailed accounts: Morgenthau, op. cit., pp. 311–12.

103. Bryce Report's descriptions: Viscount Bryce, The Treatment of Armenians in the Ottoman Empire, 1915–1916 (London, 1916), passim.

104. "Please sir, do not wait": Arshag Mahdesian, "A Probable Source of 'Forty Days of Musa Dagh,'" Armenian Review, I (Winter 1948), 108–9.

104. Several members of liberal Opposition expressed outrage: Lepsius, Der Todesgang des armenischen Volkes, pp. 265–8.

104. "German associates begged me": Morgenthau, op. cit., p. 328.

105. "Inevitability of the historical process": Ibid., pp. 337–9.

105. Wangenheim received detailed reports: Lepsius, Deutschland und Armenien, p. lxx ff.

105. "Which menace the existence of Turkey": Ibid.

105. "[Wangenheim's] antipathy to the Armenians": Morgenthau, op. cit., p. 372.

105. "I think that . . . [the Turks] are entirely justified": Stuermer, op. cit., pp. 72–4; see also Trumpener, Germany and the Ottoman Empire, 1914–1918, pp. 204–5 ff.

106. By end of year largest number of Armenians wiped out: Lepsius, Deutschland und Armenien, p. 256.

106. Billion marks of Armenian property confiscated: Lepsius, Der Todesgang des armenischen Volkes, pp. 301–4.

106–7. Toynbee estimated between 800,000 and 1,000,000 killed: Arnold Toynbee, in Introduction to The Bryce Report.

108. "According to specified pattern": Morgan D. Price, War and Revolution in Asiatic Russia (London, 1918), p. 171.

110. Turks lost ten thousand men in four days: Larcher, op. cit., pp. 402–3.

112. Deserters living as brigands in mountains: Guse, op. cit., pp. 94–5.

112. Russian Revolution saved Turks: Pomiankowski, op. cit., p. 439.

112. 300,000 men lost against the Russians: Allen and Muratoff, op. cit., pp. 438–40.

112. Turkish military strength destroyed: Ibid.

113. Thousands of Turkish soldiers starving: Larcher, op. cit., p. 396.

113. "It is remarkable": Liman von Sanders, op. cit., p. 156.

113. "It is almost like a nemesis": Ibid., p. 157.

113–14. "Decide what measures to take": Price, op. cit., pp. 142–3.

114. Retaliatory atrocities described by Turks: Ahmed Rustem Bey, *La guerre mondiale et la question turco-arménienne* (Berne, 1918), *passim*.

114. Russian officers threatened to use artillery: Djemal, op. cit., pp. 281–5.

115. Instructive precedent for later German campaign: *Trial of the Major War Criminals before the International Military Tribunal* (Nuremberg, 1947), X, 411.

V. The Arab Revolt (pages 116–51)

118. Four thousand Turkish casualties: Larcher, op. cit., p. 161; Cyril Falls and Sir George F. MacMunn, *Military Operations: Egypt and Palestine* (London, 1928), I, 199.

119. Kitchener ordered Storrs to remain in contact with Abdullah: Sir Ronald Storrs, *Orientations* (London, 1937), p. 142.

121. Morgenthau recalled Djemal's energy: Morgenthau, op. cit., pp. 172–83.

121. "I myself": Djemal, op. cit., pp. 200–1.

122. 100,000 Lebanese died: Edouard Brémond, *Le Hedjaz dans la guerre mondiale* (Paris, 1931), p. 27.

125. "He would immerse": Sir G. Arthur, *Life of Lord Kitchener* (London, 1920), III, 153–4.

125. "It may be": Kedourie, op. cit., p. 49.

126. Hussein's conditions those of "Damascus Protocol": J. C. Hurewitz, *Diplomacy in the Near and Middle East: A Documentary Record* (Princeton, 1956), II, 13–17.

127. Sykes viewed Ottoman minorities as Levantine melange: See Sir Mark Sykes, *Through Five Turkish Provinces* (London, 1900), p. 80; *Dar ul Islam* (London, 1904), p. 178; *The Caliph's Last Heritage* (London, 1915), p. 441.

127. "Seek the advice": Hurewitz, loc. cit.

128. Faruqi agreed to priority of French influence: Jukka Nevakivi, *Britain, France, and the Arab Middle East, 1914–1920* (London, 1969), p. 28.

128. Hogarth testified on British-Arab candor: Sir Harold Temperley, *History of the Peace Conference of Paris* (London, 1924), VI, 126.

129. "Their business, not ours": Storrs, op. cit., p. 178.

130. "By the glorious soul": Djemal, op. cit., p. 213.

130. "How could we be traitors": Ibid., p. 221.

130. Religious grievances of manifesto: André Mandelstam, *Le sort de l'Empire Ottoman* (Paris, 1917), p. 260.

133. Some Harb leaders remained loyal: Brémond, op. cit., p. 32.

134. Syria not responsive to Arab Revolt: David Lloyd George, *Memoirs of the Peace Conference* (London, 1938), II, 665–8.

136. Ja'far al-Askari ablest Arab officer: Lowell Thomas, *With Lawrence in Arabia* (New York, 1924), p. 269.

137. "White figure waiting tensely": T. E. Lawrence, *Seven Pillars of Wisdom* (London, 1935), p. 99.
137. "Feisal [was] a timid man": B. H. Liddell Hart, "T. E. Lawrence"—*In Arabia and After* (London, 1934), p. 188.
138. Blowing up Turkish trains: Falls and MacMunn, op. cit., p. 230.
138. Medina not captured until after war: Richard Aldington, *Lawrence of Arabia* (London, 1955), pp. 174–5.
140. Lawrence's memoirs imply Hogarth singled him out: *Times* (London), June 5, 1968.
140. "[Lawrence's] enduring world-fame": Storrs, op. cit., pp. 199–200.
141. "Raced through a driving sandstorm": T. E. Lawrence, *Revolt in the Desert* (London, 1927), p. 116.
141. Longest way proved easiest: Liddell-Hart, op. cit., p. 201.
142. "Shy showoff": Richard M. Meinertzhagen, *Middle East Diary 1917–1956* (London, 1956), p. 20.
142. "Tin-pot exhibitionist": quoted in ibid.
143. Turks numbered 33,000: Falls and MacMunn, op. cit., pp. 218–19.
144. Murray sustained 2,700 casualties: Ibid., p. 219.

144. Turkish losses a third British: Kress von Kressenstein, *Zwischen Kaukasus und Sinai* (Berlin, 1922), p. 20.
145. "An obstinate . . . character": Lawrence, *Revolt in the Desert*, p. 124.
145–6. "Before them into safety": Ibid., pp. 144–7.
146. Arab ambushes took toll by 1918: George Antonius, *The Arab Awakening* (Philadelphia, 1938), p. 231.
146. Arab uprising a painful harrassment: Larcher, op. cit., p. 502.
147. "We knew": Lawrence, *Revolt in the Desert*, p. 152.
147. "Deraa's sudden capture": Ibid.
147. "I decided to postpone": Lawrence, *Seven Pillars of Wisdom*, pp. 240–1.
149. Feisal threatened negotiations with Constantinople: Ibid., p. 571.
149. Auda threatened to hand back Aqaba: Liddell-Hart, op. cit., "A New War."
150. "Mosaic of provisional administrations": T. E. Lawrence, *Secret Dispatches from Arabia* (London, 1939), p. 39.
151. "The success or failure": David Garnett (ed.), *Letters of T. E. Lawrence* (London, 1939), p. 196.

VI. Inducements for Each Other: The Secret Treaties
(pages 152–86)

154. Enemy must be defeated in Europe, Yanushkevich emphasized: Michael T. Florinsky, "A Page of Diplomatic History: Russian Military Leaders and the Problem of Constantinople during the War," *Political Science Quarterly*, XLIV (March 1929), 111.
154. Sazanov knew how much

Straits worth: W. W. Gottleib, *Studies in Secret Diplomacy during the First World War* (London, 1957), p. 63.

154. "The war will have no meaning for us": Maurice Paléologue, *An Ambassador's Memoirs* (London, 1923), I, 153.

154. "Russia's historic mission": Gottlieb, op. cit., p. 90.

154. "In conformity with [Russian] interests": Ibid., p. 70.

154–5. "Yes, certainly": Jean Pichon, *Le partage du Proche-Orient* (Paris, 1938), pp. 38–9.

155. "When the Gallipoli expedition was finally decided upon": Sazanov, op. cit., p. 255.

155. "The realization of their secular dream": A. Pingaud, *Histoire diplomatique de la France pendant la grande guerre* (Paris, 1938), pp. 38–9.

155. Sazanov presented terms of "Great Memorandum": Evgenii A. Adamov, *Constantinople et les détroits* (Paris, 1930), I, 12.

155. "Was what we are to demand in return": Herbert Asquith, *Memories and Reflections* (Boston, 1928), II, 65.

155. British war committee discussions of March 10–19 reach agreement on Moslem political entity: Nevakivi, op. cit., 15–18.

155–6. Ambassador wished to incorporate Persian neutral zone: Pingaud, op. cit., p. 252; J. Polonsky (ed.), *Documents diplomatiques secrets russes* (Paris, 1928), p. 292. Cited hereafter as *Doc. dip. sec. russes*.

156. Tsar Nicholas smilingly accepted them: Sir George Buchanan, *My Mission to Russia* (London, 1924), II, 226–7.

156. Great Memorandum "stupefied" him: Pingaud, op. cit., p. 248.

156. French investments exceeded German: Henry H. Cumming, *Franco-British Rivalry in the*

Post-War Near East (New York, 1938), p. 11.

156. French citizens held most shares of Ottoman Public Debt: D. C. Blaisdell, *European Financial Control in the Ottoman Empire* (New York, 1929), p. 219.

156. "Everything is linked": R. Poincaré, *Au service de la France* (Paris, 1937), VI, 94–5.

156. Armenians of Cilicia objects of Russian "solicitude": *Doc. dip. sec. russes*, p. 299.

156. Russian government unofficially approved on March 18: Hurewitz, op. cit., II, 10.

156–7. Negotiations and terms of Turco-German proposal of April 18, 1915: Trumpener, *Germany and the Ottoman Empire, 1914–1918*, pp. 142–4.

157. Offer made little impression on St. Petersburg: Gottlieb, op. cit., pp. 112–31.

157. Inducement existed for continued military effort: Ibid., p. 11.

157. "The question is settled now": Paléologue, op. cit., II, 150.

158. "Several months ago": Ibid., III, 110–11.

158. Grey intimated existence of special British "arrangements": Viscount Grey of Falloden, *Twenty-Five Years* (London, 1928), II, 211–12.

158. "[Grey] has hinted": Poincaré, op. cit., VII, 206.

158. "Certain areas" were Damascus, Homs, Hama and Aleppo: Nagib Sadaka, *La question syrienne pendant la guerre de 1914* (Paris, 1940), p. 95.

158. Paris vetoed Alexandretta landing: Arthur, op. cit., p. 193.

159. Anglo-French discussions significantly hastened thereby: Smith, op. cit., pp. 356–7.

159. Asquith and Grey hesitant to speak in imperialist terms: Asquith, op. cit., p. 69.

160. Nicolson and Georges-Picot initially clashed: Nevakivi, op. cit., p. 31.

160. Sykes demonstrated sympathy for French interests: Ibid., p. 32.

160–1. Report of the De Bunsen Committee and its later modification: See A. S. Kleiman, "Britain's War Aims in the Middle East in 1915," *Journal of Contemporary* History, III (July 1968), 242–51.

161. "A right of priority": Antonius, op. cit., p. 429.

162. "Anti-clericalism is not an export article": F. Charles-Roux, *La France et les chrétiens d'Orient* (Paris, 1939), p. 232.

163. French economic interests totaled 200,000,000 francs: R. de Caix, H. Deberain, and G. Hardy, *Histoire des colonies françaises* (Paris, 1931), III, 486.

163. Railroad investments 100,-000,000 francs: R. de Gontaut-Biron, *Comment la France s'est installée en Syrie, 1918–1919* (Paris, 1923), pp. 8–9.

163. French capitalists owned 472 miles of track: Sadaka, op. cit., p. 44.

163. "The ports of Jaffa": Ibid., pp. 35–6.

163. Projected boundaries of Flandin Report: Etienne Flandin: *"La force brutale": rapport au sénat sur la Syrie et la Palestine* (Paris, 1915), *passim*.

164. "Complete in the east the defenses of Toulon": Ibid., p. 116.

164. "The axis of French policy": quoted in Cumming, op. cit., pp. 18–19.

164. Later Cyprus was added to list: Nevakivi, op. cit., p. 41.

164. Sykes shrewdly played on French Catholic fears: Ibid., p. 33.

164. French emissary agreed to "sacrifice": E. L. Woodward and R. Butler (eds.), *Documents on British Foreign Policy, 1919–1939* (London, 1952), 1st Ser., IV, No. 334. Cited hereafter as *Doc. Br. For. Pol.*

166. "Why Palestine?": Flandin, op. cit., pp. 173–5.

167. Russian Orthodox interests hardly less extensive: Theofanis G. Stavrou, *Russian Interests in Palestine, 1882–1914* (Salonica, 1963), *passim*.

167. Orthodox interests extended throughout Holy Land: H. F. Frischwasser-Ra'anan, *Frontiers of a Nation* (London, 1955), p. 63.

167. Grey asked Cabinet's support: Viscount Herbert L. S. Samuel, *Memoirs* (London, 1955), pp. 140–5.

168. Grey complained that British interests sacrificed: Lloyd George, *War Memoirs*, III, 1089.

168. Sykes agreed: Ibid., p. 1025.

168. "Poor Mark Sykes!": Lord Bertie, *Diary, 1914–1918* (London, 1924), III, 317.

168–9. Britain achieved the more dramatic advance: Frischwasser-Ra'anan, op. cit., p. 73.

169. Blueprint transparently Russian device: *Doc. dip. sec. russes*, pp. 293–4.

169. For the while Sazanov allowed matter to rest: Ibid., pp. 295–6.

170. "Personally, I am not contemplating": Smith, op. cit., pp. 367–8.

171. Foreign minister to assure Armenians religious and cultural rights: Ibid., pp. 380–1.

171. "A foolish document": Lloyd George, *Memoirs of the Peace Conference*, II, 664–5.

172. "That the late Sir Mark Sykes himself": Shane Leslie, *Mark Sykes: His Life and Letters* (London, 1923), pp. 664–5.

172. Some evidence British government shared this view: *Doc.*

Br. For. Pol., 1st Ser., IV, 247–50.

172. Difference between McMahon letter and Sykes-Picot agreement one of spirit: Elizabeth Munroe, *Britain's Moment in the Middle East, 1914–1956* (Baltimore, 1963), p. 35.

172. "The Sykes-Picot Agreement . . . was the last responsible attempt": Kedourie, op. cit., p. 65.

173. The Sherif Hussein well aware: Ibid., p. 39.

173. "As the British did in Baghdad": Lloyd George, *Memoirs of the Peace Conference*, II, 664–5.

173. "To the fold of the Caliph": Antonius, op. cit., p. 256.

174. "Stand by the Arab peoples": Ibid., pp. 431–2.

174. "Surviving parties": Ibid., p. 434.

174. "Created an altogether different situation": Ibid., p. 257.

174. "It is the wish and desire": *Foreign Office Doc. No. 4. Misc.* (London, 1939).

176. Imperiali demanded recognition of Italian claims: Gottleib, op. cit., p. 200.

176. Foreign Office wanted no challenge in eastern Mediterranean: Grey, op. cit., II, 207.

176. Sonnino willing to be patient: Gottlieb, op. cit., pp. 317–19.

176. Grey reconsidered his options: Grey, op. cit., II, 206.

177. "No discussion had taken place": Antonio Salandra, *Italy and the Great War* (London, 1932), p. 283.

177. "The reasons he then ad-

vanced": Ibid., p. 291.

177. "Of existing interests of France and Great Britain": Hurewitz, op. cit., II, 11–12.

177. Briand promised to protect Italian rights: L. Eisenmann, A. de Lapradelle, P. Renouvin, and B. Markine-Guetzévitch, *Constantinople et les détroits* (Paris, 1932), II, 299.

177–8. "The equality of Italian rights": Ibid., p. 306.

178. The request had to be honored: Lloyd George, *Memoirs of the Peace Conference*, II, 505–6.

179. Sonnino extracted assurance of parity for Italy: Hurewitz, op. cit., p. 399.

179. "It has been agreed": Ibid.

182. Ottoman Second and Third Armies decimated: Pomiankowski, op. cit., p. 399.

182. Revolutions eroded Russian strength on Turkish front: Allen and Muratoff, op. cit., p. 441.

183. "A peace without annexations": quoted in Harry N. Howard, *The Partition of Turkey* (Norman, Oklahoma, 1931), p. 176.

183. "We declare that the division of Turkey": quoted in ibid.

185. Dispatch of even one of these six divisions: Larcher, op. cit., p. 417.

186. British sailed off amid curses of citizenry: F. Kazemzadeh, *The Struggle for Transcaucasia, 1917–1921* (New York, 1951), p. 140.

VII. An Inducement for the Jews (pages 187–222)

187. "That we can rush right up to Damascus": David Garnett (ed.), *The Essential T. E. Lawrence* (New York, 1951), pp.

76–7.

187. "For my part": Lawrence, *Seven Pillars of Wisdom*, p. 168.

187. War Cabinet vetoed French

demands: Lloyd George, *Memoirs of the Peace Conference*, II, 1825–8.

187. Curzon committee urged British control of Palestine: Nevakivi, op. cit., p. 46.

187. "The French will have to accept": quoted in Frischwasser-Ra'anan, op. cit., pp. 75–6.

188. "Would be quite intolerable to ourselves": Ibid.

188. "The presence of a foreign Power": Lloyd George, *Memoirs of the Peace Conference*, II, 1144.

189. Jewish nationalism similar to Balkan and other awakenings: Howard M. Sachar, *The Course of Modern Jewish History* (Cleveland, 1958), pp. 263–4.

190. Numbered 20,000 by 1876: Yitzhak Ben-Zvi, *Eretz Yisrael v'Yishah b'y'mai HaShilton HaOttomani* (Jerusalem, 1955), p. 315.

192–3. An effective naturalization campaign: Rahel Yannait, *Anu Olim* (Tel Aviv, 1963), pp. 237–8.

193. Jewish land titles called into question: N. M. Gelber, *Hatzharath Balfour v'Toldoteha* (Jerusalem, 1939), p. 191.

194. Morgenthau bound to be taken seriously: Frank E. Manuel, *The Realities of American-Palestine Relations* (Washington, D.C., 1949), p. 13.

195. "Exalted British Government": Pesah Lipovetzky, *Joseph Trumpeldor, Life and Works* (Jerusalem, 1953), p. 50.

195. German Zionists urge "bastion" of German influence in Palestine: Leonard Stein, *The Balfour Declaration* (London, 1961), p. 213.

195. "The advance guard of German influence": Anna and Maxa Nordau, *Max Nordau* (New York, 1943), p. 207.

196–7. "From the well-ordered": Asquith, op. cit., p. 59.

197. "[He] was almost frighteningly convincing": A. L. Sachar, *Sufferance is the Badge* (New York, 1940), p. 464.

197. "I sometimes wonder": Stein, op. cit., p. 129.

197. Veneration of Protestants for Holy Land: See Barbara Tuchman, *Bible and Sword* (New York, 1956), Chapters I, II.

197. "More familiar to me": Ibid., p. 24.

199. "A virtuous and simple agrarian population": quoted in Christopher Sykes, op. cit., p. 154.

199. Sykes admired Zionist colonies: Kedourie, op. cit., p. 86.

199. Although initially reluctant, Sykes accepted need for revisionist imperial policy: Nevakivi, op. cit., pp. 47–8.

199. Sykes saw Zionist Jews as Britain's logical allies: Christopher Sykes, op. cit., p. 154.

199. "That Jewish haute finance": Stein, op. cit., p. 395.

200. French and Italians expressed friendly interest: Gelber, op. cit., pp. 75–6.

200. "Where Sykes again prepared my way": Nahum Sokolow, *History of Zionism* (London, 1918), I, xxx.

200. "[Picot] is convinced": Poincaré, op. cit., IX, 109.

201. "It was *not* from [Sykes]": Chaim Weizmann, *Trial and Error* (Philadelphia, 1949), I, 188.

201. "Because the wealth they would bring": Harold Temperley, *England and the Near East* (London, 1936), 444.

202. "If the great force of Judaism": Stein, op. cit., p. 280.

202. Lloyd George expressed prevailing conviction of Jewish "influence": Lloyd George,

Memoirs of the Peace Conference, II, 722.

202. "In the solution": Ibid., p. 724.

206. Deeply impressed by Aaronsohn the man: Weizmann, op. cit., I, 181.

207. "It was very largely": Anita Engel, *The Nili Spies* (London, 1959), p. 301.

208. "Is thus annihilated": Weizmann, op. cit., I, 238.

209. Morgenthau returned to the United States: Manuel, op. cit., pp. 155–8.

209. "It was from that talk": Stein, op. cit., p. 152.

210. "In bidding me goodbye": Ibid., p. 155.

210. Balfour remorseful about Christendom's treatment of Jews: Blanche E. C. Dugdale, *Arthur James Balfour* (London, 1936), I, 217.

210. "Will burst forth and propagate": Stein, op. cit., p. 152.

210. "Methods and means": Ibid., p. 470.

210. "It would affect": Lloyd George, *Memoirs of the Peace Conference*, II, 1650.

211. Raised embarrassing questions of Jewish dual loyalty: Stein, op. cit., pp. 497–8.

211. "Mr. Montagu could not extend": Dugdale, op. cit., p. 214.

211. "I missed a great opportunity": Weizmann, op. cit., I, 206.

212. "I believe that we shall be good neighbours": Stein, op. cit., p. 408.

212. Equally friendly statements by Allied ambassadors: Ibid., p. 408.

213. House dropped anti-Zionist misgivings: Manuel, op. cit., p. 168.

213. "I find in my pocket": Ibid., p. 169.

213–14. "They kept their word": Lloyd George, *Memoirs of the Peace Conference*, II, 733.

214. "Near the end of his days": Dugdale, op. cit., p. 235.

214. Text of Balfour Declaration in Hurewitz, op. cit., II, 25.

215. "My personal hope": Meinertzhagen, op. cit., pp. 8–9.

215. "To whom we were appealing": Lloyd George, *Memoirs of the Peace Conference*, II, 737.

216. Copies of Declaration dropped from aid: Ibid.

216. Jews acclaimed British consul in Odessa: Dugdale, op. cit., p. 234.

216–17. "The world is now contemplating": Storrs, op. cit., p. 404.

218. "The anticipation [of Jabotinsky's arrival]": Joseph B. Schechtman, *Vladimir Jabotinsky: Rebel and Statesman* (New York, 1956), p. 262.

218. Patterson threatened to resign: Colonel J. H. Patterson, *With the Judeans in the Palestine* (New York, 1922), p. 169.

218. Thirty-eighth Battalion one of first to enter Transjordan: Storrs, op. cit., p. 410.

218–19. Zionist leadership ignored Arab misgivings: Richard Lichtheim, *Sh'ar Yishuv* (Tel Aviv, 1938), Chapter XII.

219. This was the Arab contention: Antonius, op. cit., pp. 176–9.

219. The "vilayet" extended to the sea: Kedourie, op. cit., pp. 89–90.

219. Line drawn west of vicinities of four cities excluded Palestine: Paul L. Hanna, *British Policy in Palestine* (Washington D.C., 1942), 66.

220. "It was not intended by me": *Times* (London), July 23, 1937.

220. Arabs aware there was no likelihood of their control over Palestine: Stein, op. cit., p. 268.

220. "To be lightly thrown aside": M. Pearlmann, "Chapters of

Arab-Jewish Diplomacy, 1918–1922," *Jewish Social Studies*, VI (1944), 127.

220. "[Hussein] probably knows little": Ibid.

221. "You want to know the Arab is free": Sokolow, op. cit., p. 107.

221–2. "I explained to [Feisal]": Weizmann, op. cit., I, 234–5.

222. "The first meeting": Ibid.

VIII. The Death of the Sick Man (pages 223–51)

223. An army of civilian labor: Wilson, op. cit., p. 194.

225. Organized resistance ceased entirely: Roger Evans, *A Brief Outline of the Campaign in Mesopotamia, 1914–1918* (London, 1926), 114.

225. "The War Office could not ignore": Lloyd George, *War Memoirs*, IV, 1816.

225. "Half-starved dogs": Frederick J. Moberly, *The Campaign in Mesopotamia, 1914–1918* (London, 1927), IV, 248–9.

226. Supreme command committed 447,000 men: Wilson, op. cit., p. 271.

227. "Attrition": Lloyd George, *War Memoirs*, I, 899.

228. Troops on half-rations: Colonel Mehmet Emin, *La campagne turco-anglaise en Iraq et nos fautes* (Stamboul, 1919), p. 251.

228. In Palestine soldiers received little bread: Ibid.

228. Medical equipment limited: Kressenstein, op. cit., p. 213.

228. 300,000 deserted by 1917: Emin, op. cit., p. 202.

228. Ludendorff opposed to diversion of troops: Liman von Sanders, op. cit., p. 173.

229. By September 1917 death and desertion rate high: Maurice Larcher, "La campagne du général de Falkenhayn en Palestine," *Revue militaire française*, XXVI (October 1925), 30.

230. Robertson accepted the inevitable: Field Marshal Sir W. Robertson, *Soldiers and Statesmen* (London, 1926), pp. 147–8.

230. Talked Smuts out of accepting the offer: Lloyd George, *War Memoirs*, IV, 1833.

230. "Jerusalem before Christmas": Ibid., p. 1835.

231. "His manner is brusk": Meinertzhagen, op. cit., p. 117.

231. "Every infantryman in the line": Brian Gardner, *Allenby of Arabia* (New York, 1966), pp. 120–1.

232. Seventh Army ordered to move on September 28: Larcher, "La campagne du général de Falkenhayn en Palestine," p. 43.

232. Falkenhayn did not reach headquarters until November 1: Ibid., p. 46.

233. "Thus even before a shot was fired": Lord Archibald Wavell, *Allenby: Soldier and Statesman* (London, 1940), p. 203.

233. "The navel of the Turkish armies": Liddell-Hart, op. cit., p. 240.

234. "With a band of scantily clad dancing-girls": Ibid., pp. 246–7.

234. Falkenhayn eventually extricated bulk of his forces: Kressenstein, op. cit., p. 262; Larcher, *La guerre turque dans la guerre mondiale*, p. 314.

236. "Starve her to death": Storrs, op. cit., p. 301.

237. This information known to

British Intelligence: Robertson, op. cit., p. 187.

238. Only 25,000 British troops deployed inland: Wavell, op. cit., p. 203.

238. Arabs began guerrilla forays: Lawrence, *Revolt in the Desert*, pp. 274–5.

239. Liman escaped in nick of time: Larcher, *La guerre turque dans la guerre mondiale*, p. 314.

240. "Every fold of the vast hills": Lawrence, *Revolt in the Desert*, pp. 294–5.

240. Seventy thousand Turks captured and killed: Lord Hankey, *The Supreme Command* (London, 1961), II, 839.

240. "In a madness": Lawrence, *Revolt in the Desert*, p. 309.

242. "Round us by the citadel": Ibid., pp. 321–2.

243. Small force of Arabs occupied Lebanese capital: Nevakivi, op. cit., p. 71.

243. 1,192,000 Allied troops in Near East: Robertson, op. cit., p. 187.

243. "In uncoordinated fashion": Wavell, op. cit., p. 241.

246. French suffered thirty thousand casualties: Larcher, *La guerre turque dans la guerre mondiale*, p. 634.

246. French attempted to send admiral to Mudros negotiations: Nevakivi, op. cit., p. 69.

246–7. "Let England do things quietly": Townshend, op. cit., p. 380.

247. Turkish losses 1,400,000 casualties: Larcher, *La guerre turque dans la guerre mondiale*, p. 634.

247–8. Seriously ill and disappeared numbered 2,290,000: Ibid., p. 662.

248. Losses exclusive of Armenian deportations: Ibid.

248. Public debt 454,163,925 Turkish pounds: Ibid., p. 604.

249. "I trust that God": Liman von Sanders, op. cit., p. 320.

250. Djemal killed in 1922: Ibrahim Alaettin Gösa, *Turk Meshur Lari* (Istanbul, 1946), pp. 80–2.

250. Talaat begged Herbert to interpret Turkish revival: George R. Montgomery, "Why Talaat's Assassin was Acquitted," *Current History*, XIV (July 1921), 551–6.

IX. The Partition of the Levant (pages 252–90)

252. "The world at large": Sir Arnold T. Wilson, *A Clash of Loyalties: Mesopotamia, 1917–1920* (London, 1931), II, 104.

253. "Without any hesitation he agreed": Lloyd George, *Memoirs of the Peace Conference*, II, 1038. Except where otherwise noted, all Lloyd George citations henceforth refer to this work.

253–4. "It was a question": Cumming, op. cit., pp. 62–3.

254. Clemenceau received compensations: Poincaré, op. cit., VIII, 97.

254. "The abandonment of Damascus": Kedourie, op. cit., p. 122.

254. "France and Great Britain are at one": Zeine N. Zeine, *The Struggle for Arab Independence* (Beirut, 1960), pp. 47–8.

254. British officers did not protest Feisal's enjoinders: Gontaut-Biron, op. cit., p. 188.

255. "Treat the Emir Feisal": Brémond, op. cit., pp. 310–11.

255. "That Armenia, Syria, etc.": *Foreign Relations of the United States: Paris Peace Conference*

(Washington, D.C., 1942–7), III, 787–91. Hereafter cited as *For. Rel. PPC.*

256. "People and territories": See David Hunter Miller, *The Drafting of the Covenant* (New York, 1928), II, 65–6.

256. Feisal demanded full Arab independence: David Hunter Miller, *My Diary at the Peace Conference* (New York, 1921), IV, 297–9.

256. "[The] Arabs asked for freedom only": *Lloyd George*, op. cit., pp. 1043–4.

256. Lebanese delegation rejected Hashemite dynasty: Ibid., p. 1055. Americans recognized need to qualify Feisal's claims: Miller, *My Diary at the Peace Conference*, IV, 262.

258. "If the British were dealing": Kedourie, op. cit., p. 133.

258. Milner warned Lloyd George of French rigidity: Lloyd George, op. cit., pp. 1046–8.

258. Pichon's disquisition on French-Syrian connections: Ibid., pp. 1058–9.

258. "Invaluable": Zeine, op. cit., p. 78.

259. Clemenceau threatened to resign: Paul Cambon, *Correspondance, 1870–1924* (Paris, 1946), III, 333.

259. Clemenceau assumed a *quid pro quo:* Zeine, op. cit., pp. 79–82.

259. Catholic determination to ensure French "presence": Pierre Lyautey, *Le drame oriental et le rôle de la France* (Paris, 1923), p. 158.

259–60. "Of her new-felt colonies": Stephen H. Roberts, *A History of French Colonial Policy* (London, 1928), II, 605.

260. French claimed right of native conscription: See C. Régismenset, *Questions coloniales* (Paris, 1923), I, 51.

260–1. "National cohesion in the race": Lloyd George, op. cit., pp. 1026–7.

261. "I am totally opposed": Ibid., pp. 1046–8.

261. Lawrence's views at March 25 conference: H. Wickham-Steed, *Through Thirty Years* (London, 1922), II, 323.

262. Curzon scotched the proposal: *Doc. Br. For. Pol.*, 1st Ser., IV, No. 276.

262. Lloyd George warned Allenby: Ibid., No. 298.

262. "General Allenby's serious attention": Ibid., No. 326.

262. Instruction forbidden in French language: Gontaut-Biron, loc. cit.

263. British administered railroad system: Ibid.

263. "The brutal fact remains": *Doc. Br. For. Pol.*, 1st Ser., IV, 320.

263. Arab press reissued anti-French propaganda: Gontaut-Biron, loc. cit.

263. Progaganda leaders often British agents: Ibid., p. 206.

264. French foreign ministry used public figures as spokesmen: See Lyautey, op. cit., p. 125; also André Bruneau, *Traditions et politique de la France en Levant* (Paris, 1932), pp. 295–7.

264. "Which they inspired": *Doc. Br. For. Pol.*, 1st Ser., IV, 335–6.

264–5. "But I shall never accept slavery": Brémond, op. cit., p. 326.

265. "The Turkish portions": Charles Seymour (ed.), *The Intimate Papers of Colonel House* (Boston, 1928), IV, 199.

266. Feisal threw cushions at Crillon: Antonius, op. cit., p. 288.

267. Clemenceau would not appoint delegates to commission: Lloyd George, op. cit., p. 1078.

267. "He would no longer associate": Nevakivi, op. cit., p. 160.

268. Pro-French elements fearful of speaking: Gontaut-Biron, op. cit., pp. 286–9.

268. "Common emphases are unmistakable": Harry N. Howard, "An American Experiment in Peace-Making: The King Crane Commission," *Moslem World,* XXXII (April 1942), 132.

268. "Except through the support": Ibid., p. 133.

268. "For women at Mecca": Lloyd George, op. cit., p. 1079.

269. President campaigning for League: Howard, "King Crane Commission," p. 136.

270. "This morning": Earl of Ronaldshay, *The Life of Lord Curzon* (London, 1928), III, 204.

270. "It will be difficult": *Doc. Br. For. Pol.,* 1st Ser., IV, 373.

271. Feisal's letters to Lloyd George: Ibid., pp. 406–9.

271. Foreign secretary suggested man-to-man meeting: Ibid., p. 475.

271. "Never had any intention": Ibid., pp. 252–3.

271. French would not have accepted Feisal's conditions: Gontaut-Biron, op. cit., p. 8.

272. "Prepared to accord them": *Doc. Br. For. Pol.,* 1st Ser., IV, 512.

273. "Harmony of views": Ibid., pp. 625–7.

273. "This agreement was largely distasteful": Ibid., p. 630.

273. Leading spirit in nationalist movement was Yasin Pasha al-Hashimi: Nevakivi, op. cit., p. 210.

273. Feisal asked for confidence: Zeine, op. cit., p. 132.

274. Proclamation of independence of Iraq: Ibid., pp. 138–41.

275. "Public security nil": Desmond McCallum, "The French in Syria, 1919–1924," *Journal of the Central Asian Society,* XXXIII (October 1923), 8.

276. "France knows how": *Doc. Br. For. Pol.,* 1st Ser., IV, 492.

276. Meinertzhagen confirmed French belligerency: Ibid., p. 591.

277. "Integral part of the Empire": Lloyd George, op. cit., pp. 1089–91.

277. "Ipso facto, lapse": Ibid., pp. 1107–8.

279. Long-Berenger agreement: *Doc. Br. For. Pol.,* 1st Ser., IV, 1089–91.

279. Britain presented additional request: Ibid., p. 1092.

280. Balfour, Lloyd George equivocal on British control of Palestine: Nevakivi, op. cit., pp. 94–5.

280. "Mediterranean Sephardic Union": Frank E. Manuel, "The Palestine Question in Italian Diplomacy, 1917–1920," *Journal of Modern History,* XXVII (September 1944), 278.

281. Millerand and Berthelot accepted compromise: *Doc. Br. For. Pol.,* 1st Ser., VIII, 165.

281. Mandatory Power to establish "viable" Jewish national home: Paul L. Hanna, *British Policy in Palestine* (Washington, D.C., 1942), p. 5.

282. Zionists had offered advantages to Feisal: Frischwasser-Ra'anan, op. cit., pp. 167–8.

281. General staff stressed importance of extending Palestine frontiers: Nevakivi, op. cit., pp. 121–2.

283. Clemenceau and Lloyd George almost came to blows: Georges Suarez, *Clemenceau* (Paris, 1930), p. 287.

283. Pichon intent on carving away northern area: Ibid., pp. 115–16.

284. France's single concession to Britain: Ibid., p. 131.

285. Arab guerrillas terrorized: McCallum, op. cit., pp. 7–8: Lyautey, op. cit., pp. 167–8.

286. French troops trapped: Lyautey, op. cit., p. 164.
286. Gouraud's five conditions: Zeine, op. cit., pp. 171–3.
286. Gouraud appealed to Feisal: Jean Pichon, *Sur la route des Indes* (Paris, 1932), p. 362.
287. Yasin al-Hashimi warned Feisal: Paul de Rémusat, "Les cent jours du roi de Syrie," *Extrait de la revue des études historiques*, XIV (April 1924), 1.

288. Azme Bey was blown to pieces: McCallum, op. cit., pp. 10–11.
289. Feisal boarded the train with retinue: Robert Morris, *The Hashemite Kings* (New York, 1959), p. 51.
289. "To help the Arabs in the matter": Lloyd George, op. cit., pp. 1113–14.
290. Feisal seated upon his baggage: Morris, loc. cit.

X. The Partition of Turkey and the Rise of the Greek Empire (pages 291–335)

291. Turks subdued before Allied might: Edgar Pech, *Les alliés et la Turquie* (Paris, 1925), p. 5.
291. Inflation destroyed value of Turkish currency: See remarks of Commissioner Lewis Heck in *For. Rel. PPC.*, II, 231–83, II, 231–83.
292. "Our old friend England": Churchill, op. cit., IV, 367.
292. "Bane of civilization": *Doc. Br. For. Pol.*, 1st Ser., IV, 652–4.
293. "Every nation": Lloyd George, op. cit., II, 1010.
293. "A. J. B. is in Paris": Harold Nicolson, *Curzon: The Last Phase* (London, 1934), pp. 109–110.
293. Curzon determined to amputate Constantinople: Ronaldshay, op. cit., p. 265.
293. Lloyd George and Balfour hesitant about expelling caliph: Temperley, *History of the Peace Conference of Paris*, VI, 27. Hereafter Temperley citations refer to this volume.
293–4. "Of races and religions": Lloyd George, op. cit., p. 1002.
294. U.S. was Britain's first choice as mandatory: Miller, *My Diary at the Peace Conference*, I, 27–8.

295. "If it is a question": Pichon, *Le Partage du Proche-Orient*, p. 166.
296. Allies complained that Italy contributed nothing to war against Turkey: Lloyd George, op. cit., p. 783.
296. Venizelos's network of Greek agents informed him: A. F. Frangulis, *La Grèce et la crise mondiale* (Paris, 1926), II, 61–62.
297. Wilson declined action on legal grounds: *For. Rel. PPC*, III, 482.
299. "And without friends?": D. Alastos, *Venizelos* (London, 1942), p. 145.
299. Kaiser offered gains at Serbian expense: C. N. Brown and T. P. Ion (eds.), *The Greek White Book* (New York, 1919), p. 52.
299. "Let Athens know": Edouard Driault and Michel Lhéritier, *Histoire diplomatique de la Grèce de 1821 à nos jours* (Paris, 1926), V, 162.
300. "Both France and Russia": Lloyd George, op. cit., p. 1210.
301. Metaxas unimpressed: Alexander A. Pallis, *Greece's Ana-*

tolian Venture and After (London, 1937), pp. 22–3.

301. King also unimpressed: Driault and Lhéritier, op. cit., p. 177.

301. "Could almost hear": Ibid., p. 180.

301. "The territorial acquisitions": Lloyd George, op. cit., pp. 1211–1212.

302. "We are prepared": Ibid., p. 1212.

304. Venizelos secretly invited Allied landing: *Greek White Book*, Doc. No. 4.

305. "Too late": Ibid., Doc. No. 177 ff.

307. "I fully understand": Lloyd George, op. cit., pp. 1230–1.

307. Venizelos's statistics on Greek settlement: Temperley, op. cit., p. 39.

308. "Glorious renaissance": Driault and Lhéritier, op. cit., pp. 362–3.

308. Asia Minor pulsated with Greek life: Arnold J. Toynbee, *The Western Question in Turkey and Greece* (London, 1923), p. 125 ff.

308. Turkish handbooks admitted large Greek population: *For. Rel. PPC.*, II, 871.

308. Allied commission estimated 509,000 Greeks in Smyrna: Temperley, op. cit., p. 39.

309. Venizelos proposed separation of plateau and valleys: Driault and Lhéritier, op. cit., p. 362.

309. Greeks herded into interior: Lloyd George, op. cit., p. 1240.

310. "L.G. beams at this": Harold Nicolson, *Peacemaking, 1919* (London, 1933), p. 255.

310. "[Venizelos] was the greatest statesman": Lloyd George, op. cit., p. 1204.

310. "Met few men": Francesco S. Nitti, *Peaceless Europe* (London, 1922), pp. 168–9.

312. Venizelos cabled instructions: Alastos, op. cit., p. 192.

313. Clergy blessed the troops: Jean C. E. Bujac, *Les campagnes de l'armée hellénique, 1918–1922* (Paris, 1930), p. 231.

313. Four hundred Turkish casualties: Driaut and Lhéritier, op. cit., p. 369.

313. Greeks encountered Turkish Nationalist resistance: Bujac, op. cit., p. 40.

314. Venizelos ordered offensive across Meander: *Doc. Br. For. Pol.*, 1st Ser., IV, 862–7.

314. Supreme Council prohibited further advances: Ibid.

314. "The Greek Occupation, far from presenting itself": Ibid.; see also Jacques Kayser, *L'Europe et la Turquie nouvelle* (Paris, 1922), p. 38.

315. "One of the greatest modern statesmen": Nicolson, *Curzon: The Last Phase*, pp. 96–7.

315. "Assured to us": Ibid., p. 47.

316. Italian agents encouraged Turkish Nationalist movement: *Doc. Br. For. Pol.*, 1st Ser., IV, 831–3.

316. Lloyd George warned Orlando: *For. Rel. PPC.*, IV, 716–723.

316. "Should be asked clearly": Ibid., p. 721.

316. "Not being treated": Lloyd George, op. cit., p. 874.

317. "Liberty of action": Frangulis, op. cit., pp. 98–101.

317. "This occupation has only": *Doc. Br. For. Pol.*, 1st Ser., IV, 691–2.

317. Wilson protested *Realpolitik*: *For. Rel. PPC.*, V, 200.

320. Allied force limited to 75,000 Greek troops: *Doc. Br. For. Pol.*, 1st Ser., IV, 971.

320. "Terms may impose": Ibid., p. 809.

321. French restored Cilicia's economic life: Paul de Véou, *La*

passion de Cilicie (Paris, 1938), pp. 91–8.

321. Marash captured, its population slaughtered: Edouard Brémond, *La Cilicie en 1919–1920* (Paris, 1921), p. 41.

321. Ali Riza declined responsibility: Pech, op. cit., pp. 111–12.

321. De Robeck asked permission for strong measures: *Doc. Br. For. Pol.*, 1st Ser., IV, 1086–7.

321–2. "The Turks": Ibid., p. 362.

322. "The Allies must": Ibid., p. 416.

322–3. Paris resented British influence: Lloyd George, *War Memoirs*, V, 3311–13.

323. Loss of face rankled in Paris: Ibid., p. 777.

323. "Priority of influence": See Berthe Georges-Gaulis, *Angora, Constantinople, Londres* (Paris, 1922), p. 60; also Julien Viaud (Pierre Loti), *La mort de notre chère France en Orient* (Paris, 1920), pp. 153–5.

323. Talks not productive then: Pichon, *Le partage du Proche-Orient*, p. 203.

323. "The important thing": Lloyd George, op. cit., p. 1273.

323. France needed contact with Turkish Nationalists: Frangulis, op. cit., p. 143.

324. Constantinople issue resolved over Curzon's protest: Ronaldshay, op. cit., p. 270.

325–6. Terms of Sèvres treaty: Hurewitz, op. cit., pp. 81–7.

326. "In peace and war": Temperley, op. cit., p. 62.

328. Two thirds of Asia Minor's

Greeks outside Smyrna: Ibid., p. 71.

328. Smyrna largest manufacturing community: Nitti, op. cit., pp. 168–9.

328. "His own foreign secretary": Frangulis, op. cit., p. 128.

328–9. "Thankfulness to you": Lloyd George, op. cit., p. 1340.

330. Damad Farid pleaded for treaty modification: *Doc. Br. For. Pol.*, 1st Ser., VII, 73.

331. Curzon warned sultan would be evicted: Ibid., VIII, 444.

331. "Extraordinary fusillade": Pech, op. cit., p. 140.

332. "We are not told": Stephen Bonsal, *Suitors and Suppliants: The Little Nations at Versailles* (New York, 1946), pp. 177–8.

332. Venizelos's great ambitions: Driault and Lhéritier, op. cit., p. 390.

332. "I take the responsibility": Frangulis, op. cit., p. 122.

332. Churchill echoed these misgivings: Churchill, op. cit., IV, 384.

332–3. "They hate the Greeks": Lord Riddell, *Intimate Diary of the Peace Conference* (London, 1933), p. 208.

333. Greeks annihilated Kemalist force: Bujac, op. cit., p. 237.

334. "I do not think": *Doc. Br. For. Pol.*, 1st Ser., VII, 113.

334. "Superb elan": Bujac, op. cit., p. 349.

334. Damad Farid accepted treaty on his own authority: Claire Price, *The Rebirth of Turkey* (New York, 1923), p. 154.

XI. Armenia and America (pages 336–65)

336. Russian Armenia glutted with refugees: A. Poidebard, *Le rôle militaire des Arméniens sur le front du Caucase* (Paris, 1920),

23–39.

337. "Cried out from the very earth": Rita Jerrehian, "From the Armistice to the Treaty of

Sèvres," *Armenian Review*, IX (Summer 1956), 126.

337. Aharonian and Venizelos supported each other: *For. Rel. PPC.*, III, 877.

337–8. Dashnak parliament proclaimed unity of Russian and Turkish Armenia: Firuz Kazemzadeh, *The Struggle for Transcaucasia, 1917–1921* (New York, 1951), pp. 214–15.

338. "Must be completely severed": *For. Rel. PPC.*, XII, 813.

338. "On the clear understanding": Ibid., p. 902.

340. America's "disinterest" in Middle East: Miller, *My Diary at the Peace Conference*, I, 74.

340. "Until such time": E. M. House and C. Seymour (eds.), *What Really Happened at Paris?* (New York, 1921), p. 179.

341. American educational institutions in Turkey: American Board of Commissioners for Foreign Missions, *Annual Report: 1914* (Boston, 1915), Chapter I *ff.*

341. "I gave my chief attention": Morgenthau, op. cit., p. 203.

342. Mass sympathy meetings in U.S.: See, as example, a report in *The New York Times*, October 8, 1918, devoting fully two pages to excerpts of Bryce Report.

342. "It makes me sick at heart": Woodrow Wilson, *Papers*, Ser. VIII-A, July 12, 1915.

343. Sums raised in 1915–1916: James L. Barton, *History of the Near East Relief* (Boston, 1924), *passim.*

343. NER kept half-million refugees alive: See *U.S. Dept. of State Archives*, Ser. 867.4016/.

343. Wilson resisted declaration of war: *Foreign Relations of the United States* (Washington, D.C.), 2nd Ser., I (1917), 450; also Ray S. Baker, *Woodrow*

Wilson, Life and Letters (New York, 1929), VII, 392.

344. NER's quota oversubscribed: *The New York Times*, March 11, 1919.

344. American Relief Administration provided supplementary help: F. M. Surface and R. L. Bland, *American Food in the World War and Reconstruction Period* (Palo Alto, California, 1931), pp. 149–52 and 200–5.

344. NER operated hospitals, orphanages: Near East Relief, *Annual Reports to Congress* (Washington, D.C., 1920–9), *passim.*

347. Formidable appeal of March 5, 1919: *The New York Times*, March 5, 1919.

347. Monographs of authorities: See *Inquiry* Docs. Nos. 17, 29, 43, 81, 137, 331, 602, 876.

348. "Our people": *For. Rel.*, 2nd Ser., I (1917), 169–70.

349. Westermann took president to task: *Wilson Papers*, Ser. VIII-A, April 27, 1919.

349. Lybyer's proposal went further: Ibid.

349. "There is a fairly overwhelming": Ibid.

350. "The American eagle": *The New York Times*, March 6, 1919.

350. "Acceptance of a mandate": Miller, *My Diary at the Peace Conference*, XVIII, 213; see also *The New York Times*, March 15, 1917.

350. U.S. protectorate in Asia Minor logical: Jackson Fleming, "Mandates for Turkish Territory," *Asia*, XIX (December 1918), 1195–203.

350–1. "Merely as a work of altruism": Henry Morgenthau, "Why the Ottoman Empire Must be Dissolved," *World's Work*, XXXVIII (December 1918), 205.

351. Shotwell endorsed the idea: *Inquiry* Doc. No. 526.

351. "But what": "America and Armenia,'" *New Republic*, XVIII

(March 8, 1919), 169.

351. Missionaries cherished American protection: See *Wilson Papers*, Ser. VIII-A, April and May 1919 *ff*.

351. "From becoming": *Henry White Papers*, Paris Peace Conference Series, 1919, April 14, 1919.

351. Entire hinterland of Western Asia": *Inquiry* Doc. No. 633.

352. "Portion of the world": *Wilson Papers*, Ser. VIII-A, May 23, 1919.

352. "On this assurance": Lloyd George, op. cit., pp. 814–17.

353. Hearings lasted ten days: *U.S. Dept. of State Archives*, Ser. 181.91/.

353. President appointed Harbord: *Wilson Papers*, Ser. VIII-A, August 13, 1919.

354. Mission studied files: *U.S. Dept. of State Archives, Paris Peace Conference*, Ser. 184.021/.

354. "We literally dreamed": James G. Harbord, "My Mission to Armenia," *World's Work*, XLII (1932), 94–5.

354. Turks dismissed atrocities as "incidents": James H. Tashjian, "The American Military Mission to Armenia," *Armenian Review*, II (Winter 1949–50), Part IV.

354. "No cheap political adventurer": Harbord, op. cit., p. 96.

355. "We knew that much": Alexander Khatissian, *The Origin and Development of the Armenian Republic* (Athens, 1930), p. 163 (in Armenian).

355. Report compendium of specialized monographs: *For. Rel.*, 2nd Ser., II (1919), 850–72.

356. "As in the case": Ibid., p. 862.

356. "Our national doorstep": *The New York Times*, February 22, 1920.

357. Magazines devoted issues to mandatory question: *Asia*, XX (January 1920), *passim*.

357. Flood of pro-mandate petitions: *House of Reps., April 13, 16th Congr., 2nd Sess.* (1920).

357. Curzon's appeal for American mandate: *British and Foreign State Papers*, 113 (1920), pp. 71–2.

358. Adana nearly overrun: Brémond, *La Cilicie en 1919–1920*, p. 66.

358. Communists fled to Azerbaijan: Simon Vratzian, *Armenia and the Armenian Question* (Boston, 1943), p. 88.

358. "It our clear duty": *Wilson Papers*, Ser. II, March 8, 1920.

359. Wilson prepares mesage: Ibid., May 11.

359. "Greatest of the Christian peoples": *S. Doc. No. 791*, 66th Cong., 2nd Sess. (1920).

360. "To do some fighting": *The New York Times*, May 26, 1920.

361. Lodge rejected mandatory scheme: *Cong. Res. 27*, 66th Cong., 2nd Sess. (1920).

361. "Condemn President Wilson": *The New York Times*, June 11, 1920.

361. Harding challenged Cox: Ibid., June 21, 1920.

362. "I shall be glad": *Wilson Papers*, Ser. II, May 11, 1920.

362. "To the said frontier": *British and Foreign State Papers*, No. 113 (1920), pp. 72–3.

362. Turkey renounced its rights in Article Ninety: Ibid., p. 73.

363. Soviets rounded up Dashnak leaders: Jerrehian, op. cit., p. 122.

364. Kemalists disdained offer of mediation: Ibid., pp. 118–19.

364. Provisions of Treaty of Moscow: Poidebard, op. cit., pp. 58–63.

364. Reaffirmed in Treaty of Kars: Ibid., pp. 68–77.

365. "I do not know": *Wilson Papers*, Ser. II, December 16, 1920.

XII. The Second Arab Revolt: Iraq (pages 366–82)

366. "To be administered": Philip Graves, *The Life of Sir Percy Cox* (London, 1941), pp. 219–220.

367. "To preserve peace and order": Lady Gertrude Bell, *Letters* (London, 1941), pp. 219–220.

368. "More has been done": quoted in Monroe, op. cit., p. 60.

368. Proposal for "Lower" and "Upper" Mesopotamia: Philip Ireland, *Iraq: A Study in Political Development* (London, 1937), p. 148.

368. "In Mesopotamia [the Arabs] want us": Lady Bell, op. cit., p. 464.

368. Wilson's instructions: Ireland, op. cit., p. 161.

369. "No word of criticism": Wilson, op. cit., II, 164.

369. Arab misgivings: Stephen H. Longrigg, *Iraq: 1900–1950* (London, 1953), p. 113.

370. "It was clear": Sir Hubert Young, *The Independent Arab* (London, 1933), p. 294.

370. "We must therefore": Ibid., pp. 302–3.

371. "There's a lot": E. Burgoyne (ed.), *Gertrude Bell: From Her Personal Papers, 1914–1926* (London, 1961), p. 137.

371. Churchill's warning on expense of occupation: General Aylmer Haldane, *A Soldier's Saga* (London, 1948), p. 371.

372. Wilson certain his troops doomed: Wilson, op. cit., II, 289.

373. Ringleaders shot down: Ibid., p. 302.

373. Uprising cost forty million pounds: Longriff, op. cit., p. 123.

374. "Not to cry": Burgoyne, op. cit., pp. 172–3.

375. Military government terminated: Graves, op. cit., p. 265.

376. "How long": Garnett, *Letters of T. E. Lawrence*, p. 317.

378. Abdullah promised not to oppose Feisal's candidature: Graves, op. cit., p. 281.

378. Churchill's speech received with applause: Meinertzhagen, op. cit., p. 298.

379. Lady Bell organized Feisal's reception: R. Bodley and L. Hearst, *Gertrude Bell* (New York, 1940), pp. 207–8.

381. "It is not intended": Jacob Stoyanovsky, *The Mandate for Palestine* (London, 1928), p. 34.

381. Subsidiary agreements of Anglo-Iraqi treaty: Ireland, op. cit., p. 346.

381. "Difficulties there would certainly be": Young, op. cit., p. 338.

382. Treaty ratified by Iraqi Assembly: Longrigg, op. cit., p. 151.

XIII. The Second Arab Revolt (continued): Palestine (pages 383–410)

384. "Homeland be a viable one": *Doc. Br. For. Pol.*, 1st Ser., IV, 347.

384. "I never dreamed": Ibid., p. 262.

385. Boundary questions to be

settled directly between Jews and Arabs: Frischwasser-Ra'-anan, op. cit., p. 104.

385. "Arabs are not jealous": Pearlman, op. cit., p. 133.

385. "No true Arab": Ibid., p. 134.

385–6. Feisal-Weizmann agreement: quoted in Antonius, op. cit., pp. 437–9.

386. Zionists offered concessions: Frischwasser-Ra'anan, op. cit., p. 105.

386. Arab proposals for joint stand against France: Ibid., p. 107; see also Garnett, *Letters of T. E. Lawrence*, pp. 268–9.

387. "We will do our best": Pearlman, op. cit., pp. 139–40.

387. "As a representative of Palestinian Arabs": *Doc. Br. For. Pol.*, 1st Ser., IV, 364–5.

388. "But when some Zionists": Pearlman, op. cit., p. 144.

388. Ussishkin's demands: Storrs, op. cit., p. 354.

388–9. "A people can be": Ibid., p. 358.

389. Bols complained of Zionist accusations: Arab Higher Committee for Palestine, *A Collection of Official Documents Relating to the Palestine Question, 1917–1947* (New York, 1947), p. 87.

389. "Fear and distrust": *Doc. Br. For. Pol.*, 1st Ser., IV, 364.

389. Graves's warning: Philip Graves, *Palestine, The Land of Three Faiths* (London, 1923), p. 52.

390. "Holy Places and the Holy Land": *Doc. Br. For. Pol.*, 1st Ser., IV, 364.

390. Growth of Arab population: Esco Foundation for Palestine, *Palestine: A Study of Jewish, Arab and British Policies* (New Haven, 1947), I, 463.

390. Local *mukhtars* initially grateful: Graves, *Palestine, The Land of Three Faiths*, p. 115.

391. Resolution of "All-Arab Palestine Conference": Esco, op. cit., p. 474.

391. "Which I do not share": Meinertzhagen, op. cit., p. 58.

391. "There *can* be no trouble": Weizmann, op. cit., I, 254.

391–2. "He forgot": Storrs, op. cit., p. 347.

392. A number of Jews and Arabs killed: Hanna, op. cit., p. 49.

393. "Encouraging the Arabs": Meinertzhagen, op. cit., pp. 81–82.

394. British public opinion unsettled: Viscount Herbert L. S. Samuel, *Memoirs* (London, 1955), p. 183.

394. "Outrages against Jews": *Doc. Br. For. Pol.*, 1st Ser., XIII, 284.

394. "The Arabs would inevitably regard": Ibid.

394. "A mere cover": "Letter to the Editor," *Spectator*, CXXV (July 3, 1920), 3.

395. "His self is honourable": Norman Bentwich, *England in Palestine* (London, 1932), p. 413.

395. "To oppress others": Samuel, op. cit., p. 205.

397. "Without mincing words": Meinertzhagen, op. cit., p. 98.

398. Mobs killed thirty-five Jews: Horace Samuel, *Unholy Memories of the Holy Land* (London, 1930), p. 70.

398. Forty-seven Jews, forty-eight Arabs killed: *Palestine: Disturbances in May, 1921. Reports of the Commission of Inquiry with Correspondence Relating Thereto. Cmd. 1540* (London, 1921), p. 112.

399. "The feeling": Ibid., p. 40.

399. Report listed Arab grievances: Ibid., pp. 43–60.

401. Arab crowds demanding murder of Jews: *T. E. Lawrence by His Friends* (London, 1937), p. 142.

401. "My heart is full": Bentwich, op. cit., pp. 63–4.
402. "It , . . . result[s] in anarchy": *Doc. Br. For. Pol.*, 1st Ser., XIII, 334.
402. Ammonite and Moabite Governments: Alec S. K. Kirkbride, *A Crackle of Thorns* (London, 1956), p. 22.
403. Abdullah asked "true Arabs" for support: Morris, op. cit., p. 88.
403. "Cheery-faced, shrewd": quoted in C. R. Ashbee, *A Palestine Notebook, 1918–1923* (New York, 1923), p. 214.
404. Balfour emphasized need of good frontiers: *Doc. Br. For. Pol.*, 1st Ser., IV, 347.

404. "He [God] granted me": Abdullah, King of Jordan, *My Memoirs Completed* (Washington, D.C., 1954), pp. 91–2.
405–6. "Not on sufferance": *Statement of Policy Regarding the Future Disposition of Palestine.* Cmd. 1700 (London, 1922), pp. 17–21.
406. "Non-Jews": Great Britain, *Parliamentary Papers*, 1922. Cmd. 1785 (London, 1922), pp. 10–11.
407. "What I mistook": Meinertzhagen, op. cit., p. 134.
408–9. Arab-Jewish conversations inconclusive: Esco, op. cit., pp. 566–7.

XIV. The Rise of Turkey (pages 411–56)

412. Vote overwhelmingly in favor of royalists: C. F. Abbott, *Greece and the Allies, 1914–1922* (London, 1922), p. 224.
412. Anglo-French warnings: Frangulis, op. cit., pp. 172–3.
412. Greeks voted to invite Constantine back: Alastos, op. cit., p. 207.
413. "Even isolated": Toynbee, op. cit., p. 125.
414. 110,000 Greeks in Asia Minor: Frangulis, op. cit., p. 190.
414. "The friendship": Temperley, op. cit., p. 32.
415. "I felt": Kinross, *Ataturk* (New York, 1965), p. 176.
415. Ankara a squalid town: Ibid., p. 246.
416. "In terms of vitality, he wasn't": Halidé Edib (Adivar), *The Turkish Ordeal* (New York, 1928), p. 195.
418. Zinoviev issued message of sympathy: Ivar Spector, *The So-viet Union and the Muslim World, 1917–1956* (Seattle, 1958), p. 49.
418. Terms of Treaty of Moscow: R. H. Davison, "From Mudros to Lausanne," in G. A. Craig and F. Gilbert (eds.), *The Diplomats, 1919–1939* (Princeton, 1953), I, 191.
419. Russian supplies for Turks: Louis Fischer, *The Soviets in World Affairs* (London, 1930), I, 391.
419. Hellenic Army grew rapidly: Bujac, op. cit., p. 260.
420. Gounaris rejected compromise: Frangulis, op. cit., pp. 216–18.
420. "An interminable procession": Toynbee, op. cit., p. 233.
420. "Attaining the objectives": Bujac, op. cit., pp. 269–70.
421. "Nothing struck me": Toynbee, op. cit., pp. 98–9.

421–2. "And Australasia": Churchill, op. cit., IV, 391.

422. Gounaris ordered destruction of Kemalist armies: Bujac, op. cit., p. 284.

424. "As yet undergone": Edib, op. cit., p. 284.

425. Turkish officers killed in great numbers: Kinross, op. cit., pp. 315–18.

425. Battle continued for three weeks: H. C. Armstrong, *Grey Wolf, Mustafa Kemal* (London, 1937), p. 148.

425. Greeks lost eighteen thousand men: Laura M. Adkinson, *Great Britain and the Kemalist Movement for Turkish Independence, 1919–1923* (unpublished doctoral dissertation, University of Texas, 1958), p. 148.

425. "Like a wrathful Achilles": Andrew, Prince of Greece, *Towards Disaster: The Greek Army in Asia Minor in 1921* (London, 1930), p. 203.

425. Constantine returned to Athens: Bujac, op. cit., p. 135.

426. "The treachery": Lloyd George, op. cit., pp. 1242–3.

426. Sforza made private deal with Turks: Count Carlo Sforza, *Bâtisseurs de l'Europe moderne* (Paris, 1931), p. 347.

426–7. "Neither financially": quoted in Frangulis, op. cit., p. 135.

428. Catholic resentment of Greek Orthodox penetration: Ibid., p. 141.

428. French resentment of Anglo-Soviet trade pact: "Text of the Russo-British Trade Agreement," *Current History*, XIV (April 1921), 1257–9.

428–9. Paris and Ankara maintained contact: Davison, "From Mudros to Lausanne," pp. 189–190.

429. Briand's reassuring answers: Nicolson, *Curzon: The Last Phase*, p. 261. Hereafter listed as op. cit.

429. Terms of Treaty of Ankara: Ibid., p. 262.

430. Thousands of Turkish troops freed: Davison, "From Mudros to Lausanne," p. 193.

430. Curzon's indictment: Nicolson, op. cit., pp. 262–3.

430. French turned over equipment to Turks: *British and Foreign State Papers*, 114 (1921), pp. 293–323.

430. Britain's "compromise" peace plan: Bujac, op. cit., pp. 304–5.

430. Pressure exerted on Greek Government: Driault and Lhéritier, op. cit., p. 411.

431. Ukranian Soviet Mission: Fischer, op. cit., pp. 393–4.

431. Constantine visited troops: Bujac, op. cit., pp. 339–40.

432. "The little country": Kinross, op. cit., p. 456.

433. Eighty thousand Turks concentrated against Greeks: Churchill, op. cit., p. 418.

434. Hellenic Army destroyed or driven back: Bujac, op. cit., pp. 339–40.

434. Anathematizing Lloyd George: Edib, op. cit., p. 376.

434. Armenian homes looted: Arnold Toynbee and K. D. Kirkwood, *Turkey* (New York, 1927), pp. 106–7.

435. "Were really corpses": Clare Sheridan, *Nuda Veritas* (London, 1927), pp. 282–3.

436. 400,000 Greeks descended on Smyrna: Charles B. Eddy, *Greece and the Greek Refugees* (London, 1931), pp. 53–4.

437. "The Government might break up": Churchill, op. cit., p. 423.

437. "The announcement": Ibid., p. 425.

438. "Complaining, hectoring": Lord Beaverbrook, *The Decline and Fall of Lloyd George* (London, 1963), p. 161.

438. Lloyd George in condition of stunned incoherence: Ibid., p. 163.

438. French and Italian press castigated England: Adkinson, op. cit., p. 405.

438. Curzon staggered from room: Nicolson, op. cit., pp. 283–4.

438. Foreign secretary managed to resume discussion: Churchill, op. cit., p. 431.

439. Kemal's army maneuvers intended for political advantage: Kinross, op. cit., p. 383.

440. Ismet finally accepted the proposal: Sir Charles Harington, *Tim Harington Looks Back* (London, 1941), p. 69.

440. "Everyone showed signs": Sheridan, op. cit., pp. 296–7.

440. "Man, woman and child on shore": Kinross, op. cit., p. 392.

441–2. "He plunders": Lloyd George, op. cit., pp. 1361–2.

442–3. Curzon's advantages in diplomacy: Nicolson, op. cit., pp. 283–4.

443. "On the day": Ibid., p. 288.

444. "And her allies": Jane Degras (ed.), *Soviet Documents on Foreign Policy* (London, 1951), Doc. No. 398.

444. "Based on the principle": *Lausanne Conference on Near Eastern Affairs, 1922–1923.* Cmd. 1914 (London, 1923), p. 139.

444. "M. Chicherin must have mistaken": Ibid., p. 143.

444. Evidence Ismet hinted compromise on Straits in advance: Fischer, op. cit., p. 404.

445. Straits commission to govern transportation, navigation: *Lausanne Conference*, p. 109 *et seq.*

445. Stunning victory for the West: For another view, see E. H. Carr, *The Bolshevik Revolution, 1917–1923* (London, 1953), III, 486.

446. Greek refugees in Old Kingdom reached 1,200,000: Pallis, op. cit., p. 167.

446. Nansen suggested mutual exchange: *Lausanne Conference*, pp. 204–7.

447. Ismet agreed to exceptions: Driault and Lhéritier, op. cit., pp. 425–7.

447. Both nations granted minorities amnesty: *British and Foreign State Papers*, 118 (1923), Pt. II, 1048–53.

449. "Ismet, you remind me": Joseph C. Grew, *Turbulent Era* (Boston, 1952), I, 525.

449. "Done our best": Ibid., p. 551.

451. *"C'est la paix!"*: D. Caclamanes, *Eleutherios Venizelos* (London, 1936), as quoted in Alastos, op. cit., pp. 227–9.

451. "To a smile": Grew, op. cit., p. 578.

452–3. "Faithful to their orders": Prince Andrew, op. cit., pp. 297–298.

453. Old Kingdom became compact, viable: Eddy, op. cit., p. 250.

Bibliography

THE BIBLIOGRAPHY for each topic is presented as a self-contained unit. Whenever relevant, occasional listings of material are repeated under various subjects.

The Ottoman Empire Enters the War

Documentary and Semi-Documentary Sources

Great Britain, Foreign Office Publication. *Collected Diplomatic Documents Relating to the Outbreak of the European War.* London, 1915.

Gooch, G. P., and H. Temperley, eds. *British Documents on the Origins of the War.* First Series, Vol. V, London, 1928; Vol. IX, London, 1933.

Die grosse Politik der europäischen Kabinette, 1872–1914. Vol. XXXVII. Berlin, 1926.

Hurewitz, J. C. *Diplomacy in the Near and Middle East: A Documentary Record.* Vol. II. Princeton, 1956.

Imperial Russian Ministry of Foreign Affairs. *Diplomatic Documents: Negotiations covering the period from July 19–August 1 to October 19–November 1, 1914.* London, 1915.

République française Ministère des affaires étrangères. *Documents diplomatiques.* Vol. III. Paris, 1922.

Mirkine-Guetsévitch, B. "Documents: Russie et Turquie en août 1914," *Le monde slave,* IV (March 1928), 422–51.

Polonsky, J. *Documents diplomatiques secrets russes.* Paris, 1928.

Non-Official Sources

Abbott, G. F. *Turkey in Transition.* London, 1909.

Adamov, Evgenii A. *Die europäischen Mächte und die Türkei während des Weltkrieges.* Dresden, 1932.

Anderson, George W. *Russia in Middle Asia on the eve of the First World War.* Unpublished doctoral dissertation, University of Minnesota, 1945.

Benson, Edward F. *Crescent and Iron Cross*. London, 1918.

Birge, J. K. *A Guide to Turkish Area Study*. Washington, D.C., 1944.

Blaisdell, D. C. *European Financial Control in the Ottoman Empire*. New York, 1929.

Bompard, M. "L'entrée en guerre de la Turquie," *Revue de Paris*, XXVIII (July 1–15, 1921), 61–85, 261–88.

Davison, R. H. "Turkish Attitudes Concerning Christian-Muslim Equality in the Nineteenth Century," *American Historical Review*, LIX (1953–4), 844–64.

Deak, F., and J. T. Shotwell. *Turkey at the Straits*. New York, 1940.

Djemal Pasha, Ahmed. *Memories of a Turkish Statesman, 1913–1919*. New York, 1922.

Donitz, K. *Die Fahrten der Breslau*. Berlin, 1918.

Einstein, Lewis. *Inside Constantinople*. London, 1917.

Grothe, Hugo. *Deutschland, die Türkei und der Islam*. Berlin, 1914.

Helfferich, K. T. *Die deutsche Türkenpolitik*. Berlin, 1921.

Howard, Harry N. *The Partition of Turkey*. Norman, Oklahoma, 1931.

Hüber, R. *Die Bagdadbahn*. Berlin, 1943.

Hubert, Lucien. *L'Islam et la guerre*. Paris, 1918.

Jäckh, Ernst. *The Rising Crescent*. New York, 1944.

Kerner, R. J. "The Mission of Liman von Sanders. (I) Its Origin," *Slavonic Review*, VI (June 1927), 12–27; (II) "The Crisis," ibid., VI (December 1927), 344–63; (III) ibid., VI (March 1928), 543–60; (IV) "The Aftermath," ibid., VIII (June 1928), 90–112.

———. "Russia, the Straits and Constantinople, 1915–1917," *Journal of Modern History*, I (September 1929), 400–15.

Key, Kerim K. *Origins of the Young Turk Movement, 1889–1908*. Washington, D.C., 1955.

Kopp, Georg. *Das Teufelschiff und seine kleine Schwester*. Berlin, 1930.

Kunke, Max. *Die Kapitulationen der Türkei, deren Aufhebung, und die neuen deutsch-türkischen Rechtvertrage*. Munich, 1918.

Liman von Sanders, O. V. K. *Five Years in Turkey*. Annapolis, 1927.

Ludwig, Emil. "Les croisières du 'Goeben' et du 'Breslau'," *Les archives de la grande guerre*, V (March 1920), 68–87; (April 1920), 243–56.

Mandelstam, André. *Le sort de l'Empire Ottoman*. Paris, 1917.

Milne, Admiral Sir Archibald. *The Flight of the Goeben and the Breslau*. London, 1921.

Moukhtar, Mahmoud. *La Turquie, l'Allemagne et l'Europe depuis le traité de Berlin jusqu'à la guerre mondiale*. Paris, 1924.

Bibliography

Morgenthau, Henry. *Ambassador Morgenthau's Story*. New York, 1922.

Pears, Sir Edwin. *Forty Years in Constantinople*. London, 1916.

Pomiankowski, Lt. General Joseph. *Der Zusammenbruch des ottomanischen Reiches: Erinnerungen an die Türkei der Zeit des Weltkrieges*. Vienna, 1928.

Silbert, R. *Entente Diplomacy and the World War*. New York, 1921.

Snively, Marjorie K. *Russia and the Straits, 1914–1932*. Unpublished doctoral dissertation, Ohio State University, 1932.

Souchon, Admiral Wilhelm. "Der Durchbruch S.M. Schiffe *Goeben* und *Breslau* nach den Dardanellen," in *Die deutschen Flotte in grosser Zeit unter mitwirking deutschen Seehelden*. Berlin, 1926.

Talaat Pasha. "Posthumous Memoirs," *Current History*, XV (November 1921), 279–301.

Trietsch, D. *Deutschland und der Islam*. Berlin, 1912.

Trumpener, Ulrich. "German Military Aid to Turkey in 1914: An Historical Re-evaluation," *Journal of Modern History*, XXXII (June 1960), 145–9.

———. *Germany and the Ottoman Empire, 1914–1918*. Princeton, 1968.

———."Liman von Sanders and the German-Ottoman Alliance," *Journal of Contemporary History*, I (October 1966), 179–93.

———. "Turkey's Entry into World War I: An Assessment of Responsibilities," *Journal of Modern History*, XXXIV (December 1962), 369–80.

Wittlin, Alma. *Abdul Hamid: The Shadow of God*. London, 1940.

Military Campaigns: I. Mesopotamia

Non-Official Sources

Adamov, Evgenii A. *Die europaischen Mächte und die Türkei während des Weltkrieges*. Dresden, 1932.

Barker, A. J. *The Bastard War*. New York, 1967.

Bird, Wilkinson D. *A Chapter of Misfortunes: the Battles of Ctesiphon and of the Diyailah in Mesopotamia*. London, 1923.

Bourget, J. M. "Les opérations contre la Turquie," *Journal des débats*, XXXIII (October 22, 1926), 667–77.

Buchanan, Sir George C. *The Tragedy of Mesopotamia*. London, 1938.

Burne, Alfred H. *Mesopotamia, the Last Phase*. London, 1936.

Cato, Conrad. *The Navy in Mesopotamia, 1914 to 1917*. London, 1922.

Dane, Edmund. *British Campaigns in the Nearer East, 1914–1918.* London, 1918.

Emin, Colonel Mehmet. *La campagne turco-anglaise en Iraq et nos fautes.* Stambuol, 1919.

Evans, Roger. *A Brief Outline of the Campaign in Mesopotamia, 1914–1918.* London, 1926.

Gleich, Gerold von. *Vom Balkan nach Bagdad.* Berlin, 1921.

Herbert, Aubrey. *Mons, Anzac and Kut.* London, 1930.

Kearsey, A. H. C. *A Study of the Strategy and Tactics of the Mesopotamian Campaign, 1914–1917.* London, 1934.

Kiesling, Colonel H. von. *Mit Feldmarshall V. d. Goltz Pacha in Mesopotamia und Persien.* Leipzig, 1922.

Larcher, Maurice. *La guerre turque dans la guerre mondiale.* Paris, 1926.

Liman von Sanders, O. V. K. *Five Years in Turkey.* Annapolis, 1927.

Massey, W. T. *The Desert Campaigns.* New York, 1918.

Mikusch, Dagobert von. *Wassmuss, der deutsche Lawrence.* Berlin, 1939.

Moberly, Frederic J. *The Campaign in Mesopotamia, 1914–1918.* 4 vols. London, 1923–7.

Parfit, J. T. *Serbia to Kut.* London, 1917.

Pitman, I., and sons. *The Campaign of the British Army in Mesopotamia, 1914–1918.* London, 1926.

Sandes, E. W. C. *In Kut and Captivity with the Sixth Indian Division.* London, 1919.

Schweder, Paul. *Im türkischen Hauptquartier.* Leipzig, 1916.

Stuermer, Harry. *Two War Years in Constantinople.* New York, 1917.

Sykes, Christopher. *Wassmus, "The German Lawrence."* London, 1939.

Townshend, Sir Charles. *My Campaign in Mesopotamia.* London, 1920.

Wilson, Sir Arnold T. *Loyalties: Mesopotamia, 1914–1917.* Vol. I. London, 1930.

II. Dardanelles

Documentary and Semi-Documentary Sources

Aspinall-Oglander, Brig. General C. F. *Military Operations: Gallipoli;* History of the Great War based on Official Documents by direction of the Historical Section Committee of Imperial Defense. Vol. I. London, 1929.

Corbett, Sir Julian. *Naval Operations in the Great War;* based on Official Documents by direction of the Historical Committee of Imperial Defense. Vols. II, III. London, 1920–5.

"Historique officiel de l'état-major général turc: la campagne des Dardanelles." Tr. Captain Maurice Larcher, in *Les archives de la grande guerre et de l'histoire contemporaine,* XVII (1929), 129–79.

Polonsky, J. *Documents diplomatiques secrets russes.* Paris, 1928.

Non-Official Sources

Ashmead-Barlett, Ellis. *The Uncensored Dardanelles.* London, 1928.

Bean, C. E. W. *Gallipoli Mission.* Canberra, 1948.

Bluck-Schlombach, E. *Allah il Allah; mit den Siegesfahnen an den Dardanellen und auf Gallipoli.* Leipzig, 1916.

Bossert, Obermaat Erwin. *Der Kampf um die Dardanellen von einem Mitkämpfer.* Leipzig, 1925.

Chack, Paul. *Des Dardanelles aux brumes du nord.* Paris, 1937.

Chatterton, E. K. *Dardanelles Dilemma: The Story of the Naval Operations.* London, 1935.

Churchill, Winston. *The World Crisis.* Vol. II. London, 1923.

"Cromer Report," *Current History,* XI (March 1917), 167–70.

Darlington, Sir Henry. *Letters from Hellas.* London, 1936.

Einstein, Lewis. *Inside Constantinople.* London, 1917.

Emin, Ahmed. *Turkey in the World War.* New Haven, 1930.

Emin, Colonel Mehmet. *Les événements sur les fronts ottomans pendant la grande guerre.* Istanbul, 1922.

Falkenhayn, General Erich von. *General Headquarters and its Critical Decisions.* London, 1919.

Florinsky, Michael T. "A Page of Diplomatic History: Russian Military Leaders and the Problem of Constantinople during the War," *Political Science Quarterly,* XLIV (March 1929), 108–15.

Germains, Victor W. *The Tragedy of Winston Churchill.* London, 1931.

Hamilton, General Sir Ian. *Gallipoli Diary.* 2 vols. London, 1920.

Hargrave, John. *The Suvla Bay Landing.* London, 1964.

Higgins, Trumbull. *Winston Churchill and the Dardanelles.* New York, 1963.

James, Robert R. *Gallipoli.* London, 1965.

491

Kannengiesser, General Hans. *The Campaign in Gallipoli*. London, 1928.

Keyes, R. V. B. K. *The Fight for Gallipoli*. London, 1941.

Larcher, Maurice. *La guerre turque dans la guerre mondiale*. Paris, 1926.

Liman von Sanders, O. V. K. *Five Years in Turkey*. Annapolis, 1927.

Lloyd George, David. *War Memoirs*. Vol. I. London, 1933.

Lorey, Hermann. *Der Krieg in den türkischen Gewassern*. Vol. I. Berlin, 1928.

Mackenzie, Compton. *Gallipoli Memories*. London, 1929.

Marguerite, Victor, ed. *Les alliés contre la Russie*. Paris, 1927.

Masefield, John. *Gallipoli*. London, 1916.

Moorhead, Alan. *Gallipoli*. London, 1956.

Morgenthau, Henry. *Ambassador Morgenthau's Story*. New York, 1919.

Mühlmann, C. *Der Kampf um die Dardanellen*. Oldenburg, 1927.

Paléologue, Maurice. *An Ambassador's Memoirs*. 3 vols. London, 1923.

Prigge, E. R. *Der Kampf um die Dardanellen*. Weimar, 1916.

Potts, J. M. *Russian Diplomacy and Bulgaria, 1914–1915*. New York, 1951.

Sazanov, S. D. *Fateful Years*. New York, 1928.

Shankland, Peter. *Dardanelles Patrol*. New York, 1964.

Snively, Marjorie K. *Russia and the Straits, 1914–1932*. Unpublished doctoral dissertation, Ohio State University, 1932.

Tirpitz, Admiral Alfred P. von. *My Memoirs*. Vol. II. London, 1919.

Trumpener, Ulrich. *Germany and the Ottoman Empire, 1914–1918*. Princeton, 1968.

Wedgwood, J. C. *With Machine Guns in Gallipoli*. London, 1915.

Weldon, L. F. B. *"Hard Lying": Eastern Mediterranean, 1914–1919*. London, 1926.

Wester-Wemyss, Lord. *The Navy in the Dardanelles Compaign*. London, 1924.

III. Trans-Caucasus

Non-Official Sources

Adamov, Evgenii A. *Die europaischen Mächte und die Türkei während des Weltkrieges*. Dresden, 1932.

Allen, W. E. D., and Muratoff, Paul. *Caucasian Battlefields*. London, 1953.

Bibliography

Anderson, George W. *Russia in Middle Asia on the eve of the First World War*. Unpublished doctoral dissertation, University of Minnesota, 1945.

Burr, M. "Note on the History of the Turko-Caucasian Border," *Asiatic Review*, XLIII (October 1947), 351–6.

Danilov, U. N. *La Russie dans la guerre mondiale, 1914–1917.* Paris, 1927.

Drujina, Gleb. *The History of the North-West Army of General Yudenich*. Unpublished doctoral dissertation, Stanford University, 1950.

Ellis, C. H. "The Trans-Caspian Episode," *Royal Central Asian Journal*, XLVI (April 1959), 69–78.

Falkenhayn, General Erich von. *General Headquarters and its Critical Decisions*. London, 1919.

Florinsky, Michael T. *The End of the Russian Empire*. London, 1931.

Frankenberg, General L. von, and Colonel A. von Proschitz. *Deutsche Asienkämpfer*. Munich, 1920.

Golovin, Lt. General Nicholas N. *The Russian Army in the World War*. New Haven, 1931.

Guse, Felix. *Die Kaukasusfront im Weltkrieg*. Leipizig, 1940.

Heyd, Uriel. *The Foundations of Turkish Nationalism*. London, 1950.

Hostler, C. W. "Trends in Pan-Turanism," *Middle East Affairs*, III (January 1952), 3–13.

Jaschke, G. "Der Turanismus der Jungtürken; Zur osmanischen Aussenpolitik im Weltkriege," *Welt des Islam*, XXIII (1941), 1–54.

Kazara, Osman N. "Georgia and Turkey: The Historical Background," *Royal Central Asian Journal*, XXXIV (January 1947), 69–78.

Kazemzadeh, F. *The Struggle for Transcaucasia, 1914–1921*. New York, 1951.

Köprülü, Lt. Colonel Serif. *Sarikamis Ihata Manevrasi*. Istanbul, 1922.

Larcher, Maurice. *La guerre turque dans la guerre mondiale*. Paris, 1926.

Papazian, B. "The Situation in the Caucasus, 1910–1920," *Armenian Review*, XII (October 1959), 76–86.

Pomiankowski, Lt. General Joseph. *Der Zusammenbruch des ottomanischen Reiches: Erinnerungen an die Türkei der Zeit des Weltkrieges*. Vienna, 1928.

493

Price, Morgan P. *War and Revolution in Asiatic Russia*. London, 1918.

Schweder, Paul. *Im türkischen Hauptquartier*. Leipzig, 1916.

Smith, C. V., Jr. *The Russian Struggle for Power, 1914–1917*. New York, 1956.

Trumpener, Ulrich. *Germany and the Ottoman Empire, 1914–1918*. Princeton, 1968.

Zenkovsky, Serge A. *Pan-Turkism and Islam in Russia*. Cambridge, Mass., 1960.

IV. Suez, Palestine, Syria

Non-Official Sources

"The Campaign in Palestine from the Enemy's Side," *Royal United Service Institution Journal*, LXVII (October–November 1925), 2–46.

Dane, Edmund. *British Campaigns in the Nearer East, 1914–1918*. London, 1918.

Djemal Pasha, Ahmed. *Memories of a Turkish Statesman, 1913–1919*. New York, 1922.

Drexler, R. *Mit Jilderim ins Heilige Land*. Ravensburg, 1919.

Eisgruber, H. *Angriff auf den Suezkanal*. Berlin, 1939.

Falkenhayn, General Erich von. *General Headquarters and its Critical Decisions*. London, 1919.

Falls, Cyril, and MacMunn, Sir George F. *Military Operations: Egypt and Palestine*. 2 vols. London, 1928–30.

Gardner, Brian. *Allenby of Arabia*. New York, 1966.

Graves, P. *Briton and Turk*. London, 1941.

Hankey, Lord. *The Supreme Command, 1914–1918*. 2 vols. London, 1961.

Hedin, Sven. *Jerusalem*. Leipzig, 1918.

Kressenstein, Kress von. *Mit den Türken zum Suezkanal*. Berlin, 1938.

———. *Zwischen Kaukasus und Sinaï*. Berlin, 1922.

Larcher, Maurice. "La campagne du général de Falkenhayn en Palestine," *Revue militaire française*, XXVI (November 1925), 11–66.

———. *La guerre turque dans la guerre mondiale*. Paris, 1926.

Liman von Sanders, O. V. K. *Five Years in Turkey*. Annapolis, 1927.

Lloyd George, David. *War Memoirs*. Vols. I–IV. London, 1933.

Bibliography

Massey, W. T. *The Desert Campaigns*. New York, 1918.

Mühlmann, C. *Das deutsch-türkische Waffenbundnis im Welt-kriege*. Leipzig, 1940.

Petrie, C. "The Mediterranean in Two Wars," *Quarterly Review*, CCLXXXI (October 1943), 164–75.

Pomiankowski, Lt. General Joseph. *Der Zusammenbruch des otto-manischen Reiches: Erinnerungen an die Türkei der Zeit des Weltkrieges*. Vienna, 1928.

Robertson, Field Marshal Sir W. *Soldiers and Statesmen*. London, 1926.

Rovin, Georges. *Un épisode de la guerre mondiale; l'attaque du canal de Suez*. Paris, 1922.

Wavell, Lord Archibald. *Allenby: Soldier and Statesman*. London, 1940.

Wiegand, Theodor. *Sinaï*. Berlin, 1920.

The Armenian Question

Documentary and Semi-Documentary Sources

Archival Materials, United States Government

United States, Department of State Files. *Dispatches between Wash-ington and Constantinople, 1919 to 1924. Especially Series* 86oj.o1; and 867.oo1.

Files of the Paris Peace Conference. Especially Series 123H.271.

The Inquiry. A collection of 902 documents.

Collections of Papers

Letters of the American Board of Commissioners for Foreign Mis-sions, 1910–1919. 81 vols. Houghton Library, Harvard Univer-sity.

Papers of Tasker Bliss, 1918–1920. Manuscript Division, Library of Congress.

Papers of Mark Bristol, 1918–1927. Manuscript Division, Library of Congress.

Papers of Robert Lansing, 1915–1920. Manuscript Division, Library of Congress.

Papers of Henry White. Paris Peace Conference Series. Manuscript Division, Library of Congress.

Papers of Woodrow Wilson. Series II, VI, and VIII-A of the Paris Peace Conference. Manuscript Division, Library of Congress.

Bibliography

Published Material

Viscount Bryce. *The Treatment of Armenians in the Ottoman Empire, 1915–1916:* Documents Presented to Viscount Grey of Falloden, Secretary of State for Foreign Affairs. Misc. 31. London, 1916.
Hurewitz, J. C. *Diplomacy in the Near and Middle East: A Documentary Record.* Vol. II. Princeton, 1956.
In Behalf of Armenians. Hearings before the Committee on Foreign Affairs. 67th Cong., 2d Sess., H. Res. 244 (March 7, 1922).
Miller, David Hunter. *My Diary at the Conference of Paris.* 21 vols. New York, 1928.
Poidebard, A. *Le Transcaucase et la république d'Arménie dans les textes diplomatiques du traité de Brest-Litovsk au traité du Kars, 1918–1921.* Paris, 1924.
United States Department of State. *Foreign Relations of the United States: The Paris Peace Conference.* 13 vols. Washington, D.C., 1942–7.

Non-Official Sources

(Not including the extensive polemical literature on the Armenian Question in United States newspapers and magazines.)

Aknouni, E. *Germany, Turkey, Armenia.* London, 1917.
———. *Political Persecution.* New York, 1911.
Armenian Historical Research Association. *The Turkish Armenocide.* New York, 1921.
Armenian Special Mission to the United States. *The Republic of Armenia.* Washington, D.C., 1919.
Aslan, Kevork. *Armenia and the Armenians.* New York, 1920.
Aspirations et agissements révolutionnaires des comités arméniens. Constantinople, 1917.
Atabinen, R. S. *Turcs et Arméniens devant l'histoire.* Geneva, 1919.
Atamian, Sarkis. *The Armenian Community.* New York, 1955.
Barton, James L. *History of the Near East Relief.* Boston, 1924.
Berkes, Niryazi, ed. *Turkish Nationalism and Western Civilization: Selected Essays of Zia Gökalp.* New York, 1959.
Bland, R. L., and F. M. Surface. *American Food in the World War and Reconstruction Period.* Palo Alto, California, 1931.
Brémond, Edouard. *La Cilicie en 1919–1920.* Paris, 1921.
Burr, M. "Note on the History of the Turko-Caucasian Border," *Asiatic Review,* XLIII (October 1947), 351–6.
Burtt, Joseph. *The People of Ararat.* London, 1926.

496

Bibliography

Caramen, Elizabeth. *Daughter of the Euphrates*. New York, 1939.

Chambers, W. N. *Yoljulak: Random Thoughts on a Life in Imperial Turkey*. New York, 1917.

Davison, R. H. "The Armenian Crisis, 1912–1914," *American Historical Review*, XLIII (April 1948), 481–505.

DeNovo, John. *American Interests and Policies in the Middle East, 1900–1939*. Minneapolis, 1963.

Djemal Pasha, Ahmed. *Memories of a Turkish Statesman, 1913–1919*. London, 1923.

Eby, B. R. *At the Mercy of Turkish Brigands*. New Carlisle, Ohio, 1922.

Einstein, Lewis. *Inside Constantinople*. London, 1917.

Emin, Colonel Mehmet. *Les événements sur les fronts ottomans pendant la grande guerre*. Istanbul, 1922.

Falkenhayn, General Erich von. *General Headquarter and its Critical Decisions*. London, 1919.

Gibbons, Herbert A. *Armenia in the World War*. New York, 1923.

Gidney, James B. *A Mandate for Armenia*. Oberlin, Ohio, 1967.

Gottlieb, W. W. *Studies in Secret Diplomacy during the First World War*. London, 1957.

Guse, Felix. *Die Kaukasusfront im Weltkrieg*. Leipzig, 1940.

Haydar, Bammate. *Le Caucase et la révolution russe*. Paris, 1929.

Heyd, Uriel. *The Foundations of Turkish Nationalism*. London, 1950.

Harbord, Lt. General James. "My Mission to Armenia," *World's Work*, XLII (March 1932), 91–5.

Hostler, C. W. "Trends in Pan-Turanism," *Middle East Affairs*, III (January 1952), 3–13

House, E. M., and C. Seymour, eds. *What Really Happened at Paris?* New York, 1921.

Hovannisian, Richard G. *Armenia on the Road to Independence*. Berkeley, 1967.

Jäckh, Ernst. *The Rising Crescent*. New York, 1944.

Jerrehian, Rita, "From the Armistice to the Treaty of Sèvres," *Armenian Review*, IX (summer 1956), 123–32.

Kazemzadeh, F. *The Struggle for Transcaucasia, 1917–1921*. New York, 1951.

Khatissian, Alexander. *The Origins and Development of the Armenian Republic*. Athens, 1920 (in Armenian).

Kongre, Milli. *The Turco-Armenian Question: The Turkish Point of View*. London, 1919.

Korganoff, G. *La participation des Arméniens à la guerre mondiale sur le front du Caucase (1914–1918)*. Paris, 1927.

497

Krischtschian, Melkon. *Deutschland und die Ausrottung der Armenier in der Türkei.* Potsdam, 1930.

La Chesnais, V. P. G. *Les peuples de la Transcaucasie.* Paris, 1921.

Larcher, Maurice. *La guerre turque dans la guerre mondiale.* Paris, 1926.

Lepsius, Johannes. *Deutschland und Armenien, 1914–1918.* Potsdam, 1919.

———. *Der Todesgang des armenischen Volkes.* Potsdam, 1930.

Levine, Isaac Don. "Armenia Resurrected," *Asia,* XIX (April 1919), 323–30.

Levison, Leon. *How the Turk Makes War.* New York, 1918.

Liman von Sanders, O. V. K. *Five Years in Turkey.* Annapolis, 1927.

Macler, Frédéric. *Autour de l'Arménie.* Paris, 1917.

Mahdesian, Arshag. "A Probable Source of 'Forty Days of Musa Dagh'," *Armenian Review,* I (winter 1948), 108–9.

Maloumian, Khatchadour. *Political Persecution.* New York, 1919.

Mandelstam, André. *La société des nations et les puissances devant le problème arménien.* Paris, 1927.

Mécérian, Jean. *Le génocide du peuple arménien.* Beirut, 1955.

"The Memoirs of Naim Bey," in *The Turkish Armenocide.* Newton Square, Pennsylvania, 1965.

Menardos, Sinos. *Greece and Armenia.* London, 1919.

Miller, David Hunter. *The Drafting of the Covenant.* Vol. II. New York, 1928.

Minasian, R. Ter. *Armenian Freedom Fighters.* Boston, 1963.

Missakian, J. A. *A Searchlight on the Armenian Question.* Boston, 1950.

Montgomery, George R. "Why Talaat's Assassin was Acquitted," *Current History,* XIV (July 1921), 551–6.

Morgenthau, Henry. *Ambassador Morgenthau's Story.* New York, 1919.

Nalbandian, Louise. *The Armenian Revolutionary Movement.* Berkeley, 1963.

Nansen, Fridtjof. *Armenia and the Near East.* London, 1928.

Naslian, Jean. *Mémoires . . . sur les événements politico-religieux en Proche-Orient de 1914 à 1928.* 2 vols. Beirut, 1955.

Papazian, Bertha. *The Tragedy of Armenia.* Boston, 1918.

Papazian, K. S. *Patriotism Perverted.* Boston, 1934.

Pasdermadjian, Hrant. *Histoire de l'Arménie depuis les origines jusqu'au traité de Lausanne.* Paris, 1949.

Pernot, M. "La question turque: les minorités nonmusulmanes en Turquie," *Revue des deux mondes,* VIII (April 1922), 918–25.

Bibliography

Pingaud, A. *Histoire diplomatique de la France pendant la grande guerre.* Vols. I, III. Paris, 1940.

Poidebard, A. *Le rôle militaire des Arméniens sur le front du Caucase.* Paris, 1920.

Pomiankowski, Lt. General Joseph. *Der Zusammenbruch des ottomanischen Reiches: Erinnerungen an die Türkei der Zeit des Weltkrieges.* Vienna, 1928.

Price, Morgan D. *War and Revolution in Asiatic Russia.* London, 1918.

Rustem Bey, Ahmed. *La guerre mondiale et la question turco-arménienne.* Berne, 1918.

Sachar, Howard M. *The Origins of Near Eastern Policy: The United States and Turkey, 1914–1927.* Unpublished doctoral dissertation, Harvard University, 1953.

Sanjian, Avedis K. *The Armenian Communities in Syria under Ottoman Domination.* Cambridge, Mass., 1965.

Sazanov, S. D. *Fateful Years, 1909–1916.* London, 1928.

Silberstein, G. E. "The Central Powers and the Second Turkish Alliance," *Slavonic Review*, XXIV (March 1965), 77–89.

Smith, C. J., Jr. *The Russian Struggle for Power, 1914–1917.* New York, 1956.

Sumner, B. H. *Tsardom and Imperialism in the Far East and Middle East, 1880–1914.* London, 1940.

Talaat Pasha. "Posthumous Memoirs," *Current History*, XV (November 1921), 279–301.

Tashjian, James H. "The American Military Mission to Armenia," *Armenian Review*, II (winter 1949–50), Part IV.

Tekeian, C. D. *Quatre ans de guerre en Orient; l'action franco-arménienne pendant la guerre.* Paris, 1919.

Totmiants, Vakhan F. *L'Arménie économique.* Paris, 1920.

Trial of the Major War Criminals before the International Military Tribunal. Vol. X. Nuremburg, 1947.

Trumpener, Ulrich. *Germany and the Ottoman Empire, 1914–1918.* Princeton, 1968.

Varandian, M. *Le conflit arméno-georgien et la guerre du Caucase.*
———. *Histoire de la Dashnagtzoutune.* 2 vols. Paris, 1932.

Véou, Paul de. *La Passion de Cilicie.* Paris, 1954.

Vratzian, Simon. *Armenia and the Armenian Question.* Boston, 1943.

Wee, Morris. *Great Britain and the Armenian Question, 1878–1914.* Unpublished doctoral dissertation, University of Wisconsin, 1930.

The Arab Revolt

Documentary and Semi-Documentary Sources

Correspondence between Sir Henry McMahon and the Sharif of Mecca. Cmd. 5957. London, 1938.

Hurewitz, J. C. *Diplomacy in the Near and Middle East: A Documentary Record.* Vol. II. Princeton, 1956.

Jewish Agency for Palestine. *Documents Relating to the McMahon Letters.* London, 1939.

Report of a Committee Set Up to Consider Certain Correspondence Between Sir Henry McMahon and the Sharif of Mecca in 1915 and 1916. Cmd. 5974. London, 1938.

Non-Official Sources

Abdullah, King of Jordan. *Memoirs.* New York, 1950.

Aldington, Richard. *Lawrence of Arabia.* London, 1955.

Antonius, George. *The Arab Awakening.* Philadelphia, 1938.

Al-Saïd, Nuri. *Arab Independence and Unity.* Baghdad, 1943.

Arthur, Sir G. *Life of Lord Kitchener.* Vol. III. London, 1920.

Bray, N. N. E. *Shifting Sands.* London, 1934.

Brémond, Edouard. *Le Hedjaz dans la guerre mondiale.* Paris, 1931.

Bullard, Sir Reader. *Britain and the Middle East.* London, 1951.

Carrington, C. E. *T. E. Lawrence.* New York, 1936.

Dane, Edmund. *British Campaigns in the Nearer East, 1914–1918.* London, 1918.

Djemal Pasha, Ahmed. *Memoirs of a Turkish Statesman, 1913–1919.* New York, 1922.

Falls, Cyril, and Sir George F. MacMunn. *Military Operations: Egypt and Palestine.* 2 vols. London, 1928–30.

Frischwasser-Ra'anan, H. F. *The Frontiers of a Nation.* London, 1955.

Gardner, Brian. *Allenby of Arabia.* New York, 1966.

Garnett, David, ed. *The Letters of T. E. Lawrence.* London, 1938.

Gottlieb, W. W. *Studies in Secret Diplomacy during the First World War.* London, 1951.

Graves, Robert. *Lawrence and the Arabian Adventure.* New York, 1928.

Hankey, Lord. *The Supreme Command, 1914–1918.* 2 vols. London, 1951.

Hazam, John G. *Arab Nationalism and Anglo-French Imperialism on the Eve of the World War.* Unpublished doctoral dissertation, University of California, 1933.

Hogarth, D. G. *Arabia.* London, 1922.

Hourani, A. H. *Great Britain and the Arab World.* London, 1945.

Hurgronje, C. S. *The Revolt in Arabia.* New York, 1917.

Jacob, Harold F. *Kings of Arabia.* London, 1923.

Jung, Eugene. *Les puissances devant la révolte arabe.* Paris, 1924.

Kedourie, Elie. *Britain and the Middle East, 1914–1921.* London, 1956.

Kressenstein, Kress von. *Zwischen Kaukasus und Sinaï.* Berlin, 1922.

Lammens, Henri. *La Syrie, précis historique.* 2 vols. Beirut, 1921.

Larcher, Maurice. *La guerre turque dans la guerre mondiale.* Paris, 1926.

Lawrence, T. E. *Revolt in the Desert.* London, 1927.

———. *Secret Dispatches from Arabia.* London, 1939.

———. *Seven Pillars of Wisdom.* London, 1935.

Leslie, Shane. *Mark Sykes, His Life and Letters.* London, 1923.

Lloyd, G. A. L. *Egypt Since Cromer.* 2 vols. London, 1933–4.

Lloyd George, David. *Memoirs of the Peace Conference.* Vol. II. London, 1938.

Liddell Hart, B. H. *Colonel Lawrence.* London, 1935.

———. *"T. E. Lawrence"—In Arabia and After.* London, 1934.

Liman von Sanders, O. V. K. *Five Years in Turkey.* Annapolis, 1927.

Mandelstam, André. *Le sort de l'Empire Ottoman.* Paris, 1917.

Marlowe, John. *Arab Nationalism and British Imperialism.* London, 1961.

Meinertzhagen, Richard. *Middle East Diary, 1917–1956.* London, 1959.

Mousa, Suleiman. *T. E. Lawrence: An Arab View.* London, 1966.

Nevakivi, Jukka. *Britain, France, and the Arab Middle East, 1914–1920.* London, 1969.

Nuseibeh, Hazem Zaki. *The Ideas of Arab Nationalism.* Ithaca, New York, 1956.

Philby, H. St. J. *Saudi Arabia.* New York, 1955.

Pingaud, A. *Histoire diplomatique de la France pendant la grande guerre.* Vols. I, III. Paris, 1940.

Robinson, Edward. *Lawrence the Rebel.* London, 1946.

Sauvaget, Jean. *La culture française et la renaissance arabe.*

Storrs, Sir Ronald. *Orientations.* London, 1937.

Sykes, Christopher. *Four Studies in Loyalty.* London, 1948.

Sykes, Sir Mark. *The Caliph's Last Heritage.* London, 1915.

———. *Dar ul Islam.* London, 1904.

————. *Through Five Turkish Provinces*. London, 1900.

Temperley, Harold. *A History of the Peace Conference of Paris*. Vol. VI. London, 1924.

Thomas, Lowell. *With Lawrence in Arabia*. New York, 1924.

Tibawi, A. L. "Syria in The McMahon Correspondence: Fresh Evidence from the British Foreign Office Records," *Middle East Forum*, XLII (1966), 5–32.

Villars, Jean Berand. *Le colonel Lawrence*. Paris, 1955.

Wavell, Sir Archibald. *Allenby: Soldier and Statesman*. London, 1940.

Wingate, Sir Ronald. *Wingate of the Sudan*. London, 1955.

Young, Sir Hubert. *The Independent Arab*. London, 1933.

The Secret Treaties

Documentary and Semi-Documentary Sources

Brown-Scott, J., ed. *The Italian Green Book*. New York, 1916.

Eisenmann, L., A. de Lapradelle, P. Renouvin, and B. Markine-Guétzévitch. *Constantinople et les détroits*. 2 vols. Paris, 1932.

Die grosse Politik der Mächte im Weltkrieg. Vol. IV. Dresden, 1932.

Hurewitz, J. C. *Diplomacy in the Near and Middle East: A Documentary Record*. Vol. II. Princeton, 1956.

République française, Ministère des affaires étrangères. *Documents diplomatiques: les affaires balkaniques, 1914–1916. Vol. III*. Paris, 1922.

Polonsky, J. *Documents diplomatiques secrets russes*. Paris, 1928.

Woodward, E. L., and R. Butler, eds. *Documents on British Foreign Policy, 1919–1939*. 1st Series, Vol. IV. London, 1952.

Non-Official Sources

Adamov, Evgenii A. *Constantinople et les détroits*. 2 vols. Paris, 1930–2.

————. *Die europaische Mächte und die Türkei während des Weltkrieges*. Dresden, 1932.

Albrecht-Carrié, R. *Italy at the Peace Conference*. New York, 1938.

Antonius, George. *The Arab Awakening*. Philadelphia, 1938.

Asquith, Herbert. *Memories and Reflections*. 2 vols. Boston, 1928.

Avram, Benno. *The Evolution of the Suez Canal Status from 1869 to 1956*. New York, 1959.

Bernardy, A. A. *Vie d'Italia in Levante*. Bologna, 1933.

Bertie, Lord. *Diary, 1914–1918*. 3 vols. London, 1924.

Bibliography

Blaisdell, D. C. *European Financial Control in the Ottoman Empire.* New York, 1929.

Booth, C. C., and I. B. Booth. *Italy's Aegean Possessions.* London, 1928.

British Foreign Office. *France and the Levant.* London, 1920.

Bruneau, André. *Traditions et politique de la France au Levant.* Paris, 1932.

Buchanan, Sir George. *My Mission to Russia.* Vol. II. London, 1924.

Bullard, Sir Reader. *Britain and the Middle East.* London, 1951.

Caix, Robert de., H. Deberain, and G. Hardy. *Histoire des colonies françaises.* Vol. III. Paris, 1931.

Cambon, Paul. *Correspondance, 1870–1924.* Vol. III. Paris, 1946.

Charles-Roux, F. *La France et les chrétiens d'Orient.* Paris, 1939.

Cocks, F. Seymour. *The Secret Treaties and Understandings.* London, 1918.

Cremona, Paul, and M. H. A. Macartney. *Italy's Foreign and Colonial Policy, 1914–1937.* London, 1938.

Cumming, Henry H. *Franco-British Rivalry in the Post-War Near East.* New York, 1938.

Currey, Muriel. *Italian Foreign Policy, 1918–1932.* London, 1932.

Danilov, U. N. *La Russie dans la guerre mondiale (1914–1917).* Paris, 1927.

Ehrmann, Howard M. *The London Agreement and the Entrance of Italy into the World War.* Unpublished doctoral dissertation, Yale University, 1927.

Feis, Herbert. *Europe the World's Banker, 1870–1914.* New Haven, 1930.

Flandin, Etienne. *La force brutale: rapport au sénat sur la Syrie et la Palestine.* Paris, 1915.

Florinsky, Michael T. "A Page of Diplomatic History: Russian Military Leaders and the Problem of Constantinople during the War," *Political Science Quarterly,* XLIV (March 1929), 108–15.

Frischwasser-Ra'anan, H. F. *Frontiers of a Nation.* London, 1955.

Gontaut-Biron, R. de. *Comment la France s'est installée en Syrie, 1918–1919.* Paris, 1923.

Gooch, G. P. *Recent Revelations of European Diplomacy.* London, 1927.

Gottlieb, W. W. *Studies in Secret Diplomacy during the First World War.* London, 1957.

Grey, Viscount of Falloden. *Twenty-Five Years.* 2 vols. London, 1925–8.

Headlam-Morley, J. *Studies in Diplomatic History.* London, 1930.

Hoskins, Halford L. *British Routes to India.* New York, 1928.

Hourani, A. H. *Great Britain and the Arab World.* London, 1945.

Howard, Harry N. *The Partition of Turkey.* Norman, Oklahoma, 1931.

Kazara, Osman Nuri. "Georgia and Turkey: The Historical Background," *Royal Central Asian Journal,* XXXIV (January 1947), 69–78.

Kazemzadeh, F. *The Struggle for Transcaucasia, 1917–1921.* New York, 1951.

Kedourie, Elie. *Britain and the Middle East, 1914–1921.* London, 1956.

Kleiman, A. S. "Britain's War Aims in The Middle East in 1915," *Journal of Contemporary History,* III (July 1968), 242–51.

Krajewski, Leon. "La politique anglaise en Arabie (1915–1927)," *Revue de Paris,* VI (March 1928), 378–419.

Krepulski, L. "Levant," *Asie française,* XIV (April 1924), 157.

Leslie, Shane. *Mark Sykes: His Life and Letters.* London, 1923.

Lloyd George, David. *Memoirs of the Peace Conference.* Vol. II.

———. *War Memoirs.* Vols. IV, V, VI. London, 1933.

Loder, J. de V. *The Truth about Mesopotamia, Syria and Palestine.* London, 1923.

Macler, Frédéric. *La France et l'Arménie à travers l'art et l'histoire.* Paris, 1917.

Magnus, Philip. *Kitchener, Portrait of an Imperialist.* London, 1964.

Manuel, Frank E. "The Palestine Question in Italian Diplomacy," *Journal of Modern History.* XXVII (September 1955), 263–80.

Marguerite, Victor, ed. *Les alliés contre la Russie.* Paris, 1927.

Martel, René. "L'Orient et la guerre après les archives diplomatiques russes," *Le monde slave,* III (October 1926), 118–55.

Masi, Corredo. *Italia e Italiani nell'Oriente vicino e lontano.* Bologna, 1936.

Mayer, Arno J. *Political Origins of the New Diplomacy, 1917–1918.* New Haven, 1959.

McCurdy, C. A. *The Truth about the "Secret Treaties."* London, 1918.

Monroe, Elizabeth. *The Mediterranean in Politics.* London, 1938.

———. *Britain's Moment in the Middle East, 1914–1956.* Baltimore, 1963.

Nenni, P. *The Years of Tyranny in Italy.* London, 1932.

Nevakivi, Jukka. "Lord Kitchener and The Partition of the Ottoman Empire," in *Studies in International History; Essays Presented to W. Norton Medlicott.* London, 1967.

———. *Britain, France, and the Arab Middle East, 1914–1921.* London, 1969.

Page, Ambassador T. N. *Italy and the World War*. London, 1921.

Paléologue, Maurice. *An Ambassador's Memoirs*. 3 vols. London, 1923.

Pic, P. *Syrie et Palestine*. Paris, 1924.

Pichon, Jean. *Le partage du Proche-Orient*. Paris, 1938.

Pingaud, A. *Histoire diplomatique de la France pendant la grande guerre*. Vols. I, III. Paris, 1938–40.

Poincaré, Raymond. *Au service de la France*. Vols. VI, VII, VIII. Paris, 1937.

Pokrowski, M. N., ed. *Die internationalen Beziehungen im Zeitalter des Imperialismus*. Vol. VII. Berlin, 1934.

Porter, C. W. *The Career of Theophile Delcassé*. Philadelphia, 1936.

Puryear, N. J. *International Economics and Diplomacy in the Near East*. Palo Alto, California, 1939.

Roberts, Stephen A. *A History of French Colonial Policy*. Vol. II. London, 1928.

Roederer, Carle. *La Syrie et la France*. Paris, 1917.

Rondot, J. "Les intérêts pétroliers français dans le Proche-Orient," *Politique étrangère*, No. 4 (October 1932).

Royal Institute of International Affairs. *Great Britain and Palestine*. London, 1947.

Sadaka, Nagib. *La question syrienne pendant la guerre de 1914*. Paris, 1940.

Salandra, Antonio. *Italy and the Great War*. London, 1932.

Samuel, Viscount Herbert L. S. *Memoirs*. London, 1955.

Savinski, A. *Recollections of a Russian Diplomat*. London, 1922.

Seton-Watson, R. W. "Italian Intervention and the Secret Treaty of London," *Slavonic Review*, V (December 1926), 271–97.

Shatzky, B. E. "La question de Constantinople et les détroits," *Revue d'histoire de la guerre mondiale*, IV (October 1926), 289–311; V (January 1927), 19–43.

Shliapnikov, Aleksandre G. *Les alliés contre la Russie avant, pendant et après la guerre mondiale*. Paris, 1926.

Smith, Clarence J., Jr. "Great Britain and the 1914–1915 Straits Agreement with Russia: The British Promise of November, 1914," *American Historical Review*, LXX (July 1965), 1015–34.

———. *The Russian Struggle for Power, 1914–1917*. New York, 1956.

Snively, Marjorie K. *Russia and the Straits, 1914–1932*. Unpublished doctoral dissertation, Ohio State University, 1932.

Stavrou, Theofanis G. *Russian Interests in Palestine, 1882–1914*. Salonica, 1963.

Stein, Leonard. *Syria*. London, 1936.

Suarez, G. *Briand, sa vie, son oeuvre avec son journal.* Vol. III. Paris, 1939.

Sykes, Christopher. *Two Studies in Virtue.* London, 1953.

Sykes, Sir Mark. *The Caliph's Last Heritage.* London, 1915.

Taube, Baron M. de. *La politique russe d'avant-guerre et la fin de l'empire des tsars (1904–1917).* Paris, 1928.

Trumpener, Ulrich. *Germany and the Ottoman Empire, 1914–1918.* Princeton, 1968.

The Partition of the Levant

Documentary and Semi-Documentary Sources

Hurewitz, J. C. *Diplomacy in the Near and Middle East: A Documentary Record,* Vol. II. Princeton, 1956.

Miller, David Hunter. *My Diary at the Peace Conference.* 21 vols. New York, 1928.

United States Department of State. *Foreign Relations of the United States: The Paris Peace Conference.* 13 vols. Washington, D.C., 1942–7.

Woodward, E. L., and R. Butler, eds. *Documents on British Foreign Policy, 1919–1939.* 1st Series, Vol. IV. London, 1952.

The Papers of Woodrow Wilson. Series II, VI, and VIII-A (of the Paris Peace Conference). Manuscript Division, Library of Congress.

Non-Official Sources

Abdullah, King of Jordan. *Memoirs.* New York, 1950.

Abouchid, Eugenie E. *Thirty Years of Lebanon and Syria (1917–1947).* Beirut, 1948.

Achkar, J. *L'évolution politique de la Syrie et du Liban, de la Palestine, et de l'Iraq.* Paris, 1935.

Al-Husri, Abu Khaldun Sati. *The Day of Maysalun: A Page from the Modern History of the Arabs.* Washington, D.C., 1966.

Antonius, George. *The Arab Awakening.* Philadelphia, 1938.

Baker, Ray Stannard. *Woodrow Wilson and the World Settlement.* Vol. II. New York, 1922.

Bardoux, Jacques. *Lloyd George et la France.* Paris, 1923.

Batsell, Walter R. *The United States and the System of Mandates.* New York, 1925.

Bruneau, André. *Traditions et politique de la France au Levant.*

Bibliography

Bullard, Sir Reader. *Britain and the Middle East.* New York, 1951.

Cambon, Paul. *Correspondance, 1870–1924.* Vol. III. Paris, 1946.

Catroux, General G. *Deux missions en Moyen-Orient, 1919–1922.* Paris, 1958.

Churchill, Winston. *The World Crisis.* Vol. IV ("The Aftermath"). London, 1929.

Cumming, Henry H. *Franco-British Rivalry in the Post-War Near East.* New York, 1938.

David, Philippe. *Un gouvernement arabe à Damas: le congrès syrien.* Paris, 1923.

Fitzsimmons, Matthew A. *Empire by Treaty: Britain and the Middle East in the Twentieth Century.* South Bend, Indiana, 1964.

Frischwasser-Ra'anan, H. F. *The Frontiers of a Nation.* London, 1955.

Gontaut-Biron, R. de. *Comment la France s'est installée en Syrie, 1918–1919.* Paris, 1925.

Hanna, Paul L. *British Policy in Palestine.* Washington, D.C., 1942.

Hourani, A. H. *Minorities in the Arab World.* London, 1947.

———. *Syria and Lebanon.* London, 1946.

House, E. M., and C. Seymour, eds. *What Really Happened at Paris?* New York, 1921.

Howard, Harry N. "An American Experiment in Peace Making: The King Crane Commission," *Moslem World,* XXXII (April 1942), 122–46.

———. *The Partition of Turkey.* Norman, Oklahoma, 1931.

Kedourie, Elie. *Britain and the Middle East, 1914–1921.* London, 1956.

Khairallah, K. T. *Le problème du Levant: les régions arabes 'libérées.* Paris, 1919.

Lenczowski, George. *The Middle East in World Affairs.* Ithaca, New York, 1952.

Lloyd George, David. *Memoirs of the Peace Conference.* 2 vols. London, 1938.

Loder, J. de V. *The Truth about Mesopotamia, Syria and Palestine.* London, 1923.

Longrigg, Stephen. *Syria and Lebanon under French Mandate.* London, 1958.

Luquet, Jean. *La politique des mandats dans le Levant.* Paris, 1924.

Lyautey, Pierre. *Le drame oriental et le rôle de la France.* Paris, 1923.

Manuel, Frank E. "The Palestine Question in Italian Diplomacy,"

Journal of Modern History, XXVII (September 1955), 263–80.

Marlowe, John. *Arab Nationalism and British Imperialism*. London, 1954.

Massey, W. T. *Allenby's Final Triumph*. London, 1920.

McCallum, D. "The French in Syria, 1919–1924," *Journal of the Central Asian Society*, XXXIII (October 1923), 2–49.

Meinertzhagen, Richard. *Middle East Diary, 1917–1956*. London, 1959.

Monroe, Elizabeth. *Britain's Moment in the Middle East, 1914–1956*.

Morand, Edmond. *L'Angleterre, Maîtresse des destinées françaises*. Paris, 1939.

Nevakivi, Jukka. *Britain, France, and The Arab Middle East, 1914–1920*. London, 1969.

Nicolson, Harold. *Peacemaking, 1919*. London, 1933.

Pichon, Jean. *Le partage du Proche-Orient*. Paris, 1938.

———. *Sur la route des Indes*. Paris, 1932.

Poincaré, R. *Au service de la France*. Vol. VIII. Paris, 1933.

Puryear, Vernon J. *France and the Levant*. Berkeley, 1941.

Régismanset, C. *Questions coloniales*. Vol. I. Paris, 1923.

Rémusat, Paul. "Les cent jours du roi de Syrie," *Extrait de la revue des études historiques*, XIV (spring 1924), 1–27.

Riddel, Lord. *Intimate Diary of the Peace Conference and After, 1918–1923*. London, 1923.

Roberts, Stephen H. *A History of French Colonial Policy*. Vol. II. London, 1928.

Ronaldshay, Earl of. *The Life of Lord Curzon*. Vol. III. London, 1928.

Sadaka, Naguib. *La question syrienne pendant la guerre de 1914*. Paris, 1940.

Selsam, John P. *The Attempts to Form an Anglo-French Alliance, 1919–1924*. Philadelphia, 1936.

Stein, Leonard. *Syria*. London, 1926.

Storrs, Sir Ronald. *Orientations*. London, 1937.

Suarez, Georges. *Clemenceau*. Paris, 1930.

Temperley, Harold. *A History of the Peace Conference of Paris*. Vol. VI. London, 1924.

Wickham-Steed, Henry. *Through Thirty Years*. Vol. II. London, 1932.

Wright, Quincy. *Mandates Under the League of Nations*. Chicago, 1930.

Zeine, Z. N. *The Struggle for Arab Independence*. Beirut, 1960.

Bibliography

Disposing of Iraq

Documentary and Semi-Documentary Sources

Hurewitz, J. C. *Diplomacy in the Near and Middle East*: A Documentary Record. Vol. II. Princeton, 1956.

Woodward, E. L., and R. Butler, eds. *Documents on British Foreign Policy, 1919–1939.* 1st Series, Vols. IV, VII, XIII.

Non-Official Sources

Antonius, George. *The Arab Awakening.* Philadelphia, 1938.

Bell, Lady Gertrude L. *Letters.* Vol. II. London, 1927.

Bodley, R., and L. Hearst. *Gertrude Bell.* New York, 1940.

Bullard, Sir Reader. *Britain and the Middle East.* New York, 1951.

Burgoyne, E. *Gertrude Bell: From Her Personal Papers, 1914–1926.* London, 1961.

Fitzsimmons, M. A. *Empire by Treaty: Britain and the Middle East in the Twentieth Century.* South Bend, Indiana, 1964.

Graves, P. *The Life of Sir Percy Cox.* London, 1941.

Haim, Sylvia. *Arab Nationalism: An Anthology.* London 1962.

Haldane, General Aylmer. *The Insurrection in Mesopotamia.* London, 1922.

———. *A Soldier's Saga.* London, 1948.

Ireland, Philip. *Iraq: A Study in Political Development.* London, 1937.

Kedouri, Elie. *Britain and the Middle East, 1914–1921.* London, 1956.

Lloyd George, David. *Memoirs of the Peace Conference.* Vol. II. London, 1938.

Loder, J. de V. *The Truth About Mesopotamia, Syria and Palestine.* London, 1923.

Longrigg, Stephen H. *Four Centuries of Modern Iraq.* London, 1925.

———. *Iraq: 1900–1950.* London, 1953.

Luquet, Jean. *La politique des mandats dans le Levant.* Paris, 1924.

Marlowe, John. *Arab Nationalism and British Imperialism.* London, 1954.

Monroe, Elizabeth. *Britain's Moment in the Middle East, 1914–1956.* Baltimore, 1963.

Nicolson, Harold. *Peacemaking, 1919.* London, 1933.

Pichon, Jean. *Le partage du Proche-Orient.* Paris, 1938.

Ronaldshay, Earl of. *The Life of Lord Curzon.* Vol. III. London, 1924.

Seton-Williams, M. V. *Britain and the Arab States, 1920–1948.* London, 1948.

Temperley, Harold. *A History of the Peace Conference of Paris.* Vol. VI. London, 1924.

Wilson, Sir Arnold T. *Loyalties: Mesopotamia, 1914–1917.* Vol. I. London, 1930.

———. *A Clash of Loyalties: Mesopotamia, 1917–1920.* Vol. II. London, 1931.

Wright, Quincy. *Mandates Under the League of Nations.* Chicago, 1930.

Young, Sir Hubert. *The Independent Arab.* London, 1933.

Zionism and Palestine

Documentary and Semi-Documentary Sources

Arab Higher Committee for Palestine. *A Collection of Official Documents Relating to the Palestine Question, 1917–1947.* New York, 1947.

Correspondence with the Palestine Arab Delegation and the Zionist Occupation. Cmd. 1700. London, June, 1922.

Hurewitz, J.C. *Diplomacy in the Near and Middle East: A Documentary Record.* Vol. II. Princeton, 1956.

An Interim Report on the Civil Administration of Palestine During the Period of 1st July, 1920–30th June, 1921. Cmd. 1499. London, 1921.

Palestine: Disturbances in May, 1921; Reports of the Commission of Inquiry with Correspondence Relating Thereto. Cmd. 1540. London, 1921.

Report of the Palestine Royal Commission. Cmd. 5479. London, 1937.

Woodward, E. L., and R. Butler, eds. *Documents on British Foreign Policy, 1919–1939.* 1st Series, Vols. IV, VII, XIII. London, 1952.

Non-Official Sources

Aaronsohn, Alexander. *With the Turks in Palestine.* Boston, 1916.

Abdullah, King of Jordan. *Memoirs.* New York, 1950.

———. *My Memoirs Completed.* Washington, D.C., 1954.

Andrews, Fannie Fern. *The Holy Land Under the Mandate.* 2 vols. Boston, 1931.

Bibliography

Antonius, George. *The Arab Awakening*. Philadelphia, 1938.

Ashbee, C. R. *A Palestine Notebook, 1918–1923*. New York, 1923.

Assaf, Machael. *The Arab Movement in Palestine*. New York, 1937.

Bentwich, Norman. *England in Palestine*. London, 1932.

Ben-Zvi, Yitzhak. *Eretz Yisrael v'Yishuvah b'y'mai HaShilton HaOttomani*. Jerusalem, 1955.

Bonsal, Stephen. *Suitors and Suppliants: The Little Nations at Versailles*. New York, 1946.

Bowles, John. *Viscount Samuel*. London, 1957.

Burstein, Moshe. *Self-Government of the Jews in Palestine since 1900*. Tel Aviv, 1934.

De Haas, Jacob. *A History of Palestine*. New York, 1934.

———. *Louis D. Brandeis*. New York, 1929.

Dugdale, Blanche F. C. *Arthur James Balfour*. 2 vols. London, 1936.

Elath, Eliahn. *Haj Mohammed el Husseini*. Jerusalem, 1968.

Elmalah, Avraham. *Eretz Yisrael v'Suriyah b'y'mai Milhemet HaOlam*. Jerusalem, 1927.

Engel, Anita. *The Nili Spies*. London, 1959.

Esco Foundation for Palestine. *Palestine: A Study of Jewish, Arab and British Policies*. 2 vols. New Haven, 1947.

Franco, Moïse. *Essai sur l'histoire des Israélites de l'Empire Ottoman depuis les origines jusqu'à nos jours*. Paris, 1897.

Frischwasser-Ra'anan, H. F. *The Frontiers of a Nation*. London, 1955.

Gabbay, Rony E. *A Political Study of the Arab-Jewish Conflict*. New York, 1959.

Galanté, Abraham. *Turcs et Juifs: étude historique, politique*. Istanbul, 1932.

Garnett, David, ed. *The Essential T. E. Lawrence*. New York, 1951.

Gelber, N. M. *Hatzharath Balfour v'Toldoteha*. Jerusalem, 1939.

Granott, Abraham. *Agrarian Reform and the Record of Israel*. London, 1956.

Graves, Philip. *Palestine, The Land of Three Faiths*. London, 1923.

Hanna, Paul L. *British Policy in Palestine*. Washington, D.C., 1942.

Hyamson, Albert. *Palestine Under the Mandate*. London, 1950.

Jabotinsky, Vladimir. *Ne'umim, 1905–1926*. Jerusalem, 1947.

———. *The Story of the Jewish Legion*. New York, 1945.

Kedourie, Elie. *Britain and the Middle East, 1914–1921*. London, 1956.

———. "Sir Herbert Samuel and the Government of Palestine," *Middle East Studies*, V (January, 1969), 44–65.

Kirkbride, Sir Alan. *A Crackle of Thorns*. London, 1956.

Kisch, Frederick H. *Palestine Diary*. London, 1938.

Lichtheim, Richard. *Sh'ar Yishuv.* Tel Aviv, 1938.

Lipovetzky, Pesah. *Joseph Trumpeldor, Life and Works.* Jerusalem, 1953.

Lloyd George, David. *Memoirs of the Peace Conference.* Vol. II. London, 1938.

Mandel, Neville. "Turks, Arabs, and Jewish Immigration into Palestine, 1882–1914," in *St. Antony's Papers, No. 17. Middle East Affairs, No. 4.* London, 1968.

Manuel, Frank E. "The Palestine Question in Italian Diplomacy," *Journal of Modern History,* XXVII (September 1955), 263–80.

———. *The Realities of American-Palestine Relations.* Washington, D.C., 1949.

Medzini, Moshe. *Eser Shanim shel Mediniut Eretz Yisrael.* Tel Aviv, 1928.

Meinertzhagen, Richard. *Middle East Diary, 1917–1956.* London, 1959.

Nevakivi, Jukka. *Britain, France, and the Arab Middle East, 1914–1920.* London, 1969.

Nordau, Anna, and Maxa Nordau. *Max Nordau.* New York, 1943.

Patterson, Colonel J. H. *With the Judeans in the Palestine Campaign.* New York, 1922.

———. *With the Zionists in Gallipoli.* New York, 1916.

Pearlman, M. *Ben-Gurion Looks Back.* New York, 1965.

———. "Chapters of Arab-Jewish Diplomacy, 1918–1922," *Jewish Social Studies,* VI (April 1944), 123–54.

———. *The Mufti of Jerusalem.* London, 1947.

Pingaud, A. *Histoire diplomatique de la France pendant la grande guerre.* Vols. I, III. Paris, 1940.

Poznansky, Menahem. *Me-Hayye Yosef Trumpeldor.* Tel Aviv, 1945.

Rabinowicz, Oskar. *Fifty Years of Zionism: A Historical Analysis of Dr. Weizmann's "Trial and Error."* London, 1951.

Roli, Yaacov. "The Zionist Attitude to the Arabs, 1908–1914," *Middle Eastern Studies,* IV (April 1968), 198–242.

Royal Institute of International Affairs. *Great Britain and Palestine.* London, 1947.

Ruppin, Arthur. *The Agricultural Colonization of the Zionist Organization in Palestine.* London, 1956.

———. *Three Decades of Palestine.* Jerusalem, 1936.

Sachar, A. L. *Sufferance Is the Badge.* New York, 1940.

Sachar, Howard M. *Aliyah: The Peoples of Israel.* Cleveland, 1961.

Samuel, Viscount Herbert L. S. *Grooves of Change.* Indianapolis, 1946.

———. *Memoirs.* London, 1955.

Bibliography

Schechtman, Joseph B. *Vladimir Jabotinsky: Rebel and Statesman.* New York, 1956.
Sefer Toldot HaHagana. Vol. I. Tel Aviv, 1954.
Shimoni, Ya'akov. *Arvei Eretz-Yisrael.* Tel Aviv, 1947.
Sidebotham, Herbert. *Great Britain and Palestine.* London, 1937.
Sokolow, Nahum. *History of Zionism.* 2 vols. London, 1918–1919.
Stein, Leonard. *The Balfour Declaration.* London, 1961.
Storrs, Sir Ronald. *Orientations.* London, 1937.
Stoyanovsky, Jacob. *The Mandate for Palestine.* London, 1928.
Sykes, Christopher. *Crossroads to Israel.* New York, 1965.
————. *Two Studies in Virtue.* New York, 1953.
Sykes, Sir Mark. *Dar ul Islam.* London, 1904.
Temperley, Harold. *England and the Near East.* London, 1936.
Tuchman, Barbara. *Bible and Sword.* New York, 1956.
Vlavianos, B. J., and Gross, Feliks. *Struggle for Tomorrow: Modern Political Ideologies of the Jewish People.* New York, 1954.
Weizmann, Chaim. *Trial and Error.* New York, 1949.
Yaari-Poleskin, Ya'akov. *Meraglim o G'borei HaMoledet?* Tel Aviv, 1930.
Yehuda, A. S. *HaHagana shel HaYishuv b'Milhamah HaRishonah.* Jerusalem, 1952.
Yannait, Rahel. *Anu Olim.* Tel Aviv, 1963.
Zeine, Zeine N. *The Struggle for Arab Independence.* Beirut, 1960.

The Partition and Rebirth of Turkey:
The Rise and Fall of the Greek Empire

Documentary and Semi-Documentary Sources

Brown, C. N., and T. P. Ion, eds. *The Greek White Book.* New York, 1919.
Convention between Turkey and Greece Concerning the Exchange of Greek and Turkish Nationals—Lausanne, January 30, 1923. British and Foreign State Papers, CXIII (1923), Part II, 1048–53.
Degras, Jane, ed. *Soviet Documents on Foreign Policy.* London, 1951.
Great Britain, Foreign Office Publication. *Treaty of Peace with Turkey, and Other Instruments Signed at Lausanne . . . and Subsidiary Documents Forming Part of the Turkish Peace Settlement.* London, 1923.
Die grosse Politik der Mächte im Weltkrieg. Vol. IV. Dresden, 1932.
Hurewitz, J. C. *Diplomacy in the Near and Middle East: A Documentary Record.* Vol. II. Princeton, 1956.

513

Lausanne Conference on Near Eastern Affairs, 1922–1923. Cmd. 1814. London, 1923.

League of Nations. *Greek Refugee Settlement.* Geneva, 1926.

United States Department of State. *Foreign Relations of the United States: The Paris Peace Conference.* 13 vols. Washington, D.C., 1942–1947.

Woodward, E. L., and R. Butler, eds. *Documents on British Foreign Policy, 1919–1939.* 1st Series, Vols. VII, XIII. London, 1952.

Non-Official Sources

Abbott, C. F. *Greece and the Allies, 1914–1922.* London, 1922.

Adamov, Evgenii A. *Die europäischen Mächte und Griechenland während des Weltkrieges.* Dresden, 1932.

Adivar, Halidé Edib. *The Daughter of Smyrna.* Lahore, 1940.

———. *The Turkish Ordeal.* New York, 1928.

Adkinson, Laura M. *Great Britain and the Kemalist Movement for Turkish Independence, 1919–1923.* Unpublished doctoral dissertation, University of Texas, 1958.

Ahmed, Gulzar. *Turkey: Rebirth of a Nation.* Karachi, 1961.

Alastos, D. *Venizelos.* London, 1942.

Albrecht-Carrié, R. *Italy at the Peace Conference.* New York, 1938.

Ancel, Jacques. "Les bases géographiques de la question des détroits," *Le monde slave,* V (February 1920), 238–53.

Andrew, Prince of Greece. *Towards Disaster: The Greek Army in Asia Minor in 1921.* London, 1930.

———. *War Memoirs.* London, 1928.

Armstrong, H. C. *Grey Wolf, Mustafa Kemal.* London, 1937.

———. *Turkey in Travail.* London, 1925.

Atabinen, Resit Saffet. *Les Turcs et le panhellénisme.* Geneva, 1918.

Bardoux, Jacques. *Lloyd George et la France.* Paris, 1923.

Barker, E. *Macedonia, Its Place in Balkan Power Politics.* London, 1950.

Bazhdaroff, G. *The Macedonian Question Yesterday and Today.* Sofia, 1926.

Beaverbrook, Lord. *The Decline and Fall of Lloyd George.* London, 1963.

Bennett, J. G. *Witness.* London, 1926.

Benoist-Méchin, Jacques. *Mustapha Kemal.* Paris, 1954.

Bierstadt, Edward H. *The Great Betrayal.* New York, 1924.

Bigelow, Richard, ed. *Turkey Reborn.* Scotch Plains, N.J., 1941.

Bisbee, Eleanor. *The New Turks.* Philadelphia, 1951.

Bischoff, Norbert de. *La Turquie dans le monde.* Paris, 1936.

Bibliography

"Le bolchevisme et l'Islam, II. Hors de Russie; les relations russo-turques depuis l'avènement du bolchevisme," *Revue du monde musulman*, LII (1922), 181–206.

Bompard, Maurice. *Impressions sur la conférence de Lausanne*. Paris, 1923.

Bonsal, Stephen. *Suitors and Suppliants: The Little Nations at Versailles*. New York, 1946.

Booth, C. D., and I. B. Booth. *Italy's Aegean Possessions*. London, 1928.

Brémond, Edouard. *La Cilicie en 1919–1920*. Paris, 1921.

Bujac, Jean L. E. *Les campagnes de l'armée hellénique, 1918–1922*. Paris, 1930.

Bullard, Sir Reader. *Britain and the Middle East*. New York, 1951.

Carr, E. H. *The Bolshevik Revolution, 1917–1923*. Vol. III. London, 1953.

Catroux, Georges. *Deux missions en Moyen-Orient*. Paris, 1958.

Chester, S. B. *The Life of Venizelos*. New York, 1921.

Churchill, Winston S. *The World Crisis*. Vol. IV ("The Aftermath"). New York, 1929.

Ciasca, Raffaele. *Storia coloniale dell'Italia contemporanea da Assab all'impero*. Milan, 1940.

Combothecra, X. S. *La Grèce loyale*. Geneva, 1919.

Cummings, Henry H. *Franco-British Rivalry in the Post-War Near East*. New York, 1938.

Davison, R. H. "From Mudros to Lausanne," in G. A. Craig and F. Gilbert, eds. *The Diplomats, 1919–1939*. Vol. I. Princeton, 1953.

Deak, F., and J. T. Shotwell. *Turkey at the Straits*. New York, 1940.

DeNovo, John. *American Interests and Policies in the Middle East, 1900–1939*. Minneapolis, 1963.

Deny, Jean. *Souvenirs du Gazi Moustafa Kemal Pasha*. Paris, 1927.

Driault, Edouard, and Lhéritier, Michel. *Histoire diplomatique de la Grèce de 1821 à nos jours*. Vol. V. Paris, 1926.

Eddy, Charles B. *Greece and the Greek Refugees*. London, 1931.

Fischer, Louis. *The Soviets in World Affairs*. Vol. I. London, 1930.

Forster, Edward S. *A Short History of Modern Greece, 1821–1945*. London, 1956.

Fournet, Louis Dartige du. *Souvenirs de guerre d'un amiral*. Paris, 1920.

Frangulis, A. F. *La Grèce et la crise mondiale*. 2 vols. Paris, 1926.

Fuad, Ali. *La question des détroits*. Paris, 1928.

Gauvain, A. "Five Years of French Policy in the Near East," *Foreign Affairs*, III (December 1924), 277–92.

Gentizon, Paul. *Mustapha Kemal, où l'Orient en marche*. Paris, 1929.

Georges-Gaulis, Berthe. *Angora, Constantinople, Londres*. Paris, 1922.

Gontaut-Biron, R. de. *D'Angora à Lausanne*. Paris, 1924.

Goüsa, Ibrahim Alaettin. *Turk Meshur Lari*. Istanbul, 1946.

Graves, Philip. *Briton and Turk*. London, 1941.

Graves, R. W. *Storm Centers of the Near East, 1879–1929*. London, 1933.

Grew, Joseph C. *Turbulent Era*. Vol. I. Boston, 1952.

Harington, Sir Charles. *Tim Harington Looks Back*. London, 1941.

Haslip, Joan. *The Sultan*. London, 1958.

Heyd, Uriel. *Foundations of Turkish Nationalism*. London, 1950.

Hostler, C. W. *Turkism and the Soviets*. London, 1957.

Howard, Harry N. "An American Experiment in Peace Making: The King Crane Commission," *Moslem World*, XXXII (April 1942), 122–46.

———. *The King Crane Commission*. Beirut, 1963.

———. *The Partition of Turkey*. Norman, Oklahoma, 1931.

———. *The Problem of the Turkish Straits*. Washington, D.C., 1947.

Hudson, G. F. *Turkey, Greece and the Eastern Mediterranean*. London, 1939.

Jäckh, Ernst. *The Rising Crescent*. New York, 1944.

———. "Mustafa Kemals Sendung nach Anatolien," in *Aus der Geschichte des islamischen Orients*. Tübingen, 1949.

Jäschke, Gotthard, and Pritsch, Erich. *Die Türkei seit dem Weltkriege*. Vol. I. Berlin, 1929.

Kayser, Jacques. *L'Europe et la Turquie nouvelle*. Paris, 1922.

Kerofilas, C. *Eleftherios Venizelos: His Life and Work*. New York, 1915.

Kiliç, Altemur. *Turkey and the World*. Washington, D.C., 1959.

Kinross, Lord. *Ataturk*. New York, 1965.

Kirkwood, K. D., and Toynbee, Arnold. *Turkey*. New York, 1927.

Krüger, Karl. *Kemalist Turkey and the Middle East*. London, 1932.

Ladas, Stephen P. *The Exchange of Minorities: Bulgaria, Greece and Turkey*. New York, 1932.

Larcher, Maurice. *La grande guerre dans les Balkans*. Paris, 1929.

Lawson, J. C. *Tales of Aegean Intrigue*. London, 1920.

Lewis, Bernard. *The Emergence of Modern Turkey*. London, 1961.

Lloyd George, David. *Memoirs of the Peace Conference*. Vol. II. London, 1938.

Bibliography

Lybyer, Albert H. "Turkey Under the Armistice," *Journal of International Relations*, XII (April 1922), 447–73.

Mavris, N. G. *Wilson, Greece, Sforza and the Truth*. New York, 1944.

Mavrogordato, John. *Modern Greece, A Chronicle and Survey, 1800–1931*. New York, 1931.

Nicolson, Harold. *Curzon: The Last Phase*. London, 1934.

———. *Peacemaking, 1919*. London, 1933.

Nitti, Francesco S. *Peaceless Europe*. London, 1922.

Noble, G. B. *Policies and Opinions at Paris, 1919*. New York, 1935.

Oeconomos, L. *The Martyrdom of Smyrna and Eastern Christendom*. London, 1922.

Orga, Irfan, and Margarete Orga. *Ataturk*. London, 1962.

———. *Phoenix Ascendant*. London, 1958.

Paillarès, Michel. *Le Kemalisme devant les alliés*. Paris, 1922.

Pallis, Alexander A. *Greece's Anatolian Venture and After*. London, 1937.

Palmer, Alan. *The Gardeners of Salonika*. New York, 1965.

Park, Alexander G. *Bolshevism in Turkestan, 1917–1927*. New York, 1957.

Pech, Edgar. *Les alliés et la Turquie*. Paris, 1925.

Pentzopoulos, Dimitri. *The Balkan Exchange of Minorities and its Impact upon Greece*. The Hague, 1967.

Pernot, Maurice. "Constantinople sous le contrôle interallié," *Revue des deux mondes*, VII (January 1922), 276–314.

Phocas-Cosmetatos, S. P. *L'Entente et la Grèce pendant la grande guerre*. 2 vols. Paris, 1926.

Pichon, Jean. *Le partage du Proche-Orient*. Paris, 1938.

Platykas, R. D. *La Grèce pendant la guerre de 1914–1918*. Berne, 1918.

Pokrovsky, M. N. *Pages d'histoire*. Paris, 1929.

Price, Claire. *The Rebirth of Turkey*. New York, 1923.

Radoslavov, Basil. *Bulgarien und die Weltkrise*. Berlin, 1923.

Recouly, Raymond. *M. Jonnart en Grèce et l'abdication de Constantin*. Paris, 1918.

Riddell, Lord. *Intimate Diary of the Peace Conference*. London, 1933.

Ronaldshay, Earl of. *The Life of Lord Curzon*. Vol. II. London, 1928.

Rustow, Dankwart A. "The Army and the Foundation of the Turkish Republic," in *World Politics*. Vol. XL. New Haven, 1959.

Sakellarion, M. B., and N. G. Svoronos. "Greece: Culture of the Turkish Period," in *The Encyclopedia Americana*. Vol. XIII. New York, 1953.

Sarrail, P. E. *Mon commandement en Orient, 1916–1918*. Paris, 1920.

Schramm, E. S. K. *Griechenland und die grossen Mächte, 1913–1923*. Göttingen, 1933.

Seyfullah, Ibrahim. *Italien im östlichen Mittelmeer*. Berlin, 1930.

Sforza, Count Carlo. *Bâtisseurs de l'Europe moderne*. Paris, 1931.

Shatzky, B. E. "La question de Constantinople et des détroits," *Revue d'histoire de la guerre mondiale*, IV (October 1926), 289–311; V (January 1927), 19–43.

Sheridan, Clare. *Nuda Veritas*. London, 1927.

Smith, Elaine K. *Origins of the Kemalist Movement*. Washington, D.C., 1959.

Spector, Ivar. *The Soviet Union and the Muslim World, 1917–1956*. Seattle, 1958.

Street, C. J. C. *Lord Reading*. London, 1928.

Tardieu, André. *The Truth About the Treaty*. New York, 1921.

Temperley, Harold. *A History of the Peace Conference of Paris*. Vol. VI. London, 1924.

Thomson, Sir Basil H. *The Allied Secret Service in Greece*. London, 1931.

Toynbee, Arnold J. *The Western Question in Turkey and Greece*. London, 1923.

Vaka, Demetra. *Les intrigues germaniques en Grèce*. Paris, 1918.

Véou, Paul de. *La passion de Cilicie*. Paris, 1938.

Vere-Hodge, E. R. *Turkish Foreign Policy, 1918–1948*. Geneva, 1950.

Viaud, Julien (Pierre Loti). *La mort de notre chère France en Orient*. Paris, 1920.

Vopicka, C. J. *Secrets of the Balkans*. Chicago, 1921.

Walder, David. *The Chanak Affair*. London, 1969.

Willmore, J. S. *The Story of King Constantine*. London, 1919.

Yalman, Ehmed Emin. *Turkey in My Time*. Norman, Oklahoma, 1956.

Index

Index

A NOTE ABOUT THE AUTHOR

BORN IN ST. LOUIS, Missouri, in 1928, and reared in
Champaign, Illinois, Howard Morley Sachar received
his undergraduate education at Swarthmore and took
his graduate degrees at Harvard. He has taught extensively in the fields of Modern European and Middle
Eastern History, and lived in the Middle East for six
years, two of them on fellowship, the rest as director
of Brandeis University's Hiatt Institute in Jerusalem.
He has contributed to many scholarly journals, and is
the author of three previous books: *The Course of
Modern Jewish History* (1958), *Aliyah* (1961), and
From the Ends of the Earth (1964). Currently, Dr.
Sachar is Professor of Modern History at George Washington University. He lives with his wife and two
daughters in Kensington, Maryland.

A NOTE ON THE TYPE

THE TEXT of this book was set in a typeface called Primer, designed by Rudolph Ruzicka for the Merganthaler Linotype Company and first made available in 1949. Primer, a modified modern face based on Century broadface, has the virtue of great legibility and was designed especially for today's methods of composition and printing.

Primer is Ruzicka's third typeface. In 1940 he designed Fairfield, and in 1947 Fairfield Medium, both for the Merganthaler Linotype Company.

Ruzicka was born in Bohemia in 1883 and came to the United States at the age of eleven. He attended public schools in Chicago and later the Chicago Art Institute. During his long career he has been a wood engraver, etcher, cartographer, and book designer. For many years he was associated with Daniel Berkeley Updike and produced the annual keepsakes for The Merrymount Press from 1911 until 1941.

This book was composed, printed, and bound by the Haddon Craftsmen, Inc., Scranton, Pa. *Typography and binding design by*

WARREN  CHAPPELL

A NOTE ON THE TYPE

THE TEXT of this book was set in a typeface called Primer, designed by Rudolph Ruzicka for the Merganthaler Linotype Company and first made available in 1949. Primer, a modified modern face based on Century broadface, has the virtue of great legibility and was designed especially for today's methods of composition and printing.

Primer is Ruzicka's third typeface. In 1940 he designed Fairfield, and in 1947 Fairfield Medium, both for the Merganthaler Linotype Company.

Ruzicka was born in Bohemia in 1883 and came to the United States at the age of eleven. He attended public schools in Chicago and later the Chicago Art Institute. During his long career he has been a wood engraver, etcher, cartographer, and book designer. For many years he was associated with Daniel Berkeley Updike and produced the annual keepsakes for The Merrymount Press from 1911 until 1941.

This book was composed, printed, and bound by the Haddon Craftsmen, Inc., Scranton, Pa. *Typography and binding design by*

WARREN  CHAPPELL